WITHDRAWN

D1075499

WITHDRAWN

THE POTTER'S
COMPLETE BOOK
OF CLAY AND GLAZES

THE POTTER'S COMPLETE BOOK OF CLAY AND GLAZES

BY JAMES CHAPPELL

738.1
C 467p

WATSON-GUPTILL PUBLICATIONS/NEW YORK

27,522

Copyright © 1977 by James Chappell

First published 1977 in the United States and Canada by Watson-Guptill Publicatic
a division of Billboard Publications, Inc.
1515 Broadway, New York, N.Y. 10036

Library of Congress Cataloging in Publication Data
Chappell, James, 1942–
 The potter's complete book of clay and glazes.
 Bibliography: p.
 Includes index.
 1. Pottery craft—Equipment and supplies. 2. Clay.
3. Glazes. I. Title.
TT921.5.C48   738.1   76-42212
ISBN 0-8230-4202-2

All rights reserved. No part of this publication
may be reproduced or used in any form or by any means—graphic,
electronic, or mechanical, including photocopying, recording, taping,
or information storage and retrieval systems—without
written permission of the publishers.

Manufactured in U.S.A.

First Printing, 1977

DEDICATION

This book has a triple dedication—it is for the
three people who have had the most profound influence in
the shaping of my life, all of whom I respect greatly and
love dearly.

For

My beloved art teacher, Helen Marshall ("Mama B."), who
got me into this adult version of "mud pie creativity"
in the first place.

And for

My good friend and "adopted brother" Ron Pittman, who
showed me by the example of his own life that there is
more to life than playing in the "mud."

And for

My wise and humble friend Roy Cain, who helped me through
a very difficult time and through his talent for simplification
led me to discover the true meaning of "Thou art the Potter—
I am the clay."

ACKNOWLEDGMENTS

This book has passed through many stages of development in which old and new ideas were added and many discarded or reorganized in an effort to make it more cohesive. In this effort to achieve a better organized collection of material I would like to acknowledge the invaluable help of my editors, Diane Hines and especially my in-house editor, Sarah Bodine, for their advice on style, format, and material.

For those potters who so unselfishly shared their knowledge, ideas, and formulas to use in the book—deepest thanks. They are: Gordon Beaver of Kingston, Arkansas; Don Curtis of the University of Arkansas; Sue Garner of Springfield, Missouri; David Greer of Prague, Oklahoma; Neil Nulton of Branson, Missouri; Ron Pittman of Kingston, Arkansas; Rich and Kay West of Rimstone Pottery in Jasper, Arkansas; and Pal Wright of Ottawa, Kansas.

I am also deeply indebted to my photographer, Arleen Olson, for her conscientious efforts to achieve the best possible quality and esthetic display of the pottery used on the jacket of the book.

I owe a special debt of gratitude to my former art teacher, Helen Marshall, first of all for steering my interest in the area of pottery, and secondly for her encouragement, sound artistic advice and assistance in selecting the photographs which would best serve as a broad example of a few of the glazes given in this book.

My thanks also to Beverly Maddox, who very bluntly told me at the beginning of the manuscript that I was a man of too many words—I shudder to think how long this book might have been had it not been for her kind but pointed advice.

I am similarly indebted to Glynda Bunch for her time-saving aid in the organization and completion of the Dictionary of Clay and Glaze Compounds and the glossary.

My very *special* thanks to my secretary and typist, Mary Cline, for her patience, hard work, and endless smiles, in the face of an almost endless manuscript. Without her tireless help to put on paper my unrelenting flow of material, this book (and I mean this literally) would never have been finished.

And finally and foremost I am deeply grateful to a young apprentice potter, Ron Pittman, who came into my studio and brought a wealth of new ideas, thus getting me out of a "rut of contentment" with my own style. He gave me a burning desire to try new unorthodox areas of pottery—all of which I very self-righteously told him would never work—but usually did. My thanks to him for showing me that too much knowledge of a medium can sometimes stifle new areas of creativity.

CONTENTS

Introduction, 10

PART ONE. CLAYS

1. Clay and Clay Body Types, 14

Primary Clays, 14
Secondary Clays, 14
Clay Body Types, 16

2. Native Clays: Digging Your Own, 17

Why Dig, 17
Where to Look, 17
What to Look for, 19
Spot Testing: Is it Clay? 19
Testing for Impurities, 19
Testing for Lime Content, 19
Granular Impurities, 19
Testing for Organic Impurities, 19
Testing Colors of Native Clays, 20
Testing for Plasticity, 20
Taking Samples, 20
Preparing the Clay, 20
Processing Step-by-Step, 20
Simple Test Firing, 21
Accurate Testing, 21
Adjusting and Improving Clay, 22
The Aging of Clay, 23
Aging and Wedging Step-by-Step, 24

3. Clay Body Preparation, 25

Choosing a Clay Body, 25
Mixing, 25
Formulating Clays for Specific Uses, 27
Testing, Adjusting, and Improving, 28

4. Data on Clay Body Formulas, 29

Clay Body Rating Scale, 29
Glaze Rating Scale, 30
Color, 30
Categories and Labels, 30
Test Batches, 30

5. Earthenware Clay Bodies: Cone 09–04, 31

Earthenware Throwing Bodies, 31
Earthenware Casting Bodies, Cone 08–04, 31
Earthenware Sculpture Bodies, 31
Formulas for Earthenware Throwing Bodies, 32
Formulas for Earthenware Casting Bodies, 40
Formulas for Earthenware Sculpture Bodies, 43

6. Soft Stoneware Clay Bodies: Cone 03–4, 46

Formulas for Soft Stoneware Throwing Bodies, 46
Formulas for Soft Stoneware Casting Bodies, 53
Formulas for Soft Stoneware Sculpture Bodies, 56

7. Stoneware Clay Bodies: Cone 4–12, 58

Formulas for Stoneware Throwing Bodies, 46
Formulas for Stoneware Casting Bodies, 75
Formulas for Stoneware Sculpture Bodies, 77

8. Porcelain Clay Bodies: Cone 9–14, 82

Formulas for Porcelain Throwing Bodies, 83
Formulas for Porcelain Casting Bodies, 89
Formulas for Porcelain Sculpture Bodies, 91

9. Raku Clay Bodies and Glazes: Cone 016–03, 93

Raku Glazes, 93
Formulas for Raku Bodies, 94
Formulas for Raku Glazes, 97

10. Egyptian Paste: Cone 016–04, 107

Formulas for Egyptian Paste Bodies, 107
Chart of Colorants for Egyptian Paste, 111

11. Ovenware and Rangetop Bodies and Glazes:
Cone 04–09, 112

Forming, 112
Formulas for Ovenware and Rangetop Bodies and Glazes, 113

12. Coloring Clay Bodies, 116

Chart of Clay Body Colorants and Percentages, 117

13. Clay Body Defects and Adjustments, 118

14. Engobes, 120

Formulas for Engobes, 120
Chart of Engobe Colorants and Percentages, 126

15. Stains: Cone 09-10, 127

Formulas for Stains, 127

PART TWO. GLAZES

16. Glaze Types, 140

Glaze Classification, 140

17. Glaze Preparation, 144

Simple Mixing Methods, 144
Ball Milling, 144
Adding Water, 144
Using Floatatives, 145
Using Gums, 145
Using Flocculants, 145

18. Single Firing: Cone 06-9, 146

Single-Fire Clay Bodies, 146
Glazing the Ware, 146
Single-Fire Glazes, 146
Formulas for Single-Fire Glazes, 147

19. Wide-Firing-Range Glazes: Cone 06-9, 152

Formulas for Wide-Firing-Range Glazes, 152

20. Cup and Spoon Measure Glazes: Cone 014-6, 157

Materials Needed, 157
Measuring, 157
Formulas for Cup and Spoon Measure Glazes, 157

21. Special-Effect Glazes, 161

Break-Through Glazes, 161
Formulas for Break-Through Glazes, 162
Chart of Break-Through Glaze Colorants, 166
High-Fire Boiling Glaze, 167
Formula for High-Fire Boiling Glaze, 167
Chart of High-Fire Boiling Glaze Colorants, 168
Crackle Glaze Effects, 169
Formulas for Crackle Glaze Clay Bodies, 169
Formulas for Crackle Glazes, 170
Chart of Crackle Glaze Colorants, 176
Crater Glazes, 177
Suggested Uses for Crater Glazes, 177
Formulas for Crater Glazes, 177
Chart of Crater Glaze Colorants, 181
Crystalline Glazes, 182
Formulas for Crystalline Glazes, 182
Floating Glaze, 186
Formula for Floating Glaze, 186
Flowing Glazes, 187
Formulas for Flowing Glazes, 187

22. Special Effects with Commercial Glazes, 190

Single Commercial Glazes, 190
Commercial Glaze Combinations, 191
Duncan Glaze Combinations, 191
Ceramichrome Glaze Combinations, 196

Amaco Glaze Combinations, 197
Suggested Variations, 197

23. Earthenware Glazes: Cone 020-05, 199

Formulas for Earthenware Glazes, 199

24. Soft Stoneware Glazes: Cone 04-4, 232

Formulas for Soft Stoneware Glazes, 232

25. Stoneware Glazes: Cone 5-10, 284

Formulas for Stoneware Glazes, 284

26. Porcelain Glazes: Cone 10-15, 354

Formulas for Porcelain Glazes, 354

27. Celadon Glazes: Cone 010-11, 365

Formulas for Celadon Glazes, 365

28. Copper Red Glazes: Cone 04-10, 374

Formulas for Copper Red Glazes, 374

29. Ash Glazes: Cone 06-10, 385

Preparing Ashes for Use, 385
Formulas for Ash Glazes, 386

30. Slip Glazes: Cone 4-9, 394

Formulas for Slip Glazes, 394

31. Salt and Vapor Glazing, 401

Chart of Clay Bodies Suitable for Salt Glazing, 403

32. Glaze Defects and Adjustments, 404

33. Glaze Colorants, 408

Chrome Oxide, 408
Cobalt Oxide, 408
Copper Oxide, 408
Ilmenite, 409
Iron Oxide, 409
Manganese Oxide, 410
Nickel Oxide, 410
Rutile, 410
Using Single Colorants, 410
Chart of Colorant Blends, 411
Chart of Colorants for Base Glazes, 412

34. Dictionary of Clay and Glaze Compounds, 418

APPENDIX

Clay Analysis Chart (America), 428
Feldspar Analysis Chart (America), 428
Commercial Frit Chart (America), 429
Colorant Chart for Oxidation Glazes, 430
Colorant Chart for Reduction Glazes, 431
Heat Color/Temperature Chart, 432
Clay Analysis Chart (United Kingdom), 433
Feldspar Analysis Chart (United Kingdom), 434
Commercial Frits Chart (United Kingdom), 435
Health and Safety (United Kingdom), 437
Suggested Reading, 438
Glossary/Index, 440

INTRODUCTION

There is magic in clay and fire, or so it sometimes seems. Even now that I can call myself a professional potter, I am still amazed and thrilled to find that it is possible to take a sticky, dirty, slimy substance that is generally considered worthless, or at best a nuisance, and turn it into an object of art. This does indeed seem magical. No wonder the ancient Chinese set such store by their ceramic creations.

But this magical transformation of clay into art object is not easily attainable. It lies hidden beneath a mass of technical jargon, which must either be studied and digested or bypassed in some manner to obtain that first success. My own first attempts at making pottery were successful enough to lead me to want to do and learn more.

Since those early successes, however, the floor of my studio has often been littered with the fragments of my failures, smashed in anger and frustration. But you can learn a great deal from failure, provided you can face it. If at first you feel that you cannot, the best antidote is to indulge yourself dramatically in an ecstasy of self-pity, curse your wheel and kiln for conspiring against you, and smash a few more pots (preferably the bad ones). Then resolutely lift your head above the dismay and the shards, pick up the pieces, and go back to work. Having thus rid yourself of frustration (and pots), you can get back to the business of experimenting, examining your mistakes, and learning your art. I have been through this process repeatedly and have managed to

retain my love of potting and my sense of humor, because for every mistake I have made, I have also made a discovery that led me on to more daring experiments. And from it all I have gleaned those technical skills that make advancement possible.

Forming clay, creating something that has form and beauty, is a fever in the blood, but one that is deeply satisfying to the soul and pleasing to the eye. Some catch it; some are immune. And usually those who catch it cannot help but feel that those who are immune are also a little deprived. Therefore this book is first and foremost for the lover of clay and fire—the potter. It has been written with great difficulty and a great deal of experimentation, alone. The information on these pages has grown despite a lack of the solid background in chemistry and mathematics that is almost indispensable to the potter who wishes to work from scratch. It is a book for all the hidden potters, for those who labor outside the system without benefit of teachers, masters, professional studios, or even knowledgeable friends to help them.

Many books have been written on the subject of clay and glazes; even more have been written on the general subject of pottery with small sections devoted to clay body and glaze formulation. But I have never found a book on clay bodies or glazes that did not leave me in a wasteland of technical jargon.

My purpose in writing this book is to present in as clear and understandable a form as possible the end result of what those complicated, confusing, and highly technical books on clays and glazes seek to give, *a collection of clay body and glaze recipes for immediate use.*

I do not intend to overwhelm the reader with details of how clays came to be or how and why glazes were invented and evolved. There are many good books in print on the subject, the best of which are listed in the suggested reading in the appendix of this book.

My intention is to give the aspiring potter the immediate tools with which to have some measure of success and perhaps to open his eyes to the magic of clay and fire. Too many potential potters, unschooled in the technical and chemical aspects of pottery making, become discouraged when they attempt to compound their own clay bodies and glazes. If some measure of success comes to the potter in the beginning, he will then have something on which to build a more stable and more complete knowledge of the science and art of making pottery.

This book, therefore, has abundant information for those who, from a lack of technical skill, background, patience, or time, do not seek to develop their own formulas. It contains numerous formulas for clay bodies, glazes, stains, engobes, and slips with color oxide charts to meet the needs of a broad range of firing temperatures. In addition it includes sections on testing and adjustment of glaze and body defects, as well as how to avoid mistakes that are caused by a lack of understanding of the limitations of the medium itself. And for those lovers of nature, there is a section on the joys and rewards of digging one's own clays and using organic materials for body and glaze composition.

Although designed to meet the needs of the beginning potter who may be weak in the technical side of pottery, I believe this book may also be of value to those professionals who do not have the time or the patience to develop their own formulas or who want to learn more about the possibilities of the materials they are currently using. Some of the formulas have been collected over a period of years from other potters or adapted from research on glazes. Most of them, however, are the result of many years of experimentation in developing glazes to be as reliable as possible under the various firing conditions I have encountered.

No doubt the reader will find glazes in other pottery books that resemble those listed here; the primary difference will be in the proportions of ingredients given or in the addition of a chemical to stabilize the glaze. This is only natural, for as the potter gains in experience he will find that what works well for one potter or one type of kiln may not work as well for another. He will also find that ceramic compounds used in pottery will vary in composition from one location to another—hence the many versions of what appears to be one basic clay body or glaze formula. I believe that in this book the aspiring ceramics student will be able to find a clay body or glaze recipe that will fit his needs with a minimum of adjustment.

Note. Some of the chemicals used in clay preparation are potentially dangerous. Safety precautions should be taken when weighing out and mixing clay bodies. These precautions are listed under each series of clay formulas. (See also Chapter 3 on Clay Body Preparation.)

Cone numbers throughout this book refer to Orton Standard cones.

PART ONE
CLAYS

1
CLAY AND CLAY BODY TYPES

Clay is the single most important material in the time-honored art of pottery making. It is the first thing one must consider in the creation of that art form that is as old as civilization itself. To understand clay body types one must first gain some measure of knowledge of the types of clays themselves.

Clay is basically a powdery form of rock which has been broken into fine particles by the action of millions of years of decomposition by the forces of nature. Stated more scientifically it is a hydrous silicate of alumina, that is to say, a compound of alumina and silica chemically combined with water. A theoretical formula for this substance might read $Al_2O_3 . 2SiO_2 . 2H_2O$.

Clay is very seldom found in this pure form. However the forces of nature and numerous geological upheavals have taken care of that, adding various impurities in the form of minerals and metals and leaching out others which were soluble. Thus it is the variation of impurities in the basic formula that accounts for the different types of clay and consequently of clay bodies.

Clays are usually classified into two types according to their geological origin. These are then subdivided by particle size and variation of impurities inherent in the native form of the clay. The two basic geological types of clay to be found in nature are primary clays and secondary clays.

PRIMARY CLAYS

Primary clays, sometimes known as residual clays, are those which are to be found in the same location as the parent rock from which they came. They have not been moved by the forces of nature and are thus more pure and true to the theoretical formula. The primary clays are basically of one type, the kaolins.

Kaolin, taking its name from the Chinese word meaning "high ridge," is without doubt the most plentiful and valuable of the primary clays. It was first discovered and used by the ancient Chinese as early as the beginning of the Han Dynasty, which dates back to 200 B.C.

The United States is quite fortunate to have several good deposits of this clay type. The major residual deposits are in North Carolina. The lesser depostis in South Carolina and Georgia are of the sedementary type and the Florida deposits are more plastic and often termed "ball kaolins" (see the Clay Chart in the Appendix).

Kaolin is an extremely refractory clay with a melting point of over 3200°F./1260°C. It is never used alone for making clay bodies because it is too difficult to shape due to its nonplastic quality and too refractory to fire to a hard, dense body at acceptable temperature ranges for the potter. Consequently it is generally used in combination with various other clays and compounds which increases its plasticity and lowers its maturing temperature. This is necessary to produce a hard, durable, and dense body. Due to its whiteness and low shrinkage it is often used to produce porcelain or white earthenware.

The major uses of kaolin for the potter are listed below according to their importance:

1. A main ingredient in the making of porcelain and whiteware bodies.

2. A clay body additive to raise the maturing point of the clay.

3. A glaze ingredient to furnish alumina and silica.

4. A glaze ingredient for stabilizing glazes to prevent excessive flowing or running.

5. An ingredient of kiln wash to protect kiln shelves and furniture from glaze drippings.

SECONDARY CLAYS

Secondary clays are those which have been removed from the site of the parent rock by the forces of water, wind, or glacial action. This transporting of the clay by the forces of nature has had two basic effects on it. First of all, the action of water in streams full of rocks and pebbles tended to grind the coarse materials of the clay into smaller and finer particles and deposit them in beds along with various other eroded materials. This then would explain the complex makeup of secondary clays as compared to the kaolins which remained on the site of the parent rock, uncontaminated by other materials both organic and inorganic.

As might be expected, clays which have been transported by the action of nature contain many impurities such as iron, quartz, mica, alkalies, and carbonaceous matter. Depending upon the variation of impure matter content, secondary clays can be further classified into types. These types are: ball clays, fire clays, stoneware clays, earthenware clays, slip clays, and bentonite.

Ball clays are so named because they were first sold in that shape at English clay mines. In property content they are practically the opposite of the kaolins. They are plastic, more fusible, and have an iron content slightly higher than that of kaolin.

It is this property content that actually makes them complementary in character. Consequently they are often used in combination with each other to produce a workable and more practical clay body.

Although ball clays are not as pure as kaolins they are relatively free of iron and other mineral contamination and fire to body colors ranging from dense gray to light buff at about 2300°F./ 1260°C. They can be used to lower the firing temperature of kaolins or raise the maturing temperature of lower-firing clays, such as earthenware.

Ball clays are used mainly to impart plasticity and workability to other, less plastic clays. However, they are seldom used alone due to the excessive shrinkage during firing which is the result of this plasticity. Therefore ball clays are not usually added to clay bodies in percentages above 10% to 20%.

In the unfired state ball clays are usually dark gray to bluish black, due to the presence of organic and carbonaceous matter. Although they are a product of a granite-type parent rock much like kaolin, through the actions of nature they were deposited in swampy areas where they became contaminated with decaying organic materials—hence their high carbon content and gray color in the raw state. During firing, however, this organic matter burns out and does not affect the final color of the fired clay.

Ball clays are often used in glazes as a source of alumina and silica where they also act as a

good binding agent. Such glazes, however, store badly if a ball clay high in carbon is used, for the decaying carbon tends to produce gases in solution that leads to defects in the fired glaze. A few drops of formaldehyde will prevent the growth of these gas-forming bacteria. A better solution is to use a ball clay low in carbon, such as those mined in Tennessee or Kentucky.

The major uses of ball clay for the potter are listed below according to their importance:

1. A plasticizing agent in clay bodies.

2. An agent to lower firing temperatures of the more refractory clays such as kaolin and fire clay.

3. A body ingredient in stoneware to raise firing temperatures and increase plastic qualities.

4. A glaze ingredient to furnish alumina and silica.

5. A glaze stabilizer to prevent flowing.

6. A binding agent in glazes to improve their adhesive qualities.

Fire Clays obtain their name from their high refractory character which enables the potter to fire them as high as 2800°F./1538°C. without deformation or fusion taking place. They may vary widely in their properties. They may be high in mineral content and low in plasticity or vice versa, but their refractory quality remains the same. As such they are a good source of materials for raising the firing temperature of lower-firing clays, especially in stoneware bodies. In such cases they can be used in amounts up to 30%.

The major uses of fire clay for the potter are listed below according to their importance:

1. A body ingredient to increase the firing range and temperature of other clays.

2. A body stabilizer to prevent deforming or distortion at vitrification levels.

3. A body ingredient to improve thermal shock resistance in some clay body types.

Stoneware clays are plastic, workable clays which can be fired to vitrification at temperatures ranging from 2200° to 2300°F./1204° to 1260° C. As such they are ideal for the potter.

In many parts of the country deposits of such clays can be found that are usable without additions of other compounds or alterations to the body proper. They may range in color from gray to buff to darker browns. As they are usually the result of sedimentary depositing by nature, they can vary widely in composition. In many cases they closely resemble fire clays. Their very classification as stoneware clays often hinges on whether they are suitable to use in the making of pottery without considerable alterations to the natural body.

The major uses of stoneware clays for the potter are listed below in order of their importance:

1. A main body ingredient in stoneware clay bodies.

2. A clay body ingredient to increase the temperature of lower-firing clays without detracting from their plasticity.

3. A stabilizer in higher-fire earthenware clays.

Earthenware is the most common of all the secondary clay types to be found in the natural state. Earthenware makes up a group of variously colored clays in the temperature range of 1700° to 2100° F./927° to 1149° C. As such these clays may be of the greatest interest to the beginning potter. Their low fusion point is the result of the mineral content, usually in the form of alkalies and iron oxide.

Generally they are red in color but may range from red to greenish black to brown in the raw state. Their fired color will range from pink to dark brown, depending upon the iron content of the clay.

The major uses of earthenware clays for the potter are listed below according to their importance:

1. A main body ingredient in earthenware clay bodies.

2. An ingredient in slip glazes to lower the melting point.

3. An ingredient to lower temperatures of more refractory clays such as fire clay.

4. A source of color in lighter clay bodies.

Slip clays are naturally occuring clays which can function as a glaze without any additional fluxing agents being added, for they contain their own flux, usually in the form of iron oxide. They are tan to dark brown in the fired state; other colors are very rare. Their firing range is 2200° F./1204° C. and up. Many earthenware clays can function as slip clays very satisfactorily when fired in this temperature range.

The major uses of slip clays for the potter are listed below according to their importance:

1. An independent glaze material.

2. A glaze colorant.

Bentonite is a clay which has its origins in the volcanic activity during the time when the crust of the earth was being formed. This highly plastic clay was formed from the air-borne dust of volcanic eruptions. It is most commonly used as a plasticizer in clay bodies: one gram of bentonite is equal in plasticity to five grams of ball clay. It is also used quite commonly in glazes to improve adhesion—1% to 3% can be used without affecting the glaze to any noticeable extent. If used in higher amounts it can cause cracking and crawling of the glaze.

The major uses of bentonite for the potter are listed below according to their importance:

1. A plasticizing agent in all types of clay bodies.

2. A binding agent in glazes to improve the adhesive qualities.

3. A glaze ingredient to retard settling and lumping.

CLAY BODY TYPES

A perfect clay body seldom occurs in the natural state. Though earthenwares that can be fired unaltered are quite common, stonewares are less so, and natural porcelains are nonexistent. For that reason the clay bodies used by the professional potter are usually manufactured ones, either by the potter himself or by commercial clay companies.

Earthenware has been the most commonly made type of pottery down through history. The ancient Egyptians were making it well before 2500 B.C. and it remained the most common type of pottery even after the advent of stoneware and porcelain.

Earthenware is commonly made of a naturally occuring clay and fired in the temperature range of 1730° to 2075° F./943° to 1135° C. (cone 08 to 02). Most of it is fired in the 1940° F./1060° C. (cone 04) range. The fired body is non-vitreous, and if left unglazed most bodies are not waterproof due to the porous nature of the clay. This results from the low firing temperature in which the clay particles are not sufficiently compressed to prevent the penetration of liquids into the body proper. The higher the firing the more compressed the particles of clay will be. The porosity of earthenware does have its advantages, however. This allows it to resist thermal shock (a sudden change in temperature) and is thus of value in the production of baking utensils. In practical terms earthenware is also quite adaptable to the forming methods of the potter, whether throwing, casting, or sculpting. It has a pleasant tactual nature and a feeling of lightness unlike the denser forms of stoneware and porcelain, and it is far less brittle. The range of colors possible in earthenware includes warm colors possible in earthenware includes warm grays through reds, yellows, oranges, buffs, browns, and deep browns. When this wide variety of body colors is combined with the brilliant colors made possible with low-fire glazes, earthenware makes an excellent medium for the potter who tends toward esthetic expression in color.

Soft stoneware, or medium-temperature clay bodies, is something of a newcomer in the area of pottery and should be of interest to many potters concerned with the rising cost of firing. It is not a natural body, but a compounded one with a firing range of 2014° to 2165°F./1101° to 1185°C. (cone 03 to 4).

It is a semivitreous type of body that is only slightly less resistant to thermal shock than earthenware. It can be produced in the same variety of colors and the glaze color range is practically as wide as that of the earthenwares. It can also be made quite plastic and workable for any method of forming, and due to its lower maturing temperature it has a lower shrinkage rate than the more vitreous stoneware.

Stoneware clay bodies are fired to the 2200° to 2400°F./1204° to 1315°C. (cone 5 to 11) temperature range to become vitreous and thus waterproof, even when left unglazed. The name of course comes from stoneware's dense, hard, and impervious characteristics, similar to stone. Not all natural clays can be employed to make stoneware bodies. Many of them, particularly the iron-bearing red ones, would melt or seriously deform at temperatures necessary for making stoneware.

These are in nature stoneware clays that are usable for bodies without alteration. They are, however, much less common than those of the earthenware category. Therefore it is often necessary to make additions and alterations to the natural stoneware clay to make it an acceptable and workable medium for the potter.

For a stoneware body to be an acceptable medium for the potter, it should exhibit the qualities of plasticity, minimum possible shrinkage, freedom from scum-forming impurities, vitrification without distortion or deformation,

and acceptable earth colors when fired in an oxidizing or reducing atmosphere. To the novice this might sound impossible. Not true, it is indeed possible as the wares of today's potters give proof.

Porcelain and fine stoneware stand on two sides of a very subtle dividing line. Actually porcelain is a refinement of stoneware. It exhibits the same qualities of hardness, vitrification, and durability, but with the difference that unlike stoneware porcelain can only be made of several selected ingredients. No one single clay found in nature—even a refined one—will make porcelain. It is in actuality a compound of three ingredients: kaolin, feldspar, and silica. When fired to temperatures of above 2300°F./1260°C. (cone 8), it will produce a ware that is white, dense, completely vitrified, and translucent where thin. And though it is made of only three basic ingredients, they must be carefully balanced in such a way that the formed pieces will fire to the very threshold of the melting point without actually melting or even distorting.

By the standards of European porcelain makers, this clay body type must be white, completely vitrified, and translucent where thin. However, the Chinese potters, who developed it, feel that translucency is unnecessary, pure whiteness is not mandatory, and in some cases they will add color to the body to make a glaze more acceptable. They only demand that the porcelain be completely vitrified and ring sharply when struck.

In practice it takes great skill to work with a porcelain body. The three materials of which it is made are very nonplastic. And if enough plastic material is added to make it easily workable on the potter's wheel, it ceases to be porcelain. This is the reason why most porcelain pieces are made by casting or turning, a process which involves cutting away the excess clay until the necessary thinness is achieved to make the ware translucent when fired.

Despite all the problems of working with such a body, there are many fine porcelains being made today by professional potters using hand-forming methods.

2
NATIVE CLAYS: DIGGING YOUR OWN

Clay is deceptive in its simplicity. It is cheap and plentiful, and can be found all around us. It is, geologists tell us, the most abundant material on the face of the earth. Scrape off the topsoil in almost any location and you will find clay of some type. Frequently it can be found already softened by geological forces and moisture, ready for use by the potter.

This is a book for lovers of clay, therefore, it is only natural that a chapter should be devoted to the product in its natural state and how the potter can go about preparing it. I believe that every potter should know how to dig, prepare, and adjust clay, not just for the sake of knowing, but to experience the joy of creating a work from natural clays taken from the earth with his or her own hands. It is deeply rewarding and gives one a "feel" for the clay.

WHY DIG

Clay is one of those few natural materials which has no perceptible value of its own in an undeveloped state, yet it can be transformed into objects of beauty. Clay itself is amorphous and the forms the potter makes are wholly of his own invention, drawing little from the intrinsic form of the clay. Its properties however, while imposing certain limitations, also offer challenge and discipline to the potter. Hand-dug clay provides an extra thrill to the potter who can take immeasurable pride in experiencing the full challenge of forming a work directly from its natural source. Consequently, I am often surprised and irritated to discover that many writers of books on ceramics do not refer to the rewards of working with native clays; and those who do caution that it is hardly worth the effort.

It is, indeed, worth the effort. Not only is native clay cheap and abundant, but it is a rich source of various colors and textures.

Although the two main components of clay, silica and alumina, are fairly uniform from one location to another, it is the organic matter—

roots, decayed or decaying vegetable matter, impurities of trace metals, and alkalies—that varies greatly from location to location. These variations can be of enormous interest and importance to the potter, as they are major factors in enhancing and enriching a piece.

It is absurd to think that clay can or should only be purchased from ceramic suppliers, that complicated equipment and a great deal of effort are needed, or that commercial clays are superior in quality to native clays. Clay is the most abundant of materials, and the dealer's source of clay is the same as that of the prospector— it all comes from the earth. And while it is true that most commercial clays will tolerate a much higher firing, it is also true that the user of native clays can adjust them to do the same, for the higher-firing clay is only the result of simple chemical adjustments to the clay body, a process the potter can do for himself if he so desires. Any potter who is earnestly interested in broadening his outlook should have the practical experience of finding, digging, and using a native clay. Although this experience may have no commercial significance, it is certain to give the potter new insights in dealing with the medium.

WHERE TO LOOK

The presence of clay in nature is so common that finding deposits of it is quite easy in most any location, provided one knows how and where to look. Usually any farmer or road-builder can tell you where clay can be found. Another good prospect is to look in a place that has been excavated or where a stream or other natural occurrence has cut into the land. These areas are good prospects because clay is usually covered with loam and/or topsoil which conceals it from immediate view. Perhaps the most simple method of prospecting for clay is to drive slowly along the highway, observing the terrain and watching for road cuts and outcroppings in the landscape. Surface clays may be recognized by their irregular and hexangular cracking patterns and their rather crumbly surface, produced by the slaking properties of the clay when exposed to the elements. Once these patterns are known they become obvious and clays can be easily located.

WHAT TO LOOK FOR

Look for strongly developed patterns. These indicate the more useful clays. Weaker cracking patterns indicate the presence of soils and sand contamination. Another characteristic to look for is the presence of wavelike contours in the landscape. These undulating outlines are the result of weathering of the clay; only clay will weather in this particular fashion.

SPOT TESTING: IS IT CLAY?

If you suspect that an outcropping is usable clay, closer inspection for the cracking patterns and crumbly surface plus a few simple tests will quickly determine whether your prospecting has borne fruit. Once a likely spot has been found it should be given the simple "feel test." From a small sample that appears to be pure, form a ball of clay in the palm of your hand. If the sample, when moistened, adheres and forms a sticky and somewhat slimy ball, moisten the sample further and rub a bit of it between the thumb and forefinger. If it feels very slick and somewhat soapy, then the prospector can be fairly certain the deposit is usable clay. If the test sample refuses to adhere into a ball and remains crumbly and nonplastic, the deposit is not usable clay.

Clay in the larger deposits usually bears a close resemblance to soft rock. Often it has been deposited by geological forces in layers. If this is the case, the best place to obtain a sample is where the rock shapes seem to be most concentrated. When the sample is taken it should exhibit the same characteristics as those given above.

TESTING FOR IMPURITIES

When some clay has been located, the next step is to determine whether the clay is contaminated with soluble impurities. The presence of such impurities can usually be detected by scum or white staining on the clay. This can generally be noticed at the base of the contours or walls of the deposit. Failing this, a small sample can be moistened and allowed to dry. If the presence of scum or white discoloration is noticed on the surface, then soluble impurities are present and will render the deposit less useful, since the clay will be less susceptible to adjustment for firing

temperature, shrinkage, aging, and body color. Such alkaline clays can be corrected, however, without too much difficulty. Since alkalies are soluble in water, one need only wash the clay by mixing it after drying with an excess of water, letting it set for a day or two to allow the soluble impurities to dissolve into suspension, and decanting the excess water. This can be done numerous times to remove the maximum amount of solubles, but once or twice should be sufficient. You can usually determine when most of the impurities have been removed when the white scum no longer forms on the top of the water.

TESTING FOR LIME CONTENT

While the presence of alkalies in clay can be tolerated the presence of lime cannot, for when such clay is fired lime turns to calcium oxide which will absorb water, expand inside the pot, and cause it to crack, flake, or chip. A simple test to reveal if lime is present is to drop a small marble-sized sample into a 25% to 50% solution of hydrochloric acid (*Important:* This is a potentially dangerous chemical and should be used with caution.) If lime impurities are present effervescence or bubbling will take place. If the effervescence is minimal the clay may be usable in higher-fired bodies above cone 4.

GRANULAR IMPURITIES

Even if the deposit of clay is not rendered useless by a pronounced contamination of lime, it may be difficult to use if granular materials such as sand and rock fragments in large amounts are present. These of course can be screened from the clay, but this only necessitates an extra step in refining the clay for use.

If the only granular material is sand, and it is not present in amounts above 25%, the clay may be used for handbuilt work provided it is screened to remove the larger granules. The sand content will act as a grog additive to promote better drying and strength in large or thick pieces. To test for usefulness form a ball in your hand to make sure it adheres properly. Be certain that the granules are sand, for if they are not of silica content they may cause cracking or explosions during firing of the ware.

TESTING FOR ORGANIC IMPURITIES

Some clay deposits may also be impractical due to the presence of decayed organic matter. While this does not disqualify such clay for use, it can cause excessive shrinkage and adjustment problems, particularly if the clay is not aged for a prolonged period. (Aging will be discussed at the end of this chapter.) Such clays are usually very sticky and quite dark in color, ranging from dark browns through greens to black. Consequently it is advisable for the beginning prospector to avoid them at first.

TESTING COLORS OF NATIVE CLAYS

In the natural state clays range greatly in color. They may be gray, tan, red, brown, greenish, pink, brown, brown-black, black, and white. One may even find marbleized deposits of two or three of these colors. In any case, colors in natural clay almost always indicate the presence of iron or decayed organic matter, which will usually fire to tan, brown, red, rust, or dark brown, depending on the amount of iron present and whether other trace metal impurities are present. Usually the iron content is 2% to 5%. Those clays with darker colors will usually mature at a lower temperature requiring adjustment if higher firing is desired. If the deposit of clay is lighter or even white in color, it will withstand a higher firing temperature than the darker clays, particularly the dark earth red ones. It will, however, be less workable and much less plastic—an important point to consider. The beginning prospector should probably avoid the lighter clays at first, until more experience in handling native clays has been achieved. Consequently the medium-colored earth clays are probably best for the beginner—those ranging in color from tans to red-browns.

TESTING FOR PLASTICITY

The amount of plasticity in clay can be determined by rolling a moistened sample into a pencil-sized rope and coiling it around a finger. If in the coiling process the rope shows little or no sign of cracking, the clay can be considered plastic and thus quite workable. If cracking to a medium degree does take place, do not despair, plasticity can be improved by the addition of those darker sticky clays or by aging. Extreme stickiness in clay is also an indication of plasticity.

TAKING SAMPLES

When prospecting for clays, it is advisable to have several containers available to collect enough samples to make the expedition worthwhile; heavy plastic bags will also work for this purpose. A small shovel, pickax, and notebook for recording sample locations are useful also. But remember the testing procedure, summarized below, should be done successfully before any clay is transported to the studio:

1. The "feel test."

2. The test for soluble impurities.

3. The test for sand and rock fragments.

4. The test for lime contamination.

5. The test for plasticity and workability.

With the accumulated data derived from these tests, together with the experience gained from working samples of native clay by handbuilding or on the potter's wheel, the potter will be in a more informed position to estimate the value and usefulness of the clay.

PREPARING THE CLAY

No involved or complicated procedures are required in preparing native clay for use by the potter. As a natural material it is fundamentally prepared by the geological forces of nature itself and needs only to be mixed with the right amount of water and cleaned of foreign matter such as sand and rock fragments. I have on several occasions discovered a deposit so pure that it required only the addition of water to be made workable. However, it is generally advisable to follow the step-by-step procedure that follows until the prospector has had enough experience to determine whether clays need to go through the complete process of refinement:

PROCESSING STEP-BY-STEP

1. All clays should be allowed to dry completely before processing begins. This generally takes one to two weeks.

2. Remove manually the more visible rock fragments, roots, twigs, or leaves from the clay.

3. Using a hammer or mallet, break the larger lumps into smaller pieces. None should be larger than a baseball. Although some potters urge breaking the lumps into much smaller pieces, it is not really necessary, for the clay, if completely dry, will crumble to its finest particles due to the expansion which takes place when the water is being absorbed by the clay.

4. Place the dry clay in large plastic containers and cover it completely with water. Do not use metal containers for sooner or later they will oxidize and contaminate the clay. Allow the mixture to soak overnight to break down the lumps. If the clay is very fine in particle size, this step may take two days or more. It may also be necessary to add more water to the containers.

5. When the clay has soaked enough to break down all the lumps, stir it thoroughly until it reaches the creamlike consistency called slip, adding more water if necessary. This can be done manually or by any type of mixing machine.

I dump the entire softened contents of the containers into an old wringer-type washing machine and add water while agitating mechanism of the machine does the work for me.

6. When the clay has been worked to a cream-like slip, it should be poured through a sieve to remove the larger sand and pebbles—an ordinary kitchen sieve will do. The finer particles of sand will not harm the clay's usefulness. In fact they act as grog in the clay to retard cracking and shrinkage during drying and firing.

7. After sieving the slip can be allowed to stand and settle overnight. The next day the excess water on top of the clay is decanted and the thickened slip can be poured on plaster bats to remove the excess moisture. There is no magic number of minutes or hours to leave the clay on the bats. This will depend upon the amount of humidity in your area and how often you use the plaster bats for drying clay (the more you use them, the more moisture they will retain and the slower the clay will dry).

8. When the clay has been dried by the plaster bats to the point where it can be removed without sticking and remaining on the fingers, it is ready for wedging.

9. Wedging the clay on a plaster or a canvas-covered wedging board will remove more of the moisture. It will also improve the workability of the clay. If the clay is to be used for modeling, sculpting, or coiling it need not be heavily wedged. But if it is to be used for throwing on the wheel more intensive wedging is necessary.

10. At this point the potter must decide if the clay is plastic enough to be used immediately. No one else can do this for you. As you gain in skill and experience you will know by feel whether the clay is ready for throwing. If in the beginning you are not sure, put the clay aside in an airtight container to age at least two to three weeks. Aging always improves the plasticity and quality of clay. The proper procedure for aging is given in detail at the end of this chapter.

11. If you are fortunate enough to own a pug mill steps 3 through 10 can be omitted. Simply follow the same procedure for processing as those for milling and mixing commercial clays. Greater care however must be taken to remove the more obvious pieces of foreign matter discussed in step 2.

When you have completed the previous steps, you should have a workable clay which you can use immediately if you wish. It would be wise, however, to test the clay further to determine its possibilities during firing and whether adjustments to the clay body will be necessary.

SIMPLE TEST FIRING

Should you be impatient to test the clay, you must be cautious initially not to fire the sample piece above cone 04. Although I have found clays that would withstand a firing of cone 8 without adjustments, the beginning prospector cannot always expect to be that fortunate. There are two simple tests which can be employed to determine what temperature the fired clay will withstand:

1. Drop a few drops of water on the surface of the cone 04 bisque-fired pot. If the water is readily absorbed it is probable that the piece will withstand a higher firing.

2. With a sharp metal object, give the bisque-fired pot a scratch test. This is usually done on the bottom of the piece to avoid marring the surface. If the piece scratches easily with a minimum of pressure, underfiring is again indicated.

If both tests are affirmative, fire the pot to a higher temperature. I recommend one cone higher. When this has been done repeat the above tests. If they are again positive, fire the pot one cone higher still and test again. This procedure can be followed until the tests are negative or the pot shows signs of warping, distortion, or bloating. When the pot has been fired to the point where absorption is minimal and scratching is difficult, it is certain that the maturing point of the clay has been reached and possibly passed by one cone. This rather "hit or miss" method will reveal the maturing point and fired colors of the clay, but it will not give an accurate measure of the percentage of shrinkage that takes place during drying and firing.

ACCURATE TESTING

The most acceptable method for complete and accurate testing of clay bodies is as follows:

1. Using a rolling pin or similar round object, roll the clay into a slab about ½" (1.3 cm) thick.

2. With a ruler for measuring, cut several strips of clay 1" (2.5 cm) wide and 10" (25 cm) long. If several clay types are to be tested at one time, label the samples by scratching the surface with a pencil to indicate which sample is which. Also label each set with the cone number at which they are to be fired. Start with cone 04 and label successive sets cone 02, cone 1, cone 2, cone 3, cone 4, cone 5, cone 6, etc.

3. Lay the precut strips or test bars aside to dry completely for at least two days.

4. Lay the bars of clay gently across two kiln

posts with the middle of the bars unsupported and fire the first test set of bars to cone 04.

5. After firing, check the test bars carefully for the following points: Did slumping occur in the middle of the bars where they were unsupported? If so, the maturing temperature has been reached and passed by one cone. If no slumping has occurred, higher firing tests are indicated. Employ the absorption and scratch test. Carefully measure the fired test bars to determine the percentage of shrinkage. If, for example, the bars measure 9'' (22.5 cm) after firing, the bars have shrunk 1'' (2.5 cm) thus indicating that the clay has a drying and firing shrinkage of 10%; 8 1/2'' (21.6 cm) would indicate 15%, etc. Carefully note the color of the test bars. After having studied these results, lay the bars aside for future reference.

6. If the results from step 5 indicate that the maturing point of the clay has not been achieved, repeat the test using the test set of clay bars labeled cone 02, studying and recording the results after each firing test. It is unlikely, unless you have been lucky in your prospecting, that your tests will have to go past the cone 2 or cone 4 range. For this is well within the range at which most native earthenware bodies mature.

7. Do not trust any of these results to memory, write them down in a notebook to record your tests from the very beginning of your experiments to the finish, for without accurate records you may not be able to repeat the process of locating and reclaiming a particular clay that has pleased you.

8. After each test firing, carefully examine the test bars for the points indicated in step 5 saving the test bars for future reference as to shrinkage, color, maturing temperature, etc. You will find that you will be pleased with some of the sample bodies and will want to gather more of those particular clays. If you have kept accurate records there will be no problem in reproducing the clays for further use in the studio. Do not be discouraged if some of the samples did not perform well—clays can be adjusted to do what you want them to do within those limitations imposed by the very nature of the clay itself.

ADJUSTING AND IMPROVING CLAY

Once the native clay has been tested to determine its good properties and its defects, the potter is in a more educated position to make any adjustments which may be necessary, and in practice it is generally necessary to undertake some improvements to make the clay better serve the needs of good forming techniques and firing. In the science of adjusting clays, there are generally five areas in which clays are adjusted: color, texture, plasticity, shrinkage, and maturing temperature. Following are the ways in which these adjustments may be made.

Color changes may be made in the shade of clay. To change the color of a particular clay, minute amounts of coloring oxides may be added. A chart of the percentages needed will be found in Chapter 12 on Coloring Clay bodies. Listed below are the steps for changing body colors of natural clays.

1. To darken native clay, the coloring oxides of iron, manganese, rutile, ilmenite, or nickel are more suitable to native clays. Cobalt oxide in amounts of .5% can be used with any of the above colorants to give more subtle hues. The percentages of any coloring oxide are minute. Therefore, Chapter 12 on Coloring Clay Bodies should be consulted before proceeding with color changes.

2. To lighten colors of clay bodies, add lighter colors of clay, usually ball clays or white-burning clays. These can be used in percentages up to 24%.

Texture alteration is often more desirable than altering the color, and unlike the latter is far simpler to do.

1. The addition of aggregates—the most common being grog or sand—will produce a rougher texture. For large sculptured pieces having walls thicker than 1'' (2.5 cm), the addition of coarse grog or sand is mandatory to prevent cracking, warping, or even explosions in improperly dried pieces. Although 20% to 30% additions are best, additions up to 40% are not uncommon; for wheel work, add finer grog or sand of approximately 60 to 80 mesh in amounts not exceeding 10%. The subject of texture will be discussed at greater length in Chapter 12 on Coloring Clay Bodies.

2. A smoother texture in a clay body can be produced by screening the clay through a fine mesh sieve while in the slip state.

Plasticity is not an uncommon feature in native clays. However, plasticity can be improved in the following ways:

1. The addition of a more plastic clay high in organic matter in percentages up to 50% is the most obvious method of improving plasticity. This, however, can cause undue shrinkage during drying and firing.

2. Adding 2% bentonite by dry body weight will also increase plasticity. Bentonite, an extremely plastic clay formed by decomposed volcanic ash and glass, is often used by commercial clay plants for this purpose.

3. Perhaps the most common and practical way to achieve plasticity is to add 5% to 20% ball clay, but this too can cause shrinkage.

4. Bentonite and ball clay can be combined although the bentonite portion should not rise above 2% and the entire combination of additives should not exceed 25%.

5. The most time-honored method of increasing the plasticity of a clay body is aging, which will be discussed in greater detail toward the end of this chapter.

Shrinkage is one of the major problems the user of native clays may encounter. The only way to handle this problem is in the addition of more nonplastic materials to the clay body.

1. The method most often used today is to add grog in percentages up to 10% to 30%. This method is preferable because it reduces the plasticity of the clay less than other methods.

2. A less useful method is to increase the silica, kaolin, or fire clay in amounts up to 20%, either separately or in combination.

Raising or lowering the maturing temperature of the clay body is the final area of adjustment which the user of native clays may find desirable. This, too, is fairly simple to achieve.

1. The most desirable way to raise the maturing point of a clay body is to add up to 20% of a good ball clay, fire clay, or stoneware clay. The main advantage of using ball clay for this purpose is that it will not destroy the plasticity and workability of the clay. It will, however, increase the shrinkage of the fired piece to a small degree. The potter can get around part of this problem of shrinkage of the ball clay by calcining about half of the amount that is to be added to the clay.

2. Adding a good stoneware clay to the body in amounts up to 25% has the advantage of raising the maturing point without increasing the shrinkage. In some cases, this addition will actually aid in retarding shrinkage if the stoneware clay is top quality—Jordan clay or Monmouth clay is a good additive here.

3. Combining all five of the additives mentioned above is another possibility. An example of such a combination is stoneware, 6%; ball clay, 7%; silica, 3%; kaolin, 2%; fire clay, 2%.

THE AGING OF CLAY

To the uninitiated, the aging of clays may seem more like a medieval superstition than a practical method of improving the plasticity and workability of clay. Such is not the case. It is an accepted fact among "organic potters" and those who know the history of pottery that one of the most important adjustments that will increase the overall workability of freshly prepared native clays—in fact any clay—is the process of aging the clay body itself.

Potters and ancient craftsmen often aged their clay for months, perhaps even years; this was the only known method to improve the malleable qualities of clay. In the Orient, it is written, the aging of clay sometimes took a generation or more, with Chinese potters storing clay for their grandchildren and using clay which was probably prepared for them by their grandparents.

The importance of aging cannot be overemphasized, even though this process is grossly ignored by many potters and professional studios. Although the subtle quality of plasticity cannot be measured exactly, it is true that clay, like a good wine, improves with age, sometimes dramatically so. Any potter who has employed this practice can readily tell the difference by that certain feeling.

Moisturizing the clay is one method of aging. Since clays are already ancient beyond reckoning, having lain in the earth for eons, how can it be that further aging will improve the working qualities of the clay? The primary reason for this overall improvement of plasticity and workability during studio aging is that over a period of time a more thorough wetting of the clay particles takes place under controlled conditions, whereas in nature the conditions are not constant. The complete moisturizing of clay is something that cannot easily be rushed for it takes time for water to reach and permeate each individual particle of clay. It should be pointed out, however, that this moisturizing does not require generations. A significant difference is noticable in even two weeks. Mixing the new clay well with a liberal amount of water will speed up the process to a degree. And new clays which have first been put to the slip state then stiffened to the plastic stage on plaster bats will mature more quickly that those which have been mixed with only enough water to make them workable.

Bacterial growth is another outcome of aging clay. Moist clay is a very good culture medium for the growth of bacteria, especially if it is kept damp and warm. If this growth is allowed to take place the bacterial action within the clay will produce acid residues and gel-like substances which affect the clay in a favorable manner. Bacterial aging can be promoted in new batches of clay by adding and thoroughly mixing and wedging some old clay which has aged, or even scraps that have been lying around, provided they are in the moist state. Even placing new clays in containers which have the remains of some older clay will help the "working" process to get started more quickly. Covering or wrapping the new clay with old cloths or towels that have been around older clay will help also.

Some potters, working on the theory that a little acid residue is a step in the right direction, add a bit of vinegar or citric acid. Others have been known to add organic materials or small amounts of starch to aid bacterial growth. Some potters dissolve a small amount of soap in the water which is used for wetting the clay.

AGING AND WEDGING STEP-BY-STEP

Each potter will, over the years, evolve his own particular method for handling the aging process. Provided the clay is supplied with enough water and not allowed to dry out, the moisturizing process will take care of itself, if the clay balls are thoroughly wedged and aged. Since I am a thorough believer in the aging of clay, especially native clays, I have developed my own method which works very well for me, unorthodox though it may seem. For those potters who want to work with native clays, it is presented below.

1. To make sure that sufficient bacteria is present to break down the organic materials naturally inherent in native clays, I often add some old clay which has been aged and mix it thoroughly with the new clay. This will introduce a good strain of the aging bacteria into the new clay and thus get the working of the clay started much sooner.

2. If no aged clay is available, bacteria of the type needed can be supplied by dissolving compost bacterial tablets, of the type used by organic gardeners, in the water which is used for wetting the clay in the first step of preparation. These tablets can be found at any nursery or plant store. If these are not obtainable, or if the potter wishes to use more natural methods, bacteria can be obtained as follows: Obtain a small quantity of humus, rotten wood, or any organic material which has decayed or become partially decayed. Soak this material in warm water for an hour or so. Then strain the water to remove the organic material. Finally add this "bacteria water" to the tap water you are using to soak the new clay.

3. To aid the growth of bacteria in producing the acid residues and gels which lead to greater plasticity, add a cup or so of powdered starch or any other fine-grained carbohydrate material.

4. Allow this mixture of new clay to soak overnight, as the instructions in Chapter 3 on Clay Body Preparation direct, decant the excess water, and prepare the clay to a workable state using the plaster bats.

5. At this point the clay should be thoroughly wedged, for to age effectively, one must always remember that clay will age well only if it has first been properly and thoroughly wedged. Clay begins to come alive on the wedging board. This is accomplished by repeatedly cutting the clay in two and slamming the pieces forcefully on top of one another. This action is used to thoroughly mix the various components of the clay and remove any air pockets in the clay. You can alternately knead the clay thoroughly to accomplish this wedging process.

6. Once the wedging is completed the clay should be shaped into balls about 5" to 6" (13 to 15 cm) in diameter, wrapped in old damp cloth, and stored in a place where they will remain moist. A good storage place is in a plastic bag in a lidded garbage can or in a large plastic container.

7. Check the stored clay every day or two to make sure it remains moist. If drying is discernible, moisten the cloths again.

8. Allow the stored clay to age for at least two weeks, a month or even more if possible.

9. The mellowing and ripening of the clay is signaled by a rich musty scent arising from the place of storage. This perfume which seems to speak of the cool dark bowels of the earth signals that the clay is ready.

10. Unwrap a ball of the aged clay and work it in your hands. The improvement in plasticity and workability is immediately and unmistakably noticeable. After a second spiral wedging, or kneading, the clay is ready for use.

11. The potter should always remember and take into consideration that clays vary from location to location. Consequently, methods that work well for one potter and the local native clays of one area may not work as well for another. Therefore, one must experiment; if a particular step in the above process does not work well for you, discard it and try another method.

If the steps outlined in this chapter on finding, preparing, and using native clays are followed, there is no reason why anyone cannot be successful. A word of caution though, do not go into this experiment expecting it to be a "cinch." It is not. It takes time, devotion, effort, and a curious nature on the part of the potter. The rewards to be found, however, are well worth the effort.

3
CLAY BODY PREPARATION

The preparation of a clay body from scratch is a skill in itself. Although there are commercial clay suppliers who sell excellent prepared clays in ready-to-use form, it is important for the potter to know how to mix his own, either from prepared commercial clays in powder form or from the basic ingredients. From the standpoint of cost, it is usually cheaper for the professional potter to mix his own clay body from the dry powdered ingredients for a number of reasons: the freight costs are less on dry ingredients because you aren't paying for all that water, the ingredients are always cheaper if bought in large bulk amounts, and the potter can make up a clay that is suited exactly to his needs.

CHOOSING A CLAY BODY

The process of clay body preparation must begin with a decision as to the type of clay the potter desires and the forming method he plans to use. For within any clay body type there are the further categories of throwing clay bodies, casting clay bodies, and sculpture clay bodies. With the exception of casting clays which are liquid in form, they are all mixed in much the same manner.

In the mixing of a clay body one must generally start with the clays that are available to the potter in his area at a reasonable price, have no major faults, and are reasonably plastic. A clay which does not possess this quality of workability should not be seriously considered, for plasticity is the prime quality of any throwing or sculpture clay. When purchasing a commercially prepared throwing or sculpture clay in powder form, the potter need not worry about plasticity, for most commercial clays are well balanced in this respect. But for the potter who is mixing his own, clay body plasticity must be a prime concern.

Plasticity of any clay body can be improved by the addition of a good ball clay or bentonite or by the process of wedging and aging as discussed in Chapter 2. In some rare cases a clay may be so plastic and fine in particle size that it will not dry uniformly or easily without cracking. In such cases a nonplastic coarser material must be added to "open up" the clay so it will dry properly. Such materials as fine sand, grog, or a less plastic clay can be used for this purpose. Usually a 10% addition by dry body weight will suffice. Even a combination of all these openers can be used if the total combination does not exceed 10%. The openers also strengthen the clay so it will hold its shape better as it is worked.

Fluxes aid the clay body in fusing or melting at the desired maturing temperature. If the clay body lacks the proper melting properties for a certain temperature, fluxing agents can be added in the form of talc, alkalies, dolomite, nepheline syenite, feldspars, and at higher temperatures, whiting. If a deeper color is desirable, iron oxide may be used. Even lower-firing clays may be used and are usually more economical. They have the added advantage of not altering the plasticity of the original clay.

Alternately there may be occasions when the clay may be overendowed with fluxes, causing the body to bloat or deform at the desired temperature. In this case, compounds which are more refractory must be added such as clays high in aluminum and silica, kaolin, or better still a plastic fire clay with a high maturing point.

MIXING

There are three main methods for mixing clay: pug milling, soaking, or the slip method. All three are thorough and will produce a good clay mix, but of the three the first involves less work and is probably the best. The following formula for a stoneware body will be used to illustrate all three examples of mixing.

Jordan clay	50%
Redart clay	25%
Plastic fire clay	25%

The pug mill owner is indeed fortunate for this clay-mixing machine reduces the work to a minimum. In general the steps taken to mix a clay body with a pug mill are as follows.

1. Place 4 parts Jordan clay, 2 parts Redart clay, and 2 parts plastic fire clay in the mill hopper.

2. Pour water in the amount of 1/3 of the total dry body weight of the ingredients into the hopper. For example, if you have 50 lbs. (21 kg) of ingredients in the mill, you will need 16 2/3 lbs. (7 kg) of water.

3. Turn on the pug mill and the machine will do the rest.

4. If the material extruded from the mill is too dry, throw it back into the hopper and add a bit more water. This can be repeated until the clay reaches the right consistency.

5. If the clay extruded from the mill is too wet, throw it back into the hopper and add more dry material, making sure the ingredients you add are in the 4:2:2 ratio.

6. When the mill at last extrudes a clay of the proper consistency, it is ready for use without further mixing or wedging.

The soaking method involves more work but no complicated and expensive equipment is necessary. In general the steps taken to mix clay by the soaking method are as follows.

1. Obtain a large, durable plastic trash can.

2. Place the can where you want to store the clay while it is soaking for it will be quite heavy when full and you may not be able to move it.

3. Fill the can 2/3 full of water.

4. Add a cup of vinegar, organic compost agent, or some old clay to the water and mix it thoroughly with the water. This will encourage the growth of bacteria to help age the clay for greater plasticity and workability as mentioned in Chapter 2.

5. Using a large basin (a large plastic dishpan will do) premix in dry form 5 lbs. (2 kg) of Jordan clay, 2 1/2 lbs. (1 kg) of Redart clay, and 2 1/2 lbs. (1 kg) of plastic fire clay.

6. Gently sift or sprinkle the premixed dry clay on top of the water.

7. Continue adding more of the dry ingredients until the water stops absorbing the clay. Premix more dry material as you use it.

8. Cover the can with a cloth to keep out foreign matter.

9. Allow the mixture to soak for two weeks for the clay to become completely saturated with water.

10. At the end of the soaking period, remove any excess water by dipping or with a syphon.

11. If the clay is very wet and sticky, allow it to dry for a few days in the can.

12. Place the wet clay on plaster bats to remove the excess moisture. The drying time will vary depending upon the amount of clay, the temperature and humidity level.

13. Test the clay occasionally by manipulation. When it no longer sticks to the fingers or the bats it is ready. Usually a 5 lb. (2 kg) lump of clay will dry on the bats in 30 minutes to an hour.

14. Wedge the clay thoroughly as described in Chapter 2.

15. If the clay is not sufficiently plastic or workable it can be aged in the manner described in Chapter 2.

The slip method of mixing clay is closely akin to the soaking method. It is basically the same method used for preparing native clays mentioned in Chapter 2. In general the steps taken to mix clay by this method are as follows.

1. Follow steps 1 through 6 of the instructions for mixing clay by the soaking method.

2. Allow the clay and water to set for a few hours then stir thoroughly to obtain a thick creamy slip.

3. Allow the slip to set for a week or so to allow the bacteria to work on the organic content of the clay. This growth usually takes place much faster in a liquid clay than in a denser mix.

4. Dip or syphon off the excess water from the top of the can.

5. Pour the liquid slip on plaster bats to dry. This will usually take longer than for the denser clay due to the increased amount of water in the slip.

6. When the clay will pull loose from the bats without sticking it is ready to be wedged.

7. Wedge the clay in the manner described in Chapter 2.

8. Test the clay for plasticity. If it is plastic and easily workable it can be used at once. If more plasticity is desired, put the clay away in a damp place to age in the manner described in Chapter 2.

NORTHEAST NEBRASKA TECHNICAL COMMUNITY COLLEGE·LIBRARY

FORMULATING CLAYS FOR SPECIFIC USES

Usually the potter has a particular forming technique for which he wants to use a clay body. Following are three types of clay bodies and their basic characteristics.

A throwing clay body must above all have excellent workability. While it is possible to throw simple objects of coarse nonplastic clays, the potter will be severely limited to shapes that are short and thick. The complete range of possible shapes open to the skilled potter demands a clay body which is highly plastic, dense, cohesive, and formulated with enough coarse material such as sand or grog to give the body strength to hold its shape during the forming process on the wheel. The drawback of such a clay is its high rate of shrinkage.

Due to this demand for plasticity, throwing bodies are made with as little nonplastic content as possible. Materials such as the feldspars, kaolins, and silicas are held to a minimum. The main ingredients are natural stoneware clay, fire clays, and ball clays. The latter, however, should never be used in amounts exceeding 30% lest shrinkage become excessive and drying become a problem.

To enable the clay to hold its shape, 80-mesh grog is added in amounts not exceeding 10%. Larger amounts cause the clay to soak up water too readily during the forming on the wheel, and cuts down on the plasticity of the clay body.

Despite the skill of the potter, only so large and tall a pot can be thrown at one time with any given clay. For each clay body will in time reach the point where the stresses of weight and pull will cause the pot to slump. That is why the potter must be concerned with the composition of the clay body. It is vital to have a clay body that will allow the potter to use his skills to the fullest. Once the potter has found and become dependent on its strength, he may find it impossible to work well with any other clay body. Very often, beginning students of throwing will struggle fruitlessly with a clay that a professional would find impossible to use, and in their lack of knowledge of clays will needlessly blame themselves for their failures rather than the medium. To find the right clay body for throwing is all important. The clay throwing bodies discussed in Chapters 5 through 8 were designed with this in mind and the potter who concentrates on throwing should be able to find one that will amply fit his needs.

Mixing throwing bodies can be done by any of the three methods mentioned previously in this chapter. Although pug milling is the superior method due to its thoroughness, the soak method or slip method will work well provided the clay is thoroughly mixed and wedged, especially the latter.

A casting clay body designed for use with molds, like that of throwing clays, must be designed for the purpose it is to serve. Unlike throwing bodies, however, plasticity is not a prime concern. Such a body requires the liquid suspension of clay in water. This mixture must flow readily and smoothly and remain in suspension without settling either in the mold or in storage. It must be designed with only enough shrinkage to allow it to pull itself free of the mold without sticking and to dry without excessive warpage or cracking. The casting body recipes to be found in Chapters 5 through 8 were designed with all these considerations in mind.

For mixing let us assume for the purpose of illustration that the potter is working in 100 lb. (45 kg) lots of clay. The dry ingredients would then total 100 lbs. (45 kg) before any water is added. To this amount of dry clay ingredients the potter must add 40 lbs. (18 kg) of water to make a slip of the proper consistency for casting.

Weigh out the dry ingredients and place them in a large plastic container where they can be premixed in dry form. Set these aside for a moment while the water is prepared.

Into a large plastic trash can that is very durable, pour 40 lbs. (18 kg) of water. Into the water add a deflocculant; usually sodium carbonate or sodium silicate is employed. The deflocculant increases fluidity and helps particle suspension in the slip. According to our imaginary recipe for the slip the potter will need 4.8 oz. (135 gr) of this material. Weigh this amount of sodium carbonate out on the scale and add it to the water, then stir the mixture with a paddle, the hand, or an electric rotary mixer of some type while adding the dry ingredients. Once all the dry ingredients have been added to the water let the mixture set for about 4 hours. This will give the mixture time for the water to reach and be absorbed by the clay particles. At the end of the waiting period, stir the mixture until it is smooth and free of any lumps. This is best done with an electric rotary mixer of some type. A paint-mixing attachment for an electric drill will work quite well for amounts not exceeding 100 lbs. After this final mixing, allow the mixture to set overnight—it improves greatly with a little aging. If all the above procedures have been done thoroughly in the right order the potter should be able to produce an excellent casting slip to fit any of his needs with any category of working clay: earthenware, soft stoneware, stoneware, or porcelain.

Sculpture clay bodies are relatively simple to formulate. This body requires plasticity, though not as much as throwing clays, tooth to give it strength to stand alone, and openess to allow it to dry rapidly and thoroughly without cracking or warping. The answer to all these demands is grog. Additions of 20% to 30% may be used in preparing such clays. Even sand in amounts up to 10% can be used. The grog may be anywhere from fine to coarse depending upon the texture the potter wishes the clay to have.

In making lighter-weight sculpture clays where weight of the final piece may be a problem, fine-grained organic material may be added to the clay to reduce the weight of the clay. Materials such as coffee grounds and sawdust can be used for this purpose. During the firing these organic materials burn out leaving a lighter-weight clay. Additions of up to 15% are possible.

All the clay body recipes for sculpture clay bodies in Chapters 5 through 8 should serve well for any type of modeling or sculpture work.

For mixing sculpture bodies use any of the three mixing methods previously outlined in this chapter. Here again the pug milling method is better because it is less work and much more thorough. The other two methods, however, will work too if they are done properly and the clay is thoroughly mixed, wedged, and aged.

These latter two processes cannot be over stressed for a sculpture body. For more information on wedging and aging consult Chapter 2 on Native Clays.

TESTING, ADJUSTING, AND IMPROVING

In the event the potter wishes to test, adjust, or improve one of these clay types for plasticity, color, firing temperature, shrinkage, texture, warping, or cracking Chapter 2 on Native Clay Bodies may be consulted, for the basic procedures are the same for testing and changing these types of clay as they are for native clays. Consult especially the sections on Accurate Testing, Adjusting and Improving Clays, and The Aging of Clays. Chapter 1 on Clays may also be useful and Chapter 13 on Clay Body Defects should be consulted to help the potter to correct any major body defects.

4
DATA ON CLAY BODY FORMULAS

There are in the world of pottery many professional potters who have neither the time nor the desire to dig and process their own clay. There are also potters who do not care to use the commercially prepared clays, especially in ready-to-use wet form, due to cost, dislike of available colors, or unsuitable preparation. Still others do not care to wrestle with the complex mathematical and chemical problems involved in formulating a clay body. And finally there is the potter who wants a clay body that is exclusively his. In the following chapters which contain clay body formulas there is a clay body recipe to fit every need, whatever it may be, in the temperature range desired.

CLAY BODY RATING SCALE

All the clay bodies in Chapters 5 through 11 were tested in the studio with the following questions in mind.

1. What was the degree of plasticity of the clay body?

2. What was the proper firing temperature for maturity of the clay body?

3. Did cracking or distortion of the clay body take place at maturity of the body?

4. What were the colors of the body when fired to maturity, oxidation and/or reduction?

5. Did the clay body have a good surface quality at maturity?

6. What was the percentage of shrinkage?

7. Did the glaze fuse with the clay body?

8. Did the clay body hold the glaze without crawling?

9. Did the glaze retain a smooth surface quality?

10. Did the clay body alter the semi-opaque quality of the glaze?

From the above tests, five categories of ratings were derived for each clay body: temperature range, shrinkage, plasticity, glaze rating, and color.

The temperature range which was considered best suited to a particular clay body gave the proper balance of these qualities: body maturity without cracking or distortion; minimum porosity; and minimum shrinkage. For the convenience of the potter, the body maturity temperature will be listed both in the glaze title and in the fired results for each body. Temperature levels are indicated by Orton Standard pyrometric cones.

The shrinkage rating is based on the amount of shrinkage of the clay body from the wet forming stage to the fired finished stage. The percentage of shrinkage is given for each clay body.

The plasticity of each clay body was tested thoroughly in the studio and is based on a 0–12 rating scale. In the formulas it is given for each clay body immediately after the shrinkage rating. The code for the rating scale is given below:

12. Too plastic—clay would be too sticky to handle and drying and firing would be a problem, resulting in much cracking and warping of the ware.

10. Very plastic—excellent for wheel work.

8. Plastic—adequate for wheel work for smaller pieces, larger pieces if grog is added in 10% amounts, excellent for sculpture and coil building.

6. Adequate plasticity—good for sculpture and coil building, good for slab work.

4. Semiplastic—cracking takes place in coil building, adequate for sculpture and slab work.

2. Nonplastic—cracks easily and tends to crumble with any type of forming method except press molds.

0. Unusable for any type of pottery forming.

GLAZE RATING SCALE

The glaze rating scale was based on a test in which a semi-opaque glaze was placed over the clay body then checked for the following points:

1. Did the body hold the glaze without crawling?

2. Did the glaze fuse to the body at maturity?

3. Did the body promote crazing, shivering, or blistering? (see Glossary)

4. Did the clay color bleed through the glaze during firing?

5. Did the glaze retain its smooth surface quality?

The information from the above tests was then put into a glaze rating scale of 0–12 which is explained below.

12. Perfect—body holds the glaze without crawling, proper fusion takes place without cracking or blistering, and glaze surface remains smooth.

10. Nearly perfect—some slight crazing takes place.

8. A few cracks and/or bubbles take place.

6. Glaze does not always fuse and surface roughness is indicated, some color bleed-through takes place.

4. Many cracks, blisters, and some craters appear, glaze surface becomes rough as if overfired.

2. Excess cracking or pulling away of the glaze from the body.

0. Shivering takes place—the clay body is unusable with this particular glaze.

COLOR

All the clay body recipes were tested for color at the maturing point of the clay. They are given in the glaze title and further information is given in the fired results of the instructions for each clay body.

CATEGORIES AND LABELS

The succeeding chapters on clay body formulas will be divided into three sections for three types of clay bodies: throwing bodies, casting bodies, and sculpture bodies. The recipes are listed first by firing temperature then by color, from light to dark, within each chapter. They are also labeled with capital letters and numbers for identification. For example, a glaze labeled ET-1 would be an earthenware throwing body and SC-1 would be a stoneware casting body.

TEST BATCHES

It would probably be wise for the potter to make a small test batch of each clay body to determine if it is suitable or desirable for his needs before making larger amounts.

5
EARTHENWARE CLAY BODIES
CONE 09-04

All of the clay bodies in this chapter were designed for three specific purposes: throwing, casting, or sculpture. It is not advised that the potter use a clay body for a forming method for which it was not designed unless the instructions indicate that it can be done successfully.

The clay bodies were also designed for a particular temperature range and it is not advised that the potter exceed this unless the instructions indicate it can be done.

The formulas in this chapter are arranged first by forming type: throwing, casting, or sculpture, and then by temperature and color, light to dark, within each category.

The reader will find possible substitutions for most of the chemicals in Chapter 34, Dictionary of Clay and Glaze Compounds, under each individual heading.

EARTHENWARE THROWING CLAY BODIES

All of the clay bodies in this section of the chapter were specifically designed for wheel work. And while some are more workable than others all of the formulas, ET-1—35, will produce a clay body that will work well for throwing.

EARTHENWARE CASTING BODIES
CONE 08—04

Casting slips are used for casting pottery or other ceramic ware in plaster molds. As there is no manipulation of the clay by hand during the forming process, plasticity is not a prime concern. Therefore, no plasticity rating is given for these casting bodies. The rating however, for those who might be curious, is an average of 2 on the scale.

In preparing these casting formulas the general amount of water to use is 40% of the dry body weight of the total dry ingredients. For example, if the potter has weighed out 100 lbs. (45 kg) of dry ingredients then 40 lbs. (18 kg) of water would be used to make the casting slip.

The mixing of a casting body is done in much the same manner as the slip method of preparing clay outlined in Chapter 3, Clay Body Preparation. The main difference is that it is left in the slip form.

EARTHENWARE SCULPTURE BODIES

The composition of a sculpture body for handbuilding lies somewhere between throwing and casting bodies. In the formulation of a sculpture body the potter must be concerned with plasticity, but only to the extent that his clay is workable and holds together. Excess plasticity in this type of body would lead to excess shrinkage, uneven drying, and consequently firing problems. So to insure minimum shrinkage and even drying, a sculpture body must be semiplastic and contain a minimum of 20% grog to allow even drying and thereby prevent cracking and firing problems.

All the bodies in this section were designed with these qualities in mind and are therefore excellent for any type of sculpture, coil work, slab work, or handforming.

If large pieces are to be built where the weight of the clay may prove a problem, the fired weight of the clay can be reduced by the 10% addition of a finely ground organic material. Sawdust or coffee grounds are the materials most commonly used for this purpose. The addition of such materials does not affect the quality of the clay, fired or unfired, because organic materials will burn out during the firing.

Note. The ingredients in the formulas in this chapter can be weighed out in either grams or pounds. It is recommended that the potter first make a 100-gram test batch of the clay body that interests him to insure that it is suitable before making larger amounts. Any of the lighter firing bodies can be colored by the use of coloring oxides. See Chapter 12 for further information. The clay bodies are listed here by firing temperature from lower to higher cones.

ET-1 **Brick Red Throwing Body   Cone 09–04**
shrinkage 9%, plasticity 9.5, glaze rating 11

Redart clay	70.0
Fire clay	10.0
Kentucky ball clay #4	5.0
Tennessee ball clay #4	5.0
Silica	8.0
Bentonite	2.0
Red iron oxide	2.0
Grog (60–80 mesh)	10.0

Mixing. Weigh out the ingredients by grams for test batches and by pounds for larger batches. Mix the clay using any of the three methods outlined in Chapter 3 on Clay Body Preparation. The clay may be used at once or stored to age for a couple of weeks for even greater plasticity. If a pug mill is not used for mixing, take care that the clay is thoroughly wedged to increase its workability and to remove any trapped air bubbles which might lead to cracking or explosions during the firing. This clay is a highly plastic one and probably will not need aging. It is good for all wheel work and with the addition of 20% more grog it can be used for sculpture or coil building.

Drying. Place the wet pieces in a location free of drafts and allow to dry thoroughly. Drafts can lead to uneven drying and consequent warping or cracking. Test for dryness by placing the base of the piece against your cheek. If it feels even faintly moist or cool to the touch, it still contains moisture and should dry further. This is known as the "cheek test" and it is a very reliable test for dryness in unfired pottery. Drying time will vary according to the size and thickness of the ware, the temperature, and the humidity. In general most pieces will dry and be ready for firing in a week, if kept in a warm, dry room.

Bisque Firing. Fire the ware to at least cone 06. First fire slowly to 500° F./260° C. to allow any latent moisture to be removed slowly, then fire normally to the desired bisque temperature. If a raw alkaline glaze is to be used the bisque firing should be to cone 04 to prevent the ware from absorbing the soluble alkaline materials in the glaze, for this can lead to glaze failure in the form of a dry nonglassy surface, pinholing, or blisters in the surface.

Fired Results. At cone 09 this body is a brick orange and will do quite well for flowerpots. As the firing temperature increases toward cone 04 the color darkens to a brick red-brown.

ET-2 **White Throwing Body   Cone 08–04**
shrinkage 6.5%, plasticity 9.5, glaze rating 11.4

Silica	33.5
Kentucky ball clay #4	32.5
Kaolin (Florida)	20.0
Feldspar (soda)	14.0
Bentonite	1.0

Mixing. Mix in the manner of ET-1.

Drying. Dry carefully, this body is more dense than ET-1.

Bisque Firing. Bisque fire in the same manner as ET-1.

Fired Results. Fired to cone 08 the body is off-white and approaches a pure white toward cone 04. This is a very good body for transparent or translucent colors, especially the turquoises.

ET-3 **White Throwing Body   Cone 08-06**
shrinkage 7%, plasticity 10, glaze rating 10

Mixing. Mix in the manner of ET-1.

Drying. Dry in the manner of ET-1.

Bisque Firing. Bisque fire in the manner of ET-1.

Fired Results. Fires to a pure white at cone 06. This is a very good body for transparent or translucent glazes which mature at cone 06.

Tennessee ball clay #1	62.5
Ferro frit #3150	22.5
Nepheline syenite	5.0
Talc	10.0

ET-4 **Brick Orange-Red Throwing Body   Cone 08-04**
shrinkage 5.5%, plasticity 10, glaze rating 11.5

Mixing. Mix in the same manner as ET-1.

Drying. This body will dry more quickly than the previous ones due to the grog content.

Bisque Firing. Fire in the manner of ET-1.

Fired Results. This body fires to a brick orange at cone 08 and darker orange-red at cone 04. At cone 06 it is excellent for flowerpots that are to be left unglazed or even for sculpture if 20% more grog is added.

Local red clay (native)	60.0
Fire clay	10.0
Kaolin	10.0
Silica	8.0
Grog (40–60 mesh)	10.0
Jordan clay	2.0

ET-5 **Red-Brown Throwing Body   Cone 08-04**
shrinkage 5.5%, plasticity 10, glaze rating 10.5

Mixing. Mix in the manner of ET-1.

Drying. Dry in the manner of ET-4.

Bisque Firing. Fire in the manner of ET-1.

Fired Results. This body fires to a red-brown at cone 08 and darker brown at cone 04.

Redart clay	60.0
Fire clay (plastic)	10.0
Kaolin (Florida)	10.0
Silica	8.0
Grog (40–60 mesh)	10.0
Red iron oxide	2.0
Barnard slip	2.0

ET-6 **White Throwing Body   Cone 06-04**
shrinkage 7.2%, plasticity 10, glaze rating 11

Mixing. Mix in the same manner as ET-1.

Drying. Dry in the manner of ET-4.

Bisque Firing. Fire in the manner of ET-1.

Fired Results. This body fires to a dense semiporous white at cone 04.

Tennessee ball clay #1	65.0
Ferro frit #3150	7.5
Nepheline syenite	5.0
Whiting	5.0
Silica	16.5
Bentonite	1.0

ET-7 **White Throwing Body   Cone 06-04**
shrinkage 8%, plasticity 9.5, glaze rating 9

Mixing. Mix in the same manner as ET-1.

Drying. Dry in the manner of ET-1.

Bisque Firing. Fire in the manner of ET-1.

Fired Results. This body fires to a strong pure white at cone 04.

Tennessee ball clay #1	65.0
Ferro frit #3150	24.0
Talc	3.0
Nepheline syenite	3.0
Fine grog	5.0

ET-8 **Cream Throwing Body** **Cone 06-04**
shrinkage 8.6%, plasticity 8, glaze rating 9

Mixing. Mix in the manner of ET-1.

Drying. Dry in the manner of ET-1.

Bisque Firing. Fire in the manner of ET-4.

Fired Results. This body fires to a cream-yellow at cone 06 and cream at cone 04.

Kaolin (Florida)	25.0
Kentucky ball clay #4	25.0
Ferro frit #3150	20.0
Silica	15.0
Jordan clay	7.0
Monmouth clay	3.0

ET-9 **Pink Throwing Body** **Cone 06**
shrinkage 8%, plasticity 10, glaze rating 11

Mixing. Mix in the manner of ET-1.

Drying. Dry in the manner of ET-1.

Bisque Firing. Fire in the manner of ET-1, but not exceeding cone 06.

Fired Results. This body fires to an earthy pink at cone 06.

Tennessee ball clay #1	65.0
Local red clay	7.5
Nepheline syenite	5.0
Whiting	5.0
Silica	16.5
Bentonite	1.0

ET-10 **Buff Throwing Body** **Cone 06**
shrinkage 9%, plasticity 10.5, glaze rating 11

Mixing. Mix in the manner of ET-1.

Drying. Dry in the manner of ET-1.

Bisque Firing. Fire in the manner of ET-9.

Fired Results. This body fires to a tan-buff at cone 06. For a more rustic look add a different colored grog in the amount of 10%.

Tennessee ball clay #1	60.0
Jordan clay	8.0
Nepheline syenite	5.0
Whiting	4.0
Silica	16.0
Talc	5.0
Bentonite	2.0

ET-11 **Buff Throwing Body** **Cone 06-04**
shrinkage 9.5%, plasticity 10, glaze rating 9

Mixing. Mix in the manner of ET-1.

Drying. Dry in the manner of ET-1.

Bisque Firing. Fire in the manner of ET-1.

Fired Results. This body fires to a more reddish buff than ET-10.

Local red clay	50.0
Any commercial cone 06 clay	50.0

ET-12 **Gray Throwing Body** **Cone 06-04**
shrinkage 8%, plasticity 9, glaze rating 10.5

Mixing. Mix in the manner of ET-1.

Drying. Dry in the manner of ET-1.

Bisque Firing. Fire in the manner of ET-1.

Fired Results. This body fires to a light slate gray at cone 04.

Kentucky ball clay #4	10.0
Soda feldspar	10.0
Kaolin (EPK)	45.0
Silica	25.0
Talc	3.0
Iron chromate	7.0

ET-13   Brick Orange Throwing Body   Cone 06-04

shrinkage 13.5%, plasticity 11, glaze rating 11.7

Red brick clay	75.0
Kentucky ball clay #4	7.5
Tennessee ball clay #5	7.5
Silica	8.0
Talc	2.0

Mixing. Mix in the manner of ET-1.

Drying. Dry in the manner of ET-1.

Bisque Firing. Fire in the manner of ET-1.

Fired Results. This body fires to a brick orange at cone 06 and a darker orange at cone 04. It is very effective used with white or a lighter grog. It is also good used under a glaze with silicon carbide content, for this gives an artificial reduction and allows the iron red to bleed through the glaze. The glaze, of course, should be opaque and of a lighter color.

ET-14   Red Throwing Body   Cone 06-04

shrinkage 14.5%, plasticity 8, glaze rating 10.6

Red earthenware clay	75.0
Volcanic ash	20.0
Talc	5.0

Mixing. Mix in the manner of ET-1. This clay may be aged with some organic content to improve its plasticity.

Drying. Dry in the manner of ET-1.

Fired Results. This body fires an earthy red at cone 06 and darker at cone 04. It is a good body for burnishing. It is also good for sculpture with a 20% addition of 40- to 60-mesh grog.

ET-15   Red Heat-Resistant Throwing Body   Cone 06

shrinkage 14.7%, plasticity 10, glaze rating 9.2

Local red clay	70.0
Grog (20 mesh)	10.0
Grog (40 mesh)	10.0
Grog (60 mesh)	10.0

Mixing. Mix in the manner of ET-1.

Drying. Dry in the manner of ET-4.

Bisque Firing. If this body is to be used for a heat-resistant purpose, firing should be normal but the cooling should be slowed down particularly in the early stages. Under no circumstances should the peep holes be opened during cooling. This may lead to dunting at temperatures above 500° F./260° C.

Fired Results. This body fires to a brick red at cone 06. This body is highly resistant to thermal shock and can be used to make ovenware of the lighter types. That is to say, ovenware that goes from the room into the oven, not from the freezer to the oven. Its best use would be for beanpots.

ET-16   White Throwing Body   Cone 04

shrinkage 8.5%, plasticity 10, glaze rating 10.5

Kaolin (EPK)	39.0
Kentucky ball clay #4	32.0
Ferro frit #3150	10.0
Silica	10.0
Talc	7.0
Bentonite	1.0

Mixing. Mix in the manner of ET-1.

Drying. Dry in the manner of ET-1.

Bisque Firing. Fire in the manner of ET-1.

Fired Results. This body fires to a pure white at cone 04. With the addition of white grog, very large pieces can be made with this throwing body.

ET-17 White Throwing Body Cone 04
shrinkage 7%, plasticity 11, glaze rating 11.5

Mixing. Mix in the manner of ET-1.

Drying. Dry in the manner of ET-1.

Bisque Firing. Fire in the manner of ET-1.

Fired Results. This body fires to a pure white at cone 04. It is a very dense body and therefore good for utility ware, particularly since it has a high glaze rating.

Kentucky ball clay #4	42.0
Kaolin (EPK)	18.0
Silica	16.0
Cornwall stone	12.0
Bentonite	2.0
Grog (very fine)	2.0

ET-18 White Throwing Body Cone 04-2
shrinkage 12.5%, plasticity 11, glaze rating 11.5

Mixing. Mix in the manner of ET-1.

Drying. Dry in the manner of ET-1.

Bisque Firing. Bisque fire to cone 06 unless an alkaline glaze is to be used. If so, bisque fire to cone 04.

Fired Results. Due to the volcanic ash content of this body it can be fired past the earthenware range to cone 2 if the potter wishes. At cone 04 it fires to a slightly off-white color. This body is excellent for utility ware.

Tennessee ball clay #1	35.0
Kentucky ball clay #4	35.0
Volcanic ash	30.0

ET-19 White Talc Throwing Body Cone 04
shrinkage 11.6%, plasticity 11, glaze rating 11.6

Mixing. Mix in the manner of ET-1.

Drying. Dry in the manner of ET-1.

Bisque Firing. Fire to cone 06 for nonalkaline glazes and to cone 04 for alkaline glazes.

Fired Results. This body fires to a pure white. It is excellent for transparent or translucent colors.

Tennessee ball clay #1	30.0
Kentucky ball clay #4	30.0
Talc	30.0
Ferro frit #3150	15.0
Fine sand (60–80 mesh)	5.0

ET-20 White Talc Throwing Body Cone 04
shrinkage 7%, plasticity 11, glaze rating 11.5

Mixing. Mix in the manner of ET-1.

Drying. Dry in the manner of ET-1.

Bisque Firing. Fire to cone 06 for all glazes if grog is not used. If grog is used bisque fire to cone 04 for alkaline glazes.

Fired Results. Fires to a pure white at cone 04. It is good for utility ware.

Kentucky ball clay #4	58.0
Talc	36.0
Kaolin	7.0
White grog or sand (optional)	10.0

ET-21 **Imitation Procelain Throwing Body   Cone 04**
shrinkage 5.5%, plasticity 8.5, glaze rating 11.5

Mixing. Mix in the manner of ET-1. Care should be taken that residue from other clays in your mixing utensils will not contaminate this mixture if a pure white translucent body is desired.

Drying. Dry in the manner of ET-1.

Bisque Firing. Fire to cone 06.

Fired Results. This will produce a pure white body of the porcelain type with thin areas being slightly translucent. To take advantage of this effect only transparent or translucent glazes should be used over this body.

Kaolin (Florida)	36.0
Feldspar (Kona F-4)	34.0
Silica	25.0
Bentonite	3.0
Bone ash	1.0
Whiting	1.0

ET-22 **White Throwing Body   Cone 04**
shrinkage 6%, plasticity 8, glaze rating 11.5

Mixing. Mix in the manner of ET-1.

Drying. Dry in the manner of ET-1.

Bisque Firing. Fire to cone 06, cone 04 for alkaline glazes.

Fired Results. This body produces a pure white ware which is semivitreous in character. As such it is excellent for utility ware.

Kaolin (EPK)	40.0
Silica	27.0
Feldspar (soda)	15.0
Kentucky ball clay PX	15.0
Bentonite	3.0
Bone ash	1.0

ET-23 **White Throwing Body   Cone 04**
shrinkage 8.5%, plasticity 9, glaze rating 11.7

Mixing. Mix in the manner of ET-1.

Drying. Dry in the manner of ET-1.

Bisque Firing. Fire to cone 06, cone 04 for alkaline glazes.

Fired Results. This body fires to a slightly off-white at cone 04.

Tennessee ball clay #5	25.0
Kentucky ball clay #4	25.0
Kaolin (EPK)	20.0
Talc	15.0
Nepheline syenite	10.0
Cornwall stone (or Godfrey feldspar)	5.0

ET-24 **Off-White Throwing Body   Cone 04**
shrinkage 5%, plasticity 11, glaze rating 11.9

Mixing. Mix in the manner of ET-1.

Drying. Dry in the manner of ET-1.

Bisque Firing. Fire to cone 06, cone 04 for alkaline glazes.

Fired Results. This body fires to an off-white at cone 04.

Tennessee ball clay #1	48.0
Kaolin (Florida)	24.0
Cornwall stone	24.0
Flint	4.0

ET-25 **White Throwing Body   Cone 04**
shrinkage 7%, plasticity 11.4, glaze rating 11

Mixing. Mix in the manner of ET-1.

Drying. Dry in the manner of ET-1.

Bisque Firing. Fire to cone 06.

Fired Results. This body fires to a pure white at cone 04.

Kentucky ball clay #4	38.0
Kaolin (Georgia)	28.0
Cornwall stone	12.0
Silica	10.0
Soda feldspar	9.0
Grog (very fine)	3.0

ET-26 **Dense White Throwing Body   Cone 04**
shrinkage 6.5%, plasticity 8.5, glaze rating 12

Mixing. Mix in the manner of ET-1.

Drying. Dry in the manner of ET-1.

Bisque Firing. Fire to cone 06, cone 04 for alkaline glazes.

Fired Results. This body fires to a very dense pure white at cone 04. This body produces a ware that is semivitreous, very much like the quality of hotel china though not as hard. As such it is very good for utility ware.

Kentucky ball clay #4	30.0
Talc	24.5
Kaolin	14.5
Flint	14.8
Feldspar (soda)	8.2
Ferro frit #3150	6.0
Bentonite	2.0

ET-27 **Off-White Throwing Body   Cone 04**
shrinkage 5%, plasticity 11.2, glaze rating 12

Mixing. Mix in the manner of ET-1.

Drying. Dry in the manner of ET-1.

Bisque Firing. Fire to cone 06.

Fired Results. This body fires to a slightly off-white at cone 04. It is very dense, takes a glaze perfectly, and is very good used as a body for utility ware.

Kentucky ball clay #4	22.0
Tennessee ball clay #1	22.0
Kaolin	25.0
Silica	20.0
Cornwall stone	8.0
Flint grog	3.0

ET-28 **Creamy White Throwing Body   Cone 04**
shrinkage 2.9%, plasticity 9, glaze rating 11.3

Mixing. Mix in the manner of ET-1.

Drying. Dry in the manner of ET-1.

Bisque Firing. Fire to cone 06.

Fired Results. This body fires to a creamy white at cone 04. It is consequently a very good body for ivory to light yellow glazes.

Kaolin (EPK)	35.0
Talc	20.0
Ferro frit #3150	20.0
Nepheline syenite	10.0
Kentucky ball clay #4	5.0
Jordan clay	5.0

ET-29 **Buff-White Throwing Body   Cone 04–03**
shrinkage 8.2%, plasticity 9, glaze rating 10.1

Mixing. Mix in the manner of ET-1.

Drying. Dry in the manner of ET-1.

Bisque Firing. Fire to cone 06.

Fired Results. This body fires to a buff-white color at cone 04; at cone 03 it fires slightly darker. As this body tends to be slightly porous it is not recommended for utility ware. Before glazing this ware should be dampened slightly by dipping in water then allowing the body to absorb the moisture. This assures that the glaze coat will not be too thick.

Kentucky ball clay #4	22.0
Tennessee ball clay #1	20.0
Kaolin (EPK)	30.0
Silica	19.0
Cornwall stone	5.0
Grog (60–80 mesh)	4.0

ET-30 **Cream Throwing Body   Cone 04**
shrinkage 4.5%, plasticity 7.5, glaze rating 10

Mixing. Mix in the manner of ET-1.

Drying. Drying should be slowed down for thicker pieces.

Bisque Firing. Fire to cone 06, cone 04 for alkaline glazes unless they are alkaline frits.

Fired Results. This body fires to a cream color at cone 04. This body, if made to a creamy liquid, can also be used as an engobe over darker clays with the same plasticity rating.

Kaolin (Florida)	25.0
Kentucky ball clay #4	15.0
Tennessee ball clay #1	10.0
Talc	15.0
Nepheline syenite	20.0
Cornwall stone	5.0
Jordan clay	5.0

ET-31 **Buff-White Throwing Body   Cone 04**
shrinkage 10%, plasticity 10.5, glaze rating 11.5

Mixing. Mix in the same manner as ET-1.

Drying. Dry in the same manner as ET-1.

Bisque Firing. Fire to cone 06.

Fired Results. This body fires to a light buff at cone 04.

Kaolin (EPK)	25.0
Kentucky ball clay #4	25.0
Ferro frit #3150	25.0
Silica	10.0
Jordan clay	10.0
Flint grog (60–80 mesh)	5.0

ET-32 **Buff Throwing Body   Cone 04**
shrinkage 6.2%, plasticity 10.9, glaze rating 11.9

Mixing. Mix in the manner of ET-1.

Drying. Dry in the manner of ET-1.

Bisque Firing. Fire to cone 06.

Fired Results. This body fires to a medium buff at cone 04. With the addition of 20% 40- to 60-mesh grog it can work very well for sculpture.

Kaolin (EPK)	25.0
Kentucky ball clay #4	10.0
Tennessee ball clay #5	10.0
Ferro frit #3150	10.0
Monmouth clay	15.0
Talc	18.0
Silica	10.0
Bentonite	2.0

ET-33 **Pink-Buff Throwing Body   Cone 04**
shrinkage 5.5%, plasticity 11.4, glaze rating 12

Mixing. Mix in the manner of ET-1.

Drying. Less drying time is needed for this body, but it should be kept out of drafts.

Bisque Firing. Fire to cone 06.

Fired Results. This body fires to a buff-pink at cone 04. It makes a good body for pinks or translucent reds.

Kentucky ball clay #4	30.0
Kaolin	30.0
Silica	15.0
Feldspar (soda)	15.0
Grog (60–80 mesh)	6.0
Redart clay	9.0

ET-34 **Long-Range Throwing Body   Cone 04–5**
shrinkage 8.5%, plasticity 11, glaze rating 11.3

Mixing. Mix in the manner of ET-1.

Drying. Dry in the manner of ET-4.

Bisque Firing. Fire to 04. This body tends to be too porous if bisque fired to cone 06 and will lead to faulty glaze results.

Fired Results. This body is a creamy tan when fired to cone 04. If it is fired higher, and it can be due to its fire clay content, it gets darker and more gray in color.

Jordan clay	55.0
Redart clay	20.0
Fire clay	15.0
Barnard clay	5.0
Grog	5.0

ET-35 **Imitation Stoneware Throwing Body   Cone 04**
shrinkage 5%, plasticity 11, glaze rating 11.9

Mixing. Mix in the manner of ET-1. Be sure to wedge this body thoroughly.

Drying. Dry in the manner of ET-4.

Bisque Firing. Fire to cone 06, cone 04 for alkaline glazes.

Fired Results. This body fires to a tan color at cone 04. It is very hard and dense like stoneware. However, it is not completely vitrified. It is a good body for utility ware.

Tennessee ball clay #1	30.0
Kentucky ball clay #4	30.0
Ferro frit #3150	10.0
Nepheline syenite	5.0
Talc	15.0
Fire clay	10.0
Grog (60–80 mesh)	10.0

FORMULAS FOR EARTHENWARE CASTING BODIES

Note. No plasticity rating is given for casting bodies.

EC-1 **White Casting Body   Cone 08–06**
shrinkage 6%, glaze rating 12

Mixing. Mix these casting bodies according to the procedure outlined in Chapter 3 under the subheading Mixing Casting Bodies.

Casting. You will probably be using a large pitcher of some type to pour the molds. In filling the pitcher, pour the slip through a kitchen sieve. This will break up any air bubbles and remove any foreign matter or lumps you might have missed in the mixing process.

First of all, make sure that the mold is tightly and securely banded. Having a mold open during the pouring can be extremely messy and wasteful of the slip. Pour the slip gently into the center of the mold. Do not allow the slip to run down the inside of the mold if you can avoid it—this can lead to trapped air bubbles and consequently cracking or explosions during firing. Keep refilling the mold as the slip level in the mold drops due to the absorption of water by the mold.

Casting time will vary; usually it does not take over 15 minutes, but this depends on the temperature and humidity. A simple test is to pour a little on the top level of the mold to a thickness of 1/4" (6mm). When the moist sheen disappears from the top of the sample the mold is usually ready to be emptied.

The emptying process should be done gently to avoid pulling away the layer of built-up slip that has attached itself to the inside wall of the mold. If the mold is emptied too quickly a vacuum is created and the still delicate layer on the mold wall will pull away. Allow the mold to drain slowly and completely to remove excess slip that would otherwise flow back to the bottom of the cast piece and result in uneven drying problems, namely cracking or warping of the ware.

Set the mold aside to dry. Check it about every half hour. When you notice that the slip is setting and pulling away from the mold it can then be opened and the piece carefully removed.

Kentucky ball clay #4	40.0
Silica	28.0
Kaolin	16.0
Cornwall stone	14.7
Sodium carbonate	0.3

To open the mold lay it on its side, remove the bands, and gently lift up the top half. If it offers any resistance wait another hour then try again. When the top half of the mold will remove without difficulty do so, then gently remove the piece and set it aside to dry to a leatherhard stage before paring or trimming the seam marks and the top.

Drying. Place the piece in a place that is free of drafts to dry for several days. Use the cheek test outlined in the drying instructions for ET-1 to determine dryness.

Bisque Firing. Fire to cone 06, cone 04 for alkaline glazes.

Fired Results. This body fires to a pure white at cone 04.

EC-2　　**White Casting Body　Cone 06–04**
shrinkage 3%, glaze rating 12

Mixing. Mix in the manner of EC-1.

Casting. Cast using the same procedure outlined in EC-1.

Drying. Dry in the manner of EC-1.

Bisque Firing. Fire to cone 06.

Fired Results. This body fires to a pure white at cone 06–04.

Kentucky ball clay #4	45.0
Talc	40.0
Kaolin	15.0
Sodium carbonate	0.3

EC-3　　**Gray Casting Body　Cone 06–04**
shrinkage 4.2%, glaze rating 12

Mixing. Mix in the manner of EC-1.

Casting. Cast in the manner of EC-1.

Drying. Dry in the manner of EC-1.

Bisque Firing. Fire to cone 06, cone 04 for alkaline glazes.

Fired Results. This body fires to a light slate gray at cone 04. This body is good for utility ware as it is quite dense.

Kentucky ball clay #4	30.0
Tennessee ball clay #1	20.0
Talc	35.0
Kaolin (EPK)	14.0
Iron chromate	1.0
Sodium carbonate	0.3
Optional:	
Flint grog (very fine)	10.0

EC-4　　**Pink Casting Body　Cone 06–04**
shrinkage 3.6%, glaze rating 11.9

Mixing. Mix in the manner of EC-1.

Casting. Cast in the manner of EC-1.

Drying. Dry in the manner of EC-1.

Bisque Firing. Fire to cone 06.

Fired Results. This body fires to a light pink at cone 04. It makes a good body to use for transparent or translucent earth-colored glazes.

Kentucky ball clay #4	30.0
Tennessee ball clay #5	20.0
Talc	30.0
Red iron oxide	5.0
Sodium carbonate	0.3

EC-5

White Casting Body   Cone 04
shrinkage 5.5%, glaze rating 18

Mixing. Mix in the manner of EC-1.

Casting. Cast in the manner of EC-1.

Drying. This is a denser body than EC-1 through EC-4 and should be dried more slowly.

Bisque Firing. Fire to cone 06.

Fired Results. This body fires to a pure white at cone 04.

Nepheline syenite	50.0
Kaolin (EPK)	25.0
Kentucky ball clay #4	15.0
Silica	5.0
Talc	5.0
Sodium carbonate	0.3

EC-6

Off-White Casting Body   Cone 04
shrinkage 5.5%, glaze rating 11.8

Mixing. Mix in the manner of EC-1.

Casting. Cast in the manner of EC-1.

Drying. Dry in the manner of EC-5.

Bisque Firing. Fire to cone 06, cone 04 for alkaline glazes.

Fired Results. This body fires to a creamy off-white at cone 04.

Kentucky ball clay PX	25.0
Tennessee ball clay #5	25.0
Talc	35.0
Kaolin (Georgia)	15.0
Sodium carbonate	0.3

EC-7

Off-White Casting Body   Cone 04
shrinkage 5.5%, glaze rating 12

Mixing. Mix in the manner of EC-1.

Casting. Cast in the manner of EC-1.

Drying. Dry in the manner of EC-5.

Bisque Firing. Fire to cone 06.

Fired Results. This body fires to a slightly off-white color at cone 04.

Kentucky ball clay #4	30.4
Talc	25.0
Cornwall stone	5.0
Soda feldspar	7.5
Ferro frit #3150	7.2
Sodium carbonate	0.3

EC-8

Buff Casting Body   Cone 04
shrinkage 3%, glaze rating 12

Mixing. Mix in the manner of EC-1.

Casting. Cast in the manner of EC-1.

Bisque Firing. Fire to cone 06.

Fired Results. This body fires to light buff at cone 04. It is a very good body for the mass production of such items as flowerpots or any ware that is to be left unglazed. The addition of 10% 60- to 80-mesh grog will give it a more rustic appearance.

Kentucky ball clay #4	25.0
Tennessee ball clay #5	25.0
Talc	35.0
Kaolin	10.0
Jordan clay	5.0
Sodium carbonate	0.3

FORMULAS FOR EARTHENWARE SCULPTURE BODIES

Note. The clay bodies in this section are excellent for handbuilding. They are not recommended for throwing.

ES-1

Off-White Sculpture Body   Cone 04
shrinkage 3%, plasticity 5.6, glaze rating 11.1

Kaolin (EPK)	25.0
Talc	18.0
Nepheline syenite	18.0
Kaolin (Georgia)	15.0
Kentucky ball clay #4	7.5
Tennessee ball clay #5	7.5
Ferro frit #3150	8.0
Grog (60–80 mesh)	10.0

Mixing. Mix this body according to the instructions in Chapter 3, Clay Body Preparation, using any of the three methods for clay body preparation. The grog can be added in the mixing or during the wedging process. In cases where the clay may be too wet to handle, the addition of the grog will help to dry out the clay to the proper working consistency. In any case all sculpture bodies should be thoroughly wedged if the soaking or the slip method is used. If plasticity seems to be a problem, a couple of weeks of aging will raise the plasticity by almost one point.

Drying. Allow all sculpture and handbuilt pieces to dry thoroughly. Sculpture pieces are usually thicker and consequently need more drying time. Use the cheek test to check for dryness.

Bisque Firing. Bisque fire sculpture pieces only if they are to be glazed. If they are not then fire them to maturity with the first firing. This body is bisque fired at cone 06.

Fired Results. This body fires to a slightly off-white color at cone 04.

ES-2

Cream Terracotta Sculpture Body   Cone 04
shrinkage 4.2%, plasticity 5, glaze rating 11

Kaolin (EPK)	25.0
Kentucky ball clay #4	10.0
Tennessee ball clay #5	10.0
Talc	10.0
Nepheline syenite	20.0
Plastic fire clay	15.0
Jordan clay	5.0
Grog (40–60 mesh)	10.0

Mixing. Mix in the manner of ES-1.

Drying. Dry in the manner of ES-1.

Bisque Firing. Fire in the manner of ES-1.

Fired Results. This body fires to an earthy cream color at cone 04. It is especially good with the application of metal washes.

ES-3

Buff Sculpture Body   Cone 04
shrinkage 3%, plasticity 5.9, glaze rating 10.8

Kaolin (EPK)	25.0
Talc	25.0
Nepheline syenite	5.0
Redart clay	10.0
Jordan clay	10.0
Plastic fire clay	15.0
Grog (40–60 mesh)	10.0
Optional:	
Grog (60–80 mesh)	15.0

Mixing. Mix in the manner of ES-1.

Drying. Dry in the manner of ES-1.

Bisque Firing. Fire in the manner of ES-1.

Fired Results. This body fires to a medium buff color at cone 04.

ES-4   Tan-Gray Sculpture Body   Cone 04
shrinkage 6%, plasticity 7.3, glaze rating 10.8

Mixing. Mix in the manner of ES-1.

Drying. Dry in the manner of ES-1.

Bisque Firing. Fire in the manner of ES-1.

Fired Results. This body fires to a tan-gray color at cone 04. This is a good body for coil building as its plasticity is a little higher than average for a sculpture body.

Tennessee ball clay #1	15.0
Kentucky ball clay (any)	15.0
Feldspar (soda)	10.0
Kaolin (EPK)	10.0
Silica	20.0
Talc	10.0
Jordan clay	10.0
Grog (40–60 mesh)	10.0

ES-5   Yellow-Orange Terracotta Sculpture Body   Cone 04
shrinkage 4%, plasticity 7, glaze rating 11

Mixing. Mix in the manner of ES-1.

Drying. Dry in the manner of ES-1.

Bisque Firing. Fire in the manner of ES-1.

Fired Results. This body fires to light yellow-orange at cone 04. This is an excellent body for earthy pieces which are to be left unglazed.

Kaolin (EPK)	25.0
Talc	25.0
Nepheline syenite	12.0
Kentucky ball clay PX	10.0
Jordan clay	15.0
Plastic fire clay	13.0
Grog (40–60 mesh)	10.0

ES-6   Brick Orange Terracotta Sculpture Body   Cone 04
shrinkage 6%, plasticity 7, glaze rating 11.5

Mixing. Mix in the manner of ES-1.

Drying. Dry in the manner of ES-1.

Bisque Firing. Fire in the manner of ES-1.

Fired Results. This body fires to an earthy brick orange at cone 04. This is a good body for coil building due to its higher plasticity.

Redart clay	60.0
Plastic fire clay	10.0
Jordan clay	10.0
Silica	5.0
Talc	5.0
Kentucky ball clay #4	10.0
Grog (40–60 mesh)	10.0

ES-7   Orange-Red Sculpture Body   Cone 04–02
shrinkage 2.5%, plasticity 4, glaze rating 11.5

Mixing. Mix in the manner of ES-1.

Drying. Dry in the manner of ES-1.

Bisque Firing. Fire in the manner of ES-1.

Fired Results. This body fires to a darker orange-red at cone 04. Fired to cone 02 it becomes a brown orange-red. It is very attractive left unglazed.

Grog (20–40 mesh)	30.0
Monmouth clay	14.0
Jordan clay	14.0
Red brick clay	22.0
Silica	12.0
Plastic fire clay	6.0
Red iron oxide	2.0

ES-8   Orange-Red Terracotta Sculpture Body   Cone 04
shrinkage 3.5%, plasticity 6, glaze rating 9

Mixing. Mix in the manner of ES-1.

Drying. Dry in the manner of ES-1.

Bisque Firing. Fire in the manner of ES-1.

Fired Results. This body fires to a dark orange-red at cone 04. It is very earthy and rustic if left unglazed, especially if the grog is allowed to show through and some texture is used.

Monmouth clay	15.0
Jordan clay	15.0
Local red clay	25.0
Silica	15.0
Grog (60–80 mesh)	10.0
Grog (40–60 mesh)	10.0
Sawdust (60–80 mesh)	10.0

ES-9 **Brick Red Terracotta Sculpture Body   Cone 04**
shrinkage 3%, plasticity 5, glaze rating 10.2

Monmouth clay	20.0
Grog (40–60 mesh)	30.0
Local red clay	25.0
Silica	15.0
Jordan clay	10.0

Mixing. Mix in the manner of ES-1.

Drying. Dry in the manner of ES-1.

Bisque Firing. Fire in the manner of ES-1.

Fired Results. This body fires to a dark brick red at cone 04. It is more effective if a lighter color grog is used.

ES-10 **Red-Brown Sculpture Body   Cone 04**
shrinkage 3%, plasticity 8.5, glaze rating 10.2

Monmouth clay	30.0
Kentucky ball clay #4	10.0
Redart clay	20.0
Jordan clay	15.0
Silica	10.0
Grog (40–60 mesh)	10.0
Red iron oxide	5.0

Mixing. Mix in the manner of ES-1.

Drying. Dry in the manner of ES-1.

Bisque Firing. Fire in the manner of ES-1.

Fired Results. This body fires to a rich red-brown at cone 04. It is excellent for coil work due to its higher plasticity rating.

6
SOFT STONEWARE CLAY BODIES
CONE 03-4

This category of clay bodies is sometimes called medium temperature. The author has chosen to label them soft stoneware for two reasons: first, they are of such quality and are coming into more general use by potters that they deserve a special name of their own, and second, they are in many cases 90% to 95% vitreous and thus resemble the higher-fired stoneware more than the porous earthenwares.

All of the clay bodies in this chapter were designed for three specific purposes: throwing, casting, or sculpture. It is not advised that the potter use a clay body for a forming method for which it was not designed unless the instructions indicate that it can be done successfully.

The clay bodies were also designed for a particular temperature range and it is not advised that the potter exceed this unless the instructions indicate it can be done.

The recipes in this chapter are arranged first by forming type: throwing, casting, or sculpture, and then by temperature and color, light to dark, within each category.

The reader will find possible substitutions for most of the chemicals in Chapter 34, Dictionary of Clay and Glaze Compounds, under each individual heading.

Note. The ingredients in the formulas in this chapter can be weighed out in either grams or pounds. It is recommended that the potter first make a 100-gram test batch of the clay body that interests him to insure that it is suitable before making larger amounts. Any of the lighter firing bodies can be colored by the use of coloring oxides. See Chapter 12 for further information. The clay bodies are listed here by firing temperature from lower to higher cones.

FORMULAS FOR SOFT STONEWARE THROWING BODIES

SST-1

Light Tan Imitation Stoneware Throwing Body Cone 03-04
shrinkage 11.5%, plasticity 9.5, glaze rating 10

Tennessee ball clay #5	35.0
Kentucky ball clay #4	30.0
Ferro frit #3150	20.0
Nepheline syenite	5.0
Talc	8.0
Bentonite	2.0
Add:	
Grog (40–60 mesh)	10.0

Mixing. Weigh out the ingredients by grams for test batches and by pounds for larger batches. Mix the clay using any of the three methods outlined in Chapter 3 on Clay Body Preparation. The clay can be used at once or stored to age for a couple of weeks for even greater plasticity. If a pug mill is not used for mixing, take care that the clay is thoroughly wedged to increase its workability and to remove any trapped air bubbles which might lead to cracking or explosions during the firing. This particular clay is highly plastic and probably will not need aging. It is good for all wheel work and with the addition of 20% to 30% more grog, it can be used for sculpture or coiling.

Drying. Place the wet pieces in a location that is free of drafts and allow them to dry thoroughly. Drafts can lead to uneven drying and consequently warping or cracking. Test for dryness by placing the base of the piece against your cheek. If it feels even faintly moist or cool to the touch, it still contains moisture and should dry further. Drying time will vary according to the size and thickness of the ware, the temperature, and the humidity. In general most pieces will dry and be ready for firing in a week if kept in a warm, dry place.

Bisque Firing. Soft stoneware should have a bisque firing of at least cone 04. First fire the kiln slowly to 500° F./260° C. to allow any latent moisture to be removed slowly, then fire normally to the desired bisque temperature. If an alkaline glaze is to be used, particularly a raw alkaline one, the bisque fire should be one cone higher as the more porous bisque has a tendency to absorb the soluble alkaline materials and leave the glaze rough and unmatured. This will also cut down on pinholing and blisters in the alkaline glazes.

Fired Results. Fired to cone 4 this body is a light tan, about 98% vitreous, and strongly resembles the higher-fired stonewares. It is a very good body for throwing bells and wind chimes, due to its high vitrification.

SST-2

Medium Cream Throwing Body   Cone 03–4
shrinkage 10.2%, plasticity 9.3, glaze rating 11.5

Mixing. Mix in the manner of SST-1.

Drying. Dry in the manner of SST-1.

Bisque Firing. Fire in the manner of SST-1.

Fired Results. This body fires to a medium cream color at cone 4. It is quite dense and makes a good body for utility ware—not ovenware.

Tennessee ball clay #5	40.0
Kentucky ball clay #4	30.0
Volcanic ash	20.0
Plastic fire clay	5.0
Grog (40–60 mesh)	5.0
Add:	
Grog (60–80 mesh)	10.0

SST-3

Light Red Throwing Body   Cone 03–4
shrinkage 10.3%, plasticity 10.5, glaze rating 10.7

Mixing. Mix in the manner of SST-1.

Drying. Dry in the manner of SST-1.

Bisque Firing. Fire in the manner of SST-1.

Fired Results. This body fires to a light red at cone 4.

Native red clay	50.0
Silica	20.0
Kaolin (EPK)	14.0
Plastic fire clay	10.0
Grog (40–60 mesh)	6.0

SST-4

Light Cream Throwing Body   Cone 03–5
shrinkage 12.5%, plasticity 11.2, glaze rating 11.6

Mixing. Mix in the manner of SST-1.

Drying. Dry in the manner of SST-1.

Bisque Firing. Fire in the manner of SST-1.

Fired Results. At cone 03–5 this body fires to a light cream color.

Jordan clay	40.0
Tennessee ball clay #5	20.0
Redart clay	20.0
Plastic fire clay	15.0
Barnard clay	5.0
Add:	
Grog (20–40 mesh)	10.0

SST-5   **Light Brown Throwing Body**   **Cone 02-5**
shrinkage 10.8%, plasticity 10.5, glaze rating 10.7

Mixing. Mix in the manner of SST-1.

Drying. Dry in the manner of SST-1.

Bisque Firing. Fire in the manner of SST-1.

Fired Results. This body fires to a light brown at cone 5.

Jordan clay	55.0
Redart clay	11.0
Local red clay	11.0
Plastic fire clay	13.0
Barnard clay	5.0
Kentucky ball clay #4	5.0
Add:	
Grog (60–80 mesh)	10.0

SST-6   **Light Buff Throwing Body**   **Cone 02**
shrinkage 9.5%, plasticity 11.6, glaze rating 11

Mixing. Mix in the manner of SST-1.

Drying. Dry in the manner of SST-1.

Bisque Firing. Fire in the manner of SST-1.

Fired Results. This body fires to a light buff at cone 02. It is very dense and makes a good body for low-fired utility ware.

Plastic fire clay	70.0
Jordan clay	20.0
Feldspar (potash)	6.0
Silica	4.0
Add:	
Grog (60–80 mesh)	10.0

SST-7   **White Throwing Body**   **Cone 01-3**
shrinkage 5.5%, plasticity 11.5, glaze rating 11

Mixing. Mix in the manner of SST-1.

Drying. Dry in the manner of SST-1.

Bisque Firing. Fire in the manner of SST-1.

Fired Results. This body fires to a slightly off-white at cone 3. It makes a good body for utility ware.

Silica	30.0
Kentucky ball clay #4	22.0
Kaolin (Georgia)	25.0
Cornwall stone	18.0
Add:	
Grog (40–60 mesh)	10.0

SST-8   **Creamy Tan Throwing Body**   **Cone 1**
shrinkage 11.3%, plasticity 11.4, glaze rating 11.5

Mixing. Mix in the manner of SST-1.

Drying. Dry in the manner of SST-1.

Bisque Firing. Fire in the manner of SST-1.

Fired Results. This body fires to a creamy tan at cone 1. It very strongly resembles the higher-fired stoneware.

Tennessee ball clay #1	37.5
Kentucky ball clay #4	6.0
Nepheline syenite	5.5
Ferro frit #3150	5.5
Talc	16.5
Silica	5.0
Add:	
Grog (20–40 mesh)	10.0

SST-9   **Light Red Throwing Body**   **Cone 1**
shrinkage 11.2%, plasticity 11, glaze rating 10.5

Mixing. Mix in the manner of SST-1.

Drying. Dry in the manner of SST-1.

Bisque Firing. Fire in the manner of SST-1.

Fired Results. This body fires to a light brick red at cone 1.

Redart clay	65.0
Silica	20.0
Kaolin (EPK)	15.0
Add:	
Grog (60–80 mesh)	10.0

SST-10   **Cream Throwing Body   Cone 2**
shrinkage 10.7%, plasticity 11.5, glaze rating 11

Mixing.   Mix in the manner of SST-1.

Drying.   Dry in the manner of SST-1.

Bisque Firing.   Fire in the manner of SST-1.

Fired Results.   This body fires to a cream color at cone 2.

Tennessee ball clay #1	7.0
Kentucky ball clay #4	5.0
Kaolin (EPK)	2.0
Feldspar (soda)	7.0
Silica	5.0
Red art clay	1.0
Bentonite	.5
Grog (60–80 mesh)	3.0

SST-11   **Light Tan Throwing Body   Cone 2**
shrinkage 11.2%, plasticity 11.6, glaze rating 11

Mixing.   Mix in the manner of SST-1.

Drying.   Dry in the manner of SST-1.

Bisque Firing.   Fire in the manner of SST-1.

Fired Results.   This body fires to a light, cool tan at cone 2. It strongly resembles the higher-fired stoneware and is about 95% vitreous.

Silica	33.0
Kentucky ball clay #4	16.0
Tennessee ball clay #5	10.0
Cornwall stone	9.0
Feldspar (Godfrey)	9.0
Bentonite	11.0
Add:	
Grog (60–80 mesh)	10.0

SST-12   **Creamy Tan Throwing Body   Cone 2**
shrinkage 12%, plasticity 11.3, glaze rating 11.4

Mixing.   Mix in the manner of SST-1.

Drying.   Dry in the manner of SST-1.

Bisque Firing.   Fire in the manner of SST-1.

Fired Results.   This body fires to a creamy tan at cone 2 and is about 95% vitreous.

Kentucky ball clay #4	45.5
Feldspar (soda)	24.5
Silica	14.5
Kaolin (EPK)	8.4
Local red clay	7.3
Bentonite	.1
Add:	
Grog (60–80 mesh)	10.0

SST-13   **Buff Imitation Stoneware Throwing Body   Cone 2**
shrinkage 9.6%, plasticity 11, glaze rating 9.5

Mixing.   Mix in the manner of SST-1.

Drying.   Dry in the manner of SST-1.

Bisque Firing.   Fire in the manner of SST-1.

Fired Results.   This body fires to a dense buff color at cone 2. The body is about 96% vitreous.

Kentucky ball clay #4	38.7
Tennessee ball clay #5	30.0
Nepheline syenite	5.3
Ferro frit #3150	4.0
Talc	10.0
Silica	7.0
Grog (20–40 mesh)	5.0
Add:	
Grog (60–80 mesh)	5.0

SST-14   **Burnt Orange Terracotta Throwing Body   Cone 2**
shrinkage 9.3%, plasticity 10.6, glaze rating 11

Mixing.   Mix in the manner of SST-1.

Drying.   Dry in the manner of SST-1.

Bisque Firing.   Fire in the manner of SST-1.

Fired Results.   This body fires to a hard dense burnt orange at cone 2.

Local red clay	51.5
Redart clay	20.0
Plastic fire clay	28.5
Add:	
Grog (40–60 mesh)	10.0

SST-15

Bright Earth Red Throwing Body   Cone 2
shrinkage 14.6%, plasticity 10, glaze rating 11.2

Mixing. Mix in the manner of SST-1.

Drying. Dry in the manner of SST-1.

Bisque Firing. Fire in the manner of SST-1.

Fired Results. This body fires to a bright earth red at cone 2.

Local red brick clay	70.0
Plastic fire clay	17.0
Tennessee ball clay #1	11.0
Bentonite	2.0
Add:	
Grog (40–60 mesh)	10.0

SST-16

White Throwing Body   Cone 2–3
shrinkage 6.6%, plasticity 10.1, glaze rating 12

Mixing. Mix in the manner of SST-1.

Drying. Dry in the manner of SST-1.

Bisque Firing. Fire in the manner of SST-1.

Fired Results. This body fires to a dense white at cone 2 and a slightly off-white at cone 3.

Kaolin (Georgia)	54.0
Kentucky ball clay #4	18.0
Feldspar (Custer)	18.0
Silica	9.0
Bentonite	1.0
Add:	
Grog (20–40 mesh)	10.0

SST-17

Tan Throwing Body   Cone 2–3
shrinkage 12.3%, plasticity 10.5, glaze rating 10.4

Mixing. Mix in the manner of SST-1.

Drying. Dry in the manner of SST-1.

Bisque Firing. Fire in the manner of SST-1.

Fired Results. This body fires to a light tan at cone 2 and a slightly darker tan at cone 3.

Jordan clay	60.0
Silica	28.0
Native red clay	10.0
Bentonite	2.0
Add:	
Grog (40–60 mesh)	10.0

SST-18

White Vitreous Throwing Body   Cone 3
shrinkage 9%, plasticity 9.6, glaze rating 12

Mixing. Mix in the manner of SST-1.

Drying. Dry in the manner of SST-1.

Bisque Firing. Fire in the manner of SST-1.

Fired Results. The body fires to a vitreous white at cone 3.

Nepheline syenite	55.0
Kentucky ball clay #4	11.0
Kaolin (EPK)	25.0
Silica (calcined)	10.0
Bentonite	2.0

SST-19

White Vitreous Throwing Body   Cone 4
shrinkage 9.2%, plasticity 8, glaze rating 12

Mixing. Mix in the manner of SST-1.

Drying. Dry in the manner of SST-1.

Bisque Firing. Fire in the manner of SST-1.

Fired Results. This body fires to a vitreous white at cone 3.

Tennessee ball clay #1	30.0
Nepheline syenite	60.0
Bentonite	4.0
Talc	4.0

SST-20 **Tan-Cream Throwing Body   Cone 4**
shrinkage 10%, plasticity 11, glaze rating 11

Mixing. Mix in the manner of SST-1.

Drying. Dry in the manner of SST-1.

Bisque Firing. Fire in the manner of SST-1.

Fired Results. This body fires to a tan-cream at cone 4. This makes a good body for pottery which is to be used for wax-resist decoration.

Jordan clay	20.0
Tennessee ball clay #5	15.0
Kentucky ball clay #4	10.0
Plastic fire clay	30.0
Nepheline syenite	10.0
Silica	5.0
Grog (60–80 mesh)	12.0

SST-21 **Tan Imitation Stoneware Throwing Body   Cone 4**
shrinkage 9.4%, plasticity 11, glaze rating 12.

Mixing. Mix in the manner of SST-1.

Drying. Dry in the manner of SST-1.

Bisque Firing. Fire in the manner of SST-1.

Fired Results. This body fires to a vitreous tan at cone 4.

Plastic fire clay	9.5
Redart clay	5.0
Tennessee ball clay	2.0
Plastic vitrox	3.0
Grog	1.0
Nepheline syenite	1.0
Silica	.5

SST-22 **Tan Throwing Body   Cone 4**
shrinkage 8.6%, plasticity 10.1, glaze rating 11.5

Mixing. Mix in the manner of SST-1.

Drying. Dry in the manner of SST-1.

Bisque Firing. Fire in the manner of SST-1.

Fired Results. This body fires to medium tan at cone 4.

Plastic fire clay	10.0
Redart clay	10.0
Tennessee ball clay #1	5.0
Kentucky ball clay #4	5.0
Grog (60–80 mesh)	1.0
Talc	1.0

SST-23 **Buff Throwing Body   Cone 4**
shrinkage 11.7%, plasticity 11, glaze rating 12

Mixing. Mix in the manner of SST-1.

Drying. Dry in the manner of SST-1.

Bisque Firing. Fire in the manner of SST-1.

Fired Results. This body fires to a light buff at cone 4.

Tennessee ball clay #5	35.0
Kentucky ball clay #4	30.0
Nepheline syenite	5.0
Ferro frit #3150	3.5
Talc	10.5
Silica	10.0
Add:	
Grog (20–40 mesh)	10.0

SST-24 **Red-Brown Throwing Body   Cone 1–5**
shrinkage 10.8%, plasticity 10.5, glaze rating 11.7

Mixing. Mix in the manner of SST-1.

Drying. Dry in the manner of SST-1.

Bisque Firing. Fire in the manner of SST-1.

Fired Results. This body fires to an earthy red-brown at cone 1 and a darker red-brown at cone 5. At cone 5 it is about 97% vitreous.

Redart clay	40.0
Jordan clay	20.0
Talc	15.0
Silica	15.0
Nepheline syenite	10.0
Grog (60–80 mesh)	5.0

SST-25   **White Throwing Body   Cone 1–5**
shrinkage 5.4%, plasticity 11.5, glaze rating 11.2

Mixing. Mix in the manner of SST-1.

Drying. Dry in the manner of SST-1.

Bisque Firing. Fire in the manner of SST-1.

Fired Results. This body fires to a dense hard white at cone 1 and gives increasingly darker colors to off-white at cone 5.

Kaolin (EPK)	35.0
Silica	20.0
Kentucky ball clay #5	12.0
Tennessee ball clay #1	8.0
Talc	15.0
Plastic vitrox	5.0
Cornwall stone	5.0
Add:	
Bentonite	2.0

SST-26   **Medium Tan Throwing Body   Cone 1–5**
shrinkage 11%, plasticity 11.5, glaze rating 11

Mixing. Mix in the manner of SST-1.

Drying. Dry in the manner of SST-1.

Bisque Firing. Fire in the manner of SST-1.

Fired Results. This body fires to a light tan at cone 1 and to medium tan at cone 5. It is very attractive if a lighter type of grog is used.

Jordan clay	33.0
Redart clay	26.0
Kentucky ball clay #4	11.0
Tennessee ball clay #5	10.0
Silica	9.0
Plastic vitrox	8.0
Nepheline syenite	3.0
Add:	
Grog (40–60 mesh)	10.0

SST-27   **Brick Red Throwing Body   Cone 1–5**
shrinkage 14.3%, plasticity 9.2, glaze rating 11

Mixing. Mix in the manner of SST-1.

Drying. Dry in the manner of SST-1.

Bisque Firing. Fire in the manner of SST-1.

Fired Results. This body fires to a brick red at cone 2 and a red-brown at cone 5.

Redart clay	70.0
Kentucky ball clay #4	20.0
Fire clay	10.0
Add:	
Grog (40–60 mesh)	10.0

SST-28   **Dark Tan Throwing Body   Cone 2–5**
shrinkage 11.2%, plasticity 10.2, glaze rating 11

Mixing. Mix in the manner of SST-1.

Drying. Dry in the manner of SST-1.

Bisque Firing. Fire in the manner of SST-1.

Fired Results. This body fires to a light tan at cone 2 and a dark tan at cone 5.

Redart clay	25.0
Stoneware clay (any)	25.0
Kentucky ball clay #4	25.0
Fire clay	15.0
Silica	10.0
Add:	
Grog (60–80 mesh)	10.0

FORMULAS FOR SOFT STONEWARE CASTING BODIES

Note. No plasticity rating is given for casting bodies.

SSC-1

Red-Brown Casting Body   Cone 03–3
shrinkage 11.6%, glaze rating 10.6

Mixing. Mix all the casting clay bodies in this section according to the outlined procedure in Chapter 3 under Mixing Casting Bodies.

Casting. Use the same casting procedure outlined in the casting body section of Chapter 5, under clay body EC-1.

Drying. Dry in the manner of SST-1.

Bisque Firing. Fire in the manner of SST-1.

Fired Results. This body fires to an orange-brown at cone 03 and a red-brown at cone 3.

Kentucky ball clay #4	22.0
Kaolin (calcined)	20.0
Tennessee ball clay #5	18.0
Fire clay	15.0
Barnard clay	5.0
Sodium carbonate	0.3
Add:	
Water	25%

SSC-2

White Casting Body   Cone 1–4
shrinkage 6.6%, glaze rating 11.8

Mixing. Mix in the manner of SSC-1.

Casting. Cast in the manner of SSC-1.

Drying. Dry in the manner of SST-1.

Bisque Firing. Fire in the manner of SST-1.

Fired Results. This body fires to a 95% vitreous white at cone 4.

Kaolin (Georgia)	30.0
Nepheline syenite	26.0
Kentucky ball clay #4	10.0
Tennessee ball clay #5	10.0
Silica	11.0
Talc	12.0
Sodium carbonate	0.3

SSC-3

Rusty Tan Casting Body   Cone 1–4
shrinkage 10.2%, glaze rating 11

Mixing. Mix in the manner of SSC-1.

Casting. Cast in the manner of SSC-1.

Drying. Dry in the manner of SST-1.

Bisque Firing. Fire in the manner of SST-1.

Fired Results. This body fires to an earthy rust color at cone 1 and a rusty tan at cone 4.

Kaolin (calcined)	30.0
Nepheline syenite	26.0
Silica	11.0
Talc	12.0
Tennessee ball clay #1	10.0
Kentucky ball clay #4	5.0
Tennessee ball clay #5	5.0
Rutile	2.0
Sodium carbonate	0.3
Add:	
Water	25%

SSC-4

Light Brown Casting Body   Cone 1–4
shrinkage 11%, glaze rating 11

Mixing. Mix in the manner of SSC-1.

Casting. Cast in the manner of SSC-1.

Drying. Dry in the manner of SST-1.

Bisque Firing. Fire in the manner of SST-1.

Fired Results. This body fires to a pink-brown at cone 1 and a light brown at cone 4.

Nepheline syenite	25.0
Kaolin (Georgia)	24.0
Tennessee ball clay #5	20.0
Redart clay	10.0
Silica	10.0
Talc	5.0
Cornwall stone	4.0
Barnard clay	2.0
Sodium carbonate	0.3
Add:	
Water	25%

SSC-5 **Translucent White Casting Body   Cone 2–4**
shrinkage 11.3%, glaze rating 11.6

Mixing. Mix in the manner of SSC-1.

Casting. Cast in the manner of SSC-1.

Drying. Dry in the manner of SST-1.

Bisque Firing. Fire in the manner of SST-1.

Fired Results. This body fires to a vitreous translucent white at cone 4. It is a good casting body for tableware including coffee and tea sets.

Nepheline syenite	36.0
Kentucky ball clay #4	30.0
Kaolin (EPK)	18.0
Feldspar (Custer)	9.0
Silica	7.0
Sodium carbonate	0.3
Add:	
Water	25%

SSC-6 **Vitreous White Casting Body   Cone 4**
shrinkage 11.4%, glaze rating 11.9

Mixing. Mix in the manner of SSC-1.

Casting. Cast in the manner of SSC-1.

Drying. Dry in the manner of SST-1.

Bisque Firing. Fire in the manner of SST-1.

Fired Results. This body fires to a vitreous white at cone 4. It makes a good body for heavy-duty utility ware, especially tableware.

Kentucky ball clay #4	22.0
Tennessee ball clay #1	20.0
Nepheline syenite	58.0
Sodium carbonate	1.6
Add:	
Water	40%

SSC-7 **Speckled Buff Casting Body   Cone 4**
shrinkage 6.6%, glaze rating 12

Mixing. Mix in the manner of SSC-1.

Casting. Cast in the manner of SSC-1.

Drying. Dry in the manner of SST-1.

Bisque Firing. Fire in the manner of SST-1.

Fired Results. This body fires to a speckled buff color at cone 4. It is very attractive left unglazed or partially unglazed.

Kaolin (Georgia)	28.0
Nepheline syenite	24.0
Kentucky ball clay #4	10.0
Tennessee ball clay #5	10.0
Silica	11.0
Talc	10.0
Ilmenite	6.0
Sodium carbonate	0.3
Add:	
Water	25%

SSC-8 **Gray-Brown Vitreous Casting Body   Cone 4**
shrinkage 11.5%, glaze rating 11.6

Mixing. Mix in the manner of SSC-1.

Casting. Cast in the manner of SSC-1.

Drying. Dry in the manner of SST-1.

Bisque Firing. Fire in the manner of SST-1.

Fired Results. This body fires to a vitreous gray-brown at cone 4. It is very attractive used with a wax-resist decoration.

Kentucky ball clay #4	42.0
Nepheline syenite	58.0
Iron chromate	6.0
Sodium carbonate	1.6
Add:	
Grog (60–80 mesh)	10.0

SSC-9 **Medium Brown Casting Body   Cone 4**
shrinkage 11.2%, glaze rating 11.4

Mixing. Mix in the manner of SSC-1.

Casting. Cast in the manner of SSC-1.

Drying. Dry in the manner of SST-1.

Bisque Firing. Fire in the manner of SST-1.

Fired Results. This body fires to a medium brown at cone 4. It is more attractive if a lighter color grog is used in the slip. The surface of the ware should be slightly burnished with a damp sponge or cloth to allow the grog to show through.

Fire clay	29.0
Redart clay	25.8
Jordan clay	19.0
Nepheline syenite	11.2
Grog (60–80 mesh)	12.0
Silica	3.0
Sodium carbonate	0.3
Add:	
Water	25%

SSC-10 **Dark Brown Casting Body   Cone 4**
shrinkage 11.4%, glaze rating 11.3

Mixing. Mix in the manner of SSC-1.

Casting. Cast in the manner of SSC-1.

Drying. Dry in the manner of SST-1.

Bisque Firing. Fire in the manner of SST-1.

Fired Results. This body fires to a dark brown at cone 4. Use a lighter color grog in the body for a more attractive and rustic effect. The surface of the ware should be burnished as in the instructions for SSC-9,

Fire clay	29.0
Redart clay	25.7
Jordan clay	19.0
Nepheline syenite	11.0
Grog (60–80 mesh)	12.3
Silica	10.0
Red iron oxide	2.0
Sodium carbonate	0.3
Add:	
Water	25%

FORMULAS FOR SOFT STONEWARE SCULPTURE BODIES

Note. The clay bodies in this section are excellent for handbuilding. They are not recommended for throwing.

SSS-1. **Brick Red Sculpture Body   Cone 03–4**
shrinkage 10.3%, plasticity 10, glaze rating 10.5

Mixing. Mix this body according to the instructions in Chapter 3, Clay Body Preparation, using any of the three methods described. Grog can be added in the mixing or during the wedging process. In cases where the clay may be too wet to handle the addition of the grog at this point will help to dry out the clay to the proper working consistency. In any case all sculpture bodies should be thoroughly wedged if the soaking or the slip method of mixing are used. If plasticity seems to be a problem, a couple of weeks of aging will raise the plasticity by almost one point on the rating scale.

Drying. Allow all sculpture and handbuilt pieces to dry thoroughly. Sculpture pieces are usually thicker and consequently need more drying time. Use the cheek test to check for dryness.

Bisque Firing. Bisque fire sculpture pieces only if they are to be glazed later. If they are not, then fire them to maturity with the first firing. This body should be bisque fired to at least cone 03.

Fired Results. At cone 03 this body is an orange-red. It fires increasingly darker and is a brick red at cone 4.

Red brick clay or native red clay	40.0
Jordan clay	30.0
Volcanic ash	20.0
Talc	5.0
Feldspar (Kingman)	3.0
Plastic vitrox	2.0
Add:	
Grog (60–80 mesh)	10.0

SSS-2 **Off-White Sculpture Body   Cone 1–4**
shrinkage 6.1%, plasticity 8.8, glaze rating 9.7

Mixing. Mix in the manner of SSS-1.

Drying. Dry in the manner of SSS-1.

Bisque Firing. Fire in the manner of SSS-1.

Fired Results. This body fires to an off-white at cones 1–4.

Kaolin (EPK)	30.0
Kentucky ball clay #4	25.0
Talc	15.0
Volcanic ash	5.0
Cornwall stone	5.0
Plastic vitrox	5.0
Add:	
Grog (60–80 mesh)	10.0

SSS-3 **Tan Sculpture Body   Cone 1–4**
shrinkage 7.6%, plasticity 9, glaze rating 10.8

Mixing. Mix in the manner of SSS-1.

Drying. Dry in the manner of SSS-1.

Bisque Firing. Fire in the manner of SSS-1.

Fired Results. This body fires to a light tan at cone 1 and gets increasingly darker up to cone 4. At this level it is a rich tan color.

Jordan clay	34.0
Native red clay	26.0
Kentucky ball clay #4	20.0
Silica	10.0
Volcanic ash	8.0
Nepheline syenite	2.0
Add:	
Grog (60–80 mesh)	10.0
Grog (20–40 mesh)	10.0

SSS-4 **Light Brown Sculpture Body   Cone 2–3**
shrinkage 9.7%, plasticity 8.4, glaze rating 11.4

Mixing. Mix in the manner of SSS-1.

Drying. Dry in the manner of SSS-1.

Bisque Firing. Fire in the manner of SSS-1.

Fired Results. This body fires to a light brown at cones 2–4.

Kaolin (EPK)	20.0
Plastic fire clay	22.0
Kentucky ball clay #4	18.0
Nepheline syenite	5.0
Barnard clay	5.0
Talc	5.0
Add:	
Grog (20–40 mesh)	10.0
Grog (60–80 mesh)	10.0

SSS-5 **Orange-Red Sculpture Body   Cone 2–4**
shrinkage 8.6%, plasticity 10.1, glaze rating 11

Mixing. Mix in the manner of SSS-1.

Drying. Dry in the manner of SSS-1.

Bisque Firing. Fire in the manner of SSS-1.

Fired Results. This body fires to an earthy orange-red at cones 2–4. It is slightly darker at cone 4.

Plastic fire clay	40.0
Native red clay	30.0
Kentucky ball clay #4	17.0
Volcanic ash	10.0
Red Iron Oxide	2.0
Bentonite	1.0
Add:	
Grog (60–80 mesh)	10.0

SSS-6 **Buff Sculpture Body   Cone 2–4**
shrinkage 9.4%, plasticity 8.5, glaze rating 11

Mixing. Mix in the manner of SSS-1.

Drying. Dry in the manner of SSS-1.

Bisque Firing. Fire in the manner of SSS-1.

Fired Results. This body fires to a buff color at cones 2–4.

Plastic fire clay	30.0
Native red clay	16.0
Kentucky ball clay #4	15.0
Tennessee ball clay #5	15.0
Tennessee ball clay #1	4.0
Add:	
Grog (60–80 mesh)	18.0

SSS-7

Cream Sculpture Body   Cone 4
shrinkage 9.6%, plasticity 10, glaze rating 11.5

Mixing. Mix in the manner of SSS-1.

Drying. Dry in the manner of SSS-1.

Bisque Firing. Fire in the manner of SSS-1.

Fired Results. This body fires to a rich cream color at cone 4. It is very attractive if a darker grog is used.

Plastic fire clay	22.0
Kaolin (EPK)	18.0
Kentucky ball clay #4	10.0
Tennessee ball clay #5	10.0
Nepheline syenite	5.0
Whiting	5.0
Talc	5.0
Add:	
Grog (20–40 mesh)	12.5
Grog (60–80 mesh)	12.5

SSS-8

Light Buff Sculpture Body   Cone 4
shrinkage 11%, plasticity 9, glaze rating 11

Mixing. Mix in the manner of SSS-1.

Drying. Dry in the manner of SSS-1.

Bisque Firing. Fire in the manner of SSS-1.

Fired Results. This body fires to a light buff at cone 4. It is more attractive if a lighter or darker grog is used. For an even more rustic effect use both a lighter and a darker grog in this body and leave it unglazed.

Plastic fire clay	30.0
Kentucky ball clay #4	20.0
Tennessee ball clay #5	20.0
Native red clay	20.0
Jordan clay	10.0
Add:	
Grog (20–40 mesh)	20.0
Grog (60–80 mesh)	10.0

SSS-9

Brick Orange-Red Terracotta Sculpture Body   Cone 4
shrinkage 5.6%, plasticity 10, glaze rating 9

Mixing. Mix in the manner of SSS-1.

Drying. Dry in the manner of SSS-1.

Bisque Firing. Fire in the manner of SSS-1.

Fired Results. This body fires to a brick orange-red at cone 4. It will stand higher firing—as much as cone 6. At this cone level it is a brick red-brown.

Native red clay	30.0
Jordan clay	20.0
Kentucky ball clay #4	10.0
Tennessee ball clay #5	10.0
Plastic fire clay	10.0
Kaolin (EPK)	10.0
Bentonite	6.0
Talc	4.0
Add:	
Grog (20–40 mesh)	10.0
Grog (60–80 mesh)	10.0

SSS-10

Brick Red-Orange Rustic Terracotta Sculpture Body Cone 4
shrinkage 6.9%, plasticity 9, glaze rating 9.4

Mixing. Mix in the manner of SSS-1.

Drying. Dry in the manner of SSS-1.

Bisque Firing. Fire in the manner of SSS-1.

Fired Results. This body is quite rough. It fires to a rustic red-orange at cone 4. It can be fired as high as cone 6 where it is a darker brick red.

Redart clay	22.0
Kentucky ball clay #4	10.0
Kaolin (EPK)	10.0
Bentonite	4.0
Talc	4.0
Add:	
Grog (20–40 mesh)	10.0
Grog (60–80 mesh)	10.0

7
STONEWARE CLAY BODIES
CONE 4-12

Stoneware is probably the most popular of all the clay body types with artist potters, partly because of its fired strength but mainly because of the character of the finished ware which can range from the refined to the subtle to the highly rustic, depending on the whim of the potter.

The colors of fired stoneware objects can range from cream to a brown-black. There are two things that can affect the color of fired stoneware pottery: the inherent metallic oxides in the clay and the firing atmosphere used to mature the finished ware—oxidation or reduction (see Glossary).

All of the clay bodies in this chapter were designed for three specific purposes: throwing,

casting, or sculpture. It is not advised that the potter use a clay body for a forming method for which it was not designed unless the instructions indicate that it can be done successfully.

The clay bodies were also designed for a particular temperature range and it is not advised that the potter exceed this unless the instructions indicate it can be done safely.

The recipes in this chapter are arranged first by forming type: throwing, casting, or sculpture, then by temperature and color, light to dark, within each category.

The reader will find possible substitutions for most of the chemicals in Chapter 34, Dictionary of Glaze and Clay Compounds, under each individual heading.

Note. The ingredients in the formulas in this chapter can be weighed out in either grams or pounds. It is recommended that the potter first make a 100-gram test batch of the clay body that interests him to insure that it is suitable before making larger amounts. Any of the lighter firing bodies can be colored by the use of coloring oxides. See Chapter 12 for further information. The clay bodies are listed here by firing temperature from lower to higher cones.

FORMULAS FOR STONEWARE THROWING BODIES

ST-1

Tan-Brown Stoneware Throwing Body   Cone 4-9
shrinkage 12.5%, plasticity 8.9, glaze rating 9.4

Mixing. Weigh out the ingredients by grams for test batches and by pounds for larger batches. Mix the clay using any of the three methods outlined in Chapter 3 on Clay Body Preparation. The clay can be used at once or stored to age for a couple of weeks for even greater plasticity. If a pug mill is not used for mixing, take care that the clay is thoroughly wedged to increase its workability and to remove any trapped air bubbles which might lead to cracking or explosions during the firing. This particular clay is highly plastic and probably will not need aging. It is good for all wheel work and with the addition of 20% to 30% more grog, it can be used for sculpture or coil building.

Ingredient	Amount
Monmouth clay	25.0
Jordan clay	20.0
Kentucky ball clay #4	20.0
Silica	15.0
Feldspar (Custer)	5.0
Tennessee ball clay	10.0
Barnard clay	2.5
Redart clay	2.5
Add:	
Grog (60–80 mesh)	10.0

Drying. Place the wet pieces in a location that is free of drafts and allow them to dry thoroughly. Drafts can lead to uneven drying and consequent warping or cracking. Test for dryness by placing the base of the piece against your cheek. If it feels even faintly moist or cool to the touch, it still contains moisture and should dry further. Drying time will vary according to the size and thickness of the ware, the temperature, and the humidity. In general most pieces will dry and be ready for firing in a week if kept in a warm, dry place.

Bisque Firing. Stoneware should have a bisque firing of at least cone 06, cone 04 is even better. First fire the ware slowly to 500° F./260° C. to allow any latent moisture to be removed slowly, then fire normally to the desired bisque temperature. If a raw alkaline glaze is to be used the ware should be bisque fired to cone 04.

Fired Results. When fired in oxidation this stoneware body produces a light warm tan; reduction gives a light toast brown with occasional iron spots. It is good used under ash glazes.

ST-2 **Tan-Gray Stoneware Throwing Body   Cone 5**
shrinkage 12.3%, plasticity 9.9, glaze rating 9.5

Mixing. Mix in the manner of ST-1.

Drying. Dry in the manner of ST-1.

Bisque Firing. Fire in the manner of ST-1.

Fired Results. When fired in oxidation this body is a soft tan; reduction gives a cool gray-tan. This body is completely vitreous at cone 5.

Redart clay	25.0
Jordan clay	26.0
Kentucky ball clay #4	25.0
Plastic fire clay	26.0
Silica	9.0
Add:	
Grog (60–80 mesh)	10.0

ST-3 **Cream/Tan-Gray Stoneware Throwing Body   Cone 5**
shrinkage 10.8%, plasticity 9.5, glaze rating 8.8

Mixing. Mix in the manner of ST-1.

Drying. Dry in the manner of ST-1.

Bisque Firing. Fire in the manner of ST-1.

Fired Results. When fired in oxidation this body is a light cream color; reduction produces a cool tan-gray body. It is completely vitreous at cone 5.

Kentucky ball clay (PX)	28.3
Tennessee ball clay #5	20.4
Kaolin (EPK)	31.0
Potash feldspar (Kona A-3)	3.1
Add:	
Grog (60–80 mesh)	10.0

ST-4 **Brown Stoneware Throwing Body   Cone 5–6**
shrinkage 10.5%, plasticity 10.3, glaze rating 11.5

Mixing. Mix in the manner of ST-1.

Drying. Dry in the manner of ST-1.

Bisque Firing. Fire in the manner of ST-1.

Fired Results. When fired in oxidation this body is a light brown with darker specks; reduction gives clay body a rich dark brown.

Native red clay	38.0
Kaolin (EPK)	24.0
Feldspar (Kona A-3)	13.5
Cornwall stone	10.0
Silica	12.5
Bentonite	2.0
Add:	
Grog (60–80 mesh)	10.0

ST-5

Brown Stoneware Throwing Body Cone 5–6
shrinkage 9.9%, plasticity 9.0, glaze rating 8.8

Mixing. Mix in the manner of ST-1.

Drying. Dry in the manner of ST-1.

Bisque Firing. Fire in the manner of ST-1.

Fired Results. Fired in oxidation this clay body is a toast brown color; reduction gives a charcoal brown with hints of metallic highlights. It iron spots well in heavy reduction firing.

Kentucky ball clay #4	18.0
Tennessee ball clay #1	12.0
Tennessee ball clay #5	8.0
Nepheline syenite	25.0
Feldspar (Kingman)	6.0
Silica	20.0
Red iron oxide	8.0
Bentonite	3.0
Add:	
Grog (60–80 mesh)	10.0

ST-6

Speckled Tan Stoneware Throwing Body Cone 5–8
shrinkage 11.1%, plasticity 9.4, glaze rating 8.5

Mixing. Mix in the manner of ST-1.

Drying. Dry in the manner of ST-1.

Bisque Firing. Fire in the manner of ST-1.

Fired Results. When fired in oxidation this body is a light tan; reduction gives a speckled tan of a darker hue. This body iron spots well in heavy reduction firing. Being completely vitreous at cone 8 it performs well for utility ware.

Fire clay (any)	21.4
Goldart clay	8.0
Jordan clay	19.4
Grog (60–80 mesh)	12.0
Nepheline syenite	9.8
Silica	2.9
Bentonite	2.0

ST-7

Brown/Gray-Brown Stoneware Throwing Body Cone 5–8
shrinkage 10%, plasticity 9.1, glaze rating 9.3

Mixing. Mix in the manner of ST-1.

Drying. Dry in the manner of ST-1.

Bisque Firing. Fire in the manner of ST-1.

Fired Results. Fired in oxidation this body is a light brown; reduction gives a gray-brown with occasional metallic highlights. It iron spots well in heavy reduction. This body is also good for utility ware.

Native red clay	24.0
Jordan clay	11.0
Monmouth clay	10.0
Goldart clay	20.0
Grog (40–60 mesh)	10.0
Plastic fire clay	10.0
Nepheline syenite	11.0
Silica	4.0

ST-8

Tan-Brown Stoneware Throwing Body Cone 6
shrinkage 13%, plasticity 8.8, glaze rating 9.5

Mixing. Mix in the manner of ST-1.

Drying. Dry in the manner of ST-1.

Bisque Firing. Fire in the manner of ST-1.

Fired Results. When fired in oxidation this body is a tan-brown; reduction produces a warm darker brown which iron spots very well when the reduction is heavy.

Jordan clay	33.5
Lincoln fire clay	10.0
Plastic fire clay	9.5
Feldspar (Custer)	16.0
Nepheline syenite	4.0
Tennessee ball clay #5	16.0
Silica	9.0
Red iron oxide	2.0
Add:	
Grog (60–80 mesh)	10.0

ST-9

Cream-Tan Stoneware Throwing Body   Cone 6
shrinkage 14%, plasticity 9, glaze rating 9.5

Mixing. Mix in the manner of ST-1.

Drying. Dry in the manner of ST-1.

Bisque Firing. Fire in the manner of ST-1.

Fired Results. When fired in oxidation this body is a warm cream color; reduction gives a creamy tan color of a darker hue. This body does not iron spot well. It is completely vitreous at cone 6 and is good for utility ware.

Plastic fire clay	58.0
Kentucky ball clay #4	38.0
Goldart clay	4.0
Add:	
Grog (60–80 mesh)	10.0

ST-10

Brown Stoneware Throwing Body   Cone 6
shrinkage 11.3%, plasticity 11.2, glaze rating 11.5

Mixing. Mix in the manner of ST-1.

Drying. Dry in the manner of ST-1.

Bisque Firing. Fire in the manner of ST-1.

Fired Results. When fired in oxidation this body produces a soft warm brown; reduction gives a nice metallic brown. This body iron spots well in heavy reduction firing and vitrifies well for wind chimes or wind bells.

Hawthorn bond clay	30.0
Monmouth fire clay	15.0
Redart clay	40.0
Kentucky ball clay #4	15.0
Add:	
Grog (60–80 mesh)	10.0

ST-11

Tan-Gray Stoneware Throwing Body   Cone 6
shrinkage 10%, plasticity 11.3, glaze rating 11.5

Mixing. Mix in the manner of ST-1.

Drying. Dry in the manner of ST-1.

Bisque Firing. Fire in the manner of ST-1.

Fired Results. When fired in oxidation this body gives a warm cream color; reduction gives a creamy gray of a cooler hue.

Jordan clay	20.0
Tennessee ball clay #1	10.0
Kentucky ball clay #4	10.0
Plastic ball clay	30.0
Nepheline syenite	10.0
Silica	5.0
Grog (60–80 mesh)	10.0

ST-12

Off-White Stoneware Throwing Body   Cone 6
shrinkage 11.9%, plasticity 11.3, glaze rating 11.5

Mixing. Mix in the manner of ST-1.

Drying. Dry in the manner of ST-1.

Bisque Firing. Fire in the manner of ST-1.

Fired Results. When fired in oxidation this body gives an off-white which is good for utility ware of the hotel china type; reduction produces a light gray body.

Tennessee ball clay #1	49.0
Kaolin (EPK)	29.0
Talc	7.0
Nepheline syenite	5.0
Silica	10.0
Add:	
Grog (60–80 mesh)	10.0

ST-13

Pink Stoneware Throwing Body   Cone 6
shrinkage 11.3%, plasticity 11.5, glaze rating 10.9

Mixing. Mix in the manner of ST-1.

Drying. Dry in the manner of ST-1.

Bisque Firing. Fire in the manner of ST-1.

Fired Results. When fired in oxidation this body gives an earthy pink color; reduction gives an earthy pink-brown hue.

Red earthenware clay	20.0
Kaolin (EPK)	15.0
Kentucky ball clay #4	35.0
Red brick grog	10.0
Red iron oxide	3.0
Silica	7.0
Talc	7.0
Nepheline syenite	3.0
Grog (60–80 mesh)	10.0

ST-14 **Black-Brown Stoneware Throwing Body Cone 6**
shrinkage 12.5%, plasticity 8.5, glaze rating 9.3

Mixing. Mix in the manner of ST-1.

Drying. Dry in the manner of ST-1.

Bisque Firing. Fire in the manner of ST-1.

Fired Results. When fired in oxidation this body produces a black-brown color; reduction gives a metallic brown-black which iron spots very well, even in lighter reduction firings.

Red earthenware clay	40.0
Kaolin	18.0
Kentucky ball clay #4	15.0
Red iron oxide	16.0
Manganese dioxide	6.0
Bentonite	3.0
Nepheline syenite	2.0

ST-15 **Warm-Toned Buff Stoneware Throwing Body Cone 6**
shrinkage 12.5%, plasticity 10.7, glaze rating 9.7

Mixing. Mix in the manner of ST-1.

Drying. Dry in the manner of ST-1.

Bisque Firing. Fire in the manner of ST-1.

Fired Results. When fired in oxidation this body gives a warm-toned buff color; reduction gives a buff-brown color. This body has a marvelous warm quality which makes it good for pieces which are to be left unglazed.

Kentucky ball clay #4	20.0
Tennessee ball clay #5	20.0
Kaolin	20.0
Red earthenware clay	15.0
Talc	5.0
Nepheline syenite	5.0
Grog (60–80 mesh)	15.0

ST-16 **Off-White Stoneware Throwing Body Cone 6–8**
shrinkage 12.5%, plasticity 9.3, glaze rating 7.0

Mixing. Mix in the manner of ST-1.

Drying. Dry in the manner of ST-1.

Bisque Firing. Fire in the manner of ST-1.

Fired Results. When fired in oxidation this body produces an off-white which is excellent for utility ware; reduction gives a light gray color.

Kaolin (EPK)	35.0
Nepheline syenite	25.0
Silica	20.0
Kaolin (Georgia)	15.0
Kentucky ball clay #4	6.0
Tennessee ball clay #1	4.0
Godfrey feldspar	2.0
Feldspar (Kona A-3)	3.0

ST-17 **Creamy/Speckled Tan Stoneware Throwing Body
Cone 6–8**
shrinkage 12.5%, plasticity 9.5, glaze rating 8.2

Mixing. Mix in the manner of ST-1.

Drying. Dry in the manner of ST-1.

Bisque Firing. Fire in the manner of ST-1.

Fired Results. When fired in oxidation this body gives a warm cream color; reduction produces a speckled tan which spots moderately well in heavy reduction.

Jordan clay	30.0
Westko clay	10.0
Kentucky ball clay #4	10.0
Feldspar (Buckingham)	12.0
Silica	8.0

ST-18 **Gray-Brown Stoneware Throwing Body Cone 6–8**
shrinkage 12.5%, plasticity 8.3, glaze rating 8.5

Mixing. Mix in the manner of ST-1.

Drying. Dry in the manner of ST-1.

Bisque Firing. Fire in the manner of ST-1.

Fired Results. When fired in oxidation this clay produces a body which is light gray; reduction produces a light brown body. This body has a cool gray-brown quality which is good for pieces which are to be unglazed or decorated with wax resist. At cone 8 it is completely vitreous.

Tennessee ball clay #5	20.0
Kentucky ball clay #4	15.0
Kaolin (EPK)	27.0
Plastic fire clay	14.0
Silica	10.0
Feldspar (Custer)	8.0
Nepheline syenite	2.0
Black iron oxide	2.0
Grog (80–100 mesh)	2.0
Add:	
Grog (60–80 mesh)	10.0

ST-19 **Gray Stoneware Throwing Body   Cone 6–10**
shrinkage 13.0%, plasticity 9, glaze rating 8.6

Mixing. Mix in the manner of ST-1.

Drying. Dry in the manner of ST-1.

Bisque Firing. Fire in the manner of ST-1.

Fired Results. When fired in oxidation this clay produces a body which is light gray in color; reduction gives a darker gray body.

Plastic vitrox	43.0
Kentucky ball clay #4	11.2
Tennessee ball clay #5	10.0
Kaolin (EPK)	5.2
Grog (80–100 mesh)	6.2
Talc	5.2
Bentonite	3.4

ST-20 **Off-White/Gray Stoneware Throwing Body   Cone 6–10**
shrinkage 12.5%, plasticity 10, glaze rating 8.5

Mixing. Mix in the manner of ST-1.

Drying. Dry in the manner of ST-1.

Bisque Firing. Fire in the manner of ST-1.

Fired Results. When fired in oxidation this body is an off-white; reduction produces a light gray body of excellent quality for any type of utility ware.

Kentucky ball clay #4	12.0
Tennessee ball clay #1	18.0
Kaolin (EPK)	32.0
Feldspar (Kona A-3)	20.0
Nepheline syenite	12.0
Silica	4.0
Fire clay	2.0
Add:	
Grog (60–80 mesh)	10.0

ST-21 **Orange Spotted/Brick Stoneware Throwing Body Cone 6–10**
shrinkage 11%, plasticity 9, glaze rating 9.5

Mixing. Mix in the manner of ST-1.

Drying. Dry in the manner of ST-1.

Bisque Firing. Fire in the manner of ST-1.

Fired Results. When fired in oxidation this body gives a brick orange color that is excellent for outdoor flowerpots; reduction gives a spotted orange-brown color that is very good for unglazed wares.

Jordan clay	35.0
Westko clay	6.4
Plastic fire clay	30.3
Grog (40–60 mesh)	9.3
Silica	19.0
Grog (60–80 mesh)	10.0

ST-22 **Buff-Brown Stoneware Throwing Body   Cone 6–10**
shrinkage 11.3%, plasticity 10.9, glaze rating 11.2

Mixing. Mix in the manner of ST-1.

Drying. Dry in the manner of ST-1.

Bisque Firing. Fire in the manner of ST-1.

Fired Results. When fired in oxidation this clay produces a warm buff; reduction gives a buff-brown color which is excellent for pieces which are to be left unglazed or used for wax resist.

Plastic fire clay	50.0
Redart clay	25.0
Kentucky ball clay (any)	10.0
Plastic vitrox	15.0
Add:	
Grog (60–80 mesh)	10.0

ST-23 **Tan-Brown Stoneware Throwing Body   Cone 6–10**
shrinkage 11%, plasticity 9.5, glaze rating 8.9

Mixing. Mix in the manner of ST-1.

Drying. Dry in the manner of ST-1.

Bisque Firing. Fire in the manner of ST-1.

Fired Results. When fired in oxidation this clay gives a warm tan; reduction gives a warm, light brown color.

Jordan clay	14.0
Plastic fire clay	40.0
Sand (60–80 mesh)	14.0
Grog (60–80 mesh)	14.0
Kentucky ball clay #4	11.0
Barnard clay	4.2
Bentonite	2.8

ST-24   **Cool Tan/Gray Stoneware Throwing Body   Cone 7**
shrinkage 9.5%, plasticity 9.1, glaze rating 9.0

Mixing. Mix in the manner of ST-1.

Drying. Dry in the manner of ST-1.

Bisque Firing. Fire in the manner of ST-1.

Fired Results. When fired in oxidation this clay gives a body with a cool tan hue; reduction produces a cool gray body. This also a good body for pieces which are to be left unglazed or used for wax-resist decoration.

Jordan clay	58.0
Kentucky ball clay #4	10.0
Tennessee ball clay #5	9.0
Silica	9.0
Plastic fire clay	10.0
Kaolin (EPK)	5.0
Add:	
Grog (60–80 mesh)	10.0

ST-25   **Cream-Tan Stoneware Throwing Body   Cone 7–8**
shrinkage 10.4%, plasticity 9.4, glaze rating 9.2

Mixing. Mix in the manner of ST-1.

Drying. Dry in the manner of ST-1.

Bisque Firing. Fire in the manner of ST-1.

Fired Results. When fired in oxidation this clay gives a cream color; reduction gives a warm earthy tan.

Kentucky ball clay #4	26.0
Kentucky ball clay PX	20.0
Kaolin (EPK)	26.0
Plastic fire clay	19.0
Silica	14.0
Add:	
Grog (60–80 mesh)	10.0

ST-26   **Gray-Brown Stoneware Throwing Body   Cone 7–9**
shrinkage 11.4%, plasticity 9.1, glaze rating 8.2

Mixing. Mix in the manner of ST-1.

Drying. Dry in the manner of ST-1.

Bisque Firing. Fire in the manner of ST-1.

Fired Results. When fired in oxidation this body is a warm light gray; reduction gives a grayed brown. It iron spots very well in heavy reduction firing.

Plastic fire clay	62.7
Jordan clay	9.3
Monmouth clay	10.3
Nepheline syenite	4.8
Silica	5.0
Grog (40–60 mesh)	5.9
Grog (60–80 mesh)	5.9
Iron chromate	1.9

ST-27   **Orange Stoneware Throwing Body   Cone 7–9**
shrinkage 7.8%, plasticity 8.2, glaze rating 9.3

Mixing. Mix in the manner of ST-1.

Drying. Dry in the manner of ST-1.

Bisque Firing. Fire in the manner of ST-1.

Fired Results. When fired in oxidation this clay gives a pink-tan color; heavy reduction produces a spotted orange color of great beauty. This body is at its best when used for pieces to be left completely or partially unglazed.

Jordan clay	28.0
Monmouth clay	30.0
Silica	28.0
Redart clay	12.0
Barium carbonate	2.0
Add:	
Grog (60–80 mesh)	10.0

ST-28   **Tan-Brown Stoneware Throwing Body   Cone 7–9**
shrinkage 14.2%, plasticity 9.0, glaze rating 9.3

Mixing. Mix in the manner of ST-1.

Drying. Dry in the manner of ST-1.

Bisque Firing. Fire in the manner of ST-1.

Fired Results. When fired in oxidation this clay will give a cool tan color; reduction produces a cool gray-brown with darker specks. It iron spots well in heavy reduction.

Tennessee ball clay #5	22.5
Kentucky ball clay #4	18.5
Plastic fire clay	36.0
Native red clay	20.0
Kaolin (EPK)	3.0
Add:	
Grog (60–80 mesh)	10.0

ST-29

Gray-Brown Stoneware Throwing Body   Cone 7–9
shrinkage 14%, plasticity 9.0, glaze rating 9.3

Mixing. Mix in the manner of ST-1.

Drying. Dry in the manner of ST-1.

Bisque Firing. Fire in the manner of ST-1.

Fired Results. When fired in oxidation this clay will give a warm gray color; reduction gives a warm gray-brown color.

Tennessee ball clay #5	20.5
Kentucky ball clay #4	14.5
Tennessee ball clay #1	6.5
Redart clay	19.5
Kaolin	2.5
Silica	1.0
Add:	
Grog (60–80 mesh)	10.0

ST-30

Off-White/Gray-Tan Stoneware Throwing Body Cone 7–10
shrinkage 13%, plasticity 9.4, glaze rating 9.0

Mixing. Mix in the manner of ST-1.

Drying. Dry in the manner of ST-1.

Bisque Firing. Fire in the manner of ST-1.

Fired Results. When fired in oxidation this body produces an off-white; reduction gives a cool grayed tan color. When fired in the cone 8–10 range the body vitrifies and is excellent for making wind chimes or wind bells.

Kaolin (EPK)	41.0
Kentucky ball clay PX	15.0
Kentucky ball clay #4	16.0
Feldspar (Custer)	16.0
Silica	9.0
Redart clay	3.0
Add:	
Grog (60–80 mesh)	10.0

ST-31

Off-White/Warm Gray Stoneware Throwing Body Cone 7–10
shrinkage 13.1%, plasticity 8.0, glaze rating 9.4

Mixing. Mix in the manner of ST-1.

Drying. Dry in the manner of ST-1.

Bisque Firing. Fire in the manner of ST-1.

Fired Results. When fired in oxidation this body gives a nice off-white; reduction gives a light warm gray.

Kaolin (Georgia)	43.6
Kentucky ball clay #4	10.0
Tennessee ball clay #5	7.0
Feldspar (Kingman)	17.8
Monmouth fire clay	11.6
Silica	10.0

ST-32

Off-White/Gray Stoneware Throwing Body   Cone 8
shrinkage 11.3%, plasticity 10.6, glaze rating 11.3

Mixing. Mix in the manner of ST-1.

Drying. Dry in the manner of ST-1.

Bisque Firing. Fire in the manner of ST-1.

Fired Results. When fired in oxidation this clay gives an excellent off-white; reduction produces a cool gray color.

Tennessee ball clay #1	40.0
Kaolin	29.0
Talc	7.0
Nepheline syenite	5.0
Silica	19.0

ST-33

Cream/Speckled Buff Stoneware Throwing Body Cone 8
shrinkage 10.3%, plasticity 9.4, glaze rating 9.0

Mixing. Mix in the manner of ST-1.

Drying. Dry in the manner of ST-1.

Bisque Firing. Fire in the manner of ST-1.

Fired Results. When fired in oxidation this clay gives a warm cream color; reduction produces a warm speckled buff color of great beauty. It is excellent for pieces to be left unglazed or partially glazed. Due to its lower glaze rating however it is not recommended for utility ware.

Jordan clay	17.0
Monmouth clay	25.0
Goldart clay	5.0
Kentucky ball clay #4	33.0
Silica	20.0
Add:	
Grog (60–80 mesh)	10.0

ST-34 **Cream-Tan Stoneware Throwing Body   Cone 8**
shrinkage 11%, plasticity 9, glaze rating 9

Mixing. Mix in the manner of ST-1.

Drying. Dry in the manner of ST-1.

Bisque Firing. Fire in the manner of ST-1.

Fired Results. When fired in oxidation this body is a warm cream color; reduction gives a warm tan. It is an excellent body for utility ware of the rustic type for it is completely vitreous at cone 8.

Monmouth clay	40.0
Goldart clay	10.0
Kentucky ball clay PX	15.0
Talc	5.0
Silica	5.0
Add:	
Grog (60–80 mesh)	10.0

ST-35 **Gray-Tan Stoneware Throwing Body   Cone 8**
shrinkage 10.5%, plasticity 9.5, glaze rating 9.5

Mixing. Mix in the manner of ST-1.

Drying. Dry in the manner of ST-1.

Bisque Firing. Fire in the manner of ST-1.

Fired Results. When fired in oxidation this body is a cool gray color; reduction gives a cool grayed-tan color of great beauty. This body is also excellent for utility ware of the rustic type.

Jordan clay	75.0
Kentucky ball clay #4	14.0
Feldspar (Custer)	9.0
Goldart clay	2.0
Add:	
Grog (60–80 mesh)	10.0

ST-36 **Gray-Tan Stoneware Throwing Body   Cone 8**
shrinkage 10.3%, plasticity 9.6, glaze rating 9.5

Mixing. Mix in the manner of ST-1.

Drying. Dry in the manner of ST-1.

Bisque Firing. Fire in the manner of ST-1.

Fired Results. When fired in oxidation this body is a cool gray; reduction gives a cool tan of a grayer hue. It is excellent for utility ware of the rustic type.

Monmouth clay	75.0
Tennessee ball clay (any)	12.0
Feldspar (Kona A-3)	11.0
Plastic fire clay	2.0
Grog (60–80 mesh)	10.0

ST-37 **Buff-Brown Stoneware Throwing Body   Cone 8**
shrinkage 11.6%, plasticity 10.7, glaze rating 11.5

Mixing. Mix in the manner of ST-1.

Drying. Dry in the manner of ST-1.

Bisque Firing. Fire in the manner of ST-1.

Fired Results. When fired in oxidation this clay gives a warm speckled buff color; reduction gives a warm toast brown color which iron spots well in heavy reduction.

Jordan clay	50.0
Kentucky ball clay #4	22.0
Feldspar (Buckingham)	10.0
Silica	18.0
Add:	
Grog	10.0

ST-38 **Rich Earth Red Stoneware Throwing Body   Cone 8**
shrinkage 12.1%, plasticity 10.9, glaze rating 11.3

Mixing. Mix in the manner of ST-1.

Drying. Dry in the manner of ST-1.

Bisque Firing. Fire in the manner of ST-1.

Fired Results. When fired in oxidation this clay will produce a rich earth red body of great beauty; reduction gives a rich red-brown which iron spots exceptionally well even in a light reduction firing.

Jordan clay	30.0
Redart clay	30.0
Kentucky ball clay #4	20.0
Feldspar (Buckingham)	3.0
Silica	15.0
Fire clay (any)	3.0
Add:	
Red iron oxide	3.0
Add:	
Grog	10.0

ST-39   **Cream-Gray Stoneware Throwing Body**   **Cone 8–9**
shrinkage 12%, plasticity 9.5, glaze rating 7.5

Mixing.   Mix in the manner of ST-1.

Drying.   Dry in the manner of ST-1.

Bisque Firing.   Fire in the manner of ST-1.

Fired Results.   When fired in oxidation this clay will produce a warm cream color; reduction gives a warm gray color that is exceptionally beautiful if left unglazed or partially glazed.

Kentucky ball clay #4	25.3
Plastic vitrox	5.0
Feldspar (Kingman)	26.5
Kaolin (EPK)	23.2
Silica	20.0
Add:	
Grog (60–80 mesh)	10.0

ST-40   **Tan-Gray Stoneware Throwing Body**   **Cone 8–10**
shrinkage 10.9%, plasticity 10.7, glaze rating 10.7

Mixing.   Mix in the manner of ST-1.

Drying.   Dry in the manner of ST-1.

Bisque Firing.   Fire in the manner of ST-1.

Fired Results.   When fired in oxidation this clay will produce a body that is a cool tan color; reduction gives a cool gray of exceptional beauty. Due to its high glaze rating this body is good for utility ware of the more rustic type.

Kaolin (Florida)	25.0
Ball clay (any)	30.0
Redart clay	10.0
Fire clay (any)	15.0
Silica	10.0
Feldspar (potash)	10.0

ST-41   **Gray/Gold-Brown Stoneware Throwing Body**   **Cone 8–10**
shrinkage 10.9%, plasticity 9.0, glaze rating 9.5

Mixing.   Mix in the manner of ST-1.

Drying.   Dry in the manner of ST-1.

Bisque Firing.   Fire in the manner of ST-1.

Fired Results.   When fired in oxidation this clay will give a body that is a warm, medium gray; reduction gives a golden brown. It is an excellent clay body for pottery that is to be left unglazed.

Goldart clay	22.0
Lincoln clay	40.0
Kentucky ball clay #4	16.0
Grog (60–80 mesh)	7.5
Silica	4.6
Feldspar (Custer)	4.8
Kaolin (EPK)	2.3
Ilmenite (powdered)	0.9
Ilmenite (granular)	1.0
Red iron oxide	0.9

ST-42   **Gray-Brown Stoneware Throwing Body**   **Cone 8–10**
shrinkage 10.9%, plasticity 9.4, glaze rating 8.5

Mixing.   Mix in the manner of ST-1.

Drying.   Dry in the manner of ST-1.

Bisque Firing.   Fire in the manner of ST-1.

Fired Results.   When fired in oxidation this body is a warm gray; reduction produces a warm toast brown.

Plastic fire clay	60.0
Plastic vitrox clay	4.0
Jordan clay	11.0
Monmouth clay	9.0
Nepheline syenite	5.0
Silica	5.0
Grog (40–60 mesh)	2.5
Grog (60–80 mesh)	2.5
Iron chromate	3.0
Add:	
Bentonite	1.0

ST-43　**Buff-Gray Stoneware Throwing Body　Cone 8–10**
shrinkage 11.3%, plasticity 11.5, glaze rating 11.1

Mixing.　Mix in the manner of ST-1.

Drying.　Dry in the manner of ST-1.

Bisque Firing.　Fire in the manner of ST-1.

Fired Results.　When fired in oxidation this clay gives a warm buff color; reduction produces a warm gray-brown which is excellent for unglazed pieces.

Jordan clay	62.0
Kentucky ball clay #4	18.0
Silica	10.0
Feldspar (Custer)	10.0
Red iron oxide	1.0
Add:	
Grog (60–80 mesh)	10.0

ST-44　**Buff/Dark Gray Stoneware Throwing Body　Cone 8–10**
shrinkage 12.3%, plasticity 11.5, glaze rating 11.1

Mixing.　Mix in the manner of ST-1.

Drying.　Dry in the manner of ST-1.

Bisque Firing.　Fire in the manner of ST-1.

Fired Results.　When fired in oxidation this clay produces a warm buff-colored body of excellent quality; reduction gives a warm darker gray-colored body which is suitable for unglazed pieces or wax resist.

Jordan clay	60.0
Ball clay (any)	20.0
Silica	10.0
Feldspar (potash)	10.0

ST-45　**Buff/Warm Brown Stoneware Throwing Body　Cone 8–10**
shrinkage 11.2%, plasticity 11.5, glaze rating 11.5

Mixing.　Mix in the manner of ST-1.

Drying.　Dry in the manner of ST-1.

Bisque Firing.　Fire in the manner of ST-1.

Fired Results.　When fired in oxidation this clay produces a buff-colored body; reduction produces a warm buff-brown of excellent quality for pieces which are to be left unglazed or partially unglazed.

Hawthorne stoneware clay	100.0
Monmouth fire clay	35.0
Feldspar (Custer)	10.0
Kentucky ball clay #4	25.0
Add:	
Redart clay	3%
Grog (60–80 mesh)	10.0

ST-46　**Pink/Gray-Brown Stoneware Throwing Body　Cone 8–10**
shrinkage 10.5%, plasticity 11.5, glaze rating 11.3

Mixing.　Mix in the manner of ST-1.

Drying.　Dry in the manner of ST-1.

Bisque Firing.　Fire in the manner of ST-1.

Fired Results.　When fired in oxidation this clay gives an earthy pink body; reduction produces a warm gray-brown of exceptional quality. Due to its high glaze rating it is an excellent body to use for utility ware of the more rustic type.

Red earthenware clay	40.0
Kaolin	18.0
Kentucky ball clay #4	15.0
Red iron oxide	15.0
Manganese dioxide	6.0
Bentonite	3.0
Nepheline syenite	2.0
Add:	
Grog (60–80 mesh)	10.0

ST-47　**Tan/Spotted Orange-Brown Stoneware Throwing Body Cone 8–10**
shrinkage 11.4%, plasticity 9.0, glaze rating 9.4

Mixing.　Mix in the manner of ST-1.

Drying.　Dry in the manner of ST-1.

Bisque Firing.　Fire in the manner of ST-1.

Fired Results.　When fired in oxidation this clay produces a warm tan-colored body; reduction gives an excellent spotted orange-brown color of great beauty. It is excellent for pottery which is to be left unglazed.

Lincoln clay	24.0
Kentucky ball clay #4	16.0
Tennessee ball clay #5	15.0
Jordan clay	25.0
Redart clay	12.0
Silica	8.0
Add:	
Grog (60–80 mesh)	10.0

ST-48 **Tan/Spotted Brown Stoneware Throwing Body**
Cone 8–10
shrinkage 10.4%, plasticity 8.2, glaze rating 9.4

Mixing. Mix in the manner of ST-1.

Drying. Dry in the manner of ST-1.

Bisque Firing. Fire in the manner of ST-1.

Fired Results. When fired in oxidation this body is a warm tan; reduction gives a beautiful spotted brown.

Lincoln fire clay	32.4
Monmouth fire clay	20.3
Tennessee ball clay #5	19.0
Ilmenite (powdered)	5.0
Ilmenite (granular)	5.0
Red iron oxide	5.0
Manganese dioxide	1.0
Add:	
Grog (60–80 mesh)	10.0

ST-49 **Tan/Dark Tan Stoneware Throwing Body   Cone 8–10**
Courtesy of Gordon Beaver, Kingston, Arkansas
shrinkage 11%, plasticity 11.5, glaze rating 11.3

Mixing. Mix in the manner of ST-1.

Drying. Dry in the manner of ST-1.

Bisque Firing. Fire in the manner of ST-1.

Fired Results. When fired in oxidation this clay will produce a warm tan-colored body which is exceptionally good for utility ware of the more rustic type; reduction gives a darker tan color which is also good for utility ware due to its high glaze rating.

Kaiser fire clay	60.0
Kentucky ball clay #4	20.0
Redart clay	20.0

ST-50 **Tan-Brown Stoneware Throwing Body   Cone 8–10**
shrinkage 14.2%, plasticity 9.0, glaze rating 9.3

Mixing. Mix in the manner of ST-1.

Drying. Dry in the manner of ST-1.

Bisque Firing. Fire in the manner of ST-1.

Fired Results. When fired in oxidation this clay produces a body that is a warm tan in color; reduction gives a warm brown with occasional metallic highlights.

Jordan clay	17.0
Monmouth clay	15.0
Plastic fire clay	28.0
Kentucky ball clay #4	14.0
Tennessee ball clay #5	14.0
Redart clay	10.0
Sand (80–100 mesh)	2.0
Add:	
Grog (60–80 mesh)	10.0

ST-51 **Buff-Tan Stoneware Throwing Body   Cone 8–10**
Courtesy of Neil Nulton, "Mutton Hollow," Branson, Missouri
shrinkage 10%, plasticity 11.5, glaze rating 11.5

Mixing. Mix in the manner of ST-1.

Drying. Dry in the manner of ST-1.

Bisque Firing. Fire in the manner of ST-1.

Fired Results. When fired in oxidation this clay produces a buff tan body color; reduction gives a grayer tan color.

Goldart clay	100.0
Kentucky ball clay #4	50.0
Silica	25.0
Redart clay	25.0

ST-52 **Tan-Brown Stoneware Throwing Body   Cone 8–10**
shrinkage 11.5%, plasticity 8.8, glaze rating 9.3

Mixing. Mix in the manner of ST-1.

Drying. Dry in the manner of ST-1.

Bisque Firing. Fire in the manner of ST-1.

Fired Results. When fired in oxidation this body produces a warm tan color; reduction gives a warm toast brown.

Plastic fire clay	24.0
Lincoln fire clay	10.0
Kentucky ball clay #4	30.0
Redart clay	11.0
Silica	10.0
Feldspar (Kingman)	10.0
Jordan clay	5.0
Add:	
Grog (60–80 mesh)	10.0

ST-53 **Tan-Brown Stoneware Throwing Body   Cone 8–10**
shrinkage 11.4%, plasticity 8.7, glaze rating 9.4

Mixing. Mix in the manner of ST-1.

Drying. Dry in the manner of ST-1.

Bisque Firing. Fire in the manner of ST-1.

Fired Results. When fired in oxidation this clay gives a warm tan-colored body; reduction produces a warm brown of a medium hue. It is excellent when used unglazed or for wax resist.

Plastic fire clay	15.3
Lincoln fire clay	15.2
Kentucky ball clay #4	10.4
Tennessee ball clay #1	6.1
Silica	13.2
Feldspar (Custer)	16.6
Grog (60–80 mesh)	13.0
Kaolin (EPK)	8.2
Red iron oxide	2.0

ST-54 **Tan-Brown Stoneware Throwing Body   Cone 8–10**
shrinkage 13%, plasticity 7.5, glaze rating 9.3

Mixing. Mix in the manner of ST-1.

Drying. Dry in the manner of ST-1.

Bisque Firing. Fire in the manner of ST-1.

Fired Results. When fired in oxidation this clay body is a cool tan, almost gray in hue; reduction gives a cool gray-brown color. This body is not recommended for utility ware, but is better used for unglazed pottery.

Kaolin (EPK)	26.0
Kentucky ball clay #4	19.0
Tennessee ball clay #5	10.0
Plastic fire clay	16.0
Redart clay	9.0
Feldspar (Custer)	9.0
Silica	9.0
Bentonite	2.0
Add:	
Grog	10.0

ST-55 **Brown/Dark Brown Stoneware Throwing Body
Cone 8–10**
shrinkage 12.1%, plasticity 8.8, glaze rating 9.0

Mixing. Mix in the manner of ST-1.

Drying. Dry in the manner of ST-1.

Bisque Firing. Fire in the manner of ST-1.

Fired Results. When fired in oxidation this body is a medium brown color; reduction gives a dark toast brown with occasional metallic hues showing on the surface. This clay body is excellent when used for unglazed pottery or wax-resist decoration.

Native red clay	24.0
Redart clay	16.0
Plastic fire clay	20.0
Tennessee ball clay #5	12.0
Kentucky ball clay #4	15.0
Grog (60–80 mesh)	13.0

70

ST-56

Buff-Brown Stoneware Throwing Body   Cone 8–10
shrinkage 12.1%, plasticity 11.5, glaze rating 11.3

Mixing.   Mix in the manner of ST-1.

Drying.   Dry in the manner of ST-1.

Bisque Firing.   Fire in the manner of ST-1.

Fired Results.   When fired in oxidation this clay body is
a warm buff color; reduction produces a warm toast
brown of excellent quality. This clay body is at its best
when used with a lighter or a darker colored grog and
left unglazed. It is also works well for wax resist with
a light-colored glaze.

Hawthorne clay	30.0
Monmouth fire clay	60.0
Ball clay (any)	50.0
Red clay	10.0

ST-57

**Brown/Dark Brown Stoneware Throwing Body
Cone 8–10**
shrinkage 10%, plasticity 11.5, glaze rating 11.2

Mixing.   Mix in the manner of ST-1.

Drying.   Dry in the manner of ST-1.

Bisque Firing.   Fire in the manner of ST-1.

Fired Results.   When fired in oxidation this clay body
is a warm toast brown; reduction gives a darker toast-
brown color with some metallic highlights.

Fire clay (any)	40.0
Ball clay (any)	30.0
Redart clay	10.0
Silica	10.0
Feldspar (potash)	10.0

ST-58

Buff/Red Brown Stoneware Throwing Body   Cone 8–10
shrinkage 10.0%, plasticity 11.5, glaze rating 11.1

Mixing.   Mix in the manner of ST-1.

Drying.   Dry in the manner of ST-1.

Bisque Firing.   Fire in the manner of ST-1.

Fired Results.   When fired in oxidation this body is a
warm buff; reduction gives a warm earthy red-brown.

Kentucky ball clay #4	40.0
Kaolin	20.0
Red clay	15.0
Talc	5.0
Nepheline syenite	5.0
Grog	15.0

ST-59

Firebrick Stoneware Throwing Body   Cone 8–10
Courtesy of Gordon Beaver, Kingston, Arkansas
shrinkage 10.0%, plasticity 11.5, glaze rating 11.5

Mixing.   Mix in the manner of ST-1.

Drying.   Dry in the manner of ST-1.

Bisque Firing.   Fire in the manner of ST-1.

Fired Results.   When fired in oxidation this clay body
is a firebrick color; reduction gives a dark metallic red.

Monmouth fire clay	60.0
Kentucky ball clay #4	20.0
Redart clay	10.0
Talc	2.5
Iron oxide	1.0

ST-60

**Red/Metallic Dark Brown Stoneware Throwing Body
Cone 8–10**
Courtesy of Sue Garner, Springfield, Missouri.
shrinkage 11.2%, plasticity 11, glaze rating 10.6

Mixing.   Mix in the manner of ST-1.

Drying.   Dry in the manner of ST-1.

Bisque Firing.   Fire in the manner of ST-1.

Fired Results.   When fired in oxidation this body is a
dark earth red; reduction produces a metallic dark
brown.

Fire clay (Okmulgee Red-Barnes Brick Co.)	66.7
Bells dark ball clay	33.3

ST-61   **Red-Brown Stoneware Throwing Body   Cone 8–10**
shrinkage 12%, plasticity 11.4, glaze rating 11.2

Mixing. Mix in the manner of ST-1.

Drying. Dry in the manner of ST-1.

Bisque Firing. Fire in the manner of ST-1.

Fired Results. When fired in oxidation this body is a warm earth red color; reduction gives a red-brown color. This is an excellent clay for outdoor flowerpots or other types of rustic pottery if left unglazed or partially unglazed.

Red earthenware clay	20.0
Kaolin (EPK)	15.0
Kentucky ball clay #4	35.0
Red brick grog	10.0
Silica	7.0
Talc	7.0
Red iron oxide	3.0
Nepheline syenite	3.0

ST-62   **Red-Brown Stoneware Throwing Body   Cone 8–10**
shrinkage 12.5%, plasticity 11.5, glaze rating 11.2

Mixing. Mix in the manner of ST-1.

Drying. Dry in the manner of ST-1.

Bisque Firing. Fire in the manner of ST-1.

Fired Results. When fired in oxidation this clay is a red earthy brown; reduction gives a dark red-brown with metallic highlights. This body is good for all types of rustic utility ware due to its high glaze rating.

Monmouth clay	50.0
Jordan clay	50.0
Silica	50.0
Kentucky ball clay #4	25.0
Tennessee ball clay #5	25.0
Grog (60–80 mesh)	25.0
Red iron oxide	25.0

ST-63   **White-Gray Stoneware Throwing Body   Cone 9**
shrinkage 12.3%, plasticity 11.5, glaze rating 11.2

Mixing. Mix in the manner of ST-1.

Drying. Dry in the manner of ST-1.

Bisque Firing. Fire in the manner of ST-1.

Fired Results. When fired in oxidation this body is an off-white; reduction produces a light cool gray color.

Feldspar (potash)	11.0
Kaolin (EPK)	24.0
XX sagger clay	30.0
Kentucky ball clay	20.0
Flint	15.0

ST-64   **Off-White/Gray Stoneware Throwing Body   Cone 9**
shrinkage 11.4%, plasticity 11.5, glaze rating 11.2

Mixing. Mix in the manner of ST-1.

Drying. Dry in the manner of ST-1.

Bisque Firing. Fire in the manner of ST-1.

Fired Results. When fired in oxidation this body is an off-white; reduction gives a cool gray. This body is excellent for all types of utility ware.

Kaolin (EPK)	20.0
Kentucky ball clay #4	40.0
Talc	35.0
Bentonite	5.0
Add:	
Grog	10.0

ST-65   **Off-White/Gray Stoneware Throwing Body   Cone 9**
shrinkage 10.6%, plasticity 11.5, glaze rating 11.2

Mixing. Mix in the manner of ST-1.

Drying. Dry in the manner of ST-1.

Bisque Firing. Fire in the manner of ST-1.

Fired Results. When fired in oxidation this body is an off-white; reduction gives a cool light gray. This body is excellent for all types of utility ware.

Kaolin (EPK)	40.0
Kentucky ball clay #4	30.0
Silica	15.0
Feldspar (potash)	2.5
Talc	12.5
Add:	
Grog (optional)	10.0

ST-66 **Warm Gray/Speckled Gray Stoneware Throwing Body**
Cone 9
shrinkage 13.5%, plasticity 9.4, glaze rating 8.7

Mixing. Mix in the manner of ST-1.

Drying. Dry in the manner of ST-1.

Bisque Firing. Fire in the manner of ST-1.

Fired Results. When fired in oxidation this body is a
light warm-gray color; reduction gives a warm speckled
gray of a darker hue. This clay body is not recommended
for utility ware due to its low glaze rating.

Jordan clay	25.0
Monmouth clay	25.0
Tennessee ball clay #5	10.0
Kentucky ball clay #4	10.0
Feldspar (Kingman)	18.5
Silica	11.5

ST-67 **Black-Brown Stoneware Throwing Body** **Cone 9**
shrinkage 10.5%, plasticity 11.3, glaze rating 10.6

Mixing. Mix in the manner of ST-1.

Drying. Dry in the manner of ST-1.

Bisque Firing. Fire in the manner of ST-1.

Fired Results. When fired in oxidation this body is dark
brown; reduction gives a black-brown with metallic
highlights.

Kaolin (EPK)	40.0
Kentucky ball clay #4	30.0
Silica	5.0
Red iron oxide	15.0
Magnesium oxide	10.0
Grog	10.0

ST-68 **Buff-Brown Stoneware Throwing Body** **Cone 9–10**
Courtesy of Pal Wright, Ottawa, Kansas
shrinkage 9.6%, plasticity 10.5, glaze rating 11.5

Mixing. Mix in the manner of ST-1.

Drying. Dry in the manner of ST-1.

Bisque Firing. Fire in the manner of ST-1.

Fired Results. When fired in oxidation this body is a
warm earthy buff color; reduction gives a warm buff-
brown which is excellent for unglazed ware.

Jordan clay	53.0
Kentucky ball clay #4	22.0
Feldspar (Buckingham)	5.0
Silica	20.0

ST-69 **Brown/Gray-Brown Stoneware Throwing Body** **Cone 10**
shrinkage 9.6%, plasticity 10.5, glaze rating 11.5

Mixing. Mix in the manner of ST-1.

Drying. Dry in the manner of ST-1.

Bisque Firing. Fire in the manner of ST-1.

Fired Results. When fired in oxidation this body gives
a warm brown color; reduction gives a gray-brown. Due
to the very high glaze rating this clay body is excellent
for utility ware of the rustic type.

Hawthorne stoneware clay	30.0
M & M fire clay	40.0
Kentucky ball clay #4	20.0
Redart clay	10.0

ST-70 **Buff-Pink/Gray-Tan Stoneware Throwing Body** **Cone 10**
shrinkage 10.5%, plasticity 9.6, glaze rating 11.6

Mixing. Mix in the manner of ST-1.

Drying. Dry in the manner of ST-1.

Bisque Firing. Fire in the manner of ST-1.

Fired Results. When fired in oxidation this body is a
buff-pink color; reduction gives a gray-tan. Due to its
high glaze rating this clay body is excellent for utility
ware.

Plastic fire clay	41.0
Tennessee ball clay #5	12.0
Kentucky ball clay #4	12.0
Redart clay	10.0
Silica	10.0
Feldspar (potash)	10.0
Add:	
Grog	15.0

ST-71 Red-Buff-Brown Stoneware Throwing Body   Cone 10
shrinkage 11.4%, plasticity 10, glaze rating 10.9

Mixing. Mix in the manner of ST-1.

Drying. Dry in the manner of ST-1.

Bisque Firing. Fire in the manner of ST-1.

Fired Results. When fired in oxidation this clay is an earthy buff-orange; reduction gives a red-buff-brown of great beauty. It is most effective if left unglazed.

Plastic fire clay	50.0
Redart clay	25.0
Kentucky ball clay #4	20.0
Tennessee ball clay #5	20.0
Grog	16.0

ST-72 Orange-Brown/Red-Brown Stoneware Throwing Body Cone 10
shrinkage 11.4%, plasticity 10.4, glaze rating 11.8

Mixing. Mix in the manner of ST-1.

Drying. Dry in the manner of ST-1.

Bisque Firing. Fire in the manner of ST-1.

Fired Results. When fired in oxidation this body is an orange-brown of exceptional beauty; reduction gives an earth red-brown which is more effective if left unglazed.

Jordan clay	32.0
Monmouth clay	10.0
Redart clay	25.0
Kentucky ball clay #4	18.0
Feldspar (Buckingham)	5.0
Silica	20.0

ST-73 Red-Brown Stoneware Throwing Body   Cone 10
shrinkage 9.8%, plasticity 11, glaze rating 11.1

Mixing. Mix in the manner of ST-1.

Drying. Dry in the manner of ST-1.

Bisque Firing. Fire in the manner of ST-1.

Fired Results. When fired in oxidation this body is a rich earth red of great beauty; reduction gives a dark earth red-brown with metallic highlights. It is excellent for any type of rustic pottery. This body iron spots exceptionally well even in light reduction.

Jordan clay	30.0
Redart clay	27.0
Kentucky ball clay #4	18.0
Feldspar (Buckingham)	5.0
Silica	15.0
Fire clay (calcined)	5.0

ST-74 Red-Brown Stoneware Throwing Body   Cone 10
shrinkage 11%, plasticity 10.2, glaze rating 11.9

Mixing. Mix in the manner of ST-1.

Drying. Dry in the manner of ST-1.

Bisque Firing. Fire in the manner of ST-1.

Fired Results. When fired in oxidation this body is a rich earth red which will sometimes bleed through even in an oxidation firing; reduction produces a dark earthy brown which iron spots well even in light reduction.

Redart clay #93	70.0
Kentucky ball clay #4	18.0
Plastic fire clay	12.0

ST-75 Red-Brown/Brown-Black Stoneware Throwing Body Cone 12
shrinkage 12.3%, plasticity 10, glaze rating 11.3

Mixing. Mix in the manner of ST-1.

Drying. Dry in the manner of ST-1.

Bisque Firing. Fire in the manner of ST-1.

Fired Results. When fired in oxidation this body is a rich red-brown; reduction gives a brown-black color.

Jordan clay	25.0
Redart clay	25.0
Goldart clay	5.0
Kentucky ball clay #4	18.0
Feldspar (Buckingham)	5.0
Silica	15.0
Sagger clay	5.0
Red iron oxide	2.0

FORMULAS FOR STONEWARE CASTING BODIES

Note. No plasticity rating is given for casting bodies.

SC-1

Brown/Gray-Brown Stoneware Casting Body   Cone 5–9
shrinkage 10.9%, glaze rating 9.0

Mixing. Mix all the casting bodies in this section according to the procedure outlined in Chapter 3 under Mixing Casting Bodies.

Casting. Use the same casting procedure outlined in the casting body section of Chapter 5 under Clay Body EC-1.

Drying. Dry in the manner of ST-1.

Bisque Firing. Fire in the manner of ST-1.

Fired Results. Fired in oxidation this body gives a light brown; reduction produces a dark gray-brown. This body iron spots well if reduction is heavy.

Lincoln clay	30.5
Native red clay	24.0
Jordan clay	20.8
Grog (60–80 mesh)	12.0
Feldspar (Custer)	6.0
Nepheline syenite	4.0
Silica	3.4
Sodium carbonate	0.3

SC-2

Tan/Light Brown Stoneware Casting Body   Cone 6–8
shrinkage 10.9%, glaze rating 9

Mixing. Mix in the manner of SC-1.

Casting. Cast in the manner of SC-1.

Drying. Dry in the manner of SC-1.

Bisque Firing. Fire in the manner of SC-1.

Fired Results. When fired in oxidation this body is tan; reduction gives a light brown.

Kaolin	28.0
Feldspar (Custer)	21.0
Tennessee ball clay #1	15.5
Monmouth clay	15.0
Silica	15.2
Native red clay	5.0
Sodium carbonate	0.3

SC-3

**Red-Brown/Deep Brown Stoneware Casting Body
Cone 6–8**
shrinkage 11.5%, glaze rating 11.2

Mixing. Mix in the manner of SC-1.

Casting. Cast in the manner of SC-1.

Drying. Dry in the manner of SC-1.

Bisque Firing. Fire in the manner of SC-1.

Fired Results. When fired in oxidation this body is red-brown; reduction gives a deep brown. This body iron spots well.

Kaolin	25.0
Feldspar (Custer)	20.0
Tennessee ball clay #1	15.0
Monmouth clay	15.0
Silica	10.0
Redart clay	20.0
Sodium carbonate	0.3

SC-4

Off-White/Gray Stoneware Casting Body   Cone 6–10
shrinkage 14%, glaze rating 9.3

Mixing. Mix in the manner of SC-1.

Casting. Cast in the manner of SC-1.

Drying. Dry in the manner of SC-1.

Bisque Firing. Fire in the manner of SC-1.

Fired Results. When fired in oxidation this body is off-white; reduction gives a gray.

Kaolin (Georgia)	28.0
Feldspar (Custer)	21.0
Silica	18.0
Jordan clay	16.5
Kentucky ball clay #4	8.2
Tennessee ball clay #5	6.0
Soda ash	0.3

SC-5

White/Off-White Stoneware Casting Body   Cone 7–9
shrinkage 11.46%, glaze rating 9.3

Mixing. Mix in the manner of SC-1.

Casting. Cast in the manner of SC-1.

Drying. Dry in the manner of SC-1.

Bisque Firing. Fire in the manner of SC-1.

Fired Results. When fired in oxidation this body is white; reduction gives an off-white.

Jordan clay	20.0
Monmouth clay	20.0
Kaolin (Georgia)	20.0
Kentucky ball clay #4	8.0
Tennessee ball clay #1	8.0
Silica	14.0
Feldspar (Custer)	9.7
Sodium carbonate	0.3

SC-6

Tan-Gray Stoneware Casting Body   Cone 8–10
shrinkage 12.5%, glaze rating 9.5

Mixing. Mix in the manner of SC-1.

Casting. Cast in the manner of SC-1.

Drying. Dry in the manner of SC-1.

Bisque Firing. Fire in the manner of SC-1.

Fired Results. When fired in oxidation this body is tan; reduction gives a gray.

Kaolin	30.0
Kentucky ball clay #4	15.0
Stoneware clay	15.0
Red clay	5.0
Silica	15.0
Feldspar (soda)	20.0
Sodium carbonate	0.3

SC-7

Tan-Brown Stoneware Casting Body   Cone 8–10
shrinkage 12.6%, glaze rating 11.5

Mixing. Mix in the manner of SC-1.

Casting. Cast in the manner of SC-1.

Drying. Dry in the manner of SC-1.

Bisque Firing. Fire in the manner of SC-1.

Fired Results. When fired in oxidation this body is tan; reduction gives a brown. This body iron spots well.

Kaolin	31.3
Feldspar (potash)	18.0
Kentucky ball clay #4	15.4
Jordan clay	15.0
Silica	16.0
Red clay (any 06 type)	4.0
Sodium carbonate	0.3

SC-8

Tan-Gray Stoneware Casting Body   Cone 8–10
shrinkage 12%, glaze rating 11.5

Mixing. Mix in the manner of SC-1.

Casting. Cast in the manner of SC-1.

Drying. Dry in the manner of SC-1.

Bisque Firing. Fire in the manner of SC-1.

Fired Results. When fired in oxidation this body is tan; reduction gives a gray.

Jordan clay	40.0
Kaolin (Georgia)	20.0
Kentucky ball clay #4	15.0
Silica	15.0
Feldspar (soda)	10.0
Red iron oxide	1.5
Sodium carbonate	0.5

SC-9

Red/Red-Brown Stoneware Casting Body   Cone 8–10
shrinkage 12.6%, glaze rating 12

Mixing. Mix in the manner of SC-1.

Casting. Cast in the manner of SC-1.

Drying. Dry in the manner of SC-1.

Bisque Firing. Fire in the manner of SC-1.

Fired Results. When fired in oxidation this body gives a red; reduction gives a red-brown.

Kaolin	35.0
Feldspar (Buckingham)	18.0
Kentucky ball clay #4	5.0
Jordan clay	4.0
Silica	18.0
Redart	20.0
Sodium carbonate	0.3

NORTHEAST NEBRASKA TECHNICAL
COMMUNITY COLLEGE-LIBRARY

SC-10   **Light Gray/Gray Stoneware Casting Body   Cone 10–12**
shrinkage 13%, glaze rating 9.5

Mixing. Mix in the manner of SC-1.

Casting. Cast in the manner of SC-1.

Drying. Dry in the manner of SC-1.

Bisque Firing. Fire in the manner of SC-1.

Fired Results. When fired in oxidation this body gives a light gray; reduction gives a gray.

Kaolin	30.0
Feldspar (Kingman)	17.0
Silica	20.0
Jordan clay	15.5
Tennessee ball clay #1	9.2
Kentucky ball clay #4	8.0
Sodium carbonate	0.3
Add:	
Grog (80–100 mesh)	8.0

FORMULAS FOR STONEWARE SCULPTURE BODIES

Note. The clay bodies in this section are excellent for handbuilding. They are not recommended for throwing.

SS-1   **Off-White/Gray Stoneware Sculpture Body   Cone 6**
shrinkage 8.8%, plasticity 9.0, glaze rating 11.2

Mixing. Mix this body according to the instructions in Chapter 3 on Clay Body Preparation. The grog can be added during the mixing or in the wedging process. In cases where the clay may be too wet to handle, the addition of grog at the wedging stage will help to dry it out to the proper working consistency. In any case all sculpture bodies should be thoroughly wedged if the soaking or slip method is used. If plasticity seems to be a problem, a couple of weeks of aging will raise the plasticity by almost one point on the rating scale.

Drying. Allow all sculpture and handbuilt pieces to dry thoroughly. Sculpture pieces are usually thicker and consequently need more drying time. Use the cheek test to check for dryness.

Bisque Firing. Bisque fire sculpture pieces only if they are to be glazed later. If they are not, then fire them to maturity with the first firing. This body should be bisque fired to at least cone 03.

Fired Results. When fired in oxidation this body produces an off-white; reduction produces a cool gray which is very effective for unglazed pieces if a lighter grog is used.

Kentucky ball clay #4	14.0
Tennessee ball clay #5	14.0
Plastic vitrox	26.0
Feldspar (Custer)	8.0
Whiting	5.0
Talc	4.0
Bentonite	2.0
Grog (60–80 mesh)	10.0
For heavier bodies add:	
Grog (40–60 mesh)	10.0

SS-2   **Tan-Cream Stoneware Sculpture Body   Cone 6**
shrinkage 9.4%, plasticity 8.4, glaze rating 11.4

Mixing. Mix in the manner of SS-1.

Drying. Dry in the manner of SS-1.

Bisque Firing. Fire in the manner of SS-1.

Fired Results. When fired in oxidation this body produces a tan-cream; reduction produces a toast brown.

Hawthorne bond clay	70.0
M & M fire clay	15.0
Redart clay	40.0
Kentucky ball clay #4	15.0
Grog (40–60 mesh)	10.0

SS-3

Brick Red/Metallic Red-Brown Stoneware Sculpture Body   Cone 6

shrinkage 8%, plasticity 10.9, glaze rating 10.7

Mixing. Mix in the manner of SS-1.

Drying. Dry in the manner of SS-1.

Bisque Firing. Fire in the manner of SS-1.

Fired Results. When fired in oxidation this body gives a brick red; reduction gives a metallic red-brown. This body iron spots well.

Plastic fire clay	28.0
Redart clay	24.0
Monmouth clay	18.0
Kentucky ball clay #4	4.0
Nepheline syenite	10.0
Silica	6.0
Grog (60–80 mesh)	10.0

SS-4

Brown/Charcoal Brown Stoneware Sculpture Body   Cone 6–7

shrinkage 8%, plasticity 11, glaze rating 10.5

Mixing. Mix in the manner of SS-1.

Drying. Dry in the manner of SS-1.

Bisque Firing. Fire in the manner of SS-1.

Fired Results. When fired in oxidation this body is brown; reduction produces a charcoal brown body which iron spots well.

Nepheline syenite	32.0
Tennessee ball clay #5	20.0
Silica	20.0
Red iron oxide	8.0
Bentonite	2.0
Add:	
Grog (40–60 mesh)	10.0
Grog (60–80 mesh)	10.0

SS-5

Tan/Warm Gray Stoneware Sculpture Body   Cone 7–9

shrinkage 10.0%, plasticity 11.2, glaze rating 11.5

Mixing. Mix in the manner of SS-1.

Drying. Dry in the manner of SS-1.

Bisque Firing. Fire in the manner of SS-1.

Fired Results. When fired in oxidation this body gives a tan; reduction produces a warm gray.

Jordan clay	56.0
Kentucky ball clay #4	8.0
Tennessee ball clay #5	8.3
Silica	9.0
Feldspar (Custer)	10.7
Kaolin (EPK)	5.0
Add:	
Grog (40–60 mesh)	10.0
Grog (60–80 mesh)	10.0

SS-6

Brown/Metallic Brown Stoneware Sculpture Body   Cone 6–8

shrinkage 7.2%, plasticity 9.2, glaze rating 11.2

Mixing. Mix in the manner of SS-1.

Drying. Dry in the manner of SS-1.

Bisque Firing. Fire in the manner of SS-1.

Fired Results. When fired in oxidation this body produces a brown; reduction produces a metallic brown. This body iron spots very well.

Plastic fire clay	46.0
Kentucky ball clay #4	15.0
Tennessee ball clay #1	10.2
Whiting	2.8
Wollastonite	13.0
Feldspar (Custer)	3.0

SS-7

Gray/Speckled Tan Stoneware Sculpture Body   Cone 6–9

shrinkage 9.5%, plasticity 11.1, glaze rating 11.1

Mixing. Mix in the manner of SS-1.

Drying. Dry in the manner of SS-1.

Bisque Firing. Fire in the manner of SS-1.

Fired Results. When fired in oxidation this body produces a gray; reduction produces a speckled tan. This body is good for utility ware.

Plastic fire clay	48.0
Kentucky ball clay #4	15.0
Tennessee ball clay #5	15.0
Silica	10.0
Manganese dioxide	4.5
Iron chromate	3.5
Grog (20–40 mesh)	7.0
Grog (40–60 mesh)	7.0
Grog (60–80 mesh)	7.0

SS-8

**Cream/Darker Cream Stoneware Sculpture Body
Cone 7–9**
shrinkage 11.5%, plasticity 8.3, glaze rating 11.2

Mixing. Mix in the manner of SS-1.

Drying. Dry in the manner of SS-1.

Bisque Firing. Fire in the manner of SS-1.

Fired Results. When fired in oxidation this body gives a cream; reduction gives a darker cream. This body is good for utility ware.

Plastic fire clay	48.0
Kentucky ball clay #4	17.0
Tennessee ball clay #5	10.0
Sand (60–80 mesh)	12.0
Red iron oxide	1.0
Grog (40–60 mesh)	12.0
Grog (60–80 mesh, optional)	12.0

SS-9

**Orange/Speckled Orange-Tan Stoneware Sculpture Body
Cone 7–10**
shrinkage 10.1%, plasticity 10.5, glaze rating 11.4

Mixing. Mix in the manner of SS-1.

Drying. Dry in the manner of SS-1.

Bisque Firing. Fire in the manner of SS-1.

Fired Results. When fired in oxidation this body produces an orange; reduction produces a speckled orange-tan. This body iron spots well and is good for utility ware but is best left unglazed.

Jordan clay	30.3
Plastic fire clay	30.0
Kentucky ball clay #4	1.3
Silica	19.4
Grog (40–60 mesh)	8.2
Grog (60–80 mesh)	8.1

SS-10

**Buff-Cream/Gray-Buff Stoneware Sculpture Body
Cone 8**
shrinkage 9.0%, plasticity 9, glaze rating 11.8

Mixing. Mix in the manner of SS-1.

Drying. Dry in the manner of SS-1.

Bisque Firing. Fire in the manner of SS-1.

Fired Results. When fired in oxidation this body produces a buff-cream; reduction produces a gray-buff.

Jordan clay	50.0
Plastic fire clay	50.0
Redart clay	25.0
Grog (60–80 mesh)	10.0

SS-11

Buff/Gray-Tan Stoneware Sculpture Body   Cone 8
shrinkage 8.6%, plasticity 9, glaze rating 11

Mixing. Mix in the manner of SS-1.

Drying. Dry in the manner of SS-1.

Bisque Firing. Fire in the manner of SS-1.

Fired Results. When fired in oxidation this body gives a buff; reduction gives a gray-tan.

Monmouth clay	50.0
Jordan clay	50.0
Plastic fire clay	50.0
Silica	50.0
Grog (60–80 mesh)	10.0

SS-12

**Dove Gray/Toast Brown Stoneware Sculpture Body
Cone 8**
shrinkage 9.7%, plasticity 11.2, glaze rating 11.4

Mixing. Mix in the manner of SS-1.

Drying. Dry in the manner of SS-1.

Bisque Firing. Fire in the manner of SS-1.

Fired Results. When fired in oxidation this body produces a dove-gray; reduction produces a toast brown.

Plastic fire clay	65.7
Monmouth clay	18.6
Kentucky ball clay #4	4.9
Nepheline syenite	4.7
Silica	10.0
Iron chromate	2.0
Grog (60–80 mesh)	10.0

SS-13

Cream-Buff Stoneware Sculpture Body   Cone 8–10
Courtesy of David Greer, Prague, Oklahoma

Mixing. Mix in the manner of SS-1.

Drying. Dry in the manner of SS-1.

Bisque Firing. Fire in the manner of SS-1.

Fired Results. When fired in oxidation this body gives a light creamy tan; medium reduction gives a creamy buff.

Stoneware clay	200.0
Kaiser fire clay	100.0
Silica	25.0
Add:	
Fire brick grog (20–30 mesh)	50.0

SS-14

Gray/Warm Speckled Gray Stoneware Sculpture Body Cone 8–10
shrinkage 10.5%, plasticity 10.8, glaze rating 11.4

Mixing. Mix in the manner of SS-1.

Drying. Dry in the manner of SS-1.

Bisque Firing. Fire in the manner of SS-1.

Fired Results. When fired in oxidation this body gives a gray; reduction gives a warm speckled gray.

Jordan clay	50.0
Kentucky ball clay #4	10.0
Tennessee ball clay #5	10.0
Feldspar (Custer)	17.0
Silica	10.0
Kaolin (EPK)	3.0
Grog (40–60 mesh)	10.0
Grog (60–80 mesh)	10.0

SS-15

Gray/Tan Speckled Stoneware Sculpture Body Cone 8–10
shrinkage 9.5%, plasticity 10.4, glaze rating 11.5

Mixing. Mix in the manner of SS-1.

Drying. Dry in the manner of SS-1.

Bisque Firing. Fire in the manner of SS-1.

Fired Results. When fired in oxidation this body gives a gray; reduction gives a speckled tan. This body is for larger pieces and will stand stress in the wet state.

Lincoln clay	48.0
Kentucky ball clay #4	8.0
Tennessee ball clay #1	8.0
Sand (40–60 mesh)	12.0
Red iron oxide	1.0
Grog (20–40 mesh)	13.0
Grog (60–80 mesh)	10.0
Grog (80–100 mesh)	10.0

SS-16

Buff/Gray-Tan Stoneware Sculpture Body   Cone 8–10
shrinkage 10.2%, plasticity 10.6, glaze rating 11.5

Mixing. Mix in the manner of SS-1.

Drying. Dry in the manner of SS-1.

Bisque Firing. Fire in the manner of SS-1.

Fired Results. Fired in oxidation this body produces a buff; reduction produces a gray-tan body.

Jordan clay	50.0
Monmouth clay	50.0
Plastic fire clay	50.0
Kentucky ball clay #4	50.0
Silica	60.0
Grog (60–80 mesh)	60.0

SS-17

Buff-Pink/Gray Stoneware Sculpture Body   Cone 10
shrinkage 10.2%, plasticity 9.8, glaze rating 11.5

Mixing. Mix in the manner of SS-1.

Drying. Dry in the manner of SS-1.

Bisque Firing. Fire in the manner of SS-1.

Fired Results. When fired in oxidation this body produces a buff-pink; reduction produces a gray. This body is good for slab construction.

Plastic fire clay	40.0
Kentucky ball clay #4	20.0
Silica sand (60–80 mesh)	10.0
Grog (60–80 mesh)	30.0

SS-18

Red/Burnt Red Stoneware Sculpture Body Cone 10

shrinkage 10.4%, plasticity 9.3, glaze rating 11.5

Mixing. Mix in the manner of SS-1.

Drying. Dry in the manner of SS-1.

Bisque Firing. Fire in the manner of SS-1.

Fired Results. When fired in oxidation this body gives a red; reduction gives a burnt red. This body iron spots well.

Plastic fire clay	85.0
Jordan clay	10.0
Grog (40–60 mesh)	20.0
Red iron oxide	5.0

SS-19

Earth Red/Brown-Black Stoneware Sculpture Body Cone 10

shrinkage 9%, plasticity 11, glaze rating 11.5

Mixing. Mix in the manner of SS-1.

Drying. Dry in the manner of SS-1.

Bisque Firing. Fire in the manner of SS-1.

Fired Results. When fired in oxidation this body produces an earth red; reduction produces a brown-black. This body iron spots very well.

Jordan clay	30.0
Redart clay	27.0
Kentucky ball clay #4	18.0
Feldspar (Buckingham)	15.0
Silica	15.0
Plastic fire clay	5.0
Grog (40–60 mesh)	10.0
Grog (60–80 mesh)	10.0

SS-20

Earth Red/Burnt Red-Brown Stoneware Sculpture Body Cone 10

shrinkage 12.3%, plasticity 10, glaze rating 12

Mixing. Mix in the manner of SS-1.

Drying. Dry in the manner of SS-1.

Bisque Firing. Fire in the manner of SS-1.

Fired Results. When fired in oxidation this body produces an earth red; reduction produces a burnt red-brown body which iron spots very well.

Jordan clay	25.0
Redart clay	25.0
Goldart clay	5.0
Kentucky ball clay #4	18.0
Feldspar (Buckingham)	5.0
Silica	15.0
Sagger clay	5.0
Iron oxide	2.0
Grog (60–80 mesh)	10.0

8
PORCELAIN CLAY BODIES
CONE 9-14

Porcelain has long been prized for its beauty. Its great appeal is due primarily to its white color, translucency, and finish—all of which are the result of its high firing and the purity of the ingredients used in its manufacture.

The artist who chooses to work with porcelain, however, must be prepared to have his patience tested to the limit—for it is a difficult medium with which to work. Even the most simple of objects require great patience and skill. Due to the nature of its makeup it is not a very plastic material. Consequently it is difficult to work on the wheel or in sculptural form. And due to its lack of strength in the raw state, one is limited in the size of wheel-made objects that can be created.

Porcelain throwing bodies enable the potter to shape simple pieces on the wheel. To make forms delicate enough to be translucent is difficult and exasperating for it requires great skill. Consequently, most pieces which are thin enough to transmit light (about 1/4" or 6 mm thick) are usually thrown thicker, then tooled to the desired thinness with a sharp instrument on the wheel when leatherhard.

Despite all the difficulties the medium presents, it is an interesting one with which to work and every potter should try it at least once for the experience.

The throwing bodies given in this chapter are designed to be as workable and plastic as the medium will allow and still remain porcelain.

All of the clay bodies in this chapter were designed for three specific purposes: throwing, casting, or sculpture. It is not advised that the potter use a clay body for a forming method for which it was not designed unless the instructions indicate that it can be done successfully.

The clay bodies were also designed for a particular temperature range and it is not advised that the potter exceed this unless the instructions indicate it can be done.

The formulas in this chapter are arranged first by forming type: throwing, casting, or sculpture, then by temperature and color, light to dark, within each category.

The reader will find possible substitutions for most of the chemicals in Chapter 34, Dictionary of Clay and Glaze Compounds, under each individual heading.

IMPROVING THE PLASTICITY OF PORCELAIN BODIES

There is a traditional method which can be used to make the porcelain body more workable and give it more strength for throwing larger forms. It is achieved by aging the body for more plasticity and by adding porcelain grog which is made of the same material as the body itself for more strength. This is a time-consuming process, but for those who wish to try it, it is given here, step-by-step:

1. Mix up the porcelain clay to a workable consistency.

2. Make several flat slabs of the porcelain clay about 1/4" (6 mm) thick. This can be done by rolling or cutting.

3. Allow these slabs to dry completely.

4. Crumble the dry slabs into grog-sized particles with a rolling pin.

5. Pass the raw porcelain clay particles through a 80- 100-mesh screen.

6. When all the particles have been screened through the 100-mesh sieve pass them again through a finer screen to remove the finer dust.

7. Keep only the 80- 100-mesh-sized particles, for the grog should be no larger than 80 mesh and no finer than 100 mesh.

8. Place the raw grog in a bisque dish and fire it in the kiln to one cone below the final maturing point of the porcelain body.

9. Mix the fired grog with the clay body in amounts not exceeding 15% by dry body weight.

10. Mix the porcelain body in the following fashion by weighing out the ingredients and placing them in the mixing container. Add 1% by dry body weight of cornstarch or flour. Then add water which contains aging bacteria from an organic composting agent (see Chapter 2 under Aging the Clay).

11. When the clay and fired grog has been thoroughly mixed, dry it on plaster bats to a workable consistency and wedge it thoroughly.

12. Put the clay away to age for at least a month in a warm, moist place where it will not dry out.

13. At the end of a month the aged clay should have at least a slight sour smell signaling that it has aged and is ready to use.

14. Wedge the clay again very thoroughly.

If this process is followed the potter will have a porcelain clay body with which he can produce larger pieces more easily than before. And while the improvement in plasticity and strength will not be vast, it will allow the potter more latitude in working with this particular medium.

Note. The ingredients in the formulas in this chapter can be weighed out in either grams or pounds. It is recommended that the potter first make a 100-gram test batch of the clay body that interests him to insure that it is suitable before making larger amounts. Any of the lighter firing bodies can be colored by the use of coloring oxides. See Chapter 12 for further information. The clay bodies are listed here by firing temperature from lower to higher cones.

FORMULAS FOR PORCELAIN THROWING BODIES

PT-1 **White-Gray Porcelain Throwing Body   Cone 6**
shrinkage 14%, plasticity 9.8, glaze rating 11.2

Ingredient	Amount
Kaolin (Georgia)	40.0
Feldspar (potash)	25.0
Kentucky ball clay #4	10.0
Tennessee ball clay #1	6.5
Silica	13.5
Kaolin (EPK)	5.0
Bentonite	2.0

Mixing. Weigh out the ingredients by grams for test batches and by pounds for larger batches. Mix the clay using any of the three methods outlined in Chapter 3 on Clay Body Preparation. The clay can be used at once or stored to age for a couple of weeks for even greater plasticity. If a pug mill is not used for mixing, take care that the clay is thoroughly wedged to increase its workability and to remove any trapped air bubbles which might lead to cracking or explosions during the firing. This particular clay is reasonably plastic but it still should be aged to improve its workability.

Drying. Place the wet pieces in a location that is free of drafts and allow them to dry thoroughly. Drafts can lead to uneven drying and consequently warping or cracking. Test for dryness by placing the base of the piece against your cheek. If it feels even faintly moist or cool to the touch, it still contains moisture and should dry further. Drying time will vary according to the size and thickness of the ware, the temperature, and the humidity. In general pieces will dry and be ready for firing in a week if kept in a warm, dry place.

Bisque Firing. Porcelain should have a bisque firing of at least cone 04, if the ware is to be matured in the glaze firing. First fire the kiln slowly to 500° F./260° C. to allow any latent moisture to be removed slowly, then fire normally to the desired bisque temperature. If a less absorbent bisque ware is desired the ware may be fired to cone 02.

Fired Results. This body is a low-fire porcelain and as such is not quite as vitreous as higher-fired porcelain. It does, however, resemble the higher-grade porcelain and is excellent for utility ware. Fired in oxidation it is a slightly off-white; reduction gives a light gray.

PT-2   **White/Light Gray Porcelain Throwing Body   Cone 8**
shrinkage 13.2%, plasticity 8.9, glaze rating 11.5

Mixing. Mix in the manner of PT-1.

Drying. Dry in the manner of PT-1.

Bisque Firing. Fire in the manner of PT-1.

Fired Results. When fired in oxidation this body is pure white; reduction produces a very light gray.

Kaolin (Georgia)	25.0
Kaolin (Florida)	15.0
Tennessee ball clay #1	10.0
Feldspar (potash)	17.0
Nepheline syenite	10.0
Silica	22.0
Whiting	2.0

PT-3   **White/Light Gray Porcelain Throwing Body   Cone 8–10**
shrinkage 17.7%, plasticity 9.3, glaze rating 9.5

Mixing. Mix in the manner of PT-1.

Drying. Dry in the manner of PT-1.

Bisque Firing. Fire in the manner of PT-1.

Fired Results. When fired in oxidation this body is an egg-shell white; reduction gives a light gray.

Kaolin (EPK)	55.8
Feldspar (Buckingham)	24.5
Silica	15.0
Bentonite	4.7

PT-4   **White-Gray Porcelain Throwing Body   Cone 8–11**
shrinkage 15%, plasticity 7.5, glaze rating 9.6

Mixing. Mix in the manner of PT-1.

Drying. Dry in the manner of PT-1.

Bisque Firing. Fire in the manner of PT-1.

Fired Results. When fired in oxidation this body is white; reduction gives a gray.

Kaolin (EPK)	40.0
Feldspar (potash)	25.0
Silica	25.0
Kentucky ball clay #4	7.0
Bentonite	3.0

PT-5   **White-Gray Porcelain Throwing Body   Cone 9**
shrinkage 12.5%, plasticity 8.3, glaze rating 11.5

Mixing. Mix in the manner of PT-1.

Drying. Dry in the manner of PT-1.

Bisque Firing. Fire in the manner of PT-1.

Fired Results. When fired in oxidation this body gives a white; reduction gives a gray. This body is good for utility ware.

Kaolin (EPK)	38.0
Dolomite	4.0
Feldspar (potash)	10.0
Nepheline syenite	10.0
Ball clay	20.0
Flint	20.0

PT-6   **White-Gray Porcelain Throwing Body   Cone 9**
shrinkage 12.6%, plasticity 9.1, glaze rating 11.6

Mixing. Mix in the manner of PT-1.

Drying. Dry in the manner of PT-1.

Bisque Firing. Fire in the manner of PT-1.

Fired Results. When fired in oxidation this body produces a white; reduction produces a gray.

Kaolin (English)	52.0
Feldspar (Kona F-4)	23.0
Flint	25.0
Add:	
Bentonite	2.0

PT-7

White-Gray Porcelain Throwing Body   Cone 9
shrinkage 12.3%, plasticity 8.8, glaze rating 11.5

Mixing. Mix in the manner of PT-1.

Drying. Dry in the manner of PT-1.

Bisque Firing. Fire in the manner of PT-1.

Fired Results. When fired in oxidation this body is a white; reduction gives a gray.

Kaolin (domestic)	10.0
Kaolin (English)	17.0
Kaolin (Georgia)	15.0
Kaolin (EPK)	5.0
Kentucky ball clay	3.0
Feldspar (potash)	25.0
Dolomite	2.0
Flint	25.0

PT-8

White-Gray Porcelain Throwing Body   Cone 9-10
shrinkage 13.2%, plasticity 9.0, glaze rating 11.4

Mixing. Mix in the manner of PT-1.

Drying. Dry in the manner of PT-1.

Bisque Firing. Fire in the manner of PT-1.

Fired Results. When fired in oxidation this body is white; reduction gives a light gray.

Kaolin (EPK)	50.0
Kentucky ball clay #4	15.0
Feldspar (Buckingham)	25.0
Silica	10.0

PT-9

White/Light-Gray Porcelain Throwing Body   Cone 9-11
shrinkage 13%, plasticity 7, glaze rating 9.5

Mixing. Mix in the manner of PT-1.

Drying. Dry in the manner of PT-1.

Bisque Firing. Fire in the manner of PT-1.

Fired Results. When fired in oxidation this body produces a white; reduction produces a light gray.

Kaolin	45.0
Feldspar (potash)	34.0
Kentucky ball clay #4	6.0
Tennessee ball clay #1	1.0
Silica	10.0
Add:	
Bentonite	2.0

PT-10

White/Light Gray Porcelain Throwing Body   Cone 9-11
shrinkage 15.3%, plasticity 8, glaze rating 9.8

Mixing. Mix in the manner of PT-1.

Drying. Dry in the manner of PT-1.

Bisque Firing. Fire in the manner of PT-1.

Fired Results. When fired in oxidation this body is a white; reduction gives a light gray.

Tennessee ball clay	28.0
Kaolin (EPK)	26.8
Feldspar (Custer)	25.9
Silica	18.3
Bentonite	1.0

PT-11

White-Gray Porcelain Throwing Body   Cone 9-11
shrinkage 14.3%, plasticity 7.8, glaze rating 9.2

Mixing. Mix in the manner of PT-1.

Drying. Dry in the manner of PT-1.

Bisque Firing. Fire in the manner of PT-1.

Fired Results. When fired in oxidation this body is a white; reduction gives a gray.

Feldspar (potash)	26.0
Kaolin	24.0
Silica	21.0
EPK	17.0
Tennessee ball clay #1	10.0
Add:	
Bentonite	2.0

PT-12

White-Gray Porcelain Throwing Body   Cone 9–11
shrinkage 12.8%, plasticity 7.2, glaze rating 9.8

Mixing. Mix in the manner of PT-1.

Drying. Dry in the manner of PT-1.

Bisque Firing. Fire in the manner of PT-1.

Fired Results. When fired in oxidation this body produces a white; reduction produces a gray. This body is good for utility ware.

Feldspar (Custer)	30.0
Kentucky ball clay #4	16.7
Tennessee ball clay #1	10.3
Silica	20.0
Kaolin (Georgia)	18.0
Kaolin (EPK)	6.0
Add:	
Bentonite	2.0

PT-13

White-Gray Porcelain Throwing Body   Cone 9–12
shrinkage 13.5%, plasticity 7.3, glaze rating 9.5

Mixing. Mix in the manner of PT-1.

Drying. Dry in the manner of PT-1.

Bisque Firing. Fire in the manner of PT-1.

Fired Results. When fired in oxidation this body is a white; reduction gives a gray.

Silica	25.0
Tennessee ball clay #1	15.0
Kentucky ball clay #4	10.0
Feldspar (Kona F-4)	18.0
Kaolin (Georgia)	12.0
Kaolin (EPK)	10.0
Nepheline syenite	4.0
Bentonite	2.0
Dolomite	2.0
Talc	2.0

PT-14

White-Gray Porcelain Throwing Body   Cone 9–12
shrinkage 14.3%, plasticity 8.2, glaze rating 9.7

Mixing. Mix in the manner of PT-1.

Drying. Dry in the manner of PT-1.

Bisque Firing. Fire in the manner of PT-1.

Fired Results. When fired in oxidation this body is white; reduction gives a gray.

Kaolin (EPK)	30.0
Feldspar (Buckingham)	25.0
Silica	25.0
Kentucky ball clay #4	6.0
Tennessee ball clay #1	4.0
Kaolin (Georgia)	5.0
Add:	
Bentonite	2.0

PT-15

White-Gray Porcelain Throwing Body   Cone 9–14
shrinkage 12.8%, plasticity 7, glaze rating 9.4

Mixing. Mix in the manner of PT-1.

Drying. Dry in the manner of PT-1.

Bisque Firing. Fire in the manner of PT-1.

Fired Results. When fired in oxidation this body is white; reduction gives a gray. This body is good for utility ware.

Feldspar (Buckingham)	25.0
Silica	25.0
Kentucky ball clay #4	12.5
Tennessee ball clay #1	12.5
Kaolin (EPK)	23.0
Bentonite	2.0

PT-16

White/Off-White Porcelain Throwing Body   Cone 10
shrinkage 12.6%, plasticity 9.1, glaze rating 11.3

Mixing. Mix in the manner of PT-1.

Drying. Dry in the manner of PT-1.

Bisque Firing. Fire in the manner of PT-1.

Fired Results. When fired in oxidation this body produces a white; reduction produces an off-white.

Kaolin	30.0
Kentucky ball clay #4	12.5
Tennessee ball clay #1	12.5
Feldspar (potash)	20.0
Silica	20.0
Bentonite	2.5

PT-17   **White/Light Gray Porcelain Throwing Body   Cone 10**
shrinkage 12.6%, plasticity 9.1, glaze rating 11.4

Mixing. Mix in the manner of PT-1.

Drying. Dry in the manner of PT-1.

Bisque Firing. Fire in the manner of PT-1.

Fired Results. When fired in oxidation this body is
white; reduction gives a light gray.

Kaolin (Georgia)	25.0
Kaolin (Florida)	15.0
Tennessee ball clay #1	10.0
Feldspar (Kingman)	24.0
Silica	22.0
Whiting	2.0

PT-18   **White/Off-White Porcelain Throwing Body   Cone 10**
shrinkage 12.6%, plasticity 9.2, glaze rating 11.3

Mixing. Mix in the manner of PT-1.

Drying. Dry in the manner of PT-1.

Bisque Firing. Fire in the manner of PT-1.

Fired Results. When fired in oxidation this body produces a white; reduction gives an off-white.

Kaolin (EPK)	50.0
Feldspar (Buckingham)	37.0
Silica	12.0

PT-19   **White/Light Gray Porcelain Throwing Body   Cone 10–11**
shrinkage 14%, plasticity 7, glaze rating 9.3

Mixing. Mix in the manner of PT-1.

Drying. Dry in the manner of PT-1.

Bisque Firing. Fire in the manner of PT-1.

Fired Results. When fired in oxidation this body gives a
white; reduction a light gray. This body is good for
utility ware.

Barium carbonate	40.0
Kentucky ball clay #4	15.0
Tennessee ball clay #1	10.0
Kaolin (EPK)	20.0
Silica	12.5
Bentonite	2.5

PT-20   **White-Gray Porcelain Throwing Body   Cone 11**
shrinkage 12.2%, plasticity 9.6, glaze rating 11.5

Mixing. Mix in the manner of PT-1.

Drying. Dry in the manner of PT-1.

Bisque Firing. Fire in the manner of PT-1.

Fired Results. When fired in oxidation this body is a
white; reduction gives a light gray.

Kaolin (Georgia)	10.0
Kaolin (Florida)	15.0
Tennessee ball clay #1	25.0
Feldspar (Buckingham)	25.0
Silica	25.0

PT-21   **White/Off-White Porcelain Throwing Body   Cone 11**
shrinkage 12.6%, plasticity 9.7, glaze rating 11.6

Mixing. Mix in the manner of PT-1.

Drying. Dry in the manner of PT-1.

Bisque Firing. Fire in the manner of PT-1.

Fired Results. When fired in oxidation this body is
white; reduction gives an off-white.

Kaolin (Georgia)	10.0
Kaolin (Florida)	25.0
Tennessee ball clay #1	25.0
Feldspar (Buckingham)	25.0
Silica	10.0

PT-22 **White-Gray Porcelain Throwing Body   Cone 10–12**
shrinkage 12%, plasticity 7.2, glaze rating 9.8

Mixing. Mix in the manner of PT-1.

Drying. Dry in the manner of PT-1.

Bisque Firing. Fire in the manner of PT-1.

Fired Results. When fired in oxidation this body is a white; reduction gives a gray in color.

Silica	35.0
Kaolin (EPK)	30.0
Feldspar (potash)	20.0
Kentucky ball clay #4	7.5
Tennessee ball clay #1	7.5
Add:	
Bentonite	2.0

PT-23 **White-Gray Porcelain Throwing Body   Cone 10–12**
shrinkage 14%, plasticity 9.4, glaze rating 9.5

Mixing. Mix in the manner of PT-1.

Drying. Dry in the manner of PT-1.

Bisque Firing. Fire in the manner of PT-1.

Fired Results. When fired in oxidation this body produces a white; reduction produces a gray. This body is good for utility ware.

Kaolin (EPK)	38.0
Nepheline syenite	25.0
Silica	20.0
Tennessee ball clay #1	10.0
Kaolin (Georgia)	5.0
Bentonite	2.0

PT-24 **White/Off-White Porcelain Throwing Body   Cone 10–12**
shrinkage 13%, plasticity 7, glaze rating 9.8

Mixing. Mix in the manner of PT-1.

Drying. Dry in the manner of PT-1.

Bisque Firing. Fire in the manner of PT-1.

Fired Results. When fired in oxidation this body gives a white; reduction gives an off-white.

Kaolin	39.0
Silica	20.0
Nepheline syenite	15.0
Kentucky ball clay #4	15.0
Cornwall stone	9.0
Bentonite	2.0

PT-25 **White-Gray Porcelain Throwing Body   Cone 12–14**
shrinkage 14.5%, plasticity 6.9, glaze rating 9.6

Mixing. Mix in the manner of PT-1.

Drying. Dry in the manner of PT-1.

Bisque Firing. Fire in the manner of PT-1.

Fired Results. When fired in oxidation this body produces a white; reduction produces a gray.

Kaolin (Georgia)	31.0
Feldspar (potash)	21.0
Silica	18.0
Kaolin (EPK)	17.0
Kentucky ball clay #4	6.0
Tennessee ball clay #1	6.0
Bentonite	1.0

PT-26 **White/Off-White Porcelain Throwing Body   Cone 12**
shrinkage 13.6%, plasticity 7.4, glaze rating 11.5

Mixing. Mix in the manner of PT-1.

Drying. Dry in the manner of PT-1.

Bisque Firing. Fire in the manner of PT-1.

Fired Results. When fired in oxidation this body is a white; reduction gives an off-white. This body is good for utility ware.

Kaolin	44.0
Feldspar (potash)	30.0
Silica	25.0
Whiting	1.0

PT-27   **White/Off-White Porcelain Throwing Body   Cone 14**
shrinkage 14%, plasticity 8.4, glaze rating 11.6

Mixing. Mix in the manner of PT-1.

Drying. Dry in the manner of PT-1.

Bisque Firing. Fire in the manner of PT-1.

Fired Results. When fired in oxidation this body produces a white; reduction produces an off-white.

Kaolin	54.0
Feldspar (potash)	20.0
Silica	25.0
Whiting	1.0

FORMULAS FOR PORCELAIN CASTING BODIES

Note. No plasticity rating is given for casting bodies.

PC-1   **White/Off-White Porcelain Casting Body   Cone 6–8**
shrinkage 12.5%, glaze rating 11.7

Mixing. Mix all the casting clay bodies in this section according to the procedure outlined in Chapter 3 under Mixing Casting Bodies.

Casting. Use the same casting procedure outlined in the casting body section of Chapter 5 under clay body EC-1.

Drying. Dry in the manner of PT-1.

Bisque Firing. Fire in the manner of PT-1.

Fired Results. When fired in oxidation this body is a pure white; reduction gives an off-white. If the ware is thin and is fired to cone 8 this body is translucent in the thin areas.

Bone ash	35.7
Kaolin	29.0
Silica	21.0
Feldspar (potash)	14.0
Sodium carbonate	0.3

PC-2   **White Porcelain Casting Body   Cone 6–8**
shrinkage 18%, glaze rating 11.5

Mixing. Mix in the manner of PC-1.

Casting. Cast in the manner of PC-1.

Drying. Dry in the manner of PC-1.

Bisque Firing. Fire in the manner of PC-1.

Fired Results. When fired in oxidation this body is a white; reduction also gives a white.

Bone ash	54.0
Kaolin (EPK)	26.0
Feldspar (potash)	20.0
Sodium carbonate	0.3

PC-3   **White-Gray Porcelain Casting Body   Cone 6–9**
shrinkage 10%, glaze rating 11.6

Mixing. Mix in the manner of PC-1.

Casting. Cast in the manner of PC-1.

Drying. Dry in the manner of PC-1.

Bisque Firing. Fire in the manner of PC-1.

Fired Results. When fired in oxidation this body is a white; reduction gives a gray. This body is especially good for utility ware due to its high glaze rating.

Feldspar (Kona K-4)	44.0
Kaolin (Georgia)	33.3
Silica	19.1
Whiting	3.4
Sodium carbonate	2.0

PC-4 **White-Gray Porcelain Casting Body** **Cone 8–10**
shrinkage 10%, glaze rating 11.5

Mixing. Mix in the manner of PC-1.

Casting. Cast in the manner of PC-1.

Drying. Dry in the manner of PC-1.

Bisque Firing. Fire in the manner of PC-1.

Fired Results. When fired in oxidation this body is a white; reduction gives a gray.

Kaolin	40.5
Feldspar (Kona K-4)	39.5
Silica	25.5
Whiting	4.5
Sodium carbonate	0.2

PC-5 **White-Gray Porcelain Casting Body** **Cone 8–11**
shrinkage 13.5%, glaze rating 11.5

Mixing. Mix in the manner of PC-1.

Casting. Cast in the manner of PC-1.

Drying. Dry in the manner of PC-1.

Bisque Firing. Fire in the manner of PC-1.

Fired Results. When fired in oxidation this body is a white; reduction gives a gray.

Kaolin (Georgia)	42.0
Feldspar (potash)	22.5
Tennessee ball clay #5	13.5
Silica	13.0
Kaolin (EPK)	8.8
Sodium carbonate	0.2

PC-6 **White Porcelain Casting Body** **Cone 9–11**
shrinkage 11.5%, glaze rating 11.6

Mixing. Mix in the manner of PC-1.

Casting. Cast in the manner of PC-1.

Drying. Dry in the manner of PC-1.

Bisque Firing. Fire in the manner of PC-1.

Fired Results. When fired in oxidation this body produces a white; reduction also produces a white. This body is very good for making tableware due to its white quality.

Kaolin (EPK)	46.0
Silica	34.0
Feldspar (potash)	19.8
Sodium carbonate	1.2

PC-7 **White-Gray Porcelain Casting Body** **Cone 9–11**
shrinkage 14%, glaze rating 11.8

Mixing. Mix in the manner of PC-1.

Casting. Cast in the manner of PC-1.

Drying. Dry in the manner of PC-1.

Bisque Firing. Fire in the manner of PC-1.

Fired Results. When fired in oxidation this body gives a white; reduction gives a gray. This body is very good for utility ware.

Kentucky ball clay #4	12.5
Tennessee ball clay #5	12.4
Feldspar (potash)	25.8
Silica	25.7
Kaolin (Georgia)	15.6
Kaolin (EPK)	8.9
Sodium carbonate	2.0

PC-8 **White-Gray Porcelain Casting Body** **Cone 9–12**
shrinkage 12.5%, glaze rating 11.6

Mixing. Mix in the manner of PC-1.

Casting. Cast in the manner of PC-1.

Drying. Dry in the manner of PC-1.

Bisque Firing. Fire in the manner of PC-1.

Fired Results. When fired in oxidation this produces a white; reduction produces a gray.

Kaolin (Georgia)	34.5
Feldspar (potash)	28.5
Silica	21.5
Kaolin (EPK)	10.5
Tennessee ball clay #1	5.0
Sodium carbonate	2.0

PC-9   **White-Gray Porcelain Casting Body   Cone 10–13**
shrinkage 11.5%, glaze rating 11.5

Mixing. Mix in the manner of PC-1.

Casting. Cast in the manner of PC-1.

Drying. Dry in the manner of PC-1.

Bisque Firing. Fire in the manner of PC-1.

Fired Results. When fired in oxidation this body is
white; reduction gives a gray.

Kaolin (EPK)	42.0
Feldspar (potash)	28.0
Silica	20.0
Tennessee ball clay #1	10.0
Sodium carbonate	0.2

PC-10   **White-Gray Porcelain Casting Body   Cone 10–12**
shrinkage 11.5%, glaze rating 11.5

Mixing. Mix in the manner of PC-1.

Casting. Cast in the manner of PC-1.

Drying. Dry in the manner of PC-1.

Bisque Firing. Fire in the manner of PC-1.

Fired Results. When fired in oxidation this body gives a
white; reduction gives a gray.

Kaolin (EPK)	51.0
Feldspar (potash)	29.7
Silica	19.0
Sodium carbonate	0.3

PC-11   **White-Gray Porcelain Casting Body   Cone 10–14**
shrinkage 14%, glaze rating 11.9

Mixing. Mix in the manner of PC-1.

Casting. Cast in the manner of PC-1.

Drying. Dry in the manner of PC-1.

Bisque Firing. Fire in the manner of PC-1.

Fired Results. When fired in oxidation this body gives a
white; reduction gives a gray.

Kaolin (any)	44.0
Feldspar (potash)	30.8
Silica	23.0
Whiting	2.0
Sodium carbonate	0.2

PC-12   **White-Gray Porcelain Casting Body   Cone 10–14**
shrinkage 13.5%, glaze rating 11.5

Mixing. Mix in the manner of PC-1.

Casting. Cast in the manner of PC-1.

Drying. Dry in the manner of PC-1.

Bisque Firing. Fire in the manner of PC-1.

Fired Results. When fired in oxidation this body is a
white; reduction gives a gray.

Kaolin	54.8
Silica	26.0
Feldspar (potash)	21.0
Sodium silicate (dry)	2.0

FORMULAS FOR PORCELAIN SCULPTURE BODIES

Note. The clay bodies in this section are excellent for handbuilding. They are not recommended for throwing.

PS-1   **White/Off-White Porcelain Sculpture Body   Cone 6–8**
shrinkage 13.5%, plasticity 10.6, glaze rating 9.5

Mixing. Mix this body according to the instructions in
Chapter 3 on Clay Body Preparation, using any of the
three methods described there. The grog can be added in
the mixing or during the wedging process. In cases where
the clay may be too wet to handle, the addition of grog
at this point will help to dry out the clay to the proper
working consistency. If plasticity seems to be a pro-

Kentucky ball clay #4	32.0
Tennessee ball clay #5	32.0
Fine white grog	12.0
Kaolin (EPK)	11.0
Fine white sand	8.2
Feldspar (potash)	2.4
Silica	2.4

blem, the clay should be aged at least a month using the method outlined at the beginning of this chapter.

Drying. Allow all sculpture and handbuilt pieces to dry thoroughly. Sculpture pieces are usually thicker and consequently need more drying time. Use the cheek test to check for dryness.

Bisque Firing. Bisque fire sculpture pieces only if they are to be glazed later. If they are not, fire them to maturity with the first firing. This body should be bisque fired to at least cone 04, cone 02 is better.

Fired Results. When this body is fired in oxidation it is a pure white; reduction gives an off-white.

PS-2.

White-Gray Porcelain Sculpture Body   Cone 9–10
shrinkage 11.5%, plasticity 9.8, glaze rating 11.8

Mixing. Mix in the manner of PS-1.

Drying. Dry in the manner of PS-1.

Bisque Firing. Fire in the manner of PS-1.

Fired Results. When fired in oxidation this body is a white; reduction gives a gray.

Kaolin	21.0
Silica	23.0
Tennessee ball clay #5	18.0
Feldspar (potash)	18.0
White grog (40–60 mesh)	10.0
Fine silica sand	10.0

PS-3

White-Gray Porcelain Sculpture Body   Cone 10–11
shrinkage 12.0%, plasticity 9.5, glaze rating 11.5

Mixing. Mix in the manner of PS-1.

Drying. Dry in the manner of PS-1.

Bisque Firing. Fire in the manner of PS-1.

Fired Results. When fired in oxidation this body produces a white; reduction produces a gray. This body is good for figurines.

Barium carbonate	42.5
Tennessee ball clay #5	25.0
Kaolin	20.0
Fine white grog	10.0
Bentonite	2.5

PS-4

White-Tan Porcelain Sculpture Body   Cone 10–12
shrinkage 12.6%, glaze rating 11.0, plasticity rating 9.2

Mixing. Mix in the manner of PS-1.

Drying. Dry in the manner of PS-1.

Bisque Firing. Fire in the manner of PS-1.

Fired Results. When fired in oxidation this body gives a white; reduction gives a tan.

Kaolin	38.0
Silica	21.0
Whiting	5.0
Nepheline syenite	10.0
Kentucky ball clay #4	7.5
Tennessee ball clay #5	7.5
Cornwall stone	10.0
Bentonite	1.0
Add:	
White grog (60–80 mesh)	10.0

PS-5

White/Light-Green Porcelain Sculpture Body Cone 10–12
shrinkage 11.8%, glaze rating 11.1, plasticity rating 9.3

Mixing. Mix in the manner of PS-1.

Drying. Dry in the manner of PS-1.

Bisque Firing. Fire in the manner of PS-1.

Fired Results. When fired in oxidation this body is a white; reduction gives a light green.

Kaolin (EPK)	38.0
Nepheline syenite	20.0
Whiting	5.0
Kentucky ball clay #4	5.0
Tennessee ball clay #5	5.0
Kaolin (Georgia)	5.0
Bentonite	2.0
Add:	
White grog (60–80 mesh)	10.0

9
RAKU CLAY BODIES AND GLAZES
CONE 016-03

Raku is a low-fire ware which is subjected to heating and cooling stresses and tensions during firing. Beginning in the sixteenth century the Japanese used raku ware for tea ceremony vessels. The tea ceremony emphasized the beauty of the simple and the natural and so the word raku means "enjoyment of freedom."

Even today raku pieces are generally simple in form and free in design. And though the Americanized version of raku is more vigorous and striking in its conception than that of the Japanese potters, it still maintains its simple, natural, and free quality.

Much of this is due, of course, to the limitations of the medium itself. The clay used for raku which will withstand the thermal shocks inherent in the firing process is by nature less workable and less plastic than stoneware clay. Therefore there are certain limitations to the size and complexity of the pieces the potter can make with this medium. The creation of new and more adaptable clay bodies, however, has given the potter more latitude in this respect. The raku body formulas given in this chapter range from fairly plastic to nonplastic and should provide a range from which the potter can choose for throwing or handbuilding.

The procedure for making and firing raku ware will not be discussed here. There are already several books on the subject which deal at length with procedure. These are listed in the Bibliography.

The preparation of raku clay bodies, their analysis and testing are basically the same as for other clays. Therefore the information given in Chapter 3 under Clay Body Preparation should be referred to.

Only one category of raku bodies is given. The potter can decide which method he wishes to use in forming his raku pieces and choose the body characteristics best suited for that technique. A simple rule to follow is to use bodies with a high plasticity rating for throwing—at least 9.5— and those with a lower rating for handbuilt pieces.

This chapter contains clay bodies and glazes because both are unique to raku ware. All of the clay bodies and glazes were designed for raku firing only and should not be used for any other purpose unless the instructions indicate that this can be done successfully. The formulas in this chapter are arranged first by temperature range then by fired color, light to dark, within each temperature range.

The reader will find possible substitutions for most of the chemicals in Chapter 34, Dictionary of Glaze Compounds, under each individual heading.

RAKU GLAZES CONE 016–04

Raku glazes are much like any other glaze except that they are designed to reach their mature state at temperatures from 1600°F. to 2000°F./871° C. to 1093°C. This is the temperature range of most raku glazes used by potters today.

Raku glazes are generally classified by their maturing temperature. They can, however, be classified by their content such as lead or alkaline, depending upon the flux used.

Raku glazes may be opaque, transparent, or even translucent, depending on the colorant or opacifiers used. These glazes are often glassy in appearance and have a strong tendency to craze and crackle upon cooling. If the potter considers this a defect it can be remedied by adding silica, just as the glaze's tendency to run and flow can be corrected by the addition of a refractory material such as kaolin.

Much of the appeal of the raku glaze lies in the wide range of color and brilliance made possible by the addition of colorants and the low fusion point. For at this temperature range all the colorants available to the potter can be employed to their fullest, producing colors not possible in higher-fired ware.

Note. The glazes listed in this section are especially designed for raku ware. They can, however, be used on the lower-fired earthenware if crazing is not a problem or if the pottery is not to be used for utility ware.

Note. The ingredients in the formulas in this chapter can be weighed out in either grams or pounds. It is recommended that the potter first make a 100-gram test batch of the clay body that interests him to insure that it is suitable before making larger amounts. Any of the lighter firing bodies can be colored by the use of coloring oxides. See Chapter 12 for further information. The clay bodies are listed here by firing temperature from lower to higher cones.

FORMULAS FOR RAKU BODIES

RCB-1   **Tan Raku Body Cone 012–09**
shrinkage 2%, plasticity 10.8, glaze rating 10.9

Plastic fire clay	50.0
Talc	50.0
Fine sand (30 mesh)	30.0

Mixing. Weigh out the ingredients by grams for test batches and by pounds for larger batches. Mix the clay using any of the three methods outlined in Chapter 3 on Clay Body Preparation. This clay can be used at once or stored to age for a couple of weeks for even greater plasticity. If a pug mill is not used for mixing, take care that the clay is thoroughly wedged to increase its workability and to remove any trapped air bubbles which might lead to cracking or explosions during the firing.

Drying. Place the wet pieces in a location that is free of drafts and allow them to dry thoroughly. Drafts can lead to uneven drying and consequent warping or cracking. Test for dryness by placing the base of the piece against your cheek. If it feels even faintly moist or cool to the touch, it still contains moisture and should dry further. Drying time will vary according to the size and thickness of the ware, the temperature, and the humidity. In general most pieces will dry and be ready for firing if kept in a warm, dry place.

Bisque Firing. Raku ware should be bisque fired to about cone 012. First fire the kiln slowly to 500°F./260°C. to allow any latent moisture to be removed, then fire normally to the desired bisque temperature. If an alkaline glaze is to be used, particularly a raw alkaline glaze, the bisque fire should be about cone 010 as the more porous bisque has a tendency to absorb the soluble alkaline materials and leave the glaze rough and unmatured. This will also cut down on pinholing and blisters in the alkaline glazes (see Glossary).

Fired Results. This body can be glaze fired as high as cone 09. When fired in oxidation it is a light tan; reduction gives gray to black depending upon the amount of carbon absorbed by the body.

RCB-2   **Tan-Gray Raku Body Cone 012–09**
shrinkage 3%, plasticity 10.6, glaze rating 11.1

Fire clay	30.0
Ball clay	21.0
Talc	19.0
Grog	30.0

Mixing. Mix in the manner of RCB-1.

Drying. Dry in the manner of RCB-1.

Bisque Firing. Fire in the manner of RCB-1.

Fired Results. When fired in oxidation this body is a light tan; reduction gives gray to black.

RCB-3 **Red-Brown Raku Body Cone 012–09**
shrinkage 1.6%, plasticity 11.1, glaze rating 11.3

Mixing. Mix in the manner of RCB-1.

Drying. Dry in the manner of RCB-1.

Bisque Firing. Fire in the manner of RCB-1.

Fired Results. When fired in oxidation this body is a red-brown; reduction gives a darker brown with occasional metallic tints.

Local brick clay	33.5
Medium grog	33.0
Bentonite	33.5

RCB-4 **Tan-Gray Raku Body Cone 07**
shrinkage 2.6%, plasticity 9.7, glaze rating 10.6

Mixing. Mix in the manner of RCB-1.

Drying. Dry in the manner of RCB-1.

Bisque Firing. Fire in the manner of RCB-1.

Fired Results. In oxidation this body gives a light tan; reduction gives gray to black.

Lincoln fire clay	70.0
Fine grog	30.0

RCB-5 **Tan-Gray Raku Body Cone 012–07**
shrinkage 5.5%, plasticity 10.6, glaze rating 10.3

Mixing. Mix in the manner of RCB-1.

Drying. Dry in the manner of RCB-1.

Bisque Firing. Fire in the manner of RCB-1.

Fired Results. In oxidation this body is a tan; reduction gives a gray.

Jordan clay	20.0
Fire clay	60.0
Sand (40–60 mesh)	20.0

RCB-6 **Tan-Gray Raku Body Cone 06**
shrinkage 2.1%, plasticity 10.6, glaze rating 10.7

Mixing. Mix in the manner of RCB-1.

Drying. Dry in the manner of RCB-1.

Bisque Firing. Fire in the manner of RCB-1.

Fired Results. When fired in oxidation this body is tan; reduction gives a gray.

Plastic fire clay	66.6
Grog	33.3

RCB-7 **Tan-Gray Raku Body Cone 04**
shrinkage 3%, plasticity 10.5, glaze rating 11.1

Mixing. Mix in the manner of RCB-1.

Drying. Dry in the manner of RCB-1.

Bisque Firing. Fire in the manner of RCB-1.

Fired Results. In oxidation this body is a tan; reduction gives a gray.

Stoneware clay	30.0
Fire clay	25.0
Kentucky ball clay #4	15.0
Nepheline syenite	25.0
Grog (fine)	5.0

RCB-8. **Red-Brown Raku Body Cone 012–09**
shrinkage 1.9%, plasticity 11, glaze rating 11.1

Mixing. Mix in the manner of RCB-1.

Drying. Dry in the manner of RCB-1.

Bisque Firing. Fire in the manner of RCB-1.

Fired Results. When fired in oxidation this body is a red-brown; reduction also gives a red-brown.

Local red brick clay	51.0
Medium grog	49.0
Bentonite	2.0

RCB-9. **Tan-Gray Raku Body Cone 012–09**
shrinkage 1.3%, plasticity 10.6, glaze rating 11.1

Mixing. Mix in the manner of RCB-1.

Drying. Dry in the manner of RCB-1.

Bisque Firing. Fire in the manner of RCB-1.

Fired Results. In oxidation this body is a tan; reduction gives a gray.

Plastic fire clay	50.0
Talc	20.0
Fine sand or grog	30.0

RCB-10 **Tan-Gray Raku Body Cone 012–09**
shrinkage 2.1%, plasticity 10.8, glaze rating 11.1

Mixing. Mix in the manner of RCB-1.

Drying. Dry in the manner of RCB-1.

Bisque Firing. Fire in the manner of RCB-1.

Fired Results. In oxidation this body is a tan; reduction gives a gray.

Fire clay (Lincoln)	30.0
Kentucky ball clay #4	20.0
Talc	20.0
Grog	30.0

RCB-11 **Buff/Gray-Black Raku Body Cone 04**
shrinkage 4.5%, plasticity 8.2, glaze rating 11.2

Mixing. Mix in the manner of RCB-1.

Drying. Dry in the manner of RCB-1.

Bisque Firing. Fire in the manner of RCB-1.

Fired Results. When fired in oxidation this body is a buff; reduction gives gray to black.

Kaolin	25.0
Kentucky ball clay #4	25.0
Plastic fire clay	28.0
Talc	12.0
Grog (40–60 mesh)	10.0

RCB-12 **Off-White/Gray Raku Body Cone 03**
shrinkage 3.5%, plasticity 7.3, glaze rating 11.2

Mixing. Mix in the manner of RCB-1.

Drying. Dry in the manner of RCB-1.

Bisque Firing. Fire in the manner of RCB-1.

Fired Results. In oxidation this body is an off-white; reduction gives a gray.

Silica	26.0
Kentucky ball clay #4	24.0
Kaolin	16.0
Plastic vitrox	14.0
Feldspar (soda)	10.0
Grog (40–60 mesh)	10.0

RCB-13 **Off-White/Gray Raku Body Cone 04–01**
shrinkage 5.1%, plasticity 9.2, glaze rating 11.1

Mixing. Mix in the manner of RCB-1.

Drying. Dry in the manner of RCB-1.

Bisque Firing. Fire in the manner of RCB-1.

Fired Results. In oxidation this body is an off-white; reduction gives a gray.

Stoneware clay	29.0
Fire clay	27.0
Grog (40–60 mesh)	20.0
Kentucky ball clay #4	16.0
Feldspar (soda)	5.0
Silica	5.0

RCB-14 **Buff/Dark Buff Raku Body   Cone 04-01**
shrinkage 1.0%, plasticity 7.5, glaze rating 11.3

Mixing. Mix in the manner of RCB-1.

Drying. Dry in the manner of RCB-1.

Bisque Firing. Fire in the manner of RCB-1.

Fired Results. When fired in oxidation this body is a buff; reduction gives a dark buff.

Lincoln fire clay	55.0
Grog (40–60 mesh)	25.0
Talc	20.0

RCB-15 **Buff-Brown Raku Body Cone 04-03**
shrinkage 1.5%, plasticity 11, glaze rating 11

Mixing. Mix in the manner of RCB-1.

Drying. Dry in the manner of RCB-1.

Bisque Firing. Fire in the manner of RCB-1.

Fired Results. In oxidation this body is a buff color; reduction gives a brown.

Fire clay	58.0
Spodumene	31.0
Talc	5.0
Add:	
Grog (60–80 mesh)	10-20

FORMULAS FOR RAKU GLAZES

Note. The ingredients in the glaze formulas in this section can be weighed out in either grams or pounds. It is recommended that the potter first make a 100-gram test batch of the glaze that interests him to insure that it is suitable before making larger amounts. The glazes are listed here by firing temperature from lower to higher cones. Important: Do not spray glazes that have a toxic rating. Do not use a glaze with a toxic rating on any piece that might be used as utility ware.

RG-1 **Raku Base Glaze Cone 016-012**
lead, transparent, clear gloss, toxic

Mixing. Weigh out the ingredients as indicated in the formula and place them in a jar. (A pint or quart, half-liter or liter, jar can be used for this purpose.) Premix the dry contents by rotating the jar several times, then add water in the following ratio:

For a brushing glaze — 1 to 2 oz. (30 to 60 ml) per 100 grams of glaze

For a dipping glaze — 2 to 3 oz. (60 to 90 ml) per 100 grams of glaze

For a spraying glaze — 4 to 6 oz. (120 to 180 ml) per 100 grams of glaze

Red lead	88.0
Silica	12.0
C.M.C.	1 tsp
Add:	
Bentonite	2.0

These measurements are not absolute, so it would be wise for the potter to train himself by sight, feel, and consistency of the glaze whether it is right for use. For example, a brushing glaze should be about the consistency of ketchup, a dipping glaze that of cream, and a spraying glaze about that of milk.

Once the water is added and the jar given a brief shaking to mix the ingredients, add a teaspoon of C.M.C. per 100 grams of glaze by dry measure and shake the jar vigorously until the contents are thoroughly mixed. Sieve the glaze twice through a 60- to 80-mesh screen, using a stiff brush to break up any resistant lumps. Once these steps have been followed, the glaze is ready for use.

Exercise caution in handling RG-1, for it contains red lead, a compound which is very toxic. Check the entry on lead compounds in the Dictionary of Clay and Glaze Compounds in Chapter 34 for further information.

Application. Brush, dip, or spray the number of desired coats on the bisque ware. Allow the different coatings to dry to the point that the surface loses its moist sheen before applying another coat of glaze. Each coating should be about the thickness of a playing card. Allow the glazed ware to dry completely before firing. The ware should also be protected from dust or air-borne clay particles in the studio.

Fired Results. This glaze can be fired in oxidation or reduction. Fired as it is, it is a clear gloss glaze. For possible color variations consult RG-1a through RG-1m below.

Color Variations for RG-1

A. Light Green to Red-Brown Luster. In oxidation this glaze variation is a light green. In reduction it is a red-brown luster with occasional green tints.

B. Light Green to Maroon-Brown Luster. In oxidation this glaze variation is a light green. In reduction it is a maroon-brown luster. If the reduction is not heavy it produces a maroon-brown luster with occasional green tints.

C. Medium Yellow to Black. In oxidation this glaze variation is a medium yellow. In reduction it is gray to black depending on the intensity of the reduction.

D. Speckled Yellow to Black. In oxidation this glaze variation is a speckled yellow. In reduction it is gray to black depending on the intensity of the reduction.

E. Burnt Golden-Umber Brown. In oxidation this glaze variation is a golden-umber brown. In reduction it is a burnt golden-umber brown.

F. Yellow-Brown. In oxidation this glaze variation is a light yellow-brown. In reduction it is a darker yellow-brown with gray to black areas depending on the amount of carbon absorbed in the glaze during reduction.

G. Olive Green. In oxidation this glaze variation is a true olive green. In reduction it is a darker hue of olive green.

H. Forest Green. In oxidation this glaze variation is a true forest green. In reduction it is a darker shade of forest green.

I. Muddy Copper Luster. In oxidation this glaze variation is a muddy brown color. It is much better when fired in reduction where it becomes a more attractive muddy copper luster.

J. Reddish Orange. In oxidation this glaze is a light orange with occasional greenish tints. In reduction it is a red-orange with mottled areas of red and orange-brown.

A.	Copper carbonate	3.1%
	Red iron oxide	1.3%
B.	Copper carbonate	3.2%
C.	Sodium uranate	8.6%
D.	Uranium oxide	5.3%
E.	Antimony oxide	4.9%
	Nickel oxide	2.1%
F.	Tin oxide	4.0%
	Manganese dioxide	3.9%
G.	Cobalt carbonate	0.5%
	Uranium oxide	3.0%
	Red iron oxide	2.1%
H.	Lead chromate	3.0%
I.	Manganese dioxide	3.0%
	Copper carbonate	3.1%
J.	Potassium bichromate	8.0%
K.	Potassium bichromate	5.5%
L.	Tin oxide	8.1%
	Manganese dioxide	0.6%
M.	Burnt umber	8.3%

K. Brown-Orange. In oxidation this glaze variation is a light brown-orange. In reduction it is a darker brown-orange with areas of gray to black depending upon the amount of carbon absorbed during the reduction.

L. Pale Yellow. In oxidation this glaze variation is a pale yellow. In reduction it is a slightly darker yellow with large crackles which tend to absorb carbon during the reduction process.

M. Soft Brown. In oxidation this glaze variation is a medium brown of a very soft hue. In reduction it is a darker brown with areas of gray to black depending upon the amount of carbon absorbed during reduction.

RG-2

Light Cool Gray/Dark Cool Gray Raku Glaze Cone 016–012
leadless, cool gray, opaque, nontoxic

Mixing. Mix in the manner of RG-1.

Application. Apply in the manner of RG-1.

Fired Results. In oxidation this glaze is a light cool gray in color. In reduction it is a darker gray with areas of black from the carbon absorbed during reduction.

Colemanite	74.0
Silica	21.0
Kaolin	5.0
Bentonite	2.0
Umber	6.2
Tin oxide	8.1
C.M.C.	1 tsp

RG-3

Soft Gray/Soft Dark Gray Raku Glaze Cone 016–012
leadless, opaque, soft gray, nontoxic

Mixing. Mix in the manner of RG-1.

Application. Apply in the manner of RG-1.

Fired Results. In oxidation this glaze is a soft light gray. In reduction it is a darker soft gray with areas of darker gray to black due to the carbon absorbed during the reduction process.

Colemanite	62.0
Feldspar (potash)	38.0
C.M.C.	1 tsp
Add:	
Bentonite	2.0

RG-4

Barium Crackle White Raku Glaze Cone 016–012
barium, opaque, crackle white, toxic

Mixing. Mix in the manner of RG-1.

Application. Apply in the manner of RG-1.

Fired Results. In oxidation this glaze is a crackle white with uncolored cracks. In reduction it is a crackle white with black crackles due to the absorption of carbon during the reduction process.

Colemanite	62.0
Feldspar (potash)	48.0
Barium carbonate	22.0
Silica	16.0
C.M.C.	1 tsp

RG-5

Metallic Raku Glaze Cone 016–010
leadless, opaque, tan luster, nontoxic

Mixing. Mix in the manner of RG-1.

Application. Apply in the manner of RG-1.

Fired Results. In oxidation this glaze is a tan metallic luster. In reduction it is a darker tan metallic luster.

Colemanite	64.0
Borax	24.0
Nepheline syenite	6.0
Kaolin	4.0
Rutile	4.0
Copper oxide	2.0
C.M.C.	1 tsp

RG-6

Transparent Raku Base Glaze Cone 016–010
leadless, transparent, clear gloss, nontoxic

Mixing. Mix in the manner of RG-1.

Application. Apply in the manner of RG-1.

Fired Results. This glaze is clear in both oxidation and reduction. Use the suggested color variations below for best results.

Pemco frit #25	42.5
Ferro frit #3134	27.4
Lithium carbonate	9.8
Kaolin (EPK)	6.3
Silica	14.0
C.M.C.	1 tsp
Add:	
Bentonite	2.0

Color Variations for RG-6

A. For yellow use 5% to 7% praseodymium stain.

B. For Naples yellow use 3.2% Naples yellow stain.

C. For oranges use 5% to 7% uranium oxide.

D. For pure blues use 0.5% to 1.5% cobalt oxide plus 1% iron oxide for better hues.

E. For light blues use 0.5% cobalt carbonate.

F. For medium blues use 1% cobalt carbonate.

G. For darker blues use 1.5% cobalt carbonate

H. For green-blues use the same amounts as in E, F, and G plus 1.6% copper carbonate.

I. For mottled blues use 0.5% to 1.5% cobalt carbonate plus rutile in amounts of 2% to 3%.

J. For turquoise use copper carbonate in amounts of 2.5% to 3.5%. Add tin oxide in amounts of 4.5% if the glaze is to be opaque.

K. For silver lusters use silver nitrate in the amount of 2.1% and soda ash in the amount of 1 gram per mix.

L. For a silver luster with greenish tints add chrome oxide in the amount of 1.2% to K above.

M. For silver lusters with bluish tints use K above and add 1.1% of cobalt carbonate.

RG-7

Dark Turquoise/Rainbow Metallic Raku Glaze Cone 012
lead, opaque, turquoise, toxic

Mixing. Mix in the manner of RG-1.

Application. Apply in the manner of RG-1.

Fired Results. In oxidation this glaze is a dark turquoise. In reduction it is turquoise with a rainbow metallic sheen luster over it. Caution: this glaze is fluid at cone 012.

Ferro frit #5301	38.4
White lead	26.1
Silica	10.3
Boric acid	11.3
Borax	7.4
Copper oxide	4.7
Tin oxide	1.8
C.M.C.	1 tsp
Bentonite	2.0

RG-8

Clear Gloss Raku Glaze Base   Cone 012
alkaline, transparent, clear to milky, nontoxic

Mixing. Mix in the manner of RG-1.

Application. Apply in the manner of RG-1.

Fired Results. This glaze fires to a clear gloss in both oxidation and reduction. It is a good base glaze for the colorants listed at the end of the chapter. Caution: this glaze is slightly fluid.

Ferro frit #5301	73.8
Borax	17.0
Bentonite	4.0
Selenium	5.0
Bentonite	2.0
C.M.C.	1 tsp

RG-9

Clear Gloss Raku Glaze   Cone 012
lead, transparent, clear gloss, toxic

Mixing. Mix in the manner of RG-1.

Application. Apply in the manner of RG-1.

Fired Results. This glaze fires to a clear gloss in both oxidation and reduction. Caution: this glaze is slightly fluid.

White lead	60.0
Silica	18.0
Ferro frit #3134	14.0
Sodium carbonate	8.0
C.M.C.	1 tsp

RG-10.

Silver-White Gloss Raku Glaze   Cone 012
lead, translucent, white to yellow, toxic

Mixing. Mix in the manner of RG-1.

Application. Apply in the manner of RG-1.

Fired Results. In oxidation this glaze is a silver-white. In reduction it is white to yellow.

White lead	47.0
Ferro frit #5301	26.0
Silica	11.0
Tin oxide	8.0
Feldspar (soda)	5.0
Zircopax	3.0
C.M.C.	1 tsp

RG-11

Streaked Burgundy Raku Glaze   Cone 012–09
alkaline, opaque, streaked burgundy, nontoxic

Mixing. Mix in the manner of RG-1.

Application. Apply in the manner of RG-1.

Fired Results. In oxidation and reduction this glaze is a streaked burgundy.

Ferro frit #3134	24.0
Colemanite	26.0
Nepheline syenite	24.0
Red lead	26.0
Tin oxide	4.0
Manganese dioxide	4.0
C.M.C.	1 tsp

RG-12

Black Semi-Matt Raku Glaze   Cone 012–09
lead, alkaline frit, opaque, black, toxic

Mixing. Mix in the manner of RG-1.

Application. Apply in the manner of RG-1.

Fired Results. In oxidation and reduction this glaze is a black semi-matt.

Ferro frit #3134	44.0
White lead	42.0
Silica	14.0
Red iron oxide	4.0
Manganese dioxide	3.0
Cobalt oxide	2.0
C.M.C.	1 tsp

RG-13

White Cloud Raku Base Glaze   Cone 012–09
alkaline, translucent, milky, nontoxic

Mixing. Mix in the manner of RG-1.

Application. Apply in the manner of RG-1.

Fired Results. This glaze resembles a white cloud when fired in oxidation or reduction.

Colemanite	75.0
Feldspar (soda)	25.0
C.M.C.	1 tsp

A. Copper carbonate	3.0%
Manganese dioxide	1.5%
B. Copper carbonate	3.0%
Cobalt oxide	0.1%
C. Manganese dioxide	1.5%
Cobalt oxide	0.1%

A. Pale Lemon Luster. In oxidation this glaze is a pale lemon luster. In reduction it is a darker lemon luster.

B. Pale Aqua Luster. In oxidation this glaze is a pale aqua luster. In reduction it is a darker aqua luster.

C. Purple-Amber. In oxidation this glaze is a purple-amber. In reduction it is a darker purple-amber.

RG-14

Cloudy White Raku Base Glaze Cone 012–09
lead, alkaline, translucent, cloudy white, toxic

Colemanite	58.0
Red lead	32.0
Nepheline syenite	5.0
Kaolin	5.0
C.M.C.	1 tsp

Mixing. Mix in the manner of RG-1.

Application. Apply in the manner of RG-1.

Fired Results. In both oxidation and reduction this glaze is a cloudy white.

Color Variations for RG-14

| A. Red iron oxide | 7.5-8% |
| B. Black copper oxide | 2.5% |

A. Brandy. In oxidation this glaze is a brandy. In reduction it is a darker brandy.

B. Copper Luster. In oxidation this glaze is a cerebral luster. In reduction it is a darker copper luster.

RG-15

Raku Base Glaze Cone 012–09
alkaline, transparent, cloudy white, nontoxic

Ferro frit #3134	48.0
Colemanite	50.0
Kaolin (EPK)	2.0
C.M.C.	1 tsp

Mixing. Mix in the manner of RG-1.

Application. Apply in the manner of RG-1.

Fired Results. In oxidation and reduction this glaze is a cloudy white.

Color Variations for RG-15

A. Black copper oxide	2.5%
Manganese dioxide	1.0%
B. Tin oxide	3.0%
Black copper oxide	2.5%

A. Oil Luster. In oxidation this glaze is an oil luster. In reduction it is a darker oil luster color.

B. Red-Bronze. In oxidation this glaze is a red-bronze. In reduction it is a darker red-bronze.

RG-16

Clear Gloss Raku Glaze Cone 012–09
lead, transparent, clear gloss, toxic

Ferro frit #3134	40.0
Red lead	39.0
Silica	26.0
C.M.C.	1 tsp

Mixing. Mix in the manner of RG-1.

Application. Apply in the manner of RG-1.

Fired Results. In oxidation and reduction this glaze is clear.

Color Variations for RG-16

A. Manganese dioxide	5.0%
Copper carbonate	3.0%
B. Black copper oxide	4.0%
C. Black uranium oxide	3.0%
Black copper oxide	2.0%

A. Celadon Luster. In oxidation this is a celadon luster. In reduction it is a darker celadon.

B. Puce Copper Luster. In oxidation this glaze is a puce copper luster. In reduction it is a darker puce luster.

C. Metallic Red Luster. In oxidation this glaze is a red metallic luster. In reduction it is a darker red.

RG-17 **Cloudy White Raku Glaze Cone 012–09**
alkaline, translucent, cloudy white, nontoxic

Mixing. Mix in the manner of RG-1.

Application. Apply in the manner of RG-1.

Fired Results. In oxidation this glaze is a cloudy white. In reduction this glaze is a cloudy translucent white.

Colemanite	76.0
Feldspar (potash)	24.0
C.M.C.	1 tsp

RG-18 **Rabbit's Fur Raku Glaze Cone 012–06**
alkaline, opaque, streaked tan, toxic

Mixing. Mix in the manner of RG-1.

Application. Apply in the manner of RG-1.

Fired Results. In oxidation this glaze is a rabbit's fur tan. In reduction it is a streaked rabbit's fur tan.

Borax	52.0
Ferro frit #3134	39.0
Kaolin	9.0
Antimony oxide	5.0
Nickel oxide	3.0
C.M.C.	1 tsp

RG-19 **Smoky Metallic Raku Glaze Cone 012–06**
alkaline, opaque, smoky metallic, nontoxic

Mixing. Mix in the manner of RG-1.

Application. Apply in the manner of RG-1.

Fired Results. In oxidation and reduction this glaze is a smoky metallic.

Colemanite	42.0
Ferro frit #3134	28.0
Silica	18.0
Kentucky ball clay #4	7.0
Whiting	5.0
C.M.C.	1 tsp

RG-20 **Soft White Raku Glaze Cone 012–06**
alkaline, opaque, white, nontoxic

Mixing. Mix in the manner of RG-1.

Application. Apply in the manner of RG-1.

Fired Results. In oxidation this glaze is a soft white. In reduction it is a white.

Colemanite	55.0
Nepheline syenite	19.0
Lithium carbonate	16.0
Kaolin (EPK)	5.0
Tin oxide	5.0
C.M.C.	5.0

RG-21 **Soft Transparent Base Raku Glaze Cone 012**
lead, transparent, clear gloss, toxic

Mixing. Mix in the manner of RG-1.

Application. Apply in the manner of RG-1.

Fired Results. In oxidation and reduction this glaze is a clear gloss.

Ferro frit #3134	46.0
White lead	44.0
Silica	10.0
C.M.C.	1 tsp
Add:	
Bentonite	2.0

Color Variations for RG-21

A. Soft Blue. In oxidation this glaze is a soft blue. In reduction it is a slightly darker blue.

B. Soft Yellow Copper. In oxidation this glaze is a soft yellow copper. In reduction it is a slightly darker yellow copper.

C. Soft Blue Copper. In oxidation this glaze is a soft blue copper. In reduction it is a darker blue copper.

D. Soft Black. In oxidation this glaze is a soft black. In reduction it is a black.

A.	Tin oxide	7.5%
	Cobalt oxide	0.4%
B.	Tin oxide	2.5%
	Copper oxide	1.9%
C.	Copper oxide	2.0%
	Cobalt carbonate	0.5%
D.	Yellow ochre	32.0%
	Tin oxide	5.0%

RG-22

White Raku Glaze   Cone 010–06
alkaline, translucent, white, nontoxic

Mixing. Mix in the manner of RG-1.

Application. Apply in the manner of RG-1.

Fired Results. In oxidation and reduction this glaze is a white.

Colemanite	82.0
Cornwall stone	18.0
C.M.C.	1 tsp

Color Variations for RG-22

A. Deep Purple. In oxidation and reduction this glaze is a deep purple.

B. Copper Luster. In oxidation and reduction this glaze is a copper luster.

C. Copper Luster. In oxidation and reduction this glaze is a copper luster.

D. Copper Luster. In oxidation and reduction this glaze is a copper luster.

E. Gray. In oxidation this glaze is a gray. In reduction it is a darker gray.

F. Blue Copper Luster. In oxidation this glaze is a blue copper luster. In reduction it is a darker blue copper luster.

G. Light Copper Luster. In oxidation this glaze is a light copper luster. In reduction it is a copper luster.

H. Gold Luster. In oxidation this glaze is a gold luster. In reduction this glaze is a darker shade of gold luster.

A.	Manganese dioxide	2.5%
	Cobalt oxide	0.5%
B.	Yellow ochre	7.8%
	Copper oxide	2.1%
	Cobalt oxide	1.1%
C.	Copper carbonate	2.3%
D.	Copper oxide	0.5%
	Cobalt carbonate	0.3%
E.	Red iron oxide	1.0%
	Cobalt carbonate	0.3%
F.	Cobalt carbonate	0.3%
	Copper carbonate	2.1%
G.	Copper carbonate	1.0%
	Milled rutile	4.1%
H.	Silver nitrate	2.1%
	Tin oxide	1.1%

RG-23

Transparent Base Raku Glaze   Cone 010–06
alkaline, transparent, clear, nontoxic

Mixing. Mix in the manner of RG-1.

Application. Apply in the manner of RG-1.

Fired Results. In both oxidation and reduction this glaze is clear.

Colemanite	48.0
Borax	52.0
C.M.C.	1 tsp
Add:	
Bentonite	2.0

RG-24

Raku Base Glaze   Cone 09–06
lead, transparent, clear, toxic

Mixing. Mix in the manner of RG-1.

Application. Apply in the manner of RG-1.

Fired Results. In oxidation and reduction this glaze is clear.

White lead	65.0
Kaolin (EPK)	5.0
Silica	30.0
C.M.C.	1 tsp

RG-25

Alkaline Blue Raku Glaze   Cone 09–06
lead, alkaline, opaque, blue, toxic

Mixing. Mix in the manner of RG-1.

Application. Apply in the manner of RG-1.

Fired Results. In oxidation this glaze is an alkaline blue. In reduction it is a blue.

Ferro frit #5301	52.0
White lead	28.0
Borax	10.0
Silica	10.0
Copper oxide	2%–5%
Tin oxide	2.0
C.M.C.	1 tsp

RG-26

Silver-White Raku Glaze   Cone 09–06
lead, opaque, silver-white, toxic

Mixing. Mix in the manner of RG-1.

Application. Apply in the manner of RG-1.

Fired Results. In oxidation and reduction this glaze is a silver-white.

White lead	52.0
Ferro frit #5301	28.0
Feldspar (potash)	5.0
Silica	14.0
Tin oxide	6.0
C.M.C.	1 tsp

RG-27

Black Luster Raku Glaze   Cone 09–06
lead, opaque, black luster, toxic

Mixing. Mix in the manner of RG-1.

Application. Apply in the manner of RG-1.

Fired Results. In oxidation and reduction this glaze is a black luster.

White lead	62.0
Ferro frit #5301	18.0
Silica	20.0
Copper oxide	4.0
Cobalt oxide	3.0
Red iron oxide	4.0
C.M.C.	1 tsp

RG-28

Raku Base Glaze   Cone 09–06
lead, alkaline, transparent, clear, toxic

Mixing. Mix in the manner of RG-1.

Application. Apply in the manner of RG-1.

Fired Results. In oxidation and reduction this glaze is clear.

White lead	65.0
Borax	14.0
Kaolin	3.0
Silica	40.0
C.M.C.	1 tsp

RG-29

Raku Base Glaze   Cone 09–06
lead, transparent, clear gloss, toxic

Mixing. Mix in the manner of RG-1.

Application. Apply in the manner of RG-1.

Fired Results. In oxidation and reduction this glaze is a clear gloss.

White lead	58.0
Ferro frit #3124	22.0
Silica	20.0
C.M.C.	1 tsp

RG-30

Transparent Raku Glaze   Cone 06–04
alkaline, transparent, clear gloss, nontoxic

Mixing. Mix in the manner of RG-1.

Application. Apply in the manner of RG-1.

Fired Results. In oxidation and reduction this glaze is a clear gloss.

Colemanite	76.0
Nepheline syenite	24.0
C.M.C.	1 tsp
Add:	
Bentonite	2.0

RG-31

Translucent Raku Glaze   Cone 06–04
alkaline, translucent, cloudy, nontoxic

Mixing. Mix in the manner of RG-1.

Application. Apply in the manner of RG-1.

Fired Results. In oxidation and reduction this glaze is a cloudy color.

Colemanite	76.0
Plastic vitrox	14.0
Kentucky ball clay #4	10.0
C.M.C.	1 tsp
Add:	
Bentonite	2.0

RG-32

Clear Gloss Raku Glaze   Cone 06
alkaline, transparent, clear gloss, nontoxic

Mixing. Mix in the manner of RG-1.

Application. Apply in the manner of RG-1.

Fired Results. This glaze is a clear gloss in both oxidation and reduction. This glaze is nonfluid.

Colemanite	70.0
Plastic vitrox	30.0
C.M.C.	1 tsp

RG-33

Transparent Raku Glaze   Cone 04
alkaline, transparent, clear gloss, nontoxic

Mixing. Mix in the manner of RG-1.

Application. Apply in the manner of RG-1.

Fired Results. This glaze is a clear gloss in both oxidation and reduction.

Colemanite	81%
Feldspar (potash)	19%
C.M.C.	1 tsp

10
EGYPTIAN
PASTE
CONE 016-04

Egyptian Paste originated in Egypt, as the name implies, about 5000 B.C. and ornaments made from this clay have been found in the most ancient burial tombs of the Egyptians. Among these are scarabs, amulets, beaded jewelry, and small figurines.

Egyptian Paste is actually a clay body with certain inherent ingredients which allow the clay to glaze itself during the firing process. These ingredients are all members of the sodium family. The clay mixture has unusual properties which permit the sodium to rise to the surface of the pottery and recrystallize during the drying process. During firing the sodium fuses with the silica and colorants to create a glaze on the surface and vitrification within the clay body itself.

The present-day version of Egyptian Paste is usually made from feldspar, silica, ball clay, some form of sodium, and a colorant. In color Egyptian Paste can be turquoise, blue, green, yellow, pink, purple, tan, brown, and black.

Generally plasticity is a problem due to the nonplastic materials used in the makeup of the body. Therefore objects made with Egyptian Paste are usually limited in size and include beads and small wheelthrown forms.

The utmost care must be taken in the handling of the dried ware as the sodium compounds recrystallize on the surface and must not be disturbed or brushed off if a satisfactory glaze is to result.

The formulas listed in this chapter should provide the potter with a variety of bodies to use for wheel work, handbuilding, or press molding.

Note. The ingredients in the formulas in this section can be weighed out in either grams or pounds. It is recommended that the potter first make a 100-gram test batch of the body that interests him to insure that it is suitable before making larger amounts. The bodies are listed here by firing temperature from lower to higher cones. In the formulas below, glaze surface refers to the surface hardness of the fired body. The listings are on a 1–12 basis: 1–4, soft; 5–8, medium; 9–12, hard.

FORMULAS FOR EGYPTIAN PASTE BODIES

EP-1

White Egyptian Paste Body   Cone 016
shrinkage 2.5%, plasticity 9.5, glaze surface 7

Mixing. Weigh out the ingredients by grams for small test batches and pounds for larger batches. Mix the Egyptian Paste using any of the three methods outlined in Chapter 3 on Clay Body Preparation. The Egyptian Paste body should be aged at least one week—two is better.

Forming Methods. This body is sufficiently plastic to allow the throwing of smaller objects. It is good for all handbuilt forms or for press molding.

Drying. Place the wet piece in a location free of drafts to allow even and thorough drying. As drying takes place the sodium compounds within the body will rise to the surface and recrystallize in the form of a white fuzzy substance. Take great care not to disturb these crystals or to brush any of them from the surface, for it is these crystals that unite with the silica in the body to form the glaze.

Nepheline syenite	24.0
Ferro frit #3134	16.0
Silica	20.0
Sand or grog (50 mesh)	5.0
Tennessee ball clay #1	26.0
Borax	2.0
Soda ash	4.0
Bentonite	3.0

Fired Results. Fire this body to cone 016. Make sure that the piece is well stilted to prevent excess running or sticking to the kiln shelf. When fired to the proper cone this body is a glossy off-white. Overfired it is a stony matt and if copper is used as a colorant it tends to become a mottled white and metallic color.

Suggested Colorants.

1. Use 1% cobalt carbonate for a beautiful deep blue reminiscent of Persian blues.

2. Use 3% copper carbonate for turquoise.

3. Use 1% green chrome oxide for Egyptian green.

4. Use 5% lead chromate for yellows (caution: lead chromate is toxic).

See the chart at the end of the chapter for further information on colorants.

EP-2

Gloss White Egyptian Paste Body   Cone 010
shrinkage 2.3%, plasticity 8.6%, glaze surface 7.9

Mixing. Mix in the manner of EP-1.

Forming Methods. The same methods listed in EP-1 can be employed for this body.

Drying. Dry in the manner of EP-1.

Fired Results. Fired to cone 010 this body is a glossy white.

Suggested Colorants. This body will take any of the colorants listed at the end of the chapter, but works best with copper or cobalt.

Nepheline syenite	20.0
Ferro frit #3134	20.0
Silica	20.0
Silica sand (60–80 mesh)	5.0
Tennessee ball clay #1	25.0
Borax	3.0
Sodium carbonate	4.0
Bentonite	3.0

EP-3

Gloss White Egyptian Paste Body   Cone 08
shrinkage 2.9%, plasticity 6.1, glaze surface 9.9

Mixing. Mix in the manner of EP-1.

Forming Methods. This body is not sufficiently plastic to allow successful throwing and should be used primarily for handformed pieces. It is particularly good for beadmaking.

Drying. Dry in the manner of EP-1.

Fired Results. This body fires to a glossy white at cone 08. It will take on a matt surface if desired at higher temperatures.

Suggested Colorants. Use the same colorants listed for EP-1 for best results.

Feldspar (soda)	40.0
Silica	20.0
Kaolin (EPK)	15.0
Kentucky ball clay #4	5.0
Sodium carbonate	6.0
Sodium bicarbonate	6.0
Whiting	5.0
Flint grog	8.0

EP-4

Gloss White Egyptian Paste Body   Cone 08
shrinkage 3.1%, plasticity 7.2, glaze surface 5

Mixing. Mix in the manner of EP-1.

Forming Methods. This body is best used for small objects or press molding.

Drying. Dry in the manner of EP-1.

Fired Results. Fired to cone 08 this body is a gloss white which takes colorants well.

Feldspar (soda)	38.0
Silica	18.0
Kaolin (EPK)	15.0
Fine white grog	6.0
Sodium bicarbonate	10.0
Soda ash	8.0
Kentucky ball clay	5.0

EP-5

White Egyptian Paste Body   Cone 08
shrinkage 2%, plasticity 8.5, glaze surface 7.4

Mixing. Mix in the manner of EP-1.

Forming Methods. The same methods listed in EP-1 can be employed for this body as well.

Drying. Dry in the manner of EP-1.

Fired Results. This body fires to a semi-gloss white at cone 08. It takes colorants well—particularly copper or cobalt, alone or in combinations.

Feldspar (soda)	42.0
Silica	38.0
Kaolin	10.0
Fine grog or white sand	5.0
Soda ash	3.0
Bentonite	2.0

EP-6

Dry Matt White Egyptian Paste Body   Cone 08
shrinkage 3%, plasticity 8.5, glaze surface 10.8

Mixing. Mix in the manner of EP-1.

Forming Methods. The same methods listed in EP-1 can be employed for this body.

Drying. Dry in the manner of EP-1.

Fired Results. This body fires to a dry matt white at cone 08. It takes all of the colorants listed at the end of the chapter quite well.

Silica	66.0
Hommel frit #14	20.0
Bentonite	8.0
Sodium bicarbonate	6.0

EP-7

Gloss White Egyptian Paste Body Cone 07
shrinkage 2.1%, plasticity 7.2, glaze surface 9.1

Mixing. Mix in the manner of EP-1.

Forming Methods. Form in the manner of EP-3.

Drying. Dry in the manner of EP-1.

Fired Results. This body fires to a gloss white at cone 07. At cone 06 it is a semi-matt.

Suggested Colorants. Any of the colorants at the end of the chapter will work well for this body.

Feldspar (soda)	33.7
Kaolin	22.7
Silica	16.3
Fine white sand	8.3
Soda ash	5.3
Sodium bicarbonate	5.2
Kentucky ball clay #4	4.3
Whiting	4.3

EP-8

Gloss Off-White Egyptian Paste Body   Cone 07
shrinkage 3.1%, plasticity 8.2, glaze surface 9.6

Mixing. Mix in the manner of EP-1.

Forming Methods. Form in the manner of EP-3.

Drying. Dry in the manner of EP-1.

Fired Results. This body fires to a gloss off-white at cone 07. It is a semi-matt at cone 06.

Suggested Colorants. This body works best with copper oxide, copper carbonate, or cobalt oxide. An addition of 0.5% of red iron oxide will enhance the colors in this body.

Silica	36.0
Feldspar (soda)	34.0
Kaolin	11.3
Bentonite	8.2
Soda ash	5.2
Sodium bicarbonate	5.2

EP-9 **Gloss White Egyptian Paste Body   Cone 07**
shrinkage 2.3%, plasticity 6.1, glaze surface 10.0

Mixing. Mix in the manner of EP-1.

Forming Methods. Form in the manner of EP-3.

Drying. Dry in the manner of EP-1.

Fired Results. This body fires to a gloss white at cone 07. It should not be overfired.

Suggested Colorants. Any of the colorants listed at the end of the chapter will work well with this body.

Feldspar (soda)	36.0
Silica	36.0
Kaolin	12.0
Sodium bicarbonate	5.0
Copper carbonate	3.0
Dextrine	8.0

EP-10 **Semi-Gloss White Egyptian Paste Body   Cone 07**
shrinkage 2.0%, plasticity 8.5, glaze surface 3.7

Mixing. Mix in the manner of EP-1.

Forming Methods. The methods listed for EP-1 can be employed for this body.

Drying. Dry in the manner of EP-1.

Fired Results. This body fires to a semi-gloss white at cone 07. It can be fired to cone 06 if a semi-matt glaze is desirable.

Suggested Colorants. The colorants listed for the blues and greens at the end of the chapter are best for this body. The earth colors tend to be somewhat muddy in hue.

Feldspar (soda)	36.0
Silica	32.0
Kaolin (Florida)	11.0
C.M.C.	3.0
Sodium bicarbonate	5.0
Sodium carbonate	5.0
Add:	
Bentonite	5.0

EP-11 **Gloss White Egyptian Paste Body   Cone 06**
shrinkage 3.1%, plasticity 9.5, glaze surface 10.1

Mixing. Mix in the manner of EP-1.

Forming Methods. Form in the manner of EP-1.

Drying. Dry in the manner of EP-1.

Fired Results. This body fires to a beautiful gloss white at cone 06.

Suggested Colorants. The best colorants for this body are copper oxide and cobalt carbonate. If cobalt oxide is to be added, use only half the amount.

Kaolin (EPK)	50.0
Silica	25.0
Feldspar (soda)	12.0
Kentucky ball clay #4	15.0
Tennessee ball clay #1	5.0
Add:	
Soda ash	5.0
Sodium bicarbonate	5.0
Borax	5.0

EP-12 **Gloss White Egyptian Paste Body   Cone 06**
shrinkage 2.8%, plasticity 8.9, glaze surface 9.6

Mixing. Mix in the manner of EP-1.

Forming Methods. This body is sufficiently plastic to allow the throwing of small objects, but it is best used for handbuilt pieces or press molding.

Drying. Dry in the manner of EP-1.

Fired Results. This body fires to a gloss white at cone 06.

Suggested Colorants. This body works well with any of the colorants listed at the end of the chapter. The coppers used for turquoise are especially nice.

Feldspar (soda)	30.7
Kaolin	20.7
Silica	15.7
Silica sand (80–100 mesh)	5.3
Kentucky ball clay #4	10.0
Whiting	3.3
Soda ash	4.3
Sodium bicarbonate	4.3

EP-13

Semi-Gloss White Egyptian Paste Body   Cone 06

shrinkage 2.7%, plasticity 8.4, glaze surface 9.9

Mixing. Mix in the manner of EP-1.

Forming Methods. Form in the manner of EP-3.

Drying. Dry in the manner of EP-1.

Fired Results. This body fires to a semi-gloss white at cone 06. It should not be overfired.

Suggested Colorants. Any of the colorants at the end of the chapter will work well with this body.

Feldspar (soda)	35.0
Silica	35.0
Kaolin	10.0
C.M.C.	3.0
Talc	5.0
Kentucky ball clay #4	5.0
Bentonite	5.0
Soda bicarbonate	5.0
Sodium carbonate	5.0

EP-14

Gloss White Egyptian Paste Body   Cone 04

shrinkage 1.9%, plasticity 6.3, glaze surface 8.9

Mixing. Mix in the manner of EP-1.

Forming Methods. Form in the manner of EP-3.

Drying. Dry in the manner of EP-1.

Fired Results. This body fires to a gloss white at cone 04. It should not be overfired if consistent results are expected.

Suggested Colorants. This body works well with any of the colorants listed at the end of the chapter. Some unusual and unpredictable results can be obtained with the use of copper oxide when the pieces are overfired one or two cones. In such cases the copper tends to metalize and form mottled patterns.

Kentucky ball clay #4	50.0
Kaolin (EPK)	20.0
Talc	20.0
Nepheline syenite	5.0
Cornwall stone	2.5
Tennessee ball clay #1	2.5
Add:	
Soda ash	7.5
Sodium carbonate	7.5

CHART OF COLORANTS FOR EGYPTIAN PASTE

Fired Result	Colorant	Percentage
Browns	Burnt umber	2%–3%
Light blue	Cobalt oxide	0.5%
Medium blue	Cobalt oxide	1%
Dark blue	Cobalt oxide	1.5%–2%
Green	Chrome oxide	1.5%–5%
Olive	Iron oxide	8%
Purple	Manganese dioxide	2%
Pink	Iron oxide	1%
Tan	Burnt umber	2%–3%
Tan (earthy)	Yellow ochre	4%
Tan (warm)	Rutile	3%
Turquoise	Copper oxide	2.5%–4%

Note. The percentages should always be calculated by the dry body weight of the formula.

11
OVENWARE AND RANGETOP BODIES AND GLAZES
CONE 04-9

The findings of many archeologists show that down through the ages man has used clay pots for cooking. And modern potters have continued to search for better ways to produce heat-resistant pottery cooking vessels.

The clay bodies presented in this chapter can be made into ware to be used in the oven—vessels such as casseroles, beanpots, and other baking dishes. Ware made from these bodies has the advantages of durability and heat retention—thus maintaining the warmth of the food after cooking is finished. These vessels may also be used as serving pieces.

For many years the average earthenware body was considered adequate for cooking purposes, especially if it was not fired to vitrification. Earthenware cooking pots are still made and used in primitive areas today. Such vessels, however, are not watertight and consequently present sanitation problems due to the penetration of liquids. Glazes applied to such underfired ware tend to craze, creating further problems of hygiene.

Ovenware must be designed not to crack from thermal expansion and contraction. Therefore the following factors should be taken into account while formulating and using these bodies:

1. The body should contain as little free silica as possible as it has a high reversible expansion rate when heated and cooled, thus putting great strain on the clay body.

2. Feldspar should be used as a flux to take up the free silica and incorporate it chemically into the body proper to reduce its tendency to expand and contract with oven use.

3. The ware should be high fired to help incorporate as much of the free silica as possible.

4. The ware should be designed with these expansion qualities in mind: shapes should be compact, evenly made, and spherical. Pieces with angles should be avoided due to their increased tendency to crack under stress.

5. The clay body should have some iron content, especially if the pieces are to be reduction fired.

6. Glazes should be designed to fit the ware but should not be under extreme compression or stress. The ware should be evenly glazed both inside and outside with the same glaze, and the glaze should be applied only as thickly as necessary to seal the surface of the ware.

The above requirements must be taken into consideration to achieve a satisfactory body for ovenware.

FORMING

Utilitarian pots that are made from heat-resistant clay should be well thrown. Base and wall thicknesses should be as uniform as possible to insure even heat conduction through the piece. Use well-wedged clay; make well-centered forms with base and walls of uniform thickness. Trimming must be done with care to insure uniform thickness and slow, even drying is an absolute necessity. Pieces should be carefully stacked in the kiln, slowly fired (especially during the first 800°F./427°C.) and slowly and evenly cooled after firing. In fact the ware should be absolutely cool to the touch when removed from the kiln.

The first two bodies and glazes listed here have proved consistently successful for the author. They are also designed for single firings, although they may be bisque and then glaze fired if the potter so desires.

Note. The ingredients in the formulas in this chapter can be weighed out in either grams or pounds. It is recommended that the potter first make a 100-gram test batch of the clay body that interests him to insure that it is suitable before making larger amounts. Any of the porcelain bodies can be colored by the use of coloring oxides. See Chapter 12 for further information. The clay bodies are listed here by firing temperature from lower to higher cones.

OWB-1

Cream Ovenware Body   Cone 06
shrinkage 10.3%, plasticity 9.6, glaze rating 11.2

Kentucky ball clay #4	37.0
Kaolin	16.0
Talc	15.0
Bentonite	3.0

Mixing. Weigh out the dry ingredients by grams or pounds and mix them dry. At this point any of the three methods outlined in Chapter 3 on Clay Body Preparation may be used to prepare the clay. The body can be aged if desired, but in any case it should be very thoroughly wedged before throwing.

Forming Methods. The best forming method for ovenware pottery is on the wheel, for the ware must be of even thickness throughout, well centered, and evenly trimmed.

Drying. Place the ware in a place where it can dry slowly and evenly. The drying process from start to finish should take at least a week.

Bisque Firing. This is not necessary for this body if used with glaze OWG-1. It can be done, however, if the potter desires.

Firing. The ware should be well stacked in the kiln where uneven temperatures are not a problem. Firing should proceed slowly for the first 800°F./427°C. (about 200°F./93°C. per hour), then normally to cone 06. Cooling should be done slowly all the way down to 100°F./38°C. It should take twice as long to cool as to fire, otherwise cracking or dunting may be a problem (see Glossary).

Fired Results. This body fires to a light cream at cone 06 oxidation and a darker cream in reduction.

Suggested Body Colorants

Blues	Cobalt oxide	1%-5%
Greens	Chrome oxide	3%-6%
Browns	Iron oxide	5%-8%
Tans	Iron oxide	1%-3%

OWG-1

Cream Ovenware Glaze   Cone 06
leadless, transparent, clear matt, nontoxic

Hommel frit #14	36.0
Pemco frit #25	33.0
Wollastonite #25	11.0
Kentucky ball clay #4	15.0
Tennessee ball clay	5.0
C.M.C.	1 tsp

Mixing. Weigh out the ingredients as indicated in the formula and place them in a jar. (A pint or quart/half-liter or liter fruit jar can be used for this purpose.) Premix the contents by rotating the jar several times, then add water in the following ratio:

For a brushing glaze 1 to 2 oz./30 to 60 ml per 100 grams of glaze

For a dipping glaze 2 to 3 oz./60 to 90 ml per 100 grams of glaze

For a spraying glaze 4 to 6 oz./120 to 180 ml per 100 grams of glaze

These measurements are not absolute, so it would be wise for the potter to train himself by sight, feel, and the consistency of the glaze whether it is right for use. For example, a brushing glaze should be about the consistency of ketchup, a dipping glaze about that of cream, and a spraying glaze about that of milk.

Once the water is added and the jar given a brief shaking to mix the ingredients, add a teaspoon of C.M.C. per 100 grams of glaze by dry measure and shake the jar vigorously until the contents are thoroughly mixed. Sieve twice through a 60- 80-mesh screen, using a stiff brush to break up any resistant lumps. Once these steps have been followed, the glaze is ready for use. This glaze will keep well in solution for many weeks.

Application. Brush, dip, or spray the number of coats necessary to seal the surface of the pot. Ovenware pottery should not be overglazed. Allow the different coats to dry to the point that the surface loses its moist sheen before applying another coat of glaze. Allow the glazed ware to dry completely before firing. The ware should also be protected from dust or air-borne clay particles in the studio.

Firing. See OWB-1.

Fired Results. This glaze fires to a clear matt at cone 06.

Suggested Colorants. Any of the glaze colorants listed in Chapter 33, Glaze Colorants, for leadless glazes will work well in this glaze.

OWB-2 **Cream Ovenware Body   Cone 04**
shrinkage 10.7%, plasticity 9.7, glaze rating 11.3

Mixing. Mix in the manner of OWB-1.

Forming Methods. Form in the manner of OWB-1.

Drying. Dry in the manner of OWB-1.

Bisque Firing. Fire in the manner of OWB-1.

Fired Results. This body fires to a light cream in oxidation; reduction gives a darker cream.

Suggested Colorants. See OWB-1.

Kentucky ball clay #4	39.0
Kaolin	17.0
Grog (80–100 mesh)	15.0
Talc	24.0
Feldspar (potash)	2.0
Bentonite	3.0

OWG-2 **Clear Ovenware Matt Glaze   Cone 04**
leadless, transparent, clear matt, nontoxic

Mixing. Mix in the manner of OWG-1.

Application. Apply in the manner of OWG-1.

Firing. Fire in the manner of OWG-1.

Fired Results. This glaze fires to a clear satin matt.

Suggested Colorants. See OWG-1.

Kentucky ball clay #4	24.6
Tennessee ball clay #1	20.0
Kaolin	18.5
Talc	26.0
Pemco frit #54	10.9
C.M.C.	1 tsp

FPB-1 **Cream Flameproof Body** **Cone 9**
shrinkage 12%, plasticity 9.1, glaze rating 11.5

Kentucky ball clay #4	25.0
Kaolin	34.0
Talc	35.0
Grog (80–100 mesh)	2.0
Bentonite	4.0

Mixing. Mix in the manner of OWB-1.

Forming Methods. Form in the manner of OWB-1.

Drying. Dry in the manner of OWB-1.

Bisque Firing. Fire in the manner of OWB-1.

Firing. Fire in the manner of OWB-1.

Fired Results. This body fires to a light cream at cone 9 oxidation and a darker cream at cone 9 reduction.

Suggested Colorants. See OWB-1.

FPG-1 **Cream Matt Flameproof Glaze** **Cone 9**
leadless, transparent, clear matt, nontoxic

Kentucky ball clay #4	22.7
Kaolin	29.5
Talc	30.4
Lithium carbonate	9.2
Pemco frit #54	8.2

Mixing. Mix in the manner of OWG-1.

Application. Apply in the manner of OWG-1.

Firing. Fire in the manner of OWG-1.

Fired Results. This glaze fires to a clear matt at cone 9.

Suggested Colorants. See OWG-1.

12
COLORING
CLAY BODIES

The color range of fired clay is vast even in the natural state—from pure white and gray through tans, buff, earth reds or orange-red, and browns to carbon black. And though the range is mainly of warm earth tones it is sufficiently vast to give the potter a wide selection of color possibilities for many kinds of pottery.

There are times, however, when the potter may wish to alter the color of any given clay body to a different tone or hue. This can be done quite simply by the addition of various coloring oxides.

The chemicals listed in this chapter have certain coloring powers when added to a clay body. When using them the potter should keep in mind that they were tested on a white body. And this should be taken into account when adding oxides to a body which is already colored.

The usual procedure for coloring clay bodies is to add the dry colorants to the dry body formula and mix them thoroughly in the dry state before mixing with water.

CHART OF CLAY BODY COLORANTS AND PERCENTAGES

Fired Body Color	Colorant	Percentages
Black	Black iron oxide	8.0%
	Manganese dioxide	3.0%
	Cobalt oxide	1.0%
Blue (light)	Cobalt oxide	2.5%
Blue (medium)	Cobalt oxide	5.0%
Blue (dark)	Cobalt oxide	7.5%
Brown (light with specks)	Manganese dioxide	3.2%
Brown (medium)	Red iron oxide	8.2%
Brown (medium with specks)	Manganese dioxide	6.2%
Brown (dark hue with specks)	Manganese dioxide	8.5%
Buff (with specks)	Ilmenite	6.0%
	Ilmenite granular	2.0%
Buff (yellowish)	Yellow ochre	2.0%
Cream	Antimony	5.0%
Gray-blue	Black base stain	
Gray (light hue with specks)	Manganese dioxide	2.5%
	Iron chromate	2.1%
Gray (brown hue)	Copper oxide	3.1%
	Cobalt oxide	0.9%
Gray (brown hue)	Copper oxide	2.2%
	Red iron oxide	2.1%
Gray (cool brown hue)	Iron chromate	6.1%
Gray (brown hue with specks)	Iron chromate	3.1%
	Ilmenite	2.1%
Gray (charcoal)	Copper oxide	5.0%
Gray (cool)	Uranium oxide	5.0%
Green (light)	Chrome oxide	2.5%
Green (medium)	Chrome oxide	5.0%
Green (dark)	Chrome oxide	7.5%
Green (gray hue)	Green chrome oxide	3.1%
Green (medium spring hue)	Potassium carbonate	5.0%
Green (spring hue)	Potassium carbonate	3.2%
Olive (pale)	Black copper oxide	2.5%
Olive (medium gray hue)	Green chromium oxide	5.1%
Olive green (dark)	Potassium carbonate	7.5%
Pink (cool)	Black iron oxide	2.0%
Pink (earth)	Red iron oxide	2.0%
Rust-tan	Yellow ochre	5.5%
Rust (tan hue)	Black iron oxide	5.0%
Tan (medium hue)	Nickel oxide	2.1%
Tan (warm)	Rutile	3.0%
Tan (medium warm)	Rutile	6.0%
Tan (dark-warm)	Rutile	8.5%–9.0%
Tan (dark hue)	Nickel oxide	5.2%
Tan-rust (light)	Red iron oxide	2.5%
Tan-rust (medium)	Red iron oxide	5.0%
White (off-white)	Antimony oxide	2.0%
White (eggshell)	Cadmium sulfide	4.2%

Note. The percentages should always be calculated by the dry body weight of the formula.

13
CLAY BODY DEFECTS AND ADJUSTMENTS

Though the clay body formulas in this book were designed, tested, and adjusted to work as well as possible, the potter may now and then encounter a clay body which has defects of one type or another. It is therefore important that the potter learn to recognize these defects and be able to take the proper methods for correcting them. The most common defects and methods for correcting them are listed in this chapter in alphabetical order.

Bloating is usually caused by overfiring the ware. It can be recognized as blistering and slumping of the ware. The major way to correct this fault is to fire the ware at a lower temperature or add more refractory materials to the clay body such as fire clay, ball clay, silica, kaolin, or feldspar.

Color defects may appear in the form of a scum-like substance on the surface of the fired bisque ware. This is usually caused by alkalies or other soluble substances in the clay. It is more common in native clays, therefore Chapter 2 should be consulted for more information on the remedy for this defect.

Cracking occurs in two instances in the pottery process: one during the drying stage and the other during the firing stages. Of the first category the following are the most common:

1. Overwetting the pot in one area, an example of which is leaving water in the bottom of the pot after throwing.

2. Overstretching the clay during the forming process—do not try to make the clay form larger or wider than it is capable of and do not try to pull the pieces too thin.

3. Uneven drying—place the clay in an area where it will dry evenly, especially avoid drafts.

4. Forced drying can cause the clay to dry unevenly—allow the clay to dry evenly without forcing it.

5. Wetting of the piece which is past the leather-hard stage by the application of slip or engobes or by adding handles—use slips and engobes at the leatherhard stage.

6. Uneven thickness in walls or especially the base—keeps walls and base as uniform in thickness as possible.

7. Joining wetter clay to a dryer clay—join only pieces of clay which are uniform in wetness.

8. Very high shrinkage rates of clays during drying can cause cracking because the clay cannot dry evenly—add some less plastic material to the clay body such as kaolin, silica, feldspar, whiting, or fire clay.

9. Overwedging the clay may cause the clay to become short—wedge the clay well, but only enough to remove air bubbles and to make the clay workable.

10. Working clay which has dried beyond the plastic stage can cause cracks during drying—use wetter clay.

Cracks of the second category are listed as follows:

1. Thicker glazes on one side of the ware may put undue strain on the ware—keep glazes on the inside and outside of the ware uniform in thickness.

2. A too rapid rise of the temperature in the bisque or glaze firing during the first 1000° F./ 538° C. can cause tension cracks—slow down the firing rate.

3. Pieces of lime or pebbles in the clay which do not shrink with the pot during firing may cause cracking or dunting of the ware—use some sort of screening process to remove foreign material such as this from the dry clay body before mixing with water.

4. Cooling the body too rapidly after firing can cause cracking or dunting—the ware should be cooled twice as slowly as it is fired.

5. An excess of silica in the body can cause cracking if heating or cooling of the ware is too rapid—use less free silica in the body.

6. Weight from stacking greenware pieces too high on top of one another without shelves in the bisque firing can cause bottom pieces to sag or crack—do not overstack the pieces during bisque firings.

7. Firing ware that is not completely dry—be sure that the pieces are completely dry before attempting to fire them and give the greenware a slow prefiring before allowing the kiln to rise above 200° F./93° C.

Deformation is like bloating in that it usually is caused by firing a body above its vitrification point—fire the ware lower or add more refractory material to the body such as kaolin, fire clay, or silica.

Dunting is a type of cracking that is most often caused by cooling ware to quickly, putting uneven stress on the piece. Cool the kiln more slowly after firing, keeping it tightly sealed to prevent crafts from entering the firing chamber.

Glaze fit if bad can cause shivering of the glaze and/or cracking of the pot due to the stress between the contraction of glaze and clay body—use a different glaze.

Plasticity is the ease of workability of a clay body. Bodies which are not plastic enough to be easily workable may be corrected by aging and/or adding more plastic clays to the body, as discussed in Chapter 2. Bodies which are too plastic and do not dry evenly or shrink too much during the drying and firing may be made less plastic by the addition of less-plastic materials such as kaolin, feldspar, silica, or whiting.

Porosity may be excessive in fired bodies due to underfiring or the addition of too much grog to the body—fire the body to a higher temperature and/or use less grog.

Shrinkage can be excessive when the body contains too much fine-grained materials such as ball clay—add some less-plastic material to the body such as fire clay, silica, kaolin, or grog.

Vitrification involves two stages: one is when a clay body becomes vitrified at a temperature lower than desired—add some more refractory materials such as kaolin, silica, fire clay, or fine grog. And the second is when a body vitrifies at a temperature higher than desired—clay bodies may be made to mature and vitrify at a lower temperature by adding less-refractory materials such as talc (above cone 6), nepheline syenite, or other fluxing agents.

14
ENGOBES
CONE 04-11

An engobe is basically a liquid clay or slip which is painted over another clay. This thin layer of slip which provides a base for decoration, gives texture, or improves the surface of the piece is a mixture of metallic oxides, fluxing agents, and clays similar to the body to which it is applied.

Needless to say the engobe must match the shrinkage rate of the pot to which it is applied or flaking or cracking will take place. For that reason the following engobe formulas are divided into four categories. These are engobes for use on: wet clays, leatherhard clays, greenware, and bisque. In this chapter they are presented in these groupings by temperature.

All the formulas given can be colored to suit the needs of the potter with any of the colorants given at the end of the chapter.

Note. The ingredients in the formulas in this section can be weighed out in either grams or pounds. It is recommended that the potter first make a 100-gram test batch of the engobe that interests him to insure that it is suitable before making larger amounts. The engobes are listed here by firing temperature from lower to higher cones.

FORMULAS FOR ENGOBES

E-1　　　**White Engobe, wet clay　Cone 04-9**

Mixing. Weigh out the ingredients, premix them dry, then add enough water and the C.M.C. to mix the engobe to a creamy consistency, about the consistency of ketchup. Mix the engobe either by hand or by a rotary beater until thoroughly blended. Allow the mixture to stand for at least an hour to insure that all the particles of clay have been thoroughly moisturized.

Application. Apply the engobe evenly with a large, soft brush, two to three coats is usually sufficient. Each coating should dry to the point that it has lost its surface sheen before adding another coat.

Drying. Allow the piece to dry in a place which is free of drafts until it is completely dry before firing.

Bisque Firing. If the piece is to be glazed later, fire to cone 06-04. If it is to be left unglazed, fire it to maturity in the first firing.

Fired Results. This engobe fires to a pure white at cone 04-9 oxidation or reduction, or darker depending on the clay used.

Clay (same as body)	28.0
Silica	20.0
Nepheline syenite	14.5
Kaolin	10.5
Tennessee ball clay #1	10.0
Talc	5.0
Zircopax	7.0
Sodium carbonate	2.5
Borax	2.5

E-2   White Engobe, wet clay   Cone 04–9

Mixing. Mix in the manner of E-1.

Application. Apply in the manner of E-1.

Drying. Dry in the manner of E-1.

Bisque Firing. Fire in the manner of E-1.

Fired Results. See E-1 for fired results.

Clay (same as body— grogless)	44.0
Silica	28.0
Feldspar (Custer)	16.5
Magnesium carbonate	6.5
Whiting	2.0
Borax	3.0
Add:	
C.M.C.	1 tsp

E-3   White Engobe, wet clay   Cone 04–11

Mixing. Mix in the manner of E-1.

Application. Apply in the manner of E-1.

Drying. Dry in the manner of E-1.

Bisque Firing. Fire in the manner of E-1.

Fired Results. This engobe fires to a pure white at cone 04–11 or darker depending on the clay used.

Clay (same as body)	51.0
Feldspar (Custer)	19.0
Silica	20.0
Zircopax	5.0
Borax	2.5
Sodium carbonate	2.5
Add:	
C.M.C.	1 tsp

E-4   White Engobe, wet clay   Cone 05–9

Mixing. Mix in the manner of E-1.

Application. Apply in the manner of E-1.

Drying. Dry in the manner of E-1.

Bisque Firing. Fire in the manner of E-1.

Fired Results. This engobe fires to a pure white at cone 05–9 or darker depending on the clay used.

Clay (same as body)	52.0
Tennessee ball clay #1	23.0
Kaolin (EPK)	19.0
Silica	6.0
Add:	
Bentonite	1.0
C.M.C.	1 tsp

E-5   White Engobe, leatherhard clay   Cone 08–1

Mixing. Mix in the manner of E-1.

Application. Apply in the manner of E-1.

Drying. Dry in the manner of E-1.

Bisque Firing. Fire in the manner of E-1.

Fired Results. This engobe fires to a pure white at cone 08–1 oxidation or reduction.

Kaolin	24.0
Tennessee ball clay #1	26.0
Ferro frit #3134	14.0
Talc	6.0
Silica	20.0
Zircopax	5.0
Borax	5.0
Add:	
C.M.C.	1 tsp

E-6   White Engobe, leatherhard clay   Cone 04–6

Mixing. Mix in the manner of E-1.

Application. Apply in the manner of E-1.

Drying. Dry in the manner of E-1.

Bisque Firing. Fire in the manner of E-1.

Fired Results. This engobe fires to a pure white at cone 04–6 oxidation or reduction.

Ferro frit #3134	44.5
Kaolin	11.5
Silica	11.5
Tennessee ball clay #1	10.0
Tin oxide	10.0
Feldspar (Custer)	8.5
Whiting	2.5
Borax	1.5
Add:	
C.M.C.	1 tsp

E-7 **White Engobe, leatherhard clay   Cone 04–6**

Mixing. Mix in the manner of E-1.

Application. Apply in the manner of E-1.

Drying. Dry in the manner of E-1.

Bisque Firing. Fire in the manner of E-1.

Fired Results. This engobe fires to a pure white at cone 04–6 oxidation or reduction.

Silica	30.5
Nepheline syenite	24.5
Tennessee ball clay #1	20.0
Kaolin (EPK)	10.0
Tin oxide	2.0
Borax	3.0
Add:	
C.M.C.	1 tsp

E-8 **White Engobe, leatherhard clay   Cone 04–9**

Mixing. Mix in the manner of E-1.

Application. Apply in the manner of E-1.

Drying. Dry in the manner of E-1.

Bisque Firing. Fire in the manner of E-1.

Fired Results. This engobe fires to a pure white at cone 04–9 oxidation or reduction.

Fire clay (80–100 mesh)	49.0
Silica	19.0
Feldspar (Custer)	10.0
Kaolin (EPK—calcined)	10.0
Zircopax	10.0
Borax	2.0
Add:	
C.M.C.	1 tsp

E-9 **White Engobe, leatherhard clay   Cone 1–6**

Mixing. Mix in the manner of E-1.

Application. Apply in the manner of E-1.

Drying. Dry in the manner of E-1.

Bisque Firing. Fire in the manner of E-1.

Fired Results. This engobe fires to a pure white at cone 1–6 oxidation or reduction.

Kaolin	26.0
Tennessee ball clay #1	24.0
Nepheline syenite	15.5
Talc	4.5
Silica	20.0
Zircopax	2.5
Tin oxide	2.5
Borax	5.0
Add:	
C.M.C.	1 tsp

E-10 **White Engobe, leatherhard clay   Cone 6–11**

Mixing. Mix in the manner of E-1.

Application. Apply in the manner of E-1.

Drying. Dry in the manner of E-1.

Bisque Firing. Fire in the manner of E-1.

Fired Results. This engobe fires to a pure white at cone 6–11 oxidation or reduction.

Kaolin	24.0
Tennessee ball clay #1	26.0
Feldspar (Custer)	19.0
Silica	21.0
Zircopax	2.5
Tin oxide	2.5
Borax	5.0
Add:	
C.M.C.	1 tsp

E-10 **White Engobe, leatherhard clay   Cone 6–11**

Mixing. Mix in the manner of E-1.

Application. Apply in the manner of E-1.

Drying. Dry in the manner of E-1.

Bisque Firing. Fire in the manner of E-1.

Fired Results. This engobe fires to a pure white at cone 6–11 oxidation or reduction.

Kaolin	24.0
Tennessee ball clay #1	26.0
Feldspar (Custer)	19.0
Silica	21.0
Zircopax	2.5
Tin oxide	2.5
Borax	5.0
Add:	
C.M.C.	1 tsp

E-12

White Engobe, greenware   Cone 08–1

Mixing. Mix in the manner of E-1.

Application. Apply in the manner of E-1.

Drying. Dry in the manner of E-1.

Bisque Firing. Fire in the manner of E-1.

Fired Results. This engobe fires to a pure white at cone 08–1 oxidation or reduction.

Kaolin	14.0
Tennessee ball clay #1	16.0
Kaolin (calcined)	21.0
Ferro frit #3134	14.0
Talc	5.0
Silica	18.0
Zircopax	3.0
Tin oxide	3.5
Borax	5.0
Add:	
C.M.C.	1 tsp

E-13

White Engobe, greenware   Cone 04–6

Mixing. Mix in the manner of E-1.

Application. Apply in the manner of E-1.

Drying. Dry in the manner of E-1.

Bisque Firing. Fire in the manner of E-1.

Fired Results. This engobe fires to a pure white at cone 04–6 oxidation or reduction.

Kaolin (EPK—calcined)	18.5
Silica	21.5
Tennessee ball clay #1	15.0
Nepheline syenite	7.5
Whiting	7.5
Kaolin (Georgia)	15.0
Talc	5.0
Tin oxide	2.5
Zircopax	2.5
Sodium carbonate	5.0
Add:	
C.M.C.	1 tsp

E-14

White Engobe, greenware   Cone 04–9

Mixing. Mix in the manner of E-1.

Application. Apply in the manner of E-1.

Drying. Dry in the manner of E-1.

Bisque Firing. Fire in the manner of E-1.

Fired Results. This engobe fires to a pure white at cone 04–9 oxidation or reduction or darker depending on the clay used.

Clay (same as body)	32.0
Kaolin (Florida—calcined)	18.0
Silica	20.0
Pemco frit #54	15.0
Talc	5.0
Tin oxide	2.5
Zircopax	2.5
Borax	5.0
Add:	
C.M.C.	1 tsp

E-15

White Engobe, greenware   Cone 04–10

Mixing. Mix in the manner of E-1.

Application. Apply in the manner of E-1.

Drying. Dry in the manner of E-1.

Bisque Firing. Fire in the manner of E-1.

Fired Results. This engobe fires to a pure white at cone 04–10 oxidation or reduction or darker depending on the clay used.

Clay (same as body)	28.0
Kaolin (EPK—calcined)	22.0
Feldspar (Custer)	20.0
Silica	20.0
Zircopax	5.0
Borax	2.5
Sodium carbonate	2.5
Add:	
C.M.C.	1 tsp

E-16   **White Engobe, greenware   Cone 1–6**

Mixing. Mix in the manner of E-1.

Application. Apply in the manner of E-1.

Drying. Dry in the manner of E-1.

Bisque Firing. Fire in the manner of E-1.

Fired Results. This engobe fires to a pure white at cone 1–6 oxidation or reduction.

Kaolin	16.0
Tennessee ball clay #1	14.0
Kaolin (calcined)	21.0
Nepheline syenite	14.0
Talc	5.0
Silica	21.0
Tin oxide	4.0
Zircopax	4.0
Borax	5.0
Add:	
C.M.C.	1 tsp

E-17   **White Engobe, greenware   Cone 6–11**

Mixing. Mix in the manner of E-1.

Application. Apply in the manner of E-1.

Drying. Dry in the manner of E-1.

Bisque Firing. Fire in the manner of E-1.

Fired Results. This engobe fires to a pure white at cone 6–11 oxidation or reduction.

Kaolin	16.0
Tennessee ball clay #1	14.0
Kaolin (calcined)	20.0
Feldspar (Custer)	22.0
Silica	18.0
Tin oxide	2.5
Zircopax	2.5
Borax	5.0
Add:	
C.M.C.	1 tsp

E-18   **White Engobe, bisque   Cone 08–1**

Mixing. Mix in the manner of E-1.

Application. Apply in the manner of E-1.

Drying. Dry in the manner of E-1.

Bisque Firing. Fire in the manner of E-1.

Fired Results. This engobe fires to a pure white at cone 08–1 oxidation or reduction.

Kaolin	5.5
Tennessee ball clay #1	14.5
Kaolin (EPK—calcined)	19.0
Ferro frit #3134	16.0
Talc	15.0
Silica	20.0
Tin oxide	5.0
Borax	5.0
Add:	
C.M.C.	1 tsp

E-19   **White Engobe, bisque   Cone 04–6**

Mixing. Mix in the manner of E-1.

Application. Apply in the manner of E-1.

Drying. Dry in the manner of E-1.

Bisque Firing. Fire in the manner of E-1.

Fired Results. This engobe fires to a pure white at cone 04–6 oxidation or reduction.

Tennessee ball clay #1	46.0
Silica	20.0
Kaolin	15.0
Nepheline syenite	10.0
Whiting	8.0
Borax	1.0
Add:	
Tin oxide	3.0
C.M.C.	1 tsp

E-20

White Engobe, bisque   Cone 04–9

Mixing. Mix in the manner of E-1.

Application. Apply in the manner of E-1.

Drying. Dry in the manner of E-1.

Bisque Firing. Fire in the manner of E-1.

Fired Results. This engobe fires to a pure white at cone 04–9 oxidation or reduction.

Kaolin (EPK)	55.6
Feldspar (Custer)	26.0
Kaolin (Georgia)	17.2
Borax	1.2
Add:	
C.M.C.	1 tsp

E-21

White Engobe, bisque   Cone 04–10

Mixing. Mix in the manner of E-1.

Application. Apply in the manner of E-1.

Drying. Dry in the manner of E-1.

Bisque Firing. Fire in the manner of E-1.

Fired Results. This engobe fires to a pure white at cone 04–10 oxidation or reduction or darker depending on the clay used.

Clay (same as body)	28.0
Feldspar (Custer)	18.0
Silica	22.0
Kaolin	12.0
Tennessee ball clay #1	10.0
Zircopax	2.5
Tin oxide	2.5
Sodium carbonate	2.5
Borax	2.5

E-22

White Engobe, bisque   Cone 04–10

Mixing. Mix in the manner of E-1.

Application. Apply in the manner of E-1.

Drying. Dry in the manner of E-1.

Bisque Firing. Fire in the manner of E-1.

Fired Results. This engobe fires to a pure white at cone 04–10 oxidation or reduction.

Feldspar (Custer)	34.0
Kaolin	34.0
Silica	22.0
Whiting	4.0
Tin oxide	4.0
Borax	2.0
Add:	
C.M.C.	1 tsp

E-23

White Engobe, bisque   Cone 6–11

Mixing. Mix in the manner of E-1.

Application. Apply in the manner of E-1.

Drying. Dry in the manner of E-1.

Bisque Firing. Fire in the manner of E-1.

Fired Results. This engobe fires to a pure white at cone 6–11 oxidation or reduction.

Kaolin	6.0
Tennessee ball clay #1	14.0
Kaolin (calcined)	20.5
Ferro frit #3134	4.5
Nepheline syenite	5.0
Feldspar (Custer)	19.0
Silica	21.0
Zircopax	2.5
Tin oxide	2.5
Borax	5.0
Add:	
C.M.C.	1 tsp

White Engobe, bisque   Cone 6–11

Mixing. Mix in the manner of E-1.

Application. Apply in the manner of E-1.

Drying. Dry in the manner of E-1.

Bisque Firing. Fire in the manner of E-1.

Fired Results. This engobe fires to a pure white at cone 6–11 oxidation or reduction.

Kaolin	6.0
Tennessee ball clay #1	14.0
Kaolin (calcined)	20.0
Ferro frit #3134	4.0
Nepheline syenite	21.0
Talc	5.0
Silica	19.5
Tin oxide	3.0
Zircopax	2.5
Borax	5.0
Add:	
C.M.C.	1 tsp

CHART OF ENGOBE COLORANTS AND PERCENTAGES

Fired Result	Oxide	Percentage
Black	Iron oxide	3.0%
	Cobalt oxide	2.0%
	Manganese dioxide	2.0%
	Nickel oxide	2.0%
Blue (light)	Cobalt oxide	0.5%
Blue (medium)	Cobalt oxide	1.0%
Blue (dark)	Cobalt oxide	1.5%
Blue (gray hue)	Cobalt oxide	1.0%
	Iron oxide	2.0%
	Copper oxide	1.5%
Brown (light)	Iron oxide	3.0%
Brown (medium)	Iron oxide	4.5%
Brown (dark)	Iron oxide	6.0%
Brown (speckled)	Manganese dioxide (granular)	3.0%
Brown (purple hue)	Manganese dioxide	6.0%
Cream	Antimony oxide	5.0%
Gray (light)	Iron chromate	1.0%
Gray (medium)	Iron chromate	2.0%
Gray (dark)	Iron chromate	3.0%
Green (light)	Copper oxide	1.5%
Green (medium)	Copper oxide	3.0%
Green (dark)	Copper oxide	4.5%
Tan (light)	Iron oxide	2.0%
Tan (medium)	Iron oxide	3.0%
Tan (dark)	Iron oxide	4.0%
Tan (creamy)	Rutile	6.0%
Tan (creamy and spotted)	Rutile	6.0%
	Rutile (granular)	6.0%
Yellow (light)	Vanadium stain	5.0%
Yellow (medium)	Vanadium stain	10.0%
Yellow (dark)	Vanadium stain	15.0%
Yellow (ochre)	Yellow ochre	4.5%

Note. The percentages should always be calculated by the dry body weight of the formula.

15
STAINS
CONE 09-10

The word "stain" as used in pottery is almost self-explanatory for it is a composition of coloring oxides and clays which can be used to stain and color other clays. It may be used under glazes or left unglazed to suit the whim of the potter. Stains of various types can be made in many colors and shades. The final color of most stains is determined by the colorant oxide in the stain, the stain compound itself, the way in which it is used in the compound, the firing technique, whether oxidation or reduction fired, and the type of overglaze used.

Some types of stains are relatively simple and can be mixed and used immediately on clay bodies.

Other types, and particularly some colors, demand more time and are more complicated to prepare. The process requires weighing out the ingredients, dry-mixing them by hand or in a ball mill, calcining them in a crucible, wet or dry grinding them in a ball mill for several hours, washing, sieving, and sometimes ball milling again before they can be used as a stain. Such colors as red, yellow, and orange must be prepared in this manner.

The stains presented in this chapter are of both types with directions given for each individual type. If the directions are followed faithfully they should perform as indicated.

Note. The stains in this chapter are listed alphabetically by color rather than by temperature range.

FORMULAS FOR STAINS

S-1   **Black Stain   Cone 6–8**

Mixing. Weigh out the ingredients by grams or pounds, dry-mix by hand or in a ball mill for five minutes, place in a crucible, and calcine to cone 8. After calcining, place the compound in a ball mill and dry-grind for four to five hours. Do not undergrind this or any stain for most stains of this type must be finely ground to give true colors. After grinding is completed mix the stain with water to the consistency of milk and sieve it through a 200-mesh screen. At this point the stain is ready to use for spraying or brushing over the entire body of the pot to be stained. If the stain is to be used for underglaze painting it should be mixed thicker (about the consistency of condensed milk) and a teaspoon of C.M.C. added for each pint (half-liter) of stain.

Application. If the entire body of the pot is to be stained, apply by spraying or brushing, allow the stain to dry, then sponge off the excess with a wet sponge or cloth. For underglaze painting apply with a brush of your choice.

Firing. Fire this stain to the cone 6–8 range. If the pot is to be overglazed the stain should be prefired to cone

Chrome oxide	54.0
Red iron oxide	26.0
Manganese dioxide	15.0
Cobalt oxide	5.0

06–04 before the glaze is applied to avoid the risk of smearing the stain design. If the glaze is to be sprayed on the pot the prefiring can be omitted.

Fired Results. This stain fires to a true black at cone 6–8 oxidation or reduction, and black metallic above cone 8.

S-2

Black Stain   Cone 6-8

Mixing. Mix in the manner of S-1.

Application. Apply in the manner of S-1.

Firing. Fire in the manner of S-1.

Fired Results. This stain fires to a true black at cone 6–8 oxidation or reduction, and black metallic above cone 8.

Chrome oxide	64.0
Red iron oxide	36.0

S-3

Blue-Black Stain   Cone 09-9

Mixing. Mix in the manner of S-1.

Application. Apply in the manner of S-1.

Firing. Fire in the manner of S-1.

Fired Results. This stain fires to a black at cone 09–6, blue-black at cone 7–9 oxidation or reduction.

Cobalt oxide	40.0
Aluminum oxide	40.0
Chrome oxide	18.0
Zircopax	2.0

S-4

Black Metallic Stain   Cone 8-10
Courtesy of Neil Nulton, "Mutton Hollow," Branson, Missouri

Mixing. Mix thoroughly by hand or rotary beater, then use.

Application. This stain may be applied by brush but it is more successful if sprayed.

Firing. Fire in the manner of S-1.

Fired Results. This stain fires to a beautiful metallic black at cone 8–10 oxidation or reduction.

Albany slip	260.0
Cobalt oxide	24.0
Copper oxide	24.0
Red iron oxide	24.0
Manganese dioxide	25.0

S-5

Light Blue Stain   Cone 09-9

Mixing. Mix in the manner of S-1.

Application. Apply in the manner of S-1.

Firing. Fire in the manner of S-1.

Fired Results. This stain fires to a light blue at cone 09–9, a slightly darker blue if an overglaze is used, and burns out completely above cone 9 reduction.

Tin oxide	96.0
Antimony oxide	4.0

S-6

Light Blue Stain   Cone 09-9

Mixing. Mix in the manner of S-1 but calcine only to cone 6.

Application. Apply in the manner of S-1.

Firing. Fire in the manner of S-1.

Fired Results. This stain fires to a light blue at cone 09–9, darker if an overglaze is used.

Aluminum oxide	50.0
Tin oxide	35.0
Zinc oxide	9.5
Cobalt carbonate	5.5

S-7 **Medium Blue Stain Cone 09–9**

Mixing. Mix in the manner of S-1.

Application. Apply in the manner of S-1.

Firing. Fire in the manner of S-1.

Fired Results. This stain fires to a medium blue at cone 09–9 oxidation or reduction, slightly darker if an overglaze is used.

Alumina oxide	87.0
Zinc oxide	11.2
Cobalt oxide	3.5
Tin oxide	0.3

S-8 **Medium Blue Stain Cone 09–9**

Mixing. Mix in the manner of S-1 but calcine only to cone 6.

Application. Apply in the manner of S-1.

Firing. Fire in the manner of S-1.

Fired Results. This stain fires to a medium blue at cone 09–9 oxidation or reduction, darker if an overglaze is used.

Alumina oxide	75.0
Zinc oxide	13.0
Cobalt oxide	12.0

S-9 **Medium Blue Stain Cone 09–9**

Mixing. Mix in the manner of S-1 but calcine only to cone 6.

Application. Apply in the manner of S-1.

Firing. Fire in the manner of S-1.

Fired Results. This stain fires to a medium blue at cone 09–9 oxidation or reduction. At cone 9 reduction the stain has a lavender hue to it. With an overglaze the stain is a lighter, fuller blue.

Zinc oxide	50.1
Zircopax	3.0
Silica	35.5
Cobalt oxide	11.4

S-10 **Dark Blue Stain Cone 09–9**

Mixing. Weigh out the ingredients as in S-1, wet-grind, dry, calcine to cone 02, dry-grind for four to five hours, screen, then add water as directed in S-1.

Application. Apply in the manner of S-1.

Firing. Fire in the manner of S-1.

Fired Results. This stain fires to a darker shade of cerulean blue at cone 09–9 oxidation or reduction, darker if an overglaze is used.

Kaolin (EPK)	75.0
Cobalt oxide	15.0
Chrome oxide	10.0

S-11 **Ultramarine Blue Stain Cone 6–9**

Mixing. Mix in the manner of S-1.

Application. Apply in the manner of S-1.

Firing. Fire in the manner of S-1.

Fired Results. This stain fires to a beautiful ultramarine blue at cone 6–9 oxidation or reduction, slightly darker if an overglaze is used.

Chrome oxide	48.0
Silica	14.0
Cobalt oxide	38.0

S-12 **Light Rusty Brown Stain Cone 09–9**

Mixing. Mix in the manner of S-1 but calcine only to cone 6, wet-grind for four to five hours then sieve.

Application. Apply in the manner of S-1.

Firing. Fire in the manner of S-1.

Fired Results. This stain fires to a light rusty brown at cone 09–6 oxidation or reduction, darker above cone 6, and darker still at cone 9 reduction if an overglaze is used.

Zinc oxide	50.0
Iron oxide	18.0
Chrome oxide	16.0
Aluminum oxide	14.0
Tin oxide	2.0

S-13 **Rust Brown Stain Cone 09–9**

Mixing. Mix in the manner of S-1, but calcine only to cone 6.

Application. Apply in the manner of S-1.

Firing. Fire in the manner of S-1.

Fired Results. This stain fires to a rust color at cone 09 and increasingly darker up to cone 9 oxidation or reduction. With an overglaze at cone 9 reduction it is a medium tan color with occasional spotting.

Zinc oxide	56.0
Chrome oxide	22.0
Iron oxide	22.0
Zircopax	6.0

S-14 **Gray-Brown Stain Cone 09–9**

Mixing. Mix in the manner of S-1, but calcine only to cone 6.

Application. Apply in the manner of S-1.

Firing. Fire in the manner of S-1.

Fired Results. This stain fires to a gray with brown overtones at cone 09, increasing brownish gray above this temperature, and a dark brown with green overtones at cone 9 reduction. With an overglaze it is green with brown overtones at cone 9 reduction.

Zinc oxide	52.0
Chrome oxide	48.0

S-15 **Green-Brown Stain Cone 09–9**

Mixing. Mix in the manner of S-1, but calcine only to cone 6.

Application. Apply in the manner of S-1.

Firing. Fire in the manner of S-1.

Fired Results. This stain fires to a pure brown up to cone 2 with increasing green overtones above this temperature. At cone 9 reduction it is green, and it is green-brown with an overglaze.

Zinc oxide	50.0
Zircopax	20.0
Chrome oxide	30.0

S-16 **Brown Stain Cone 6–8**

Mixing. Mix in the manner of S-1.

Application. Apply in the manner of S-1.

Firing. Fire in the manner of S-1.

Fired Results. This stain fires to a medium dark brown at cone 6–8 oxidation. With an overglaze it is slightly darker.

Zinc oxide	10.0
Chrome oxide	15.0
Red iron oxide	25.0
Red lead	10.0
Boric acid	10.0

S-17

Red-Brown Stain   Cone 4–8

Mixing. Mix in the manner of S-1.

Application. Apply in the manner of S-1.

Firing. Fire in the manner of S-1.

Fired Results. This stain fires to an earth red-brown at cone 6–8 oxidation or reduction. Above this it tends to burn and give metallic overtones which are also quite attractive on unglazed pieces.

Chrome oxide	10.0
Red iron oxide	25.0
Zinc oxide	10.0

S-18

Deep Brown Stain   Cone 09–9

Mixing. Mix in the manner of S-1.

Application. Apply in the manner of S-1.

Firing. Fire in the manner of S-1.

Fired Results. This stain fires to a medium dark-brown at cone 09–6 and increasingly darker up to cone 9–10. The colors are generally the same in oxidation or reduction. With an overglaze the stain is a black-brown above cone 6 oxidation or reduction.

Zinc oxide	60.0
Iron oxide	26.0
Chrome oxide	15.0

S-19

Dove Gray Stain   Cone 06–9

Mixing. Mix in the manner of S-1, but calcine only to cone 6.

Application. Apply in the manner of S-1.

Firing. Fire in the manner of S-1.

Fired Results. This stain fires to a beautiful dove gray at cone 06 and gets increasingly darker up to cone 9 oxidation or reduction. At cone 9 reduction with an overglaze it is a medium gray with occasional spotting.

Silica	58.0
Nickel oxide	22.0
Whiting	11.0
Cobalt oxide	6.0
Chromium oxide	3.0

S-20

Chrome Green Stain   Cone 08–9

Mixing. Mix in the manner of S-1, but calcine only to cone 6.

Application. Apply in the manner of S-1.

Firing. Fire in the manner of S-1.

Fired Results. This stain fires to a chrome green at cone 08 with increasingly darker shades of green at each cone level above cone 08, oxidation or reduction. With an overglaze at cone 9 reduction it is more of an olive green.

Kaolin	60.0
Silica	5.0
Chrome oxide	35.0

S-21   **Light Green Stain (Celadon) Cone 08–8**

Potassium bichromate	34.0
Silica	18.0
Whiting	18.0
Fluorspar	17.0
Chrome oxide	6.0
Tin oxide	5.0
Zircopax	2.0

Mixing. Weigh out the ingredients as directed in S-1, mix, dry, calcine to cone 04, rinse with cold water, wet-grind for five hours, rinse again, dry, and screen. Then mix with water as directed in S-1.

Application. Apply in the manner of S-1.

Firing. Fire in the manner of S-1.

Fired Results. This stain fires to a light celadon green at cone 08–6 then increasingly darker above this temperature level, oxidation or reduction. With an overglaze it is slightly darker.

S-22   **Light Gray-Green Stain Cone 08–9**

Silica	30.0
Feldspar (potash)	22.0
Whiting	18.0
Fluorspar	10.0
Red lead	8.0
Calcium carbonate	9.0
Copper oxide	7.0

Mixing. Mix in the manner of S-1, but calcine only to cone 6 then wet-grind, dry, and screen.

Application. Apply in the manner of S-1.

Firing. Fire in the manner of S-1.

Fired Results. This stain fires to a light gray-green at cone 08 oxidation or reduction with increasingly darker shades of this color being obtained above this cone level. With an overglaze it is always slightly darker than unglazed.

S-23   **Blue-Green Stain Cone 4–8**

Cobalt oxide	41.8
Chromium oxide	20.3
Aluminum oxide	38.0

Mixing. Mix in the manner of S-1.

Application. Apply in the manner of S-1.

Firing. Fire in the manner of S-1.

Fired Results. This stain fires to a blue-green at cone 4 and increasingly darker above this, oxidation or reduction. Above cone 8 it takes on metallic overtones. With a glaze it is slightly darker at all cone levels.

S-24   **Orange Stain Cone 2–6**

Antimony oxide	28.8
Tin oxide	13.8
Red iron oxide	14.9
Red lead	42.5

Mixing. Mix in the manner of S-1, but calcine only to cone 6.

Application. Apply in the manner of S-1.

Firing. Fire in the manner of S-1.

Fired Results. This stain fires to a medium orange at cone 2 and increasingly darker with each cone level above cone 2. The results are generally the same in oxidation or reduction firing. With an overglaze the shades are always slightly darker.

S-25

Medium Orange Stain   Cone 09-9

Mixing. Mix in the manner of S-1, but calcine only to cone 6, then wet-grind, dry, and screen. Mix with water as directed in S-1.

Application. Apply in the manner of S-1.

Firing. Fire in the manner of S-1.

Fired Results. This stain fires to orange-beige at cone 08–2, orange at cone 3–9 with increasingly darker shades with each increasing cone level. At cone 9 reduction it is a light yellow-orange. Except at cone 9 reduction the shades are generally the same whether fired oxidation or reduction. All shades are darker if an overglaze is used.

Aluminum oxide	58.0
Zinc oxide	23.0
Zircopax	2.0
Whiting	11.0
Red iron oxide	6.0

S-26

Pink Stain   Cone 08-9

Mixing. Mix in the manner of S-1, but wet-grind, dry, calcine to cone 02, dry grind for five hours, and screen.

Application. Apply in the manner of S-1.

Firing. Fire in the manner of S-1.

Fired Results. This stain fires pink at cone 08–9 with purple overtones if an overglaze is used. The shades are basically the same in oxidation or reduction firings.

Tin oxide	70.0
Zircopax	18.0
Boric acid	8.0
Lead chromate	4.0

S-27

Pink Stain   Cone 6-8

Mixing. Mix in the manner of S-1, then add the CMC to the finished mix.

Application. Apply in the manner of S-1.

Firing. Fire in the manner of S-1.

Fired Results. This stain fires pink at cone 6–8 oxidation or reduction. With an overglaze it is slightly darker.

Tin oxide	49.5
Whiting	19.5
Fluorspar	8.0
Silica	20.5
Potassium dichromate	7.5
Add:	
C.M.C.	1 tsp

S-28

Pink Stain   Cone 6-10

Mixing. Pre-grind in a mortar to break up any lumps then mix in the manner of S-27.

Application. Apply in the manner of S-1.

Firing. Fire in the manner of S-1.

Fired Results. This stain fires a pure light pink at cone 6–8 and darker at cone 10. The colors are relatively the same in oxidation or reduction. With an overglaze the colors are slightly darker.

Tin oxide	52.0
Whiting	25.0
Silica	16.0
Borax	4.0
Potassium dichromate	3.0
Add:	
C.M.C.	1 tsp

S-29   Red Stain   Cone 08–6

Mixing. Premix in the manner of S-1, but dry-grind, calcine, dry-grind again, screen, wet-grind for five to six hours and sieve.

Application. Apply in the manner of S-1.

Firing. Fire in the manner of S-1.

Fired Results. This stain fires blood red at cone 08 oxidation or reduction. With an overglaze at cone 08 it is a red-violet. Above cone 6 the color tends to burn out leaving deeper earth red with metallic overtones.

Tin oxide	48.0
Whiting	22.0
Silica	20.0
Fluorspar	7.0
Lead chromate	3.0

S-30   Crimson Red Stain   Cone 4–8

Mixing. Mix in the manner of S-1.

Application. Apply in the manner of S-1.

Firing. Fire in the manner of S-1.

Fired Results. This stain fires to a crimson red at cone 4 oxidation or reduction and darker with each rise in temperature. At cone 8 it is a deep crimson red in oxidation or reduction. With an overglaze it is almost blood red.

Whiting	23.9
Calcium sulfate	6.5
Fluorspar	4.5
Silica	20.8
Tin oxide	43.7
Zinc oxide	1.0
Potassium dichromate	1.6

S-31   Red Stain   Cone 08–8

Mixing. Mix in the manner of S-1, but calcine only to cone 7.

Application. Apply in the manner of S-1.

Firing. Fire in the manner of S-1.

Fired Results. This stain fires blood red at cone 08–2. It begins to lighten to pink with each rise in cone level. At cone 9 it is a pure light pink. The colors are basically the same in oxidation or reduction.

Tin oxide	44.0
Calcium sulfate	65.0
Silica	21.0
Whiting	21.0
Calcium fluoride	4.7
Potassium bichromate	2.0

S-32   Earth Red Stain   Cone 06–8

Mixing. Weight out the ingredients, mix them dry, add water and C.M.C., and use.

Application. Apply in the manner of S-1.

Firing. Fire in the manner of S-1.

Fired Results. This stain fires to an earth red at cone 06–8 oxidation or reduction. With an overglaze it is darker and less attractive.

Kaolin	65.0
Red iron oxide	35.0
C.M.C.	1 tsp

S-33   Tan Stain   Cone 08–8

Mixing. Mix in the manner of S-1, but calcine to cone 1 only.

Application. Apply in the manner of S-1.

Firing. Fire in the manner of S-1.

Fired Results. This stain fires to yellow-tan at cone 08–8 with darker shades of tan being obtained at the higher cone levels. With an overglaze it darkens slightly.

White lead	58.0
Antimony oxide	23.0
Potassium nitrate	10.0
Red iron oxide	5.0
Zircopax	4.0

S-34 **Turquoise Stain Cone 4-6**

Mixing. Mix in the manner of S-1, but calcine only to cone 6.

Application. Apply in the manner of S-1.

Firing. Fire in the manner of S-1.

Fired Results. This stain fires to pure bright turquoise at cone 4–6 oxidation or reduction. At temperatures above cone 6 the color tends to burn out leaving mixtures of turquoise and metallic overtones. This can however be quite attractive and rustic at cones not exceeding 8.

Copper phosphate	55.0
Tin oxide	43.0
Silica	2.0

S-35 **Violet Stain Cone 09-8**

Mixing. Mix in the manner of S-1, but wet-grind, calcine to cone 04, wet-grind again, and sieve.

Application. Apply in the manner of S-1.

Firing. Fire in the manner of S-1.

Fired Results. This stain fires to a light violet at cone 09–2, above this cone level the color tends to darken and go toward an ugly gray-violet. The colors tend to be the same in oxidation or reduction. With an overglaze the colors are darker.

Tin oxide	89.0
Boric acid	10.0
Lead chromate	1.0

S-36 **White Stain Cone 09-8**

Mixing. Mix in the manner of S-1, but calcine only to cone 6.

Application. Apply in the manner of S-1.

Firing. Fire in the manner of S-1.

Fired Results. This stain fires white at cone 09–8 if left unglazed. With an overglaze it fires light gray at all cone levels. The colors are basically the same in oxidation or reduction.

Tin oxide	64.0
Whiting	36.0

S-37 **White Stain Cone 09-8**

Mixing. Mix dry, add water, and use.

Application. Apply in the manner of S-1.

Firing. Fire in the manner of S-1.

Fired Results. This stain fires white at all cone levels given. Above 8 it tends to burn out and go metallic. The colors are basically the same in oxidation or reduction and the addition of an overglaze does not darken the color.

Kaolin (EPK)	39.0
White lead	39.0
Tin oxide	10.0
Zinc oxide	2.0
Silica	10.0

S-38   **Off-White Stain Cone 09–8**

Kaolin (EPK)	39.0
White lead	39.0
Tin oxide	10.0
Zinc oxide	2.0
Silica	9.0
Red iron oxide	1.0

Mixing. Mix dry, add water, and use.

Application. Apply in the manner of S-1.

Firing. Fire in the manner of S-1.

Fired Results. This stain fires to an off-white at all cone levels given. Above cone 8 it tends to burn out and go metallic. The colors are basically the same in oxidation or reduction and the addition of an overglaze does not darken the color.

S-39   **Yellow-White Cone 09–9**

Zircopax	50.0
Whiting	40.0
Tin oxide	10.0

Mixing. Mix in the manner of S-1, but calcine to cone 5.

Application. Apply in the manner of S-1.

Firing. Fire in the manner of S-1.

Fired Results. This stain fires yellow-white at all cones given in oxidation. In reduction it fires a more pure white at all cone levels given.

S-40   **Yellow Stain Cone 08–8**

Zircopax	85.0
Vanadium	12.0
Tin oxide	3.0

Mixing. Mix in the manner of S-1.

Application. Apply in the manner of S-1.

Firing. Fire in the manner of S-1.

Fired Results. This stain fires a light chrome yellow at cone 08 and gets lighter with each increase in temperature. The colors tend to be the same in oxidation or reduction and are slightly darker with an overglaze.

S-41   **Yellow Stain Cone 09–9**

Red lead	35.0
Antimony oxide	10.0
Tin oxide	10.0

Mixing. Mix in the manner of S-1, but wet-grind, calcine to cone 04, wet-grind again, dry, and screen.

Application. Apply in the manner of S-1.

Firing. Fire in the manner of S-1.

Fired Results. This stain fires a light Naples yellow at cone 09 and gets lighter with each rise in cone level. The colors are basically the same in oxidation or reduction and the addition of an overglaze tends to darken the color very slightly.

S-42   **Yellow Stain Cone 09–8**

Red lead	53.0
Antimony oxide	24.0
Tin oxide	18.0
Zircopax	3.0
Potassium nitrate	2.0

Mixing. Mix in the manner of S-1, but calcine only to cone 1.

Application. Apply in the manner of S-1.

Firing. Fire in the manner of S-1.

Fired Results. This stain fires to a light chrome yellow at cone 09–06 and gets lighter with each rise in cone level. The colors tend to be the same in oxidation and reduction and the use of an overglaze tends to darken the colors slightly.

S-43

Yellow Stain   Cone 08–8

Mixing. Mix in the manner of S-1, but calcine only to cone 5.

Application. Apply in the manner of S-1.

Firing. Fire in the manner of S-1.

Fired Results. This stain fires to a dark lemon yellow at cone 08–06 and gets lighter with each rise in cone level. The colors tend to be a shade darker in reduction and burn out at cone 9. Colors are darker with an overglaze.

Red lead	46.0
Antimony oxide	33.0
Tin oxide	17.0
Yellow ochre	4.0

S-44

Yellow Stain   Cone 4–6

Mixing. Mix in the manner of S-1, but calcine only to cone 6.

Application. Apply in the manner of S-1.

Firing. Fire in the manner of S-1.

Fired Results. This stain fires to a dark creamy yellow at cone 4–6, but tends to burn out above cone 6. The shades of color tend to be the same in oxidation or reduction. With the use of an overglaze the colors are a shade darker and less attractive.

Antimony oxide	30.0
Red lead	50.0
Tin oxide	20.0

Note. Some of the chemicals used in glaze preparation are potentially dangerous. Safety precautions should be taken when weighing out, mixing, and applying glazes. These precautions are listed under each series of glaze formulas. (See also Chapter 17 on Glaze Preparation.)

PART TWO

GLAZES

16
GLAZE TYPES

For the potter the study and use of glazes is infinitely more complex than that of clays and the formulation of clay bodies. A greater number of chemicals and materials are involved and more variables must be taken into account if the potter is to be successful. While in clay body formulation "hit or miss" methods are often successful, in glaze formulation more accurate procedures are necessary if any degree of success or predictability is to be achieved. Even the potter who uses commercially prepared glazes from a ceramic supply house must have some coherent knowledge of the areas of application and firing technique in order to achieve some measure of success.

It is therefore necessary that the potter have some basic knowledge of glaze types if he is to be successful in making his own glazes, for different types of glazes behave differently under various conditions such as application, firing, and use of oxides and colorants in the basic formulas. If the potter has some understanding of the basics of glazes and the various types he will be in a better position to control the results he wishes to achieve.

The formulation of a ceramic glaze is not really as complicated or mysterious as most beginning potters seem to believe. A glaze is a fundamentally a thin glass coating fused to the surface of the clay by the high temperature made possible by firing it in a kiln. While it is true that many glazes have a highly complicated chemical structure, a simple glaze can be formulated, for only three elements are necessary to form a glaze: silica, a flux, and a refractory element.

The silica in a glaze is the glass-forming compound. Were it not for the high melting temperature of this element it would make a fine glaze by itself. But due to the fact that it melts at 3100° F./1705° C., some means of lowering the melting point must be found. This is done by adding a flux to the formula.

A flux refers to any compound which can be added to the silica to lower its melting point. In lower-fired glazes, compounds of lead and sodium are used. In higher-fired glazes these fluxes are replaced by calcium and feldspar compounds.

A refractory element is added—to stabilize the glaze and make it less fluid and more durable. If the potter were to use only silica and a fluxing agent he would find that the resulting glaze would be rather fluid under fire and less durable than would be desirable for practical use. The element used to achieve this durability is alumina, for it readily combines with silica to form a tough glass coating which is highly resistant to abrasion and thermal shock.

GLAZE CLASSIFICATION

While it is true that a good simple glaze can be made from the three ingredients mentioned above, a greater understanding of glazes and their use can be achieved if the potter gains some basic knowledge of the various types of glazes and the characteristics exhibited by each individual type. The most important of these types are presented here for this purpose. And for the convenience of the reader they are given in alphabetical order by title.

An alkaline glaze is one which uses some alkaline compound such as sodium, lithium, or potassium as a flux to lower the fusion point of silica to form the glaze. There are two types of alkaline glazes, the low-fire type and the high-fire type.

The low-fire alkaline glaze matures at temperatures in the cone 016–02 range. This type of glaze tends to be glassy in appearance, scratches easily, crazes on most clay bodies, and produces brilliant colors with certain coloring oxides.

The usual fluxes used in low-fire alkaline glazes are sodium compounds either in the form of sodium carbonate, sodium bicarbonate, borax, or colemanite. Unfortunately most of the sodium compounds are soluble and tend to recrystallize in the glaze solution when stored for long periods. They also tend to be absorbed by the bisque ware resulting in an inferior glaze. For this reason "raw alkaline" glazes which use the first three sodium compounds above should be mixed, ground, and used at once, and then only on a bisque pot that has been fired to at least cone 04.

A better solution to these problems is to introduce the sodium into the glaze in the form of a frit, which makes the soda insoluble. There are many such soda-silica frits available from ceramic supply houses and it is generally more convenient and less expensive for the potter to use them than to try to produce his own, for it is a highly complicated and time-consuming process. Moreover, with the use of the more convenient commercial frits the results are generally more predictable and are much the same as those achieved when using raw alkaline compounds.

The high-fire alkaline glaze, which matures in the cone 4–9 range, generally uses the less-soluble lithium compounds in combination with calcium fluxes to produce its finish. In some cases the less-soluble compound colemanite is used in small amounts in combination with lithium and calcium. And due to the fact that these alkaline compounds are less soluble and will remain suspended in solution they tend to be much more stable when stored in solution form. This type of glaze is also more durable in surface quality due to its calcium content, less susceptible to crazing, and less colorful than the lower-fired alkaline glazes.

The popularity of the alkaline glazes probably comes from their ability to produce brilliant colors with the addition of certain coloring oxides. The famous Egyptian blue for example can be produced only in an alkaline glaze with the use of copper. Certain shades of blue and turquoise are likewise produced only in alkaline glazes. Cobalt compounds give beautiful intense blues, iron produces straw gold colors, and vibrant purples and violets are possible with the use of manganese. Indeed the colors produced by these colorant compounds in the alkaline glazes are more intense than in any other glaze type.

Ash glazes are probably the oldest form of glazing known to man. They were first discovered by the ancient Chinese in their wood-burning kilns where the ashes from the fire box blew through the kiln chamber, landed on the ware inside, and fused with the silica in the clay bodies to form a thin glaze coating. Although they have no commercial value in industry there seems to be a revived interest in them by today's potters for the unusual patterned surfaces and mottled effects they tend to produce when fired in a reduction atmosphere at high temperatures.

The reader will find this subject discussed at greater length in Chapter 29 on Ash Glazes.

Boron glazes are the result of the use of boric oxide as a flux. This strong flux behaves in much the same manner as the alkaline fluxes. Boron is usually introduced into the glaze in a borosilicate frit due to the fact that most forms of boric oxides are soluble. The boron compound colemanite is

also used quite commonly for it is relatively insoluble.

The typical boron glaze usually fires in the cone 016–02 temperature range. It tends to favor the production of brilliant colors much like those of the alkaline glazes except that iron tends to be rather dull and lifeless in appearance compared to its performance in an alkaline glaze.

Boron glazes often tend to give a milky opalescent quality with bluish hues, especially if colemanite is used to supply the boron content. Potters often exploit this characteristic by adding small amounts of ilmenite to promote this quality. The results are often spectacular with opalescent mottled colors and/or cloudy fluid runs breaking the surface of the glaze. Glazes which are high in boric oxide also tend to boil and bubble violently during firing then smooth out to give a broken, mottled appearance. Such effects can also be promoted to even greater advantage by the addition of rutile and/or zinc oxide.

Bristol glazes get their name from the city in England where they were first developed in the nineteenth century when lead poisoning became a problem in the pottery industry.

Bristol glazes fire at medium temperature range and use the relatively nontoxic zinc oxide as their principal flux. In combination with whiting and feldspar this chemical produces a reasonably fluid glaze which is opaque, rather stiff, and less glassy than the typical lead or alkaline glaze. Its response to the usual coloring oxides is less brilliant—more muted and subtle—than in the alkalines or lead glazes. Good green and blue hues are possible with copper compounds and cobalt respectively, good browns are produced by the addition of chrome oxide, but the iron compounds are rather muddy and insignificant.

The major faults of the bristol glazes are their tendency to crawl or crackle during firing (this can be reduced to a minimum by using calcined zinc oxide to cut the shrinkage rate of the glaze), pitting, and pinholding. And due to these faults and the fact that good nontoxic lead frits are now available at reasonable prices, bristol glazes are not real favorites with potters of today. They can be very attractive, however, when thickly applied on pottery of a light color.

Crackle glazes are actually not glaze types in themselves for they cannot be classified by composition but rather by fired effect. This is due to the fact that the crackling is simply the result of tensions developing in the fired piece when the glaze and body expand and contract at different rates during the firing and cooling process. Although this type of glaze effect has often been considered a defect by some potters, it can be a very beautiful and subtle way of decorating pottery, particularly as there are many color possibilities available.

Crackle glazes can be made to form large or small crackle patterns depending on the composition of the glaze or on the type of clay body to which it is applied. If the potter uses a clay body which has a lower expansion quality than the glaze, the crackle effect can be promoted to a much higher degree. To emphasize the crackle patterns in the glaze the pottery can be rubbed with dark colorants such as ink.

For further information about this glaze type consult Chapter 21 on Special-Effect Glazes.

Crystalline glazes are generally of two types: one has small single crystals suspended in the glaze, and the second has larger crystal clusters in or on the surface. Both types of crystals tend to catch and reflect the light.

In practice the potter will find that the composition of the crystalline glaze must be carefully related to the pot form, for the jewel-like crystals tend to float from the surface and become lost in more radical forms. Crystal formation is due to the absence of alumina in the glaze formula—its presence tends to retard the crystal development. Additions of iron, zinc, and rutile tend to promote the development of crystal formation in the glaze. Their presence also makes the glaze more opaque than usual, while the absence of alumina as a stabilizer tends to make the glaze more fluid and brilliant in surface appearance.

For the reader who is interested in this type of glaze the subject is handled in greater detail in Chapter 21.

Feldspar glazes are some of the most simple glazes known to man. First discovered in China these glazes remained the exclusive property of the Chinese for many centuries, for only they possessed the technical knowledge of kiln construction and firing to reach the high temperatures necessary to melt and fuse the feldspar. This substance in powder form melts by itself at cone 8–9. A simple glaze can even be made of this material alone, for when ground to powder and spread over the surface of the ware it produces a beautiful milky-white glaze similar to those of the early Chinese potters. Indeed some of the most beautiful glazes ever produced were compounds of three simple materials: feldspar, calcium carbonate, and silica—all of which are available in abundance everywhere.

Flowing glazes may be produced for all temperature ranges. Their composition is achieved by increasing the fluxing agent in the formula and decreasing the stabilizing agent, alumina. For when this is done the glaze tends to melt more

quickly and flow down the sides of the pot during the firing, creating unusual effects.

The subject of flowing glazes is duscussed at greater length in Chapter 21.

Frit glazes differ very little in chemical content from the alkaline or lead glazes. For the fritting process is primarily a method of rendering alkaline compounds insoluble and lead compounds nontoxic.

The basic process involves melting the toxic or soluble compounds with silica to a glassy state, cooling the mixture rapidly to force it to shatter into small pieces, then grinding the glass particles to a fine powder. The frit powder is then used as a main constituent of the glaze formula.

It is generally advisable for the potter to buy these frit compounds from commercial supply houses due to the fact that making them is a long, tedious process involving complex formulation and specialized equipment.

Lead glazes get their name from the fluxes used in their formulation which are oxides of the lead compounds. They are an extremely useful medium for the potter for they can be made to perform well in a wide range, from cone 016–6. They have many advantages: they are characteristically reliable in performance, easily controlled, quite durable in use, and brilliant in surface as well as in color.

The lead glaze does have one major disadvantage, however: it is very toxic in the raw state. Consequently the potter should exercise extreme caution in handling this compound, particularly in the raw state. Lead-based glazes should not be used on ware which is to come into contact with food, especially food with an acid content. For if the ware is improperly fired the lead can leach out into the food and contaminate it. The best way to avoid this problem is to use a lead-silicate frit which is nontoxic in this combination and thus safe to use on utility ware.

Luster glazes are generally thin metallic coatings applied on top of another glaze after firing and refired at a lower temperature than the melting point of the base glaze. Usually the base glaze is of the lead-tin type. The luster coating is usually a combination of resin, bismuth nitrate, and a metallic salt compound suspended in an oil-of-lavender base. After the solution is applied it is fired only high enough to fuse the metal to the base-glaze surface and burn out the resin and lavender-oil base. The metal compounds generally used are zinc acetate, lead acetate, copper sulfate, manganese sulfate, cobalt sulfate, silver chloride, gold chloride, and uranium nitrate. A wide variety of colors such as reds, browns, yellows, silver-whites, and clear iridescent sheens can be produced with the use of the luster glaze.

Matt glazes can most simply be described as those having a surface which reflects little or no light as compared to the glossy surfaces of the lead and alkaline glazes. Matt glazes are usually formulated by increasing the aluminum content in the formula or by substituting barium carbonate for a portion of the flux used in the glaze formula. This is the reason they are often called alumina or barium matt glazes.

True matt glazes are sometimes confused with underfired specimens of other glazes or those that have been applied too thin to produce a good glaze surface. A true matt glaze should exhibit the characteristics of smoothness of surface with no gloss present to reflect light and little or no transparent areas, except where a clear matt is used as an overglaze for a piece which has underglaze decoration.

Raku glazes are handled in Chapter 9 on Raku Bodies and Glazes.

Reduction glazes are those formulated to perform best in a kiln atmosphere which is low in oxygen during certain stages of the firing cycle. It was in this type of atmosphere that the ancient Chinese first produced their famous copper reds and iron celadons. These results are obtained through the carbon in the kiln atmosphere uniting with the iron and copper coloring oxides in the glazes, thereby altering the color of the fired result. For when iron or copper oxide loses its oxygen content it remains suspended in the glaze as a carbonate, giving green or red respectively. Alternately, if it remains oxidized it gives iron red or green respectively.

The true reduction glaze such as the copper red or celadon should not be confused with other glazes which are fired in a reducing atmosphere to achieve certain iron spotting or mottled surface colors, for many glazes will behave in this manner if used over a clay body high in iron content when fired in a heavy reduction atmosphere.

Salt glazes are one of the oldest types of glazes. They were first discovered in the twelfth century in Germany and were in common use on utility ware for many years until the middle of the nineteenth century. In recent years, however, there has been a revived interest in this type of glaze by studio potters.

The actual salting procedure is relatively simple. The pottery is put into the kiln in the greenware state and fired to its maturing point. Then ordinary salt, sodium chloride, is thrown into the kiln. The salt volatilizes and the sodium

in gas form combines with the silica content on the surface of the pottery to form a thin glaze coating on the ware. However, the process does have disadvantages: deadly chlorine gas given off during the salting is a potential health hazard; after repeated firings the kiln interior and furniture become coated with glaze. Moreover, the kiln used for salt firing cannot be used for regular firings ever again. Consequently this type of glaze firing should be done in a fuel-fired kiln with a good chimney which is located outside or in a studio which is very well ventilated. It should never be attempted in an electric kiln, for the gas would destroy the elements. The reader will find this subject discussed in greater detail in Chapter 31 on Salt and Vapor Glazing.

Slip glazes are made from low-firing raw natural clays which have natural fluxes inherent in the chemical makeup of the clay. Generally few modifications are necessary to the clay beyond preparation by washing and sieving to remove impurities. Sometimes additions of other chemicals are added to make the glaze fit better or to lower or raise the melting point of the clay. These changes however are generally minor. The color range available in slip glazes is for the most part earthy: tans, browns, and blacks. The usual firing range for most slip glazes is in the cone 6–12 range.

The reader will find this glaze type discussed at greater length in Chapter 30 on Slip Glazes.

Stoneware and porcelain glazes can be considered as any leadless glaze that can be fired above the cone 6 range. Even though many potters demand that a porcelain glaze be clear, smooth, colorless, formulated with feldspar and whiting as the major fluxes, and fired to maturity at levels above cone 9, the final definition of a stoneware or porcelain glaze depends upon the type of ware upon which they are used.

Actually it is a far simpler matter to make a glaze that matures at stoneware levels than one that matures at cone 06, for at higher temperature levels the extreme heat of the kiln works to the advantage of the potter, allowing the most simple combination of compounds to melt and fuse into a glaze.

A good stoneware glaze is characterized by its hardness, subtle color, durability, and muted surface sheen. Moreover, due to the higher cone level at which a stoneware glaze is fired, the interface or joining of the glaze layer to the clay body surface of the pot is more complete than with lower-firing glazes and clay bodies. In the final result the glaze and the pot become one united object and are therefore stronger, more durable, and completely nonporous.

17
GLAZE PREPARATION

For the potter who becomes interested in compounding his own glazes, a knowledge of the proper methods of preparation is essential. And while this is not a complex operation, there are some general rules the potter should follow if the final result is to be a success. The process of preparing a glaze is essentially one of thoroughly mixing the ingredients to form a sliplike substance of an even consistency which can be successfully applied to the bisque-fired ware. The primary reason for this thorough mixing and intermingling of the different ingredients with water is to promote a better and more uniform melting of the glaze and thus a more perfect result.

This mixing of the glaze ingredients can be accomplished by several different methods depending upon the glaze type involved. For while some glaze types can be mixed simply by placing them in a jar and shaking it for several minutes, others need to be ground and mixed in a ball mill to properly combine the ingredients.

SIMPLE MIXING METHODS

Most of the glaze materials supplied by chemical supply houses today are already so finely processed that they will pass through a 200-mesh screen. Therefore they do not require grinding. The problem then is to mix the glaze in a manner that is thorough enough to completely intermingle the ingredients and disperse any coloring oxides.

For small batches of such glazes the mixing can be done dry in a mortar and pestle or shaken in a jar for several minutes after water has been added (except the raw alkaline types which should always be ground dry). An even better method particularly for simple mixing of large glaze batches is to use an electric rotary beater of some type and beat the glaze wet for several minutes at a medium speed. A kitchen blender is also good for this purpose. Either of these latter two methods insures a better mix and helps to better disperse the coloring oxides

which sometimes have a tendency to clump together in the glaze suspension.

The mixing methods given here are the most common ones used for preparing glazes for use on pottery. If the general rules given for each individual method are followed the prepared glaze suspension should present few problems of application for the potter.

BALL MILLING

Probably the most thorough method of mixing a glaze is grinding in a ball mill. This method not only serves to thoroughly mix the ingredients but it also grinds any coarse particles to a finer size to insure better melting and fusing of the glaze. Grinding time may vary with the type of ingredients but an hour is usually sufficient. In any case the ground material should pass easily through a 100-mesh sieve before it can be considered ready for use.

For most glazes the usual procedure is to grind them wet. If this is done properly the glaze will be a smooth and uniform suspension which will spread evenly on application.

Glazes which have a tendency to fall out of solution after long periods of storage are usually dry ground in the ball mill. This is true of any glaze which has soluble ingredients, like raw alkaline glazes which tend to lump in suspension after two or three days of storage. The usual procedure is to dry-grind them, then mix with water only the amount to be used at the moment. Of course, if a soluble glaze such as this is to be used at once it can be ground wet.

ADDING WATER

The beginning potter often is confused by the problem of how much water to add to the dry glaze ingredients. This will depend on several different factors. For example, glazes which have considerable clay or colemanite in them will require a greater proportion of water.

Generally the consistency of the glaze suspension is determined by the method of application which is to be used. With experience the potter will learn how much water to use with a certain glaze formula and then it is best to add the dry ingredients to the water (preferably warm) rather than to add the water to the dry ingredients.

For brushing, glazes should be about the thickness of ketchup to insure a proper coating. Usually two to three coats should be painted on the ware to insure a uniform application.

For dipping, glazes should be about the thickness of cream if the ware is not of the porous type. For the more highly porous wares the glaze solution should be somewhat thinner to allow it to seep into and penetrate the pores of the ware.

For spraying, glazes should be about the thickness of milk and should be ground and screened through a 100-mesh sieve to remove any coarse particles which might clog the spray gun.

USING FLOATATIVES

The potter will find that many of the glazes that he mixes will contain materials which are heavy and tend to settle rapidly to the bottom of the suspension. The addition of a floatative such as bentonite in the amount of 1% will correct this defect without altering the basic formula or the fired result. This addition however does not completely correct the problem of settling, for all glazes tend to settle to some extent and consequently all glazes should be stirred thoroughly before using if they have been stored for only a day or two.

USING GUMS

Many potters like to use gums to make the glaze adhere to the ware better. Gums also insure a tougher glaze coating when the glaze is dry thus preventing crumbling or powdering of the dried glaze when handled. The addition of such gums is not harmful to the glaze for they burn out during firing.

Gums are discussed at length in Chapter 34, Dictionary of Clay and Glaze Compounds.

USING FLOCCULANTS

The potter will find the use of flocculants to thicken the glaze quite useful if he is glazing vitreous or nonporous wares where building up a thick coating of the glaze is difficult. To correct this problem the glaze can be artificially thickened with flocculants such as aluminum sulfate or magnesium sulfate in amounts of 1% by dry body weight. The addition of either of these two materials will not alter the final fired results of the glaze.

18
SINGLE FIRING
CONE 06-9

Customarily studio potters bisque fire all ware before glazing. This practice evolved as a result of the high breakage rate in the greenware state. However technological advances in clay body formulation have solved some of the problems which first made single firing of pottery unpopular. The need of the ceramic industry to cut costs in labor, energy, and kiln replacement made these advances possible. And consequently single firing in industry is now quite common. Similarly for the studio potter who is also faced with the rising cost of energy and equipment, single firing of pottery might be an attractive alternative to consider.

SINGLE-FIRE CLAY BODIES

Almost any clay body, in fact most of those being used by potters today, can be successfully single fired. This is also true of most commercially prepared clays. For clays which are plastic enough to use for wheel work are also plastic enough to dry to a durable, less porous greenware state. The addition of organic binders, borax, or bentonite in small amounts will produce an even more durable greenware body. Additions of these materials should not exceed 1% to 1-1/2% and clay bodies with organic binders require a slower firing rate in the first 1000° F./538° C. to allow the gases to escape slowly. A second method of increasing the durability of greenware is to increase the amount of plastic material in the body formula.

For such bodies tend to shrink more, are less porous in the dry state, and are thus more durable.

GLAZING THE WARE

Any piece of pottery that is to be single fired should be thoroughly dry before the glaze is applied. The best methods of application are brushing or spraying as these require less handling of the ware and permit less water to be absorbed by the ware. This in turn reduces the chance of breakage or cracking of the ware. Glazes used for greenware should also be somewhat thicker than those used on bisque ware for the prevention of excess absorption of water into the ware.

SINGLE-FIRE GLAZES

Many glazes designed for bisque ware can be used on greenware if they contain a major portion of clay and if the firing cycle is carried out slowly. For the clay in the glaze will tend to shrink as the greenware shrinks thus lessening the chance of glaze defects.

All of the glazes listed here have been tested for single firing and have proved quite reliable when handled in the manner described in the directions.

The reader will find possible substitutions for many of the glaze chemicals used in Chapter 34, Dictionary of Clay and Glaze Compounds.

Note. The glazes in this chapter are labeled toxic or nontoxic. Toxic glazes should be carefully handled both in formulation and in application. During preparation the potter should wear a dust mask to prevent inhalation of toxic materials and not allow these materials to come into prolonged contact with the skin. Frequent washing of the hands when handling these glazes is a wise precaution. Toxic glazes should be applied by brushing and dipping—never spraying. For even under the best conditions some inhalation of the toxic mist from the spray is bound to take place or, equally bad, the mist from the spray gun can settle on the skin and be absorbed into the body system.

FORMULAS FOR SINGLE-FIRE GLAZES

SFG-1 **Satin Matt Glaze   Cone 06**
alkaline, transparent, clear matt, nontoxic

Mixing. Weigh out the ingredients and mix by using one of the methods outlined in Chapter 17.

Application. Apply the glaze to thoroughly dry greenware by brushing, dipping, or spraying. See Chapter 17 for details.

Firing. Allow the ware to dry completely before firing. Fire the greenware slowly in the first 1000° F./538° C. to allow the chemically bonded water to escape; then fire normally to the maturing point of the glaze.

Fired Results. This glaze fires to a clear satin matt at cone 06. It is an excellent base for the colorants listed in Chapter 33 which are appropriate for alkaline-type glazes.

Sodium fluosilicate	14.3
Lithium carbonate	7.0
Whiting	10.4
Kentucky ball clay #4	13.6
Silica	54.7
Add:	
C.M.C.	1 tsp

SFG-2 **Clear Glaze Base   Cone 06**
alkaline, transparent, clear gloss, nontoxic

Mixing. Mix in the manner of SFG-1.

Application. Apply in the manner of SFG-1.

Firing. Fire in the manner of SFG-1.

Fired Results. This glaze fires to a transparent gloss at cone 06. It can be used well as a color base for any colorants appropriate for alkaline glazes.

Pemco frit #54	36.0
Sodium fluosilicate	36.0
Tennessee ball clay #1	18.3
Silica	9.1
Add:	
C.M.C.	1 tsp

SFG-3 **Clear Glaze Base   Cone 1**
alkaline-frit, transparent, clear gloss, nontoxic

Mixing. Mix in the manner of SFG-1.

Application. Apply in the manner of SFG-1.

Firing. Fire in the manner of SFG-1.

Fired Results. This glaze fires to a clear gloss at cone 1. It makes a good color base for the alkaline colorants.

Ferro frit #3134	61.0
Tennessee ball clay #1	18.5
Kaolin (Georgia)	20.5
Add:	
C.M.C.	1 tsp

SFG-4 **Opaque Matt Glaze   Cone 1**
alkaline, opaque, off-white, slightly toxic

Mixing. Mix in the manner of SFG-1.

Application. Apply in the manner of SFG-1.

Firing. Fire in the manner of SFG-1.

Fired Results. This glaze fires to an opaque off-white at cone 1. It is a good color base for any alkaline colorant.

Sodium fluosilicate	10.8
Lithium carbonate	12.8
Tin oxide	11.9
Albany slip	18.5
Tennessee ball clay #1	46.0
Add:	
C.M.C.	1 tsp

SFG-5 **Bright Matt Glaze   Cone 1**
alkaline-frit, translucent, bright matt, nontoxic

Mixing. Mix in the manner of SFG-1.

Application. Apply in the manner of SFG-1.

Firing. Fire in the manner of SFG-1.

Fired Results. This glaze fires to a bright translucent matt at cone 1.

Pemco frit #54	30.8
Lithium carbonate	2.2
Magnesium carbonate	2.6
Whiting	12.3
Tennessee ball clay #1	24.0
Silica	28.1
Add:	
C.M.C.	1 tsp

SFG-6 **Semitranslucent Gloss Glaze   Cone 1**
alkaline-frit, translucent, gloss, nontoxic

Mixing. Mix in the manner of SFG-1.

Application. Apply in the manner of SFG-1.

Firing. Fire in the manner of SFG-1.

Fired Results. This glaze fires to a translucent gloss at cone 1.

Hommel frit #242	40.5
Lithium carbonate	3.2
Magnesium carbonate	2.8
Whiting	15.1
Kentucky ball clay #4	33.8
Silica	4.6
Add:	
C.M.C.	1 tsp

SFG-7 **Satin Matt Glaze   Cone 1**
alkaline, transparent, satin matt, nontoxic

Mixing. Mix in the manner of SFG-1.

Application. Apply in the manner of SFG-1.

Firing. Fire in the manner of SFG-1.

Fired Results. This glaze fires to a clear satin matt at cone 1. It is a good color base.

Lithium carbonate	2.8
Magnesium carbonate	2.9
Whiting	18.5
Feldspar (potash)	32.8
Kentucky ball clay #4	30.0
Silica	14.2
Add:	
C.M.C.	1 tsp

SFG-8 **Clear Glaze Base   Cone 4**
alkaline-frit, transparent, clear gloss, nontoxic

Mixing. Mix in the manner of SFG-1.

Application. Apply in the manner of SFG-1.

Firing. Fire in the manner of SFG-1.

Fired Results. This glaze fires to a clear gloss at cone 4.

Ferro frit #3134	15.9
Magnesium carbonate	4.6
Whiting	2.5
Feldspar (potash)	27.7
Kentucky ball clay #4	25.7
Silica	24.6
Add:	
C.M.C.	1 tsp

SFG-9 **Golden Brown Satin Matt Glaze   Cone 4**
alkaline, semi-opaque, satin matt, nontoxic

Mixing. Mix in the manner of SFG-1.

Application. Apply in the manner of SFG-1.

Firing. Fire in the manner of SFG-1.

Fired Results. This glaze fires to a golden brown satin matt at cone 4. It fires darker if used over dark clay.

Lithium carbonate	9.9
Albany slip	77.6
Tin oxide	12.5
Add:	
C.M.C.	1 tsp

SFG-10

Bright Yellow Transparent Gloss Glaze   Cone 4
alkaline, transparent, yellow gloss, nontoxic

Mixing. Mix in the manner of SFG-1.

Application. Apply in the manner of SFG-1.

Firing. Fire in the manner of SFG-1.

Fired Results. This glaze fires to a clear yellow gloss at cone 4.

Colemanite	52.0
Barnard slip	24.0
Kentucky ball clay #4	24.0
Add:	
C.M.C.	1 tsp

SFG-11

Transparent Satin Matt Glaze   Cone 4
alkaline, transparent, satin matt, nontoxic

Mixing. Mix in the manner of SFG-1.

Application. Apply in the manner of SFG-1.

Firing. Fire in the manner of SFG-1.

Fired Results. This glaze fires to a clear satin matt at cone 4.

Colemanite	52.0
Tennessee ball clay #1	48.0
Add:	
C.M.C	1 tsp

SFG-12

Clear Gloss Glaze   Cone 4
alkaline, transparent, clear gloss, nontoxic

Mixing. Mix in the manner of SFG-1.

Application. Apply in the manner of SFG-1.

Firing. Fire in the manner of SFG-1.

Fired Results. This glaze fires to a clear gloss at cone 4. It is a good base for alkaline colors.

Colemanite	52.0
Albany slip	23.5
Kentucky ball clay #4	24.5
Add:	
C.M.C.	1 tsp

SFG-13

Opaque Crater Glaze   Cone 4
alkaline, opaque, crater surface, nontoxic

Mixing. Mix in the manner of SFG-1.

Application. Apply in the manner of SFG-1.

Firing. Fire in the manner of SFG-1.

Fired Results. This glaze fires to an opaque crater type at cone 4. It is best used over a darker clay body.

Sodium fluosilicate	23.2
Volcanic ash	21.0
Tennessee ball clay #1	56.6
Add:	
C.M.C.	1 tsp

SFG-14

Dry Matt Glaze   Cone 4
alkaline, semi-opaque, dry matt surface, nontoxic

Mixing. Mix in the manner of SFG-1.

Application. Apply in the manner of SFG-1.

Firing. Fire in the manner of SFG-1.

Fired Results. This glaze fires to an opaque dry matt at cone 4.

Sodium fluosilicate	14.0
Whiting	46.0
Add:	
C.M.C.	1 tsp

SFG-15　　**Transparent Gloss Glaze　Cone 6**
alkaline-barium, transparent, gloss, toxic

Mixing. Mix in the manner of SFG-1.

Application. Apply in the manner of SFG-1.

Firing. Fire in the manner of SFG-1.

Fired Results. This glaze fires to a transparent gloss at cone 6. At cone 4 it is a semi-matt which is semitranslucent.

Feldspar (Kona F-4)	46.5
Colemanite	16.4
Barium carbonate	15.5
Silica	11.5
Whiting	7.7
Kaolin (EPK)	2.5
Add:	
C.M.C.	1 tsp

SFG-16　　**Opaque Carmel Semi-Matt Glaze　Cone 6**
alkaline-ash, opaque, semi-matt, nontoxic

Mixing. Mix in the manner of SFG-1.

Application. Apply in the manner of SFG-1.

Firing. Fire in the manner of SFG-1.

Fired Results. This glaze fires to a carmel semi-matt at cone 6.

Barnard clay	44.0
Wood ash	44.0
Lithium carbonate	10.0
Bentonite	2.0
Add:	
C.M.C.	1 tsp

SFG-17　　**Chocolate Brown Semi-Matt Glaze　Cone 6**
alkaline, semi-opaque, semi-matt, nontoxic

Mixing. Mix in the manner of SFG-1.

Application. Apply in the manner of SFG-1.

Firing. Fire in the manner of SFG-1.

Fired Results. This glaze fires to a chocolate brown semi-matt at cone 6.

Albany slip	84.0
Lithium carbonate	11.5
Tin oxide	4.0
Bentonite	1.5
Add:	
C.M.C.	1 tsp

SFG-18　　**Transparent Bright Matt Glaze　Cone 9**
alkaline, transparent, bright matt, nontoxic

Mixing. Mix in the manner of SFG-1.

Application. Apply in the manner of SFG-1.

Firing. Fire in the manner of SFG-1.

Fired Results. This glaze fires to a transparent bright matt at cone 9 oxidation or reduction.

Colemanite	15.5
Lithium carbonate	27.0
Tennessee ball clay #1	56.5
Add:	
C.M.C.	1 tsp

SFG-19　　**Stony Matt Glaze　Cone 9**
alkaline, semi-opaque, stony matt, nontoxic

Mixing. Mix in the manner of SFG-1.

Application. Apply in the manner of SFG-1.

Firing. Fire in the manner of SFG-1.

Fired Results. This glaze fires to a semi-opaque stony matt at cone 9 oxidation or reduction. It can be used as a base for any of the colorants except iron which tends to be rather muddy and unattractive.

Colemanite	19.5
Barium carbonate	18.5
Tennessee ball clay #1	62.0
Add:	
C.M.C.	1 tsp

SFG-20. **Deep Brown Semi-Gloss Glaze   Cone 9**
alkaline, semi-opaque, semi-gloss, nontoxic

Mixing. Mix in the manner of SFG-1.

Application. Apply in the manner of SFG-1.

Firing. Fire in the manner of SFG-1.

Fired Results. This glaze fires to a deep brown semi-gloss which is semi-opaque at cone 9 oxidation or reduction.

Colemanite	22.0
Barnard slip	48.5
Kentucky ball clay #4	29.5
Add:	
C.M.C.	1 tsp

SFG-21 **Stony Matt Glaze   Cone 9–10**
alkaline, semitransparent, stony matt, nontoxic

Mixing. Mix in the manner of SFG-1.

Application. Apply in the manner of SFG-1.

Firing. Fire in the manner of SFG-1.

Fired Results. This glaze fires to a semitransparent stony matt at cone 9 oxidation or reduction. At cone 10 oxidation or reduction it is a smooth stony matt.

Colemanite	11.4
Barium carbonate	34.5
Tennessee ball clay #1	54.1
Add:	
C.M.C.	1 tsp

SFG-22 **Bright Stony Matt Glaze   Cone 9–10**
alkaline, semitransparent, bright stony matt, nontoxic

Mixing. Mix in the manner of SFG-1.

Application. Apply in the manner of SFG-1.

Firing. Fire in the manner of SFG-1.

Fired Results. This glaze fires to a bright stony matt at cone 9 oxidation or reduction. At cone 10 oxidation or reduction it fires to a satin matt glaze.

Colemanite	14.5
Whiting	33.5
Tennessee ball clay #1	52.0
Add:	
C.M.C.	1 tsp

19
WIDE-FIRING-RANGE GLAZES
CONE 06-7

There have been many advances in the science of glaze formulation in the last two decades. And as a result potters have found that it is now possible to compound glazes that are functional and predictable throughout a wide range of firing temperatures. Such glazes can give great flexibility to the potter's work and help to overcome many studio problems in allocating work time and firing. They are also of use in kilns that do not fire evenly.

It has been found through much experimentation that glaze formulas which contain larger amounts of alumina and/or multiple metal compounds will stand a wider range of firing temperatures than the average glaze.

The glazes listed in this chapter have been found to perform well in a wide temperature range and should thus be of great aid to the potter who needs multiple-use glazes.

It is not advised that the potter substitute for any of chemicals listed in the formulas except the frits. Listings of such possible substitutions can be found under individual titles in Chapter 34, Dictionary of Clay and Glaze Compounds.

Note. The glazes in this chapter are labeled toxic or nontoxic. Toxic glazes should be carefully handled both in formulation and in application. During preparation the potter should wear a dust mask to prevent inhalation of toxic materials and not allow these materials to come into prolonged contact with the skin. Frequent washing of the hands when handling these glazes is a wise precaution. Toxic glazes should be applied by brushing and dipping—never spraying. For even under the best conditions some inhalation of the toxic mist from the spray is bound to take place or, equally bad, the mist from the spray gun can settle on the skin and be absorbed into the body system.

FORMULAS FOR WIDE-FIRING-RANGE GLAZES

WFG-1   **Clear Glaze Base   Cone 018–010**
alkaline-lead frit, transparent, clear matt, nontoxic

Mixing. Weigh out the ingredients and wet-grind by hand or ball mill for several minutes until all the material will pass through a 100-mesh screen.

Application. Apply to bisque by brushing, dipping, or spraying to the thickness of 1/16" (1.6 mm). Allow to dry slightly between coats, then dry completely before firing, taking care that the glazed ware does not collect studio dust while stored to dry.

Firing. Fire the ware to the selected temperature range using normal firing procedures.

Fired Results. This glaze fires to a bright matt at cone 018 and to a clear semi-gloss at cone 010. It will fire to a bright gloss at cone 08 but tends to run excessively beyond this point. It is a good color base for the alkaline colorants listed in Chapter 33 on Glaze Colorants.

Hommel frit #259	42.6
Ferro frit #3134	27.5
Lithium carbonate	10.8
Kaolin (EPK)	6.0
Silica	14.0
Add:	
C.M.C.	1 tsp

WFG-2

Clear Matt Glaze   Cone 018–014
alkaline-frit, transparent, matt to clear, nontoxic

Mixing. Mix in the manner of WFG-1.

Application. Apply in the manner of WFG-1.

Firing. Fire in the manner of WFG-1.

Fired Results. This glaze fires to a good clear matt at cone 018 to a clear gloss at cone 014. It can be used as a running glaze at cone 06 for run and mottled effects.

Ferro frit #3819	56.0
Ferro frit #3223	33.8
Lithium carbonate	7.8
Kaolin	2.0
Add:	
C.M.C.	1 tsp

WFG-3

Translucent Semi-Gloss Glaze   Cone 06–1
raw lead, translucent, semi-matt, toxic

Mixing. Mix in the manner of WFG-1.

Application. Apply in the manner of WFG-1.

Firing. Fire in the manner of WFG-1.

Fired Results. This glaze fires to a translucent semi-matt at cone 06 and goes to a gloss at cone 02–1.

White lead	37.0
Feldspar (soda)	18.0
Kaolin (EPK)	17.0
Whiting	9.0
Tin oxide	7.0
Zinc oxide	4.0
Silica	8.0
Add:	
C.M.C.	1 tsp

WFG-4

Translucent Semi-Gloss Glaze   Cone 06–1
lead-alkaline, translucent, semi-gloss, toxic

Mixing. Mix in the manner of WFG-1.

Application. Apply in the manner of WFG-1.

Firing. Fire in the manner of WFG-1.

Fired Results. This glaze fires to a semi-gloss at cone 06 and ranges to a bright gloss at cone 1. It is an excellent color base.

Silica	30.0
Borax (powdered)	26.0
White lead	15.0
Feldspar (Custer)	8.0
Tin oxide	7.0
Sodium carbonate	8.0
Kaolin (calcined)	3.0
Kaolin (EPK)	3.0
Add:	
C.M.C.	1 tsp

WFG-5

Cream Matt Glaze   Cone 06–1
lead-barium, semi-opaque, matt, toxic

Mixing. Mix in the manner of WFG-1.

Application. Apply in the manner of WFG-1.

Firing. Fire in the manner of WFG-1.

Fired Results. This glaze fires to a cream matt at cone 06 and to a cream semi-gloss at cone 1.

White lead	45.0
Feldspar (soda)	36.0
Barium carbonate	11.0
Silica	4.0
Kaolin	2.0
Zinc oxide	1.0
Add:	
C.M.C.	1 tsp

WFG-6

Transparent Matt Glaze   Cone 1–6
alkaline, transparent, matt, nontoxic

Mixing. Mix in the manner of WFG-1.

Application. Apply in the manner of WFG-1.

Firing. Fire in the manner of WFG-1.

Fired Results. This glaze fires to a transparent matt glaze at cone 1–4 and ranges to a clear semi-matt at cone 5–6.

Whiting	20.0
Lithium carbonate	4.5
Ferro frit #3293	17.2
Kaolin	15.2
Kaolin (calcined)	18.5
Silica	24.6
Add:	
C.M.C.	1 tsp

WFG-7 **Transparent Matt Glaze Cone 1–6**
alkaline-frit, transparent, matt, nontoxic

Mixing. Mix in the manner of WFG-1.

Application. Apply in the manner of WFG-1.

Firing. Fire in the manner of WFG-1.

Fired Results. This glaze fires to a transparent matt at cone 1–4 and becomes a clear semi-gloss at cone 6.

Whiting	13.7
Lithium carbonate	6.0
Ferro frit #3293	22.0
Kaolin	13.9
Kaolin (calcined)	10.0
Silica	34.4
Add:	
C.M.C.	1 tsp

WFG-8 **Transparent Matt Glaze Cone 1–6**
alkaline-frit, transparent, matt, nontoxic

Mixing. Mix in the manner of WFG-1.

Application. Apply in the manner of WFG-1.

Firing. Fire in the manner of WFG-1.

Fired Results. This glaze fires to a transparent matt at cone 1–6. It is an excellent color base.

Whiting	28.6
Lithium carbonate	5.7
Ferro frit #3293	21.8
Kaolin	19.6
Silica	24.3
Add:	
C.M.C.	1 tsp

WFG-9 **Transparent Matt Glaze Cone 1–6**
alkaline-frit, transparent, matt, nontoxic

Mixing. Mix in the manner of WFG-1.

Application. Apply in the manner of WFG-1.

Firing. Fire in the manner of WFG-1.

Fired Results. This glaze fires to a transparent matt at cone 1–4 and ranges to a clear satin matt at cone 5–6.

Whiting	18.8
Lithium carbonate	4.1
Ferro frit #3293	12.2
Kaolin	12.7
Kaolin (calcined)	12.7
Silica	41.5
Add:	
C.M.C.	

WFG-10 **Transparent Matt Glaze Cone 1–6**
barium, transparent, matt, toxic

Mixing. Mix in the manner of WFG-1.

Application. Apply in the manner of WFG-1.

Firing. Fire in the manner of WFG-1.

Fired Results. This glaze fires transparent at cone 1–6.

Amblygonite	26.5
Feldspar (Custer)	17.5
Ferro frit #3223	20.9
Dolomite	5.9
Barium carbonate	6.5
Whiting	4.7
Zinc oxide	2.6
Silica	15.4
Add:	
C.M.C.	1 tsp

WFG-11 **Clear Semi-Gloss Cone 3–7**
barium, clear, semi-gloss, toxic

Mixing. Mix in the manner of WFG-1.

Application. Apply in the manner of WFG-1.

Firing. Fire in the manner of WFG-1.

Fired Results. This glaze fires to a clear semi-gloss at cone 3–7.

Feldspar (Custer)	57.5
Silica	18.0
Kaolin	8.0
Zinc oxide	6.0
Whiting	4.5
Barium carbonate	6.0
Add:	
C.M.C.	1 tsp

WFG-12 **Clear Semi-Matt Glaze   Cone 3–7**
leadless, clear, semi-matt, nontoxic

Mixing. Mix in the manner of WFG-1.

Application. Apply in the manner of WFG-1.

Firing. Fire in the manner of WFG-1.

Fired Results. This glaze fires to a clear semi-matt at cone 3–5 and a satin matt at cone 6–7. This is an excellent glaze for utility ware.

Feldspar (Custer)	57.0
Silica	12.5
Whiting	11.5
Kaolin	11.0
Zinc oxide	6.0
Add:	
C.M.C.	1 tsp

WFG-13 **Satin Matt Glaze   Cone 01–9**
leadless, translucent, matt, slightly toxic

Mixing. Mix in the manner of WFG-1.

Application. Apply in the manner of WFG-1.

Firing. Fire in the manner of WFG-1.

Fired Results. This glaze fires to satin matt at cone 01, translucent at cone 4–6, and transparent at cone 9, oxidation or reduction. It is a good color base for any of the colorants listed in Chapter 33 on Glaze Colorants.

Zinc oxide (calcined)	9.8
Feldspar (Custer)	50.0
Whiting	10.0
Kaolin (EPK)	17.6
Silica	13.6
Add:	
Bentonite	2.0
C.M.C.	1 tsp

WFG-14 **Matt Glaze   Cone 1–9**
leadless, transparent, matt, slightly toxic

Mixing. Mix in the manner of WFG-1.

Application. Apply in the manner of WFG-1.

Firing. Fire in the manner of WFG-1.

Fired Results. This is a matt glaze at cone 1. At cone 4–6 it becomes translucent and transparent at cone 9. It like WFG-13 is also an excellent color base glaze. And as it is leadless it is good for utility ware.

Zinc oxide (calcined)	6.0
Feldspar (Kingman)	58.1
Whiting	9.0
Kaolin (EPK)	14.8
Silica	12.1
Add:	
Bentonite	2.0
C.M.C.	1 tsp

WFG-15 **Opaque Matt Glaze   Cone 1–9**
leadless, opaque, matt, slightly toxic

Mixing. Mix in the manner of WFG-1.

Application. Apply in the manner of WFG-1.

Firing. Fire in the manner of WFG-1.

Fired Results. This glaze fires to an opaque matt at cone 1, translucent at cone 6–8, and clear at cone 9. It is a good color base for the cobalt colorants.

Zinc oxide (calcined)	8.0
Feldspar (Custer)	56.3
Whiting	8.3
Kaolin (EPK)	16.2
Silica	11.2
Add:	
Bentonite	2.0
C.M.C.	1 tsp

WFG-16 **Matt Glaze   Cone 4–9**
leadless, translucent, matt, slightly toxic

Mixing. Mix in the manner of WFG-1.

Application. Apply in the manner of WFG-1.

Firing. Fire in the manner of WFG-1.

Fired Results. This glaze fires to a translucent matt at cone 4–6 and increasingly more clear up to cone 9.

Zinc oxide (calcined)	7.8
Feldspar (Custer)	59.4
Whiting	7.8
Kaolin (EPK)	13.5
Silica	11.5
Add:	
Bentonite	2.0
C.M.C.	1 tsp

WFG-17

Satin Matt Glaze   Cone 4–9
barium, opaque, matt, toxic

Mixing. Mix in the manner of WFG-1.

Application. Apply in the manner of WFG-1.

Firing. Fire in the manner of WFG-1.

Fired Results. This glaze fires to a satin matt at cone 4–9. It is a good color base for copper or cobalt colorants.

Zinc oxide (calcined)	6.6
Barium carbonate	22.0
Feldspar (Custer)	48.2
Whiting	8.8
Kaolin (EPK)	5.7
Silica	8.7
Add:	
Bentonite	2.0
C.M.C.	1 tsp

WFG-18

Translucent Semi-Gloss Glaze   Cone 6–9
leadless, translucent, semi-gloss, nontoxic

Mixing. Mix in the manner of WFG-1.

Application. Apply in the manner of WFG-1.

Firing. Fire in the manner of WFG-1.

Fired Results. This glaze fires to a translucent semi-gloss at cone 6 and a transparent gloss at cone 9. When used over white bodies it is slightly yellow.

Zinc oxide (calcined)	9.5
Volcanic ash	80.6
Whiting	9.9
Add:	
Bentonite	2.0
C.M.C.	1 tsp

20
CUP AND SPOON MEASURE GLAZES
CONE 014-6

When the beginning potter starts to formulate his own glazes he will readily discover that some expensive equipment for weighing and measuring the ingredients can be involved. If such equipment is not available the potter can use ordinary kitchen utensils at first.

MATERIALS NEEDED

For this simple type of glaze formulation the following equipment is needed: a set of measuring cups including a full cup, half-cup, third-cup, and a quarter-cup, and a set of measuring spoons including a tablespoon, teaspoon, half-teaspoon, and a quarter-teaspoon. These utensils should be of the dry-measure type that can be scraped level at the top for more accurate measuring.

MEASURING

The measuring process begins by sifting the powdered ingredients through a kitchen sifter or through a 20-mesh screen. This action will fluff up those chemicals which have a tendency to become packed and will make the measuring

by volume more accurate. When filling the cups or spoons take care not to pack the ingredients but fill them gently above the top of the measure. Then carefully scrape a straightedged stick or ruler across the top of the measuring utensil to remove the excess chemical. This operation is simpler and less wasteful if the potter works over a paper, using a different piece for each chemical so that the excess can be returned to its container thus eliminating waste.

CONCLUSION

The glazes given in this chapter range in firing temperature from cone 014–6. But due to the fact that the measuring is less accurate, they can range one cone in either direction. Each glaze formula makes approximately 1 lb. (.45 kg) of dry glaze or about 1 quart (.95 liter) of liquid glaze of the brushing type.

The reader will find listings of possible chemical substitutions in Chapter 34, Dictionary of Clay and Glaze Compounds, under each individual chemical.

Note. The glazes in this chapter are labeled toxic or nontoxic. Toxic glazes should be carefully handled both in formulation and in application. When calculating percentages for adding colorants, it would be approximately accurate to assume that one tablespoon equals 1%. The proportions of ingredients are given here in abbreviated form: C = cup, T = tablespoon, and t = teaspoon.

FORMULAS FOR CUP AND SPOON MEASURE GLAZES

CSMG-1   **Clear Semi-Gloss Glaze   Cone 014–010**
alkaline, transparent, semi-gloss, nontoxic

Mixing. Measure out the ingredients and mix them by one of the methods outlined in Chapter 17 under Glaze Preparation.

Application. Apply to bisque by brushing, dipping, or spraying. Allow each coat to dry slightly between applications before adding the next coat of glaze. Then store the glazed ware in a dust-free place to dry before firing.

Firing. Fire the ware to the selected temperature range using normal procedures.

Fired Results. This glaze fires to a clear bright gloss at cone 014–010. It is a good base for any of the alkaline colorants.

Pemco frit #25	¾ C + 2 T + ¼ t
Hommel frit #14	¾ C + ¼ t
Lithium carbonate	⅓ C + ¾ t
Silica	3 T + 2¾ t
Bentonite	1 t
C.M.C. (liquid)	1 t

CSMG-2 **Clear Gloss Glaze   Cone 014–012**
alkaline-frit, transparent, gloss, nontoxic

Mixing. Mix in the manner of CSMG-1.

Application. Apply in the manner of CSMG-1.

Firing. Fire in the manner of CSMG-1.

Fired Results. This glaze fires to a clear gloss at cone
014–012. It is a good base for the alkaline colorants.
It is not recommended for utility ware as it tends to
craze.

Pemco frit #25	2¼ C + 1 T
Pemco frit #54	½ C + ¾ t
Lithium carbonate	3 T + 3 t
Bentonite	1 T
C.M.C. (liquid)	1 t

CSMG-3. **Opaque Gloss Glaze   Cone 012–010**
alkaline-barium, opaque, gloss, toxic

Mixing. Mix in the manner of CSMG-1.

Application. Apply in the manner of CSMG-1.

Firing. Fire in the manner of CSMG-1.

Fired Results. This glaze fires to an opaque gloss at
cone 012–010. Use the usual alkaline colorants. It is
not recommended for utility ware.

Lithium carbonate	¼ C + 2 T + ½ t
Pemco frit #25	1½ C 1 T + ¼ t
Kaolin (EPK)	4 T + ¼ t
Barium carbonate	¼ C + 2 T + ½ t
Silica	2 T + ¼ t
Bentonite	1 T
C.M.C. (liquid)	1 t

CSMG-4 **Bright Matt Glaze   Cone 010**
alkaline, transparent, matt, nontoxic

Mixing. Mix in the manner of CSMG-1.

Application. Apply in the manner of CSMG-1.

Firing. Fire in the manner of CSMG-1.

Fired Results. This glaze fires to a bright matt at cone
010. It is a particularly good base for the copper
colorants.

Colemanite	1¾ C + 1½ t
Lithium carbonate	1 T + 1¼ t
Kaolin	¼ C + 2 T
Silica	½ C + ⅓ C + 2 t
Bentonite	1 T
C.M.C. (liquid)	1 t

CSMG-5 **Transparent Semi-Gloss Glaze   Cone 010**
alkaline-frit, transparent, semi-gloss, nontoxic

Mixing. Mix in the manner of CSMG-1.

Application. Apply in the manner of CSMG-1.

Firing. Fire in the manner of CSMG-1.

Fired Results. This glaze fires to a bright clear semi-gloss
glaze at cone 010. This is an especially good base for the
copper colorants.

Ferro frit #3134	1¼ C + 1¾ t
Nepheline syenite	½ C + ⅓ C + 1 T
Whiting	¼ C + 3 T
Kaolin	1 T + ¼ t
Bentonite	1 T
C.M.C. (liquid)	1 t

CSMG-6. **Transparent Patterned Gloss Glaze   Cone 08**
colemanite, transparent, patterned gloss, nontoxic

Mixing. Mix in the manner of CSMG-1.

Application. Apply in the manner of CSMG-1.

Firing. Fire in the manner of CSMG-1.

Fired Results. This glaze fires to a bright patterned
semi-gloss at cone 08. This glaze is a good base for copper
and cobalt colorants.

Colemanite	1½ C + ⅓ C + 2 T
Kaolin (EPK)	½ C + 2¼ t
Silica	⅓ C + 1½ t
Bentonite	1 T
C.M.C. (liquid)	1 t

CSMG-7. **Transparent Gloss Glaze   Cone 06**
colemanite-frit, transparent, gloss, nontoxic

Mixing. Mix in the manner of CSMG-1.

Application. Apply in the manner of CSMG-1.

Firing. Fire in the manner of CSMG-1.

Fired Results. This glaze fires to a clear gloss at cone 06. It is a good base for copper and cobalt colorants.

Colemanite	½ C + ⅓ C + 1 t
Pemco frit #25	1 C + 2 T + ¼ t
Kaolin (EPK)	1½ C + 1 T + ½ t
Bentonite	1 T
C.M.C. (liquid)	1 t

CSMG-8 **Transparent Gloss Glaze   Cone 04**
alkaline-frit, transparent, gloss, nontoxic

Mixing. Mix in the manner of CSMG-1.

Application. Apply in the manner of CSMG-1.

Firing. Fire in the manner of CSMG-1.

Fired Results. This glaze fires to a transparent gloss at cone 04. It is a good base for any of the alkaline colorants.

Nepheline syenite	1 C + 2 T + 1½ t
Pemco frit #54	2½ C + 2 T + 2 t
Whiting	1 T + 1 t
Bentonite	1 T
C.M.C. (liquid)	1 t

CSMG-9 **Dry Matt Glaze   Cone 1**
alkaline-barium, semi-opaque, dry matt, toxic

Mixing. Mix in the manner of CSMG-1.

Application. Apply in the manner of CSMG-1.

Firing. Fire in the manner of CSMG-1.

Fired Results. This glaze fires to a dry matt at cone 1. It is a good base for the copper and cobalt colorants.

Ferro frit #3134	¾ C + 1½ T + 1 t
Colemanite	⅓ C
Whiting	3 t
Barium carbonate	¼ C + 2¼ t
Kaolin (EPK)	⅓ C + 2 T + 1¼ t
Silica	⅓ C + 1 T
Bentonite	1 T
C.M.C. (liquid)	1 t

CSMG-10 **Satin Matt Glaze   Cone 1**
alkaline-barium, semi-opaque, satin matt, toxic

Mixing. Mix in the manner of CSMG-1.

Application. Apply in the manner of CSMG-1.

Firing. Fire in the manner of CSMG-1.

Fired Results. This glaze fires to a satin matt at cone 1. It produces good turquoise and blues with copper and cobalt colorants respectively.

Nepheline syenite	1 C + 3 T + 1½ t
Lithium carbonate	3 T + 1 t
Barium carbonate	¼ C + 1 T + 1 t
Whiting	¼ C + 1¾ t
Zinc oxide	¼ C
Tin oxide	2 T
Silica	⅓ C + 2 T + ½ t
Bentonite	1 T
C.M.C. (liquid)	1 t

CSMG-11 **Transparent Semi-Gloss Glaze   Cone 1**
alkaline-frit, transparent, semi-gloss, nontoxic

Mixing. Mix in the manner of CSMG-1.

Application. Apply in the manner of CSMG-1.

Firing. Fire in the manner of CSMG-1.

Fired Results. This glaze fires to a transparent gloss at cone 1. This is a good glaze for utility ware.

Nepheline syenite	1¾ C + 2 T + 1 t
Pemco frit #54	1¼ C + 1 t
Whiting	½ C
Silica	1 T
Bentonite	1 T
C.M.C. (liquid)	1 t

CSMG-12 **Satin Matt Glaze   Cone 4**
alkaline, translucent, satin matt, slightly toxic

Mixing. Mix in the manner of CSMG-1.

Application. Apply in the manner of CSMG-1.

Firing. Fire in the manner of CSMG-1.

Fired Results. This glaze fires to a satin matt at cone 4.
It is a good glaze for utility ware.

Zinc oxide	½ C + 2 T
Whiting	2 T + ¼ t
Lithium carbonate	¼ C + 1 t
Kaolin (EPK)	⅓ C + 2 T
Tin oxide	2 T
Titanium oxide	⅓ C + 1 t
Silica	1 T
Bentonite	1 T
C.M.C. (liquid)	1 t

CSMG-13 **Semi-Opaque Matt Glaze   Cone 4**
leadless, semi-opaque, matt, nontoxic

Mixing. Mix in the manner of CSMG-1.

Application. Apply in the manner of CSMG-1.

Firing. Fire in the manner of CSMG-1.

Fired Results. This glaze fires to a semi-opaque matt at
cone 4. It is a good colorant base.

Feldspar (Custer)	1¼ C + 1¾ t
Zinc oxide	⅓ C + 1 T
Tin oxide	2 T
Whiting	⅓ C + 2 T + ½ t
Kaolin (EPK)	½ C + 2 T + ¾ t
Silica	2 T + 1½ t
Bentonite	1 T
C.M.C. (liquid)	1 t

CSMG-14 **Opaque Matt Glaze   Cone 6**
leadless, opaque, matt, nontoxic

Mixing. Mix in the manner of CSMG-1.

Application. Apply in the manner of CSMG-1.

Firing. Fire in the manner of CSMG-1.

Fired Results. This glaze fires to an opaque matt at
cone 6. It is a good base for most colorants except the
coppers which tend to burn out.

Feldspar (Custer)	
	½ C + ⅓ C + 1 T + 2½ t
Lithium carbonate	3 T + 1½ t
Whiting	¼ C + 2½ t
Kaolin (EPK)	2½ C + ⅓ C + ½ t
Silica	½ C + 2¼ t
Tin oxide	3 T
Zircopax	1 t
Bentonite	2 T
C.M.C. (liquid)	1 t

CSMG-15 **Dry Matt Glaze   Cone 6**
leadless, semi-opaque, dry matt, nontoxic

Mixing. Mix in the manner of CSMG-1.

Application. Apply in the manner of CSMG-1.

Firing. Fire in the manner of CSMG-1.

Fired Results. This glaze fires to a semi-opaque dry matt
at cone 6. It is a good base for most colorants. It is also
a good glaze for utility ware.

Whiting	½ C + 1 T
Feldspar (Custer)	2 t
Lithium carbonate	3 T + 1 t
Kaolin (EPK)	2½ C + ⅓ C + 1 t
Silica	½ C + 3 T + 1 t
Bentonite	1 T
C.M.C. (liquid)	1 t

21
SPECIAL-EFFECT GLAZES

Special-effect glazes can be classified as those which give effects that are extraordinary, due either to their composition or the firing technique used by the potter. This uniqueness may manifest itself in the color, crazing, or textured glaze surface, appearance of crystal formations within the glaze, or broken and mottled color combinations. Listed within this chapter are five categories of such glazes with several glaze formulas given for each category.

The reader will notice that the glaze instructions give the type of glaze, its degree of opacity, its fired natural color without color oxides, and the degree of toxicity in parentheses beside the glaze number. These listings are made to enable the potter to better choose the type of glaze needed and to determine which colorants will work well with the glaze and whether adjustments will have to be made to correct any flaws. In addition, warnings are given of the possible toxic effects of those glazes which do contain poisonous compounds so the potter can take proper precautions in handling and using the glaze. For further information Chapter 34, Dictionary of Clay and Glaze Compounds, can be consulted.

All the glaze formulas in this chapter are given in grams unless otherwise indicated. They will be labeled SEG for Special Effect Glazes, plus the number, to avoid confusion with other glazes in the book.

BREAK-THROUGH GLAZES

I have labeled this category "break-through" because that is exactly what happens to the glaze in the firing process. It is actually a combination of two glazes applied to the ware, one over the other. During firing the base glaze breaks through the top glaze giving a variety of mottled colored effects. Seldom are any two of the fired pieces alike, but the results are always spectacular.

It has been found by much glaze experimentation that any glaze containing the compound Albany slip will bubble and boil due to the volatile gases which are released during the firing. Usually this takes place in the cone 2–5 range. In a normal firing above this range the bubbling will expend itself and the glaze surface will smooth out to give a normal glaze. If a less fluid glaze is placed over the base glaze, however, the bleeding and breaking-through process will reveal its effects in an endless variety of mottled color combinations.

Listed here are several Albany slip glazes and several top glazes which can be used to create these marvelous glaze effects, all of which can be fired in the cone 6 range. The formulas for the base and top glazes which follow can be used as listed or in any combination the potter might wish to try.

One coat of the base glaze will give a moderate boil and break-through effect, while two coats will give a more violent boil which sometimes results in a lacy mottled effect. The results are not always predictable, but they are always unique.

Two coats of the top glaze over one or two coats of the base glaze will give a textured surface along with the mottled color.

I recommend mixing small amounts of these glazes. If the potter finds the glaze is a desirable one, it is always possible to mix more. If the glaze does not fit the needs of the potter or requires some adjustment, there is less waste with the smaller batches of glaze.

The reader will find listings of possible chemical substitutions in Chapter 34, Dictionary of Clay and Glaze Compounds, under each individual chemical.

Note. The glazes in this chapter are labeled toxic or nontoxic. Toxic glazes should be carefully handled both in formulation and in application. During preparation the potter should wear a dust mask to prevent inhalation of toxic materials and not allow these materials to come into prolonged contact with the skin. Frequent washing of the hands when handling these glazes is a wise precaution. Toxic glazes should be applied by brushing and dipping—never spraying. For even under the best conditions some inhalation of the toxic mist from the spray is bound to take place or, equally bad, the mist from the spray gun can settle on the skin and be absorbed into the body system.

SEG-1
SEG-1a

1. Albany Slip Base Glaze   Cone 6
lead, transparent, gloss brown, toxic

1a. Translucent Matt Top Glaze   Cone 6
leadless, semi-opaque, off-white, nontoxic

Mixing. Weigh out the ingredients as indicated in the recipe and place them in a jar. (A pint or quart/half-liter or liter fruit jar can be used for this purpose.) Premix the contents by rotating the jar several times, then add water in the following ratio:

For brushing	1–2 oz. (30–60 ml) per 100 grams of glaze
For dipping	2–3 oz. (60 to 90 ml) per 100 grams of glaze
For spraying	4–6 oz. (120 to 180 ml) per 100 grams of glaze

These measurements are not absolute, so it would be wise for the potter to train himself by sight, feel, and the consistency of the glaze whether it is right for use. For example, a brushing glaze should be about the consistency of ketchup, a dipping glaze about the consistency of cream, and a spraying glaze about the consistency of milk.

Once the water is added, and the jar given a brief shaking to mix the ingredients, add a teaspoon of C.M.C. per 100 grams of glaze by dry measure and shake the jar vigorously until the contents are thoroughly mixed. Sieve the glaze twice through a 60- to 80 mesh screen, using a stiff brush to break up any resistant lumps. Once these steps have been followed, the glaze is ready for use. These glazes keep well in solution for many weeks.

Exercise caution in handling SEG-1, for it contains red lead, a compound which is very toxic. Check the entry on lead compounds in the Dictionary of Clay and Glaze Compounds in Chapter 34 for further information.

Application. Brush, dip, or spray the number of desired coats on cone 06 bisque only—the number depending on the fired results desired (see fired results for possibilities.) Allow the different coatings to dry to the point that the surface loses its moist sheen before applying another coat of glaze. Each coating should be about the thickness of a playing card. Allow the glazed ware to dry completely before firing. The ware should also be protected from dust or air-borne clay particles in the studio.

Caution should be taken if SEG-1 is sprayed, for the vapor should not be breathed into the lungs or allowed to settle on the skin and remain there for any length of time, due to its possible toxic effects. It would also be unwise to use this glaze on the inside of utility ware that would come into contact with foods that might contain any type of acid—even a mild one.

Albany slip	55.4
Red lead	16.2
Cornwall stone	7.1
Silica	8.0
Kaolin	2.9
Whiting	3.2
Zinc oxide	1.3
Manganese dioxide	2.6
Red iron oxide	0.5
Bentonite	2.0
C.M.C.	1 tsp

Nepheline syenite	58.0
Whiting	11.5
Zinc oxide	9.5
Kaolin	19.0
Silica	2.0
Bentonite	2.0
C.M.C.	1 tsp

Fired Results. Fire this glaze to cone 6 oxidation and allow the kiln to cool normally. The possibilities for combinations of these two glazes are listed below.

1. Use one coat of SEG-1 and one coat of SEG-1a for a moderate boil and break-through effect.

2. Use one coat of SEG-1 and two coats of SEG-1a for a glaze surface that will have the appearance of iron spotting characteristic of reduction firing.

3. Use two coats of SEG-1 and one coat of SEG-1a for a more violent boil and break-through effect which often gives a lacy, mottled effect.

4. Use two coats of SEG-1 and two coats of SEG-1a for a slightly textured surface with mottled colors and crater impressions with darker centers.

5. Two coats of SEG-1 and three coats of SEG-1a will give a textured surface that is more on the rustic side than the preceding combination. This combination too will give the mottled color and crater impressions.

6. Use three coats of SEG-1 and three or four coats of SEG-1a for a glaze surface that has fissures and crater impressions. Use this combination over a darker clay for more interesting and dramatic effects.

7. The above combinations can all be used over dark or light clays. The only difference is that lighter shades will result with lighter clays and darker shades with darker clays.

SEG-2
SEG-2a

2. Albany Slip Base Glaze   Cone 6
alkaline, transparent, gloss brown, nontoxic

2a. Translucent Matt Top Glaze   Cone 6
leadless, transparent, clear, nontoxic

Mixing. Weigh out the ingredients and mix these two glazes in the same manner as outlined for glazes SEG-1 and 1a. These two glazes keep well in solution for many weeks.

Application. Brush, dip, or spray the number of desired coats to the ware according to the instructions given for SEG-1 and 1a.

Fired Results. Fire the bisque ware to cone 6 oxidation. Both of these glazes have a tendency to craze with the passage of time. They can be mixed in the same combination as SEG-1 and 1a but the final color will be mottled cordovan brown instead of the darker glossy brown of the previous glaze combination.

Albany slip	75.2
Lithium carbonate	15.8
Kaolin	5.0
Bentonite	2.0
C.M.C.	1 tsp

Volcanic ash	35.0
Whiting	35.0
Silica	25.0
Kaolin	15.0
Bentonite	2.0
C.M.C.	1 tsp

SEG-3
SEG-3a

3. Albany Slip Base Glaze   Cone 6
alkaline, transparent, gloss brown, nontoxic

3a. Satin Matt Top Glaze   Cone 6
alkaline, opaque, off-white, nontoxic

Mixing. Mix these two glazes according to the procedure for SEG-1 and 1a. SEG-3a is an excellent color base and both glazes keep well in solution. For color selections refer to the colorant chart at the end of the Break-Through Glaze section.

Application. Apply these glazes in the same manner as SEG-1 and 1a.

Fired Results. Fire to cone 6 oxidation. These two glazes can be used in the same combinations as SEG-1 and 1a. The colemanite, however, will give a figured pattern to the boil and break-through effect not present in the other combinations.

Albany slip	88.0
Colemanite	8.0
Kaolin	4.0
Bentonite	2.0
C.M.C.	1 tsp

Feldspar (potash)	9.4
Lithium carbonate	2.6
Whiting	15.8
Zinc oxide	16.8
Kaolin	32.4
Silica	23.0
Bentonite	2.0
C.M.C.	1 tsp

SEG-4
SEG-4a

4. Albany Slip Base Glaze   Cone 6
leadless, transparent, mottled gloss brown, nontoxic

4a. Smooth Matt Top Glaze   Cone 6
alkaline, opaque, off-white, nontoxic

Mixing. Use the same procedure as listed for SEG-1 and 1a. SEG-4a is a good base for the colorants listed at the end of this glaze section. Both glazes keep well in solution.

Application. Apply in the same manner as for SEG-1 and 1a.

Fired Results. Fire to cone 6 oxidation. When these two glazes are used in combination, the rutile content of SEG-4 will give a caramel hue to the browns with the boil and break-through effect.

Albany slip	92.0
Titanium dioxide (rutile)	6.0
Kaolin	2.0
Bentonite	2.0
C.M.C.	1 tsp

Lithium carbonate	6.9
Whiting	6.0
Rutile	11.1
Zinc oxide	19.9
Silica	22.6
Bentonite	2.0
C.M.C.	1 tsp

SEG-5
SEG-5a

5. Albany Slip Base Glaze   Cone 6
alkaline, transparent, mottled brown, nontoxic

5a. Off-White Matt Top Glaze   Cone 6
alkaline, transparent, clear, nontoxic

Mixing. Mix in the same manner as SEG-1 and 1a. When mixing SEG-5a, Hommel frit #242, Ferro frit #134, or Pemco frit #54 can be substituted for Hommel frit #14. The colorants listed at the end of the section work well with SEG-5a. Both glazes keep well in solution.

Application. Apply in the same manner as SEG-1 and 1a.

Fired Results. Fire to cone 6 oxidation or reduction. In an oxidation firing the cryolite content will generally produce antique gold hues with the boil and break-through effect. When this combination is used over a clay body with high iron content and fired in a reducing atmosphere, the glaze will iron spot well and the break-through effect will be enhanced even more.

Albany slip	84.0
Cryolite	14.0
Kaolin	2.0
Bentonite	2.0
C.M.C.	1 tsp

Spodumene	56.0
Talc	43.8
Hommel frit #14	2.2
Bentonite	2.0
C.M.C.	1 tsp

Optional Top Glazes

The following glazes can be used as optional top glazes. They are given for the purpose of producing increasingly more rustic glazes. Although they are listed as SEG-5b-5e, they may be used with any of the five Albany slip base glazes given. The effects, however, are more predictable if SEG-5 is used as a base glaze.

SEG-5b.

Waxy Matt Top Glaze   Cone 6
leadless, opaque, off-white, nontoxic

Mixing. Mix in the manner of SEG-1a.

Application. Apply in the manner of SEG-1a.

Fired Results. Fire to cone 6 oxidation. This glaze will produce a mottled surface with alternate areas of gloss brown to waxy matt surface which is off-white to tan in color. If applied more heavily it will give the same colors and surface but the areas of opaque matt will have a flowing drifted effect.

Nepheline syenite	35.4
Magnesium carbonate	17.6
Dolomite	12.9
Kaolin	2.5
Silica	31.6
Whiting	20.0
Bentonite	2.0
C.M.C.	1 tsp

SEG-5c

Smooth Stony Matt Top Glaze   Cone 6
leadless, opaque, off-white, toxic in unfired state

Mixing. Mix in the manner of SEG-1a. Some caution should be taken, however, in handling this glaze due to its barium carbonate content which is toxic in the unfired state.

Application. Apply in the manner of SEG-1a but take precautions against the toxic barium carbonate content.

Fired Results. Fire in the same manner as SEG-5b. This glaze will produce surfaces varying from mottled with alternate flowing areas of smooth browns to a stony matt surface and is off-white to tan in color. If applied heavily it will flow and form ridged surfaces and fissures.

Nepheline syenite	41.7
Whiting	8.1
Zinc oxide	2.9
Magnesium carbonate	3.6
Barium carbonate	13.5
Kaolin (Florida)	4.8
Silica	25.4
Bentonite	2.0
C.M.C.	1 tsp

SEG-5d.

Stony Matt Top Glaze   Cone 6
leadless, opaque, stony white, nontoxic

Mixing. Mix in the same manner as SEG-1a.

Application. Apply in the same manner as SEG-1a.

Fired Results. Fire in the same manner as 5c. The finished colors will be similar to SEG-5c, but the surface will be more ridged, fissured, and rustic.

Bone ash	7.0
Nepheline syenite	24.1
Magnesium carbonate	3.6
Wollastonite	12.0
Kaolin (EPK)	15.2
Whiting	31.6
Tin oxide	5.6
Bentonite	2.0
C.M.C.	1 tsp

SEG-5e.

Dry Stony Matt Top Glaze   Cone 6
leadless, opaque, stony off-white to purple tans, nontoxic

Mixing. Mix in the same manner as SEG-5c.

Application. Apply in the same manner as SEG-5c.

Fired Results. Fire in the same manner as SEG-5c. This glaze will produce an extremely rustic effect of gloss browns with dry stony ridges which are off-white to tan to dull purple in color.

Feldspar (potash)	39.2
Silica	28.0
Whiting	27.5
Kaolin	12.5
Bentonite	2.0
C.M.C.	1 tsp

COLORANTS

When selecting colorants the potter should be aware that every colorant does not behave in the same manner in every type of glaze base. Listed here for the aid of the potter are a few precautions that should be taken when selecting colorants—the potter should also remember that glaze colorant, when given in percentages, should be calculated from the dry body weight of the glaze.

Browns. A variety of brown can be produced in any glaze base if sufficient iron oxide is used.

Barium blues. This is a blue of great depth and richness. It can only be produced in a barium glaze and only with copper carbonate or copper oxide. If copper oxide is used, use half the amount given for the copper carbonate.

Blues. Many hues of this color can be produced in any glaze base with the use of cobalt oxide. The addition of 0.5% to 1% iron oxide will make them more subtle.

Grays. The most pleasing grays for these glazes are produced with iron chromate and iron oxide in any glaze given in this section.

Greens. Chrome oxide will produce green in any base if tin or zinc are not present in large amounts. If tin oxide is present, pink hues may result. If zinc oxide is present, brown hues may result. However, some interesting mottled results can be produced in this manner.

Blue-greens. The combination of copper carbonate, cobalt oxide, and iron oxide will produce nice blue-greens provided tin and zinc are not present in amounts above 5% and 7% respectively.

Tans. Many shades of this color can be produced with iron oxide in any nonlead glaze, or in any type of base if rutile or ilmenite is used as a colorant.

Turquoise. This color can only be produced with copper carbonate or copper oxide and only in an alkaline glaze. If copper oxide is used, add half the amount given for the copper carbonate.

Yellows. Citron, lemon, and primrose yellow can be produced in any of the base glazes and with only subtle differences. Straw yellow, however, can only be produced with iron oxide and only in a lead-base glaze. Some interesting effects can be gained with the straw yellow by sponging a rutile wash over it for limited crystal effects.

CHART OF BREAK-THROUGH GLAZE COLORANTS

Fired Result	Colorant	Percentage
Browns	Iron oxide	5%–10%
Barium blues	Copper carbonate	5%–10%
Light blue	Cobalt oxide	0.5%
Medium blue	Cobalt oxide	1.0%
Dark blue	Cobalt oxide	2.0%
Greens	Chrome oxide	3%–5%
Gray	Iron chromate	3%–5%
	Iron oxide	1.0%
Blue-green	Copper carbonate	10.0%
	Cobalt oxide	1.0%
	Iron oxide	1.0%
Tans	Ilmenite (powdered)	5.0%–10.0%
Golden tans	Rutile	3.0%–7.0%
Speckled tans	Ilmenite (powdered)	5.0%–10.0%
	Ilmenite (granular)	0.5%
Turquoise	Copper carbonate	3.0%–7.0%
Citron yellow	Praseodymium stain	3.0%–7.0%
Lemon yellow	Vanadium stain	3.0%–5.0%
Primose yellow	Naples yellow stain	2.0%–5.0%
Straw yellow	Iron oxide	1.0%–3.0%

Note. The percentages should always be calculated by the dry body weight of the formula.

HIGH-FIRE BOILING GLAZE

A second type of special-effect boiling glaze with a wide firing range cone 018–10 is presented here. Each firing temperature can give exotic though not always predictable results.

The reader will find a list of possible chemical substitutions in Chapter 34, Dictionary of Clay and Glaze Compounds, under each individual chemical.

FORMULA FOR HIGH-FIRE BOILING GLAZE

SEG-6

High-Fire Boiling Glaze   Cone 4–10
lead, alkaline, transparent, clear

White lead	150.0
Feldspar (soda)	32.0
Ferro frit #3134	55.0
Kaolin	44.0
Silica	47.0
Bentonite	2.0
C.M.C.	1 tsp

Mixing. Use the same mixing procedure for this glaze as for glaze SEG-1. Hommel frit #242, Hommel frit #14, or Pemco frit #54 can be substituted for Ferro frit #3134.

Application. This glaze can be applied in the same manner as SEG-1. If, however, it is to be used over a wash or sponged design of colorant oxides, dipping or spraying would be preferable as brushing might tend to destroy or alter the wash or sponged design.

Fired Results. The following are possible variations with this versatile glaze:

1. Use over a wash of rutile and water with a tablespoon of C.M.C. per half-pint (quarter-liter) of wash. The C.M.C. will help set the design or wash so the dipping or spraying will not alter it. Fire to cone 6 oxidation and cool slowly for tan crystalline break-through effects.

2. Use over a wash of Barnard slip for unusual bleed-through effects. Fire to cone 6-8.

3. Use over a darker clay that is heavily grogged for interesting textural bleed-through effects. Fire to cone 4–10.

4. For interesting artificial reduction effects, add 5–10 grams of silicon carbide.

5. Use over lighter clays with grog and fire reduction to cone 10.

6. Use over buff clay for an unusual rust-colored bleed-through effect.

7. Use over an iron oxide engobe or wash. This gives a very beautiful combination of rust, white, and translucent colors. Fire in reduction or artificial reduction to cone 6–10.

8. Use a darker form of this glaze over a lighter clay body which has been textured heavily. Fire to cone 4–10. Each firing range gives a different result and no two pieces are ever quite the same.

9. Add 1 tablespoon of granular ilmenite for spotted effects.

10. Use lighter colors of the glaze over darker clays which have been textured. Fire to cone 4–10. This variation allows the texture and the color of the clay to show through for more rustic effects.

11. Use one of the previously mentioned top glazes in the Break-Through section over the top of a good coating of the boiling glaze. Remember to alternate the colors—light over dark, dark over light. Fire to cone 6. This variation not only gives break-through effects but texture and fissures appear in the surface of the glaze. Fire to cone 6–8.

12. Try all the above experiments except 11 at different temperatures, oxidation or reduction firing, cone 2–10.

CHART OF HIGH-FIRE BOILING GLAZE COLORANTS

Fired Result	Colorant	Percentage
Light blue	Cobalt oxide	2.0%
Medium blue	Cobalt oxide	3.5%
Dark blue	Cobalt oxide	7.5%
Gray	Iron chromate	10.0%
	Iron oxide	3.0%
Blue-green	Copper carbonate	10.8%
	Cobalt oxide	1.0%
	Iron oxide	1.2%
Opaque	Tin oxide	30.0%
Rust	Iron oxide	13.9%
Golden tans	Rutile	10.0%–15.0%
Gray tans	Iron oxide	5.0%
	Iron chromate	2.0%
Rusty tans	Iron oxide	8.0%
	Ilmenite (powdered)	4.0%
Speckled tans	Ilmenite (powdered)	10.0%
	Ilmenite (granular)	5.0%
Turquoise	Copper carbonate	8.0%
Translucent	Tin oxide	15.0%

Note. The percentages should always be calculated by the dry body weight of the formula.

CRACKLE GLAZE EFFECTS

An effective but simple method of obtaining unusual effects is through the use of a crackle glaze. This type of glaze cannot be characterized by its composition but rather by its effect, due to the fact that the crackling is merely the result of tension developing in the fired piece when the glaze and body expand and contract at different rates during the firing and cooling process. Although this type of glaze has often been considered defective, it can be a very beautiful and subtle way of decorating pottery, particularly as there are many color possibilities available.

Crackle glazes can be made to form large or fine crackle patterns depending on the composition of the glaze or on the body to which it is applied. If one uses a clay body which has lower or higher expansion rate than the glaze, the crackle effect can be promoted to a much higher degree. To emphasize the crackle patterns in the glaze, the pottery can be rubbed with dark colorants such as tea, coffee, ink, or coloring oxides. If one wishes to emphasize a larger crackle pattern the ware should be rubbed with colorant soon after the firing. If smaller crackle patterns are to be emphasized the piece can be allowed to set for a week or so then rubbed, the reason being that more and more crackles tend to appear as time passes due to the tensions in the piece. Strong crackle patterns can even be produced artificially by throwing the hot pottery into a bucket of very cold water. This can

be done when the pottery is about 200° to 300° F./94° to 149°C., but this should never be attempted if the temperature of the ware is higher than this or the entire piece might crack.

It should be pointed out, however, that crackle glazes are mainly decorative and should not be used on practical ware which is to come into contact with food or drink. From a sanitary standpoint, dishes, cups, or casseroles should not be glazed with crackle glazes. They can, of course, be used on the outside of such pieces, provided they are glazed on the inside with a practical, noncrackle glaze. The reason for this precaution is that bacteria tend to find their way into the crackles and out again into the food or drink, giving rise to the possibility of food poisoning.

Listed here for the use of the potter who wants to experiment are several glazes of the crackle type in a wide range of firing temperatures. Also listed are four clay body types which can be used to promote better crackle patterns. To avoid confusion with other clay bodies in the book, they will be labeled SE, for Special Effects. They should not be used with glazes where crackling of the glaze is not desired.

The reader will find possible substitutions for many of the glaze chemicals used in these glazes in Chapter 34, Dictionary of Clay and Glaze Compounds.

FORMULAS FOR CRACKLE GLAZE CLAY BODIES

SECB-1   Crackle Glaze Clay Body   Cone 08–06

Mixing. The formulas as stated will make only small batches of clay. For larger amounts, the formula should probably be multiplied by 10 or 20. All four of these clay bodies should be mixed thoroughly, either by hand or pug mill, wedged thoroughly, and allowed to age for at least two weeks. Chapter 3 on Clay Body Preparation or Chapter 2 on Native Clays can be consulted for further information on the aging of clay. Tennessee ball clay #5 can be substituted for Kentucky ball clay #4 if necessary.

Kentucky ball clay #4	56.5
Talc	35.0
Colemanite	4.5
Bentonite	2.0

Forming Techniques. These clay bodies are good for slab or wheel forming. With the addition of 10% grog they can be used for sculptured pieces.

Fired Results. Allow the pieces to dry completely before firing the bisque to cone 06. Never use these clays for glazing in the greenware state for they tend to pinhole on greenware. Fire to cone 010–06. Cool slowly from the maturing point at cone 06 to 100°F./38°C. to avoid dunting or cracking. This body fires to a pure white bisque.

SECB-2 **Crackle Glaze Clay Body   Cone 06–02**

Mixing. Mix in the manner of SECB-1.

Forming Techniques. Use the techniques given for SECB-1.

Fired Results. Fire to cone 06–02 and cool in the manner of SECB-1. This body fires to a pure white.

Kentucky ball clay #4	60.0
Talc	35.0
Colemanite	3.0
Bentonite	2.0

SECB-3 **Crackle Glaze Clay Body   Cone 02–06**

Mixing. Mix in the manner of SECB-1.

Forming Techniques. Use the techniques given for SECB-1.

Fired Results. Fire to cone 02–6. Cool in the manner of SECB-1. This body fires to a pure white.

Kentucky ball clay #4	58.0
Talc	39.5
Bentonite	2.0

SECB-4 **Crackle Glaze Clay Body   Cone 6–8**

Mixing. Mix in the manner of SECB-1.

Forming Techniques. Use the techniques given for SECB-1.

Fired Results. Fire to cone 6–8 and cool more carefully than the other SECB bodies. This body fires to a creamy off-white bisque.

Kentucky ball clay #4	70.0
Talc	20.0
Kaolin	2.0
Bentonite	2.0
Fine grog or sand	6.0

FORMULAS FOR CRACKLE GLAZES

SEG-7 **Crackle Glaze   Cone 015**
alkaline, transparent, clear, nontoxic

Mixing. Weigh out and mix this glaze in the same manner as directed for SEG-1 at the beginning of the chapter. When mixing this glaze, Ferro frit #3259, Hommel frit #259 or #25, or Pemco frit #25 can be substituted for Ferro frit #3134. This is a nontoxic glaze which stores exceptionally well.

Application. Brush, dip, or spray until the final glaze coating reaches the thickness of a dime. Usually two to three coatings will suffice. Allow the coatings to dry moderately between applications.

Fired Results. Fire SEG-7 to cone 015 oxidation. If not overfired it will produce a high gloss glaze with a fine mesh of crackles. It is an excellent color base for the colorants listed at the end of the crackle glaze section.

Ferro frit #3293	40.0
Ferro frit #3819	38.3
Ferro frit #3134	21.7
Bentonite	2.0
C.M.C.	1 tsp

SEG-8 **Crackle Glaze   Cone 012**
alkaline-barium, transparent, clear, toxic

Mixing. Weigh out and mix as with the previous glaze, SEG-7. However, as barium carbonate sometimes has a tendency to lump in solution, it would be best to grind this glaze wet in a mortar or ball mill and use it within a week of mixing. If it is to be used after sitting for a long period, it should be reground and sieved carefully through a 60- to 80-mesh screen. Better still, mix only the amount with water and C.M.C. that you anticipate

Ferro frit #3819	57.3
Whiting	7.0
Barium carbonate	12.7
Silica	23.0
Bentonite	2.0
C.M.C.	1 tsp

using. For possible frit substitutions, see the mixing instructions for SEG-7. Handle this glaze with caution—barium carbonate is toxic if breathed or taken internally. It should not be allowed to settle on the skin for any length of time.

Application. Apply SEG-8 in the same manner as SEG-7. Use over a white body unless the glaze is to be made opaque.

Fired Results. Fire to cone 012 oxidation for a brilliant gloss surface. Do not overfire as this glaze tends to oxidize badly producing a scumlike formation on the surface.

SEG-9

Crackle Glaze   Cone 08
raw alkaline, transparent, clear, nontoxic

Mixing. This is a raw alkaline glaze and such glazes tend to lump if allowed to set in solution for more than a week. Therefore only the amount needed should be weighed out and mixed at one time. An addition of a tablespoon of alcohol per 100 grams of glaze will help to retard the lumping somewhat, but it is still better to mix this glaze, grind it well in a mortar or ball mill, and use it within a few days.

Application. Apply in the same manner as SEG-7. Use only over white clay unless the glaze is to be translucent or opaque.

Fired Results. Fire this glaze to cone 08. The fired results are similar to SEG-8; the main difference being that SEG-9 is less expensive to make. This glaze is nontoxic. It produces a medium crackle effect.

Soda ash	63.0
Whiting	20.0
Feldspar (potash)	110.0
Silica	25.0
Bentonite	2.0
C.M.C.	1 tsp

SEG-10

Crackle Glaze   Cone 06
alkaline-barium, semitransparent, clear to milky, toxic

Mixing. Mix this glaze in the same manner as SEG-7 but do not substitute different frits for those listed. Caution: this glaze contains barium carbonate.

Application. Apply in the same manner as SEG-7 to white clay bodies only, unless the glaze is to be opaque.

Fired Results. Fire to cone 06 oxidation. This glaze matures to a brilliant surface with larger crackle patterns. It makes an excellent base for the colorants at the end of this section. Do not overfire or oxidizing will take place in the form of a white scum on the surface of the piece. This can be removed with vinegar and salt but it always seems to return with the passage of time.

Hommel frit #259	43.9
Zinc oxide	3.0
Barium carbonate	43.0
Silica	33.0
Bentonite	4.0
C.M.C.	1 tsp

SEG-11.

Crackle Glaze   Cone 06
alkaline-barium, transparent, clear, nontoxic

Mixing. Mix in the manner of SEG-7. This glaze keeps well in solution for about a month.

Application. Apply in the same manner as SEG-7 to a white body.

Fired Results. Fire this glaze to cone 06. It produces a semi-gloss surface with medium to large crackle patterns.

Pemco frit #25	47.0
Lithium carbonate	8.0
Wollastonite	22.0
Kaolin	21.0
Silica	2.0
Bentonite	2.0
C.M.C.	1 tsp

SEG-12   **Crackle Glaze   Cone 04**
alkaline-barium, transparent, clear to milky, toxic

Feldspar (potash)	102.0
Colemanite	123.3
Barium carbonate	43.0
Silica	33.0
Bentonite	4.0
C.M.C.	1 tsp

Mixing. Due to the barium carbonate content as well as the colemanite this glaze should be mixed dry and only the amount needed at the time should be mixed with water. Add the C.M.C. after the water. The potter will notice that this glaze recipe is not based on the usual 100 gram batch. Therefore the colorants added to this glaze should be double the amount listed for the 100 gram batches. Caution: this glaze is toxic due to its barium content.

Application. Apply this glaze in the same manner as SEG-7. Use only over a white body unless the glaze is to be opaque.

Fired Results. Fire to cone 04 oxidation for a brilliant gloss surface with a fine mesh of crackles. This glaze makes an excellent base for the turquoise and blue colorants provided it is not overfired.

SEG-13   **Crackle Glaze   Cone 04**
lead-barium-alkaline, transparent, clear, toxic

White lead	26.0
Barium carbonate	11.0
Zinc oxide	3.0
Colemanite	84.0
Feldspar (potash)	60.0
Kaolin	10.0
Silica	75.0
Bentonite	4.0
C.M.C.	1 tsp

Mixing. Mix and grind this glaze in dry form and add the water and C.M.C. to only the amount needed. Handle this glaze carefully because it contains two toxic compounds, white lead and barium carbonate. This glaze is at its best when used as a base for the turquoise and blue colorants.

Application. Apply in the same manner as SEG-7. When using the turquoise colorants, use only over a white body—SEC-2 is best for this glaze.

Fired Results. Fire to cone 04 oxidation. This glaze will give a semi-gloss surface with fine to medium crackles. Due to the mixed base the colors will be unique.

SEG-14   **Crackle Glaze   Cone 04–02**
raw alkaline, transparent, clear to milky, nontoxic

Borax	105.0
Feldspar (potash)	60.0
Whiting	25.0
Kaolin	10.0
Silica	76.0
Zinc oxide	25.0
Bentonite	5.0
C.M.C.	1 tsp

Mixing. This, like SEG-9, is a raw alkaline glaze so grind it dry after mixing and use immediately to prevent lumping, or mix with water only the amount you plan to use. Double colorants.

Application. Apply in the manner as SEG-7. For transparents or translucents use a white body for best results.

Fired Results. Fire to cone 04–02. This glaze gives a semi-gloss surface with medium crackles. It is best used as a base for the Egyptian blue, Persian blue, or Indian turquoise colorants listed at the end of the section. If these colorants are used, they should not be made opaque but left transparent or slightly translucent and used only over a white body. This glaze is nontoxic.

SEG-15.   **Crackle Glaze   Cone 02**
alkaline-boro-silicate, transparent, clear to milky,
nontoxic

Ferro frit #3134	13.0
Pemco frit #25	42.0
Colemanite	17.7
Kaolin	11.5
Silica	15.8
Bentonite	2.0
C.M.C.	1 tsp

Mixing. This glaze should be mixed in the same manner
as SEG-7. That glaze can also be consulted for possible
frit substitutions. This glaze stores quite well in solution.

Application. Apply this glaze in the same manner as
SEG-7.

Fired Results. Fire to cone 02. This glaze matures to a
brilliant gloss surface with small crackles. It makes an
excellent base for all the colorants listed at the end of
the section. Use only over a white body unless the glaze
is to be made opaque.

SEG-16   **Crackle Glaze   Cone 4**
alkaline, transparent, clear, nontoxic

Hommel frit #259	52.4
Whiting	8.0
Kaolin	3.6
Kaolin (calcined)	3.0
Silica	33.0
Bentonite	2.0
C.M.C.	1 tsp

Mixing. This glaze should be mixed in the same manner
as SEG-7. Also see that glaze for possible frit substitutions. This glaze keeps well in solution and is not subject
to lumping. It also makes a good base for opaque glazes
of any color.

Application. Apply in the same manner as SEG-7 and
use only over a white body unless the glaze is to be
opaque.

Fired Results. Fire this glaze to cone 4 for a gloss surface with larger crackles. It makes an excellent base for
the earth colors provided they are opaque, in which case
it can be used over darker-colored clays to give more
subtle hues to the final finish.

SEG-17   **Crackle Glaze   Cone 4–6**
alkaline, semitransparent, clear to milky, nontoxic

Lithium carbonate	25.0
Colemanite	25.0
Zinc oxide (calcined)	5.0
Calcium fluoride	5.0
Silica	25.0
Bentonite	2.0
C.M.C.	1 tsp

Mixing. Mix this glaze in the same manner as SEG-7.
The potter should probably mix only small amounts of
this glaze as it tends to age badly, giving a very blistered
surface after about a week in solution.

Application. Apply in the same manner as SEG-7.

Fired Results. Fire this glaze cone 4–6 oxidation for
a semi-gloss surface with beautiful medium crackle
patterns.

SEG-18 **Crackle Glaze   Cone 6**
alkaline, transparent, clear, nontoxic

Volcanic ash	52.5
Ferro frit #3134	28.0
Kaolin	5.3
Kaolin (calcined)	4.0
Bentonite	2.0
C.M.C.	1 tsp

Mixing. Mix in the same manner as SEG-7 and refer to that glaze for possible frit substitutions. If the volcanic ash tends to be lumpy in solution the glaze should probably be ground wet. This glaze is better used as a color base than used alone.

Application. Apply in the same manner as SEG-7. It can be applied over darker clays with good results if the glaze is opaque. Glaze the pieces less heavily at the base for this glaze tends to be rather fluid.

Fired Results. Fire to cone 6 oxidation for a brilliant glossy surface with fine crackles. Stilt the piece carefully in the kiln as this glaze tends to be rather fluid at maturity.

SEG-19 **Crackle Glaze   Cone 8**
alkaline, transparent, clear, nontoxic

Lepidolite	60.0
Feldspar (potash)	140.0
Cryolite	20.0
Bone ash	20.0
Whiting	40.0
Colemanite	40.0
Bentonite	6.0
C.M.C.	1 tsp

Mixing. Mix this glaze in the same manner as SEG-7. It keeps well in solution for many weeks without lumping.

Application. Apply in the same manner as SEG-7.

Fired Results. Fire to cone 8 oxidation for a semi-gloss surface with large crackle patterns reminiscent of the "Crab's Claw" patterns produced by the ancient Chinese potters.

SEG-20 **Crackle Glaze   Cone 8**
alkaline, transparent, clear, nontoxic

Pemco frit #25	15.1
Nepheline syenite	73.1
Whiting	8.0
Kaolin (EPK)	3.8
Bentonite	2.0
C.M.C.	1 tsp

Mixing. Weigh out the ingredients and mix them in a dry state before adding water, then the C.M.C. See SEG-7 for possible frit substitutions.

Application. Brush, dip, or spray three coats on the bisque to the thickness of a quarter. This glaze can be used over darker clays if it is opaque.

Fired Results. Fire to cone 8 oxidation for a semi-gloss surface with large crackle patterns. Copper is not an ideal colorant for this glaze as it has a tendency to burn out. However, this in itself can give some unusual metallic effects.

SEG-21 **Crackle Glaze   Cone 8**
alkaline, transparent, clear, nontoxic

Ferro frit #3819	11.3
Lithium carbonate	6.6
Kaolin (calcined)	14.0
Kaolin (EPK)	8.0
Silica	60.0
Bentonite	2.0
C.M.C.	1 tsp

Mixing. Mix this glaze in the same manner as SEG-7, also see that glaze for possible frit substitutions. This glaze is very stable and keeps well in solution for several weeks.

Application. Apply in the same manner as SEG-7. For the best crackle effects use on SEC-4.

Fired Results. Fire to cone 8 oxidation for a semimatt surface with large irregular crackle patterns. This glaze can be very effective if made opaque and used over a darker body. The glaze, of course, should be several shades lighter than the body.

SEG-22   **Crackle Glaze   Cone 9**
alkaline, transparent, clear to milky, nontoxic

Hommel frit #25	9.9
Lithium carbonate	4.6
Kaolin (calcined)	16.0
Kaolin (EPK)	8.0
Silica	61.5
Bentonite	2.0
C.M.C.	1 tsp

Mixing. Mix this glaze in the same manner as SEG-7. The frit substitutions given for SEG-7 will also work here. This is a frit glaze and keeps well in solution for several weeks.

Application. Apply in the same manner as SEG-20.

Fired Results. Fire to cone 9 oxidation for a bright subtle glaze surface with medium to large crackle patterns. More crackles tend to develop with the passage of time.

SEG-23   **Crackle Glaze   Cone 9**
alkaline, translucent, milky white, nontoxic

Pemco frit #25	7.4
Spodumene	48.0
Kaolin (EPK)	8.0
Silica	41.4
Bentonite	2.0
C.M.C.	1 tsp

Mixing. Mix according to the instructions for SEG-7, using the same frit substitutions if necessary. This glaze is nontoxic and keeps well in solution for many weeks.

Application. Apply in the same manner as SEG-20. This glaze works best if it is opaque and used on a lighter body.

Fired Results. Fire to cone 9 for a semi-matt surface that has large irregular crackle patterns much like those produced by the ancient Chinese potters.

COLORANTS

The potter should always remember that colorant percentages are calculated by the dry body weight of the glaze batch.

Barium blues can only be produced in a glaze with a high barium content. SEG-8, 12, and 13 will work well for this color.

Chinese blue can be produced only in an alkaline glaze. Number 14 is the best one for this purpose.

Dynasty blue can only be produced in an alkaline glaze—here again number 14 is the best for this purpose.

Egyptian blue can only be produced in an alkaline glaze. SEG-13, 14, or 15 work well for this color.

Persian blue is best produced in an alkaline glaze but some exceptional hues are possible with an alkaline-barium glaze.

Royal blue can be produced in any glaze base with only slightly different hues resulting.

Blue-green can be produced in any glaze base. The best hues seem to result in the alkaline glazes or in high-fire leadless glazes with a high feldspar content.

Browns can be produced with iron oxide in any glaze base.

Creamy tans can best be produced in a nonalkaline glaze.

Golden tans are best when produced with an alkaline glaze.

Gray-tan can be produced in any glaze base but the best hues are in the high-fire leadless glazes with a high calcium content.

Rusty tan can be produced in a nonalkaline glaze.

Speckled tan is best if produced in a nonalkaline glaze.

Turquoise can only be produced in a high alkaline glaze.

Desert turquoise can only be produced in an alkaline glaze; SEG-14 is best for this.

Indian turquoise can only be produced in an alkaline glaze; SEG-14 is best for this purpose.

Citron yellow should be produced with SEG-11.

Chrome yellow is best if produced with SEG-11, although any alkaline-frit glaze will work reasonably well.

Primrose yellow should be made using SEG-11.

Straw yellow can only be made with iron oxide and in a high-lead glaze such as SEG-13.

CHART OF CRACKLE GLAZE COLORANTS

Fired Result	Colorant	Percentage
Barium blues	Copper oxide	5.0%–10.0%
Chinese blue	Copper oxide	3.0%
	Iron oxide	0.5%
Dynasty blue	Copper oxide	1.0%
	Cobalt oxide	0.5%
	Iron oxide	0.5%
Egyptian blue	Copper oxide	5.0%
	Iron oxide	1.0%
Royal blue	Cobalt oxide	5.0%
	Iron oxide	1.0%
Blue-green	Copper carbonate	10.8%
	Cobalt oxide	1.0%
	Iron oxide	1.2%
Browns	Iron oxide	5.0%–10.0%
Creamy tan	Iron oxide	3.0%
Golden tan	Iron oxide	5.0%
	Rutile	2.0%
Gray tan	Iron oxide	3.0%
	Iron chromate	1.5%
Rusty tan	Iron oxide	3.0%
Speckled tan	Ilmenite (powdered)	5.0%
	Ilmenite (granular)	3.0%
Turquoise	Copper carbonate	10.0%
	Iron oxide	0.5%
Desert turquoise	Copper oxide	3.0%
	Copper carbonate	5.0%
	Iron oxide	0.5%
	Tin oxide	10.0%
Indian turquoise	Copper oxide	2.0%
	Copper carbonate	5.0%
	Iron oxide	0.5%
Citron yellow	Praseodymium stain	10.0%
Chrome yellow	Vanadium stain	10.0%
Primrose yellow	Naples yellow stain	5.0%
Straw yellow	Iron oxide	3.0%

Note. The percentages should always be calculated by the dry body weight of the formula.

CRATER GLAZES

One of the most unusual and intriguing areas for the potter today to explore is that of bubbling glazes to create texture. These glazes, sometimes known as crater glazes, take their name from the craterlike texture that they form on the surface of the pottery, reminiscent of the craters of the moon. It was only in the second quarter of this century that these glazes began to be considered favorably rather than as faults. Thus it may be difficult for some potters to break with tradition and strive for this glaze fault. For those who do, however, the possibilities are endless.

Crater glazes are generally produced by adding compounds to the glaze which will liberate gases during the firing cycle. As the volatile gases strive to reach the surface of the glaze, they tend to form bubbles which break through the surface and pop, leaving craters in the glaze. If the firing and cooling are done rather rapidly, these depressions do not heal over, but leave craterlike cavities in the surface of the glaze.

Various granular substances can be introduced into the glazes to make the effect more prominent. At earthenware temperatures manganese dioxide, silicon carbide, or magnesium carbonate are used. At stoneware levels granular gypsum is frequently employed. In both cases the amounts should not exceed 3% of the dry body weight of the glaze.

The selection of glaze formulas given here should produce excellent results provided they are not overfired. The potter will probably have better control over the final result if the process is observed through the peep hole of the kiln, and any temperature rise is immediately stopped if it appears that the craters may be healing over. In fact several firings may be necessary to ascertain the proper conditions for the potter's own individual kiln.

The colorants given for this glaze are primarily earth colors which the author feels are more in keeping with the rustic nature of the glaze type. In fact the best effects to be gained are those in which the potter uses darker or heavily grogged clays and allows the natural colorants of the clay to bleed or show through during the firing process.

The reader will find possible substitutions for many of the glaze chemicals used in these glazes in Chapter 34, Dictionary of Clay and Glaze Compounds.

SUGGESTED USES FOR CRATER GLAZES

The variations given below can be used with all the crater glazes given, SEG-24 to 36.

1. Use over smooth bisque ware for moderate crater effects.

2. Use over dark-colored clay bodies for more prominent crater effects.

3. Use over textured bodies for more rustic effects.

4. Use different thicknesses of glaze for more prominent craters combined with texture.

5. Use those crater glazes which contain silicon carbide over heavily grogged or textured bodies to obtain an artificial reduction in addition to the cratering effect.

FORMULAS FOR CRATER GLAZES

SEG-24 **Crater Glaze Cone 015**
alkaline, translucent, clear to milky, nontoxic

Mixing. Mix this glaze in the same manner as SEG-1 of this chapter. It does not store well beyond two to three weeks, but has a tendency to lump in solution.

Application. Brush, dip, or spray to form a coating of glaze about the thickness of a dime. Allow to dry completely before firing.

Fired Results. Fire to cone 015 oxidation exactly. This glaze will produce large craters in the surface that have a softened time-eroded appearance. It gives its best effect over an off-white to buff clay body. If a darker clay body is used the glaze should be opaque or colored to a shade lighter than the clay.

Lithium carbonate	12.0
Sodium silicofluoride	29.0
Alumina hydrate	15.3
Silica	43.7
Silicon carbide (granular)	2.0
Bentonite	2.0
C.M.C.	1 tsp

SEG-25   **Crater Glaze   Cone 08–06**

alkaline-frit, semi-opaque, clear to milky, nontoxic

Sodium silicofluoride	42.9
Whiting	15.0
Kaolin	21.4
Silica	20.7
Manganese dioxide (granular)	2.0
Bentonite	2.0
C.M.C.	1 tsp

Mixing. Mix this glaze in the same manner as SEG-1. It keeps well in solution for many weeks.

Application. Apply in the same manner as SEG-14.

Fired Results. Fire to cone 08–06. This glaze should be observed through the peep hole during the last stage of firing to determine when the bubbling is at its height. When this happens turn off the kiln and reduce the heat rapidly by cracking the kiln lid about a 1/4" (6mm) and opening one peep hole—preferably the bottom one. By stopping the bubbling at various stages the potter can determine which effect he prefers. Using this process, the glaze can be made to give a variety of crater surfaces.

If very large blisters result, they can be broken and ground down with an old piece of broken stoneware, kiln shelf, or fire brick for an interesting surface of opaque ridges surrounding darker areas.

Fired at cone 06 and cooled normally this glaze will give a good variety of small to medium craters. Increasing the thickness of the glaze will give a more violent boil and result in a more rustic glaze surface.

SEG-26   **Crater Glaze   Cone 04**

alkaline, semi-opaque, off-white, nontoxic

Cryolite	17.8
Calcium fluoride	3.9
Magnesium carbonate	2.9
Kaolin (Georgia)	12.8
Silica	69.6
Silicon carbide	2.0
C.M.C.	1 tsp

Mixing. Mix in the manner of SEG-1. This glaze is stable and keeps well in solution for two to three weeks.

Application. Apply in the same manner as SEG-24. For a more rustic effect double the thickness of the application.

Fired Results. Fire to cone 04 oxidation. This glaze gives a good variety of craters on a somewhat smooth background. The effect is better over buff to dark clay bodies especially if the glaze is made translucent or opaque.

SEG-27   **Crater Glaze   Cone 1**

alkaline frit, transparent, semiclear, nontoxic

Ferro frit #3134	39.4
Nepheline syenite	49.6
Whiting	18.0
Silicon carbide (granular)	2.0
Bentonite	2.0
C.M.C.	1 tsp

Mixing. Mix in the same manner as SEG-1, also see that glaze for possible frit substitutions. It keeps well in solution for several weeks.

Application. Apply in the same manner as SEG-24 or thicker for more rustic effects.

Fired Results. Fire to cone 1. With a normal application this glaze will give a lavalike texture with scattered craters of small to medium size. With thicker applications the surface will resemble pumice stone with an uneven surface.

SEG-28

Crater Glaze Cone 4
alkaline, semi-opaque, off-white, nontoxic

Mixing. Mix in the same manner as SEG-1. If mixed with care it keeps well in solution. See SEG-1 for possible frit substitutions.

Application. Apply in the manner of SEG-24 for moderate effects. For more rustic effects double or triple the thickness.

Fired Results. Fire to cone 4 oxidation. Unusual small craterlike depressions are formed in this glaze, generally having darker centers. Using darker clay bodies will accentuate this effect.

Cryolite	35.3
Calcium fluoride	20.0
Kaolin	7.0
Silica	37.0
Alumina oxide	0.7
Manganese dioxide (granular)	2.0
Bentonite	2.0
C.M.C.	1 tsp

SEG-29

Crater Glaze Cone 4
alkaline, translucent, milky white, nontoxic

Mixing. Mix in the same manner as SEG-1. This glaze keeps very well in solution for several weeks.

Application. Apply in the same manner as SEG-24.

Fired Results. Fire to cone 4 oxidation. Do not overfire. This glaze normally gives smaller but very prominent craters on a textured background. For more rustic effects double the thickness, but glaze more lightly at the base of the bisque to avoid possible running of the glaze.

Lepidolite	50.5
Calcium fluoride	12.6
Sodium silicofluoride	3.6
Silica	30.3
Kaolin	3.0
Manganese dioxide (granular)	1.0
Silicon carbide (granular)	1.0
Bentonite	2.0
C.M.C.	1 tsp

SEG-30

Crater Glaze Cone 4–5
alkaline, semi-opaque, off-white, nontoxic

Mixing. Mix in the same manner as SEG-1. This glaze does not keep well in solution beyond a month.

Application. Apply to the thickness of a dime by brushing, dipping, or spraying.

Fired Results. Fire to cone 4 oxidation. This glaze utilizes all three crater-forming compounds for a variety of crater effects, from small to large. But watch its firing carefully for the crater effects are fugitive above cone 4.

Cryolite	10.6
Calcium fluoride	13.3
Magnesium carbonate	2.9
Zinc oxide	4.0
Kaolin (calcined)	14.0
Silica	53.0
Silicon carbide (granular)	1.5
Manganese dioxide (granular)	1.5
Bentonite	2.0
C.M.C.	1 tsp

SEG-31

Crater Glaze Cone 4–5
alkaline, semi-opaque, milky white, nontoxic

Mixing. Mix in the manner as SEG-1. It keeps well in solution for about two weeks without lumping.

Application. Apply in the same manner of SEG-24.

Fired Results. Fire to cone 4–5 oxidation. At cone 4 this glaze gives a more rustic and violent crater surface, while at cone 5 the surface of the ware will have a smoother, weathered appearance with larger craters which are usually darker in the center. If a darker clay body is used here the effects in both cases will be more rustic and interesting.

Calcium fluoride	10.0
Lepidolite	52.0
Sodium fluoride	2.0
Cryolite	3.0
Silica	32.8
Bentonite	2.0
C.M.C.	1 tsp

SEG-32

Crater Glaze   Cone 4

alkaline, semi-opaque, milky white, nontoxic

Mixing. Mix in the same manner as SEG-1. This glaze keeps well in solution for at least a month without lumping.

Application. Apply in the manner of SEG-30.

Fired Results. Fire to cone 4 oxidation. This glaze gives a slight textured crater surface. More texture can be achieved if it is used over a buff textured clay body.

Cryolite	27.4
Calcium fluoride	15.6
Kaolin	20.0
Silica	37.0
Magnesium carbonate	2.0
Bentonite	2.0
C.M.C.	1 tsp

SEG-33

Crater Glaze   Cone 4

alkaline, semi-opaque, milky white, nontoxic

Mixing. Mix in the same manner as SEG-1. This glaze keeps moderately well in solution for several months.

Application. Apply in the same manner as SEG-30.

Fired Results. Fire to cone 4 oxidation. If this glaze is made opaque, it closely resembles the craters of the moon. It is at its best if used over a buff to light brown grogged clay body.

Lepidolite	5.0
Cryolite	45.0
Talc	50.0
Bentonite	2.0
Manganese dioxide (granular)	2.0
C.M.C.	1 tsp

SEG-34

Crater Glaze   Cone 4

alkaline, semi-opaque, off-white, nontoxic

Mixing. Mix in the same manner as SEG-1. It keeps well in solution for two to three weeks without lumping.

Application. Apply in the same manner as SEG-30.

Fired Results. Fire to cone 4 oxidation. Very large and prominent craters are possible with this glaze. It should be carefully watched to insure that it does not overfire. Its effects are at their best if used over a buff to brown grogged clay body.

Cryolite	40.8
Calcium fluoride	5.3
Lepidolite	2.0
Magnesium carbonate	1.2
Zinc oxide	1.6
Kaolin	3.7
Kaolin (calcined)	2.2
Silica	43.4
Bentonite	2.0
C.M.C.	1 tsp

SEG-35

Crater Glaze   Cone 4

alkaline, translucent to opaque, milky white, nontoxic

Mixing. Mix in the same manner as SEG-1. This glaze keeps well in solution for two to three weeks.

Application. Apply in the same manner as SEG-30.

Fired Results. Fire to cone 4 oxidation for a variety of large to small craters in a lavalike background. For the most interesting results, use this glaze over a textured, grogged brown clay body.

Cryolite	41.8
Calcium fluoride	7.3
Magnesium carbonate	1.2
Zinc oxide	1.7
Kaolin	1.6
Silica	43.4
Manganese dioxide (granular)	2.0
Bentonite	2.0
C.M.C.	1 tsp

SEG-36

Crater Glaze   Cone 5
lead-alkaline, opaque, mottled gloss and matt brown, toxic

Use SEG-1 and SEG-1a

Mixing. Use SEG-1 and 1a combination in the Break-Through Glaze section of this chapter. Caution: SEG-1 is quite toxic.

Application. Apply SEG-1 to the thickness of a dime and allow it to dry. On top of SEG-1 apply SEG-1a to the same thickness and allow the glaze combination to dry completely before firing.

Fired Results. Fire to cone 5 oxidation. Be careful not to overfire this glaze combination; the crater effect is fugitive above cone 5. This glaze combination is very unpredictable; results can vary from large blisters to medium craters to a lavalike surface. If large blisters result, finish the ware in the same manner as listed for SEG-25.

CHART OF CRATER GLAZE COLORANTS

Fired Result	Colorant	Percentage
Browns	Iron oxide	5.0%–10.0%
Opaque	Tin oxide	20.0%
Tans	Iron oxide	1.0%–5.0%
Speckled tans	Iron oxide	1.0%–5.0%
	Ilmenite (granular)	5.0%
Translucent	Tin oxide	10.0%
Yellows	Vanadium stain	5.0%–15.0%
	Iron oxide	1.0%–5.0%

Note. The percentages should always be calculated by the dry body weight of the formula.

CRYSTALLINE GLAZES

Crystalline glazes are of two types: one has small single crystals suspended in the glaze, and the second has large crystal clusters in or on the surface. Both types of crystal tend to catch and reflect the light. In practice their composition has to be carefully related to the pot form, for the jewel-like clusters seem to float from the surface of the more radical forms. Higher additions of the compounds zinc, rutile, and iron oxide tend to favor the development of crystals in the glaze. The presence of these compounds makes the glaze more opaque than usual and the absence of aluminum tends to make them quite fluid and brilliant in surface effect.

The most critical part of producing crystalline glazes is in the firing cycle. The heating phase is carried out in the normal fashion, but the cooling must be slowed to about 100°F./38°C. above the maturing point, then held there several hours before slowly cooling in the last stages of firing. A pyrometer is almost indispensible for the proper firing and cooling of the crystalline glaze, for without an instrument to indicate the rise and fall of the temperature inside the kiln the process cannot be properly controlled.

Due to the fluidity of this glaze type, the pottery is usually fired sitting on a pedestal of insulating brick or on a high stilt within a shallow dish. After firing, the brick or stilt can be easily ground from the base of the pot on a carborundum grinding stone.

Since this glaze type is the most difficult of all the special-effect glazes to use successfully, I have listed eight recipes which are the least difficult of all those I have encountered.

The reader will notice that included after the firing instructions is a list of the other possible colorants that may be used with each individual glaze. The colorants have been listed in this manner because not every one of the eight glazes in this section will tolerate a colorant change. For example copper oxide and copper carbonate will work well in one glaze and burn out in another higher-fired glaze. For this reason and to save the potter possible failures, there will be no separate color chart listed at the end of the glaze section.

The reader will find possible substitutions for many of the glaze chemicals used in these glazes in Chapter 34, Dictionary of Clay and Glaze Compounds.

FORMULAS FOR CRYSTALLINE GLAZES

SEG-37 **Crystalline Glaze Cone 06–04**
lead-frit, translucent, light green, nontoxic

Lead sesquisilicate	76.5
Zinc oxide	6.0
Kaolin (calcined)	7.5
Ilmenite (powdered)	5.0
Copper oxide	2.5
Rutile	3.0
Bentonite	2.0
C.M.C.	1 tsp

Mixing. Mix this glaze in the same manner as SEG-1. It keeps well in solution for long periods.

Application. Apply by brushing, dipping, or spraying to the thickness of a dime toward the top of the piece and thinner at the base. Leave at least 3/4″ (19mm) of the base of the ware unglazed to prevent excessive running.

Fired Results. Fire to cone 06–04 oxidation; quickly reduce the temperature of the kiln to about cone 08–09; maintain this temperature for two to three hours, then cool very slowly to 100°F./38°C. before opening the kiln. The slow-cooling process allows the crystal formation to take place. This glaze used as it is given is a light green with lighter green crystals. Caution: this glaze is quite fluid, so take care to stilt it properly in a shallow bisque dish during firing.

Suggested Variations.

1. Omit the copper oxide for a glaze that is tan with cream-colored crystals.

2. Substitute 1 gram of cobalt oxide for a glaze that is medium blue with lighter blue crystals.

SEG-38

Crystalline Glaze   Cone 05
raw alkaline, semi-opaque, rust brown, nontoxic

Borax	172.9
Barium carbonate	10.8
Boric acid	12.6
Kaolin	6.2
Silica	176.0
Red iron oxide	67.0
Bentonite	2.0
C.M.C.	1 tsp

Mixing. This glaze should be mixed, ground dry, and used immediately. If this is not possible, mix only the amount you anticipate using with water and C.M.C. and store the remainder dry. It does not store well in solution, having a tendency to lump badly.

Application. Apply to the thickness of a dime at the top and lighter toward the base of the pot to avoid excessive running onto the kiln shelf or stilt in a shallow bisque dish which can be discarded later.

Fired Results. Fire to cone 05 oxidation, cool quickly to cone 04 for two to three hours, then cool slowly to 100°F./38°C. before opening the kiln. This adventurine crystal glaze produces a rust-colored surface with tan to off-white crystals. Other colorants cannot be substituted for the iron oxide in this glaze as the iron also acts as a fluxing agent of this glaze.

SEG-39

Crystalline Glaze   Cone 3–4
lead-frit, transparent, cream with light crystals, nontoxic

Ferro frit #3304	80.5
Iron oxide	15.0
Kaolin (calcined)	4.5
Bentonite	2.0
C.M.C.	1 tsp

Mixing. Mix this glaze in the same manner as SEG-1. It keeps very well in solution for long periods.

Application. Apply in the same manner as SEG-37.

Fired Results. Fire to cone 3–4 oxidation; cool rapidly to cone 1; maintain this temperature for two to three hours, then cool slowly about 100°F./38°C. per hour until cone 06 is reached; then cool normally. This glaze produces a cream-yellow color with lighter crystals.

Suggested Variations

1. Substitute 15 grams of copper carbonate for the iron oxide for a medium-green glaze with lighter crystals.

2. Use 14 grams of copper oxide for a darker green glaze with medium green crystals.

3. Add 1 to 2 grams cobalt oxide for a dark blue glaze with lighter blue to off-white crystals.

SEG-40

Crystalline Glaze   Cone 3–4
raw alkaline, translucent, tan, nontoxic

Soda ash	15.3
Boric acid	14.2
Zinc oxide	21.5
Silica	47.8
Rutile	6.6
Ball clay (Kentucky #4)	6.0
Bentonite	2.0
C.M.C.	1 tsp

Mixing. Mix in the same manner as SEG-38.

Application. Apply in the same manner as SEG-38.

Fired Results. Fire to cone 3–4 oxidation, cool the kiln 100°F./38°C.; maintain this temperature for two hours; then cool normally. This glaze gives a translucent tan with off-white crystals.

Suggested Variations

1. Add 5 grams of copper oxide for a medium green glaze with off-white crystals.

2. Add 1 gram of cobalt oxide for a medium blue glaze with blue to off-white crystals.

SEG-41

Crystalline Glaze   Cone 8
alkaline, semi-opaque, off-white with light crystals, nontoxic

Sodium carbonate	11.2
Whiting	6.2
Zinc oxide	21.3
Silica	39.1
Rutile	5.1
Kaolin (EPK)	17.3
Bentonite	2.0
C.M.C.	1 tsp

Mixing. Mix in the same manner as SEG-38.

Application. Apply in the same manner as SEG-38.

Fired Results. Fire to cone 8 oxidation; cool quickly to cone 5; maintain this temperature for two to three hours; then cool slowly to cone 06 before allowing the kiln to cool normally. Allow the kiln to cool to 100° F./ 38°C. before opening. The pot should be well stilted on a "china cookie" inside a shallow bisque dish to catch the excess run-off of the glaze. The cookie can later be chipped and ground from the base.

Suggested Variations

1. Add 4 grams of iron oxide for a yellow-tan glaze with off-white to silver-colored crystals.

2. Add 1 gram of cobalt oxide for a light blue glaze with lighter blue to silver crystals.

SEG-42

Crystalline Glaze   Cone 9
leadless, translucent, milky white, nontoxic

Feldspar (potash)	41.0
Silica	29.5
Whiting	19.5
Kaolin (EPK)	10.0
C.M.C.	1 tsp

Mixing. Mix in the same manner as SEG-1. This glaze keeps well in solution for long periods without lumping.

Application. Apply in the same manner as SEG-38.

Fired Results. Fire to cone 9 oxidation and cool about 100° F./38°C. per hour until the kiln has reached the temperature of cone 6, then cool normally. This glaze produces a translucent milky white glaze with silver crystals. The pottery should be well stilted.

Suggested Variations

1. Add 0.5 grams of cobalt oxide for a light milky blue with silver-colored crystals.

2. Add 1 gram of cobalt oxide for a translucent blue with lighter-blue to silver-colored crystals.

3. Add 2 to 3 grams of cobalt oxide for a dark translucent blue with lighter blue to silver-colored crystals.

SEG-43

Crystalline Glaze   Cone 11
leadless, transparent, clear, nontoxic

Feldspar (potash)	105.0
Whiting	35.0
Silica	35.0
Zinc oxide	25.0
Bentonite	2.0
C.M.C.	1 tsp

Mixing. Mix in the same manner as SEG-1. This glaze stores well in solution for long periods of time without lumping.

Application. Apply in the same manner as SEG-38.

Fired Results. Fire to cone 11 oxidation. Cool about 100° F./38°C. per hour until cone 7 is reached, then cool normally. This glaze used as it is given is rather mediocre. Use the suggested variations for SEG-42 for some interesting effects.

SEG-44   **Crystalline Glaze   Cone 11**
raw alkaline, semi-opaque, off-white, nontoxic

Mixing. Mix in the same manner as SEG-38.

Application. Apply in the same manner as SEG-38.

Fired Results. Fire in the same manner as SEG-43. Be careful to stilt the ware properly as this glaze is very fluid. It produces an off-white surface with pearly white crystals of various sizes. Used over an off-white to buff clay body, it produces a more subtle type of crystalline coloration. The suggested variations for SEG-42 can also be used very effectively with this glaze.

Soda ash	46.5
Silica	104.0
Zinc oxide	49.5
Titanium dioxide (rutile)	20.0
Bentonite	2.0
C.M.C.	1 tsp

FLOATING GLAZE

Listed here is one separate glaze that is so spectacular in its effect that it must be classified as a special-effect glaze. I have labeled it a floating glaze because the colors seem to float on the surface of a darker background of great depth, reminiscent of a deep pool of water.

The potter who tries it, however, should heed this warning: it is a very fickle glaze and does not always produce the desired effect. Many things have to be taken into account when trying it; even the mineral content of the water the potter uses can alter the results. Firing it in the same kiln with bisque or with other glazes with a copper content can adversely affect it. But if the complete instructions are followed faithfully, you should be able to produce a glaze well worth the efforts involved.

The potter should not attempt to substitute any of the chemicals in this glaze with other chemicals.

FORMULA FOR FLOATING GLAZE

SEG-45   **Floating Blue Glaze   Cone 6**
leadless, semi-opaque to opaque, mottled blue, nontoxic

Nepheline syenite	47.3
Colemanite	27.0
Silica	20.3
Kaolin (EPK)	5.4
Red iron oxide	2.0
Cobalt oxide	1.0
Rutile (milled)	4.0
C.M.C.	1 tsp

Mixing. Weigh the ingredients very carefully and mix them in a clean jar. Premix the contents and add distilled water, or water that is known to have a low mineral content, then add two teaspoons of C.M.C. and shake vigorously. Sieve two or three times through a 60- to 80-mesh screen, forcing all the material through the screen with a stiff clean brush. Store the glaze in an air-tight container and it will keep well for long periods. But it should be mixed and stirred thoroughly each time it is used.

Application. The glaze should be stirred occasionally during application as the iron content has a tendency to settle rapidly. Apply to the thickness of a dime by brushing, dipping, or spraying, being careful that your tools are clean and free of other glaze materials that might contaminate this glaze. Allow the glaze to dry slightly between coatings and to dry completely before firing. Take care that dust does not settle on the surface during the drying process.

Fired Results. Fire to cone 6 oxidation exactly and cool normally. This glaze produces a deep blue-brown background of great depth with lighter mottled blues that seem to float on the very surface of the background glaze.

Suggested Variations

1. Apply the glaze as the instructions indicate then sponge or stipple with a brush one coating of the glaze over this in an uneven pattern for an even more mottled effect.

2. Apply the glaze as the instructions indicate and lightly sponge a thin wash of 3 grams of chrome oxide to 100 grams of water plus a tablespoon of C.M.C. over the top of the glaze to produce a floating blue glaze with subtle green tints.

3. After the application of the main glaze, sponge lightly with a coating of rutile wash consisting of 2 grams rutile per 100 grams of water plus a tablespoon of C.M.C. for a floating blue glaze with slight tan crystalline tints on the surface.

FLOWING GLAZES

Flowing glazes can be described as those which depend of their flowing action during the firing process for the desired effect. They may be produced in all temperature ranges. Their composition is achieved by increasing the fluxing agent in the formula and decreasing the stabilizing agent, alumina. When this is done the agent tends to melt more quickly and flow down the sides of the pot during the firing cycle, creating unusual effects in the glaze.

Flowing glazes are best used with other colored glazes to mingle colors. They may be used under, between, or over other glazes of different colors to create these flowing effects. For example, if a flowing glaze is placed between a white base glaze and a top blue glaze the result would be a marbleized mixture of blues and whites in an overall flowing pattern. They may also be used to create a flowing frosted pattern around the rims of cups and bowls.

In the following list are glazes for each cone level from 014–10, all of which may be made opaque or colored with any of the colorants listed in Chapter 34 on Clay and Glaze Colorants.

FORMULAS FOR FLOWING GLAZES

SEG-46

Transparent Flowing Glaze   Cone 014
lead, transparent, gloss, toxic

Mixing. Weigh out the ingredients and mix according to one of the methods given in Chapter 17 on Glaze Preparation.

Application. Apply one heavy coat all over the ware and a second coat on the top three quarters by dipping, brushing, or spraying. The glaze may be applied under, between, or over other glazes depending on the desired effect.

Firing. Fire to the cone level indicated then cool the kiln quickly down at least 200°F./94°C. to set the flowed pattern, otherwise the glaze will continue to flow and there will be excess flowing and dripping at the bottom of the pieces.

Fired Results. The results will depend on how the glaze is used: 1. If applied under a colored glaze it will produce mottled broken patterns of the top color. 2. If applied between two different colors or different shades of the same color it will produce a marbleized pattern of running color. 3. If applied over a colored glaze it will produce flowing streaked patterns similar to those of a milky colemanite glaze.

White lead	75.0
Silica	25.0
Kaolin	5.0
Bentonite	2.0
C.M.C.	1 tsp

SEG-47

Transparent Flowing Glaze   Cone 012
lead, transparent, gloss, toxic

Mixing. Mix in the manner of SEG-46.

Application. Apply in the manner of SEG-46.

Firing. Fire in the manner of SEG-46.

Fired Results. See *Fired Results* on SEG-46.

White lead	90.0
Kaolin	18.0
Silica	2.0
Bentonite	2.0
C.M.C.	1 tsp

SEG-48   **Transparent Flowing Glaze   Cone 010**
lead, transparent, gloss, toxic

Mixing. Mix in the manner of SEG-46.

Application. Apply in the manner of SEG-46.

Firing. Fire in the manner of SEG-46.

Fired Results. See *Fired Results* on SEG-46.

White lead	80.7
Silica	10.1
Kaolin	4.0
Boric acid	5.2
Bentonite	2.0
C.M.C.	1 tsp

SEG-49   **Transparent Flowing Glaze   Cone 08**
lead, transparent, gloss, toxic

Mixing. Mix in the manner of SEG-46.

Application. Apply in the manner of SEG-46.

Firing. Fire in the manner of SEG-46.

Fired Results. See *Fired Results* on SEG-46.

Red lead	31.0
White lead	20.0
Silica	18.5
Borax	15.0
Kaolin	4.0
Bentonite	2.0
C.M.C.	1 tsp

SEG-50   **Transparent Flowing Glaze   Cone 06**
lead, transparent, gloss, toxic

Mixing. Mix in the manner of SEG-46.

Application. Apply in the manner of SEG-46.

Firing. Fire in the manner of SEG-46.

Fired Results. See *Fired Results* on SEG-46.

White lead	64.0
Silica	26.0
Kaolin	10.0
Bentonite	2.0
C.M.C.	1 tsp

SEG-51   **Transparent Flowing Glaze   Cone 04**
lead, transparent, gloss, toxic

Mixing. Mix in the manner of SEG-46.

Application. Apply in the manner of SEG-46.

Firing. Fire in the manner of SEG-46.

Fired Results. See *Fired Results* on SEG-46.

White lead	70.0
Silica	10.0
Kaolin (EPK)	6.0
Feldspar (Kona F-4)	7.0
Borax	3.0
Zinc oxide	4.0
Bentonite	2.0
C.M.C.	1 tsp

SEG-52   **Transparent Flowing Glaze   Cone 02**
lead, transparent, gloss, toxic

Mixing. Mix in the manner of SEG-46.

Application. Apply in the manner of SEG-46.

Firing. Fire in the manner of SEG-46.

Fired Results. See *Fired Results* on SEG-46.

White lead	56.0
Silica	25.0
Kentucky ball clay #4	12.0
Whiting	4.0
Zinc oxide	3.0
Bentonite	2.0
C.M.C.	1 tsp

SEG-53   **Transparent Flowing Glaze   Cone 2**
lead, transparent, gloss, toxic

Mixing. Mix in the manner of SEG-46.

Application. Apply in the manner of SEG-46.

Firing. Fire in the manner of SEG-46.

Fired Results. See *Fired Results* on SEG-46.

White lead	55.0
Feldspar (Custer)	20.0
Whiting	15.0
Bentonite	2.0
C.M.C.	1 tsp

SEG-54

Transparent Flowing Glaze   Cone 4
lead, transparent, gloss, toxic

Mixing. Mix in the manner of SEG-46.

Application. Apply in the manner of SEG-46.

Firing. Fire in the manner of SEG-46.

Fired Results. See *Fired Results* on SEG-46.

White lead	58.0
Feldspar (Custer)	20.0
Whiting	12.0
Bentonite	2.0
C.M.C.	1 tsp

SEG-55

Transparent Flowing Glaze   Cone 6
lead, transparent, gloss, toxic

Mixing. Mix in the manner of SEG-46.

Application. Apply in the manner of SEG-46.

Firing. Fire in the manner of SEG-46.

Fired Results. See *Fired Results* on SEG-46.

White lead	65.0
Feldspar (Custer)	25.0
Silica	5.0
Whiting	5.0
Bentonite	2.0
C.M.C.	1 tsp

SEG-56

Transparent Flowing Glaze   Cone 8
leadless, transparent, gloss, nontoxic

Mixing. Mix in the manner of SEG-46.

Application. Apply in the manner of SEG-46.

Firing. Fire in the manner of SEG-46.

Fired Results. See *Fired Results* on SEG-46.

Feldspar (Custer)	60.0
Whiting	10.0
Colemanite	10.0
Silica	10.0
Kentucky ball clay #4	8.0
Kaolin	2.0
Bentonite	2.0
C.M.C.	1 tsp

SEG-57

Transparent Flowing Glaze   Cone 9
leadless, transparent, gloss, nontoxic

Mixing. Mix in the manner of SEG-46.

Application. Apply in the manner of SEG-46.

Firing. Fire in the manner of SEG-46.

Fired Results. See *Fired Results* on SEG-46.

Nepheline syenite	55.0
Silica	25.0
Whiting	10.0
Colemanite	5.0
Dolomite	4.0
Bentonite	2.0
C.M.C.	1 tsp

SEG-58

Transparent Flowing Glaze   Cone 10
leadless, transparent, gloss, nontoxic

Mixing. Mix in the manner of SEG-46.

Application. Apply in the manner of SEG-46.

Firing. Fire in the manner of SEG-46.

Fired Results. See *Fired Results* on SEG-46.

Feldspar (Kona F-4)	50.9
Silica	24.0
Whiting	18.0
Kaolin	2.7
Dolomite	2.4
Zinc oxide	1.0
Colemanite	1.0
Bentonite	2.0
C.M.C.	1 tsp

22
SPECIAL EFFECTS WITH COMMERCIAL GLAZES

One area that many professional potters tend to overlook is that of commercially prepared glazes. Many potters have developed the mistaken idea that these glazes are for beginners only. This is a fallacy, for there are several companies which produce extensive lines of glazes which are very reliable under various firing conditions. While it is true that many of them are designed for earthenware temperature levels and tend to be more glossy, they can nevertheless be so striking in result that they are indeed worthy of the potter's attention. These glazes often produce very colorful results that can be used to advantage by the imaginative potter.

SINGLE COMMERCIAL GLAZES

The three major commercial glaze companies with which the author has dealt extensively are Duncan, Ceramichrome, and AMACO, all of whose products are readily available in most larger cities. All three of these companies have single glazes that are completely reliable under the recommended firing conditions. And those recommended here for the reader are by no means the only glazes worthy of the potter's attention. To list them all would require a complete book in itself, so I have tried to point out those that have been the most successful and appealing under various testing conditions.

Duncan Ceramics has an antique glaze series that is exceptionally good and produces beautiful frosted shades and finishes ranging from two to three shades of color — all tending toward matt finishes.

Their *Art Glaze* series is also unusual. The excitement and charm of these particular glazes lie in the fact that no two firings will give exactly the same result. The thickness of application, firing temperature, and the shape of the ware all have a bearing on the end result.

The Duncan Company has recently carried out extensive tests on their glazes for high-fire capabilities and has found that many of their cone 06–05 glazes will fire successfully to cone 6 with very good results. A booklet listing these glazes is available at most ceramic supply stores handling their merchandise.

Ceramichrome has several series of glazes that would especially appeal to the potter who wants to experiment. Especially worthy of attention is the *Apollo* series which contains a wide variety of glazes with various fired results ranging from matt finishes to heavy textures, many of which will fire to cone 6 with good results.

The *Art Glaze* series is also worthy of note, for it contains many glazes which give varying results depending on the application and firing method used. Many of these are excellent for use on lower-fired stoneware bodies.

The *Exotic Glaze* series also offers a wide variety of colors for different unusual effects at firing ranges from cone 06–6. These glazes cover a range of earthy stoneware colors.

For the admirers of the beautiful stonewares of the ancient Chinese there is the *Crackle Matt* series which produces prominent crackle finishes much like those of the ancient potters of China.

AMACO (American Art Clay Company, Inc.) has several interesting glaze series. These include matt glazes which are especially reliable and the high-fire glaze series which fires to cone 4–6 with excellent results.

CONCLUSION

The glazes listed above are by no means the only glazes worthy of the potter's attention, for each of these companies has a vast range of glazes, all of which are completely reliable. Those listed here serve as an indication of the variety of glazes available which should not be overlooked by the potter.

COMMERCIAL GLAZE COMBINATIONS

Some unique and unusual color effects can be achieved by the combination of different commercial glazes. The following listings of glaze combinations have been tested for reliability and will work if the directions are followed faithfully. They are listed first by company, then by the dominant color effect, and finally in alphabetical order by color. All of the combinations can be fired in the cone 06–05 range, depending on the amount of spill effect desired.

DUNCAN GLAZE COMBINATIONS

DC-1. Amber and green in a spill pattern.

Apply 2 coats of AR603, Autumn; let dry thoroughly; then apply 2 coats of AR620, Rusty Amber.

DC-2. Basic amber color with swirls of chocolate brown.

Apply 3 coats of GL640, Foliage Green Gloss; then 1 heavy coat of 20027, Fiesta.

DC-3. Antique gold showing through light brown.

Apply 2 coats of AN324, Antique Green Art; then 2 coats of AR620, Rusty Amber.

DC-4. A mellow blend of amber, gold, and tan.

Apply 2 coats of AR620, Rusty Amber; then 2 coats of SY540, Spill Base; and finally 2 coats of GL600, Buttercup Yellow.

DC-5. Rich black and red velvet.

Apply 2 coats of GL625, Mahogany Brown; then 3 coats of GL631, Chinese Red.

DC-6. Rough black lava texture with brown overtones.

Apply 2 coats of AR684, Charcoal Lava Art; then 3 coats of AR620, Rusty Amber.

DC-7. An oriental contemporary of black and red sponge design.

Apply 2 coats of AR612, Cinnamon Brown; then 3 coats of GL632, Tangerine.

DC-8. Brown-black with iron black texture showing through top glaze.

Apply 3 coats AR684, Charcoal Lava; then 2 coats AR616, Manzanita Brown.

DC-9. Allover pattern of specks in black, gray, and white.

Apply 2 coats of GL613, Black; then 2 coats of SY541, Pattern Base; and finally 3 coats of GL638, Opaque White.

DC-10. Dull black with tan overtones.

Apply 2 coats AR684, Charcoal Lava Art; then 2 coats of SP904, Tan.

DC-11. Blue-and-white spill pattern.

Apply 2 coats GL638, Opaque White; then 2 coats of SY540, Spill Base; and finally 2 coats of AN313, Antique Blue.

DC-12. Antique blue with spots breaking the surface in a mottled pattern.

Apply 2 coats GL638, Opaque White; then 2 coats SY541, Pattern Base; and finally 2 coats of AN313, Antique Blue.

DC-13. Antique blue and opaque white in a cascade spill effect.

Apply 2 coats of GL638, Opaque White; then 2 coats of SY542, Cascade Base; and finally 2 coats of AN313, Antique Blue.

DC-14. Vibrant blend of blues and reds.

Apply 2 coats of GL634, Royal Blue; then 2 coats of GL637, Christmas Red.

DC-15. Streaks of blues and greens.

Apply 2 coats of GL601, Marigold Yellow; then 3 coats of GL628, Hawaiian Blue.

DC-16. Vibrant blue with splashes of gray-green.

Apply 2 coats of GL634, Royal Blue; then 3 coats of AN324, Antique Green Art.

DC-17. A leopard-spotted pattern in yellow and navy blue.

Apply 3 coats of SP913, Flame Yellow; then 2 coats of GL634, Royal Blue.

DC-18. Exciting blue-and-red tones.

Apply 2 coats of GL614, Matador Red; then 2 coats of GL608, Turquoise.

DC-19. Allover pattern of blue-green and yellows.

Apply 3 coats of SP913, Flame Yellow; then 2 coats of SY541, Pattern Base; and 2 coats of GL628, Hawaiian Blue.

DC-20. All the mystery and depth of raging blue-green waters.

Apply 2 coats of GL609, Emerald Green; then 2 coats of SY540, Spill Base; and finally 2 coats of GL634, Royal Blue.

DC-21. Beautiful colors from pale blue to deep green.

Apply 3 coats of GL609, Emerald Green;

then apply, by a heavy trail down the edge, CR802, White Opaque.

DC-22. Romantic splash of blues, reds, and gray.

Apply 3 coats of GL637, Christmas Red; then 2 coats of GL617, Clear Brushing; and finally 2 coats of GL638, Hawaiian Blue.

DC-23. Lovely blue-and-white fleece appearance.

Apply 2 coats of GL628, Hawaiian Blue; with 2 coats of SY541, Pattern Base; and finally 2 coats of CR802, White Opaque.

DC-24. A rough, blue-gray and black finish.

Apply 2 coats of AR684, Charcoal Lava Art; then 2 coats of GL628, Hawaiian Blue.

DC-25. Deep blue with a burst of red and grays.

Apply 2 coats of AR648, Charcoal Lava Art; then 3 coats of GL631, Chinese Red.

DC-26. Blue-green with patterns of blue and green with white spill effects.

Apply 3 coats of SP903, Blue; then 1 heavy coat of 20026, Monterey Jade.

DC-27. Blue and moss-green in a mottled pattern.

Apply 3 coats of SP903, Blue; then 1 coat of AN324, Antique Green Art, in a drop pattern.

DC-28. Tahiti Blue background with runs of red, blue, and gray.

Apply 2 coats of GL638, Opaque White; using a coarse metal scouring pad apply even daubs of GL646, Tahiti Blue; when dry, daub on GL650, Pansy, in the same manner.

DC-29. Gloss-blue background with marbleized patterns of darker and lighter blues.

Apply 3 coats of GL647, Baby Blue; using a metal scouring pad, pat on GL648, Catalina Blue, in a ''here and there'' pattern; when dry, pat on GL634, Royal Blue, in the same manner.

DC-30. Lovely blue with streaks of dark brown and white.

Apply 2 coats of GL615, Mahogany Brown; then 2 coats of SY540, Spill Base; and finally 2 coats of GL628, Hawaiian Blue.

DC-31. A marbleized effect of rich, deep blues and reds.

Apply 2 coats of GL626, Royal Ruby; then 2 coats of SY541, Pattern Base; and finally 2 coats of GL628, Hawaiian Blue.

DC-32. A blue-black surface with white starlike spots.

Apply 2 coats of GL619, Black Luster; then 2 coats of SY540, Spill Base; and finally 2 coats of SA389, White Satin.

DC-33. Deep brown with green swirl pattern.

Apply 3 coats of GL666, Walnut Brown; then 2 coats of SY540, Spill Base; and finally 2 to 3 coats of GL609, Emerald Green.

DC-34. Brown and a rouge spill effect.

Apply 2 coats of GL673, Expresso; then 3 coats of SS331, Clear; then 2 coats of GL659, Zinnia.

DC-35. Patterns of brown knots showing through orange-yellow.

Apply 2 coats of AR612, Cinnamon Brown; then 2 coats of GL602, Orange.

DC-36. Spills and speckles of brown, tan, and beige.

Apply 2 coats of AR610, Maplewood; then 2 coats of GL638, Opaque White.

DC-37. A furlike effect of brown and tan.

Apply 2 coats of AR612, Cinnamon Brown; then 2 coats of GL638, Opaque White.

DC-38. A medium speckled brown and green, very refreshing.

Apply 3 coats of AR610, Maplewood; then 1 coat of GL609, Emerald Green.

DC-39. A jewel-like radiance of warm brown and glittering pink.

Apply 2 coats of GL615, Mahogany Brown; then 2 coats SY540, Spill Base; and finally 2 coats of GL623, Rose Pink.

DC-40. Muted, creamy moonbeams through dark-brown shadows.

Apply two coats of GL615, Mahogany Brown; then 2 coats of SY540, Spill Base; and finally 2 coats of GL600, Buttercup Yellow.

DC-41. A warm contrast of brown and greens.

Apply 2 coats of AN304 Antique Beige; followed by 2 coats of GL617 Clear Brushing; then 1 coat of GL615, Mahogany Brown; and finally 1 coat of AN324, Antique Green Art.

DC-42. Golden-browns in a misty pattern.

Apply 3 coats of AR620, Rusty Amber; and then 2 coats of GL638, Opaque White.

DC-43. Dramatic browns with a filigree effect.

Apply 2 coats of AR616, Manzanita Brown; then 2 coats of SY540, Spill Base; and finally 2 coats of GL632, Tangerine.

DC-44. Shimmering beauty of variegated browns and blue.

Apply 2 coats of GL615, Mahogany Brown; then 2 coats of GL617, Clear Brushing; and finally 2 coats of GL628, Hawaiian Blue.

DC-45. Bold brown and tangerine of native handicraft.

Apply 2 coats of AR616, Manzanita Brown; then 2 coats of GL617, Clear Brushing; and finally 2 coats of GL632, Tangerine.

DC-46. A combination of the colors of all the seasons.

Apply 2 coats of AR616, Manzanita Brown; then 2 coats of SY541, Pattern Base; and finally 1 coat of GL628, Hawaiian Blue with blobs of GL632, Tangerine.

DC-47. Reddish brown under shades of light silver-green.

Apply 2 coats of AR616, Manzanita Brown; then 1 coat of GL617, Clear Brushing; and finally 2 coats of SA380, Sage Green.

DC-48. Deep-brown background with splashes of tangerine and chartreuse shades.

Apply 2 coats of AR616, Manzanita Brown, then 2 coats of SY541, Pattern Base; and finally 1 coat of GL625, Chartreuse, and blobs of GL632, Tangerine, around the edges.

DC-49. A sheen from reddish browns to pale green.

Apply 2 coats of AR616, Manzanita Brown; then 1 coat of SY540, Spill Base, and finally 2 coats of SA380, Sage Green.

DC-50. Deep-brown with an overlay of greens, browns, and orange.

Apply 2 coats of GL615, Mahogany Brown; then 2 coats of SY540, Spill Base; and then 2 coats of SP904, Tan; and finally 1 coat of SA380, Sage Green.

DC-51. Rich browns over pale green.

Apply 2 coats of GL628, Hawaiian Blue; then 3 coats of GL615, Mahogany Brown.

DC-52. Gloss-brown background with runs of matt mint green.

Apply 2 coats of GL615, Mahogany Brown; then 3 coats of AN316, Antique Mint Green.

DC-53. Tan-brown gloss background with runs of white and gold.

Apply 3 coats of AR610, Maplewood; then 1 heavy coat of 20034, Gold Rush.

DC-54. Brown gloss with red spill effects and white patterns.

Apply 2 coats of GL644, Spanish Brown; then 1 heavy coat of 20027, Fiesta.

DC-55. Basic gloss brown-red with darker brown spots breaking the surface.

Apply 2 coats of GL615, Mahogany Brown; then 2 coats of SY541, Pattern Base; and finally 2 coats of GL637, Christmas Red.

DC-56. Dark-brown matt with runs of cloudy white and darker brown spots.

Apply 2 coats of GL666, Walnut Brown; then 1 coat of GL617, Clear Brushing Glaze; and finally 1 coat of SP943, Divinity Chip.

DC-57. Brown background with heavy runs of red.

Apply 2 coats of GL666, Walnut Brown; then 2 coats of GL637, Christmas Red.

DC-58. Brown with runs of white and gold.

Apply 3 coats of GL615, Mahogany Brown; then 1 coat of 20034, Gold Rush.

DC-59. Caramel color with broken areas of amber and green.

Apply 2 coats of AR681, Red Amber; then 2 coats of AN319, Frosty Mint; and finally 2 coats of GL667, Caramel.

DC-60. Creamy caramel patterned with silvery green.

Apply 2 coats of AR610, Maplewood; then 2 coats SY540, Spill Base; 1 coat of SA380, Sage Green; and finally add blobs of GL600, Buttercup Yellow.

DC-61. Green and turquoise marbleized pattern.

Apply 2 coats GL609, Emerald Green; then 2 coats GL617, Clear Brushing; and finally 2 coats of GL608, Turquoise.

DC-62. Frosty mint green with spots of pink breaking through the surface.

Apply 2 coats of GL623, Rose Pink; then 2 coats of SY541, Pattern Base; and finally 3 coats of AN319, Frosty Mint.

DC-63. Silver-green with dark-brown spots breaking through the surface.

Apply 2 coats of GL615, Mahogany Brown; then 2 coats of SY541, Pattern Base; and finally 1 coat of MA704, Silver Green.

DC-64. Basic green background with red-amber spill effects.

Apply 2 coats of AR681, Red Amber; then 2 coats of SY540, Spill Base; and finally 2 coats of GL663, Holly Green.

DC-65. Basic dark green with heavy runs of bright golden yellow.

Apply 2 coats of GL663, Holly Green; then 2 coats of SY540, Spill Base; and finally 2 coats of GL665, Golden Yellow.

DC-66. Basic green-moss matt with patterns of pink breaking through the surface.

Apply 2 coats of GL623, Rose Pink; then 2 coats of AN324, Antique Green Art.

DC-67. Gloss mixture of green and white in a heavy spill pattern.

Apply 3 coats of AR603, Autumn; then 2 coats of SY540, Spill Base; and finally 3 coats of GL653, Downright White.

DC-68. Matt-green mixture of purples, reds, and whites.

Apply 2 coats of AN316, Antique Mint Green; then 2 coats of 20020, Plum Beautiful.

DC-69. Tan and green matt mixture of runs in an exotic pattern.

Apply 2 coats of AN315, Antique Tan; then 2 coats of AN316, Antique Mint Green.

DC-70. Green and brown pattern of matt color in a spill type of mixture.

Apply 2 coats of AN316, Antique Mint Green; then 2 coats of AN317, Antique Brown.

DC-71. Basic foliage green with spills of matt blues against a gloss-green background.

Apply 2 coats of GL640, Foliage Green; then 3 coats of AN313, Antique Blue.

DC-72. Basic green with spill effects of red and white.

Apply 2 coats of AR620, Rusty Amber; then 1 heavy coat of 20023, Windy Wheat.

DC-73. Lacy pattern of green, chartreuse, and gold.

Apply 2 coats of GL602, Orange; then 3 coats of AN324, Antique Green Art.

DC-74. Dark antique green with pools of dark brown.

Apply 2 coats of GL615, Mahogany Brown; then 2 coats of SY541, Pattern Base; and finally 2 coats of AN324, Antique Green Art.

DC-75. Dark green with patterns of light green and dots of yellow.

Apply 2 coats of GL609, Emerald Green; then 2 coats of SY541, Pattern Base; and finally 2 coats of AN324, Antique Green Art.

DC-76. Dark green with red-orange winding through it.

Apply 2 coats of GL609, Emerald Green; then 2 coats of SY541, Pattern Base; and finally 2 coats of GL614, Matador Red.

DC-77. Ranges from deep green to whispers of yellow.

Apply 2 coats of GL609, Emerald Green; then 2 coats of SY540, Spill Base; and finally 2 coats of GL601, Marigold Yellow.

DC-78. Mottled ancient look of two-toned green and yellow.

Apply 1 coat of GL600, Buttercup Yellow; and then 1 coat of SY540, Spill Base; and finally 1 coat of AN324, Antique Green Art.

DC-79. Green and brown fernlike effect.

Apply 2 coats of AR610, Maplewood; then 2 coats of SY540, Spill Base; and finally 2 coats of SA380, Sage Green.

DC-80. Greens and browns of light and dark hues.

Apply 2 coats of AR620, Rusty Amber; then 2 coats of SY540, Spill Base; and finally 2 coats of GL609, Emerald Green.

DC-81. Soft green with overtones of pink and green.

Apply 2 coats of GL623, Rose Pink; then 2 coats of SY541, Pattern Base; and 3 coats of AN324, Antique Green Art.

DC-82. Torrid jungle colors of green and yellow.

Apply 2 coats of AN324, Antique Green Art; then 2 coats of SY540, Spill Base; and finally 3 coats of SP913, Flame Yellow.

DC-83. Mystical greens, deep browns, gray, and rust color.

Apply 2 coats of AR610, Maplewood; then 2 coats of AN324, Antique Green Art.

DC-84. Filigree of light green and tan over blue-green.

Apply 2 coats of SP903, Blue; then 2 coats of AN324, Antique Green Art.

DC-85. Gray and brown spill mixture in a marbleized pattern.

Apply 3 coats of GL630, Gull Grey; then 2

coats SY540, Spill; and finally 2 coats of GL615, Mahogany Brown.

DC-86. Gray and blue patterns of marbleized color.

Apply 2 coats of GL628, Hawaiian Blue; then 2 coats 541, Cascade; and finally 2 to 3 coats of GL630, Gull Grey.

DC-87. A charming effect of pale tangerine and turquoise.

Apply 2 coats of GL632, Tangerine; then 2 coats of GL608, Turquoise.

DC-88. Mottled hues of orange and tan.

Apply 2 coats of GL602, Tangerine; then 3 coats of SP904, Tan.

DC-89. Red-orange swirls with dark brown and black undertones.

Apply 2 coats of GL615, Mahogany Brown; then 2 coats of GL631, Chinese Red.

DC-90. Light tangerine with pools of deep brown.

Apply 2 coats of AR616, Manzanita Brown; then drip a heavy coat of GL632, Tangerine, around the edges.

DC-91. Purple and blue patterns in a spill effect.

Apply 3 coats of GL633, Royal Purple; 2 coats of SY540, Spill Base; then 3 coats of GL634, Royal Blue.

DC-92. Swirls of purple and white with reds in a marbleized pattern.

Apply 2 coats of GL638, Opaque White; then 1 heavy coat of 20020, Plum Beautiful; and sponge on GL638, Opaque White.

DC-93. Red background with spots and runs of green breaking through the surface.

Apply 2 coats of GL669, Green; then 2 coats of SY541, Pattern Base; and finally 2 coats of GL614, Matador Red.

DC-94. Allover speckles and runs of red and black.

Apply 2 coats of AR612, Cinnamon Brown; then 3 coats of GL631, Chinese Red.

DC-95. Gay red and yellow of the Mardi Gras.

Apply 2 coats of GL614, Matador Red; then 2 coats of SY541, Pattern Base; and finally 2 coats of GL625, Chartreuse.

DC-96. Warm, mysterious effect of red and chartreuse.

Apply 2 coats of GL625, Chartreuse; then 1

coat of SY541, Pattern Base; then 2 coats of GL614, Matador Red; then 1 coat of Pattern Base; and finally another coat of Matador Red.

DC-97. The look of red and black molten lava.

Apply 2 coats of GL614, Matador Red; then 2 coats of SY541, Pattern Base; and finally 1 coat of AR684, Charcoal Lava Art.

DC-98. Rock like forms of red and gray.

Apply 3 coats of GL637, Christmas Red; then 3 coats of GL630, Gull Grey; around the edge then pour or drip an uneven border of GL638, Opaque White, in between colors.

DC-99. Mottled effect of raspberries and cream.

Apply 2 coats of GL626, Royal Ruby; then 1 coat of GL617, Clear Brushing; and finally 1 coat of SA381, Palomino.

DC-100. Beaded gray and white over a red base.

Apply 3 coats of GL637, Christmas Red; then 1 coat of GL638, Opaque White; and finally 2 coats of GL630, Gull Grey.

DC-101. An iridescent effect of red and orange.

Apply 2 coats of GL632, Tangerine; then 2 coats of GL614, Matador Red.

DC-102. All the fire of hot red-orange coals.

Apply 2 coats of SP913, Flame Yellow; then 2 coats of GL614, Matador Red.

DC-103. Multicolored specks over a red and yellow mottled background.

Apply 2 coats of GL614, Matador Red; then 2 coats of SP913, Flame Yellow.

DC-104. A hammered-metal pattern of red and blue.

Apply 3 coats of GL631, Chinese Red, then 2 coats of SY541, Pattern Base; and finally 2 coats of GL628, Hawaiian Blue.

DC-105. Enchanting reds with dimpled browns and tans.

Apply 3 coats of GL637, Christmas Red; then 2 coats of AR612, Cinnamon Brown.

DC-106. Tans and blues of the beach with white swirls.

Apply 2 coats of AR610, Maplewood; then 2 coats of SY541, Pattern Base; and finally 2 coats of SP903, Blue.

DC-107. Warm tans and brown tone.

Apply 2 coats of AN304, Antique Beige; then 2 coats of GL617, Clear Brushing; and finally 2 coats of GL615, Mahogany Brown.

DC-108. Irregular swirls of pinkish tan.

Apply 1 coat of GL617, Clear Brushing; then 2 coats of GL623, Rose Pink; and finally 1 coat of AR610, Maplewood.

DC-109. Basic matt turquoise with spills of purple, red, and white.

Apply 3 coats of AN314, Antique Turquoise; then 1 heavy coat of 20020, Plum Beautiful.

DC-110. Turquoise and brown in a matt mixture of spill effects.

Apply 2 coats of AN314, Antique Turquoise; then 2 coats of AN317, Antique Brown.

DC-111. Turquoise blue with small and large brown specks.

Apply 2 coats of GL615, Mahogany Brown; then 2 coats of SY540, Spill Base; and follow with 2 coats of GL608, Turquoise.

DC-112. A blend of turquoise blue and greens over black.

Apply 2 coats of SA359, Black; then 2 coats of SY541, Pattern Base; and finally 2 coats of SA356, Peacock Green.

DC-113. Beautiful turquoise with a paisley print of brown.

Apply 2 coats of AR610, Maplewood; then 2 coats of SY541, Pattern Base; and finally 2 coats of GL628, Hawaiian Blue.

DC-114. Light turquoise and tans of Persian beauty.

Apply 2 coats of GL615, Mahogany Brown; then 2 coats of GL628, Hawaiian Blue.

DC-115. Deep turquoise-green with metallic black areas.

Apply 2 coats of GL628, Hawaiian Blue; then 2 coats of AR686, Black Diamond Art.

DC-116. Turquoise blue with splashes and streaks of golden tan.

Apply 2 coats of GL628, Hawaiian Blue; then 2 coats of AN324, Antique Green Art.

DC-117. Overall white with spots of dark-brown breaking through the surface in large and small patterns.

Apply 2 coats of GL615, Mahogany Brown; then 1 coat of MA721, White.

DC-118. Dainty white, green, and rosy pink.

Apply 2 coats of GL623, Rose Pink; then 2 coats of GL617, Clear Brushing; then 2 coats of SA380, Sage Green; and finally drop a heavy coat of GL638, Opaque White, around the edge.

DC-119. Patterns of pink outlined in black.

Apply 2 coats of SA359 Black; then 2 coats of ST541, Pattern Base; and finally 2 coats of SA357, Carnation Pink.

DC-120. Yellow and brown spill effect.

Apply 2 coats of GL600, Buttercup Yellow; then 2 coats of SY540, Spill Base; and finally 2 coats of AR612, Maplewood, or AR610, Cinnamon Brown.

DC-121. Allover patterns of yellows, tans and light green.

Apply 2 coats of AR620, Rusty Amber; then 1 coat of SY541, Pattern Base; and finally 2 coats of SA380, Sage Green.

DC-122. Exotic yellow and black of a slinky jungle cat.

Apply 2 coats of SA359, Black; then 2 coats of ST541, Pattern Base; and 2 coats of SP913, Flame Yellow.

DC-123. Sponge design of yellow on a deep-brown base.

Apply 2 coats of GL615, Mahogany Brown; and then 3 coats of SP913, Flame Yellow.

DC-124. Pale yellow-green with tan streaks.

Apply 2 coats of AR610, Maplewood; then 2 coats of SY540, Spill Base; and finally 2 coats of GL625, Chartreuse.

DC-125. Yellow-brown with swirls of white.

Apply 2 coats of GL615, Mahogany Brown; then 2 coats of SY540, Spill Base; and finally 2 coats of GL601, Marigold Yellow.

CERAMICHROME GLAZE COMBINATIONS

CC-1. Amber and gold colors in a sunburst design.

Apply 4 coats of 822, Sunburst; then sponge heavily in a mottled pattern 1 heavy coat of 532, Sahara Gold.

CC-2. Amber and red in a marbleized spill pattern.

Apply 3 coats of 532, Sahara Gold; then 3 coats of 611, Harem Rose.

CC-3. Amber mosaic patterns.

Apply 4 coats of 821, Mosaic; then sponge heavily in a mottled pattern 1 heavy coat of 532, Sahara Gold.

CC-4. Black and white textured patterns.

Apply 2 coats of 425, Black Matt; then sponge on a coat of 721, Snowflake White, in a mottled pattern.

CC-5. Black and yellow textured pattern.

Apply 3 coats of 431, Black Matt; then sponge on 1 heavy coat of 723, Primrose Yellow, in a mottled pattern.

CC-6. Blue and brown mixture in a spill effect.

Apply 3 coats of 1212, Bronze Metallic Base; then 2 coats of 1213, Metallic Overtone Glaze.

CC-7. Aqua-blue and white spill effect in a fernlike pattern.

Apply 2 coats of 508, Aqua; then 3 coats of 701, White Spill.

CC-8. Blue variations with gold patterns of mottled color.

Sponge on 2 coats of 207, Light Blue, in a mottled pattern; then apply 2 heavy coats of 510, Crater Lake Art.

CC-9. Light-blue to dark-blue patterns of mottled color with gold filigree patterns floating on top of the glaze.

Apply 3 coats of 542, Sapphire Blue; then 2 coats of 521, Filigree Glaze.

CC-10. Blue textured surface with orange breaking through the surface glaze.

Apply 4 coats of 904, Brilliant Orange; then 2 coats of 404, Blue Satin Matt.

CC-11. Blue and orange mixture of swirling color.

Apply 3 coats of 204, Mandarin Blue; then 3 coats of 876, Caliph Orange.

CC-12. Blue and silver-green spill effects.

Apply 3 coats of 204, Mandarin Blue; then 3 coats of 509, Silver Spruce.

CC-13. Blue and clear mixture of color in a wavelike pattern.

Apply 1 coat of 207, Light Blue; 2 coats of 003, Clear Glaze; 2 coats of 207, Light Blue again; then finally 1 coat of 003, Clear Glaze.

CC-14. Blue with streaks of brown and turquoise.

Apply 2 coats of 751, Spiced Date; then 3 coats of 707, Turquoise Spill; and finally 2 coats of 207, Light Blue.

CC-15. Sapphire-blue and turquoise spill effects.

Apply 2 coats of 542, Sapphire Blue; then 3 coats of 707, Turquoise Spill.

CC-16. Sapphire-blue and white spill effects in flowing pattern.

Apply 2 coats of 542, Sapphire Blue; then 3 coats of 701, White Spill.

CC-17. Brown and yellow spill patterns.

Apply 2 coats of 543, Redwood Burn; then 3 coats of 703, Yellow Spill.

C-18. Brown and red spill effects.

Apply 3 coats of 543, Redwood Burn; then 3 coats of 763, Royal Crimson.

CC-19. Brown and white fissured cratered glaze effect.

Apply 4 coats of 1211, Moon Pebble; then 2 coats of 1216, Meteorite.

CC-20. Green and gray-brown with white patterns of color showing through the top glaze.

Apply 2 coats of 503, Olive Green; 2 coats of 701, White Spill, with a sponge; then 2 coats of 502, Silky Grey.

CC-21. Green and turquoise spill effect in wavy patterns.

Apply 2 coats of 614, Precious Emerald; then 3 coats of 707, Turquoise Spill.

CC-22. Green and turquoise spill effect with dark-brown streaks breaking through.

Apply 2 coats of 754, Jamica Palm; then 3 coats of 707, Turquoise Spill.

CC-23. Silver-green and clear spill patterns.

Apply 2 coats of 003, Clear Glaze; then 2 coats of 509, Silver Spruce. This combination is best used over a white body.

CC-24. Green to blue spill effects in a broken pattern.

Apply 2 coats of 541, Leaf Green; 3 coats of 003, Clear Glaze; then 3 coats of 2014, Azure.

CC-25. Green and blue patterns in a broken design.

Apply 3 coats of 2004, Teal Green; then 3 coats of 542, Sapphire Blue.

CC-26. Two-toned green spill effects.

Apply 4 coats of 212, Lettuce Green; then 3 coats of 754, Jamica Palm.

CC-27. Green and brown colors in a cascade pattern.

Apply 2 coats of 2020, Cinnamon; 2 coats of 707, Turquoise Spill; and finally 2 coats of 464, Green Moss Art.

CC-28. Moss green with gray and white tints in a flowing fissured pattern.

Apply 3 coats of 731, Silver Flame; then 4 coats of 585, Tesserae.

CC-29. Gold metallic tones with mottled patterns.

Apply 1 heavy coat of 1214, Sun Gold; then sponge on 1 coat of 796 or 797, White Brocade, in a mottled design.

CC-30. Metallic gray with white mosaic patterns which have green tints of color at the edges.

Apply 2 coats of 482, Gunmetal; then 4 coats of 585, Tesserae.

CC-31. Purple and blue spill effects.

Apply 3 coats of 762, Royal Purple; then 3 coats of 542, Sapphire Blue.

CC-32. Red marbleized mixture of different hues.

Apply 4 coats of 871, Bagdad Red; sponge on 1 coat of 763, Royal Crimson; then sponge on 1 heavy coat of 875, Flame Red.

CC-33. Turquoise and aqua in a marbleized spill pattern.

Apply 3 coats of 508, Aqua; then 3 coats of 707, Turquoise Spill.

CC-34. Turquoise and yellow in a marbleized spill pattern.

Apply 3 coats of 220, Bright Yellow; then 3 coats of 707, Turquoise Spill.

CC-35. White and orange mosaic patterns.

Apply 3 coats of 1201, Orange Glo; then 4 or 5 coats of 585, Tesserae.

CC-36. Cascade patterns of white and silver-gray.

Apply 2 coats of C40, White; then 2 coats of 509, Silver Spruce.

CC-37. White and black textured pattern.

Apply 3 coats of 421, White Matt; then sponge on 1 coat of 725, Iron Black, in a mottled pattern.

CC-38. Tropical effects of yellow, green, and brown.

Apply 4 coats of 703, Yellow Spill; then sponge on 1 coat of 1201, Orange Glo, in a mottled pattern; and finally sponge on 1 coat of 531, Sinbad Brown, also in a mottled pattern.

CC-39. Yellow and amber in a wavy mixture of spill colors.

Apply 2 coats of 220, Bright Yellow; 2 coats of 221, Honey Gold; 1 coat of 220, Bright Yellow; and finally 1 coat of 221, Honey Gold.

CC-40. Yellow-brown with swirls of yellow and white.

Apply 3 coats of 531, Sinbad Brown; then 2 coats of 701, White Spill; and finally 2 coats of 201, Lemon Yellow.

CC-41. Yellow and blue spill effects.

Apply 2 coats of 542, Sapphire Blue; then 3 coats of 703, Yellow Spill.

AMACO GLAZE COMBINATIONS

There are no individual combinations listed for this particular company. Their glazes are so completely reliable and predictable that the author has decided to give only suggested variations and leave the rest to the reader and his imagination to work out.

SUGGESTED VARIATIONS

AV-1. Apply 2 coats of any glaze as a base color in the LG series; then apply 4 coats LG10, Clear; and finally apply 2 to 3 coats of any gloss glaze that will harmonize with the base coat. Fire to cone 06-05 depending upon the amount of spill effect desired.

AV-2. Apply 2 coats of any matt glaze except the high-fire matts; then apply 4 to 5 coats of LG10, Clear; and finally apply 3 to 4 coats of any top glaze color that will harmonize well with the base coat. Fire to cone 06-04 depending on the amount of spill effect desired.

23
EARTHENWARE GLAZES
CONE 020-05

Earthenware glazes, sometimes known as soft glazes, are those that fire to maturity at cone 020-05. The typical earthenware glaze is glossy and smooth to the touch, or at least this has been so until the last decade or so. Today many semi-gloss, satin matts, and true matts are available in the earthenware glaze range due to the intense amount of research which has been done both in industry and by studio potters on the subject.

There are numerous compounds that the potter can use to formulate an earthenware glaze. Consequently many glaze varieties are possible to the potter who wishes to experiment. Even by using one formula as a base with which to work and adding varying amounts of opacifiers and colorants, many glaze varieties are possible.

The basic difference between earthenware glazes and those that fire at higher temperatures is that the former must use lead, sodium, or boron as a fluxing agent to melt the glass-forming silica which is necessary in any glaze.

The glazes in this chapter range from the high-gloss type to true matts. They are organized first by cone level, 020–05, then by color, alphabetically, and finally by surface, whether gloss, semi-gloss, satin matt, or matt.

Any of the glaze recipes can be colored or altered in color by the use of the colorants listed in Chapter 33, Glaze Colorants. And any of those that are listed as clear, translucent, or opaque make good base glazes for the colorants.

The reader will also find lists of possible chemical substitutions in Chapter 34, Dictionary of Clay and Glaze Compounds.

Note. The glazes in this chapter are labeled toxic or nontoxic. Toxic glazes should be carefully handled both in formulation and in application. During preparation the potter should wear a dust mask to prevent inhalation of toxic materials and not allow these materials to come into prolonged contact with the skin. Frequent washing of the hands when handling these glazes is a wise precaution. Toxic glazes should be applied by brushing and dipping—never spraying. For even under the best conditions some inhalation of the toxic mist from the spray is bound to take place or, equally bad, the mist from the spray gun can settle on the skin and be absorbed into the body system.

FORMULAS FOR EARTHENWARE GLAZES

EG-1

Clear Glaze   Cone 020
alkaline, transparent, gloss, nontoxic

Mixing. Weigh out the ingredients and mix by using one of the methods outlined in Chapter 17 on Glaze Preparation.

Application. Apply to cone 04 bisque by brushing, dipping, or spraying. See Chapter 17 for more details.

Firing. Fire normally in any type kiln to the cone level indicated.

Fired Results. This glaze fires to a clear gloss at cone 020. It is a good base for any of the colorants except iron oxide in amounts above .5%.

Colemanite	35.9
Pemco frit #25	52.0
Lithium carbonate	10.1
Kaolin (any)	3.0
Add:	
Bentonite	2.0
C.M.C.	1 tsp.

EG-2

Clear Glaze Cone 020

alkaline, transparent, gloss, nontoxic

Mixing. Mix in the manner of EG-1.

Application. Apply in the manner of EG-1.

Firing. Fire in the manner of EG-1.

Fired Results. This glaze fires to a clear gloss at cone 020. It is a good base for any of the alkaline colorants, especially the coppers and cobalts.

Colemanite	42.0
Pemco frit #25	26.0
Lithium carbonate	5.0
Cryolite	9.0
Silica	18.0
Add:	
Bentonite	2.0
C.M.C.	1 tsp.

EG-3

Clear Glaze Cone 018

alkaline-frit, transparent, gloss, nontoxic

Mixing. Mix in the manner of EG-1.

Application. Apply in the manner of EG-1.

Firing. Fire in the manner of EG-1.

Fired Results. This glaze fires to a clear gloss at cone 018. It is a good base for any of the alkaline colorants.

Ferro frit #3819	45.0
Ferro frit #3134	25.4
Lithium carbonate	10.3
Kaolin	4.0
Silica	15.3
Add:	
Bentonite	2.0
C.M.C.	1 tsp.

EG-4

Clear Glaze Cone 018

alkaline, transparent, gloss, nontoxic

Mixing. Mix in the manner of EG-1.

Application. Apply in the manner of EG-1.

Firing. Fire in the manner of EG-1.

Fired Results. This glaze fires to a clear gloss at cone 018. It is a good base for any of the colorants listed in Chapter 33 for earthenware glazes.

Bismuth oxide	73.4
Lithium carbonate	3.7
Hommel frit #259	15.5
Silica	6.4
Add:	
Bentonite	2.0
C.M.C.	1 tsp.

EG-5

Clear Satin-Matt Glaze Cone 018

alkaline, transparent, satin matt, nontoxic

Mixing. Mix in the manner of EG-1.

Application. Apply in the manner of EG-1.

Firing. Fire in the manner of EG-1.

Fired Results. This glaze fires to a clear satin matt at cone 018. This is an especially good base for the coppers and cobalts. The addition of .5% iron oxide can give some interesting hues.

Pemco frit #25	42.6
Pemco frit #54	27.3
Lithium carbonate	9.9
Kaolin (any)	6.1
Silica	14.1
Add:	
C.M.C.	1 tsp.

EG-6

Clear Matt Cone 018

alkaline, transparent, clear matt, nontoxic

Mixing. Mix in the manner of EG-1.

Application. Apply in the manner of EG-1.

Firing. Fire in the manner of EG-1.

Fired Results. This glaze fires to a clear matt at cone 018. The best colorants for this glaze are copper and cobalt.

Ferro frit #3819	54.4
Ferro frit #3223	35.6
Lithium carbonate	8.0
Kaolin (EPK)	2.0
Add:	
Bentonite	2.0
C.M.C.	1 tsp.

EG-7   **Clear Semi-Matt Glaze Cone 016**
alkaline, transparent, semi-matt, nontoxic

Mixing. Mix in the manner of EG-1.

Application. Apply in the manner of EG-1.

Firing. Fire in the manner of EG-1.

Fired Results. This glaze fires to a clear semi-matt at cone 016. Avoid iron as a colorant as it tends to give muddy colors in this glaze.

Hommel frit #259	54.4
Ferro frit #3223	35.6
Lithium carbonate	8.0
Kaolin	2.0
Add:	
Bentonite	2.0
C.M.C.	1 tsp.

EG-8   **Clear Satin-Matt Glaze Cone 106**
alkaline, transparent, clear satin matt, nontoxic

Mixing. Mix in the manner of EG-1.

Application. Apply in the manner of EG-1.

Firing. Fire in the manner of EG-1.

Fired Results. This glaze fires to a clear satin matt at cone 016. Iron oxide can be used in this glaze to tint other colors if it does not exceed .5% of the dry body weight of the glaze.

Pemco frit #25	42.6
Pemco frit #54	27.3
Lithium carbonate	9.8
Kaolin	6.2
Silica	14.1
Add:	
C.M.C.	1 tsp.

EG-9   **Green Gloss Glaze Cone 016**
lead, opaque, gloss, toxic

Mixing. This glaze contains a toxic chemical; it should therefore be handled with caution. (See note at the beginning of this chapter.)

Application. Apply only by dipping or brushing. (See note at the beginning of this chapter.)

Firing. Fire in the manner of EG-1.

Fired Results. This glaze fires to a dark forest-green at cone 016.

Ferro frit #5301	49.0
White lead	25.0
Copper	19.0
Silica	7.0

EG-10   **Translucent Satin Matt Cone 016**
alkaline-barium, translucent, cloudy white, toxic

Mixing. Mix in the manner of EG-9.

Application. Apply in the manner of EG-9.

Firing. Fire in the manner of EG-1.

Fired Results. This glaze fires to a translucent satin matt at cone 016.

Lithium carbonate	13.4
Ferro frit #3819	56.2
Kaolin	4.8
Barium carbonate	20.4
Silica	5.2
Add:	
Bentonite	2.0
C.M.C.	1 tsp.

EG-11   **Egyptian Blue Gloss Glaze Cone 015**
alkaline, transparent, gloss, nontoxic

Mixing. Mix in the manner of EG-1.

Application. Apply in the manner of EG-1.

Firing. Fire in the manner of EG-1.

Fired Results. This glaze fires to a lovely Egyptian blue at cone 015. It tends to crackle with age.

Ferro frit #3134	78.5
Lithium carbonate	19.5
Copper oxide	2.0
Add:	
Bentonite	1.0
C.M.C.	1 tsp.

EG-12

Clear Glaze   Cone 015
alkaline, transparent, gloss, nontoxic

Mixing. Mix in the manner of EG-1.

Application. Apply in the manner of EG-1.

Firing. Fire in the manner of EG-1.

Fired Results. This glaze fires to a clear gloss at cone 015.

Colemanite	40.0
Pemco frit #25	55.0
Kaolin (EPK)	5.0
Add:	
Bentonite	2.0
C.M.C.	1 tsp.

EG-13

Clear Glaze   Cone 015
alkaline, transparent, gloss, nontoxic

Mixing. Mix in the manner of EG-1.

Application. Apply in the manner of EG-1.

Firing. Fire in the manner of EG-1.

Fired Results. This glaze fires to a clear glaze at cone 015.

Ferro frit #3819	57.6
Ferro frit #3223	34.4
Lithium carbonate	8.0
Add:	
Bentonite	2.0
C.M.C.	1 tsp.

EG-14

Clear Glaze   Cone 015
alkaline, transparent, gloss, nontoxic

Mixing. Mix in the manner of EG-1.

Application. Apply in the manner of EG-1.

Firing. Fire in the manner of EG-1.

Fired Results. This glaze fires to a clear glaze at cone 015.

Ferro frit #3819	45.5
Ferro frit #3134	24.4
Lithium carbonate	10.1
Kaolin	6.0
Silica	14.0
Add:	
Bentonite	2.0
C.M.C.	1 tsp.

EG-15

Clear Glaze   Cone 015
lead, transparent, gloss, toxic

Mixing. Mix in the manner of EG-9.

Application. Apply in the manner of EG-9.

Firing. Fire in the manner of EG-1.

Fired Results. This glaze fires to a clear glaze at cone 015.

White lead	28.0
Ferro frit #3134	32.0
Lithium carbonate	8.0
Silica	28.0
Bentonite	2.0
Add:	
C.M.C.	1 tsp.

EG-16

Clear Matt   Cone 015
alkaline, transparent, matt, nontoxic

Mixing. Mix in the manner of EG-1.

Application. Apply in the manner of EG-1.

Firing. Fire in the manner of EG-1.

Fired Results. This glaze fires to a clear matt at cone 015.

Bismuth oxide	63.6
Colemanite	9.5
Kaolin	9.4
Silica	17.5

EG-17

Sage Green Glaze   Cone 015
alkaline, opaque, semi-gloss, nontoxic

Mixing. Mix in the manner of EG-1.

Application. Apply in the manner of EG-1.

Firing. Fire in the manner of EG-1.

Fired Results. This glaze fires to a sage green at cone 015. If overfired it turns metallic.

Hommel frit #33	45.3
Hommel frit #259	54.7
Add:	
Bentonite	2.0
Green chrome oxide	3.0
Titanium oxide	8.0
C.M.C.	1 tsp.

EG-18   Turquoise Gloss Glaze   Cone 015

alkaline, transparent, gloss, nontoxic

Mixing. Mix in the manner of EG-1.

Application. Apply in the manner of EG-1.

Firing. Fire in the manner of EG-1.

Fired Results. This glaze fires to a turquoise at cone 015. Use over a white body for best effect.

Colemanite	39.5
Ferro frit #3819	56.6
Kaolin (EPK)	3.9
Add:	
Bentonite	1.0
Copper oxide	2.5
C.M.C.	1 tsp.

EG-19   Chrome Red Gloss Glaze   Cone 015

lead, transparent, gloss, toxic

Mixing. Mix in the manner of EG-9.

Application. Apply in the manner of EG-9.

Firing. All red and orange glazes should be fired separately for best results, with the kiln vented up to at least two cones below the maturing point of the glaze. Also they should never be overfired for they tend to turn gray to green.

Fired Results. This glaze fires to a bright chrome red at cone 015.

White lead	78.5
Lithium carbonate	5.5
Silica	16.0
Add:	
Bentonite	2.0
Green chrome oxide	3.5
C.M.C.	1 tsp.

EG-20   Tangerine Gloss Glaze   Cone 015

lead, translucent, gloss, toxic

Mixing. Mix in the manner of EG-9.

Application. Apply in the manner of EG-9.

Firing. Fire in the manner of EG-19.

Fired Results. This glaze fires to a tangerine orange at cone 015.

White lead	78.5
Lithium carbonate	6.0
Silica	15.5
Add:	
Bentonite	2.0
Chrome oxide	2.0
Iron oxide	0.1
C.M.C.	1 tsp.

EG-21   Indian Red Matt Glaze   Cone 015

lead, translucent, matt, toxic

Mixing. Mix in the manner of EG-9.

Application. Apply in the manner of EG-9.

Firing. Fire in the manner of EG-19.

Fired Results. This glaze fires to an Indian red matt at cone 015.

White lead	78.5
Lithium carbonate	6.0
Silica	15.5
Add:	
Bentonite	2.0
Chrome oxide	1.0
Iron oxide	0.1
C.M.C.	1 tsp.

EG-22   Geranium Red Gloss Glaze   Cone 015

lead, semi-opaque, gloss, toxic

Mixing. Mix in the manner of EG-9.

Application. Apply in the manner of EG-9.

Firing. Fire in the manner of EG-19.

Fired Results. This glaze fires to a geranium red gloss at cone 015.

White lead	78.5
Lithium carbonate	6.0
Silica	15.5
Add:	
Bentonite	2.0
Chrome oxide	3.1
Iron oxide	0.1
C.M.C.	1 tsp.

EG-23 **Lacquer Red Gloss Glaze Cone 015**
lead, opaque, gloss, toxic

Mixing. Mix in the manner of EG-9.

Application. Apply in the manner of EG-9.

Firing. Fire in the manner of EG-1.

Fired Results. This glaze fires to a deep red at cone 015.

White lead	78.5
Lithium carbonate	6.0
Silica	15.5
Add:	
Tin oxide	6.5
Chrome oxide	3.1
Iron oxide	0.1

EG-24 **Nasturtium Red Matt Glaze Cone 015**
lead, opaque, matt, toxic

Mixing. Mix in the manner of EG-9.

Application. Apply in the manner of EG-9.

Firing. Fire in the manner of EG-19.

Fired Results. This glaze fires to a bright orange-red at cone 015.

White lead	78.5
Lithium carbonate	6.0
Silica	15.5
Add:	
Bentonite	2.0
Chrome oxide	3.0
Titanium oxide	1.6
Iron oxide	0.1
C.M.C.	1 tsp.

EG-25 **Venetian Red Gloss Glaze Cone 015**
lead, transparent, gloss, toxic

Mixing. Mix in the manner of EG-9.

Application. Apply in the manner of EG-9.

Firing. Fire in the manner of EG-19.

Fired Results. This glaze fires to a deep red gloss at cone 015.

White lead	78.5
Lithium carbonate	6.0
Silica	15.5
Add:	
Bentonite	2.0
Chrome oxide	0.5
Iron oxide	0.1
C.M.C.	1 tsp.

EG-26 **Translucent White Glaze Cone 015**
alkaline, translucent, gloss, nontoxic

Mixing. Mix in the manner of EG-1.

Application. Apply in the manner of EG-1.

Firing. Fire in the manner of EG-1.

Fired Results. This glaze fires to a translucent white gloss at cone 015.

Ferro frit #3134	25.0
Pemco frit #25	37.0
Lithium carbonate	10.0
Kaolin	9.0
Silica	19.0
Add:	
Tin oxide	2.0
Bentonite	2.0

EG-27 **Translucent Base Glaze Cone 015**
alkaline-frit, translucent, cloudy, nontoxic

Mixing. Mix in the manner of EG-1.

Application. Apply in the manner of EG-1.

Firing. Fire in the manner of EG-1.

Fired Results. This glaze fires to a cloudy translucent white at cone 015.

Pemco frit #54	25.0
Ferro frit #25	44.0
Lithium carbonate	10.0
Tennessee ball clay #1	6.0
Silica	13.5
Bentonite	1.5

EG-28　　**Opaque White Glaze   Cone 015**
alkaline-frit, opaque, gloss, nontoxic

Mixing. Mix in the manner of EG-1.

Application. Apply in the manner of EG-1.

Firing. Fire in the manner of EG-1.

Fired Results. This glaze fires to an opaque at cone 015.

Ferro frit #3134	36.4
Pemco frit #25	55.6
Kaolin	8.0
Add:	
Tin oxide	10.0
Bentonite	2.0

EG-29　　**White Majolica Glaze   Cone 015**
lead, opaque, semi-gloss, toxic

Mixing. Mix in the manner of EG-9.

Application. Apply in the manner of EG-9.

Firing. Fire in the manner of EG-1.

Fired Results. This glaze fires to a milk white at cone 015.

Hommel frit #61	38.0
White lead	28.0
Lithium carbonate	8.0
Silica	19.0
Tin oxide	10.0
Bentonite	2.0
Add:	
C.M.C.	1 tsp.

EG-30　　**Cadmium Yellow Glaze   Cone 015**
alkaline-frit, transparent, gloss, nontoxic

Mixing. Mix in the manner of EG-1.

Application. Apply in the manner of EG-1.

Firing. Fire in the manner of EG-1.

Fired Results. This glaze fires to a cadmium yellow at cone 015.

Ferro frit #3819	80.5
Lithium carbonate	19.5
Add:	
Naples yellow stain	5.0
Bentonite	2.0
C.M.C.	1 tsp.

EG-31　　**Clear Semi-Gloss Glaze   Cone 014**
alkaline, transparent, clear semi-gloss, nontoxic

Mixing. Mix in the manner of EG-1.

Application. Apply in the manner of EG-1.

Firing. Fire in the manner of EG-1.

Fired Results. This glaze fires to a clear semi-gloss at cone 014. It is a good color base.

Ferro frit #3819	54.4
Ferro frit #3223	35.6
Lithium carbonate	8.0
Kaolin	2.0
Add:	
Bentonite	2.0
C.M.C.	1 tsp.

EG-32　　**Clear Satin-Matt Glaze   Cone 014**
alkaline-barium, transparent, clear satin matt, toxic

Mixing. Mix in the manner of EG-9.

Application. Apply in the manner of EG-9.

Firing. Fire in the manner of EG-1.

Fired Results. This glaze fires to a clear satin matt at cone 014.

Lithium carbonate	13.4
Ferro frit #3819	56.2
Kaolin (EPK)	4.8
Barium carbonate	20.4
Silica	5.2
Add:	
Bentonite	2.0
C.M.C.	1 tsp.

EG-33

Orange Gloss Glaze   Cone 012
lead, translucent, gloss, toxic

Mixing. Mix in the manner of EG-9.

Application. Apply in the manner of EG-9.

Firing. Fire in the manner of EG-19.

Fired Results. This glaze fires to a translucent orange gloss at cone 012.

White lead	74.0
Silica	13.0
Kaolin (EPK)	12.0
Chrome oxide	1.0
Add:	
Bentonite	2.0
C.M.C.	1 tsp.

EG-34

Orange Gloss Glaze   Cone 012
lead, transparent, gloss, toxic

Mixing. Mix in the manner of EG-9.

Application. Apply in the manner of EG-9.

Firing. Fire in the manner of EG-19.

Fired Results. This glaze fires to a transparent orange gloss at cone 012. It tends to be somewhat fluid so pieces should be properly stilted.

Red lead	67.5
Silica	29.5
Kaolin	10.5
Potassium bichromate	6.5
Soda ash	4.5
Bentonite	2.0
Add:	
C.M.C.	1 tsp.

EG-35

Bright-Orange Gloss Glaze   Cone 012
lead, translucent, gloss, toxic

Mixing. Mix in the manner of EG-9.

Application. Apply in the manner of EG-9.

Firing. Fire in the manner of EG-19.

Fired Results. This glaze fires to a bright translucent orange gloss at cone 012.

White lead	72.0
Silica	18.0
Kaolin (EPK)	7.0
Tin oxide	1.9
Chrome oxide	1.1
Add:	
Bentonite	2.0
C.M.C.	1 tsp.

EG-36

Candy-Apple-Red Gloss Glaze   Cone 012
lead, translucent, gloss, toxic

Mixing. Mix in the manner of EG-9.

Application. Apply in the manner of EG-9.

Firing. Fire in the manner of EG-19.

Fired Results. This glaze fires to a deep red gloss at cone 012.

Read lead	82.2
Lead chromate	5.8
Silica	5.2
Kaolin (EPK)	4.2
Tin oxide	2.2
Whiting	0.4
Add:	
Bentonite	2.0
C.M.C.	1 tsp.

EG-37

Chrome-Red Semi-Gloss Glaze   Cone 012
lead, translucent, semi-gloss, toxic

Mixing. Mix in the manner of EG-9.

Application. Apply in the manner of EG-9.

Firing. Fire in the manner of EG-19.

Fired Results. This glaze fires to a bright chrome-red gloss at cone 012.

White lead	75.5
Silica	14.5
Kaolin	6.5
Tin oxide	2.1
Chrome oxide	1.4
Add:	
Bentonite	2.0
C.M.C.	1 tsp.

EG-38 **Translucent White Gloss Glaze   Cone 012**
alkaline-frit, translucent, gloss, nontoxic

Mixing. Mix in the manner of EG-1.

Application. Apply in the manner of EG-1.

Firing. Fire in the manner of EG-1.

Fired Results. This glaze fires to a translucent white gloss at cone 012.

Ferro frit #3819	40.9
Ferro frit #3134	23.8
Lithium carbonate	10.7
Kaolin (EPK)	9.7
Silica	15.9
Add:	
Bentonite	2.0
C.M.C.	1 tsp.

EG-39 **Yellow Gloss Glaze   Cone 012**
lead, transparent, gloss, toxic

Mixing. Mix in the manner of EG-9.

Application. Apply in the manner of EG-9.

Firing. Fire in the manner of EG-1.

Fired Results. This glaze fires to a light yellow at cone 012.

White lead	80.0
Silica	14.0
Colemanite	6.0
Add:	
Bentonite	2.0
C.M.C.	1 tsp.

EG-40 **Slightly Yellow Glaze   Cone 012**
lead, transparent, gloss, toxic

Mixing. Mix in the manner of EG-9.

Application. Apply in the manner of EG-9.

Firing. Fire in the manner of EG-1.

Fired Results. This glaze fires to a transparent gloss with a slightly yellow tint at cone 012. It is slightly fluid and tends to craze with age.

White lead	63.0
Silica	26.0
Colemanite	9.0
Kaolin	3.0

EG-41 **Translucent Yellow Gloss Glaze   Cone 012**
lead, translucent, gloss, toxic

Mixing. Mix in the manner of EG-9.

Application. Apply in the manner of EG-9.

Firing. Fire in the manner of EG-1.

Fired Results. This glaze fires to a translucent yellow gloss at cone 012.

Red lead	82.2
White lead	5.8
Silica	5.2
Kaolin (EPK)	4.2
Tin oxide	2.2
Whiting	0.4
Add:	
Bentonite	2.0
C.M.C.	1 tsp.

EG-42 **Black Gloss Glaze   Cone 010**
alkaline, opaque, black gloss, nontoxic

Mixing. Mix in the manner of EG-1.

Application. Apply in the manner of EG-1.

Firing. Fire in the manner of EG-1.

Fired Results. This glaze fires to an opaque-black gloss at cone 010. It may be used over light or dark bodies with equally good results.

Pemco frit #25	69.5
Lithium carbonate	24.5
Zinc oxide	2.5
Magnesium carbonate	5.0
Add:	
Bentonite	2.0
Cobalt oxide	2.0
Chrome oxide	2.0
Manganese dioxide	2.0
Nickel oxide	2.0
Iron oxide	2.0
C.M.C.	1 tsp.

EG-43 **Clear Semi-Gloss Glaze Cone 010**
alkaline, transparent, clear semi-gloss, nontoxic

Mixing. Mix in the manner of EG-1.

Application. Apply in the manner of EG-1.

Firing. Fire in the manner of EG-1.

Fired Results. This glaze fires to a clear semi-gloss at cone 010.

Pemco frit #25	42.6
Hommel frit #14	27.3
Lithium carbonate	9.8
Kaolin	6.2
Silica	14.1
Add:	
C.M.C.	1 tsp.

EG-44 **Clear Stony Matt Glaze Cone 010**
alkaline, transparent, matt, nontoxic

Mixing. Mix in the manner of EG-1.

Application. Apply in the manner of EG-1.

Firing. Fire in the manner of EG-1.

Fired Results. This glaze fires to a semiclear stony matt at cone 010.

Colemanite	76.8
Wollastonite	5.1
Kaolin (EPK)	10.2
Silica	7.9
Add:	
Bentonite	2.0
C.M.C.	1 tsp.

EG-45 **Coral Red Semi-Gloss Glaze Cone 010**
lead, translucent, semi-gloss, toxic

Mixing. Mix in the manner of EG-9.

Application. Apply in the manner of EG-9.

Firing. Fire in the manner of EG-19.

Fired Results. This glaze fires to a bright coral red semi-gloss at cone 010. It tends to be slightly fluid so pieces should be properly stilted in the kiln.

Red lead	72.5
Silica	11.5
Kaolin	4.5
Tin oxide	4.5
Chrome oxide	4.0
Whiting	2.5
Bentonite	0.5
Add:	
C.M.C.	1 tsp.

EG-46 **Blood-Red Matt Glaze Cone 010**
lead, translucent, matt, toxic

Mixing. Mix in the manner of EG-9.

Application. Apply in the manner of EG-9.

Firing. Fire in the manner of EG-19.

Fired Results. This glaze fires to a blood-red matt at cone 010.

Red lead	74.5
Feldspar (Kona F-4)	9.5
Chrome oxide	6.0
Silica	4.5
Barium carbonate	4.0
Tin oxide	1.5
Add:	
Bentonite	2.0
C.M.C.	1 tsp.

EG-47 **Chrome Flame Red Matt Glaze Cone 010**
lead-barium, translucent, matt, toxic

Mixing. Mix in the manner of EG-9.

Application. Apply in the manner of EG-9.

Firing. Fire in the manner of EG-19.

Fired Results. This glaze fires to a bright flame red matt at cone 010.

Red lead	76.0
Feldspar (Custer)	10.0
Chrome oxide	6.0
Silica	4.0
Barium carbonate	4.0
Add:	
Bentonite	2.0
Tin oxide	2.0
C.M.C.	1 tsp.

EG-48

Ochre-Orange Gloss Glaze   Cone 010–08
lead, opaque, gloss, toxic

Mixing. Mix in the manner of EG-9.

Application. Apply in the manner of EG-9.

Firing. Fire in the manner of EG-19.

Fired Results. This glaze fires to an earthy orange gloss at cone 010. It is very attractive over heavily grogged clays.

White lead	62.8
Silica	17.2
Kaolin (EPK)	9.0
Potassium bichromate	4.6
Sodium carbonate	3.8
Tin oxide	2.6
Add:	
Bentonite	2.0
C.M.C.	1 tsp.

EG-49

Opaque Orange-Red Gloss Glaze   Cone 010
lead, opaque, gloss, toxic

Mixing. Mix in the manner of EG-9.

Application. Apply in the manner of EG-9.

Firing. Fire in the manner of EG-19.

Fired Results. This glaze fires to an orange-red gloss at cone 010.

White lead	65.5
Silica	18.1
Kaolin (EPK)	9.0
Tin oxide	4.0
Sodium carbonate	1.9
Chrome oxide	0.7
Lead chromate	0.5
Add:	
Bentonite	2.0
C.M.C.	1 tsp.

EG-50

Orange-Red Translucent Gloss Glaze   Cone 010
lead, translucent, gloss, toxic

Mixing. Mix in the manner of EG-9.

Application. Apply in the manner of EG-9.

Firing. Fire in the manner of EG-19.

Fired Results. This glaze fires to a translucent orange-red gloss at cone 010.

Red lead	70.4
Silica	10.5
Kaolin (EPK)	5.3
Chrome oxide	4.3
Feldspar (Kona F-4)	3.1
Tin oxide	2.1
Whiting	2.1
Bentonite	2.2
Add:	
C.M.C.	1 tsp.

EG-51

Orange-Red Semi-Gloss Glaze   Cone 010
lead, transparent, semi-gloss, toxic

Mixing. Mix in the manner of EG-9.

Application. Apply in the manner of EG-9.

Firing. Fire in the manner of EG-19.

Fired Results. This glaze fires to a semi-gloss orange-red at cone 010.

Red lead	79.5
Silica	7.5
Chrome oxide	6.0
Kaolin	4.0
Rutile	1.0
Bentonite	2.0
Add:	
C.M.C.	1 tsp.

EG-52

Bright Opalescent Glaze   Cone 010
alkaline, translucent, gloss, nontoxic

Mixing. Mix in the manner of EG-1.

Application. Apply in the manner of EG-1.

Firing. Fire in the manner of EG-1.

Fired Results. This is a bright translucent glaze at cone 010.

Ferro frit #3134	82.5
Boric acid	7.9
Kaolin (EPK)	9.5
Add:	
Bentonite	2.0
C.M.C.	1 tsp.

EG-53

Bright Translucent Glaze   Cone 010
alkaline, translucent, gloss, nontoxic

Mixing. Mix in the manner of EG-1.

Application. Apply in the manner of EG-1.

Firing. Fire in the manner of EG-1.

Fired Results. This is a bright translucent glaze that is a cloudy white at cone 010.

Colemanite	74.8
Boric acid	12.2
Kaolin (EPK)	10.0
Silica	5.0
Add:	
Bentonite	2.0
C.M.C.	1 tsp.

EG-54

Translucent Gloss Glaze   Cone 010
alkaline, translucent, gloss, nontoxic

Mixing. Mix in the manner of EG-1.

Application. Apply in the manner of EG-1.

Firing. Fire in the manner of EG-1.

Fired Results. This glaze fires to a translucent white at cone 010.

Colemanite	85.5
Kaolin (EPK)	7.7
Silica	6.8
Add:	
Bentonite	2.0

EG-55

Translucent White Gloss Glaze   Cone 010
raw alkaline, translucent, gloss, nontoxic

Mixing. Mix in the manner of EG-1.

Application. Apply in the manner of EG-1.

Firing. Fire in the manner of EG-1.

Fired Results. This glaze fires to a translucent white gloss at cone 010.

Silica	28.2
Borax (calcined)	27.2
Potassium carbonate	10.2
Sodium carbonate	16.2
Boric acid	5.9
Aluminum oxide	4.5
Whiting	2.8
Bentonite	1.1
Add:	
C.M.C.	1 tsp.

EG-56

Yellow Translucent Gloss Glaze   Cone 010
lead, translucent, gloss, toxic

Mixing. Mix in the manner of EG-9.

Application. Apply in the manner of EG-9.

Firing. Fire in the manner of EG-1.

Fired Results. This glaze fires to a translucent yellow gloss at cone 010.

Red lead	64.7
White lead	14.0
Silica	9.1
Kaolin (EPK)	4.7
Boric acid	4.5
Bentonite	1.0
Tin oxide	4.0
Add:	
C.M.C.	1 tsp.

EG-57

Translucent White Gloss   Cone 09
alkaline, translucent, gloss, nontoxic

Mixing. Mix in the manner of EG-1.

Application. Apply in the manner of EG-1.

Firing. Fire in the manner of EG-1.

Fired Results. This glaze fires to a translucent gloss white at cone 09.

Colemanite	89.5
Whiting	4.3
Kaolin (EPK)	6.2
Add:	
Bentonite	2.0
C.M.C.	1 tsp.

EG-58

Translucent White Gloss Glaze   Cone 09
alkaline, translucent, gloss, nontoxic

Mixing. Mix in the manner of EG-1.

Application. Apply in the manner of EG-1.

Firing. Fire in the manner of EG-1.

Fired Results. This glaze fires to a translucent white gloss at cone 09. It is a very good base for copper colorants.

Ferro frit #3819	52.5
Colemanite	17.8
Whiting	10.0
Silica	19.7
Add:	
Bentonite	2.0
C.M.C.	1 tsp.

EG-59

Translucent White Gloss Glaze   Cone 09
alkaline, translucent, gloss, nontoxic

Mixing. Mix in the manner of EG-1.

Application. Apply in the manner of EG-1.

Firing. Fire in the manner of EG-1.

Fired Results. This glaze fires to a buttery translucent gloss white at cone 09.

Pemco frit #25	13.0
Colemanite	68.0
Magnesium carbonate	19.0
Add:	
Bentonite	2.0
C.M.C.	1 tsp.

EG-60

Transparent Slightly Yellow Semi-Gloss Glaze   Cone 09
lead, transparent, semi-gloss, toxic

Mixing. Mix in the manner of EG-9.

Application. Apply in the manner of EG-9.

Firing. Fire in the manner of EG-1.

Fired Results. This glaze fires to a transparent light yellow semi-gloss at cone 09.

Red lead	42.2
Silica	34.3
Borax	11.7
Boric acid	9.3
Kaolin	2.5
Add:	
Bentonite	2.0
C.M.C.	1 tsp.

EG-61

Clear Glaze   Cone 08
alkaline-zinc, transparent, gloss, slightly toxic

Mixing. Mix in the manner of EG-9.

Application. Apply in the manner of EG-9.

Firing. Fire in the manner of EG-1.

Fired Results. This glaze fires to a clear gloss at cone 08. It is slightly fluid.

Zinc oxide	17.6
Pemco frit #25	52.2
Lithium carbonate	6.4
Kaolin (EPK)	5.8
Silica	18.0
Add:	
C.M.C.	1 tsp.

EG-62

Clear Glaze   Cone 08–06
alkaline, transparent, gloss, nontoxic

Mixing. Mix in the manner of EG-1.

Application. Apply in the manner of EG-1.

Firing. Fire in the manner of EG-1.

Fired Results. This glaze fires to a clear gloss at cone 08–06.

Soda ash	62.0
Borax	30.0
Whiting	20.0
Feldspar	110.0
Silica	25.0
Add:	
Bentonite	2.0
C.M.C.	1 tsp.

EG-63 **Clear Gloss Glaze   Cone 08**
colemanite, transparent, gloss, nontoxic

Mixing. Mix in the manner of EG-1.

Application. Apply in the manner of EG-1.

Firing. Fire in the manner of EG-1.

Fired Results. This glaze fires to a clear gloss at cone 08. It is a very stable glaze which gives uniform and reliable results. It is therefore a very good base for colorants.

Colemanite	70.0
Kaolin	10.5
Silica	11.0

EG-64 **Clear Glaze   Cone 08**
colemanite, transparent, semi-gloss, nontoxic

Mixing. Mix in the manner of EG-1.

Application. Apply in the manner of EG-1.

Firing. Fire in the manner of EG-1.

Fired Results. This glaze fires to a clear semi-gloss at cone 08.

Colemanite	70.0
Kaolin (EPK)	12.5
Silica	17.5
Add:	
Bentonite	2.0
C.M.C.	1 tsp.

EG-65 **Clear Glaze   Cone 08**
alkaline, transparent, semi-gloss, nontoxic

Mixing. Mix in the manner of EG-1.

Application. Apply in the manner of EG-1.

Firing. Fire in the manner of EG-1.

Fired Results. This glaze fires to a clear semi-gloss at cone 08. It is a very good and stable alkaline color base.

Colemanite	70.0
Kaolin	12.0
Whiting	1.0
Silica	17.0
Add:	
Bentonite	2.0
C.M.C.	1 tsp.

EG-66 **Clear Matt Glaze   Cone 08**
alkaline, transparent, matt, toxic

Mixing. Mix in the manner of EG-9.

Application. Apply in the manner of EG-9.

Firing. Fire in the manner of EG-1.

Fired Results. This glaze fires to a transparent matt at cone 08.

Zinc oxide	14.4
Barium carbonate	35.7
Lithium carbonate	8.8
Kaolin	15.1
Silica	26.0
Add:	
Bentonite	2.0
C.M.C.	1 tsp.

EG-67 **Satin Matt Glaze   Cone 08**
leadless-barium, translucent, matt, toxic

Mixing. Mix in the manner of EG-9.

Application. Apply in the manner of EG-9.

Firing. Fire in the manner of EG-1.

Fired Results. This glaze fires to a translucent matt at cone 08.

Zinc oxide	5.6
Nepheline syenite	44.7
Barium carbonate	17.2
Lithium carbonate	3.0
Whiting	9.5
Silica	20.0
Add:	
Bentonite	2.0
C.M.C.	1 tsp.

EG-68 **Clear Satin Matt Glaze   Cone 08**
colemanite, transparent, clear satin matt, nontoxic

Mixing. Mix in the manner of EG-1.

Application. Apply in the manner of EG-1.

Firing. Fire in the manner of EG-1.

Fired Results. This glaze fires to a clear satin matt at cone 08.

Colemanite	69.0
Kaolin (EPK)	11.0
Silica	20.0
Add:	
Bentonite	2.0
C.M.C.	1 tsp.

EG-69 **Clear Matt Glaze   Cone 08**
leadless, transparent, matt, slightly toxic

Mixing. Mix in the manner of EG-9.

Application. Apply in the manner of EG-9.

Firing. Fire in the manner of EG-1.

Fired Results. This glaze fires to a transparent matt at cone 08.

Hommel frit #259	40.0
Zinc oxide	9.8
Whiting	13.0
Silica	37.2
Add:	
Bentonite	2.0
C.M.C.	1 tsp.

EG-70 **Clear Matt Glaze   Cone 08**
alkaline-frit, transparent, matt, nontoxic

Mixing. Mix in the manner of EG-1.

Application. Apply in the manner of EG-1.

Firing. Fire in the manner of EG-1.

Fired Results. This glaze fires to a clear matt at cone 08.

Pemco frit #25	32.6
Pemco frit #54	38.4
Lithium carbonate	5.9
Silica	23.1
Add:	
Bentonite	2.0
C.M.C.	1 tsp.

EG-71 **Chromium Red   Cone 08–09**
lead, transparent, gloss, toxic

Mixing. Mix in the manner of EG-9.

Application. Apply in the manner of EG-9.

Firing. Fire in the manner of EG-19.

Fired Results. This glaze fires to a bright chrome red at cone 08–09.

Red lead	200.6
Potassium bichromate	14.4
Soda ash	6.1
Kaolin	25.8
Silica	54.0
Add:	
Bentonite	2.0
C.M.C.	1 tsp.

EG-72 **Translucent White Glaze   Cone 08**
alkaline, translucent, gloss, nontoxic

Mixing. Mix in the manner of EG-1.

Application. Apply in the manner of EG-1.

Firing. Fire in the manner of EG-1.

Fired Results. This glaze fires to a translucent white gloss at cone 08.

Ferro frit #3819	33.5
Colemanite	27.6
Strontium carbonate	13.1
Silica	24.8
Add:	
Bentonite	2.0
C.M.C.	1 tsp.

EG-73 **Off-White Translucent Gloss Glaze   Cone 08**
lead, translucent, gloss, toxic

Mixing. Mix in the manner of EG-9.

Application. Apply in the manner of EG-9.

Firing. Fire in the manner of EG-1.

Fired Results. This glaze fires to an off-white translucent gloss at cone 08.

White lead	58.0
Feldspar (Kona F-4)	18.3
Silica	18.0
Kaolin (EPK)	2.5
Whiting	2.2
Tin oxide	1.0
Add:	
Bentonite	2.0
C.M.C.	1 tsp.

EG-74 **Cloudy Translucent White Gloss Glaze   Cone 08**
lead-colemanite, translucent, gloss, toxic

Mixing. Mix in the manner of EG-9.

Application. Apply in the manner of EG-9.

Firing. Fire in the manner of EG-1.

Fired Results. This glaze fires to a cloudy translucent white gloss at cone 08.

White lead	53.0
Feldspar (Kona F-4)	17.0
Silica	16.0
Colemanite	5.0
Whiting	3.0
Kaolin (EPK)	3.0
Tin oxide	3.0
Add:	
Bentonite	2.0
C.M.C.	1 tsp.

EG-75 **Semi-Opaque Gloss Glaze   Cone 08**
lead-colemanite, semi-opaque, gloss, toxic

Mixing. Mix in the manner of EG-9.

Application. Apply in the manner of EG-9.

Firing. Fire in the manner of EG-1.

Fired Results. This glaze fires to a semi-opaque gloss white at cone 08.

White lead	53.0
Feldspar (potash)	16.0
Silica	15.0
Colemanite	5.0
Whiting	3.0
Kaolin	3.0
Tin oxide	10.0
Add:	
C.M.C.	1 tsp.

EG-76 **Opaque White Glaze   Cone 08**
alkaline, opaque, gloss, nontoxic

Mixing. Mix in the manner of EG-1.

Application. Apply in the manner of EG-1.

Firing. Fire in the manner of EG-1.

Fired Results. This glaze fires to an opaque gloss white at cone 08.

Pemco frit #25	28.2
Colemanite	9.6
Whiting	22.7
Kaolin (EPK)	6.0
Silica	33.5
Add:	
C.M.C.	1 tsp.

EG-77 **Yellow Translucent Gloss Glaze   Cone 08**
lead, translucent, gloss, toxic

Mixing. Mix in the manner of EG-9.

Application. Apply in the manner of EG-9.

Firing. Fire in the manner of EG-1.

Fired Results. This glaze fires to a yellow translucent gloss at cone 08.

White lead	55.4
Feldspar (Kona F-4)	21.0
Silica	16.5
Whiting	4.4
Zinc oxide	1.1
Tin oxide	1.5
Add:	
Bentonite	2.0
C.M.C.	1 tsp.

EG-78

Semi-Opaque Matt Glaze   Cone 08
barium, semi-opaque, matt, toxic

Mixing. Mix in the manner of EG-9.

Application. Apply in the manner of EG-9.

Firing. Fire in the manner of EG-1.

Fired Results. This glaze fires to a semi-opaque matt at cone 08.

Nepheline syenite	42.7
Barium carbonate	17.2
Zinc oxide	10.6
Lithium carbonate	3.0
Whiting	9.5
Silica	17.0
Add:	
Bentonite	2.0
C.M.C.	1 tsp.

EG-79

Translucent Yellow Gloss Glaze   Cone 08
lead, translucent, gloss, toxic

Mixing. Mix in the manner of EG-9.

Application. Apply in the manner of EG-9.

Firing. Fire in the manner of EG-1.

Fired Results. This glaze fires to a translucent yellow gloss at cone 08.

White lead	88.0
Kaolin	8.0
Tin oxide	4.0
Add:	
Bentonite	2.0
C.M.C.	1 tsp.

EG-80

Translucent White Glaze   Cone 07
colemanite, transparent, gloss, nontoxic

Mixing. Mix in the manner of EG-1.

Application. Apply in the manner of EG-1.

Firing. Fire in the manner of EG-1.

Fired Results. This glaze fires to a translucent white gloss at cone 08.

Ferro frit #3269	20.0
Colemanite	36.9
Zinc oxide	5.0
Kaolin (EPK)	10.8
Silica	27.3

EG-81

Translucent Glaze   Cone 07
leadless, translucent, gloss, toxic

Mixing. Mix in the manner of EG-9.

Application. Apply in the manner of EG-9.

Firing. Fire in the manner of EG-1.

Fired Results. This glaze fires to a translucent gloss at cone 07. If applied heavily it is a cloudy white.

Ferro frit #3269	45.0
Nepheline syenite	11.5
Barium carbonate	3.6
Whiting	4.6
Kaolin (EPK)	10.5
Flint	24.8
Add:	
Bentonite	2.0

EG-82

Black Matt   Cone 06
alkaline, opaque, black matt, nontoxic

Mixing. Mix in the manner of EG-1.

Application. Apply in the manner of EG-1.

Firing. Fire in the manner of EG-1.

Fired Results. This glaze fires to an opaque black matt at cone 06. It can be used on any color clay body.

Pemco frit #25	42.5
Lithium carbonate	8.6
Wollastonite	13.7
Kaolin	23.5
Silica	10.7
Bentonite	2.0
Add:	
Cobalt oxide	2.0
Chrome oxide	2.0
Black iron oxide	2.0
C.M.C.	1 tsp.

EG-83 **Black Gloss   Cone 06**
alkaline, opaque, black gloss, nontoxic

Mixing. Mix in the manner of EG-1.

Application. Apply in the manner of EG-1.

Firing. Fire in the manner of EG-1.

Fired Results. This glaze fires to an opaque black gloss at cone 06.

Pemco frit #25	49.0
Lithium carbonate	8.6
Wollastonite	13.9
Kaolin	19.5
Silica	20.5
Bentonite	2.0
Add:	
Cobalt oxide	2.0
Copper oxide	2.0
Chrome oxide	2.0
Nickel oxide	1.5
C.M.C.	1 tsp.

EG-84 **Egyptian Blue Gloss Glaze   Cone 06**
raw alkaline, transparent, gloss, nontoxic

Mixing. Mix in the manner of EG-1.

Application. Apply in the manner of EG-1.

Firing. Fire in the manner of EG-1.

Fired Results. This glaze fires to a beautiful Egyptian blue gloss at cone 06. It is transparent and therefore should be used over a white body.

Sodium carbonate	30.5
Lithium carbonate	8.5
Kaolin	22.5
Silica	38.5
Add:	
Copper oxide	2.5
Bentonite	1.0
C.M.C.	1 tsp.

EG-85 **Clear Gloss Glaze   Cone 06**
alkaline, transparent, gloss, nontoxic

Mixing. Mix in the manner of EG-1.

Application. Apply in the manner of EG-1.

Firing. Fire in the manner of EG-1.

Fired Results. This glaze fires to a clear gloss at cone 06. With the addition of 8%–10% tin oxide or 10% ultrox it makes an excellent opaque white. It is also a very good color base for any of the alkaline colorants.

Colemanite	25.8
Pemco frit #25	41.6
Kaolin	32.6
Add:	
C.M.C.	1 tsp.

EG-86 **Clear Glaze   Cone 06**
alkaline-frit, transparent, gloss, nontoxic

Mixing. Mix in the manner of EG-1.

Application. Apply in the manner of EG-1.

Firing. Fire in the manner of EG-1.

Fired Results. This glaze fires to a clear gloss at cone 06.

Pyrophyllite	18.0
Pemco frit P-54	82.0
Add:	
Bentonite	2.0
C.M.C.	1 tsp.

EG-87 **Clear Glaze   Cone 06**
alkaline-frit, transparent, gloss, nontoxic

Mixing. Mix in the manner of EG-1.

Application. Apply in the manner of EG-1.

Firing. Fire in the manner of EG-1.

Fired Results. This glaze fires to a clear gloss at cone 06.

Silica	2.0
Pemco frit P-54	89.5
Kaolin (EPK)	8.5
Add:	
Bentonite	2.0
C.M.C.	1 tsp.

EG-88

Clear Glaze   Cone 06
alkaline-frit, transparent, gloss, nontoxic

Mixing. Mix in the manner of EG-1.

Application. Apply in the manner of EG-1.

Firing. Fire in the manner of EG-1.

Fired Results. This glaze fires to a clear gloss at cone 06.

Silica	1.3
Spodumene	15.0
Ferro frit #3134	83.7
Add:	
Bentonite	1.0
C.M.C.	1 tsp.

EG-89

Clear Glaze   Cone 06
alkaline-frit, transparent, gloss, nontoxic

Mixing. Mix in the manner of EG-1.

Application. Apply in the manner of EG-1.

Firing. Fire in the manner of EG-1.

Fired Results. This glaze fires to a bright clear gloss at cone 06.

Silica	1.2
Lepidolite	16.2
Pemco frit P-54	82.4
Bentonite	0.3
Add:	
C.M.C.	1 tsp.

EG-90

Clear Glaze   Cone 06
barium, transparent, gloss, toxic

Mixing. Mix in the manner of EG-9.

Application. Apply in the manner of EG-9.

Firing. Fire in the manner of EG-1.

Fired Results. This glaze fires to a clear glaze at cone 06.

Ferro frit #3819	27.3
Ferro frit #3223	26.4
Nepheline syenite	19.8
Barium carbonate	26.5
Add:	
Bentonite	1.5
C.M.C.	1 tsp.

EG-91

Clear Glaze   Cone 06
leadless, transparent, gloss, nontoxic

Mixing. Mix in the manner of EG-1.

Application. Apply in the manner of EG-1.

Firing. Fire in the manner of EG-1.

Fired Results. This glaze fires to a clear gloss at cone 06.

Ferro frit #3223	48.2
Nepheline syenite	24.9
Strontium carbonate	13.9
Whiting	13.0
Add:	
Bentonite	1.0
C.M.C.	1 tsp.

EG-92

Clear Gloss   Cone 06
barium-alkaline, transparent, clear gloss, toxic

Mixing. Mix in the manner of EG-9.

Application. Apply in the manner of EG-9.

Firing. Fire in the manner of EG-1.

Fired Results. This glaze fires to a clear gloss at cone 06. It is a very good base for the copper and cobalt colorants.

Nepheline syenite	12.1
Barium carbonate	52.4
Boric acid	19.0
Kaolin	8.9
Silica	5.6
Bentonite	2.0
Add:	
C.M.C.	1 tsp.

EG-93 **Clear Gloss Glaze   Cone 06**
raw alkaline, transparent, clear gloss, nontoxic

Mixing. Mix in the manner of EG-1.

Application. Apply in the manner of EG-1.

Firing. Fire in the manner of EG-1.

Fired Results. This glaze fires to a clear gloss at cone 06. It is most effective and successful when used on cone 04 bisque.

Sodium carbonate	30.5
Lithium carbonate	8.5
Kaolin	22.5
Silica	38.5
Add:	
Bentonite	2.0
C.M.C.	1 tsp.

EG-94 **Clear Gloss Glaze   Cone 06**
alkaline, transparent, clear gloss, nontoxic

Mixing. Mix in the manner of EG-1.

Application. Apply in the manner of EG-1.

Firing. Fire in the manner of EG-1.

Fired Results. This glaze fires to a clear gloss at cone 06. It makes an excellent base for turquoise with the addition of copper oxide.

Pemco frit #25	40.9
Lithium carbonate	7.5
Kaolin (EPK)	23.5
Silica	28.1
Add:	
Bentonite	2.0
C.M.C.	1 tsp.

EG-95 **Clear Gloss Glaze   Cone 06**
raw alkaline, transparent, gloss, nontoxic

Mixing. This glaze is a raw alkaline and should be ground dry and used at once.

Application. Apply in the manner of EG-1.

Firing. Fire in the manner of EG-1.

Fired Results. This glaze fires to a clear gloss at cone 06. It is a very good base for copper and cobalt colorants.

Lithium carbonate	10.0
Soda ash	30.0
Kaolin	20.0
Silica	40.0
Add:	
C.M.C.	1 tsp.

EG-96 **Clear Glaze   Cone 06–04**
alkaline, transparent, gloss, nontoxic

Mixing. Mix in the manner of EG-1.

Application. Apply in the manner of EG-1.

Firing. Fire in the manner of EG-1.

Fired Results. This glaze fires to a clear gloss at cone 06–04. It is a very stable glaze and can be used on utility ware.

Pemco frit #25	48.0
Lithium carbonate	8.0
Whiting	12.0
Kaolin	20.0
Silica	14.0
Add:	
Bentonite	1.0
C.M.C.	1 tsp.

EG-97 **Clear Glaze   Cone 06**
raw alkaline, transparent, gloss, nontoxic

Mixing. This is a raw alkaline, grind it dry and use immediately.

Application. Apply in the manner of EG-1.

Firing. Fire in the manner of EG-1.

Fired Results. This glaze fires to a clear gloss at cone 06. For a nice Egyptian blue add 2%–4% copper oxide. For a lovely Persian blue add 7% copper oxide and .5% cobalt oxide.

Soda ash	29.0
Kaolin	35.0
Silica	32.0
Volcanic ash	17.0
Aluminum oxide	2.0
Borax	10.0

EG-98

Clear Gloss Glaze   Cone 06
alkaline, transparent, clear gloss, nontoxic

Mixing. Mix in the manner of EG-1.

Application. Apply in the manner of EG-1.

Firing. Fire in the manner of EG-1.

Fired Results. This glaze fires to a clear gloss at cone 06. It is very stable and can be used on utility ware if the clay body is high in talc.

Pemco frit #25	45.5
Lithium carbonate	8.0
Whiting	12.0
Kaolin	21.0
Silica	13.5
Add:	
Bentonite	2.0
C.M.C.	1 tsp.

EG-99

Clear Gloss Glaze   Cone 06
lead, transparent, gloss, toxic

Mixing. Mix in the manner of EG-9.

Application. Apply in the manner of EG-9.

Firing. Fire in the manner of EG-1.

Fired Results. This glaze fires to a clear gloss at cone 06. It is a very stable base for colorants. Do not use on utility ware due to its high lead content.

White lead	44.0
Whiting	2.7
Zinc oxide	5.5
Feldspar (Custer)	15.6
Kaolin (EPK)	3.4
Silica	27.8
Add:	
Bentonite	1.0
C.M.C.	1 tsp.

EG-100

Clear Gloss Glaze   Cone 06
alkaline, transparent, gloss, slightly toxic

Mixing. Mix in the manner of EG-9.

Application. Apply in the manner of EG-9.

Firing. Fire in the manner of EG-1.

Fired Results. This glaze fires to a clear gloss at cone 06. It has a tendency to craze on high silica bodies.

Feldspar (Kona F-4)	42.0
Colemanite	33.0
Silica	10.0
Barium carbonate	6.0
Zinc oxide	5.0
Kaolin (EPK)	4.0
Add:	
Bentonite	2.0
C.M.C.	1 tsp.

EG-101

Clear Semi-Gloss Glaze   Cone 06
alkaline, transparent, semi-gloss, nontoxic

Mixing. Mix in the manner of EG-1.

Application. Apply in the manner of EG-1.

Firing. Fire in the manner of EG-1.

Fired Results. This glaze fires to a clear semi-gloss at cone 06.

Hommel frit #259	44.4
Lithium carbonate	10.0
Wollastonite	22.0
Kaolin	20.0
Silica	3.6
Add:	
Bentonite	2.0
C.M.C.	1 tsp.

EG-102

Clear Fluid Gloss Glaze   Cone 06
lead, transparent, gloss, toxic

Mixing. Mix in the manner of EG-9.

Application. Apply in the manner of EG-9.

Firing. Fire in the manner of EG-1.

Fired Results. This glaze fires to a clear gloss at cone 06. It tends to be very fluid so pieces should be well stilted in the kiln.

White lead	79.0
Whiting	13.0
Kaolin	6.0
Silica	2.0
Add:	
Bentonite	1.0
C.M.C.	1 tsp.

EG-103 **Clear Semi-Gloss Glaze   Cone 06**
lead, transparent, semi-gloss, toxic

Mixing. Mix in the manner of EG-9.

Application. Apply in the manner of EG-9.

Firing. Fire in the manner of EG-1.

Fired Results. This glaze fires to a clear semi-gloss at cone 06.

White lead	56.0
Feldspar (Kona F-4)	18.0
Silica	14.0
Whiting	9.0
Kaolin (EPK)	3.0
Add:	
Bentonite	1.0
C.M.C.	1 tsp.

EG-104. **Clear Semi-Matt Glaze   Cone 06**
alkaline, transparent, semi-matt, nontoxic

Mixing. Mix in the manner of EG-1.

Application. Apply in the manner of EG-1.

Firing. Fire in the manner of EG-1.

Fired Results. This glaze fires to a clear semi-matt at cone 06.

Pemco frit #25	48.2
Lithium carbonate	8.8
Wollastonite	13.0
Kaolin	18.0
Silica	12.0
Add:	
Bentonite	1.0
C.M.C.	1 tsp.

EG-105 **Clear Semi-Matt Glaze   Cone 06**
alkaline-frit, transparent, semi-matt, nontoxic

Mixing. Mix in the manner of EG-1.

Application. Apply in the manner of EG-1.

Firing. Fire in the manner of EG-1.

Fired Results. This glaze fires to a clear semi-matt at cone 06.

Ferro frit #3134	42.2
Wollastonite	23.3
Lithium carbonate	7.4
Kaolin (EPK)	20.5
Silica	6.6
Add:	
Bentonite	2.0
C.M.C.	1 tsp.

EG-106 **Clear Matt Glaze   Cone 06**
frit, transparent, matt, nontoxic

Mixing. Mix in the manner of EG-1.

Application. Apply in the manner of EG-1.

Firing. Fire in the manner of EG-1.

Fired Results. This glaze fires to a transparent matt at cone 06.

Ferro frit #3819	40.7
Whiting	20.0
Strontium carbonate	20.5
Kaolin	5.4
Silica	12.7
Add:	
Bentonite	2.0
C.M.C.	1 tsp.

EG-107 **Clear Stony Matt Glaze   Cone 06**
barium, transparent, clear stony matt, toxic

Mixing. Mix in the manner of EG-9.

Application. Apply in the manner of EG-9.

Firing. Fire in the manner of EG-1.

Fired Results. This glaze fires to a clear stony matt at cone 06.

Barium carbonate	22.5
Pemco frit #25	26.3
Magnesium carbonate	12.6
Boric acid	6.5
Kaolin (EPK)	6.3
Silica	25.8
Add:	
Bentonite	2.0
C.M.C.	1 tsp.

EG-108

Clear Matt Glaze   Cone 06–04
alkaline, transparent, matt, nontoxic
Mixing. Mix in the manner of EG-1.

Application. Apply in the manner of EG-1.

Firing. Fire in the manner of EG-1.

Fired Results. This glaze fires to a clear matt at cone 06–04. It tends to crackle on most bodies, except those with a high talc content.

Pemco frit #54	42.0
Whiting	12.0
Lithium carbonate	6.0
Kaolin (EPK)	20.0
Silica	18.0
Add:	
Bentonite	1.0

EG-109

Clear Matt Base Glaze   Cone 06
lead, transparent, matt, toxic

Mixing. Mix in the manner of EG-9.

Application. Apply in the manner of EG-9.

Firing. Fire in the manner of EG-1.

Fired Results. This glaze fires to a clear matt at cone 06. It is a very good base for any of the high lead glaze colorants.

White lead	41.8
Whiting	6.3
Zinc oxide	3.8
Feldspar (Custer)	27.3
Kaolin	14.2
Silica	5.6
Add:	
Bentonite	1.0
C.M.C.	2 tsp.

EG-110

Grapefruit Green Glaze   Cone 06
lead frit, transparent, gloss, toxic

Mixing. Mix in the manner of EG-9.

Application. Apply in the manner of EG-9.

Firing. Fire in the manner of EG-1.

Fired Results. This glaze fires to a transparent grapefruit green at cone 06.

Lead monosilicate	62.0
Lithium carbonate	10.7
Barium carbonate	15.5
Silica	11.8
Add:	
Green chromium oxide	0.5
Bentonite	1.0
C.M.C.	1 tsp.

EG-111

Spinach Green Glaze   Cone 06
colemanite, transparent, gloss, nontoxic

Mixing. Mix in the manner of EG-1.

Application. Apply in the manner of EG-1.

Firing. Fire in the manner of EG-1.

Fired Results. This glaze fires to a transparent spinach green gloss at cone 06.

Colemanite	25.5
Hommel frit #33	39.1
Kaolin	35.4
Add:	
Green chromium oxide	0.5
Bentonite	1.0
C.M.C.	1 tsp.

EG-112

Transparent Orange Gloss Glaze   Cone 06
lead, transparent, gloss, toxic

Mixing. Mix in the manner of EG-9.

Application. Apply in the manner of EG-9.

Firing. Fire in the manner of EG-19.

Fired Results. This glaze fires to a transparent orange gloss at cone 06.

Red lead	54.0
Uranium oxide	19.0
Silica	18.0
Feldspar (Kona F-4)	9.0
Add:	
Bentonite	2.0
C.M.C.	1 tsp.

EG-113   **Translucent Orange Matt Glaze   Cone 06**
lead, translucent, matt, toxic

Mixing. Mix in the manner of EG-9.

Application. Apply in the manner of EG-9.

Firing. Fire in the manner of EG-19.

Fired Results. This glaze fires to a translucent orange matt at cone 06.

White lead	62.5
Feldspar (Kona F-4)	16.2
Barium carbonate	9.4
Lead chromate	4.5
Kaolin (EPK)	3.7
Cornwall stone	3.7
Add:	
Bentonite	1.0
C.M.C.	1 tsp.

EG-114   **Translucent Orange-Red Gloss Glaze   Cone 06**
lead, translucent, gloss, toxic

Mixing. Mix in the manner of EG-9.

Application. Apply in the manner of EG-9.

Firing. Fire in the manner of EG-19.

Fired Results. This glaze fires to a translucent orange-red gloss at cone 06.

White lead	72.2
Silica	15.1
Feldspar (Kona F-4)	8.7
Kaolin	2.0
Green chromium oxide	2.0
Add:	
C.M.C.	1 tsp.

EG-115   **Opaque Red Matt Glaze   Cone 06**
lead, opaque, matt, toxic

Mixing. Mix in the manner of EG-9.

Application. Apply in the manner of EG-9.

Firing. Fire in the manner of EG-19.

Fired Results. This glaze fires to an opaque red matt at cone 06.

White lead	61.5
Red lead	10.5
Feldspar (Kona F-4)	17.2
Barium carbonate	9.2
Potassium bichromate	4.7
Cornwall stone	3.6
Kaolin	3.6
Bentonite	1.0
Add:	
C.M.C.	1 tsp.

EG-116   **Turquoise Gloss Glaze   Cone 06**
alkaline, transparent, gloss, nontoxic

Mixing. Mix in the manner of EG-1.

Application. Apply in the manner of EG-1.

Firing. Fire in the manner of EG-1.

Fired Results. This glaze fires to a bright turquoise gloss at cone 06. It should be used on a white body for best results.

Colemanite	23.5
Pemco frit #25	41.4
Kaolin	34.6
Add:	
Copper carbonate	5.0
Bentonite	1.0
C.M.C.	1 tsp.

EG-117   **Translucent Gloss Glaze   Cone 06**
lead-alkaline, translucent, gloss, toxic

Mixing. Mix in the manner of EG-9.

Application. Apply in the manner of EG-9.

Firing. Fire in the manner of EG-1.

Fired Results. This glaze fires to a translucent gloss at cone 06.

Silica	30.0
Borax	25.7
White lead	13.5
Feldspar (Kona F-4)	9.0
Tin oxide	7.7
Sodium carbonate	6.7
Kaolin (calcined)	4.0
Kaolin (EPK)	2.4
Bentonite	1.0

EG-118

Translucent White Glaze   Cone 06
alkaline, translucent, gloss, nontoxic

Mixing. Mix in the manner of EG-1.

Application. Apply in the manner of EG-1.

Firing. Fire in the manner of EG-1.

Fired Results. This glaze fires to a translucent white gloss at cone 06.

Pemco frit #54	52.2
Lithium carbonate	14.0
Kaolin	16.0
Flint	17.8
Add:	
Bentonite	1.0
C.M.C.	1 tsp.

EG-119

Translucent Gloss Glaze   Cone 06
raw alkaline, translucent, gloss, toxic

Mixing. Mix in the manner of EG-9.

Application. Apply in the manner of EG-9.

Firing. Fire in the manner of EG-1.

Fired Results. This glaze fires to a beautiful milky white translucent gloss at cone 06. It makes some very excellent tints of color when used as a color base.

Borax	30.2
Feldspar (soda)	
White lead	12.4
Red lead	10.0
Silica	6.4
Whiting	5.2
Kaolin	5.2
Tin oxide	4.2
Add:	
C.M.C.	1 tsp.

EG-120

White Translucent Gloss Glaze   Cone 06
lead, translucent, gloss, toxic

Mixing. Mix in the manner of EG-9.

Application. Apply in the manner of EG-9.

Firing. Fire in the manner of EG-1.

Fired Results. This glaze fires to a translucent white gloss at cone 06.

White lead	48.5
Silica	18.5
Tin oxide	10.5
Whiting	6.5
Kaolin (EPK)	6.0
Kaolin (Georgia)	4.5
Zinc oxide	4.5
Add:	
Bentonite	1.0
C.M.C.	1 tsp.

EG-121

Opaque White Gloss Glaze   Cone 06
alkaline, opaque, gloss, nontoxic

Mixing. Mix in the manner of EG-1.

Application. Apply in the manner of EG-1.

Firing. Fire in the manner of EG-1.

Fired Results. This glaze fires to an opaque white gloss at cone 06.

Feldspar (Kona F-4)	55.6
Colemanite	28.3
Tin oxide	10.0
Silica	1.1
Add:	
Bentonite	1.0
C.M.C.	1 tsp.

EG-122

Translucent White Semi-Gloss Glaze   Cone 06
lead, translucent, semi-gloss, toxic

Mixing. Mix in the manner of EG-9.

Application. Apply in the manner of EG-9.

Firing. Fire in the manner of EG-1.

Fired Results. This glaze fires to a translucent white semi-gloss at cone 06.

White lead	46.0
Feldspar (Kona F-4)	18.0
Silica	18.0
Whiting	10.0
Kaolin	6.0
Bone ash	2.0
Add:	
Bentonite	2.0
C.M.C.	1 tsp.

EG-123

Translucent Semi-Gloss Glaze   Cone 06
colemanite, translucent, semi-gloss, nontoxic

Mixing. Mix in the manner of EG-1.

Application. Apply in the manner of EG-1.

Firing. Fire in the manner of EG-1.

Fired Results. This glaze fires to a cloudy milky white translucent semi-gloss at cone 06.

Feldspar (Custer)	55.0
Colemanite	28.9
Zinc oxide	10.0
Silica	5.6
Whiting	0.5
Add:	
C.M.C.	1 tsp.

EG-124

Translucent White Semi-Gloss Glaze   Cone 06
alkaline, translucent, semi-gloss, nontoxic

Mixing. Mix in the manner of EG-1.

Application. Apply in the manner of EG-1.

Firing. Fire in the manner of EG-1.

Fired Results. This glaze fires to a translucent white semi-gloss at cone 06.

Silica	43.4
Feldspar (Custer)	12.3
Cryolite	14.4
Lithium carbonate	10.6
Bone ash	9.3
Whiting	6.4
Kaolin	3.6
Add:	
C.M.C.	1 tsp.

EG-125

Opaque White Semi-Gloss Glaze   Cone 06
alkaline, opaque, semi-gloss, nontoxic

Mixing. Mix in the manner of EG-1.

Application. Apply in the manner of EG-1.

Firing. Fire in the manner of EG-1.

Fired Results. This glaze fires to an opaque white semi-gloss at cone 06.

Colemanite	21.8
Pemco frit #25	42.8
Kaolin	35.2
Add:	
Tin oxide	4.0
Bentonite	1.0
C.M.C.	1 tsp.

EG-126

Translucent Semi-Matt Glaze   Cone 06
lead, translucent, semi-matt, toxic

Mixing. Mix in the manner of EG-9.

Application. Apply in the manner of EG-9.

Firing. Fire in the manner of EG-1.

Fired Results. This glaze fires to a translucent white semi-matt at cone 06.

White lead	46.5
Feldspar (Kona F-4)	18.0
Silica	17.5
Whiting	11.0
Kaolin	7.0
Add:	
Bentonite	1.0
C.M.C.	1 tsp.

EG-127

Translucent Matt Glaze   Cone 06
lead, translucent, matt, toxic

Mixing. Mix in the manner of EG-9.

Application. Apply in the manner of EG-9.

Firing. Fire in the manner of EG-1.

Fired Results. This glaze fires to a creamy white translucent matt at cone 06.

White lead	65.7
Feldspar (Kona F-4)	17.0
Barium carbonate	10.6
Kaolin (EPK)	2.9
Cornwall stone	3.8
Add:	
C.M.C.	1 tsp.

EG-128

Stony Matt Glaze   Cone 06
leadless, opaque, stony matt, nontoxic

Mixing. Mix in the manner of EG-1.

Application. Apply in the manner of EG-1.

Firing. Fire in the manner of EG-1.

Fired Results. This glaze fires to an opaque stony matt at cone 06. It is a very good base for earth colors.

Cryolite	18.3
Sodium fluoride	14.1
Kaolin (EPK)	11.0
Fluorspar	10.0
Silica	46.6
Add:	
Bentonite	2.0
C.M.C.	1 tsp.

EG-129

Slightly Yellow Gloss Glaze   Cone 06
alkaline-lead, transparent, gloss, toxic

Mixing. Mix in the manner of EG-9.

Application. Apply in the manner of EG-9.

Firing. Fire in the manner of EG-1.

Fired Results. This glaze fires to a transparent gloss with a slightly yellow tint.

Volcanic ash	60.0
Colemanite	20.0
White lead	10.0
Borax	10.0
Add:	
Bentonite	1.0

EG-130

Transparent Yellow Gloss Glaze   Cone 06
lead, transparent, gloss, toxic

Mixing. Mix in the manner of EG-9.

Application. Apply in the manner of EG-9.

Firing. Fire in the manner of EG-1.

Fired Results. This glaze fires to a transparent gloss with a slightly yellow tint due to its high lead content.

White lead	62.7
Silica	25.5
Kaolin	9.8
Bone ash	2.0
Add:	
Bentonite	1.0
C.M.C.	1 tsp.

EG-131

Transparent Yellow Gloss Glaze   Cone 06
lead, transparent, gloss, toxic

Mixing. Mix in the manner of EG-9.

Application. Apply in the manner of EG-9.

Firing. Fire in the manner of EG-1.

Fired Results. This glaze fires to a transparent gloss with a slightly yellow tint.

White lead	60.0
Silica	28.0
Kaolin (EPK)	12.0
Add:	
Bentonite	2.0
C.M.C.	1 tsp.

EG-132

Translucent Yellow Gloss Glaze   Cone 06
lead, translucent, gloss, toxic

Mixing. Mix in the manner of EG-9.

Application. Apply in the manner of EG-9.

Firing. Fire in the manner of EG-1.

Fired Results. This glaze fires to a translucent gloss at cone 06 with a slightly yellow tint.

White lead	62.0
Colemanite	4.0
Silica	25.0
Kaolin	9.5
Bentonite	2.5
Add:	
C.M.C.	1 tsp.

EG-133 **Chrome Yellow Gloss Glaze   Cone 06**
alkaline-frit, transparent, gloss, nontoxic

Mixing. Mix in the manner of EG-1.

Application. Apply in the manner of EG-1.

Firing. Fire in the manner of EG-1.

Fired Results. This glaze fires to a transparent chrome yellow at cone 06.

Pemco frit #25	46.4
Whiting	8.0
Lithium carbonate	8.0
Kaolin	21.0
Silica	16.6
Add:	
Vanadium stain	5.0
Bentonite	1.0
C.M.C.	1 tsp.

EG-134 **Citron-Yellow Gloss Glaze   Cone 06**
alkaline-frit, transparent, gloss, nontoxic

Mixing. Mix in the manner of EG-1.

Application. Apply in the manner of EG-1.

Firing. Fire in the manner of EG-1.

Fired Results. This glaze fires to a transparent citron-yellow at cone 06.

Pemco frit #25	46.4
Whiting	8.0
Lithium	8.0
Kaolin	21.0
Silica	16.6
Add:	
Praseodynium stain	5.0
Bentonite	1.0
C.M.C.	1 tsp.

EG-135 **Citron-Yellow Semi-Matt Glaze   Cone 06**
alkaline-frit, translucent, semi-matt, nontoxic

Mixing. Mix in the manner of EG-1.

Application. Apply in the manner of EG-1.

Firing. Fire in the manner of EG-1.

Fired Results. This glaze fires to a semi-matt citron-yellow at cone 06.

Ferro frit #3134	40.0
Wollastonite	25.5
Lithium carbonate	7.5
Kaolin	20.8
Silica	6.6
Add:	
Vanadium stain	5.0
Bentonite	1.0
C.M.C.	1 tsp.

EG-136 **Primrose Yellow Semi-Matt Glaze   Cone 06**
alkaline, translucent, semi-matt, nontoxic

Mixing. Mix in the manner of EG-1.

Application. Apply in the manner of EG-1.

Firing. Fire in the manner of EG-1.

Fired Results. This glaze fires to a light yellow semi-matt at cone 06.

Pemco frit #54	40.2
Whiting	9.4
Lithium carbonate	7.1
Kaolin	21.8
Silica	22.4
Add:	
Naples yellow stain	5.0
Bentonite	1.0
C.M.C.	1 tsp.

EG-137 **Lithium Blue Matt Glaze   Cone 06**
raw alkaline, translucent, matt, nontoxic

Mixing. Mix in the manner of EG-95.

Application. Apply in the manner of EG-1.

Firing. Fire in the manner of EG-1.

Fired Results. This glaze fires to a lovely lithium blue matt at cone 06.

Silica	52.0
Lithium carbonate	26.5
Kaolin	11.5
Copper carbonate	3.7
Sodium carbonate	3.3
Bentonite	1.0
Bone ash	1.0
Add:	
C.M.C.	1 tsp.

EG-138

Transparent Gloss Glaze Cone 05
lead, transparent, gloss, toxic

Mixing. Mix in the manner of EG-9.

Application. Apply in the manner of EG-9.

Firing. Fire in the manner of EG-1.

Fired Results. This glaze fires to a clear gloss at cone 05.

White lead	50.0
Feldspar (Custer)	16.0
Silica	15.5
Whiting	10.5
Kaolin (EPK)	4.0
Kaolin (calcined)	4.0
Add:	
Bentonite	2.0
C.M.C.	1 tsp.

EG-139

Clear Glaze Cone 05
alkaline, transparent, gloss, nontoxic

Mixing. Mix in the manner of EG-1.

Application. Apply in the manner of EG-1.

Firing. Fire in the manner of EG-1.

Fired Results. This glaze fires to a clear gloss at cone 05.

Colemanite	63.6
Wollastonite	24.4
Kaolin (EPK)	12.0
Add:	
Bentonite	1.0
C.M.C.	1 tsp.

EG-140

Clear Gloss Glaze Cone 05
raw alkaline, transparent, gloss, nontoxic

Mixing. Mix in the manner of EG-95.

Application. Apply in the manner of EG-1.

Firing. Fire in the manner of EG-1.

Fired Results. This glaze fires to a clear gloss at cone 05. It is an excellent base for copper colorants.

Borax	33.0
Feldspar (Kona F-4)	19.0
Silica	19.0
Sodium carbonate	17.0
Whiting	6.0
Kaolin (EPK)	6.0
Add:	
Bentonite	1.0
C.M.C.	1 tsp.

EG-141

Ground-Glass Gloss Glaze Cone 05
lead, translucent, gloss, toxic

Mixing. Mix in the manner of EG-9.

Application. Apply in the manner of EG-9.

Firing. Fire in the manner of EG-1.

Fired Results. This glaze fires to a clear gloss at cone 05.

Ground glass	50.0
White lead	26.0
Kaolin	12.0
Tin oxide	10.0
Bentonite	2.0
Add:	
C.M.C.	1 tsp.

EG-142

Clear Semi-Gloss Glaze Cone 05
lead-alkaline, transparent, semi-gloss, toxic

Mixing. Mix in the manner of EG-9.

Application. Apply in the manner of EG-9.

Firing. Fire in the manner of EG-1.

Fired Results. This glaze fires to a clear semi-gloss at cone 05.

White lead	26.5
Colemanite	22.6
Feldspar (Oxford)	16.0
Silica	17.0
Kaolin (EPK)	4.7
Whiting	4.7
Tin oxide	6.5
Bentonite	2.0
Add:	
C.M.C.	1 tsp.

EG-143

Clear Semi-Gloss Glaze   Cone 05
alkaline, transparent, semi-gloss, nontoxic

Mixing. Mix in the manner of EG-1.

Application. Apply in the manner of EG-1.

Firing. Fire in the manner of EG-1.

Fired Results. This glaze fires to a clear semi-gloss at cone 05.

Feldspar (Kona F-4)	40.5
Silica	28.4
Cryolite	10.4
Zinc oxide	9.6
Bone ash	2.0
Sodium carbonate	4.0
Whiting	4.0
Add:	
Bentonite	1.0
C.M.C.	1 tsp.

EG-144

Clear Semi-Gloss Glaze   Cone 05
lead, transparent, semi-gloss, toxic

Mixing. Mix in the manner of EG-9.

Application. Apply in the manner of EG-9.

Firing. Fire in the manner of EG-1.

Fired Results. This glaze fires to a clear semi-gloss at cone 05.

White lead	47.0
Feldspar (Custer)	18.0
Silica	16.5
Whiting	11.5
Kaolin	7.0
Add:	
Bentonite	1.0
C.M.C.	1 tsp.

EG-145

Clear Semi-Matt Gloss Glaze   Cone 05
lead-alkaline, transparent, semi-matt, toxic

Mixing. Mix in the manner of EG-9.

Application. Apply in the manner of EG-9.

Firing. Fire in the manner of EG-1.

Fired Results. This glaze fires to a clear semi-matt at cone 05.

Feldspar (Kona F-4)	35.5
White lead	20.3
Red lead	4.4
Colemanite	15.2
Silica	6.1
Kaolin	7.7
Whiting	2.8
Barium carbonate	2.8
Rutile	2.7
Tin oxide	2.5
Add:	
C.M.C.	1 tsp.

EG-146

Translucent Opalescent Glaze   Cone 05
alkaline, translucent, gloss, nontoxic

Mixing. Mix in the manner of EG-1.

Application. Apply in the manner of EG-1.

Firing. Fire in the manner of EG-1.

Fired Results. This glaze fires to a translucent opalescent gloss at cone 05.

Pemco frit #54	35.5
Wollastonite	14.2
Feldspar (Custer)	28.1
Kaolin (EPK)	9.3
Silica	12.9
Add:	
Bentonite	1.0
C.M.C.	1 tsp.

EG-147

Translucent Opalescent Glaze   Cone 05
colemanite, translucent, gloss, nontoxic

Mixing. Mix in the manner of EG-1.

Application. Apply in the manner of EG-1.

Firing. Fire in the manner of EG-1.

Fired Results. This glaze fires to a translucent opalescent glaze at cone 05.

Colemanite	66.5
Kaolin (EPK)	8.5
Silica	25.0
Add:	
Bentonite	1.0
C.M.C.	1 tsp.

EG-148 Yellow-Orange Matt Glaze   Cone 05
lead, translucent, matt, toxic

Mixing. Mix in the manner of EG-9.

Application. Apply in the manner of EG-9.

Firing. Fire in the manner of EG-19.

Fired Results. This glaze fires to a yellow-orange matt at cone 05.

White lead	43.3
Feldspar (Kona F-4)	17.8
Kaolin (calcined)	14.4
Whiting	10.6
Silica	6.8
Uranium oxide	5.6
Yellow stain (any)	1.5
Add:	
Bentonite	2.0
C.M.C.	1 tsp.

EG-149 Pink Semi-Gloss Glaze   Cone 05
lead, translucent, semi-gloss, toxic

Mixing. Mix in the manner of EG-9.

Application. Apply in the manner of EG-9.

Firing. Fire in the manner of EG-1.

Fired Results. This glaze fires to a pink semi-gloss at cone 05.

White lead	36.0
Silica	20.0
Feldspar (Custer)	16.0
Kaolin (EPK)	11.0
Whiting	8.0
Pink stain (any)	5.0
Tin oxide	1.0
Opax	2.0
Add:	
C.M.C.	1 tsp.

EG-150 Blue-Purple Translucent Glaze   Cone 05
alkaline, translucent, gloss, nontoxic

Mixing. Mix in the manner of EG-1.

Application. Apply in the manner of EG-1.

Firing. Fire in the manner of EG-1.

Fired Results. This glaze fires to a blue-purple translucent matt at cone 05.

Boric acid	62.0
Silica	13.0
Sodium carbonate	13.0
Magnesium carbonate	7.0
Lithium carbonate	1.2
Cobalt oxide	1.3
Iron oxide	0.5

EG-151 Translucent White Matt Glaze   Cone 05
lead, translucent, matt, toxic

Mixing. Mix in the manner of EG-9.

Application. Apply in the manner of EG-9.

Firing. Fire in the manner of EG-1.

Fired Results. This glaze fires to a translucent white matt at cone 05.

White lead	48.5
Feldspar (Custer)	23.8
Tin oxide	12.4
Kaolin	4.2
Kentucky Old Mine #4 ball clay	4.3
Zinc oxide	4.6
Silica	2.2
Add:	
Bentonite	1.0
C.M.C.	1 tsp.

EG-152 **Transparent Yellow Gloss Glaze   Cone 05**
lead, transparent, gloss, toxic

Mixing. Mix in the manner of EG-9.

Application. Apply in the manner of EG-9.

Firing. Fire in the manner of EG-1.

Fired Results. This glaze fires to a transparent yellow gloss at cone 05.

White lead	50.0
Red lead	12.0
Kaolin	24.0
Silica	18.0
Kentucky Old Mine #4 ball clay	6.0
Add:	
Bentonite	1.0
C.M.C.	1 tsp.

EG-153 **Translucent Yellow Semi-Gloss Glaze   Cone 05**
barium-alkaline, translucent, semi-gloss, toxic

Mixing. Mix in the manner of EG-9.

Application. Apply in the manner of EG-9.

Firing. Fire in the manner of EG-1.

Fired Results. This glaze fires to a translucent yellow gloss at cone 05.

Barium carbonate	6.3
Lithium carbonate	4.2
Whiting	10.8
Pemco frit #25	17.6
Alumina hydrate	3.3
Colemanite	19.0
Zinc oxide	1.7
Kaolin	10.2
Silica	26.9
Add:	
Vanadium stain	6.0

EG-154 **Opaque-Yellow Satin Matt Glaze   Cone 05**
leadless, opaque, satin matt, nontoxic

Mixing. Mix in the manner of EG-1.

Application. Apply in the manner of EG-1.

Firing. Fire in the manner of EG-1.

Fired Results. This glaze fires to an opaque-yellow satin matt at cone 05.

Lithium carbonate	3.0
Cryolite	11.0
Wollastonite	2.8
Zinc oxide	3.8
Tin oxide	5.0
Kaolin	14.0
Silica	55.0
Whiting	6.0
Add:	
Vanadium stain	6.0

EG-155 **Opaque-Yellow Matt Glaze   Cone 05**
alkaline-fluoride, opaque, matt, nontoxic

Mixing. Mix in the manner of EG-1.

Application. Apply in the manner of EG-1.

Firing. Fire in the manner of EG-1.

Fired Results. This glaze fires to an opaque-yellow matt at cone 05.

Lithium carbonate	6.2
Magnesium carbonate	3.1
Fluorspar	5.3
Colemanite	9.4
Lepidolite	24.3
Wollastonite	21.1
Kaolin	30.6
Add:	
Vanadium stain	6.0

EG-156

Opaque-Yellow Matt Glaze   Cone 05
alkaline-frit, opaque, matt, nontoxic

Mixing. Mix in the manner of EG-1.

Application. Apply in the manner of EG-1.

Firing. Fire in the manner of EG-1.

Fired Results. This glaze fires to a light opaque-yellow matt at cone 05.

Magnesium carbonate	7.3
Pemco frit #54	16.0
Lithium carbonate	10.3
Alumina oxide	4.4
Whiting	6.0
Zinc oxide	6.1
Kaolin	7.2
Silica	40.0
Bentonite	2.0
Add:	
Vanadium stain	6.0

24
SOFT STONEWARE GLAZES
CONE 04-4

The step from earthenware to soft stoneware (sometimes known as medium-temperature ware) is a gradual one and therefore the ware and glazes at this in-between stage exhibit many of the characteristics of both. Most of the colors available at the lower earthenware cone levels are still possible in the soft stoneware range and many of the more rustic earth colors of stoneware pottery are possible at this level also. The higher firing range of soft stoneware gives the clay a hardness and greater durability similar to that of true stoneware, making it more useful for utility wares as well as decorative pottery. In addition many more chemicals with high fusion points, such as the feldspar and calcium compounds which give hardness and durability to the glazes, can be brought into use that cannot be used in the lower fired earthenwares.

For these practical reasons it is an area that should be of growing interest to the potter especially in light of the increasing cost of kiln firing, whether electric or fuel. The lower firing temperatures also cause less wear and tear to the kiln.

The glazes in this chapter range from the high-gloss type to the true matts. They are organized first by cone level, 04–4, then by color, alphabetically, and finally by surface, whether gloss, semi-gloss, satin matt, or matt.

Any of the glaze recipes in this chapter can be colored or altered in color by the use of the colorants listed in Chapter 33, Glaze Colorants. And any of those that are listed as clear, translucent, or opaque makes a good base glaze for colorants.

The reader will also find lists of possible chemical substitutions in Chapter 34, Dictionary of Clay and Glaze Compounds.

Note. The glazes in this chapter are labeled toxic or nontoxic. Toxic glazes should be carefully handled both in formulation and in application. During preparation the potter should wear a dust mask to prevent inhalation of toxic materials and not allow these materials to come into prolonged contact with the skin. Frequent washing of the hands when handling these glazes is a wise precaution. Toxic glazes should be applied by brushing and dipping—never spraying. For even under the best conditions some inhalation of the toxic mist from the spray is bound to take place or, equally bad, the mist from the spray gun can settle on the skin and be absorbed into the body system.

FORMULAS FOR SOFT STONEWARE GLAZES

SSG-1   **Transparent Amber Gloss Glaze   Cone 04**
lead, transparent, gloss, toxic

Mixing. Weigh out the ingredients and mix by using one of the methods outlined in Chapter 17 on Glaze Preparation. This glaze should be handled with care as it contains a toxic chemical.

Application. Apply to cone 04 bisque by brushing or dipping. See Chapter 17 for more details.

Firing. Fire normally in any type kiln to the cone level indicated.

Fired Results. This glaze fires to a transparent amber gloss at cone 04.

Red lead	50.0
Silica	24.0
Redart clay (sieved)	24.0
Bentonite	2.0
Add:	
C.M.C.	1 tsp.

SSG-2 **Opaque Mirror-Black Glaze Cone 04**
lead, opaque, high-gloss, toxic

Mixing. Mix in the manner of SSG-1.

Application. Apply in the manner of SSG-1.

Firing. Fire in the manner of SSG-1.

Fired Results. This glaze fires to an opaque mirror black at cone 04. Best results are gained if it is used over a darker clay body.

White lead	48.4
Silica	25.4
Kaolin	8.3
Whiting	5.2
Sodium carbonate	5.0
Cobalt oxide	2.5
Red iron oxide	2.5
Manganese dioxide	2.5
Add:	
Bentonite	2.0
C.M.C.	1 tsp.

SSG-3 **Opaque Brown Goldstone Gloss Glaze Cone 04**
lead, opaque, gloss, toxic

Mixing. Mix in the manner of SSG-1.

Application. Apply in the manner of SSG-1.

Firing. Fire in the manner of SSG-1.

Fired Results. This glaze fires to an opaque brown goldstone gloss at cone 04.

White lead	58.2
Feldspar (soda)	23.0
Silica	11.1
Red iron oxide	3.5
Whiting	2.3
Bentonite	1.0
Add:	
C.M.C.	1 tsp.

SSG-4 **Brown Satin Matt Glaze Cone 04**
alkaline-barium, opaque, satin matt, toxic

Mixing. Mix in the manner of SSG-1.

Application. Apply in the manner of SSG-1.

Firing. Fire in the manner of SSG-1.

Fired Results. This glaze fires to a brown smooth satin matt at cone 04.

Lithium carbonate	10.3
Barium carbonate	6.9
Whiting	9.7
Zinc oxide	19.8
Kaolin	21.1
Silica	41.2
Add:	
Manganese carbonate	3.0
Bentonite	1.0
C.M.C.	1 tsp.

SSG-5 **Translucent Barium Blue Matt Glaze Cone 04–02**
lead-barium, translucent, matt, toxic

Mixing. Mix in the manner of SSG-1.

Application. Apply in the manner of SSG-1.

Firing. Fire in the manner of SSG-1.

Fired Results. This glaze fires to a translucent barium blue matt at cone 04–02. The best results are at cone 04.

Whiting	20.0
White lead	130.0
Feldspar (Custer)	64.0
Barium carbonate	39.0
Kaolin (calcined)	21.0
Silica	37.0
Bentonite	2.5
Copper carbonate	5.0

SSG-6	**Translucent Egyptian Blue Gloss Glaze Cone 04**

raw alkaline, translucent, gloss, nontoxic

Mixing. This is a raw alkaline glaze so it should be dry-ground and stored or wet-ground and used at once. See Chapter 17, Glaze Preparation, for further details.

Application. Apply by brushing, dipping, or spraying, and use at least a cone 04 bisque which will absorb less of the soluble sodium compounds in this glaze.

Firing. Fire in the manner of SSG-1.

Fired Results. This glaze fires to a beautiful translucent Egyptian blue gloss at cone 04. A small amount of iron oxide will mute the color if the potter desires; 1.5% should be sufficient.

Borax (calcined)	105.0
Feldspar (Custer)	60.0
Whiting	28.0
Kaolin	10.0
Silica	76.0
Zinc oxide	28.0
Copper oxide	9.5
Bentonite	2.5
C.M.C.	1 tsp.

SSG-7   Transparent Persian Blue Gloss Glaze   Cone 04

raw alkaline, transparent, gloss, nontoxic

Mixing. Mix in the manner of SSG-6.

Application. Apply in the manner of SSG-6.

Firing. Fire in the manner of SSG-1.

Fired Results. This glaze fires to a transparent Persian blue gloss at cone 04. It should be used on a white body for best results.

Borax (calcined)	36.6
Feldspar (Custer)	21.0
Whiting	9.6
Kaolin	3.5
Silica	26.5
Copper oxide	1.4
Cobalt oxide	0.7
Bentonite	0.7

SSG-8   Transparent Sapphire Blue Gloss Glaze   Cone 04

raw alkaline, transparent, gloss, nontoxic

Mixing. Mix in the manner of SSG-6.

Application. Apply in the manner of SSG-6.

Firing. Fire in the manner of SSG-1.

Fired Results. This glaze fires to a transparent sapphire blue gloss at cone 04.

Borax (calcined)	36.6
Feldspar (Custer)	21.0
Whiting	9.6
Kaolin	3.5
Silica	26.5
Cobalt oxide	1.4
Iron oxide	0.7
Bentonite	0.7

SSG-9   Translucent Ultramarine Blue Satin Matt Glaze Cone 04

lead, translucent, satin matt, toxic

Mixing. Mix in the manner of SSG-1.

Application. Apply in the manner of SSG-1.

Firing. Fire in the manner of SSG-1.

Fired Results. This glaze fires to a translucent ultramarine satin matt at cone 04.

White lead	42.2
Tennessee ball clay #1	21.0
Feldspar (Kona F-4)	17.1
Whiting	9.0
Silica	9.9
Add:	
Bentonite	1.0
C.M.C.	1 tsp.

SSG-10.   Translucent Cream Gloss Glaze   Cone 04

lead, translucent, gloss, toxic

Mixing. Mix in the manner of SSG-1.

Application. Apply in the manner of SSG-1.

Firing. Fire in the manner of SSG-1.

Fired Results. This glaze fires to a translucent cream gloss at cone 04.

White lead	56.0
Silica	19.0
Tennessee ball clay #1	9.0
Ultrox	11.0
Borax	3.0
Sodium carbonate	2.0
Add:	
Bentonite	2.0
C.M.C.	1 tsp.

SSG-11 **Translucent Cream Semi-Gloss Glaze Cone 04**
lead-alkaline, translucent, semi-gloss, toxic

Mixing. Mix in the manner of SSG-1.

Application. Apply in the manner of SSG-1.

Firing. Fire in the manner of SSG-1.

Fired Results. This glaze fires to a translucent cream semi-gloss at cone 04. It is also a good color base for earth colorants.

White lead	40.7
Borax	23.4
Sodium carbonate	2.8
Tin oxide	7.7
Ultrox	8.0
Zinc oxide	1.7
Silica	15.4
Add:	
Bentonite	2.0
C.M.C.	1 tsp.

SSG-12 **Opaque Cream Matt Glaze   Cone 04**
lead, opaque, matt, toxic

Mixing. Mix in the manner of SSG-1.

Application. Apply in the manner of SSG-1.

Firing. Fire in the manner of SSG-1.

Fired Results. This glaze fires to an opaque cream matt at cone 04.

White lead	53.5
Silica	15.4
Feldspar (Kona F-4)	11.4
Tin oxide	8.5
Rutile	5.7
Kaolin (EPK)	3.9
Borax	1.6
Add:	
Bentonite	2.0
C.M.C.	1 tsp.

SSG-13 **Transparent High-Gloss Glaze Cone 04**
lead, transparent, gloss, glaze, toxic

Mixing. Mix in the manner of SSG-1.

Application. Apply in the manner of SSG-1.

Firing. Fire in the manner of SSG-1.

Fired Results. This glaze fires to a clear high-gloss at cone 04. It is a highly stable glaze for colorants or opacifiers.

White lead	52.0
Feldspar (soda)	19.0
Silica	19.0
Whiting	5.0
Kaolin	4.0
Bentonite	1.0
Add:	
C.M.C.	1 tsp.

SSG-14 **Clear High-Gloss Glaze Cone 04**
leadless, transparent, gloss, nontoxic

Mixing. Weigh out the ingredients and mix using one of the methods in Chapter 17, Glaze Preparation.

Application. Apply by brushing, dipping, or spraying. (See Chapter 17 for more details.)

Firing. Fire in the manner of SSG-1.

Fired Results. This glaze fires to a high-gloss at cone 04. It makes a good base for the alkaline colorants.

Pemco frit #54	20.0
Kaolin	5.0
Cryolite	70.0
Silica	5.0

SSG-15 **Transparent Fluid Gloss Glaze Cone 04**
lead, transparent, gloss, toxic

Mixing. Mix in the manner of SSG-1.

Application. Apply in the manner of SSG-1.

Firing. Fire in the manner of SSG-1.

Fired Results. This glaze fires to a clear gloss at cone 04. It is very fluid, therefore pieces should be well stilted in the kiln.

White lead	71.0
Silica	10.0
Kaolin	6.0
Feldspar (Kona F-4)	7.0
Zinc oxide	6.0
Add:	
Bentonite	2.0
C.M.C.	1 tsp.

SSG-16

Transparent Fluid Gloss Glaze   Cone 04
lead, transparent, gloss, toxic

Mixing. Mix in the manner of SSG-1.

Application. Apply in the manner of SSG-1.

Firing. Fire in the manner of SSG-1.

Fired Results. This glaze fires to a clear gloss at cone 04. It is very fluid and makes a good interglaze between two other colors for spill effects.

White lead	46.0
Feldspar (soda)	30.0
Silica	12.0
Whiting	6.0
Kaolin	2.0
Add:	
Bentonite	1.0
C.M.C.	1 tsp.

SSG-17

Clear Gloss Glaze   Cone 04
colemanite, transparent, gloss, toxic

Mixing. Mix in the manner of SSG-1.

Application. Apply in the manner of SSG-1.

Firing. Fire in the manner of SSG-1.

Fired Results. This glaze fires to a clear gloss at cone 04 with a very slight yellow tint.

Volcanic ash	68.0
Colemanite	22.0
White lead	10.0
Borax	10.0

SSG-18

Clear Gloss Glaze   Cone 04
colemanite, transparent, clear gloss, nontoxic

Mixing. Mix in the manner of SSG-14.

Application. Apply in the manner of SSG-14.

Firing. Fire in the manner of SSG-1.

Fired Results. This glaze fires to a clear gloss at cone 04. It is an excellent color base for the copper colorants for making turquoise blues of various shades.

Colemanite	65.0
Kaolin (EPK)	5.0
Silica	20.0

SSG-19

Clear Gloss Glaze   Cone 04
colemanite, transparent, gloss, nontoxic

Mixing. Mix in the manner of SSG-14.

Application. Apply in the manner of SSG-14.

Firing. Fire in the manner of SSG-1.

Fired Results. This glaze fires to a clear gloss at cone 04. Its best use is either alone or as a color base for the copper or cobalt colorants.

Colemanite	61.0
Kaolin (EPK)	14.0
Silica	25.0

SSG-20

Clear Gloss Glaze   Cone 04
lead-colemanite, transparent, gloss, toxic

Mixing. Mix in the manner of SSG-1.

Application. Apply in the manner of SSG-1.

Firing. Fire in the manner of SSG-1.

Fired Results. This glaze fires to a clear gloss at cone 04.

White lead	52.0
Feldspar (Kona F-4)	17.5
Silica	17.5
Colemanite	7.0
Whiting	3.0
Kaolin	3.0
Add:	
Bentonite	2.0
C.M.C.	1 tsp.

SSG-21

Clear Glaze   Cone 04
lead, transparent, gloss, toxic

Mixing. Mix in the manner of SSG-1.

Application. Apply in the manner of SSG-1.

Firing. Fire in the manner of SSG-1.

Fired Results. This glaze fires to a clear gloss at cone 04. It is excellent for use over slip decoration.

White lead	46.4
Feldspar (soda)	31.5
Kaolin	2.8
Talc	1.7
Silica	11.8
Whiting	5.8

SSG-22

Clear Gloss Glaze   Cone 04
alkaline-frit, transparent, gloss, nontoxic

Mixing. Mix in the manner of SSG-14.

Application. Apply in the manner of SSG-14.

Firing. Fire in the manner of SSG-1.

Fired Results. This simple glaze fires to a clear gloss at cone 04.

Kaolin	20.0
Pemco frit #54	78.0
Add:	
Bentonite	2.0
C.M.C.	1 tsp.

SSG-23

Clear Gloss Glaze   Cone 04
lead, transparent, gloss, toxic

Mixing. Mix in the manner of SSG-1.

Application. Apply in the manner of SSG-1.

Firing. Fire in the manner of SSG-1.

Fired Results. This glaze fires to a clear gloss at cone 04. It is a good base for earth colors, especially iron oxide.

White lead	45.5
Silica	28.0
Feldspar (Custer)	16.8
Zinc oxide	4.5
Kaolin	3.2
Whiting	2.0
Bentonite	1.0
Add:	
C.M.C.	1 tsp.

SSG-24

Transparent Gloss Glaze   Cone 04
lead, transparent, gloss, toxic

Mixing. Mix in the manner of SSG-1.

Application. Apply in the manner of SSG-1.

Firing. Fire in the manner of SSG-1.

Fired Results. This glaze fires to a clear gloss at cone 04.

White lead	64.0
Silica	28.0
Kaolin	6.0
Whiting	1.0
Bentonite	2.0
Add:	
C.M.C.	1 tsp.

SSG-25

Transparent Gloss Glaze   Cone 04
lead, transparent, gloss, toxic

Mixing. Mix in the manner of SSG-1.

Application. Apply in the manner of SSG-1.

Firing. Fire in the manner of SSG-1.

Fired Results. This glaze fires to a clear gloss at cone 04. It is very fluid at maturity—stilt glazed wares carefully in the kiln.

White lead	54.0
Silica	28.0
Tennessee ball clay #1	10.5
Kaolin	1.5
Whiting	4.0
Zinc oxide	2.0
Tin oxide	1.0
Bentonite	1.0
Add:	
C.M.C.	1 tsp.

SSG-26
Transparent Gloss Glaze   Cone 04
colemanite, transparent, gloss, nontoxic

Mixing. Mix in the manner of SSG-14.

Application. Apply in the manner of SSG-14.

Firing. Fire in the manner of SSG-1.

Fired Results. This glaze fires to a clear gloss at cone 04. This is an especially good color base for copper or cobalt colorants especially with a 2% addition of rutile.

Colemanite	52.5
Silica	25.5
Feldspar (Custer)	10.0
Kaolin	12.0
Add:	
Bentonite	2.0
C.M.C.	1 tsp.

SSG-27
Transparent Gloss Glaze   Cone 04
lead, transparent, gloss, toxic

Mixing. Mix in the manner of SSG-1.

Application. Apply in the manner of SSG-1.

Firing. Fire in the manner of SSG-1.

Fired Results. This glaze fires to a clear gloss at cone 04.

White lead	40.0
Feldspar (Kona F-4)	28.0
Silica	16.0
Cornwall stone	8.0
Kaolin	2.0
Whiting	4.0
Bentonite	2.0
Add:	
C.M.C.	1 tsp.

SSG-28
Transparent Gloss Glaze   Cone 04
lead, transparent, gloss, toxic

Mixing. Mix in the manner of SSG-1.

Application. Apply in the manner of SSG-1.

Firing. Fire in the manner of SSG-1.

Fired Results. This glaze fires to a clear gloss at cone 04.

White lead	30.0
Feldspar (Kona F-4)	28.0
Silica	16.0
Whiting	7.5
Kaolin	7.5
Colemanite	8.0
Zinc oxide	1.0
Bentonite	2.0
Add:	
C.M.C.	1 tsp.

SSG-29
Transparent Gloss Glaze   Cone 04
colemanite-barium, transparent, gloss, toxic

Mixing. Mix in the manner of SSG-1.

Application. Apply in the manner of SSG-1.

Firing. Fire in the manner of SSG-1.

Fired Results. This glaze fires to a transparent gloss at cone 04. Try it under other colored glazes—it will boil through the top glaze and give beautiful mottled effects.

Colemanite	22.2
Feldspar (Custer)	37.3
Barium carbonate	20.2
Kaolin	4.1
Silica	17.1

SSG-30
Clear Gloss Glaze   Cone 04
alkaline-lead, transparent, gloss, toxic

Mixing. Mix in the manner of SSG-1.

Application. Apply in the manner of SSG-1.

Firing. Fire in the manner of SSG-1.

Fired Results. This glaze fires to a clear gloss at cone 04. It tends to be slightly fluid. The best colorants for this glaze as a base are copper carbonate or cobalt.

Lithium carbonate	27.9
White lead	25.0
Bone ash	12.0
Feldspar (Kona F-4)	9.0
Kaolin	14.6
Silica	53.9
Bentonite	3.0

SSG-31

Transparent Smooth Gloss Glaze   Cone 04
colemanite-barium, transparent, gloss, toxic

Mixing. Mix in the manner of SSG-1.

Application. Apply in the manner of SSG-1.

Firing. Fire in the manner of SSG-1.

Fired Results. This glaze fires to a transparent smooth gloss at cone 04. Use copper carbonate in it for beautiful barium blues.

Colemanite	38.0
Feldspar (Custer)	36.0
Barium carbonate	14.0
Silica	10.0
Whiting	1.0
Bentonite	1.0
Add:	
C.M.C.	1 tsp.

SSG-32

Transparent Smooth Gloss Glaze   Cone 04
lead-alkaline, transparent, gloss, toxic

Mixing. Mix in the manner of SSG-1.

Application. Apply in the manner of SSG-1.

Firing. Fire in the manner of SSG-1.

Fired Results. This glaze fires to a clear gloss at cone 04.

White lead	30.0
Borax	18.0
Colemanite	5.0
Feldspar (Custer)	18.0
Silica	17.0
Kaolin	8.0
Whiting	4.0
Add:	
C.M.C.	1 tsp.

SSG-33

Transparent Semi-Gloss Glaze   Cone 04
lead, transparent, semi-gloss, toxic

Mixing. Mix in the manner of SSG-1.

Application. Apply in the manner of SSG-1.

Firing. Fire in the manner of SSG-1.

Fired Results. This glaze fires to a clear semi-gloss at cone 04.

White lead	45.0
Feldspar (Kona F-4)	38.0
Kaolin	5.5
Whiting	5.5
Silica	3.0
Tin oxide	1.0
Bentonite	2.0
Add:	
C.M.C.	1 tsp.

SSG-34

Transparent Semi-Gloss Glaze   Cone 04
lead, transparent, semi-gloss, toxic

Mixing. Mix in the manner of SSG-1.

Application. Apply in the manner of SSG-1.

Firing. Fire in the manner of SSG-1.

Fired Results. This glaze fires to a clear semi-gloss at cone 04.

White lead	45.5
Feldspar (Custer)	28.0
Silica	12.5
Barium carbonate	4.4
Colemanite	2.0
Kaolin	2.8
Bentonite	1.8
Add:	
C.M.C.	1 tsp.

SSG-35

Transparent Semi-Gloss Glaze   Cone 04
colemanite-barium, transparent, semi-gloss, toxic

Mixing. Mix in the manner of SSG-1.

Application. Apply in the manner of SSG-1.

Firing. Fire in the manner of SSG-1.

Fired Results. This glaze fires to a transparent semi-gloss at cone 04. It is a good base for any of the alkaline colorants.

Colemanite	23.0
Feldspar (Custer)	35.0
Barium carbonate	20.0
Silica	18.0
Kaolin	3.0
Bentonite	1.0
Add:	
C.M.C.	1 tsp.

SSG-36

Transparent Semi-Gloss Glaze   Cone 04
lead-alkaline, transparent, semi-gloss, toxic

Mixing. Mix in the manner of SSG-1.

Application. Apply in the manner of SSG-1.

Firing. Fire in the manner of SSG-1.

Fired Results. This glaze fires to a clear semi-gloss at cone 04.

Silica	27.3
Feldspar (Kona F-4)	26.4
Borax	20.6
White lead	18.3
Colemanite	4.6
Whiting	3.5
Zinc oxide	1.9
Add:	
Bentonite	2.0

SSG-37

Clear Semi-Gloss Glaze   Cone 04
colemanite, transparent, semi-gloss, nontoxic

Mixing. Mix in the manner of SSG-14.

Application. Apply in the manner of SSG-14.

Firing. Fire in the manner of SSG-1.

Fired Results. This glaze fires to a clear semi-gloss at cone 04.

Colemanite	70.0
Kaolin (EPK)	10.0
Silica	20.0
Add:	
Bentonite	2.0
C.M.C.	1 tsp.

SSG-38

Clear Matt Glaze   Cone 04
colemanite, transparent, satin matt, nontoxic

Mixing. Mix in the manner of SSG-14.

Application. Apply in the manner of SSG-14.

Firing. Fire in the manner of SSG-1.

Fired Results. This glaze fires to a clear satin matt at cone 04.

Colemanite	70.0
Kaolin	15.0
Silica	15.0
Add:	
Bentonite	2.0
C.M.C.	1 tsp.

SSG-39

Iron Red Glaze   Cone 04
lead, translucent, gloss, toxic

Mixing. Mix in the manner of SSG-1.

Application. Apply in the manner of SSG-1.

Firing. Fire in the manner of SSG-1.

Fired Results. This glaze fires to an iron red gloss at cone 04. Try adding a little rutile to it for mottled effects—2% should be sufficient.

White lead	43.5
Whiting	6.6
Kaolin	10.1
Zinc oxide	2.5
Silica	26.5
Tin oxide	5.8
Red iron oxide	3.7
Bentonite	1.3
Add:	
C.M.C.	2 tsp.

SSG-40

Translucent Rust Semi-Gloss Glaze   Cone 04
lead, translucent, semi-gloss, toxic

Mixing. Mix in the manner of SSG-1.

Application. Apply in the manner of SSG-1.

Firing. Fire in the manner of SSG-1.

Fired Results. This glaze fires to a translucent rust semi-gloss at cone 04.

White lead	64.0
Kaolin	14.0
Silica	10.0
Rutile	7.0
Tennessee ball clay #1	2.0
Zinc oxide	1.0
Add:	
Bentonite	2.0
C.M.C.	1 tsp.

SSG-41   **Transparent Tan Gloss Glaze   Cone 04**
lead, transparent, gloss, toxic

Mixing. Mix in the manner of SSG-1.

Application. Apply in the manner of SSG-1.

Firing. Fire in the manner of SSG-1.

Fired Results. This glaze fires to a transparent tan gloss at cone 04.

White lead	60.9
Feldspar (Kona F-4)	12.7
Silica	11.5
Tin oxide	7.6
Barium carbonate	5.2
Kaolin (EPK)	2.1
Nickel oxide	0.4
Add:	
Bentonite	2.0
C.M.C.	1 tsp.

SSG-42   **Translucent Tan Semi-Gloss Glaze   Cone 04**
colemanite-lead, translucent, semi-gloss, toxic

Mixing. Mix in the manner of SSG-1.

Application. Apply in the manner of SSG-1.

Firing. Fire in the manner of SSG-1.

Fired Results. This glaze fires to a translucent tan semi-gloss at cone 04.

Volcanic ash	33.6
Colemanite	21.4
Kaolin	20.0
White lead	7.7
Tin oxide	7.7
Borax	3.4
Zinc oxide	2.3
Barium carbonate	3.8
Add:	
Bentonite	2.0

SSG-43   **Translucent Mottled Tan Matt Glaze   Cone 04**
lead, translucent, matt, toxic

Mixing. Mix in the manner of SSG-6.

Application. Apply in the manner of SSG-1.

Firing. Fire in the manner of SSG-1.

Fired Results. This glaze fires to a translucent mottled tan matt at cone 04.

White lead	60.0
Feldspar (Custer)	19.5
Borax	11.5
Rutile	4.7
Kaolin (calcined)	3.8
Zinc oxide	0.5
Add:	
Bentonite	2.0
C.M.C.	1 tsp.

SSG-44   **Transparent Tan Semi-Gloss Glaze   Cone 04**
lead, transparent, semi-gloss, toxic

Mixing. Mix in the manner of SSG-1.

Application. Apply in the manner of SSG-1.

Firing. Fire in the manner of SSG-1.

Fired Results. This glaze fires to a transparent tan semi-gloss at cone 04.

White lead	61.4
Plastic vitrox	4.4
Kaolin	14.4
Silica	12.3
Rutile	6.5
Bentonite	1.0
Add:	
C.M.C.	1 tsp.

SSG-45

Transparent Turquoise Gloss Glaze   Cone 04
lead-alkaline, transparent, gloss, toxic

Mixing. Mix in the manner of SSG-6.

Application. Apply in the manner of SSG-1.

Firing. Fire in the manner of SSG-1.

Fired Results. This glaze fires to a transparent turquoise gloss at cone 04.

Whiting	10.2
Borax	25.2
Soda ash	1.0
White lead	19.0
Feldspar (potash)	26.2
Silica	12.6
Kaolin	1.5
Copper carbonate	3.5
Bentonite	1.0

SSG-46

Translucent Turquoise Gloss Glaze   Cone 04
colemanite-lead, translucent, gloss, toxic

Mixing. Mix in the manner of SSG-1.

Application. Apply in the manner of SSG-1.

Firing. Fire in the manner of SSG-1.

Fired Results. This glaze fires to a translucent turquoise gloss at cone 04.

Colemanite	28.5
Silica	24.0
Feldspar (Kona F-4)	18.8
White lead	0.7
Tin oxide	6.5
Copper oxide	3.3
Kaolin (EPK)	3.0
Barium carbonate	3.9
Zinc oxide	1.2
Add:	
Bentonite	2.0
C.M.C.	1 tsp.

SSG-47

Translucent Turquoise Semi-Gloss Glaze   Cone 04
raw alkaline-lead, translucent, semi-gloss, toxic

Mixing. Mix in the manner of SSG-6.

Application. Apply in the manner of SSG-6.

Firing. Fire in the manner of SSG-1.

Fired Results. This glaze fires to a translucent turquoise semi-gloss at cone 04.

Borax	24.0
Feldspar (Custer)	22.2
White lead	17.7
Silica	11.8
Whiting	11.0
Tin oxide	4.0
Ultrox	4.2
Copper carbonate	3.5
Lithium carbonate	1.7
Add:	
Bentonite	2.0

SSG-48

Cloudy Imitation Stoneware Glaze   Cone 04
barium-alkaline, translucent, semi-gloss, nontoxic

Mixing. Mix in the manner of SSG-1.

Application. Apply in the manner of SSG-1.

Firing. Fire in the manner of SSG-1.

Fired Results. This glaze fires to a cloudy off-white reminiscent of higher-fire stoneware glazes. It is a good color base for earth colorants.

Lithium carbonate	10.0
Whiting	9.0
Barium carbonate	5.8
Zinc oxide	9.2
Kaolin	22.3
Silica	42.0
Bentonite	2.0

SSG-49

Cloudy Satin-Matt Imitation Stoneware Glaze Cone 04
leadless, translucent, satin matt, nontoxic

Mixing. Mix in the manner of SSG-14.

Application. Apply in the manner of SSG-14.

Firing. Fire in the manner of SSG-1.

Fired Results. This glaze fires to a cloudy off-white satin matt at cone 04 reminiscent of stoneware glazes. It is a good base for earth colorants.

Nepheline syenite	37.5
Pemco frit #54	55.9
Whiting	7.2
Bentonite	2.0
C.M.C.	1 tsp.

SSG-50

White Satin-Matt Imitation Stoneware Glaze Cone 04
barium, semi-opaque, matt, toxic

Mixing. Mix in the manner of SSG-1.

Application. Apply in the manner of SSG-1.

Firing. Fire in the manner of SSG-1.

Fired Results. This glaze fires to a white satin-matt stonewarelike glaze at cone 04.

Ferro frit #3819	36.0
Colemanite	5.3
Whiting	8.7
Barium carbonate	13.8
Kaolin	12.7
Silica	22.0
Bentonite	1.5
Add:	
C.M.C.	1 tsp.

SSG-51

Translucent White Gloss Glaze Cone 04
lead, translucent, gloss, toxic

Mixing. Mix in the manner of SSG-6.

Application. Apply in the manner of SSG-1.

Firing. Fire in the manner of SSG-1.

Fired Results. This glaze fires to a translucent white gloss at cone 04.

Red lead	37.3
Silica	31.0
Borax	10.0
Tin oxide	7.3
Kaolin (EPK)	4.5
Colemanite	5.5
Alumina oxide	4.4

SSG-52

Translucent Milky White Gloss Glaze Cone 04
alkaline-frit, translucent, gloss, nontoxic

Mixing. Mix in the manner of SSG-14.

Application. Apply in the manner of SSG-14.

Firing. Fire in the manner of SSG-1.

Fired Results. This glaze fires to a translucent milky white gloss at cone 04.

Pemco frit #25	50.0
Feldspar (Custer)	18.0
Silica	16.0
Kaolin (EPK)	6.0
Whiting	5.0
Ultrox	5.0
Add:	
Bentonite	2.0
C.M.C.	1 tsp.

SSG-53

Translucent Blue-White Gloss Glaze Cone 04
lead, translucent, gloss, toxic

Mixing. Mix in the manner of SSG-1.

Application. Apply in the manner of SSG-1.

Firing. Fire in the manner of SSG-1.

Fired Results. This glaze fires to a translucent blue-white gloss at cone 04.

White lead	44.2
Feldspar (potash)	16.9
Silica	10.9
Whiting	8.8
Ultrox	9.2
Kaolin	6.0
Colemanite	4.0
Add:	
Bentonite	2.0
C.M.C.	1 tsp.

SSG-54 **Translucent Milky Semi-Gloss Glaze   Cone 04**
lead, translucent, semi-gloss, toxic

Mixing. Mix in the manner of SSG-1.

Application. Apply in the manner of SSG-1.

Firing. Fire in the manner of SSG-1.

Fired Results. This glaze fires to a translucent milky semi-gloss at cone 04.

White lead	40.0
Feldspar (Kona F-4)	18.0
Silica	15.0
Barium carbonate	15.0
Whiting	4.0
Kaolin	4.0
Lithium carbonate	4.0
Add:	
Bentonite	2.0
C.M.C.	1 tsp.

SSG-55 **Translucent White Semi-Matt Glaze   Cone 04**
lead-feldspathic, translucent, semi-matt, toxic

Mixing. Mix in the manner of SSG-1.

Application. Apply in the manner of SSG-1.

Firing. Fire in the manner of SSG-1.

Fired Results. This glaze fires to a translucent white semi-matt at cone 04.

Feldspar (Kona F-4)	40.0
White lead	38.0
Whiting	8.0
Silica	5.0
Kaolin	5.0
Magnesium carbonate	4.0
Add:	
Bentonite	2.0
C.M.C.	1 tsp.

SSG-56 **Translucent Smooth Matt Glaze   Cone 04**
lead, translucent, smooth matt, toxic

Mixing. Mix in the manner of SSG-1.

Application. Apply in the manner of SSG-1.

Firing. Fire in the manner of SSG-1.

Fired Results. This glaze fires to a translucent white matt at cone 04.

White lead	50.2
Kaolin (calcined)	10.0
Feldspar (Kona F-4)	9.0
Nepheline syenite	8.9
Barium carbonate	7.3
Whiting	4.6
Silica	4.8
Ultrox	5.2
Add:	
Bentonite	1.0

SSG-57 **Opaque White Satin-Matt Glaze   Cone 04**
lead, opaque, satin matt, toxic

Mixing. Mix in the manner of SSG-1.

Application. Apply in the manner of SSG-1.

Firing. Fire in the manner of SSG-1.

Fired Results. This glaze fires to an opaque white satin matt at cone 04.

White lead	42.4
Tennessee ball clay #1	20.0
Feldspar (Kona F-4)	17.7
Whiting	11.5
Silica	8.6
Add:	
Bentonite	2.0
C.M.C.	1 tsp.

SSG-58 **Translucent White Matt Glaze   Cone 04**
alkaline-barium, translucent, matt, toxic

Mixing. Mix in the manner of SSG-1.

Application. Apply in the manner of SSG-1.

Firing. Fire in the manner of SSG-1.

Fired Results. This glaze fires to a translucent white matt at cone 04.

Feldspar (Kona F-4)	45.0
Whiting	12.0
Barium carbonate	12.0
Colemanite	12.0
Silica	10.0
Zinc oxide	3.0
Ultrox	5.0
Add:	
Bentonite	2.0

SSG-59 **Opaque Matt Glaze   Cone 04**
lead, opaque, matt, toxic

Mixing. Mix in the manner of SSG-1.

Application. Apply in the manner of SSG-1.

Firing. Fire in the manner of SSG-1.

Fired Results. This glaze fires to an opaque white matt at cone 04.

White lead	40.0
Feldspar (soda)	27.7
Kaolin (Georgia)	13.6
Whiting	9.5
Silica	4.5
Ultrox	4.0
Bentonite	1.0
Add:	
C.M.C.	1 tsp.

SSG-60 **Opaque Dry Matt Glaze   Cone 04**
lead, opaque, dry matt, toxic

Mixing. Mix in the manner of SSG-1.

Application. Apply in the manner of SSG-1.

Firing. Fire in the manner of SSG-1.

Fired Results. This glaze fires to an opaque dry matt at cone 04.

White lead	50.0
Feldspar (Custer)	20.0
Kaolin (calcined)	12.9
Whiting	10.0
Kaolin	4.0
Add:	
Bentonite	2.0
C.M.C.	1 tsp.

SSG-61 **Translucent Satin-Matt Glaze   Cone 04**
lead, translucent, satin matt, toxic

Mixing. Mix in the manner of SSG-1.

Application. Apply in the manner of SSG-1.

Firing. Fire in the manner of SSG-1.

Fired Results. This glaze fires to a translucent satin matt at cone 04.

White lead	29.9
Colemanite	6.1
Whiting	7.8
Zinc oxide	1.1
Feldspar (Custer)	30.1
Kaolin	6.6
Silica	18.4

SSG-62 **Semi-Opaque Frosty White Matt Glaze   Cone 04**
colemanite-barium, semi-opaque, matt, toxic

Mixing. Mix in the manner of SSG-1.

Application. Apply in the manner of SSG-1.

Firing. Fire in the manner of SSG-1.

Fired Results. This glaze fires to a frosty semi-opaque white matt at cone 04. Copper and cobalt are especially good colorants for this glaze.

Barium carbonate	13.5
Colemanite	11.4
Feldspar (Custer)	46.9
Whiting	12.8
Zinc oxide	3.9
Silica	10.5
Add:	
Bentonite	1.0
C.M.C.	1 tsp.

SSG-63 **Semi-Opaque Semi-Matt Glaze   Cone 04**
raw alkaline-lead, semi-opaque, semi-matt, toxic

Mixing. Mix in the manner of SSG-1.

Application. Apply in the manner of SSG-1.

Firing. Fire in the manner of SSG-1.

Fired Results. This glaze fires to a semi-opaque white semi-matt at cone 04.

Silica	22.0
Sodium carbonate	20.0
Borax (calcined)	16.0
Feldspar (Kona F-4)	12.0
Whiting	9.1
White lead	8.6
Kaolin	6.0
Colemanite	4.2
Add:	
Bentonite	2.0
C.M.C.	1 tsp.

SSG-64

Semi-Opaque Satin-Matt Glaze   Cone 04
lithium-lead, semi-opaque, satin matt, toxic

Mixing. Mix in the manner of SSG-1.

Application. Apply in the manner of SSG-1.

Firing. Fire in the manner of SSG-1.

Fired Results. This glaze fires to a semi-opaque white satin matt at cone 04.

Lithium carbonate	18.2
White lead	15.1
Bone ash	7.5
Feldspar (Kona F-4)	6.3
Kaolin	10.7
Silica	34.6
Bentonite	1.0
Ultrox	6.6
Add:	
C.M.C.	1 tsp.

SSG-65

Semi-Opaque Semi-Matt Glaze   Cone 04
lead, semi-opaque, semi-matt, toxic

Mixing. Mix in the manner of SSG-1.

Application. Apply in the manner of SSG-1.

Firing. Fire in the manner of SSG-1.

Fired Results. This glaze fires to a semi-opaque semi-matt white at cone 04.

White lead	54.7
Whiting	6.0
Kaolin	14.0
Silica	10.7
Titanium dioxide	4.7
Ultrox	8.7
Bentonite	1.2
Add:	
C.M.C.	1 tsp.

SSG-66

Semi-Opaque Smooth-Matt Glaze   Cone 04
lead, semi-opaque, smooth matt, toxic

Mixing. Mix in the manner of SSG-1.

Application. Apply in the manner of SSG-1.

Firing. Fire in the manner of SSG-1.

Fired Results. This glaze fires to a semi-opaque white smooth matt at cone 04.

White lead	61.0
Feldspar (Custer)	17.2
Kaolin (EPK)	1.6
Titanium dioxide	4.6
Whiting	1.5
Borax	11.6
Kaolin (calcined)	2.5
Add:	
Ultrox	8.0

SSG-67

Semi-Opaque Satin-Matt Glaze   Cone 04
colemanite-lead, semi-opaque, satin matt, toxic

Mixing. Mix in the manner of SSG-1.

Application. Apply in the manner of SSG-1.

Firing. Fire in the manner of SSG-1.

Fired Results. This glaze fires to a semi-opaque white satin matt at cone 04.

Colemanite	21.2
Whiting	5.3
Barium carbonate	2.6
White lead	6.3
Borax	4.2
Volcanic ash	31.9
Kaolin	18.7
Zinc oxide	3.1
Ultrox	6.3
Add:	
Bentonite	2.0

SSG-68

Semi-Opaque Frosty White Gloss Glaze   Cone 04
lead-barium, semi-opaque, gloss, toxic

Mixing. Mix in the manner of SSG-1.

Application. Apply in the manner of SSG-1.

Firing. Fire in the manner of SSG-1.

Fired Results. This glaze fires to a frosty white gloss at cone 04.

White lead	40.5
Barium carbonate	15.8
Feldspar (Custer)	21.4
Whiting	2.7
Kaolin	3.2
Silica	15.2
Bentonite	1.2
C.M.C.	1 tsp.

SSG-69 **Semi-Opaque White Gloss Glaze   Cone 04**
lead-high calcium, semi-opaque, gloss, toxic

Mixing. Mix in the manner of SSG-1.

Application. Apply in the manner of SSG-1.

Firing. Fire in the manner of SSG-1.

Fired Results. This glaze fires to a semi-opaque white gloss at cone 04. It is a very good base for high lead colorants.

White lead	38.3
Feldspar (Custer)	41.9
Silica	5.2
Kaolin	4.5
Whiting	7.7
Magnesium carbonate	1.4
Bentonite	1.0
Add:	
C.M.C.	1 tsp.

SSG-70 **Opaque Semi-Gloss Glaze   Cone 04**
lead-alkaline, opaque, semi-gloss, toxic

Mixing. Mix in the manner of SSG-1.

Application. Apply in the manner of SSG-1.

Firing. Fire in the manner of SSG-1.

Fired Results. This glaze fires to an opaque semi-gloss at cone 04.

Silica	35.0
Lithium carbonate	20.5
White lead	16.0
Kaolin	10.0
Bone ash	8.2
Feldspar (Kona F-4)	6.2
Bentonite	2.0
Colemanite	1.5
Add:	
Bentonite	1.0
C.M.C.	1 tsp.

SSG-71 **Opaque White Semi-Gloss Glaze   Cone 04**
alkaline-lead, opaque, semi-gloss, toxic

Mixing. Mix in the manner of SSG-1.

Application. Apply in the manner of SSG-1.

Firing. Fire in the manner of SSG-1.

Fired Results. This glaze fires to an opaque white semi-gloss at cone 04.

Silica	30.0
Borax	24.8
White lead	14.4
Feldspar (Custer)	8.0
Ultrox	8.5
Sodium carbonate	6.0
Kaolin (calcined)	4.7
Kaolin	3.3
Add:	
Bentonite	2.0
C.M.C.	1 tsp.

SSG-72 **Opaque White Smooth Gloss Glaze   Cone 04**
lead, opaque, gloss, toxic

Mixing. Mix in the manner of SSG-1.

Application. Apply in the manner of SSG-1.

Firing. Fire in the manner of SSG-1.

Fired Results. This glaze fires to an opaque white smooth gloss at cone 04.

White lead	28.0
Borax	25.0
Feldspar (Custer)	17.0
Silica	17.0
Kaolin	8.0
Whiting	3.0
Bentonite	2.0
Add:	
C.M.C.	1 tsp.

SSG-73 **Smooth Matt Opaque Glaze   Cone 04**
bristol, opaque, milky, slightly toxic

Mixing. Mix in the manner of SSG-1.

Application. Apply in the manner of SSG-1.

Firing. Fire in the manner of SSG-1.

Fired Results. This glaze fires to a smooth opaque matt at cone 04. Avoid using iron oxide as colorants for colors tend to be muddy.

Zinc oxide (calcined)	15.0
Ferro frit #3223	38.6
Pemco frit #25	24.7
Kaolin	19.9
Bentonite	2.0
Add:	
C.M.C.	1 tsp.

SSG-74 **Translucent Satin-Matt Glaze   Cone 04**
bristol, translucent, milky white, slightly toxic

Mixing. Mix in the manner of SSG-1.

Application. Apply in the manner of SSG-1.

Firing. Fire in the manner of SSG-1.

Fired Results. This glaze fires to a translucent satin matt at cone 04.

Zinc oxide (calcined)	18.4
Ferro frit #3223	36.2
Lithium carbonate	7.2
Kaolin (EPK)	18.6
Silica	17.6
Bentonite	2.0
Add:	
C.M.C.	1 tsp.

SSG-75 **Opaque Satin-Matt Glaze   Cone 04**
bristol, opaque, cloudy white, slightly toxic

Mixing. Mix in the manner of SSG-1.

Application. Apply in the manner of SSG-1.

Firing. Fire in the manner of SSG-1.

Fired Results. This glaze fires to an opaque satin matt at cone 04.

Zinc oxide (calcined)	24.5
Ferro frit #3223	43.2
Pemco frit #25	26.3
Kaolin	4.0
Bentonite	2.0
Add:	
C.M.C.	1 tsp.

SSG-76 **Opaque White Matt Volcanic Ash   Cone 04**
colemanite-lead, opaque, matt, toxic

Mixing. Mix in the manner of SSG-1.

Application. Apply in the manner of SSG-1.

Firing. Fire in the manner of SSG-1.

Fired Results. This glaze fires to an opaque white matt at cone 04.

Colemanite	40.0
Whiting	10.0
Barium carbonate	5.0
White lead	14.0
Borax	6.0
Volcanic ash	60.0
Kaolin	35.0
Zinc oxide	6.0
Tin oxide	12.0

SSG-77 **Transparent Gloss Glaze   Cone 04**
colemanite-lead, transparent, gloss, toxic

Mixing. Mix in the manner of SSG-1.

Application. Apply in the manner of SSG-1.

Firing. Fire in the manner of SSG-1.

Fired Results. This glaze fires to a transparent gloss at cone 04.

Volcanic ash	58.0
Colemanite	20.0
White lead	10.0
Borax	5.0
Feldspar (Kona F-4)	4.0
Magnesium carbonate	2.0
Bentonite	1.0

SSG-78 **Transparent Light Yellow Glaze   Cone 04**
alkaline-frit, transparent, gloss, nontoxic

Mixing. Mix in the manner of SSG-14.

Application. Apply in the manner of SSG-14.

Firing. Fire in the manner of SSG-1.

Fired Results. This glaze fires to a light transparent yellow at cone 04.

Portland cement	17.0
Pemco frit #25	76.5
Flint	4.3
Magnesium carbonate	3.5
Add:	
Bentonite	2.0
C.M.C.	1 tsp.

SSG-79 **Transparent Yellow Gloss Glaze   Cone 04**
alkaline-frit, transparent, gloss, toxic

Mixing. Mix in the manner of SSG-1.

Application. Apply in the manner of SSG-1.

Firing. Fire in the manner of SSG-1.

Fired Results. This glaze fires to a transparent yellow gloss at cone 04.

Pemco frit #54	48.0
Uranium oxide	25.0
Feldspar (Kona F-4)	12.0
Kaolin	8.7
Nepheline syenite	4.6
Bentonite	1.7
Add:	
C.M.C.	1 tsp.

SSG-80 **Opaque Bright Yellow Gloss Glaze   Cone 04**
lead, opaque, gloss, toxic

Mixing. Mix in the manner of SSG-1.

Application. Apply in the manner of SSG-1.

Firing. Fire in the manner of SSG-1.

Fired Results. This glaze fires to a bright opaque yellow gloss at cone 04.

White lead	56.0
Feldspar (Kona F-4)	31.0
Silica	4.0
Kaolin	3.6
Antimony oxide	4.0
Bentonite	2.0
Add:	
C.M.C.	1 tsp.

SSG-81 **Translucent Ochre Semi-Gloss Glaze   Cone 04**
lead, translucent, semi-gloss, toxic

Mixing. Mix in the manner of SSG-1.

Application. Apply in the manner of SSG-1.

Firing. Fire in the manner of SSG-1.

Fired Results. This glaze fires to a translucent ochre semi-gloss at cone 04.

White lead	55.0
Silica	18.0
Rutile	12.0
Feldspar (Kona F-4)	10.0
Kaolin (EPK)	3.0
Colemanite	1.6
Add:	
Bentonite	1.0
C.M.C.	1 tsp.

SSG-82 **Opaque Metallic Black Gloss Glaze   Cone 03**
lead, opaque, smooth gloss, toxic

Mixing. Mix in the manner of SSG-1.

Application. Apply in the manner of SSG-1.

Firing. Fire in the manner of SSG-1.

Fired Results. This glaze fires to an opaque metallic black gloss at cone 03.

Red lead	60.0
Silica	20.0
Kaolin	12.0
Cobalt oxide	2.3
Feldspar (Kona F-4)	1.8
Copper oxide	1.3
Manganese dioxide	1.3
Red iron oxide	1.2
Add:	
Bentonite	1.0

SSG-83   **Transparent Fluid Gloss Glaze   Cone 03**
lead, transparent, gloss, toxic

Mixing. Mix in the manner of SSG-1.

Application. Apply in the manner of SSG-1.

Firing. Fire in the manner of SSG-1.

Fired Results. This glaze fires to a clear transparent
gloss at cone 03.

Red lead	50.0
Silica	20.0
Kaolin	15.0
Whiting	10.0
Feldspar (Kona F-4)	5.0
Add:	
Bentonite	1.0
C.M.C.	1 tsp.

SSG-84   **Transparent Gloss Glaze   Cone 03**
frit, transparent, gloss, nontoxic

Mixing. Mix in the manner of SSG-14.

Application. Apply in the manner of SSG-14.

Firing. Fire in the manner of SSG-1.

Fired Results. This glaze fires to a clear transparent
gloss at cone 03.

Ferro frit #3269	36.8
Colemanite	10.4
Whiting	9.6
Alumina oxide	4.8
Kaolin (EPK)	12.6
Silica	27.8
Add:	
Bentonite	1.0
C.M.C.	1 tsp.

SSG-85   **Transparent Gloss Glaze   Cone 03**
lead, transparent, gloss, toxic

Mixing. Mix in the manner of SSG-1.

Application. Apply in the manner of SSG-1.

Firing. Fire in the manner of SSG-1.

Fired Results. This glaze fires to a transparent gloss
glaze at cone 03.

White lead	45.2
Silica	28.0
Feldspar (Custer)	16.0
Colemanite	4.6
Kaolin (calcined)	4.1
Whiting	2.0
Add:	
Bentonite	1.0
C.M.C.	1 tsp.

SSG-86   **Transparent Semi-Matt Glaze   Cone 03**
alkaline-lead, transparent, semi-matt, slightly toxic

Mixing. Mix in the manner of SSG-1.

Application. Apply in the manner of SSG-1.

Firing. Fire in the manner of SSG-1.

Fired Results. This glaze fires to a transparent semi-matt
at cone 03.

Silica	22.0
Sodium carbonate	20.0
Borax (calcined)	16.0
Feldspar (Kona F-4)	12.0
Whiting	9.1
Kaolin	6.0
Colemanite	6.0
Add:	
Bentonite	2.0
C.M.C.	1 tsp.

SSG-87   **Transparent Matt Glaze   Cone 03**
bristol, transparent, matt, slightly toxic

Mixing. Mix in the manner of SSG-1.

Application. Apply in the manner of SSG-1.

Firing. Fire in the manner of SSG-1.

Fired Results. This glaze fires to a clear matt at cone 03.

Nepheline syenite	31.1
Lithium carbonate	2.9
Zinc oxide	26.3
Whiting	5.3
Silica	33.5
Bentonite	1.0
Add:	
C.M.C.	1 tsp.

SSG-88 **Transparent Dry Matt Glaze   Cone 03**
barium, transparent, dry matt, slightly toxic

Mixing. Mix in the manner of SSG-1.

Application. Apply in the manner of SSG-1.

Firing. Fire in the manner of SSG-1.

Fired Results. This glaze fires to a clear dry matt at cone 03.

Nepheline syenite	32.5
Lithium carbonate	1.4
Zinc oxide	20.0
Barium carbonate	6.8
Whiting	6.8
Silica	32.5
Add:	
Bentonite	2.0
C.M.C.	1 tsp.

SSG-89 **Translucent Cream Semi-Matt Glaze   Cone 03**
lead, translucent, semi-matt, toxic

Mixing. Mix in the manner of SSG-1.

Application. Apply in the manner of SSG-1.

Firing. Fire in the manner of SSG-1.

Fired Results. This glaze fires to a translucent cream semi-matt at cone 03. This is a good base for iron colorants.

White lead	40.0
Feldspar (Custer)	28.7
Kaolin	14.0
Whiting	8.5
Silica	5.7
Zinc oxide	2.7
Add:	
Bentonite	2.0
C.M.C.	1 tsp.

SSG-90 **Translucent Cream Matt Glaze   Cone 03**
lead, translucent, matt, toxic

Mixing. Mix in the manner of SSG-1.

Application. Apply in the manner of SSG-1.

Firing. Fire in the manner of SSG-1.

Fired Results. This glaze fires to a translucent cream matt at cone 03. This is a good base for iron and rutile colorants.

White lead	50.2
Kaolin (calcined)	10.0
Feldspar (Kona F-4)	9.0
Nepheline syenite	8.9
Barium carbonate	7.3
Whiting	4.6
Silica	4.8
Ultrox	5.2
Add:	
C.M.C.	1 tsp.

SSG-91 **Translucent Ivory Gloss Glaze   Cone 03**
lead, translucent, gloss, toxic

Mixing. Mix in the manner of SSG-1.

Application. Apply in the manner of SSG-1.

Firing. Fire in the manner of SSG-1.

Fired Results. This glaze fires to a translucent ivory gloss at cone 03.

White lead	46.2
Feldspar (Custer)	19.4
Silica	10.4
Whiting	8.8
Ultrox	8.8
Kaolin	6.4
Add:	
Bentonite	1.0
C.M.C.	1 tsp.

SSG-92   **Translucent Semi-Gloss Glaze   Cone 03**
lead-borax, translucent, semi-gloss, toxic

Mixing. Mix in the manner of SSG-6.

Application. Apply in the manner of SSG-1.

Firing. Fire in the manner of SSG-1.

Fired Results. This glaze fires to a milky translucent semi-gloss at cone 03.

Silica	30.0
Borax	24.8
White lead	14.4
Feldspar (Kingman)	8.0
Ultrox	8.5
Sodium carbonate	6.0
Kaolin (calcined)	4.7
Kaolin (Georgia)	3.3
Add:	
Bentonite	1.0
C.M.C.	1 tsp.

SSG-93   **Translucent White Semi-Matt Glaze   Cone 03**
lead, translucent, semi-matt, toxic

Mixing. Mix in the manner of SSG-1.

Application. Apply in the manner of SSG-1.

Firing. Fire in the manner of SSG-1.

Fired Results. This glaze fires to a translucent white semi-matt at cone 03.

White lead	35.5
Feldspar (soda)	18.0
Kaolin	17.1
Whiting	10.5
Ultrox	8.0
Silica	7.0
Zinc oxide	3.7
Add:	
C.M.C.	1 tsp.

SSG-94   **White Titanium Matt Glaze   Cone 03**
leadless, semi-opaque, matt, nontoxic

Mixing. Mix in the manner of SSG-14.

Application. Apply in the manner of SSG-14.

Firing. Fire in the manner of SSG-1.

Fired Results. This glaze fires to a off-white matt at cone 03.

Nepheline syenite	39.5
Pemco frit #54	57.5
Whiting	3.0
Add:	
Titanium dioxide	7.5
Bentonite	1.5
C.M.C.	1 tsp.

SSG-95   **Opaque Black Gloss Glaze   Cone 02**
lead, opaque, gloss, toxic

Mixing. Mix in the manner of SSG-1.

Application. Apply in the manner of SSG-1.

Firing. Fire in the manner of SSG-1.

Fired Results. This glaze fires to an opaque black gloss at cone 02.

White lead	62.0
Silica	16.0
Manganese dioxide	10.0
Cornwall stone	5.0
Red clay	7.0
Add:	
Bentonite	2.0
C.M.C.	1 tsp.

SSG-96   **Lithium Blue Gloss Glaze   Cone 02**
alkaline, transparent, gloss, nontoxic

Mixing. Mix in the manner of SSG-14.

Application. Apply in the manner of SSG-14.

Firing. Fire in the manner of SSG-1.

Fired Results. This glaze fires to a beautiful lithium blue gloss at cone 02.

Lithium carbonate	26.9
Kaolin	13.6
Silica	53.5
Copper carbonate	4.1
Bentonite	2.8
Add:	
C.M.C.	1 tsp.

SSG-97

Transparent Blue Gloss Glaze   Cone 02
lead, transparent, gloss, toxic

Mixing. Mix in the manner of SSG-1.

Application. Apply in the manner of SSG-1.

Firing. Fire in the manner of SSG-1.

Fired Results. This glaze fires to a light transparent blue at cone 02.

Red lead	50.0
White lead	10.0
Colemanite	3.0
Silica	20.0
Kaolin	15.0
Feldspar (Oxford)	2.0
Add:	
Bentonite	2.0
C.M.C.	1 tsp.
Cobalt carbonate	1.0

SSG-98

Clear Gloss Glaze   Cone 02
lead, transparent, gloss, toxic

Mixing. Mix in the manner of SSG-1.

Application. Apply in the manner of SSG-1.

Firing. Fire in the manner of SSG-1.

Fired Results. This glaze fires to a clear gloss at cone 02. It is a good base for the iron colorants or the ochres.

Red lead	55.0
Silica	22.0
Kaolin	16.0
Colemanite	5.0
Feldspar (Kona F-4)	2.0
Add:	
Bentonite	2.0
C.M.C.	1 tsp.

SSG-99

Transparent Gloss Glaze   Cone 02
lithium base, transparent, gloss, nontoxic

Mixing. Mix in the manner of SSG-14.

Application. Apply in the manner of SSG-14.

Firing. Fire in the manner of SSG-1.

Fired Results. This glaze fires to a transparent gloss at cone 02.

Lithium carbonate	22.1
Whiting	11.3
Zinc oxide	7.0
Kaolin	28.1
Silica	30.0
Bentonite	1.0
Add:	
C.M.C.	1 tsp.

SSG-100

Transparent Semi-Gloss Glaze   Cone 02
lead, transparent, semi-gloss, toxic

Mixing. Mix in the manner of SSG-1.

Application. Apply in the manner of SSG-1.

Firing. Fire in the manner of SSG-1.

Fired Results. This glaze fires to a transparent semi-gloss at cone 02.

Red lead	58.0
Silica	23.0
Kaolin	12.0
Colemanite	4.6
Feldspar (Custer)	2.4
Add:	
Bentonite	1.0
C.M.C.	1 tsp.

SSG-101

Clear Matt Glaze   Cone 02
lead, transparent, matt, toxic

Mixing. Mix in the manner of SSG-1.

Application. Apply in the manner of SSG-1.

Firing. Fire in the manner of SSG-1.

Fired Results. This glaze fires to a clear matt at cone 02.

White lead	42.1
Whiting	9.9
Feldspar (potash)	36.5
Kaolin (calcined)	7.2
Kaolin	3.6
Bentonite	0.7

SSG-102   **Translucent White Gloss Glaze   Cone 02**
alkaline-frit, translucent, gloss, nontoxic

Mixing. Mix in the manner of SSG-14.

Application. Apply in the manner of SSG-14.

Firing. Fire in the manner of SSG-1.

Fired Results. This glaze fires to a translucent white gloss at cone 02.

Hommel frit #259	24.2
Ultrox	4.0
Whiting	17.2
Kaolin	17.2
Silica	39.4
Add:	
Bentonite	1.0
C.M.C.	1 tsp.

SSG-103   **Translucent White Gloss Glaze   Cone 02**
alkaline-frit, translucent, gloss, nontoxic

Mixing. Mix in the manner of SSG-14.

Application. Apply in the manner of SSG-14.

Firing. Fire in the manner of SSG-1.

Fired Results. This glaze fires to a translucent white gloss at cone 02.

Ferro #3819	21.7
Colemanite	34.6
Ultrox	5.9
Kaolin	10.8
Silica	27.0
Add:	
Bentonite	2.0
C.M.C.	1 tsp.

SSG-104   **Translucent White Matt Glaze   Cone 02**
lead, translucent, matt, toxic

Mixing. Mix in the manner of SSG-1.

Application. Apply in the manner of SSG-1.

Firing. Fire in the manner of SSG-1.

Fired Results. This glaze fires to a translucent white matt at cone 02.

White lead	45.0
Feldspar (Kona F-4)	35.0
Whiting	10.0
Kaolin (calcined)	5.0
Kaolin	5.0
Add:	
Bentonite	1.0
C.M.C.	1 tsp.

SSG-105   **Opaque White Gloss Glaze   Cone 02**
lead, opaque, gloss, toxic

Mixing. Mix in the manner of SSG-1.

Application. Apply in the manner of SSG-1.

Firing. Fire in the manner of SSG-1.

Fired Results. This glaze fires to an opaque white gloss at cone 02.

White lead	33.5
Feldspar (Kona F-4)	33.5
Tin oxide	10.0
Silica	9.0
Whiting	7.0
Zinc oxide	3.0
Kaolin	3.0
Ultrox	1.0
Add:	
Bentonite	1.0
C.M.C.	1 tsp.

SSG-106   **Opaque White Gloss Glaze   Cone 02**
lead, opaque, gloss, toxic

Mixing. Mix in the manner of SSG-1.

Application. Apply in the manner of SSG-1.

Firing. Fire in the manner of SSG-1.

Fired Results. This glaze fires to an opaque white gloss at cone 02.

White lead	32.1
Whiting	7.8
Feldspar (Custer)	34.6
Zinc oxide	3.8
Kaolin	3.9
Silica	8.4
Tin oxide	9.4
Add:	
C.M.C.	1 tsp.

SSG-107   **Opaque Dry Matt Glaze   Cone 02**
lead, translucent, matt, toxic

Mixing. Mix in the manner of SSG-1.

Application. Apply in the manner of SSG-1.

Firing. Fire in the manner of SSG-1.

Fired Results. This glaze fires to an opaque white dry matt at cone 02.

White lead	48.0
Feldspar (Custer)	24.0
Kaolin (calcined)	12.0
Whiting	10.0
Kaolin	4.0
Add:	
Bentonite	1.0
C.M.C.	1 tsp.

SSG-108   **Translucent Violet Matt Glaze   Cone 02**
barium, translucent, matt, toxic

Mixing. Mix in the manner of SSG-1.

Application. Apply in the manner of SSG-1.

Firing. Fire in the manner of SSG-1.

Fired Results. This glaze fires to a translucent violet matt at cone 02.

Barium carbonate	30.2
Lithium carbonate	2.4
Zinc oxide	5.4
Whiting	9.5
Feldspar (Custer)	36.2
Silica	16.3
Add:	
Nickel carbonate	2.0
Bentonite	1.0
C.M.C.	1 tsp.

SSG-109   **Transparent Gloss Glaze   Cone 01**
leadless, transparent, gloss, nontoxic

Mixing. Mix in the manner of SSG-14.

Application. Apply in the manner of SSG-14.

Firing. Fire in the manner of SSG-1.

Fired Results. This glaze fires to a clear gloss at cone 01.

Pemco frit #54	20.0
Nepheline syenite	70.0
Whiting	10.0
Add:	
Bentonite	2.0
C.M.C.	1 tsp.

SSG-110   **Transparent Semi-Gloss Glaze   Cone 01**
leadless, transparent, semi-gloss, nontoxic

Mixing. Mix in the manner of SSG-14.

Application. Apply in the manner of SSG-14.

Firing. Fire in the manner of SSG-1.

Fired Results. This glaze fires to a clear semi-gloss at cone 01.

Pemco frit #54	15.0
Nepheline syenite	70.0
Whiting	15.0

SSG-111   **Transparent Satin-Matt Glaze   Cone 01**
leadless, transparent, satin matt, nontoxic

Mixing. Mix in the manner of SSG-14.

Application. Apply in the manner of SSG-14.

Firing. Fire in the manner of SSG-1.

Fired Results. This glaze fires to a transparent satin matt at cone 01.

Pemco frit #54	13.3
Nepheline syenite	50.0
Feldspar (Custer)	18.4
Whiting	18.3
Add:	
Bentonite	1.0
C.M.C.	1 tsp.

SSG-112   **Translucent Matt Glaze Cone 01**
bristol, translucent, matt, nontoxic

Mixing. Mix in the manner of SSG-14.

Application. Apply in the manner of SSG-14.

Firing. Fire in the manner of SSG-1.

Fired Results. This glaze fires to a translucent matt at cone 01.

Feldspar (potash)	43.2
Lithium carbonate	4.2
Zinc oxide	29.4
Whiting	5.4
Kaolin	7.0
Silica	9.8
Add:	
Bentonite	1.0
C.M.C.	1 tsp.

SG-113   **Black Gloss Glaze Cone 1**
leadless, opaque, black gloss, nontoxic

Mixing. Mix in the manner of SSG-14.

Application. Apply in the manner of SSG-14.

Firing. Fire in the manner of SSG-1.

Fired Results. This glaze fires to an opaque black gloss at cone 1.

Nepheline syenite	78.5
Ferro frit #3134	11.0
Whiting	10.5
Bentonite	2.0
Add:	
Cobalt oxide	2.0
Chrome oxide	2.0
Black iron oxide	2.0
C.M.C.	1 tsp.

SSG-114   **Black Matt Glaze Cone 1**
leadless, opaque, black matt, nontoxic

Mixing. Mix in the manner of SSG-14.

Application. Apply in the manner of SSG-14.

Firing. Fire in the manner of SSG-1.

Fired Results. This glaze fires to an opaque black matt at cone 1.

Nepheline syenite	28.5
Ferro frit #3134	48.9
Kaolin	5.1
Whiting	3.0
Silica	14.5
Add:	
Cobalt oxide	2.0
Chrome oxide	2.0
Black iron oxide	2.0
C.M.C.	1 tsp.

SSG-115   **Opaque Gunmetal Black Semi-Gloss Glaze Cone 1**
leadless, opaque, semi-gloss, nontoxic

Mixing. Mix in the manner of SSG-14.

Application. Apply in the manner of SSG-14.

Firing. Fire in the manner of SSG-1.

Fired Results. This glaze fires to an opaque gunmetal black at cone 1.

Nepheline syenite	78.0
Ferro frit #3134	10.0
Whiting	1.0
Kaolin	3.0
Add:	
Cobalt oxide	2.0
Copper oxide	2.0
Manganese oxide	2.0
Iron oxide	2.0
C.M.C.	1 tsp.

SSG-116   **Clear Gloss Glaze Cone 1**
alkaline, transparent, gloss, nontoxic

Mixing. Mix in the manner of SSG-14.

Application. Apply in the manner of SSG-14.

Firing. Fire in the manner of SSG-1.

Fired Results. This glaze fires to a clear gloss at cone 1.

Spodumene	48.0
Ferro frit #3134	50.0
Magnesium carbonate	2.0
Add:	
Bentonite	1.0
C.M.C.	1 tsp.

SSG-117 **Clear Gloss Glaze Cone 1**
alkaline, transparent, gloss, nontoxic

Mixing. Mix in the manner of SSG-14.

Application. Apply in the manner of SSG-14.

Firing. Fire in the manner of SSG-1.

Fired Results. This glaze fires to a clear gloss at cone 1.

Kaolin (EPK)	34.0
Hommel frit #14	64.0
Magnesium carbonate	2.0
Add:	
Bentonite	2.0
C.M.C.	1 tsp.

SSG-118 **Clear Gloss Glaze Cone 1**
colemanite, transparent, gloss, nontoxic

Mixing. Mix in the manner of SSG-14.

Application. Apply in the manner of SSG-14.

Firing. Fire in the manner of SSG-1.

Fired Results. This glaze fires to a clear gloss at cone 1. It is a very good base for colorants, giving uniform results.

Colemanite	55.5
Kaolin	17.5
Silica	27.0
Add:	
Bentonite	1.0

SSG-119 **Clear Gloss Glaze Cone 1**
colemanite, transparent, gloss, nontoxic

Mixing. Mix in the manner of SSG-14.

Application. Apply in the manner of SSG-14.

Firing. Fire in the manner of SSG-1.

Fired Results. This glaze fires to a clear gloss at cone 1.

Colemanite	60.0
Kaolin	19.0
Silica	31.0

SSG-120 **Transparent Gloss Glaze Cone 1**
lead, transparent, gloss, toxic

Mixing. Mix in the manner of SSG-1.

Application. Apply in the manner of SSG-1.

Firing. Fire in the manner of SSG-1.

Fired Results. This glaze fires to a clear gloss at cone 1.

White lead	52.5
Feldspar (Kona F-4)	15.5
Cornwall stone	15.0
Silica	10.0
Whiting	4.0
Colemanite	3.0
Add:	
Bentonite	1.0
C.M.C.	1 tsp.

SSG-121 **Clear Semi-Gloss Glaze Cone 1**
colemanite, transparent, semi-gloss, nontoxic

Mixing. Mix in the manner of SSG-14.

Application. Apply in the manner of SSG-14.

Firing. Fire in the manner of SSG-1.

Fired Results. This glaze fires to a clear semi-gloss at cone 1. It is an excellent color base, giving uniform results at every firing.

Colemanite	60.0
Kaolin	15.0
Silica	25.0
Add:	
Bentonite	1.0
C.M.C.	1 tsp.

SSG-122 **Transparent Semi-Gloss Glaze Cone 1**
lead, transparent, semi-gloss, toxic

Mixing. Mix in the manner of SSG-1.

Application. Apply in the manner of SSG-1.

Firing. Fire in the manner of SSG-1.

Fired Results. This glaze fires to a clear semi-gloss at cone 1.

White lead	48.4
Feldspar (Custer)	26.7
Whiting	16.6
Kaolin (EPK)	4.3
Colemanite	2.0
Add:	
Bentonite	1.0
C.M.C.	1 tsp.

SSG-123 **Clear Satin-Matt Glaze Cone 1**
colemanite, transparent, satin matt, nontoxic

Mixing. Mix in the manner of SSG-14.

Application. Apply in the manner of SSG-14.

Firing. Fire in the manner of SSG-1.

Fired Results. This glaze fires to a clear satin matt at cone 1. It makes a very reliable color base, giving uniform results at every firing.

Colemanite	55.0
Kaolin	17.5
Silica	22.5
Add:	
Bentonite	1.0
C.M.C.	1 tsp.

SSG-124 **Clear Satin-Matt Glaze Cone 1**
frit, transparent, satin matt, nontoxic

Mixing. Mix in the manner of SSG-14.

Application. Apply in the manner of SSG-14.

Firing. Fire in the manner of SSG-1.

Fired Results. This glaze fires to a clear satin matt at cone 1 giving uniform results whether clear or colored.

Pemco frit #54	38.0
Silica	32.0
Whiting	15.0
Kaolin	10.0
Colemanite	5.0
Add:	
Bentonite	1.0
C.M.C.	1 tsp.

SSG-125 **Clear Satin-Matt Glaze Cone 1**
frit, transparent, satin matt, nontoxic

Mixing. Mix in the manner of SSG-14.

Application. Apply in the manner of SSG-14.

Firing. Fire in the manner of SSG-1.

Fired Results. This glaze fires to a clear satin matt at cone 1 giving uniform results.

Ferro frit #3134	38.0
Whiting	32.0
Silica	16.0
Kaolin	10.0
Colemanite	4.0
Bentonite	1.0
Add:	
C.M.C.	1 tsp.

SSG-126 **Clear Satin-Matt Glaze Cone 1**
zinc-feldspathic, transparent, satin matt, slightly toxic

Mixing. Mix in the manner of SSG-1.

Application. Apply in the manner of SSG-1.

Firing. Fire in the manner of SSG-1.

Fired Results. This glaze fires to a clear satin matt at cone 1. It is a highly stable glaze and is excellent for use on utility ware.

Zinc oxide	10.3
Feldspar (Kingman)	45.2
Wollastonite	13.9
Whiting	10.6
Kaolin	18.0
Colemanite	2.0
Bentonite	1.0
Add:	
C.M.C.	1 tsp.

SSG-127

Clear Semi-Matt Glaze   Cone 1
colemanite, transparent, semi-matt, slightly toxic

Mixing. Mix in the manner of SSG-1.

Application. Apply in the manner of SSG-1.

Firing. Fire in the manner of SSG-1.

Fired Results. This glaze fires to a clear semi-matt at cone 1. It is a good glaze for utility ware.

Feldspar (Custer)	20.0
Colemanite	18.4
Magnesium carbonate	4.6
Whiting	29.0
Silica	25.0
Add:	
Bentonite	2.0
C.M.C.	1 tsp.

SSG-128

Marked Clear Matt Glaze   Cone 1
bristol, transparent, matt, slightly toxic

Mixing. Mix in the manner of SSG-1.

Application. Apply in the manner of SSG-1.

Firing. Fire in the manner of SSG-1.

Fired Results. This glaze fires to a marked clear matt at cone 1.

Zinc oxide	20.0
Lithium carbonate	12.0
Titanium dioxide	7.5
Whiting	4.5
Kaolin	16.5
Silica	38.3
Bentonite	1.2
Add:	
C.M.C.	1 tsp.

SSG-129

Translucent White Gloss Glaze   Cone 1
colemanite, translucent, gloss, nontoxic

Mixing. Mix in the manner of SSG-14.

Application. Apply in the manner of SSG-14.

Firing. Fire in the manner of SSG-1.

Fired Results. This glaze fires to a cloudy translucent white at cone 1. It is quite stable and makes a good glaze for utility ware.

Colemanite	40.0
Silica	28.0
Whiting	18.0
Kaolin	8.0
Magnesium carbonate	5.0
Bentonite	1.0
Add:	
C.M.C.	1 tsp.

SSG-130

White Satin-Matt Glaze   Cone 1
leadless, translucent, satin matt, nontoxic

Mixing. Mix in the manner of SSG-14.

Application. Apply in the manner of SSG-14.

Firing. Fire in the manner of SSG-1.

Fired Results. This glaze fires to a white satin matt at cone 1.

Nepheline syenite	37.2
Kaolin (EPK)	3.1
Pemco frit #54	11.3
Whiting	17.4
Silica	29.0
Bentonite	2.0
Add:	
C.M.C.	1 tsp.

SSG-131

Semi-Opaque Matt Glaze   Cone 1
bristol, barium, semi-opaque, matt, slightly toxic

Mixing. Mix in the manner of SSG-1.

Application. Apply in the manner of SSG-1.

Firing. Fire in the manner of SSG-1.

Fired Results. This glaze fires to an opaque cloudy white at cone 1. Avoid iron as a colorant as it tends to turn an ugly muddy color in this glaze base.

Zinc oxide (calcined)	9.6
Nepheline syenite	40.8
Lithium carbonate	2.1
Barium carbonate	16.5
Whiting	11.0
Silica	20.0
Add:	
Bentonite	2.0
C.M.C.	1 tsp.

SSG-132 **Smooth Opaque Matt Glaze   Cone 1**
bristol, opaque, matt, slightly toxic

Mixing. Mix in the manner of SSG-1.

Application. Apply in the manner of SSG-1.

Firing. Fire in the manner of SSG-1.

Fired Results. This glaze fires to an opaque matt which is a lovely cloudy white at cone 1.

Zinc oxide (Calcined)	10.6
Ferro frit #3223	34.2
Lithium carbonate	7.7
Kaolin	21.0
Silica	26.4
Add:	
Bentonite	2.0
C.M.C.	1 tsp.

SSG-133 **Opaque White Matt Glaze   Cone 1**
barium, opaque, matt, toxic

Mixing. Mix in the manner of SSG-1.

Application. Apply in the manner of SSG-1.

Firing. Fire in the manner of SSG-1.

Fired Results. This glaze fires to an opaque white matt at cone 1.

Nepheline syenite	42.2
Lithium carbonate	11.5
Barium carbonate	16.5
Whiting	10.0
Zinc oxide	8.1
Silica	20.2
Bentonite	1.2
Add:	
C.M.C.	1 tsp.

SSG-134 **Opaque Milky White Matt Glaze   Cone 1**
frit, opaque, matt, nontoxic

Mixing. Mix in the manner of SSG-14.

Application. Apply in the manner of SSG-14.

Firing. Fire in the manner of SSG-1.

Fired Results. This glaze fires to an opaque milky white smooth matt at cone 1. It is highly stable and good for use on utility ware.

Pyrophyllite	34.0
Ferro frit #3134	62.0
Colemanite	3.0
Bentonite	1.0
Add:	
C.M.C.	1 tsp.

SSG-135 **Transparent Gloss Glaze   Cone 2**
frit, transparent, gloss, nontoxic

Mixing. Mix in the manner of SSG-14.

Application. Apply in the manner of SSG-14.

Firing. Fire in the manner of SSG-1.

Fired Results. This glaze fires to a clear gloss at cone 2.

Ferro frit #3134	48.3
Silica	20.4
Feldspar (Kona F-4)	15.3
Whiting	4.7
Talc	5.7
Kaolin	4.8
Add:	
Bentonite	2.0
C.M.C.	1 tsp.

SSG-136 **Transparent Gloss Glaze   Cone 2**
colemanite, transparent, gloss, nontoxic

Mixing. Mix in the manner of SSG-14.

Application. Apply in the manner of SSG-14.

Firing. Fire in the manner of SSG-1.

Fired Results. This glaze fires to a clear gloss at cone 2. It makes a good glaze for utility ware.

Feldspar (Custer)	40.2
Colemanite	24.1
Silica	18.0
Zinc oxide	9.9
Kaolin	4.8
Bentonite	2.0
Add:	
C.M.C.	1 tsp.

SSG-137   **Transparent Gloss Glaze   Cone 2**
lead, transparent, gloss, toxic

Mixing. Mix in the manner of SSG-1.

Application. Apply in the manner of SSG-1.

Firing. Fire in the manner of SSG-1.

Fired Results. This glaze fires to a clear gloss at cone 2.

White lead	42.0
Feldspar (Kona F-4)	28.0
Silica	12.0
Whiting	10.0
Kaolin	5.0
Zinc oxide	4.0
Add:	
Bentonite	1.0
C.M.C.	1 tsp.

SSG-138   **Transparent Semi-Gloss Glaze   Cone 2**
lead, transparent, semi-gloss, toxic

Mixing. Mix in the manner of SSG-1.

Application. Apply in the manner of SSG-1.

Firing. Fire in the manner of SSG-1.

Fired Results. This glaze fires to a clear gloss at cone 2.

Feldspar (Custer)	32.0
Red lead	25.0
Silica	20.0
Whiting	9.0
Tennessee ball clay #1	6.0
Kaolin	6.0
Colemanite	2.0
Add:	
Bentonite	1.0
C.M.C.	1 tsp.

SSG-139   **Transparent Bright Matt Glaze   Cone 2**
feldspathic-barium, transparent, matt, toxic

Mixing. Mix in the manner of SSG-1.

Application. Apply in the manner of SSG-1.

Firing. Fire in the manner of SSG-1.

Fired Results. This glaze fires to a clear bright matt at cone 2.

Feldspar (Custer)	71.5
Zinc oxide	10.4
Barium carbonate	7.0
Whiting	1.5
Magnesium carbonate	2.1
Add:	
Bentonite	2.0
C.M.C.	1 tsp.

SSG-140   **Transparent Satin-Matt Glaze   Cone 2**
leadless, transparent, satin matt, nontoxic

Mixing. Mix in the manner of SSG-14.

Application. Apply in the manner of SSG-14.

Firing. Fire in the manner of SSG-1.

Fired Results. This glaze fires to a clear satin matt at cone 2.

Lithium carbonate	2.0
Zinc oxide	6.0
Whiting	36.8
Kaolin	36.8
Silica	16.3
Magnesium carbonate	2.1
Add:	
Bentonite	1.0
C.M.C.	1 tsp.

SSG-141   **Translucent Orange Gloss Glaze   Cone 2**
lead, translucent, gloss, toxic

Mixing. Mix in the manner of SSG-1.

Application. Apply in the manner of SSG-1.

Firing. Fire in the manner of SSG-1.

Fired Results. This glaze fires to a translucent orange gloss at cone 2.

Red lead	64.0
Uranium oxide	17.0
Kaolin	13.0
Silica	4.0
Zinc oxide	2.0
Add:	
Bentonite	1.0
C.M.C.	1 tsp.

SSG-142

Translucent Orange-Red Gloss Glaze   Cone 2
lead, translucent, gloss, toxic

Mixing. Mix in the manner of SSG-1.

Application. Apply in the manner of SSG-1.

Firing. Fire in the manner of SSG-1.

Fired Results. This glaze fires to a translucent orange-red gloss at cone 2.

Red lead	60.0
Uranium oxide	24.5
Silica	14.5
Tin oxide	2.0
Add:	
Bentonite	1.0
C.M.C.	1 tsp.

SSG-143

Translucent Gloss Glaze   Cone 2
lead, translucent, gloss, toxic

Mixing. Mix in the manner of SSG-1.

Application. Apply in the manner of SSG-1.

Firing. Fire in the manner of SSG-1.

Fired Results. This glaze fires to a translucent gloss at cone 2.

Cornwall stone	64.0
White lead	22.0
Whiting	10.0
Ultrox	2.0
Superpax	2.0
Add:	
Bentonite	1.0
C.M.C.	1 tsp.

SSG-144

Translucent Gloss Glaze   Cone 2
colemanite, translucent, gloss, nontoxic

Mixing. Mix in the manner of SSG-14.

Application. Apply in the manner of SSG-14.

Firing. Fire in the manner of SSG-1.

Fired Results. This glaze fires to a translucent white gloss at cone 2.

Feldspar (Custer)	34.0
Colemanite	32.5
Silica	20.0
Zinc oxide	4.0
Whiting	3.8
Add:	
Bentonite	1.0

SSG-145

Translucent Semi-Gloss Glaze   Cone 2
lead, translucent, semi-gloss, toxic

Mixing. Mix in the manner of SSG-1.

Application. Apply in the manner of SSG-1.

Firing. Fire in the manner of SSG-1.

Fired Results. This glaze fires to a translucent white semi-gloss at cone 2.

White lead	43.8
Feldspar (Custer)	26.8
Whiting	12.0
Kaolin	17.7
Add:	
Bentonite	2.0
C.M.C.	1 tsp.

SSG-146

Translucent Matt Glaze   Cone 2
raw alkaline, translucent, matt, nontoxic

Mixing. Mix in the manner of SSG-14.

Application. Apply in the manner of SSG-14.

Firing. Fire in the manner of SSG-1.

Fired Results. This glaze fires to a translucent white matt at cone 2.

Feldspar (Custer)	50.0
Sodium carbonate	22.0
Silica	12.0
Whiting	10.0
Colemanite	5.0
Add:	
Bentonite	2.0
C.M.C.	1 tsp.

SSG-147 **Translucent Smooth Dry Matt Glaze   Cone 2**
lead, translucent, smooth dry matt, toxic

Mixing. Mix in the manner of SSG-1.

Application. Apply in the manner of SSG-1.

Firing. Fire in the manner of SSG-1.

Fired Results. This glaze fires to a translucent white smooth dry matt at cone 2.

White lead	34.0
Feldspar (Kona F-4)	32.2
Kaolin (EPK)	15.4
Whiting	16.4
Bentonite	1.0
Add:	
C.M.C.	1 tsp.

SSG-148 **Marked Satin-Matt Glaze   Cone 2**
bristol, transparent, clear marked, nontoxic

Mixing. Mix in the manner of SSG-14.

Application. Apply in the manner of SSG-14.

Firing. Fire in the manner of SSG-1.

Fired Results. This glaze fires to a mottled white satin matt at cone 2.

Zinc oxide	22.5
Lithium carbonate	9.5
Titanium dioxide	7.5
Whiting	4.5
Kaolin (EPK)	17.6
Silica	38.4
Add:	
C.M.C.	1 tsp.

SSG-149 **White Satin-Matt Glaze   Cone 2**
leadless, opaque, satin matt, nontoxic

Mixing. Mix in the manner of SSG-14.

Application. Apply in the manner of SSG-14.

Firing. Fire in the manner of SSG-1.

Fired Results. This glaze fires to a white opaque satin matt at cone 2.

Nepheline syenite	69.5
Ferro frit #3134	10.0
Whiting	20.5
Add:	
Titanium dioxide	5.5
Bentonite	2.0
C.M.C.	1 tsp.

SSG-150 **Transparent Gloss Glaze Base   Cone 3**
leadless, transparent, gloss, nontoxic

Mixing. Mix in the manner of SSG-14.

Application. Apply by spraying for best results.

Firing. Fire in the manner of SSG-1.

Fired Results. This is primarily a base glaze which works exceptionally well with iron and copper colorants. Add 1% iron oxide for a beige which has lighter crystals, or add 2% copper carbonate for a light green with brown spots reminiscent of iron spotting.

Whiting	32.0
Zinc oxide	13.0
Feldspar (Custer)	30.0
Kaolin (EPK)	20.6
Silica	3.0
Magnesium carbonate	1.8
Add:	
Bentonite	1.0
C.M.C.	1 tsp.

SSG-151 **Transparent Gloss Glaze   Cone 3**
colemanite-barium, transparent, gloss, toxic

Mixing. Mix in the manner of SSG-1.

Application. Apply in the manner of SSG-1.

Firing. Fire in the manner of SSG-1.

Fired Results. This glaze fires to a clear gloss at cone 3. This is a good glaze base for colorants and for use on utility ware.

Feldspar (Kingman)	36.2
Silica	22.0
Colemanite	18.4
Zinc oxide	8.2
Barium carbonate	7.6
Talc	7.3
Bentonite	2.0
Add:	
C.M.C.	1 tsp.

SSG-152

Transparent Semi-Gloss Glaze   Cone 3
leadless, transparent, semi-gloss, toxic

Mixing. Mix in the manner of SSG-1.

Application. Apply in the manner of SSG-1.

Firing. Fire in the manner of SSG-1.

Fired Results. This glaze fires to a clear semi-gloss at cone 3. It is slightly toxic in the raw state due to its barium content.

Feldspar (Kingman)	56.0
Silica	18.0
Kaolin	7.0
Zinc oxide	6.0
Whiting	6.0
Barium carbonate	7.0
Bentonite	1.0
Add:	
C.M.C.	1 tsp.

SSG-153

Transparent Semi-Matt Glaze   Cone 3
leadless, transparent, semi-matt, nontoxic

Mixing. Mix in the manner of SSG-14.

Application. Apply in the manner of SSG-14.

Firing. Fire in the manner of SSG-1.

Fired Results. This glaze fires to a clear semi-matt at cone 3.

Feldspar (Custer)	57.0
Silica	12.0
Whiting	10.0
Kaolin	10.0
Zinc oxide	8.0
Bentonite	1.0
Add:	
C.M.C.	1 tsp.

SSG-154

Clear Satin Matt Glaze   Cone 3
barium, transparent, satin matt, toxic

Mixing. Mix in the manner of SSG-1.

Application. Apply in the manner of SSG-1.

Firing. Fire in the manner of SSG-1.

Fired Results. This glaze fires to a clear satin matt at cone 3.

Feldspar (potash)	29.5
Barium carbonate	29.9
Magnesium carbonate	12.0
Whiting	9.1
Silica	18.5
C.M.C.	1 tsp.
Add:	
Bentonite	2.0

SSG-155

Translucent White Gloss Glaze   Cone 3
colemanite, translucent, gloss, nontoxic

Mixing. Mix in the manner of SSG-14.

Application. Apply in the manner of SSG-14.

Firing. Fire in the manner of SSG-1.

Fired Results. This glaze fires to a translucent white gloss at cone 3.

Pemco frit #25	37.0
Colemanite	10.6
Whiting	8.5
Alumina oxide	7.0
Kaolin	12.5
Silica	22.0
Magnesium carbonate	2.4
Add:	
Bentonite	1.0
C.M.C.	1 tsp.

SSG-156

Translucent Semi-Gloss Glaze   Cone 3
feldspar-barium, translucent, semi-gloss, toxic

Mixing. Mix in the manner of SSG-1.

Application. Apply in the manner of SSG-1.

Firing. Fire in the manner of SSG-1.

Fired Results. This glaze fires to a translucent semi-gloss white at cone 3.

Feldspar (Custer)	42.0
Silica	28.0
Kaolin	12.0
Whiting	5.0
Barium carbonate	8.0
Magnesium carbonate	3.0
Zinc oxide	2.0
Add:	
C.M.C.	1 tsp.

SSG-157   **Opaque White Semi-Gloss Glaze   Cone 3**
feldspar-barium, opaque, semi-gloss, toxic

Mixing. Mix in the manner of SSG-1.

Application. Apply in the manner of SSG-1.

Firing. Fire in the manner of SSG-1.

Fired Results. This glaze fires to an opaque egg-shell white semi-gloss at cone 3.

Feldspar (Custer)	40.0
Silica	18.0
Kaolin	14.0
Whiting	11.0
Barium carbonate	10.0
Zinc oxide	6.0
Magnesium carbonate	1.0
Add:	
Bentonite	1.0
C.M.C.	1 tsp.

SSG-158   **Black Gloss Luster Glaze   Cone 4**
leadless, opaque, black gloss, nontoxic

Mixing. Mix in the manner of SSG-14.

Application. Apply in the manner of SSG-14.

Firing. Fire in the manner of SSG-1.

Fired Results. This glaze fires to an opaque black gloss luster at cone 4.

Nepheline syenite	46.5
Ferro frit #3134	27.9
Whiting	23.6
Kaolin (EPK)	2.0
Add:	
Bentonite	2.0
Cobalt oxide	2.0
Chrome oxide	2.0
Black iron oxide	2.0
C.M.C.	1 tsp.

SSG-159   **Opaque Black Semi-Gloss Glaze   Cone 4**
barium, opaque, semi-gloss, toxic

Mixing. Mix in the manner of SSG-1.

Application. Apply in the manner of SSG-1.

Firing. Fire in the manner of SSG-1.

Fired Results. This glaze fires to an opaque black semi-gloss at cone 4.

Feldspar (Custer)	30.0
Barium carbonate	17.0
Barnard clay	17.0
Kaolin	8.0
Zinc oxide	8.0
Silica	7.0
Colemanite	7.0
Copper oxide	3.0
Cobalt oxide	2.0
Iron oxide	2.0
Add:	
Bentonite	1.0
C.M.C.	1 tsp.

SSG-160   **Translucent Barium-Blue Semi-Matt Glaze   Cone 4**
barium, translucent, semi-matt, toxic

Mixing. Mix in the manner of SSG-1.

Application. Apply in the manner of SSG-1.

Firing. Fire in the manner of SSG-1.

Fired Results. This glaze fires to a beautiful translucent barium-blue semi-matt at cone 4. It gives better results if used on a light-colored body.

Feldspar (Kona F-4)	46.8
Barium carbonate	14.2
Whiting	12.2
Colemanite	11.5
Silica	10.2
Zinc oxide	5.1
Add:	
Bentonite	1.0
C.M.C.	1 tsp.
Copper carbonate	10.0

SSG-161 Opaque Brown Gloss Glaze   Cone 4
leadless, opaque, gloss, nontoxic

Mixing. Mix in the manner of SSG-14.

Application. Apply in the manner of SSG-14.

Firing. Fire in the manner of SSG-1.

Fired Results. This glaze fires to an opaque brown gloss with antique gold hues and swirls of color in it.

Albany slip	84.0
Cryolite	15.0
Bentonite	1.0
Add:	
C.M.C.	1 tsp.

SSG-162 Autumn-Brown Glaze   Cone 4
leadless, transparent, gloss, nontoxic

Mixing. Mix in the manner of SSG-14.

Application. Apply in the manner of SSG-14.

Firing. Fire in the manner of SSG-1.

Fired Results. This glaze fires to an autumn-brown gloss at cone 4.

Albany slip	89.5
Manganese dioxide	10.5
Add:	
Bentonite	2.0
C.M.C.	1 tsp.

SSG-163 Opaque Medium-Brown Gloss Glaze   Cone 4
lead frit, opaque, gloss, nontoxic

Mixing. Mix in the manner of SSG-14.

Application. Apply in the manner of SSG-14.

Firing. Fire in the manner of SSG-1.

Fired Results. This glaze fires to an opaque medium-brown gloss at cone 4.

Lithium carbonate	4.5
Wollastonite	6.7
Lead monosilicate	70.7
Kaolin (EPK)	12.3
Silica	5.8
Add:	
Chrome oxide (green)	2.0

SSG-164 Opaque Light-Caramel-Brown Gloss Glaze   Cone 4
leadless, opaque, gloss brown, nontoxic

Mixing. Mix in the manner of SSG-14.

Application. Apply in the manner of SSG-14.

Firing. Fire in the manner of SSG-1.

Fired Results. This glaze fires to a light-caramel-brown gloss at cone 4.

Albany slip	88.5
Zinc oxide	11.5
Add:	
Bentonite	2.0
C.M.C.	1 tsp.

SSG-165 Opaque Caramel-Brown Gloss Glaze   Cone 4
leadless, opaque, gloss brown, nontoxic

Mixing. Mix in the manner of SSG-14.

Application. Apply in the manner of SSG-14.

Firing. Fire in the manner of SSG-1.

Fired Results. This glaze fires to an opaque caramel-brown gloss at cone 4.

Albany slip	93.0
Rutile	7.0
Add:	
Bentonite	2.0
C.M.C.	1 tsp.

SSG-166 Transparent Cordovan-Brown Gloss Glaze   Cone 4
leadless, transparent, gloss brown, nontoxic

Mixing. Mix in the manner of SSG-14.

Application. Apply in the manner of SSG-14.

Firing. Fire in the manner of SSG-1.

Fired Results. This glaze fires to a transparent cordovan-brown gloss at cone 4.

Albany slip	81.5
Red iron oxide	18.5
Add:	
Bentonite	2.0
C.M.C.	1 tsp.

SSG-167   **Transparent Brown Figured Gloss Glaze   Cone 4**
leadless, transparent, gloss brown, nontoxic

Mixing. Mix in the manner of SSG-14.

Application. Apply in the manner of SSG-14.

Firing. Fire in the manner of SSG-1.

Fired Results. This glaze fires to a transparent brown figured gloss at cone 4.

Albany slip	90.5
Colemanite	9.5
Add:	
Bentonite	2.0
C.M.C.	1 tsp.

SSG-168   **Transparent Moss-Brown Gloss Glaze   Cone 4**
leadless, transparent, old moss brown, nontoxic

Mixing. Mix in the manner of SSG-14.

Application. Apply in the manner of SSG-14.

Firing. Fire in the manner of SSG-1.

Fired Results. This glaze fires to a transparent old-moss-brown gloss at cone 4.

Albany slip	91.3
Lithium carbonate	8.7
Add:	
Bentonite	2.0
C.M.C.	1 tsp.

SSG-169   **Translucent Buff Semi-Gloss Glaze   Cone 4**
feldspathic, translucent, semi-gloss, nontoxic

Mixing. Mix in the manner of SSG-14.

Application. Apply in the manner of SSG-14.

Firing. Fire in the manner of SSG-1.

Fired Results. This glaze fires to a translucent buff semi-gloss at cone 4.

Feldspar (Custer)	62.0
Zinc oxide	16.0
Kaolin (EPK)	9.0
Whiting	9.0
Silica	2.0
Add:	
Nickel oxide	2.0

SSG-170   **Transparent High-Gloss Glaze Base   Cone 4**
colemanite, transparent, high-gloss, nontoxic

Mixing. Mix in the manner of SSG-14.

Application. Apply in the manner of SSG-14.

Firing. Fire in the manner of SSG-1.

Fired Results. This glaze fires to a transparent high-gloss at cone 4. It is primarily a base glaze for alkaline colorants.

Colemanite	32.0
Silica	30.0
Feldspar (Custer)	20.0
Talc	14.0
Kaolin	4.0
Add:	
Bentonite	2.0

SSG-171   **Clear Gloss Glaze   Cone 4**
alkaline, transparent, clear gloss, nontoxic

Mixing. Mix in the manner of SSG-14.

Application. Apply in the manner of SSG-14.

Firing. Fire in the manner of SSG-1.

Fired Results. This glaze fires to a clear gloss at cone 4.

Volcanic ash	63.4
Pemco frit #25	26.5
Zinc oxide	4.3
Lithium carbonate	3.7
Bentonite	2.0
Add:	
C.M.C.	1 tsp.

SSG-172 **Clear Gloss Glaze   Cone 4**
alkaline, transparent, clear gloss, nontoxic

Mixing. Mix in the manner of SSG-14.

Application. Apply in the manner of SSG-14.

Firing. Fire in the manner of SSG-1.

Fired Results. This glaze fires to a clear patterned gloss at cone 4. The patterned effects show at their best with earth colorants.

Lepidolite	49.0
Colemanite	24.0
Zinc oxide	4.5
Silica	20.5
Bentonite	2.0
Add:	
C.M.C.	1 tsp.

SSG-173 **Clear Gloss Glaze   Cone 4**
alkaline, transparent, clear gloss, nontoxic

Mixing. Mix in the manner of SSG-14.

Application. Apply in the manner of SSG-14.

Firing. Fire in the manner of SSG-1.

Fired Results. This glaze fires to a clear gloss at cone 4.

Pemco frit #25	43.5
Lithium carbonate	6.1
Whiting	14.0
Kaolin (EPK)	9.2
Silica	27.2
Add:	
Bentonite	2.0
C.M.C.	1 tsp.

SSG-174 **Clear Gloss Glaze   Cone 4**
alkaline, transparent, clear gloss, nontoxic

Mixing. Mix in the manner of SSG-14.

Application. Apply in the manner of SSG-14.

Firing. Fire in the manner of SSG-1.

Fired Results. This glaze fires to a clear gloss at cone 4.

Lithium carbonate	16.6
Nepheline syenite	29.0
Whiting	15.5
Kaolin	5.7
Silica	32.2
Add:	
Bentonite	2.0
C.M.C.	1 tsp.

SSG-175 **Clear Gloss Glaze   Cone 4**
leadless, transparent, gloss, nontoxic

Mixing. Mix in the manner of SSG-14.

Application. Apply in the manner of SSG-14.

Firing. Fire in the manner of SSG-1.

Fired Results. This glaze fires to a clear gloss at cone 4.

Spodumene	30.0
Magnesium carbonate	6.5
Zinc oxide	2.2
Hommel frit #14	13.0
Wollastonite	17.5
Kaolin	10.0
Silica	20.5
Add:	
Bentonite	2.0

SSG-176 **Clear Gloss Glaze   Cone 4**
leadless, transparent, gloss, nontoxic

Mixing. Mix in the manner of SSG-14.

Application. Apply in the manner of SSG-14.

Firing. Fire in the manner of SSG-1.

Fired Results. This glaze fires to a clear gloss at cone 4. It is very stable and reliable and therefore excellent for use on utility ware.

Lithium carbonate	5.2
Feldspar (Custer)	36.0
Strontium carbonate	15.0
Whiting	10.0
Zinc oxide	2.3
Magnesium carbonate	1.5
Kaolin	4.0
Silica	24.0
Add:	
Bentonite	1.0
C.M.C.	1 tsp.

SSG-177

Clear Gloss Glaze   Cone 4
alkaline-frit, transparent, gloss, nontoxic

Mixing. Mix in the manner of SSG-14.

Application. Apply in the manner of SSG-14.

Firing. Fire in the manner of SSG-1.

Fired Results. This glaze fires to a clear gloss at cone 4.

Kaolin (EPK)	38.0
Ferro frit #3134	60.0
Bentonite	2.0
Add:	
C.M.C.	1 tsp.

SSG-178

Clear Gloss Glaze   Cone 4
colemanite, transparent, gloss, nontoxic

Mixing. Mix in the manner of SSG-14.

Application. Apply in the manner of SSG-14.

Firing. Fire in the manner of SSG-1.

Fired Results. This glaze fires to a clear gloss at cone 4. It gives very reliable and uniform results with colorants.

Colemanite	50.5
Kaolin	16.0
Silica	33.0
Add:	
Bentonite	1.0
C.M.C.	1 tsp.

SSG-179

Clear Gloss Glaze   Cone 4
colemanite, transparent, gloss, nontoxic

Mixing. Mix in the manner of SSG-14.

Application. Apply in the manner of SSG-14.

Firing. Fire in the manner of SSG-1.

Fired Results. This glaze fires to a clear gloss at cone 4. It is an exceptionally good glaze base for alkaline colorants, giving uniform results.

Colemanite	55.0
Kaolin	10.0
Silica	40.0

SSG-180

Clear Fluid Glaze   Cone 4
raw alkaline, transparent, gloss, nontoxic

Mixing. Mix in the manner of SSG-6.

Application. Apply in the manner of SSG-6.

Firing. Fire in the manner of SSG-1.

Fired Results. This glaze fires to a clear gloss at cone 4. It has a tendency to craze with age.

Volcanic ash	60.0
Borax	30.0
Whiting	5.0
Bentonite	5.0
Add:	
C.M.C.	1 tsp.

SSG-181

Clear Gloss Glaze   Cone 4
leadless, transparent, gloss, nontoxic

Mixing. Mix in the manner of SSG-14.

Application. Apply in the manner of SSG-14.

Firing. Fire in the manner of SSG-1.

Fired Results. This glaze fires to a clear gloss at cone 4. It is highly stable and makes a good base glaze for colorants. It is also an excellent glaze to use on utility ware.

Feldspar (Kona F-4)	58.7
Kaolin (EPK)	14.8
Silica	12.4
Whiting	7.0
Zinc oxide	7.5
Add:	
Bentonite	1.0

SSG-182 **Clear Gloss Glaze   Cone 4**
colemanite, transparent, gloss, toxic

Mixing. Mix in the manner of SSG-1.

Application. Apply in the manner of SSG-1.

Firing. Fire in the manner of SSG-1.

Fired Results. This glaze fires to a clear gloss at cone 4. It has a slight tendency to craze with age.

Feldspar (Custer)	48.4
Colemanite	23.3
Silica	11.6
Barium carbonate	9.0
Kaolin	5.3
Zinc oxide	3.5
Add:	
Bentonite	1.0
C.M.C.	1 tsp.

SSG-183 **Clear Gloss Glaze   Cone 4**
barium, transparent, gloss, toxic

Mixing. Mix in the manner of SSG-1.

Application. Apply in the manner of SSG-1.

Firing. Fire in the manner of SSG-1.

Fired Results. This glaze fires to a clear gloss at cone 4.

Feldspar (potash)	10.5
Whiting	6.5
Dolomite	6.5
Barium carbonate	7.0
Kaolin	14.0
Flint	26.0
Zinc oxide	8.0

SSG-184 **Clear Gloss Glaze   Cone 4**
alkaline-frit, transparent, gloss, nontoxic

Mixing. Mix in the manner of SSG-14.

Application. Apply in the manner of SSG-14.

Firing. Fire in the manner of SSG-1.

Fired Results. This glaze fires to a clear gloss at cone 4. It is very stable and gives uniform results with colorants.

Hommel frit #14	34.3
Wollastonite	7.6
Magnesium carbonate	5.7
Feldspar (potash)	9.4
Kaolin	15.5
Flint	24.4
Zinc oxide	4.1

SSG-185 **Clear Gloss Glaze   Cone 4**
colemanite, transparent, gloss, nontoxic

Mixing. Mix in the manner of SSG-14.

Application. Apply in the manner of SSG-14.

Firing. Fire in the manner of SSG-1.

Fired Results. This glaze fires to a clear gloss at cone 4. It is very stable and reliable. The magnesium content gives a slight buttery sheen to the surface.

Colemanite	50.0
Kaolin	14.0
Silica	34.0
Magnesium carbonate	2.0
Add:	
Bentonite	1.0
C.M.C.	1 tsp.

SSG-186 **Clear Gloss Glaze   Cone 4**
raw alkaline, transparent, clear, nontoxic

Mixing. Mix in the manner of SSG-6.

Application. Apply in the manner of SSG-6.

Firing. Fire in the manner of SSG-1.

Fired Results. This glaze fires to a clear gloss at cone 4. Since it is a raw alkaline it is very good for copper colorants or cobalt colorants.

Tennessee ball clay #1	50.0
Sodium bicarbonate	24.5
Ferro frit #3134	12.9
Borax (powdered)	12.5
Add:	
Bentonite	2.0
C.M.C.	1 tsp.

SSG-187 **Clear Gloss Glaze   Cone 4**
colemanite, transparent, clear, nontoxic

Mixing. Mix in the manner of SSG-14.

Application. Apply in the manner of SSG-14.

Firing. Fire in the manner of SSG-1.

Fired Results. This glaze fires to a clear gloss at cone 4.
It is very stable and reliable. It can also be used on
greenware.

Tennessee ball clay #1	50.0
Colemanite	48.0
Bentonite	2.0
Add:	
C.M.C.	1 tsp.

SSG-188 **Transparent Gloss Glaze   Cone 4-6**
alkaline, transparent, gloss, nontoxic

Mixing. Mix in the manner of SSG-14.

Application. Apply in the manner of SSG-14.

Firing. Fire in the manner of SSG-1.

Fired Results. This glaze fires to a bright clear gloss at
cone 4-6.

Lithium carbonate	25.0
Colemanite	25.0
Zinc oxide	5.0
Calcium fluoride	5.0
Silica	25.0

SSG-189 **Clear Semi-Gloss Glaze   Cone 4**
colemanite, transparent, semi-gloss, nontoxic

Mixing. Mix in the manner of SSG-14.

Application. Apply in the manner of SSG-14.

Firing. Fire in the manner of SSG-1.

Fired Results. This glaze fires to a clear semi-gloss glaze
at cone 4. It is very stable with colorants but has a
slight tendency to craze with age.

Colemanite	55.0
Kaolin	17.0
Silica	41.0

SSG-190 **Gloss Patterned Glaze   Cone 4**
raw alkaline-clay, transparent, patterned gloss, nontoxic

Mixing. Mix in the manner of SSG-6.

Application. Apply in the manner of SSG-6.

Firing. Fire in the manner of SSG-1.

Fired Results. This glaze fires to a clear patterned gloss
at cone 4.

Tennessee ball clay #1	50.0
Sodium bicarbonate	24.0
Ferro frit #3134	13.5
Borax (powdered)	12.5
Add:	
Bentonite	2.0
C.M.C.	1 tsp.

SSG-191 **Clear Mottled Gloss Glaze   Cone 4**
raw alkaline-clay, transparent, gloss, nontoxic

Mixing. Mix in the manner of SSG-6.

Application. Apply in the manner of SSG-6.

Firing. Fire in the manner of SSG-1.

Fired Results. This glaze fires to a clear mottled gloss at
cone 4.

Tennessee ball clay #1	50.0
Sodium carbonate	20.0
Borax	17.5
Sodium fluoride	12.5
Add:	
Bentonite	2.0
C.M.C.	1 tsp.

SSG-192

Clear Gloss Patterned Glaze   Cone 4
raw alkaline-clay, transparent, clear patterned, nontoxic

Mixing. Mix in the manner of SSG-6.

Application. Apply in the manner of SSG-6.

Firing. Fire in the manner of SSG-1.

Fired Results. This glaze fires to a clear patterned gloss at cone 4. It can be used on greenware.

Tennessee ball clay #1	48.5
Sodium carbonate	23.5
Borax (powdered)	16.5
Colemanite	11.5
Add:	
Bentonite	1.2
C.M.C.	1 tsp.

SSG-193

Clear Smooth-Matt Glaze   Cone 4
lithium-barium, transparent, matt, toxic

Mixing. Mix in the manner of SSG-1.

Application. Apply in the manner of SSG-1.

Firing. Fire in the manner of SSG-1.

Fired Results. This glaze fires to a clear smooth matt at cone 4.

Lithium carbonate	3.8
Feldspar (potash)	42.3
Wollastonite	18.2
Barium carbonate	15.9
Zinc oxide	1.8
Magnesium carbonate	3.6
Flint	14.4
Add:	
Bentonite	1.0
C.M.C.	1 tsp.

SSG-194

Clear Smooth-Matt Glaze   Cone 4
raw alkaline-clay, transparent, clear, nontoxic

Mixing. Mix in the manner of SSG-6.

Application. Apply in the manner of SSG-6.

Firing. Fire in the manner of SSG-1.

Fired Results. This glaze fires to a clear smooth matt at cone 4. It can be used on greenware.

Tennessee ball clay #1	50.0
Sodium bicarbonate	24.0
Borax (powdered)	12.4
Zinc oxide	12.6
Bentonite	1.0
Add:	
C.M.C.	1 tsp.

SSG-195

Clear Smooth-Matt Glaze   Cone 4
raw alkaline-clay, transparent, clear, nontoxic

Mixing. Mix in the manner of SSG-6.

Application. Apply in the manner of SSG-6.

Firing. Fire in the manner of SSG-1.

Fired Results. This glaze fires to a clear satin matt at cone 4.

Barium carbonate	40.5
Zinc oxide	11.0
Ferro frit #3293	32.9
Lithium carbonate	1.8
Kaolin (EPK)	9.5
Silica	4.3
Add:	
Bentonite	2.0
C.M.C.	1 tsp.

SSG-196

Clear Satin-Matt Glaze   Cone 4
alkaline-frit, transparent, matt, nontoxic

Mixing. Mix in the manner of SSG-14.

Application. Apply in the manner of SSG-14.

Firing. Fire in the manner of SSG-1.

Fired Results. This glaze fires to a clear satin matt at cone 4.

Nepheline syenite	37.6
Kaolin	3.4
Hommel frit #14	13.8
Whiting	15.8
Silica	28.4
Bentonite	1.0
Add:	
C.M.C.	1 tsp.

SSG-197 **Clear Silky-Matt Glaze   Cone 4**
alkaline-frit, transparent, silky matt, toxic

Mixing. Mix in the manner of SSG-1.

Application. Apply in the manner of SSG-1.

Firing. Fire in the manner of SSG-1.

Fired Results. This glaze fires to a clear silky matt at cone 4. It makes a very good base for the alkaline colorants.

Lepidolite	13.5
Spodumene	21.0
Hommel frit #14	18.9
Whiting	4.0
Barium carbonate	16.4
Kaolin	10.1
Silica	14.1
Magnesium carbonate	2.0

SSG-198 **Clear Satin-Matt Glaze   Cone 4**
colemanite, transparent, satin matt, nontoxic

Mixing. Mix in the manner of SSG-14.

Application. Apply in the manner of SSG-14.

Firing. Fire in the manner of SSG-1.

Fired Results. This glaze fires to a clear satin matt at cone 4. It is very stable and reliable as a color base glaze.

Colemanite	50.0
Kaolin	20.0
Silica	30.0

SSG-199 **Clear Satin-Matt Glaze   Cone 4**
leadless, transparent, satin matt, nontoxic

Mixing. Mix in the manner of SSG-14.

Application. Apply in the manner of SSG-14.

Firing. Fire in the manner of SSG-1.

Fired Results. This glaze fires to a clear satin matt at cone 4.

Feldspar (Custer)	32.4
Magnesium carbonate	5.5
Wollastonite	20.0
Silica	42.1
Add:	
Bentonite	1.0
C.M.C.	1 tsp.

SSG-200 **Clear Satin-Matt Glaze   Cone 4**
alkaline-frit, transparent, satin matt, nontoxic

Mixing. Mix in the manner of SSG-14.

Application. Apply in the manner of SSG-14.

Firing. Fire in the manner of SSG-1.

Fired Results. This glaze fires to a clear satin matt at cone 4.

Hommel frit #14	11.1
Magnesium carbonate	3.8
Wollastonite	23.4
Feldspar (Custer)	27.0
Kaolin (EPK)	18.0
Kaolin (calcined)	10.6
Silica	6.1
Add:	
Bentonite	2.0
C.M.C.	1 tsp.

SSG-201 **Clear Semi-Matt Glaze   Cone 4**
lithium, transparent, semi-matt, nontoxic

Mixing. Mix in the manner of SSG-14.

Application. Apply in the manner of SSG-14.

Firing. Fire in the manner of SSG-1.

Fired Results. This glaze fires to a clear semi-matt at cone 4.

Lithium carbonate	15.0
Nepheline syenite	31.0
Whiting	15.0
Kaolin (EPK)	6.0
Silica	28.0
Magnesium carbonate	2.0
Add:	
Bentonite	1.0

SSG-202 **Clear Satin-Matt Glaze Cone 4**
colemanite, transparent, satin matt, nontoxic

Mixing. Mix in the manner of SSG-14.

Application. Apply in the manner of SSG-14.

Firing. Fire in the manner of SSG-1.

Fired Results. This glaze fires to a clear satin matt at cone 4.

Colemanite	40.0
Whiting	30.0
Silica	18.0
Kaolin (EPK)	8.0
Magnesium carbonate	4.0
Add:	
Bentonite	1.0
C.M.C.	1 tsp.

SSG-203 **Clear Satin-Matt Glaze Cone 4**
leadless, transparent, satin matt, nontoxic

Mixing. Mix in the manner of SSG-14.

Application. Apply in the manner of SSG-14.

Firing. Fire in the manner of SSG-1.

Fired Results. This glaze fires to a clear satin matt at cone 4.

Hommel frit #14	33.0
Spodumene	39.0
Whiting	28.0
Silica	20.0
Kaolin	9.0
Magnesium carbonate	1.0
Add:	
Bentonite	1.0
C.M.C.	1 tsp.

SSG-204 **Clear Matt Glaze Cone 4**
barium, transparent, matt, toxic

Mixing. Mix in the manner of SSG-1.

Application. Apply in the manner of SSG-1.

Firing. Fire in the manner of SSG-1.

Fired Results. This glaze fires to a clear matt at cone 4.

Feldspar (Custer)	31.7
Strontium carbonate	4.4
Whiting	11.4
Barium carbonate	11.4
Magnesium carbonate	2.2
Silica	36.0
Fluorspar	2.9
Add:	
Bentonite	1.0
C.M.C.	1 tsp.

SSG-205 **Clear Matt Glaze Cone 4**
leadless, transparent, matt, slightly toxic

Mixing. Mix in the manner of SSG-1.

Application. Apply in the manner of SSG-1.

Firing. Fire in the manner of SSG-1.

Fired Results. This glaze fires to a clear matt at cone 4.

Feldspar (Custer)	34.1
Strontium carbonate	10.3
Whiting	6.3
Zinc oxide	9.7
Kaolin (EPK)	10.8
Silica	28.8
Magnesium carbonate	2.0
Add:	
Bentonite	1.0
C.M.C.	1 tsp.

SSG-206

Clear Matt Glaze   Cone 4
leadless-zinc, transparent, matt, slightly toxic

Mixing. Mix in the manner of SSG-1.

Application. Apply in the manner of SSG-1.

Firing. Fire in the manner of SSG-1.

Fired Results. This glaze fires to a clear matt at cone 4.

Feldspar (Custer)	47.1
Zinc oxide	10.3
Wollastonite	14.9
Strontium carbonate	5.0
Whiting	4.6
Kaolin	16.1
Magnesium carbonate	2.0
Add:	
Bentonite	1.0
C.M.C.	1 tsp.

SSG-207

Clear Patterned Matt Glaze   Cone 4
leadless-zinc, transparent, matt, slightly toxic

Mixing. Mix in the manner of SSG-1.

Application. Apply in the manner of SSG-1.

Firing. Fire in the manner of SSG-1.

Fired Results. This glaze fires to a clear patterned matt at cone 4. It can give some various and unusual results with this glaze.

Feldspar (Custer)	50.0
Zinc oxide	10.8
Whiting	10.0
Strontium carbonate	8.6
Kaolin	12.8
Silica	5.8
Magnesium carbonate	2.0
Add:	
Bentonite	1.0
C.M.C.	1 tsp.

SSG-208

Clear Patterned Matt Glaze   Cone 4
raw alkaline-clay, transparent, clear patterned, nontoxic

Mixing. Mix in the manner of SSG-6.

Application. Apply in the manner of SSG-6.

Firing. Fire in the manner of SSG-1.

Fired Results. This glaze fires to a clear patterned matt at cone 4. It can be used on greenware.

Tennessee ball clay #1	46.5
Borax (powdered)	23.8
Lithium carbonate	28.7
Add:	
Bentonite	1.0
C.M.C.	1 tsp.

SSG-209

Clear Dry Matt Glaze   Cone 4
barium, transparent, clear dry matt, toxic

Mixing. Mix in the manner of SSG-1.

Application. Apply in the manner of SSG-1.

Firing. Fire in the manner of SSG-1.

Fired Results. This glaze fires to a clear dry matt at cone 4.

Barium carbonate	50.2
Lepidolite	34.8
Lithium carbonate	6.2
Silica	8.8
Add:	
Bentonite	2.0
C.M.C.	1 tsp.

SSG-210

Translucent Stony Matt Glaze   Cone 4
barium, translucent, dry stony matt, toxic

Mixing. Mix in the manner of SSG-1.

Application. Apply in the manner of SSG-1.

Firing. Fire in the manner of SSG-1.

Fired Results. This glaze fires to a translucent stony matt at cone 4.

Lepidolite	35.8
Wollastonite	26.0
Barium carbonate	17.8
Magnesium carbonate	4.8
Zinc oxide	3.5
Silica	12.1
Add:	
Bentonite	1.0

SSG-211 **Translucent Cream Semi-Matt Glaze Cone 4**
lead, translucent, semi-matt, toxic

Mixing. Mix in the manner of SSG-1.

Application. Apply in the manner of SSG-1.

Firing. Fire in the manner of SSG-1.

Fired Results. This glaze fires to a translucent cream semi-matt at cone 4.

Feldspar (Custer)	35.0
White lead	28.8
Whiting	18.0
Silica	9.0
Colemanite	9.1
Kaolin (calcined)	2.2
Add:	
Bentonite	1.0
C.M.C.	1 tsp.

SSG-212 **Transparent Gray Gloss Glaze Cone 4**
colemanite-barium, transparent, gloss, toxic

Mixing. Mix in the manner of SSG-1.

Application. Apply in the manner of SSG-1.

Firing. Fire in the manner of SSG-1.

Fired Results. This glaze fires to a transparent gray gloss at cone 4.

Feldspar (Kingman)	36.2
Silica	22.0
Colemanite	18.4
Zinc oxide	8.2
Barium carbonate	7.6
Talc	7.3
Bentonite	2.0
Add:	
Iron chromate	1.0

SSG-213 **Opaque Jade Green Semi-Matt Glaze Cone 4**
barium, opaque, semi-matt, toxic

Mixing. Mix in the manner of SSG-1.

Application. Apply in the manner of SSG-1.

Firing. Fire in the manner of SSG-1.

Fired Results. This glaze fires to an opaque jade green semi-matt at cone 4.

Feldspar (Custer)	37.6
Barium carbonate	18.5
Kaolin	5.6
Silica	9.5
Colemanite	10.5
Zinc oxide	8.4
Copper carbonate	4.9
Bentonite	1.0
Add:	
C.M.C.	1 tsp.

SSG-214 **Shadow Green Gloss Glaze Cone 4**
bristol, transparent, gloss, slightly toxic

Mixing. Mix in the manner of SSG-1.

Application. Apply in the manner of SSG-1.

Firing. Fire in the manner of SSG-1.

Fired Results. This glaze fires to a shadow gloss at cone 4. If overfired it turns metallic.

Zinc oxide	20.0
Whiting	5.6
Lithium carbonate	12.0
Kaolin	17.7
Silica	38.0
Titanium dioxide	7.7
Add:	
Chrome oxide	1.5
C.M.C.	1 tsp.

SSG-215 **Transparent Spinach-Green Gloss Glaze Cone 4**
colemanite, transparent, gloss, nontoxic

Mixing. Mix in the manner of SSG-14.

Application. Apply in the manner of SSG-14.

Firing. Fire in the manner of SSG-1.

Fired Results. This glaze fires to a transparent dark green gloss at cone 4.

Colemanite	52.0
Kaolin	13.0
Silica	34.0
Bentonite	1.0
Add:	
Chrome oxide	1.5

SSG-216 **Opaque Pink Semi-Gloss Glaze   Cone 4**
leadless-barium, opaque, semi-gloss, slightly toxic

Mixing. Mix in the manner of SSG-1.

Application. Apply in the manner of SSG-1.

Firing. Fire in the manner of SSG-1.

Fired Results. This glaze fires to an opaque pink semi-gloss at cone 4.

Feldspar (Custer)	23.7
Silica	22.7
Kaolin	13.5
Whiting	10.4
Pink stain (any)	10.5
Zinc oxide	6.8
Barium carbonate	6.9
Dolomite	5.3
Add:	
Bentonite	1.0
C.M.C.	1 tsp.

SSG-217 **Translucent Turquoise Gloss Glaze   Cone 4**
colemanite, translucent, gloss, nontoxic

Mixing. Mix in the manner of SSG-14.

Application. Apply in the manner of SSG-14.

Firing. Fire in the manner of SSG-1.

Fired Results. This glaze fires to a translucent turquoise gloss at cone 4.

Feldspar (Custer)	29.3
Colemanite	20.2
Silica	20.2
Kaolin	9.2
Dolomite	10.2
Copper carbonate	5.5
Ultrox	4.7
Add:	
Bentonite	2.0
C.M.C.	1 tsp.

SSG-218 **Opaque Red-Rust Gloss Glaze   Cone 4**
lead, opaque, gloss, toxic

Mixing. Mix in the manner of SSG-1.

Application. Apply in the manner of SSG-1.

Firing. Fire in the manner of SSG-1.

Fired Results. This glaze fires to an opaque red-rust gloss at cone 4.

Feldspar (Kona F-4)	29.6
Silica	22.1
Tin oxide	17.1
Whiting	10.6
Red iron oxide	7.7
White lead	7.5
Kaolin	5.1
Add:	
Bentonite	1.0
C.M.C.	1 tsp.

SSG-219 **Opaque Rust Semi-Gloss Glaze   Cone 4**
semi-lead, opaque, semi-gloss, toxic

Mixing. Mix in the manner of SSG-1.

Application. Apply in the manner of SSG-1.

Firing. Fire in the manner of SSG-1.

Fired Results. This glaze fires to an opaque rust semi-gloss at cone 4.

Feldspar (Kona F-4)	29.5
Silica	22.1
Ultrox	16.1
Whiting	12.1
Red iron oxide	7.9
White lead	7.0
Kaolin	5.1
Add:	
Bentonite	2.0
C.M.C.	1 tsp.

SSG-220   **Translucent Tan Semi-Matt Glaze   Cone 4**
raw alkaline, translucent, semi-matt, nontoxic

Mixing. Mix in the manner of SSG-14.

Application. Apply in the manner of SSG-14.

Firing. Fire in the manner of SSG-1.

Fired Results. This glaze fires to a translucent tan semi-matt at cone 4.

Silica	38.0
Zinc oxide	22.0
Boric acid	14.4
Sodium carbonate	12.3
Rutile	7.7
Tennessee ball clay #1	5.6
Add:	
Bentonite	1.0
C.M.C.	1 tsp.

SSG-221   **Translucent Gloss Glaze   Cone 4**
lead-colemanite, translucent, gloss, toxic

Mixing. Mix in the manner of SSG-1.

Application. Apply in the manner of SSG-1.

Firing. Fire in the manner of SSG-1.

Fired Results. This glaze fires to a slightly cloudy white at cone 4. It makes a good color base.

Feldspar (Kona F-4)	50.5
White lead	19.1
Colemanite	12.5
Silica	7.1
Dolomite	5.5
Ultrox	4.3
Add:	
C.M.C.	1 tsp.

SSG-222   **Translucent White Gloss Glaze   Cone 4**
frit, translucent, gloss, nontoxic

Mixing. Mix in the manner of SSG-14.

Application. Apply in the manner of SSG-14.

Firing. Fire in the manner of SSG-1.

Fired Results. This glaze fires to a translucent white at cone 4.

Ferro frit #3819	41.3
Whiting	22.6
Kaolin	17.7
Flint	16.4
Add:	
Ultrox	3.0

SSG-223   **Translucent Cloudy White Gloss Glaze   Cone 4**
alkaline-frit, translucent, gloss, nontoxic

Mixing. Mix in the manner of SSG-14.

Application. Apply in the manner of SSG-14.

Firing. Fire in the manner of SSG-1.

Fired Results. This glaze fires to a translucent cloudy white at cone 4.

Hommel frit #14	7.5
Hommel frit #259	46.4
Wollastonite	21.3
Kaolin	8.4
Silica	16.4
Ultrox	5.0

SSG-224   **Translucent Waxy-White Semi-Gloss Glaze   Cone 4**
bristol, translucent, semi-gloss, slightly toxic

Mixing. Mix in the manner of SSG-1.

Application. Apply in the manner of SSG-1.

Firing. Fire in the manner of SSG-1.

Fired Results. This glaze fires to a translucent waxy white at cone 4.

Zinc oxide	21.9
Whiting	4.0
Lithium carbonate	10.9
China clay	15.8
Cryolite	6.0
Flint	32.1
Titanium dioxide	8.1
Magnesium carbonate	2.9
Add:	
Bentonite	1.0
C.M.C.	1 tsp.

SSG-225 **Translucent Cloudy-White Smooth Matt   Cone 4**
alkaline-frit-barium, translucent, smooth matt, toxic

Mixing. Mix in the manner of SSG-1.

Application. Apply in the manner of SSG-1.

Firing. Fire in the manner of SSG-1.

Fired Results. This glaze fires to a translucent cloudy white matt at cone 4.

Hommel frit #14	28.0
Feldspar (Custer)	32.3
Silica	6.9
Kaolin	11.7
Barium carbonate	6.9
Fluorspar	2.8
Talc	8.8
Magnesium carbonate	2.6
Add:	
Bentonite	2.0
C.M.C.	1 tsp.

SSG-226 **Semi-Opaque Satin-Matt Glaze   Cone 4**
barium, semi-opaque, satin matt, toxic

Mixing. Mix in the manner of SSG-1.

Application. Apply in the manner of SSG-1.

Firing. Fire in the manner of SSG-1.

Fired Results. This glaze fires to a semi-opaque satin-matt white at cone 4.

Lepidolite	13.4
Spodumene	20.1
Pemco frit #54	17.9
Whiting	5.0
Barium carbonate	16.4
Kaolin	10.1
Silica	15.1
Magnesium carbonate	2.0
Add:	
Bentonite	1.0
C.M.C.	1 tsp.

SSG-227 **Semi-Opaque Satin-Matt Glaze   Cone 4**
barium, semi-opaque, satin matt, toxic

Mixing. Mix in the manner of SSG-1.

Application. Apply in the manner of SSG-1.

Firing. Fire in the manner of SSG-1.

Fired Results. This glaze fires to a semi-opaque satin matt at cone 4. It is a very good color base for most of the colorants listed in Chapter 33.

Lithium carbonate	2.8
Feldspar (Custer)	42.2
Wollastonite	18.4
Barium carbonate	3.8
Zinc oxide	1.6
Magnesium carbonate	3.8
Silica	15.4
Add:	
Bentonite	1.0
C.M.C.	1 tsp.

SSG-228 **Semi-Opaque Matt Glaze   Cone 4**
barium, semi-opaque, matt, toxic

Mixing. Mix in the manner of SSG-1.

Application. Apply in the manner of SSG-1.

Firing. Fire in the manner of SSG-1.

Fired Results. This glaze fires to a semi-opaque white matt at cone 4. It is a very stable glaze that is good for utility ware.

Feldspar (potash)	31.3
Strontium carbonate	4.4
Whiting	10.2
Barium carbonate	11.4
Zinc oxide	1.0
Magnesium carbonate	3.3
Flint	36.0
Fluorspar	24.0
Add:	
Bentonite	1.0

SSG-229 **Semi-Opaque Satin-Matt Glaze   Cone 4**
leadless frit, semi-opaque, satin matt, nontoxic

Mixing. Mix in the manner of SSG-14.

Application. Apply in the manner of SSG-14.

Firing. Fire in the manner of SSG-1.

Fired Results. This glaze fires to a semi-opaque satin matt at cone 4.

Nepheline syenite	38.0
Kaolin	3.0
Pemco frit #54	11.8
Whiting	15.4
Silica	29.4
Magnesium carbonate	2.4
Add:	
Bentonite	2.0
C.M.C.	1 tsp.

SSG-230 **Semi-Opaque Matt Glaze   Cone 4**
feldspathic-zinc, semi-opaque, matt, slightly toxic

Mixing. Mix in the manner of SSG-1.

Application. Apply in the manner of SSG-1.

Firing. Fire in the manner of SSG-1.

Fired Results. This glaze fires to a semi-opaque matt at cone 4. This glaze is very dependable and gives uniform results with colorants. It is also a good glaze for utility ware.

Feldspar (Custer)	48.5
Zinc oxide	8.8
Whiting	18.6
Kaolin	14.5
Silica	6.1
Colemanite	3.5
Add:	
Bentonite	1.0
C.M.C.	1 tsp.

SSG-231 **Opaque Gloss Glaze   Cone 4**
colemanite-barium, opaque, gloss, toxic

Mixing. Mix in the manner of SSG-1.

Application. Apply in the manner of SSG-1.

Firing. Fire in the manner of SSG-1.

Fired Results. This glaze fires to an opaque white gloss at cone 4.

Feldspar (Custer)	36.0
Silica	20.0
Colemanite	20.8
Zinc oxide	10.1
Barium carbonate	7.6
Talc	7.3
Add:	
Bentonite	2.0
Ultrox	10.0

SSG-232 **Opaque White Gloss Glaze   Cone 4**
colemanite, opaque, gloss, nontoxic

Mixing. Mix in the manner of SSG-14.

Application. Apply in the manner of SSG-14.

Firing. Fire in the manner of SSG-1.

Fired Results. This glaze fires to a smooth, bright opaque white gloss at cone 4. It has a beautiful smooth buttery quality and is very stable and reliable and consequently suitable for all utility ware. It takes colorants very well.

Colemanite	13.6
Feldspar (potash)	46.0
Silica	18.8
Kaolin	2.5
Whiting	8.1
Ultrox	4.0
Dolomite	6.0
Bentonite	1.0

SSG-233. **Opaque White Gloss Glaze   Cone 4**
colemanite-barium, opaque, gloss, toxic

Mixing. Mix in the manner of SSG-1.

Application. Apply in the manner of SSG-1.

Firing. Fire in the manner of SSG-1.

Fired Results. This glaze fires to a smooth opaque white gloss that is slightly milky and cloudy when applied over clays.

Colemanite	20.4
Barium carbonate	6.4
Feldspar (Custer)	43.0
Silica	24.3
Kaolin	1.0
Whiting	1.6
Zinc oxide	3.1

SSG-234

Opaque White Semi-Gloss Glaze   Cone 4
feldspathic-barium, opaque, semi-gloss, toxic

Mixing. Mix in the manner of SSG-1.

Application. Apply in the manner of SSG-1.

Firing. Fire in the manner of SSG-1.

Fired Results. This glaze fires to a smooth opaque semi-gloss white at cone 4. It is very stable and a good color base.

Feldspar (Custer)	26.1
Dolomite	7.9
Barium carbonate	7.6
Whiting	9.5
Kaolin	8.0
Silica	15.7
Zinc oxide	9.0
Ultrox	16.2

SSG-235

Smooth Patterned Semi-Gloss Glaze   Cone 4
leadless, opaque, patterned off-white, nontoxic

Mixing. Mix in the manner of SSG-14.

Application. Apply in the manner of SSG-14.

Firing. Fire in the manner of SSG-1.

Fired Results. This glaze fires to a smooth patterned white semi-gloss at cone 4.

Lepidolite	50.0
Sodium fluoride	4.8
Calcium fluoride	13.4
Silica	31.8
Add:	
Bentonite	2.0
C.M.C.	1 tsp.

SSG-236

Opaque Shiny Matt Glaze   Cone 4
bristol, opaque, milky white, slightly toxic

Mixing. Mix in the manner of SSG-1.

Application. Apply in the manner of SSG-1.

Firing. Fire in the manner of SSG-1.

Fired Results. This glaze fires to an opaque, silky matt white at cone 4. It is highly stable and makes a good color base, giving uniform results.

Zinc oxide (calcined)	9.5
Nepheline syenite	26.1
Ferro frit #3223	31.4
Kaolin	15.4
Silica	17.6
Add:	
Bentonite	2.0
C.M.C.	1 tsp.

SSG-237

White Satin-Matt Glaze   Cone 4
barium, opaque, satin matt, toxic

Mixing. Mix in the manner of SSG-1.

Application. Apply in the manner of SSG-1.

Firing. Fire in the manner of SSG-1.

Fired Results. This glaze fires to an opaque white satin matt at cone 4. It is very stable and reliable, giving uniform results with colorants.

Feldspar (Custer)	51.5
Whiting	5.0
Barium carbonate	11.2
Strontium carbonate	8.1
Zinc oxide	9.0
Kaolin	4.6
Silica	9.3
Bentonite	1.3
Add:	
C.M.C.	1 tsp.

SSG-238

White Satin-Matt Glaze   Cone 4
leadless, opaque, satin matt, nontoxic

Mixing. Mix in the manner of SSG-14.

Application. Apply in the manner of SSG-14.

Firing. Fire in the manner of SSG-1.

Fired Results. This glaze fires to an opaque white satin matt at cone 4. It gives uniform results with colorants and is excellent for utility ware.

Feldspar (potash)	48.0
Zinc oxide	10.5
Whiting	19.5
Kaolin	14.3
Silica	5.8
Bentonite	1.9
Add:	
C.M.C.	1 tsp.

SSG-239　**Mottled Matt Glaze   Cone 4**
leadless, opaque, mottled off-white, nontoxic

Mixing. Mix in the manner of SSG-14.

Application. Apply in the manner of SSG-14.

Firing. Fire in the manner of SSG-1.

Fired Results. This glaze fires to an opaque mottled matt off-white at cone 4. It is very attractive when used over a darker clay body. It gives uniform results in colorants.

Cryolite	25.2
Fluorspar	15.7
Kaolin (EPK)	21.0
Silica	36.0
Feldspar (potash)	2.1
Add:	
Bentonite	1.0
C.M.C.	1 tsp.

SSG-240　**White Matt Glaze   Cone 4**
leadless, opaque, matt, nontoxic

Mixing. Mix in the manner of SSG-14.

Application. Apply in the manner of SSG-14.

Firing. Fire in the manner of SSG-1.

Fired Results. This glaze fires to an opaque white matt at cone 4. When colorants are used and the kiln cooled slowly, it has a tendency to produce minute crystal formations in the surface.

Pemco frit #54	63.7
Lithium carbonate	2.7
Kaolin	25.0
Titanium dioxide	8.5
Add:	
Bentonite	2.0
C.M.C.	1 tsp.

SSG-241　**Translucent Buttercup-Yellow Gloss Glaze   Cone 4**
colemanite, translucent, gloss, nontoxic

Mixing. Mix in the manner of SSG-14.

Application. Apply in the manner of SSG-14.

Firing. Fire in the manner of SSG-1.

Fired Results. This glaze fires to a translucent yellow gloss at cone 4. It gives best results when used over a white or nearly white body. It can be made opaque by the addition of 5% to 8% Ultrox or tin oxide.

Lepidolite	78.0
Lithium carbonate	4.0
Colemanite	16.0
Magnesium carbonate	2.0
Add:	
Uranium oxide	10.0
Bentonite	2.0
C.M.C.	1 tsp.

SSG-242　**Translucent Sulphur-Yellow Gloss Glaze   Cone 4**
barium, translucent, gloss, toxic

Mixing. Mix in the manner of SSG-1.

Application. Apply in the manner of SSG-1.

Firing. Fire in the manner of SSG-1.

Fired Results. This glaze fires to a mellow sulphur-yellow gloss at cone 4.

Lithium carbonate	5.5
Strontium carbonate	10.0
Whiting	3.6
Barium carbonate	30.5
Nepheline syenite	23.3
Kaolin	3.8
Silica	22.3
Add:	
Praesodymium stain	10.0
Bentonite	1.0
C.M.C.	1 tsp.

SSG-243 **Translucent Pineapple-Yellow Gloss Glaze   Cone 4**
colemanite-barium, translucent, gloss, toxic

Mixing. Mix in the manner of SSG-1.

Application. Apply in the manner of SSG-1.

Firing. Fire in the manner of SSG-1.

Fired Results. This glaze fires to a translucent pineapple-yellow gloss at cone 4. It gives more satisfactory results when used over a light-colored clay body.

Pemco frit #54	38.0
Colemanite	8.0
Whiting	3.0
Barium carbonate	16.0
Kaolin	10.0
Silica	24.0
Bentonite	2.0
Add:	
Vanadium stain	10.0

SSG-244 **Translucent Straw-Yellow Gloss Glaze   Cone 4**
leadless, translucent, gloss, nontoxic

Mixing. Mix in the manner of SSG-14.

Application. Apply in the manner of SSG-14.

Firing. Fire in the manner of SSG-1.

Fired Results. This glaze fires to a translucent straw-yellow gloss at cone 4.

Portland cement	28.0
Ferro frit #3819	57.0
Silica	13.1
Magnesium carbonate	2.0
Add:	
Red iron oxide	5.0
Bentonite	2.0
C.M.C.	1 tsp.

SSG-245 **Transparent Amber-Yellow Gloss Glaze   Cone 4**
colemanite, transparent, gloss, nontoxic

Mixing. Mix in the manner of SSG-14.

Application. Apply in the manner of SSG-14.

Firing. Fire in the manner of SSG-1.

Fired Results. This glaze fires to a transparent amber-yellow gloss at cone 4. It is not recommended for utility ware as it has a tendency to craze with age.

Volcanic ash	62.0
Colemanite	35.0
Magnesium carbonate	2.0
Bentonite	1.0
Add:	
Red iron oxide	2.0

25
STONEWARE GLAZES
CONE 5-10

Stoneware glazes can be classified as those which reach maturity at the cone 5 to 10 range. The three compounds lead, sodium, and boron which figure so prominently in the lower-fired glazes have practically no place in stoneware glazes but are usually replaced by feldspar or wood ash. Though the higher firing temperatures tend to limit the color range, there are vast glaze texture and color possibilities within the subtle and more rustic stoneware range.

Due to the fact that most stoneware glaze formulas contain only a few compounds, the potter will find them much easier and faster to mix. And he need not have a vast collection of chemicals on hand. The student of glazes should always remember however that even though these glazes tend to be more simple than the lower-fired ones, proper and accurate measuring and mixing are an absolute necessity. It is all too easy and common for the potter to misread or miscalculate a formula and ruin a glaze without realizing it until the firing has taken place.

The glaze formulas are listed in this chapter first by cone level, 5 to 10, then alphabetically by color, and finally by surface: gloss, semi-gloss, satin matt, and matt, within each color division.

The potter will also find a list of possible chemical substitutions in Chapter 34, Dictionary of Clay and Glaze Compounds.

Note. The glazes in this chapter are labeled toxic or nontoxic. Toxic glazes should be carefully handled both in formulation and in application. During preparation the potter should wear a dust mask to prevent inhalation of toxic materials and not allow these materials to come into prolonged contact with the skin. Frequent washing of the hands when handling these glazes is a wise precaution. Toxic glazes should be applied by brushing and dipping—never spraying. For even under the best conditions some inhalation of the toxic mist from the spray is bound to take place or, equally bad, the mist from the spray gun can settle on the skin and be absorbed into the body system.

FORMULAS FOR STONEWARE GLAZES

SG-1

Transparent Brown Gloss Glaze   Cone 5
leadless, transparent, gloss, nontoxic

Mixing. Weigh out the ingredients and mix by using one of the methods outlined in Chapter 17 on Glaze Preparation.

Application. Apply to cone 06–04 bisque by brushing, dipping, or spraying. See Chapter 17 for more details.

Firing. Fire normally in any type kiln to the cone level indicated in the directions.

Fired Results. This glaze fires to a transparent gloss brown at cone 5.

Manganese carbonate	2.7
Whiting	10.5
Feldspar (Custer)	54.7
Kaolin (EPK)	6.3
Silica	24.9
Add:	
Red iron oxide	10.3
C.M.C.	1 tsp.

SG-2 **Translucent Brown Semi-Matt Glaze Cone 5**
leadless, translucent, semi-matt, nontoxic

Mixing. Mix in the manner of SG-1.

Application. Apply in the manner of SG-1.

Firing. Fire in the manner of SG-1.

Fired Results. This glaze fires to a translucent brown semi-matt at cone 5.

Nepheline syenite	51.5
Whiting	19.4
Silica	18.1
Kaolin	8.4
Zinc oxide	2.6
Add:	
Red iron oxide	5.1
Bentonite	1.0
C.M.C.	1 tsp.

SG-3 **Opaque Brown Matt Glaze Cone 5**
lead, opaque, matt, toxic

Mixing. Mix in the manner of SG-1, but handle with care as this glaze contains a toxic chemical.

Application. Apply by brushing or dipping. (See note at beginning of this chapter.)

Firing. Fire in the manner of SG-1.

Fired Results. This glaze fires to an opaque brown matt with darker specks at cone 5.

Feldspar (Custer)	32.0
White lead	17.2
Kaolin	14.6
Albany slip	12.0
Barnard slip	2.2
Dolomite	10.8
Whiting	5.8
Silica	5.0
Ilmenite	1.5
Add:	
C.M.C.	1 tsp.

SG-4 **Transparent Gray-Blue Gloss Glaze Cone 5**
leadless, transparent, gloss, nontoxic

Mixing. Mix in the manner of SG-1.

Application. Apply in the manner of SG-1.

Firing. Fire in the manner of SG-1.

Fired Results. This glaze fires to a transparent gray-blue gloss at cone 5.

Nepheline syenite	51.5
Whiting	19.4
Silica	18.1
Kaolin	8.4
Zinc oxide	2.6
Add:	
Iron chromate	3.0
Bentonite	1.0
C.M.C.	1 tsp.

SG-5 **Translucent Ice-Blue Matt Glaze Cone 5**
barium, translucent, matt, toxic

Mixing. Mix in the manner of SG-3.

Application. Apply in the manner of SG-3.

Firing. Fire in the manner of SG-1.

Fired Results. This glaze fires to a translucent ice-blue matt at cone 5.

Feldspar (Custer)	52.5
Barium carbonate	16.0
Zinc oxide	11.9
Whiting	5.8
Kaolin	5.0
Silica	9.0
Add:	
Nickel oxide	3.0
Bentonite	1.0
C.M.C.	1 tsp.

SG-6

Clear High-Gloss Glaze   Cone 5
leadless, transparent, high-gloss, nontoxic

Mixing. Mix in the manner of SG-1.

Application. Apply in the manner of SG-1.

Firing. Fire in the manner of SG-1.

Fired Results. This glaze fires to a clear high-gloss at cone 5.

Feldspar (Custer)	51.1
Whiting	18.6
Kaolin	10.8
Zinc oxide	8.7
Silica	5.9
Bentonite	4.9
Add:	
C.M.C.	1 tsp.

SG-7

Clear Bright Gloss Glaze   Cone 5
colemanite, transparent, gloss, nontoxic

Mixing. Mix in the manner of SG-1.

Application. Apply in the manner of SG-1.

Firing. Fire in the manner of SG-1.

Fired Results. This glaze fires to a clear bright gloss at cone 5. It is a good base glaze for copper or cobalt colorants.

Colemanite	51.0
Silica	31.0
Kaolin	16.0
Feldspar (Custer)	3.0
Add:	
Bentonite	1.0
C.M.C.	1 tsp.

SG-8

Clear Semi-Gloss Glaze   Cone 5
barium, transparent, semi-gloss, toxic

Mixing. Mix in the manner of SG-3.

Application. Apply in the manner of SG-3.

Firing. Fire in the manner of SG-1.

Fired Results. This glaze fires to a clear semi-gloss at cone 5.

Feldspar (potash)	52.0
Silica	18.0
Barium carbonate	14.0
Whiting	6.5
Kentucky ball clay #4	5.0
Kaolin	4.5
Add:	
Bentonite	1.0
C.M.C.	1 tsp.

SG-9

Clear Semi-Gloss Glaze   Cone 5
colemanite, transparent, semi-gloss, nontoxic

Mixing. Mix in the manner of SG-1.

Application. Apply in the manner of SG-1.

Firing. Fire in the manner of SG-1.

Fired Results. This glaze fires to a clear semi-gloss at cone 5.

Feldspar (Kona F-4)	45.7
Silica	15.2
Talc	12.7
Colemanite	12.9
Dolomite	9.0
Kaolin	4.5
Add:	
Bentonite	1.0
C.M.C.	1 tsp.

SG-10

Transparent Satin-Matt Glaze   Cone 5
alkaline-frit, transparent, satin matt, nontoxic

Mixing. Mix in the manner of SG-1.

Application. Apply in the manner of SG-1.

Firing. Fire in the manner of SG-1.

Fired Results. This glaze fires to a clear satin matt at cone 5.

Hommel frit #14	11.5
Feldspar (Custer)	28.0
Magnesium carbonate	3.5
Wollastonite	22.6
Kaolin (calcined)	11.8
Kaolin (Georgia)	17.1
Flint	5.5

SG-11	**Clear Matt Glaze Cone 5**
lead, transparent, matt, toxic

Mixing. Mix in the manner of SG-3.

Application. Apply in the manner of SG-3.

Firing. Fire in the manner of SG-1.

Fired Results. This glaze fires to a clear matt at cone 5.

Red lead	50.0
Feldspar (potash)	16.1
Kaolin	12.0
Tennessee ball clay #5	11.0
Whiting	6.0
Silica	4.9
Add:	
Bentonite	1.0
C.M.C.	1 tsp.

SG-12	**Translucent Cream-Matt Glaze Cone 5**
lead, translucent, matt, toxic

Mixing. Mix in the manner of SG-3.

Application. Apply in the manner of SG-3.

Firing. Fire in the manner of SG-1.

Fired Results. This glaze fires to a translucent cream matt at cone 5.

White lead	33.1
Tennessee ball clay #1	31.0
Feldspar (Custer)	17.9
Whiting	16.0
Silica	2.0
Add:	
Bentonite	1.0
C.M.C.	1 tsp.

SG-13	**Transparent Blue-Green Gloss Glaze Cone 5**
leadless, transparent, gloss, nontoxic

Mixing. Mix in the manner of SG-1.

Application. Apply in the manner of SG-1.

Firing. Fire in the manner of SG-1.

Fired Results. This glaze fires to a transparent blue-green gloss at cone 5.

Nepheline syenite	51.5
Whiting	19.4
Silica	18.1
Kaolin	8.4
Zinc oxide	2.6
Add:	
Copper carbonate	3.0
Cobalt carbonate	0.5
Bentonite	1.0

SG-14	**Translucent Gray-Green Semi-Matt Glaze Cone 5**
leadless, translucent, semi-matt, nontoxic

Mixing. Mix in the manner of SG-1.

Application. Apply in the manner of SG-1.

Firing. Fire in the manner of SG-1.

Fired Results. This glaze fires to a translucent semi-matt gray-green at cone 5.

Nepheline syenite	50.0
Whiting	19.4
Silica	18.0
Kaolin	9.0
Zinc oxide	3.6
Add:	
Copper carbonate	2.0
Bentonite	1.0
C.M.C.	1 tsp.

SG-15

Translucent Tan Semi-Matt Glaze   Cone 5
leadless, translucent, semi-matt, nontoxic

Mixing. Mix in the manner of SG-1.

Application. Apply in the manner of SG-1.

Firing. Fire in the manner of SG-1.

Fired Results. This glaze fires to a translucent warm-tan semi-matt at cone 5.

Feldspar (Custer)	36.5
Silica	25.2
Kaolin (Georgia)	17.1
Whiting	14.5
Dolomite	2.0
Red iron oxide	1.6
Rutile	1.4
Bone ash	1.0
Magnesium carbonate	0.7
Add:	
Bentonite	1.0

SG-16

Translucent Warm-Tan Semi-Matt Glaze   Cone 5
leadless, translucent, semi-matt, nontoxic

Mixing. Mix in the manner of SG-1.

Application. Apply in the manner of SG-1.

Firing. Fire in the manner of SG-1.

Fired Results. This glaze fires to a translucent warm-tan semi-matt at cone 5.

Nepheline syenite	50.5
Whiting	19.5
Silica	18.0
Kaolin	8.9
Zinc oxide	3.1
Add:	
Rutile	10.0
Bentonite	1.0
C.M.C.	1 tsp.

SG-17

Translucent Mottled-Tan Gloss   Cone 5
colemanite, translucent, gloss, nontoxic

Mixing. Mix in the manner of SG-1.

Application. Apply in the manner of SG-1.

Firing. Fire in the manner of SG-1.

Fired Results. This glaze fires to a translucent mottled-tan gloss at cone 5.

Plastic ultrox	40.0
Cornwall stone	4.0
Colemanite	30.0
Wollastonite	19.0
Feldspar (Custer)	7.0
Add:	
Iron oxide	5.0
Bentonite	1.0

SG-18

Transparent Tan Gloss Glaze   Cone 5
alkaline, transparent, gloss, nontoxic

Mixing. Mix in the manner of SG-1.

Application. Apply in the manner of SG-1.

Firing. Fire in the manner of SG-1.

Fired Results. This glaze fires to a transparent tan gloss at cone 5.

Feldspar (Custer)	34.8
Pemco frit #25	25.4
Silica	25.0
Whiting	4.8
Colemanite	6.1
Kentucky ball clay #4	3.9
Add:	
Rutile	3.0

SG-19

Transparent Turquoise Gloss Glaze   Cone 5
alkaline-frit, transparent, gloss, nontoxic

Mixing. Mix in the manner of SG-1.

Application. Apply in the manner of SG-1.

Firing. Fire in the manner of SG-1.

Fired Results. This glaze fires to a transparent turquoise gloss at cone 5.

Feldspar (Custer)	33.5
Ferro frit #3819	25.3
Silica	25.3
Whiting	5.6
Colemanite	6.5
Tennessee ball clay #1	3.8
Add:	
Copper carbonate	3.0
Bentonite	1.0
C.M.C.	1 tsp.

SG-20

Translucent White Gloss Glaze   Cone 5
alkaline-barium, translucent, gloss, toxic

Mixing. Mix in the manner of SG-3.

Application. Apply in the manner of SG-3.

Firing. Fire in the manner of SG-1.

Fired Results. This glaze fires to a translucent white gloss at cone 5.

Feldspar (Custer)	36.0
Silica	22.0
Colemanite	19.0
Zinc oxide	4.0
Opax	4.0
Barium carbonate	7.0
Talc	6.0
Ultrox	2.0
Add:	
Bentonite	1.0
C.M.C.	1 tsp.

SG-21

Translucent Blue-White Gloss Glaze   Cone 5
colemanite-barium, translucent, gloss, toxic

Mixing. Mix in the manner of SG-3.

Application. Apply in the manner of SG-3.

Firing. Fire in the manner of SG-1.

Fired Results. This glaze fires to a translucent blue-white gloss at cone 5.

Feldspar (Custer)	31.0
Silica	31.0
Colemanite	18.0
Zinc oxide	4.0
Ultrox	4.0
Barium carbonate	6.0
Talc	6.0
Add:	
Bentonite	1.0
C.M.C.	1 tsp.

SG-22

Translucent Cloudy-White Semi-Gloss Glaze   Cone 5
barium, translucent, semi-gloss, toxic

Mixing. Mix in the manner of SG-3.

Application. Apply in the manner of SG-3.

Firing. Fire in the manner of SG-1.

Fired Results. This glaze fires to a translucent cloudy-white semi-gloss at cone 5.

Feldspar (Custer)	33.0
Silica	22.0
Whiting	11.5
Barium carbonate	12.0
Kaolin	8.5
Ultrox	9.0
Zinc oxide	4.0
Add:	
Bentonite	1.0
C.M.C.	1 tsp.

SG-23

Translucent Gray-White Semi-Gloss Glaze   Cone 5
barium, translucent, semi-gloss, toxic

Mixing. Mix in the manner of SG-3.

Application. Apply in the manner of SG-3.

Firing. Fire in the manner of SG-1.

Fired Results. This glaze fires to a translucent gray-white semi-gloss at cone 5.

Feldspar (Kingman)	53.5
Silica	17.0
Barium carbonate	14.0
Whiting	6.0
Tennessee ball clay #1	5.0
Kaolin	4.5
Add:	
Bentonite	1.0
C.M.C.	1 tsp.

SG-24 **Translucent White Semi-Gloss Glaze   Cone 5**
colemanite, translucent, semi-gloss, nontoxic

Mixing. Mix in the manner of SG-1.

Application. Apply in the manner of SG-1.

Firing. Fire in the manner of SG-1.

Fired Results. This glaze fires to a translucent white semi-gloss at cone 5.

Feldspar (Kona F-4)	47.0
Silica	15.2
Talc	12.7
Colemanite	11.7
Dolomite	10.0
Kaolin	4.4
Add:	
Bentonite	1.0
C.M.C.	1 tsp.

SG-25 **Translucent White Semi-Matt Glaze   Cone 5**
leadless, translucent, semi-matt, nontoxic

Mixing. Mix in the manner of SG-1.

Application. Apply in the manner of SG-1.

Firing. Fire in the manner of SG-1.

Fired Results. This glaze fires to a translucent white semi-matt at cone 5.

Nepheline syenite	51.9
Whiting	18.5
Silica	18.0
Kaolin	9.0
Ultrox	2.6
Add:	
Bentonite	1.0
C.M.C.	1 tsp.

SG-26 **Translucent White Semi-Matt Glaze   Cone 5**
lead, translucent, semi-matt, toxic

Mixing. Mix in the manner of SG-3.

Application. Apply in the manner of SG-3.

Firing. Fire in the manner of SG-1.

Fired Results. This glaze fires to a translucent white semi-matt at cone 5.

Feldspar (Buckingham)	39.5
White lead	17.6
Kaolin	16.4
Dolomite	14.7
Whiting	6.0
Silica	5.8
Add:	
Bentonite	1.0
C.M.C.	1 tsp.

SG-27 **Opaque White Gloss Glaze   Cone 5**
alkaline, opaque, gloss, nontoxic

Mixing. Mix in the manner of SG-1.

Application. Apply in the manner of SG-1.

Firing. Fire in the manner of SG-1.

Fired Results. This glaze fires to an opaque white gloss at cone 5.

Lithium carbonate	10.8
Magnesium carbonate	10.1
Whiting	9.4
Kaolin (calcined)	7.2
Kaolin	16.8
Silica	45.7

SG-28 **Opaque White Gloss Glaze   Cone 5**
barium, opaque, gloss, toxic

Mixing. Mix in the manner of SG-3.

Application. Apply in the manner of SG-3.

Firing. Fire in the manner of SG-1.

Fired Results. This glaze fires to an opaque white gloss at cone 5.

Feldspar (Custer)	48.2
Silica	16.8
Barium carbonate	11.8
Whiting	5.9
Tennessee ball clay #1	4.1
Kaolin	4.1
Ultrox	9.1
Add:	
Bentonite	1.0
C.M.C.	1 tsp.

SG-29   **Opaque White Semi-Gloss Glaze   Cone 5**
alkaline-frit, opaque, semi-gloss, nontoxic

Mixing. Mix in the manner of SG-1.

Application. Apply in the manner of SG-1.

Firing. Fire in the manner of SG-1.

Fired Results. This glaze fires to an opaque white semi-gloss at cone 5.

Silica	51.3
Feldspar (Custer)	13.5
Hommel frit #14	14.3
Tennessee ball clay #1	9.0
Ultrox	10.0
Bentonite	2.0
Add:	
C.M.C.	1 tsp.

SG-30   **Opaque White Matt Glaze   Cone 5**
barium, opaque, matt, toxic

Mixing. Mix in the manner of SG-3.

Application. Apply in the manner of SG-3.

Firing. Fire in the manner of SG-1.

Fired Results. This glaze fires to an opaque white matt at cone 5.

Feldspar (Custer)	54.0
Kaolin (EPK)	13.6
Whiting	13.5
Barium carbonate	6.5
Silica	5.7
Ultrox	5.0
Magnesium carbonate	2.2
Add:	
Bentonite	1.0

SG-31   **Opaque Off-White Matt Glaze   Cone 5**
lead, opaque, matt, toxic

Mixing. Mix in the manner of SG-3.

Application. Apply in the manner of SG-3.

Firing. Fire in the manner of SG-1.

Fired Results. This glaze fires to an opaque matt at cone 5.

Red lead	45.4
Feldspar (Custer)	16.4
Kaolin	10.0
Tennessee ball clay #1	9.1
Whiting	5.7
Silica	4.2
Ultrox	9.2
Add:	
Bentonite	1.0
C.M.C.	1 tsp.

SG-32   **Translucent Yellow Semi-Matt Glaze   Cone 5**
barium, translucent, semi-matt, toxic

Mixing. Mix in the manner of SG-3.

Application. Apply in the manner of SG-3.

Firing. Fire in the manner of SG-1.

Fired Results. This glaze fires to a translucent yellow matt at cone 5.

Feldspar (Custer)	52.0
Silica	18.5
Barium carbonate	14.0
Ultrox	6.5
Uranium oxide	6.5
Tennessee ball clay #1	4.0
Kaolin	4.5
Add:	
Bentonite	1.0
C.M.C.	1 tsp.

SG-33   **Opaque Ochre-Yellow Matt Glaze   Cone 5**
alkaline-frit, opaque, matt, nontoxic

Mixing. Mix in the manner of SG-1.

Application. Apply in the manner of SG-1.

Firing. Fire in the manner of SG-1.

Fired Results. This glaze fires to an opaque ochre-yellow matt at cone 5.

Kaolin	30.0
Pemco frit #54	25.0
Zinc oxide	17.0
Silica	14.6
Iron oxide	4.2
Lithium carbonate	3.7
Ultrox	4.7
Yellow ochre	0.5
Copper carbonate	0.4
Add:	
Bentonite	1.0
C.M.C.	1 tsp.

SG-34   **Black Gloss Glaze   Cone 6**
leadless, opaque, black gloss, nontoxic

Mixing. Mix in the manner of SG-1.

Application. Apply in the manner of SG-1.

Firing. Fire in the manner of SG-1.

Fired Results. This glaze fires to an opaque black gloss at cone 6.

Feldspar (Buckingham)	40.5
Wollastonite	16.1
Zinc oxide	11.6
Kaolin	4.7
Silica	24.1
Whiting	2.0
Add:	
Bentonite	2.0
Cobalt oxide	2.0
Chrome oxide	2.0
Black iron oxide	2.0
C.M.C.	1 tsp.

SG-35   **Opaque Blue Semi-Gloss Glaze   Cone 6-7**
Courtesy of Kay and Rick West, Jasper, Arkansas
colemanite, opaque, semi-gloss, nontoxic

Mixing. Mix in the manner of SG-1.

Application. Apply in the manner of SG-1.

Firing. Fire in the manner of SG-1.

Fired Results. This glaze fires to an opaque blue semi-gloss at cone 6.

Colemanite	50.0
Kaolin (EPK)	15.0
Silica	35.0
Add:	
Cobalt oxide	1.0
Copper oxide	2.0
Rutile	1.0

SG-36   **Transparent Midnight-Blue Gloss Glaze   Cone 6**
alkaline, transparent, gloss, non-toxic

Mixing. Mix in the manner of SG-3.

Application. Apply in the manner of SG-3.

Firing. Fire in the manner of SG-1.

Fired Results. This glaze fires to a transparent midnight-blue gloss at cone 6.

Lithium carbonate	13.5
Feldspar (Custer)	56.0
Whiting	8.0
Kaolin	5.0
Silica	17.5
Add:	
Vanadium pentoxide	5.0
Bentonite	1.0

SG-37

Transparent Light-Blue Gloss Glaze   Cone 6
barium, transparent, gloss, toxic

Mixing. Mix in the manner of SG-3.

Application. Apply in the manner of SG-3.

Firing. Fire in the manner of SG-1.

Fired Results. This glaze fires to a transparent light-blue gloss at cone 6.

Barium carbonate	39.4
Lithium carbonate	2.2
Zinc oxide	14.1
Feldspar (Custer)	31.0
Silica	13.3
Add:	
Nickel carbonate	4.0
Bentonite	1.0

SG-38

Opaque Orange-Brown Gloss Glaze   Cone 6
leadless, opaque, gloss, nontoxic

Mixing. Mix in the manner of SG-1.

Application. Apply in the manner of SG-1.

Firing. Fire in the manner of SG-1.

Fired Results. This glaze fires to an orange-brown opaque gloss at cone 6.

Silica	36.5
Feldspar (Custer)	31.0
Whiting	14.0
Iron oxide	11.0
Kaolin	8.0
Add:	
Bentonite	1.0
Ultrox	5.0
C.M.C.	1 tsp.

SG-39

Clear Gloss Glaze   Cone 6
alkaline-frit, transparent, gloss, nontoxic

Mixing. Mix in the manner of SG-1.

Application. Apply in the manner of SG-1.

Firing. Fire in the manner of SG-1.

Fired Results. This glaze fires to a clear gloss at cone 6.

Volcanic ash	63.7
Pemco frit #54	27.3
Kaolin	9.0
Add:	
Bentonite	1.0

SG-40

Clear High-Gloss Glaze   Cone 6
lead, transparent, high-gloss, toxic

Mixing. Mix in the manner of SG-3.

Application. Apply in the manner of SG-3.

Firing. Fire in the manner of SG-1.

Fired Results. This glaze fires to a clear high-gloss at cone 6.

Cornwall stone	37.5
Red lead	37.9
Silica	19.0
Whiting	5.6
Colemanite	1.4
Add:	
Bentonite	1.0
C.M.C.	1 tsp.

SG-41

Clear Gloss Glaze   Cone 6
leadless, transparent, gloss, nontoxic

Mixing. Mix in the manner of SG-1.

Application. Apply in the manner of SG-1.

Firing. Fire in the manner of SG-1.

Fired Results. This glaze fires to a clear gloss at cone 6.

Lepidolite	42.0
Flint	30.0
Whiting	19.0
Kaolin	9.0
Add:	
Bentonite	1.0

SG-42

Clear Gloss Glaze   Cone 6
colemanite, transparent, gloss, nontoxic

Mixing. Mix in the manner of SG-1.

Application. Apply in the manner of SG-1.

Firing. Fire in the manner of SG-1.

Fired Results. This glaze fires to a clear gloss at cone 6.

Colemanite	49.5
Silica	32.0
Kaolin	16.0
Whiting	1.5
Bentonite	1.0
Add:	
C.M.C.	1 tsp.

SG-43

Clear Gloss Glaze   Cone 6
leadless, transparent, gloss, nontoxic

Mixing. Mix in the manner of SG-1.

Application. Apply in the manner of SG-1.

Firing. Fire in the manner of SG-1.

Fired Results. This glaze fires to a clear gloss at cone 6.

Nepheline syenite	35.5
Magnesium carbonate	14.6
Zinc oxide	11.9
Kaolin	2.4
Silica	35.6
Add:	
Bentonite	1.0
C.M.C.	1 tsp.

SG-44

Clear Gloss Glaze   Cone 6
leadless, transparent, gloss, nontoxic

Mixing. Mix in the manner of SG-1.

Application. Apply in the manner of SG-1.

Firing. Fire in the manner of SG-1.

Fired Results. This glaze fires to a clear gloss at cone 6.

Nepheline syenite	28.7
Magnesium carbonate	10.8
Zinc oxide	4.0
Colemanite	13.6
Silica	34.7
Kaolin	8.2
Add:	
C.M.C.	1 tsp.

SG-45

Clear Gloss Glaze   Cone 6
colemanite, transparent, gloss, nontoxic

Mixing. Mix in the manner of SG-1.

Application. Apply in the manner of SG-1.

Firing. Fire in the manner of SG-1.

Fired Results. This glaze fires to a clear gloss at cone 6.

Spodumene	51.0
Colemanite	26.0
Silica	23.0
Add:	
Bentonite	1.0
C.M.C.	1 tsp.

SG-46

Clear Gloss Glaze   Cone 6
colemanite, transparent, gloss, nontoxic

Mixing. Mix in the manner of SG-1.

Application. Apply in the manner of SG-1.

Firing. Fire in the manner of SG-1.

Fired Results. This glaze fires to a clear gloss at cone 6.

Nepheline syenite	46.2
Colemanite	28.0
Silica	20.4
Kaolin	5.4
Add:	
Bentonite	1.0
C.M.C.	1 tsp.

SG-47

Clear Gloss Glaze   Cone 6
alkaline, transparent, gloss, nontoxic

Mixing. Mix in the manner of SG-1.

Application. Apply in the manner of SG-1.

Firing. Fire in the manner of SG-1.

Fired Results. This glaze fires to a clear gloss at cone 6.

Volcanic ash	82.0
Whiting	8.3
Lithium carbonate	7.6
Colemanite	2.1
Add:	
Bentonite	1.0
C.M.C.	1 tsp.

SG-48	**Clear Gloss Glaze Cone 6** barium, transparent, gloss, toxic *Mixing.* Mix in the manner of SG-3. *Application.* Apply in the manner of SG-3. *Firing.* Fire in the manner of SG-1. *Fired Results.* This glaze fires to a clear gloss at cone 6.	Feldspar (Kona F-4)	35.9
		Kaolin	15.3
		Dolomite	11.4
		Spodumene	9.5
		Whiting	8.2
		Silica	7.0
		Barium carbonate	6.5
		Tennessee ball clay #1	3.7
		Ultrox	2.0
		Talc	1.7

SG-49	**Clear Gloss Glaze Cone 6** alkaline, transparent, gloss, nontoxic *Mixing.* Mix in the manner of SG-1. *Application.* Apply in the manner of SG-1. *Firing.* Fire in the manner of SG-1. *Fired Results.* This glaze fires to a clear gloss at cone 6.	Lepidolite	51.0
		Colemanite	25.0
		Tin oxide	4.0
		Silica	20.0

SG-50	**Clear Gloss Glaze Cone 6** alkaline, transparent, gloss, nontoxic *Mixing.* Mix in the manner of SG-1. *Application.* Apply in the manner of SG-1. *Firing.* Fire in the manner of SG-1. *Fired Results.* This glaze fires to a clear gloss at cone 6.	Lithium carbonate	5.0
		Pemco frit #25	25.0
		Zinc oxide	4.0
		Tin oxide	1.0
		Volcanic ash	65.0

SG-51	**Clear Semi-Gloss Glaze Cone 6** barium, transparent, semi-gloss, toxic *Mixing.* Mix in the manner of SG-3. *Application.* Apply in the manner of SG-3. *Firing.* Fire in the manner of SG-1. *Fired Results.* This glaze fires to a clear semi-gloss at cone 6.	Whiting	9.5
		Colemanite	15.5
		Barium carbonate	10.0
		Talc	5.0
		Nepheline syenite	29.0
		Silica	19.5
		Lithium carbonate	5.0
		Kaolin	4.5
		Bentonite	2.0
		Add:	
		C.M.C.	1 tsp.

SG-52	**Clear Semi-Gloss Glaze Cone 6** barium, transparent, semi-gloss, toxic *Mixing.* Mix in the manner of SG-3. *Application.* Apply in the manner of SG-3. *Firing.* Fire in the manner of SG-1. *Fired Results.* This glaze fires to a clear semi-gloss at cone 6.	Feldspar (Kona F-4)	44.6
		Silica	20.5
		Barium carbonate	9.4
		Zinc oxide	6.8
		Whiting	6.7
		Kaolin	5.6
		Tennessee ball clay #1	4.0
		Talc	2.4
		Add:	
		Bentonite	1.0
		C.M.C.	1 tsp.

SG-53 **Clear Semi-Matt Glaze   Cone 6**
barium, transparent, clear semi-matt, toxic

Mixing. Mix in the manner of SG-3.

Application. Apply in the manner of SG-3.

Firing. Fire in the manner of SG-1.

Fired Results. This glaze fires to a clear semi-matt at cone 6.

Barium carbonate	21.4
Nepheline syenite	24.8
Strontium carbonate	14.4
Whiting	4.8
Kaolin (EPK)	7.1
Silica	31.5
Add:	
Bentonite	2.0
C.M.C.	1 tsp.

SG-54 **Clear Semi-Matt Glaze   Cone 6**
barium, transparent, semi-matt, toxic

Mixing. Mix in the manner of SG-3.

Application. Apply in the manner of SG-3.

Firing. Fire in the manner of SG-1.

Fired Results. This glaze fires to a clear semi-matt at cone 6.

Bismuth oxide	12.0
Feldspar (Custer)	50.6
Whiting	3.3
Barium carbonate	17.9
Zinc oxide	7.2
Silica	9.0
Add:	
Bentonite	1.0
C.M.C.	1 tsp.

SG-55 **Clear Lightly Matted Glaze   Cone 6**
alkaline, transparent, light matt, nontoxic

Mixing. Mix in the manner of SG-1.

Application. Apply in the manner of SG-1.

Firing. Fire in the manner of SG-1.

Fired Results. This glaze fires to a clear light matt at cone 6.

Lithium carbonate	10.8
Feldspar (Custer)	27.3
Whiting	13.8
Kaolin	11.7
Silica	36.4
Add:	
Bentonite	1.0
C.M.C.	1 tsp.

SG-56 **Clear Smooth-Matt Glaze   Cone 6**
alkaline, transparent, smooth matt, nontoxic

Mixing. Mix in the manner of SG-1.

Application. Apply in the manner of SG-1.

Firing. Fire in the manner of SG-1.

Fired Results. This glaze fires to a clear smooth matt at cone 6.

Lepidolite	23.0
Magnesium carbonate	3.3
Colemanite	5.8
Wollastonite	20.4
Kaolin	14.5
Silica	29.2
Fluorspar	3.8
Add:	
Bentonite	1.0

SG-57 **Clear Satin-Matt Glaze   Cone 6**
leadless, transparent, satin matt, nontoxic

Mixing. Mix in the manner of SG-1.

Application. Apply in the manner of SG-1.

Firing. Fire in the manner of SG-1.

Fired Results. This glaze fires to a clear satin matt at cone 6.

Feldspar (Custer)	35.9
Whiting	10.0
Zinc oxide	24.8
Kaolin	4.1
Silica	22.6
Strontium carbonate	2.6
Add:	
Bentonite	1.0

SG-58

Clear Smooth-Matt Glaze   Cone 6
leadless, transparent, smooth matt, nontoxic

Mixing. Mix in the manner of SG-1.

Application. Apply in the manner of SG-1.

Firing. Fire in the manner of SG-1.

Fired Results. This glaze fires to a clear smooth matt at cone 6.

Lithium carbonate	6.0
Whiting	5.9
Titanium dioxide	10.5
Zinc oxide	19.5
Kaolin	19.7
Silica	37.5
Add:	
Bentonite	1.0
C.M.C.	1 tsp.

SG-59

Clear Satin-Matt Glaze   Cone 6
leadless, transparent, satin matt, nontoxic

Mixing. Mix in the manner of SG-1.

Application. Apply in the manner of SG-1.

Firing. Fire in the manner of SG-1.

Fired Results. This glaze fires to a clear satin matt at cone 6.

Feldspar (Custer)	9.4
Lithium carbonate	1.6
Whiting	16.8
Zinc oxide	17.8
Kaolin	31.4
Silica	23.0
Add:	
Bentonite	1.0

SG-60

Clear Satin-Matt Glaze   Cone 6
leadless, transparent, satin matt, nontoxic

Mixing. Mix in the manner of SG-1.

Application. Apply in the manner of SG-1.

Firing. Fire in the manner of SG-1.

Fired Results. This glaze fires to a clear satin matt at cone 6.

Feldspar (Custer)	39.7
Whiting	28.6
Kaolin (EPK)	13.8
Silica	17.9
Add:	
Bentonite	1.0
C.M.C.	1 tsp.

SG-61

Clear Satin-Matt Glaze   Cone 6
leadless, transparent, satin matt, nontoxic

Mixing. Mix in the manner of SG-1.

Application. Apply in the manner of SG-1.

Firing. Fire in the manner of SG-1.

Fired Results. This glaze fires to a clear satin matt at cone 6.

Feldspar (Custer)	34.2
Whiting	12.1
Zinc oxide	25.3
Kaolin	4.0
Silica	22.4
Bentonite	2.0
Add:	
C.M.C.	1 tsp.

SG-62

Clear Matt Glaze   Cone 6
alkaline-frit, transparent, matt, toxic

Mixing. Mix in the manner of SG-3.

Application. Apply in the manner of SG-3.

Firing. Fire in the manner of SG-1.

Fired Results. This glaze fires to a clear matt at cone 6.

Spodumene	50.9
Talc	43.0
Hommel frit #14	2.3
Bentonite	1.9
Magnesium carbonate	1.9
C.M.C.	1 tsp.

SG-63

Opaque Mottled-Cream Gloss Glaze   Cone 6
lead, opaque, gloss, toxic

Mixing. Mix in the manner of SG-3.

Application. Apply in the manner of SG-3.

Firing. Fire in the manner of SG-1.

Fired Results. This glaze fires to an opaque mottled-cream gloss at cone 6.

White lead	12.1
Red lead	12.1
Whiting	6.0
Silica	30.1
Borax	24.1
Boric acid	3.0
Sodium carbonate	4.5
Kaolin	1.5
Tin oxide	4.5
Iron oxide	2.1

SG-64

Opaque Cream-Tan Waxy Matt Glaze   Cone 6
leadless, opaque, matt, nontoxic

Mixing. Mix in the manner of SG-1.

Application. Apply in the manner of SG-1.

Firing. Fire in the manner of SG-1.

Fired Results. This glaze fires to an opaque cream-tan waxy matt at cone 6.

Nepheline syenite	35.4
Magnesium carbonate	17.6
Dolomite	17.9
Kaolin	5.0
Silica	35.6
Whiting	20.0
Ilmenite (powdered)	4.0
Ilmenite (granular)	2.0
Bentonite	2.0
C.M.C.	1 tsp.

SG-65

Translucent White Gloss Glaze   Cone 6
leadless, translucent, gloss, nontoxic

Mixing. Mix in the manner of SG-1.

Application. Apply in the manner of SG-1.

Firing. Fire in the manner of SG-1.

Fired Results. This glaze fires to a translucent white gloss at cone 6.

Volcanic ash	39.0
Whiting	29.0
Silica	18.0
Kaolin	8.0
Magnesium carbonate	4.0
Bentonite	2.0

SG-66

Translucent White Gloss Glaze   Cone 6
leadless, translucent, gloss, nontoxic

Mixing. Mix in the manner of SG-1.

Application. Apply in the manner of SG-1.

Firing. Fire in the manner of SG-1.

Fired Results. This glaze fires to a translucent white gloss at cone 6.

Lepidolite	39.0
Whiting	28.0
Silica	18.0
Kaolin	9.0
Magnesium carbonate	4.0
Bentonite	2.0

SG-67

Translucent Semi-Gloss Glaze   Cone 6
leadless, translucent, semi-gloss, nontoxic

Mixing. Mix in the manner of SG-1.

Application. Apply in the manner of SG-1.

Firing. Fire in the manner of SG-1.

Fired Results. This glaze fires to a translucent semi-gloss at cone 6.

Feldspar (Custer)	68.5
Whiting	12.0
Silica	8.0
Cornwall stone	6.5
Zinc oxide	2.0
Magnesium carbonate	2.0
Bentonite	1.0

SG-68

Translucent Semi-Gloss Glaze   Cone 6
alkaline, translucent, semi-gloss, nontoxic

Mixing. Mix in the manner of SG-1.

Application. Apply in the manner of SG-1.

Firing. Fire in the manner of SG-1.

Fired Results. This glaze fires to a translucent semi-gloss at cone 6.

Feldspar (Kona F-4)	49.0
Sodium carbonate	28.0
Silica	11.0
Whiting	8.0
Sodium borate	1.5
Magnesium carbonate	1.5

SG-69

Translucent Cloudy-White Gloss Glaze   Cone 6
barium, translucent, gloss, toxic

Mixing. Mix in the manner of SG-3.

Application. Apply in the manner of SG-3.

Firing. Fire in the manner of SG-1.

Fired Results. This glaze fires to a translucent cloudy-white gloss at cone 6.

Feldspar (potash)	37.1
Barium carbonate	13.5
Lithium carbonate	2.3
Magnesium carbonate	2.3
Whiting	13.3
Kaolin	4.4
Silica	24.1
Bentonite	2.0

SG-70

Translucent Cloudy-White Gloss Glaze   Cone 6
alkaline, translucent, gloss, nontoxic

Mixing. Mix in the manner of SG-1.

Application. Apply in the manner of SG-1.

Firing. Fire in the manner of SG-1.

Fired Results. This glaze fires to a translucent cloudy-white gloss at cone 6.

Lithium carbonate	4.7
Whiting	11.0
Zinc oxide	7.0
Volcanic ash	76.6
Bentonite	2.7
Add:	
C.M.C.	1 tsp.

SG-71

Translucent White Satin-Matt Glaze   Cone 6
leadless, translucent, satin matt, nontoxic

Mixing. Mix in the manner of SG-1.

Application. Apply in the manner of SG-1.

Firing. Fire in the manner of SG-1.

Fired Results. This glaze fires to a translucent white satin matt at cone 6.

Feldspar (Custer)	48.5
Whiting	18.0
Silica	18.5
Kaolin (EPK)	8.5
Zinc oxide	2.5
Magnesium carbonate	3.0
Bentonite	1.0

SG-72

Translucent White Matt Glaze   Cone 6
barium, translucent, matt, toxic

Mixing. Mix in the manner of SG-3.

Application. Apply in the manner of SG-3.

Firing. Fire in the manner of SG-1.

Fired Results. This glaze fires to a translucent white matt at cone 6.

Feldspar (Custer)	45.3
Barium carbonate	22.8
Tennessee ball clay #1	11.2
Whiting	9.0
Zinc oxide	9.0
Magnesium carbonate	1.7
Add:	
Bentonite	1.0
C.M.C.	1 tsp.

SG-73   **Semi-Opaque Gloss Glaze   Cone 6**
leadless, semi-opaque, patterned, nontoxic

Mixing. Mix in the manner of SG-1.

Application. Apply in the manner of SG-1.

Firing. Fire in the manner of SG-1.

Fired Results. This glaze fires to a semi-opaque gloss white at cone 6.

Lepidolite	62.5
Calcium fluoride	35.0
Bentonite	2.5
C.M.C.	1 tsp.

SG-74   **Opaque Patterned-White Gloss Glaze   Cone 6**
leadless, opaque, gloss, nontoxic

Mixing. Mix in the manner of SG-1.

Application. Apply in the manner of SG-1.

Firing. Fire in the manner of SG-1.

Fired Results. This glaze fires to an opaque patterned-white gloss at cone 6.

Zircopax	36.0
Fluorspar	51.0
Kaolin	13.0
Feldspar (potash)	2.0
Add:	
Bentonite	2.0
C.M.C.	1 tsp.

SG-75   **Opaque White Gloss Glaze   Cone 6**
alkaline, opaque, gloss, nontoxic

Mixing. Mix in the manner of SG-1.

Application. Apply in the manner of SG-1.

Firing. Fire in the manner of SG-1.

Fired Results. This glaze fires to an opaque white gloss at cone 6.

Lithium carbonate	9.5
Magnesium carbonate	10.0
Whiting	12.3
Alumina oxide	5.0
Kaolin	16.5
Silica	46.2

SG-76   **Opaque Semi-Gloss Glaze   Cone 6**
alkaline, opaque, semi-gloss, nontoxic

Mixing. Mix in the manner of SG-1.

Application. Apply in the manner of SG-1.

Firing. Fire in the manner of SG-1.

Fired Results. This glaze fires to an opaque semi-gloss white at cone 6.

Feldspar (Custer)	48.2
Lithium carbonate	6.2
Whiting	3.4
Zinc oxide	10.8
Kaolin	15.0
Silica	16.4
Add:	
Bentonite	2.0

SG-77   **Opaque White Semi-Gloss Glaze   Cone 6**
leadless, opaque, semi-gloss, nontoxic

Mixing. Mix in the manner of SG-1.

Application. Apply in the manner of SG-1.

Firing. Fire in the manner of SG-1.

Fired Results. This glaze fires to an opaque white semi-gloss at cone 6.

Feldspar (Kona F-4)	85.5
Tennessee ball clay #1	6.5
Whiting	2.5
Zinc oxide	2.4
Silica	1.8
Magnesium carbonate	1.4

SG-78   **Opaque Semi-Matt Glaze   Cone 6**
alkaline, opaque, semi-matt, nontoxic

Mixing. Mix in the manner of SG-1.

Application. Apply in the manner of SG-1.

Firing. Fire in the manner of SG-1.

Fired Results. This glaze fires to an opaque semi-matt at cone 6.

Lithium carbonate	8.9
Feldspar (Custer)	24.8
Whiting	13.4
Kaolin	11.5
Silica	32.2
Ultrox	9.2
Add:	
C.M.C.	1 tsp.

SG-79

Opaque Mottled Semi-Matt Glaze   Cone 6
bristol, opaque, mottled white, slightly toxic

Mixing. Mix in the manner of SG-3.

Application. Apply in the manner of SG-3.

Firing. Fire in the manner of SG-1.

Fired Results. This glaze fires to an opaque mottled white semi-matt at cone 6.

Zinc oxide (calcined)	9.6
Nepheline syenite	25.3
Lithium carbonate	9.7
Kaolin (EPK)	20.0
Silica	34.1
Add:	
C.M.C.	1 tsp.

SG-80

White Opaque Semi-Matt Glaze   Cone 6
leadless, opaque, semi-matt, nontoxic

Mixing. Mix in the manner of SG-1.

Application. Apply in the manner of SG-1.

Firing. Fire in the manner of SG-1.

Fired Results. This glaze fires to an opaque white semi-matt at cone 6.

Feldspar (Custer)	41.7
Whiting	14.5
Zinc oxide	12.0
Kaolin	5.9
Silica	25.9
Add:	
Titanium dioxide	5.5
Bentonite	2.0
C.M.C.	1 tsp.

SG-81

Off-White Opaque Patterned Semi-Matt Glaze   Cone 6
leadless, opaque, semi-matt, nontoxic

Mixing. Mix in the manner of SG-1.

Application. Apply in the manner of SG-1.

Firing. Fire in the manner of SG-1.

Fired Results. This glaze fires to an off-white opaque patterned semi-matt at cone 6.

Zinc oxide	22.0
Whiting	4.5
Lithium carbonate	5.5
Kaolin	20.2
Cryolite	5.7
Silica	32.0
Titanium dioxide	9.0
Bentonite	1.1
Add:	
C.M.C.	1 tsp.

SG-82

Off-White Patterned Matt Glaze   Cone 6
leadless, opaque, patterned matt, nontoxic

Mixing. Mix in the manner of SG-1.

Application. Apply in the manner of SG-1.

Firing. Fire in the manner of SG-1.

Fired Results. This glaze fires to an off-white patterned matt glaze at cone 6.

Lepidolite	49.0
Whiting	19.5
Silica	29.5
Bentonite	2.0
Add:	
C.M.C.	1 tsp.

SG-83

Semi-Opaque Matt Glaze   Cone 6
barium, semi-opaque, matt, toxic

Mixing. Mix in the manner of SG-3.

Application. Apply in the manner of SG-3.

Firing. Fire in the manner of SG-1.

Fired Results. This glaze fires to a semi-opaque white cloudy matt at cone 6.

Feldspar (Custer)	17.0
Whiting	14.5
Barium carbonate	29.4
Kaolin	21.0
Silica	16.2
Bentonite	1.6
Add:	
C.M.C.	1 tsp.

SG-84

Opaque White Matt Glaze   Cone 6
leadless, opaque, matt, nontoxic

Mixing. Mix in the manner of SG-1.

Application. Apply in the manner of SG-1.

Firing. Fire in the manner of SG-1.

Fired Results. This glaze fires to an opaque white matt at cone 6.

Feldspar (Custer)	34.0
Silica	24.0
Zinc oxide	10.0
Whiting	16.0
Tennessee ball clay #5	8.0
Ultrox	8.0
Add:	
Bentonite	1.0
C.M.C.	1 tsp.

SG-85

Opaque Mottled Matt Glaze   Cone 6
bristol, opaque, matt, toxic

Mixing. Mix in the manner of SG-3.

Application. Apply in the manner of SG-3.

Firing. Fire in the manner of SG-1.

Fired Results. This glaze fires to an opaque mottled white matt at cone 6.

Zinc oxide	12.5
Nepheline syenite	40.0
Lithium carbonate	4.8
Kaolin	7.5
Silica	35.2
Add:	
Bentonite	2.0
C.M.C.	1 tsp.

SG-86

Opaque Smooth Stony Matt Glaze   Cone 6
barium, opaque, stony matt, toxic

Mixing. Mix in the manner of SG-3.

Application. Apply in the manner of SG-3.

Firing. Fire in the manner of SG-1.

Fired Results. This glaze fires to an opaque smooth stony matt white at cone 6.

Nepheline syenite	40.5
Whiting	9.2
Zinc oxide	3.8
Magnesium carbonate	2.5
Barium carbonate	12.0
Kaolin	5.8
Silica	25.0
Bentonite	1.4
Add:	
C.M.C.	1 tsp.

SG-87

Opaque White Stony Matt Glaze   Cone 6
leadless, opaque, stony matt, toxic

Mixing. Mix in the manner of SG-3.

Application. Apply in the manner of SG-3.

Firing. Fire in the manner of SG-1.

Fired Results. This glaze fires to an opaque white stony matt at cone 6.

Bone ash	6.0
Nepheline syenite	24.6
Magnesium carbonate	2.3
Wollastonite	12.5
Kaolin	14.1
Strontium carbonate	30.0
Tin oxide	5.3
Ultrox	5.2
Add:	
C.M.C.	1 tsp.

SG-88

Opaque White Stony Matt Glaze   Cone 6
leadless, opaque, stony matt, nontoxic

Mixing. Mix in the manner of SG-1.

Application. Apply in the manner of SG-1.

Firing. Fire in the manner of SG-1.

Fired Results. This glaze fires to an opaque white stony matt at cone 6.

Feldspar (potash)	36.4
Silica	21.3
Whiting	18.2
Kaolin	9.1
Ultrox	9.0

SG-89 **Granular-Surface Glaze** **Cone 6**

leadless, opaque, sandy matt, nontoxic

Mixing. Mix in the manner of SG-1.

Application. Apply in the manner of SG-1.

Firing. Fire in the manner of SG-1.

Fired Results. This glaze fires to an opaque sandy-surface matt at cone 6.

Cryolite	44.5
Talc	53.0
Tennessee ball clay #1	2.5
Add:	
Bentonite	2.0
C.M.C.	1 tsp.

SG-90 **Stony Fissured Glaze** **Cone 6**

leadless, opaque, stony fissured matt, nontoxic

Mixing. Mix in the manner of SG-1.

Application. Apply in the manner of SG-1.

Firing. Fire in the manner of SG-1.

Fired Results. This glaze fires to an opaque stony fissured white matt at cone 6.

Cryolite	31.0
Zircopax	67.0
Kentucky ball clay #4	2.0
Add:	
Bentonite	2.0
C.M.C.	1 tsp.

SG-91 **Off-White Crater Glaze** **Cone 6**

leadless, opaque, crater, nontoxic

Mixing. Mix in the manner of SG-1.

Application. Apply in the manner of SG-1.

Firing. Fire in the manner of SG-1.

Fired Results. This glaze fires to an off-white crater surface glaze at cone 6.

Talc	44.5
Lepidolite	54.5
Bentonite	2.0
Add:	
C.M.C.	1 tsp.

SG-92 **Clear Gloss Glaze** **Cone 7**

lead, transparent, gloss, toxic

Mixing. Mix in the manner of SG-3.

Application. Apply in the manner of SG-3.

Firing. Fire in the manner of SG-1.

Fired Results. This glaze fires to a clear gloss at cone 7.

White lead	30.0
Feldspar (Kona F-4)	28.0
Silica	22.0
Kaolin (EPK)	12.0
Whiting	8.0
Add:	
Bentonite	1.0
C.M.C.	1 tsp.

SG-93 **Clear Matt Glaze** **Cone 7**

leadless, transparent, matt, nontoxic

Mixing. Mix in the manner of SG-1.

Application. Apply in the manner of SG-1.

Firing. Fire in the manner of SG-1.

Fired Results. This glaze fires to a clear matt at cone 7.

Feldspar (Custer)	48.6
Whiting	26.6
Kaolin (calcined)	19.5
Kaolin	4.3
Bentonite	1.0

SG-94 **Translucent Gloss Glaze** **Cone 7**

leadless, translucent, gloss, nontoxic

Mixing. Mix in the manner of SG-1.

Application. Apply in the manner of SG-1.

Firing. Fire in the manner of SG-1.

Fired Results. This glaze fires to a translucent gloss at cone 7.

Feldspar (Custer)	26.9
Silica	20.2
Whiting	20.2
Kaolin	10.2
Zinc oxide	6.7
Titanium dioxide	6.6
Ultrox	7.2
Bentonite	2.0

SG-95   **Translucent Semi-Gloss Glaze   Cone 7**
leadless, translucent, semi-gloss, nontoxic

Mixing. Mix in the manner of SG-1.

Application. Apply in the manner of SG-1.

Firing. Fire in the manner of SG-1.

Fired Results. This glaze fires to a translucent semi-gloss at cone 7.

Silica	36.1
Feldspar (Custer)	29.6
Whiting	16.7
Kaolin	10.2
Magnesium carbonate	5.6
Bentonite	1.8

SG-96   **Translucent White Satin-Matt Glaze   Cone 7**
leadless, translucent, satin matt, nontoxic

Mixing. Mix in the manner of SG-1.

Application. Apply in the manner of SG-1.

Firing. Fire in the manner of SG-1.

Fired Results. This glaze fires to a translucent white satin matt at cone 7.

Feldspar (Custer)	61.1
Zinc oxide	11.1
Whiting	11.1
Tennessee ball clay	9.2
Magnesium carbonate	5.6
Bentonite	1.9

SG-97   **Opaque White Gloss Glaze   Cone 7**
barium, opaque, gloss, toxic

Mixing. Mix in the manner of SG-3.

Application. Apply in the manner of SG-3.

Firing. Fire in the manner of SG-1.

Fired Results. This glaze fires to an opaque white gloss at cone 7.

Feldspar (Custer)	28.7
Silica	24.5
Whiting	14.1
Tin oxide	7.2
Barium carbonate	7.3
Kaolin	7.1
Ultrox	7.3
Magnesium carbonate	3.8

SG-98   **Opaque White Gloss Glaze   Cone 7**
colemanite, opaque, gloss, nontoxic

Mixing. Mix in the manner of SG-1.

Application. Apply in the manner of SG-1.

Firing. Fire in the manner of SG-1.

Fired Results. This glaze fires to an opaque white gloss at cone 7.

Colemanite	50.4
Alumina oxide	3.5
Kaolin	9.0
Silica	3.4
Add:	
Bentonite	1.0
Magnesium carbonate	1.9
C.M.C.	1 tsp.

SG-99   **Opaque White Semi-Gloss Glaze   Cone 7**
leadless, opaque, semi-gloss, nontoxic

Mixing. Mix in the manner of SG-1.

Application. Apply in the manner of SG-1.

Firing. Fire in the manner of SG-1.

Fired Results. This glaze fires to an opaque semi-gloss white at cone 7.

Volcanic ash	74.8
Zinc oxide	7.5
Whiting	12.2
Magnesium carbonate	1.8
Bentonite	4.7

SG-100

Opaque White Matt Glaze   Cone 7
leadless, opaque, matt, nontoxic

Mixing. Mix in the manner of SG-1.

Application. Apply in the manner of SG-1.

Firing. Fire in the manner of SG-1.

Fired Results. This glaze fires to an opaque white matt at cone 7.

Feldspar (Custer)	32.7
Silica	26.5
Whiting	11.8
Kaolin	7.2
Tin oxide	5.4
Ultrox	4.5
Dolomite	2.9
Talc	4.5
Magnesium carbonate	2.7
Bentonite	1.8

SG-101

Opaque Cream-White Matt Glaze   Cone 7
leadless, opaque, matt, nontoxic

Mixing. Mix in the manner of SG-1.

Application. Apply in the manner of SG-1.

Firing. Fire in the manner of SG-1.

Fired Results. This glaze fires to an opaque cream-white at cone 7.

Feldspar (Custer)	47.5
Tennessee ball clay #1	23.5
Whiting	21.0
Spodumene	6.0
Strontium carbonate	2.0
Add:	
Bentonite	1.0
C.M.C.	1 tsp.

SG-102

Opaque White Dry Matt Glaze   Cone 7
leadless, opaque, dry matt, nontoxic

Mixing. Mix in the manner of SG-1.

Application. Apply in the manner of SG-1.

Firing. Fire in the manner of SG-1.

Fired Results. This glaze fires to an opaque white dry matt at cone 7.

Feldspar (Custer)	48.0
Kaolin	27.5
Whiting	19.5
Spodumene	4.0
Bentonite	1.0
Add:	
C.M.C.	1 tsp.

SG-103

Clear Base Semi-Gloss Glaze   Cone 8
barium, transparent, semi-gloss, toxic

Mixing. Mix in the manner of SG-3.

Application. Apply in the manner of SG-3.

Firing. Glazes which mature at cone 8 and above should probably be fired in a nonelectric kiln, especially if they are to be fired in reduction. Reduction firing in electric kilns tends to destroy the elements rather quickly.

Fired Results. This glaze fires to a clear semi-gloss at cone 8, oxidation or reduction. The best colorants for this glaze are coppers, irons, and chromes.

Barium carbonate	24.6
Lithium carbonate	3.0
Nickel oxide	1.6
Zinc oxide	17.1
Feldspar (Custer)	31.7
Kaolin	2.1
Silica	14.2
Whiting	4.7
Bentonite	1.0

SG-104　**Clear Base Semi-Gloss Glaze　Cone 8**
barium, transparent, semi-gloss, toxic

Mixing. Mix in the manner of SG-3.

Application. Apply in the manner of SG-3.

Firing. Fire in the manner of SG-103.

Fired Results. This glaze fires to a clear semi-gloss at cone 8, oxidation or reduction. The best colorants for this base are copper and iron.

Barium carbonate	18.7
Lithium carbonate	5.3
Zinc oxide	23.1
Feldspar (Custer)	13.2
Kaolin	8.6
Titanium dioxide	2.7
Silica	22.7
Whiting	4.4
Bentonite	1.0
Add:	
For Gray Glaze	
Copper carbonate	1.0
For Brown Glaze	
Nickel carbonate	2.0
Cobalt carbonate	1.0

SG-105　**Opaque Black Semi-Gloss Glaze　Cone 8**
leadless, opaque, semi-gloss, nontoxic

Mixing. Mix in the manner of SG-1.

Application. Apply in the manner of SG-1.

Firing. Fire in the manner of SG-103.

Fired Results. This glaze fires to a very dark olive in oxidation and an opaque black in reduction in cone 8.

Feldspar (Custer)	43.0
Silica	19.0
Whiting	13.0
Kaolin	11.5
Black iron oxide	9.0
Zinc oxide	2.0
Magnesium carbonate	2.5
Add:	
Bentonite	1.0
C.M.C.	1 tsp.

SG-106　**Translucent Light-Blue Gloss Glaze　Cone 8**
raw alkaline, translucent, gloss, nontoxic

Mixing. This glaze should be dry-ground and only the amount needed should be mixed with water.

Application. Apply in the manner of SG-1.

Firing. Fire in the manner of SG-103.

Fired Results. In oxidation this glaze is a light blue gloss; in reduction it is a broken white with brown-and-black markings.

Feldspar (Kona F-4)	25.0
Boric acid	24.0
Silica	12.1
Sodium carbonate	9.7
Sodium bicarbonate	9.7
Kaolin	9.4
Magnesium carbonate	1.6
Whiting	3.0
Strontium carbonate	2.7
Tin oxide	2.5
Copper carbonate	0.3

SG-107　**Transparent Light-Blue Smooth Glaze　Cone 8**
barium, transparent, smooth gloss, toxic

Mixing. Mix in the manner of SG-3.

Application. Apply in the manner of SG-3.

Firing. Fire in the manner of SG-103.

Fired Results. This is primarily an oxidation glaze. It fires to a transparent light blue at cone 8. In reduction it is rather unattractive.

Barium carbonate	18.6
Zinc oxide	19.7
Feldspar (Custer)	49.4
Silica	12.3
Add:	
Nickel carbonate	3.2
Bentonite	1.0
C.M.C.	1 tsp.

SG-108

Opaque Chocolate-Brown Semi-Gloss Glaze   Cone 8
Courtesy of Neil Nulton, Branson, Missouri
leadless, opaque, semi-gloss, nontoxic

Mixing. Mix in the manner of SG-1.

Application. Apply in the manner of SG-1.

Firing. Fire in the manner of SG-103.

Fired Results. This glaze fires to an opaque chocolate-brown gloss at cone 8 oxidation or reduction.

Cornwall stone	330.0
Whiting	40.0
Dolomite	74.0
Bone ash	20.0
Magnesium carbonate	40.0
Kaolin (Georgia)	130.0
Rutile (milled)	32.0
Red iron oxide	13.0

SG-109

Opaque Saturated-Iron Brown Gloss Glaze   Cone 4–8
Courtesy of Kay and Rick West, Jasper, Arkansas
colemanite, opaque, gloss, nontoxic

Mixing. Mix in the manner of SG-1.

Application. Apply in the manner of SG-1.

Firing. Fire in the manner of SG-103.

Fired Results. This glaze fires to a saturated-iron brown gloss in oxidation.

Colemanite	50.0
Kaolin (EPK)	15.0
Silica	35.0
Ferro frit #3134	15.0
Tin oxide	5.0

SG-110

Opaque Gray-Brown Gloss Glaze   Cone 8
leadless, opaque, gloss, nontoxic

Mixing. Mix in the manner of SG-1.

Application. Apply in the manner of SG-1.

Firing. Fire in the manner of SG-103

Fired Results. This glaze fires to an opaque gray-brown gloss at cone 8; in reduction it is a darker grayed brown.

Feldspar (Custer)	55.5
Silica	24.5
Red iron oxide	9.0
Whiting	6.5
Kaolin	3.4
Bentonite	1.1
Add:	
C.M.C.	1 tsp.

SG-111

Opaque Metallic-Brown Matt Glaze   Cone 8
leadless, opaque, matt, nontoxic

Mixing. Mix in the manner of SG-1.

Application. Apply in the manner of SG-1.

Firing. Fire in the manner of SG-103.

Fired Results. This glaze fires to a red-brown at cone 8 oxidation; in reduction it is a metallic black semi-matt.

Hardwood ash	47.0
Yellow ochre	43.0
Whiting	9.0
Magnesium carbonate	1.0
Add:	
Bentonite	1.0
C.M.C.	1 tsp.

SG-112

Opaque Red-Brown Semi-Gloss Glaze   Cone 8
leadless, opaque, semi-gloss, nontoxic

Mixing. Mix in the manner of SG-1.

Application. Apply in the manner of SG-1.

Firing. Fire in the manner of SG-103.

Fired Results. This glaze fires to a rich red-brown in both oxidation and reduction at cone 8.

Feldspar (Custer)	30.7
Silica	23.5
Whiting	10.4
Strontium carbonate	5.3
Magnesium dioxide	11.3
Rutile	8.6
Kaolin	7.5
Vanadium stain	1.4
Yellow ochre	
Bentonite	1.0

SG-113　　**Opaque Red-Brown Matt Glaze　Cone 8**
leadless, opaque, matt, nontoxic

Mixing. Mix in the manner of SG-1.

Application. Apply in the manner of SG-1.

Firing. Fire in the manner of SG-103.

Fired Results. This glaze fires to a rich red-brown in oxidation; in reduction it is a metallic brown of great beauty.

Feldspar (Kingman)	50.0
Silica	18.3
Kaolin	16.8
Iron oxide	9.0
Whiting	5.0
Magnesium carbonate	0.9
Add:	
Bentonite	1.0
C.M.C.	1 tsp.

SSG-114　　**Clear Gloss Glaze　Cone 8**
colemanite-barium, transparent, gloss, toxic

Mixing. Mix in the manner of SG-3.

Application. Apply in the manner of SG-3.

Firing. Fire in the manner of SG-103.

Fired Results. This glaze fires to a clear gloss at cone 8; it tends to be quite fluid if overfired to the cone 9 range.

Whiting	10.0
Colemanite	12.0
Barium carbonate	8.0
Magnesium carbonate	5.0
Feldspar (potash)	30.0
Silica	30.0
Kaolin	5.0

SSG-115　　**Clear Gloss Glaze　Cone 8**
leadless, transparent, gloss, nontoxic

Mixing. Mix in the manner of SG-1.

Application. Apply in the manner of SG-1.

Firing. Fire in the manner of SG-103.

Fired Results. This glaze fires to a clear gloss at cone 8 oxidation or reduction.

Lepidolite	47.5
Whiting	18.5
Silica	33.0
Magnesium carbonate	1.0
Add:	
Bentonite	2.0
C.M.C.	1 tsp.

SSG-116　　**Clear Gloss Glaze　Cone 8**
leadless, transparent, gloss, nontoxic

Mixing. Mix in the manner of SG-1.

Application. Apply in the manner of SG-1.

Firing. Fire in the manner of SG-103.

Fired Results. This glaze fires to a bright clear gloss at cone 8 oxidation or reduction. It is a good base for most colorants.

Feldspar (Kingman)	28.5
Magnesium carbonate	2.2
Whiting	18.6
Kaolin	16.2
Silica	33.5
Bentonite	2.0

SSG-117　　**Clear Crackle Gloss Glaze　Cone 8**
leadless, transparent, crackle gloss, nontoxic

Mixing. Mix in the manner of SG-1.

Application. Apply in the manner of SG-1.

Firing. Fire in the manner of SG-103.

Fired Results. This glaze fires to a clear gloss at cone 8 oxidation or reduction. It generally forms beautiful crackle patterns over most clay bodies.

Feldspar (Oxford)	37.2
Whiting	10.4
Strontium carbonate	8.3
Cornwall stone	18.6
Tennessee ball clay #1	18.8
Zinc oxide	6.5
Bentonite	2.0

SG-118

Transparent Gloss Glaze   Cone 8
leadless, transparent, gloss, nontoxic

Mixing. Mix in the manner of SG-1.

Application. Apply in the manner of SG-1.

Firing. Fire in the manner of SG-103.

Fired Results. This glaze fires to a transparent gloss in oxidation at cone 8; in reduction it takes on a tan hue but still remains transparent.

Feldspar (Kingman)	45.8
Whiting	10.3
Strontium carbonate	6.3
Zinc oxide	13.7
Silica	11.5
Kaolin	8.6
Tin oxide	3.1
Titanium dioxide	1.7

SG-119

Clear Gloss Fluid Glaze   Cone 8
leadless, transparent, gloss, nontoxic

Mixing. Mix in the manner of SG-1.

Application. Apply in the manner of SG-1.

Firing. Fire in the manner of SG-103.

Fired Results. This glaze fires to a clear gloss at cone 8 oxidation or reduction. In both cases it tends to be rather fluid, giving some rather exotic effects over darker clay bodies.

Feldspar (Custer)	57.0
Whiting	10.0
Zinc oxide	11.0
Silica	10.0
Tennessee ball clay #1	7.5
Kaolin	1.5
Magnesium carbonate	2.0
Bentonite	1.0

SG-120

Clear Gloss Glaze   Cone 8
colemanite, transparent, gloss, nontoxic

Mixing. Mix in the manner of SG-1.

Application. Apply in the manner of SG-1.

Firing. Fire in the manner of SG-103.

Fired Results. This glaze fires to a clear gloss in both oxidation and reduction. It is somewhat fluid at a hard cone 8.

Feldspar (Custer)	62.6
Colemanite	28.1
Whiting	3.0
Kaolin	6.1
Magnesium carbonate	0.2
Add:	
Bentonite	1.0
C.M.C.	1 tsp.

SG-121

Clear Semi-Gloss Glaze   Cone 8
barium, transparent, semi-gloss, toxic

Mixing. Mix in the manner of SG-3.

Application. Apply in the manner of SG-3.

Firing. Fire in the manner of SG-103.

Fired Results. This glaze fires to a clear gloss in both oxidation and reduction at cone 8.

Feldspar (Kona F-4)	42.7
Whiting	12.1
Strontium carbonate	5.2
Kaolin (calcined)	12.5
Silica	8.7
Colemanite	9.0
Barium carbonate	5.8
Kaolin	4.1
Add:	
Bentonite	1.0

SG-122

Clear Semi-Matt Glaze   Cone 8
leadless, transparent, semi-matt, nontoxic

Mixing. Mix in the manner of SG-1.

Application. Apply in the manner of SG-1.

Firing. Fire in the manner of SG-103.

Fired Results. This glaze fires to a semitransparent semi-matt at cone 8 oxidation or reduction.

Feldspar (Custer)	46.4
Zinc oxide	23.0
Whiting	12.2
Strontium carbonate	4.0
Silica	13.4
Magnesium carbonate	0.9
Add:	
Bentonite	1.0
C.M.C.	1 tsp.

SG-123 **Clear Matt Glaze   Cone 8**
leadless, transparent, matt, nontoxic

Mixing. Mix in the manner of SG-1.

Application. Apply in the manner of SG-1.

Firing. Fire in the manner of SG-103.

Fired Results. This glaze fires to a clear matt in both oxidation and reduction.

Nepheline syenite	41.0
Silica	29.0
Whiting	19.0
Kaolin (EPK)	9.0
Magnesium carbonate	2.0
Add:	
Bentonite	1.0
C.M.C.	1 tsp.

SG-124 **Clear Matt Glaze   Cone 8**
leadless, transparent, matt, nontoxic

Mixing. Mix in the manner of SG-1.

Application. Apply in the manner of SG-1.

Firing. Fire in the manner of SG-103.

Fired Results. This glaze fires to a clear matt at cone 8 oxidation or reduction.

Volcanic ash	37.4
Silica	28.1
Whiting	18.6
Kaolin	9.3
Magnesium carbonate	4.8
Bentonite	1.8

SG-125 **Clear Dry Matt Glaze   Cone 8**
leadless, transparent, dry matt, nontoxic

Mixing. Mix in the manner of SG-1.

Application. Apply in the manner of SG-1.

Firing. Fire in the manner of SG-103.

Fired Results. This glaze fires to a clear dry matt at cone 8 oxidation or reduction. It is a good base for earth colors and is best used on rustic types of pottery.

Feldspar (potash)	14.0
Magnesium carbonate	2.0
Whiting	9.7
Alumina oxide	8.8
Kaolin	13.0
Silica	50.5
Add:	
Bentonite	1.0
C.M.C.	1 tsp.

SG-126 **Clear Stony Matt Glaze   Cone 8**
leadless, transparent, matt, nontoxic

Mixing. Mix in the manner of SG-1.

Application. Apply in the manner of SG-1.

Firing. Fire in the manner of SG-103.

Fired Results. This glaze fires to a clear stony matt at cone 8 reduction or oxidation.

Nepheline syenite	37.4
Whiting	28.1
Silica	18.6
Kaolin	9.3
Magnesium carbonate	4.8
Bentonite	1.8

SG-127 **Opaque Cream Dry Matt   Cone 8**
leadless, opaque, dry matt, nontoxic

Mixing. Mix in the manner of SG-1.

Application. Apply in the manner of SG-1.

Firing. Fire in the manner of SG-103.

Fired Results. This glaze fires to an opaque cream in oxidation and tan in reduction.

Feldspar (Kingman)	35.5
Whiting	10.6
Strontium carbonate	10.0
Kaolin	18.6
Silica	14.9
Rutile	3.8
Magnesium carbonate	4.8
Bentonite	1.8

SG-128

Translucent Cream Gloss Glaze   Cone 8
alkaline-frit, translucent, gloss, nontoxic

Mixing. Mix in the manner of SG-1.

Application. Apply in the manner of SG-1.

Firing. Fire in the manner of SG-103.

Fired Results. This glaze fires to a translucent cream gloss in oxidation and slightly darker in reduction. It iron spots well over darker bodies.

Pemco frit #54	24.9
Rutile	9.7
Whiting	14.0
Kaolin	28.6
Silica	22.8
Add:	
Ultrox	2.0
Bentonite	2.0

SG-129

Translucent Cream Gloss Glaze   Cone 8
leadless, translucent, gloss, nontoxic

Mixing. Mix in the manner of SG-1.

Application. Apply in the manner of SG-1.

Firing. Fire in the manner of SG-103.

Fired Results. This glaze fires to a cream gloss at cone 8 oxidation and cream-tan in reduction.

Nepheline syenite	22.8
Talc	32.8
Titanium dioxide	10.0
Whiting	11.0
Kaolin	16.9
Magnesium carbonate	4.7
Bentonite	

SG-130

Opaque Reduction Gray Semi-Gloss Glaze   Cone 8
barium, opaque, semi-gloss, toxic

Mixing. Mix in the manner of SG-3.

Application. Apply in the manner of SG-3.

Firing. Fire in the manner of SG-103.

Fired Results. This glaze fires to a grayed pink in oxidation and gray in reduction.

Feldspar (Custer)	33.2
Silica	24.3
Whiting	9.6
Barium carbonate	8.5
Rutile	6.3
Tin oxide	5.5
Ultrox	4.2
Kaolin (calcined)	3.5
Colemanite	4.1
Cobalt carbonate	3.0

SG-131

Opaque Charcoal-Gray Gloss Glaze   Cone 8
leadless, opaque, gloss, nontoxic

Mixing. Mix in the manner of SG-1.

Application. Apply in the manner of SG-1.

Firing. Fire in the manner of SG-103.

Fired Results. This glaze fires to a gray-tan in oxidation and charcoal-gray in reduction.

Feldspar (Kingman)	66.3
Whiting	7.2
Silica	8.2
Tin oxide	5.2
Ultrox	4.0
Red iron oxide	5.8
Zinc oxide	3.2
Add:	
Bentonite	1.0
C.M.C.	1 tsp.

SG-132

Opaque Blue-Green Semi-Gloss Glaze   Cone 8
feldspathic, opaque, semi-gloss, nontoxic

Mixing. Mix in the manner of SG-1.

Application. Apply in the manner of SG-1.

Firing. Fire in the manner of SG-103.

Fired Results. This glaze fires to a mottled blue-green in oxidation and charcoal-gray in reduction.

Feldspar (Custer)	39.8
Silica	29.7
Whiting	19.8
Kaolin	10.7
Add:	
Cobalt oxide	8.9
Rutile	8.9
Vanadium pentoxide	1.3
Bentonite	2.0

SG-133

Temmoku Green Semi-Gloss Glaze   Cone 8
leadless, opaque, semi-gloss, nontoxic

Mixing. Mix in the manner of SG-1.

Application. Apply in the manner of SG-1.

Firing. Fire in the manner of SG-103.

Fired Results. This glaze fires to an opaque dark olive in oxidation and black in reduction.

Stoneware clay (sieved)	26.4
Silica	26.4
Feldspar (Custer)	24.2
Whiting	19.8
Spodumene	3.2
Add:	
Iron oxide	9.0
Bentonite	2.0

SG-134

Transparent Medium-Green Gloss Glaze   Cone 8
raw alkaline, transparent, gloss, nontoxic

Mixing. Mix in the manner of SG-1.

Application. Apply in the manner of SG-1.

Firing. Fire in the manner of SG-103.

Fired Results. This glaze fires to a medium green in oxidation and a mottled darker green in reduction.

Silica	32.7
Cornwall stone	27.4
Borax	21.6
Barium carbonate	9.0
Soda ash	4.7
Zinc oxide	4.2
Add:	
Copper carbonate	2.0
Ultrox	

SG-135

Opaque Dark-Green Satin-Matt Glaze   Cone 8
leadless, opaque, satin matt, nontoxic

Mixing. Mix in the manner of SG-1.

Application. Apply in the manner of SG-1.

Firing. Fire in the manner of SG-103.

Fired Results. This glaze fires to a dark-green satin matt in oxidation and a dark-gray metallic green in reduction.

Feldspar (Kingman)	32.5
Silica	24.7
Whiting	16.4
Rutile	9.1
Kaolin	8.2
Copper oxide	7.3
Iron oxide	1.8
Add:	
Bentonite	2.0

SG-136

Opaque Olive-Green Gloss Glaze   Cone 8
leadless, opaque, gloss, nontoxic

Mixing. Mix in the manner of SG-1.

Application. Apply in the manner of SG-1.

Firing. Fire in the manner of SG-103.

Fired Results. This glaze fires to a dark opaque olive-green in oxidation and a metallic dark brown in reduction.

Nepheline syenite	33.5
Silica	28.7
Whiting	16.0
Iron oxide	12.3
Kaolin (calcined)	8.0
Bentonite	1.5

SG-137

Opaque Tan Matt Glaze   Cone 8
leadless, opaque, matt, nontoxic

Mixing. Mix in the manner of SG-1.

Application. Apply in the manner of SG-1.

Firing. Fire in the manner of SG-103.

Fired Results. This glaze fires to a warm tan in oxidation and a slightly darker tan in reduction.

Zinc oxide	40.0
Colemanite	1.5
Feldspar (Custer)	22.5
Silica	18.0
Whiting	13.1
Rutile	5.8
Add:	
Bentonite	2.0

SG-138   **Opaque Tan Semi-Gloss Glaze**   **Cone 8**
feldspathic, opaque, semi-gloss, nontoxic

Mixing. Mix in the manner of SG-1.

Application. Apply in the manner of SG-1.

Firing. Fire in the manner of SG-103.

Fired Results. This glaze fires to a light tan in oxidation and a slightly darker shade in reduction.

Feldspar (Kingman)	54.3
Silica	17.6
Whiting	11.0
Volcanic ash	10.4
Kaolin	3.4
Rutile	3.3
Add:	
Bentonite	2.0

SG-139   **Opaque Tan Dry Matt Glaze**   **Cone 8**
barium, opaque, matt, toxic

Mixing. Mix in the manner of SG-3.

Application. Apply in the manner of SG-3.

Firing. Fire in the manner of SG-103.

Fired Results. This glaze fires to a warm tan in oxidation and gray in reduction.

Feldspar (Custer)	42.5
Barium carbonate	26.4
Kaolin	10.2
Magnesium carbonate	2.2
Rutile	7.4
Silica	6.6
Tennessee ball clay #1	3.1
Ultrox	1.5
Whiting	0.1

SG-140   **Translucent White Gloss Glaze**   **Cone 8**
leadless, translucent, gloss, nontoxic

Mixing. Mix in the manner of SG-1.

Application. Apply in the manner of SG-1.

Firing. Fire in the manner of SG-103.

Fired Results. This glaze fires to a translucent cloudy-white in oxidation or reduction. It iron spots well in reduction over darker clay bodies.

Feldspar (potash)	46.9
Zinc oxide	10.4
Lithium carbonate	4.4
Whiting	4.1
Kaolin	17.2
Silica	16.8
Add:	
Bentonite	1.0
C.M.C.	1 tsp.

SG-141   **Translucent White Gloss Glaze**   **Cone 8**
leadless, translucent, gloss, nontoxic

Mixing. Mix in the manner of SG-1.

Application. Apply in the manner of SG-1.

Firing. Fire in the manner of SG-103.

Fired Results. This glaze fires to a translucent white in oxidation or reduction.

Feldspar (potash)	65.8
Whiting	6.4
Kaolin	14.2
Silica	11.6
Magnesium carbonate	2.0
Add:	
Bentonite	1.0
C.M.C.	1 tsp.

SG-142   **Translucent Cloudy-White Gloss Glaze**   **Cone 8**
leadless, translucent, gloss, nontoxic

Mixing. Mix in the manner of SG-1.

Application. Apply in the manner of SG-1.

Firing. Fire in the manner of SG-103.

Fired Results. This glaze fires to a cloudy translucent white in oxidation or reduction. It iron spots well and makes good pastel colors when small amounts of colorants are added.

Feldspar (potash)	51.5
Zinc oxide	9.7
Whiting	8.1
Kaolin	18.0
Silica	12.7
Add:	
Bentonite	1.0
C.M.C.	1 tsp.

SG-143 **Translucent Cloudy-White Gloss Glaze   Cone 8**
alkaline-frit, translucent, gloss, nontoxic

Mixing. Mix in the manner of SG-1.

Application. Apply in the manner of SG-1.

Firing. Fire in the manner of SG-103.

Fired Results. This glaze fires to a translucent white in oxidation or reduction.

Nepheline syenite	21.0
Pemco frit #54	10.0
Magnesium carbonate	2.7
Whiting	17.3
Kaolin	23.0
Silica	26.0
Add:	
Bentonite	1.0
C.M.C.	1 tsp.

SG-144 **Translucent White Gloss Glaze   Cone 8**
colemanite-frit, translucent, gloss, nontoxic

Mixing. Mix in the manner of SG-1.

Application. Apply in the manner of SG-1.

Firing. Fire in the manner of SG-103.

Fired Results. This glaze fires to a translucent white in oxidation or reduction.

Feldspar (potash)	21.0
Ferro frit #3819	14.0
Colemanite	23.0
Kaolin	12.5
Silica	29.5
Add:	
Bentonite	1.0
C.M.C.	1 tsp.

SG-145 **Translucent Semi-Gloss Glaze   Cone 8**
leadless, translucent, semi-gloss, nontoxic

Mixing. Mix in the manner of SG-1.

Application. Apply in the manner of SG-1.

Firing. Fire in the manner of SG-103.

Fired Results. This glaze fires to a translucent semi-gloss in oxidation or reduction.

Feldspar (potash)	41.5
Magnesium carbonate	4.0
Whiting	15.7
Kaolin	5.1
Silica	27.7
Add:	
Bentonite	2.0
C.M.C.	1 tsp.

SG-146 **Translucent White Gloss Glaze   Cone 8**
barium, translucent, gloss, toxic

Mixing. Mix in the manner of SG-3.

Application. Apply in the manner of SG-3.

Firing. Fire in the manner of SG-103.

Fired Results. This glaze fires to a translucent white gloss in oxidation or reduction.

Feldspar (Custer)	28.6
Silica	27.3
Kaolin	14.6
Whiting	9.8
Zinc oxide	6.0
Dolomite	5.8
Barium carbonate	5.4
Ultrox	2.5

SG-147 **Translucent Off-White Gloss Glaze   Cone 8**
barium, translucent, gloss, toxic

Mixing. Mix in the manner of SG-3.

Application. Apply in the manner of SG-3.

Firing. Fire in the manner of SG-103.

Fired Results. This glaze fires to a translucent off-white in oxidation or reduction.

Feldspar (Custer)	30.2
Silica	28.1
Kaolin (EPK)	14.0
Whiting	9.1
Strontium carbonate	2.0
Zinc oxide	6.1
Dolomite	5.8
Barium carbonate	4.7
Add:	
Bentonite	1.0
C.M.C.	1 tsp.

SG-148

Translucent Blue-White Semi-Gloss Glaze Cone 8
colemanite, translucent, semi-gloss, nontoxic

Mixing. Mix in the manner of SG-1.

Application. Apply in the manner of SG-1.

Firing. Fire in the manner of SG-103.

Fired Results. This glaze fires to a translucent blue-white semi-gloss in oxidation or reduction.

Cornwall stone	82.0
Whiting	13.0
Spodumene	3.0
Magnesium carbonate	2.0
Add:	
Bentonite	2.0

SG-149

Translucent Egg-Shell-White Gloss Glaze Cone 8
barium, translucent, gloss, toxic

Mixing. Mix in the manner of SG-3.

Application. Apply in the manner of SG-3.

Firing. Fire in the manner of SG-103.

Fired Results. This glaze fires to a translucent egg-shell white in oxidation or reduction.

Feldspar (Custer)	28.2
Silica	28.2
Kaolin	15.0
Whiting	11.0
Zinc oxide	7.1
Dolomite	3.1
Talc	2.0
Barium carbonate	4.6
Add:	
Bentonite	1.0
C.M.C.	1 tsp.

SG-150

Translucent Off-White Gloss Glaze Cone 8
colemanite, translucent, gloss, nontoxic

Mixing. Mix in the manner of SG-1.

Application. Apply in the manner of SG-1.

Firing. Fire in the manner of SG-103.

Fired Results. This glaze fires to a translucent off-white gloss in reduction or oxidation.

Spodumene	23.6
Feldspar (Custer)	20.4
Lepidolite	17.7
Whiting	12.4
Colemanite	11.5
Cryolite	6.3
Magnesium carbonate	1.9
Bone ash	6.1
Add:	
Bentonite	1.0

SG-151

Translucent White Semi-Gloss Glaze Cone 8
leadless, translucent, semi-gloss, nontoxic

Mixing. Mix in the manner of SG-1.

Application. Apply in the manner of SG-1.

Firing. Fire in the manner of SG-103.

Fired Results. This glaze fires to a translucent white semi-gloss in oxidation or reduction.

Feldspar (Kingman)	79.0
Whiting	9.0
Silica	9.0
Magnesium carbonate	3.0
Add:	
Bentonite	1.0
C.M.C.	1 tsp.

SG-152

Translucent White Semi-Gloss Glaze Cone 8
leadless, translucent, semi-gloss, nontoxic

Mixing. Mix in the manner of SG-1.

Application. Apply in the manner of SG-1.

Firing. Fire in the manner of SG-103.

Fired Results. This glaze fires to a translucent white semi-gloss in oxidation or reduction.

Feldspar (Custer)	78.1
Whiting	1.5
Kaolin	9.4
Magnesium carbonate	2.0
Add:	
Bentonite	1.0
C.M.C.	1 tsp.

SG-153

Translucent Off-White Semi-Gloss Glaze   Cone 8
leadless, translucent, semi-gloss, nontoxic

Mixing. Mix in the manner of SG-1.

Application. Apply in the manner of SG-1.

Firing. Fire in the manner of SG-103.

Fired Results. This glaze fires to a translucent off-white gloss in oxidation or reduction.

Feldspar (Kona F-4)	45.0
Silica	34.0
Whiting	13.0
Kaolin	6.0
Dolomite	2.0
Add:	
C.M.C.	1 tsp.

SG-154

Translucent White Semi-Matt Glaze   Cone 8
leadless, translucent, semi-matt, nontoxic

Mixing. Mix in the manner of SG-1.

Application. Apply in the manner of SG-1.

Firing. Fire in the manner of SG-103.

Fired Results. This glaze fires to a translucent white semi-matt in reduction or oxidation.

Nepheline syenite	45.0
Silica	25.0
Kaolin (EPK)	19.5
Whiting	9.5
Talc	1.0
Add:	
C.M.C.	1 tsp.

SG-155

Translucent White Semi-Matt Glaze   Cone 8
leadless, translucent, semi-matt, nontoxic

Mixing. Mix in the manner of SG-1.

Application. Apply in the manner of SG-1.

Firing. Fire in the manner of SG-103.

Fired Results. This glaze fires to a white semi-matt in oxidation or reduction.

Feldspar (Custer)	41.6
Whiting	18.0
Cornwall stone	18.5
Tennessee ball clay #1	18.5
Ultrox	3.4
Add:	
C.M.C.	1 tsp.

SG-156

Translucent White Matt Glaze   Cone 8
lead, translucent, matt, toxic

Mixing. Mix in the manner of SG-3.

Application. Apply in the manner of SG-3.

Firing. Fire in the manner of SG-103.

Fired Results. This glaze fires to a translucent white cloudy matt in oxidation or reduction.

White lead	40.9
Feldspar (Custer)	28.2
Kaolin	13.6
Whiting	8.0
Silica	4.5
Ultrox	4.8
Add:	
Bentonite	1.5
C.M.C.	1 tsp.

SG-157

Semi-Opaque Gloss Glaze   Cone 8
leadless, semi-opaque, gloss, nontoxic

Mixing. Mix in the manner of SG-1.

Application. Apply in the manner of SG-1.

Firing. Fire in the manner of SG-103.

Fired Results. This glaze fires to a semi-opaque gloss white at cone 8 in oxidation or reduction.

Whiting	7.5
Magnesium carbonate	10.0
Feldspar (Custer)	51.0
Kaolin	7.5
Silica	19.0
Ultrox	5.0
Add:	
Bentonite	2.0
C.M.C.	1 tsp.

SG-158

Semi-Opaque White Gloss Glaze   Cone 8
leadless, semi-opaque, gloss, nontoxic

Mixing. Mix in the manner of SG-1.

Application. Apply in the manner of SG-1.

Firing. Fire in the manner of SG-103.

Fired Results. This glaze fires to a semi-opaque white gloss at cone 8 reduction. It is also white in oxidation.

Feldspar (Custer)	50.0
Kaolin	8.0
Silica	24.0
Zircopax	12.0
Colemanite	16.0
Talc	16.0
Dolomite	8.0

SG-159

Opaque White Gloss Glaze   Cone 8
alkaline-frit, opaque, gloss, nontoxic

Mixing. Mix in the manner of SG-1.

Application. Apply in the manner of SG-1.

Firing. Fire in the manner of SG-103.

Fired Results. This glaze fires to an opaque white in oxidation. In reduction it is a darker off-white.

Pemco frit #54	14.4
Lithium carbonate	5.1
Magnesium carbonate	4.6
Whiting	27.1
Kaolin (calcined)	21.0
Kaolin	22.8
Silica	5.0
Add:	
Bentonite	1.0

SG-160

Opaque White Semi-Gloss Glaze   Cone 8
leadless, opaque, semi-gloss, nontoxic

Mixing. Mix in the manner of SG-1.

Application. Apply in the manner of SG-1.

Firing. Fire in the manner of SG-103.

Fired Results. This glaze fires to an opaque white semi-gloss at cone 8 oxidation. It is slightly darker in reduction.

Feldspar (Custer)	32.6
Silica	32.7
Dolomite	15.0
Kaolin	8.6
Whiting	5.7
Ultrox	5.4
Add:	
Bentonite	1.0

SG-161

Opaque White Semi-Gloss Glaze   Cone 8
leadless, opaque, semi-gloss, nontoxic

Mixing. Mix in the manner of SG-1.

Application. Apply in the manner of SG-1.

Firing. Fire in the manner of SG-103.

Fired Results. This glaze fires to a creamy buttery white in oxidation and slightly darker in reduction.

Feldspar (Custer)	38.0
Silica	20.8
Whiting	16.2
Kaolin (calcined)	8.3
Kaolin (EPK)	8.2
Spodumene	2.8
Magnesium carbonate	3.3
Ultrox	2.4
Add:	
Bentonite	1.0

SG-162

Opaque White Semi-Matt Glaze   Cone 8
leadless, opaque, semi-matt, nontoxic

Mixing. Mix in the manner of SG-1.

Application. Apply in the manner of SG-1.

Firing. Fire in the manner of SG-103.

Fired Results. This glaze fires to an opaque white in oxidation or reduction.

Feldspar (Kingman)	39.0
Silica	28.0
Whiting	10.0
Strontium carbonate	9.0
Kaolin (EPK)	10.0
Ultrox	5.0
Add:	
C.M.C.	1 tsp.

SG-163

Opaque White Gloss Glaze   Cone 8
Courtesy of Kay and Rick West, Jasper, Arkansas
colemanite, opaque, gloss, nontoxic

Mixing. Mix in the manner of SG-1.

Application. Apply in the manner of SG-1.

Firing. Fire in the manner of SG-103.

Fired Results. This glaze fires to an opaque white gloss
in oxidation or reduction.

Colemanite	50.0
Kaolin (EPK)	15.0
Silica	35.0
Tin oxide	5.0

SG-164

Opaque White Matt Glaze   Cone 8
colemanite, opaque, matt, nontoxic

Mixing. Mix in the manner of SG-1.

Application. Apply in the manner of SG-1.

Firing. Fire in the manner of SG-103.

Fired Results. This glaze fires to an opaque matt white
in oxidation or reduction.

Feldspar (Custer)	42.5
Silica	19.2
Talc	14.5
Colemanite	12.0
Dolomite	7.6
Kaolin	4.2
Add:	
Bentonite	1.0

SG-165

Opaque White Matt Glaze   Cone 8–10
Courtesy of Sue Garner, Springfield, Missouri
leadless, opaque, matt, nontoxic

Mixing. Mix in the manner of SG-1.

Application. Apply in the manner of SG-1.

Firing. Fire in the manner of SG-103.

Fired Results. This glaze fires to an opaque white matt
reduction at cone 8–10.

Dolomite	9.7
Talc	27.8
Nepheline syenite	22.6
Ball clay	11.2
Silica	26.5
Add:	
Zinc oxide	2.0
Superpax	6.0

SG-166

Opaque White Matt Glaze   Cone 8–10
Courtesy of Sue Garner, Springfield, Missouri
leadless, opaque, matt, nontoxic

Mixing. Mix in the manner of SG-1.

Application. Apply in the manner of SG-1.

Firing. Fire in the manner of SG-103.

Fired Results. This glaze fires to an opaque white in
oxidation or reduction.

Feldspar (Custer)	48.9
Kaolin (Georgia)	25.1
Dolomite	28.9
Add:	
Superpax	6.0

SG-167

Opaque White Matt Glaze   Cone 8
leadless, opaque, nontoxic

Mixing. Mix in the manner of SG-1.

Application. Apply in the manner of SG-1.

Firing. Fire in the manner of SG-103.

Fired Results. This glaze fires to an opaque white matt
in oxidation or reduction.

Feldspar (Custer)	37.2
Whiting	28.0
Silica	18.7
Kaolin (EPK)	9.3
Magnesium carbonate	4.7
Bentonite	1.9

SG-168

Opaque White Dry Matt Glaze   Cone 8
leadless, opaque, dry matt, nontoxic

Mixing. Mix in the manner of SG-1.

Application. Apply in the manner of SG-1.

Firing. Fire in the manner of SG-103.

Fired Results. This glaze fires to an opaque white dry matt in oxidation or reduction.

Feldspar (Custer)	61.5
Kaolin	23.1
Whiting	7.7
Ultrox	5.8
Bentonite	1.9
Add:	
C.M.C.	1 tsp.

SG-169

Medium-Yellow Matt Glaze   Cone 8
colemanite, translucent, matt, nontoxic

Mixing. Mix in the manner of SG-1.

Application. Apply in the manner of SG-1.

Firing. Fire in the manner of SG-103.

Fired Results. This glaze fires to a medium yellow in oxidation. In reduction it is a little darker and iron spots well.

Volcanic ash	38.5
Colemanite	21.1
Kaolin	7.7
Silica	27.0
Bentonite	1.9
Magnesium carbonate	3.8
Add:	
C.M.C.	1 tsp.

SG-170

Opaque Ochre-Yellow Dry Matt Glaze   Cone 8
leadless, opaque, dry matt, nontoxic

Mixing. Mix in the manner of SG-1.

Application. Apply in the manner of SG-1.

Firing. Fire in the manner of SG-103.

Fired Results. This glaze fires to an opaque ochre-yellow dry matt in oxidation; in reduction it is a grayed brown.

Feldspar (Custer)	38.0
Kaolin	26.1
Whiting	18.5
Silica	13.0
Spodumene	4.4
Add:	
Rutile	8.0
Yellow ochre	1.0
C.M.C.	1 tsp.

SG-171

River-Wheat Yellow Satin-Matt Glaze   Cone 8
Courtesy of Rick and Kay West, Jasper, Arkansas
leadless-slip, opaque, satin matt, nontoxic

Mixing. Mix in the manner of SG-1.

Application. Apply in the manner of SG-1.

Firing. Fire in the manner of SG-103.

Fired Results. This glaze fires to a wheat-yellow satin matt at cone 8 oxidation. In reduction it is an iron spotted yellow.

Albany slip	79.0
Lithium carbonate	7.0
Ultrox	12.0

SG-172

Ochre-Yellow Dry Matt Glaze   Cone 8
leadless, opaque, dry matt, nontoxic

Mixing. Mix in the manner of SG-1.

Application. Apply in the manner of SG-1.

Firing. Fire in the manner of SG-103.

Fired Results. This glaze fires to an opaque dry matt ochre yellow in oxidation; it is darker and spotted in reduction.

Whiting	44.5
Kaolin	40.2
Silica	4.5
Vanadium pentoxide	6.3
Red iron oxide	4.5
Add:	
Bentonite	1.0

SG-173 **Yellow Cratered Glaze   Cone 8**
leadless, opaque, crater, nontoxic

Mixing. Mix in the manner of SG-1.

Application. Apply in the manner of SG-1.

Firing. Fire in the manner of SG-103.

Fired Results. This glaze fires to an opaque yellow cratered surface in oxidation and darker in reduction.

Feldspar (Custer)	49.7
Talc	12.9
Whiting	9.9
Kaolin	3.0
Silica	17.9
Vanadium stain	4.7
Yellow ochre	0.9
Bentonite	1.0

SG-174 **Yellow Cratered Glaze   Cone 8**
leadless, opaque, crater, nontoxic

Mixing. Mix in the manner of SG-1.

Application. Apply in the manner of SG-1.

Firing. Fire in the manner of SG-103.

Fired Results. This glaze fires to an opaque yellow cratered glaze in oxidation, darker in reduction.

Feldspar (Custer)	62.3
Colemanite	5.9
Silica	27.0
Spodumene	4.8
Add:	
Bentonite	2.0
C.M.C.	1 tsp.

SG-175 **Translucent Amber Semi-Gloss Glaze   Cone 9**
leadless, translucent, semi-gloss, nontoxic

Mixing. Mix in the manner of SG-1.

Application. Apply in the manner of SG-1.

Firing. Fire in the manner of SG-103.

Fired Results. This glaze fires to an amber semi-gloss in oxidation and slightly darker in reduction.

Nepheline syenite	42.1
Silica	27.1
Dolomite	9.3
Whiting	7.5
Talc	6.5
Add:	
Bentonite	2.8
Red iron oxide	1.0
Rutile	1.0
Magnesium carbonate	0.9

SG-176 **Opaque Black Gloss Glaze   Cone 9**
leadless, opaque, gloss, nontoxic

Mixing. Mix in the manner of SG-1.

Application. Apply in the manner of SG-1.

Firing. Fire in the manner of SG-103.

Fired Results. This glaze fires to an opaque black gloss in oxidation or reduction.

Feldspar (Custer)	42.1
Silica	21.0
Whiting	14.7
Kaolin	10.0
Red iron oxide	9.0
Ultrox	2.2
Magnesium carbonate	1.0

SG-177 **Opaque Black Semi-Gloss Glaze   Cone 9**
leadless, opaque, semi-gloss, nontoxic

Mixing. Mix in the manner of SG-1.

Application. Apply in the manner of SG-1.

Firing. Fire in the manner of SG-103.

Fired Results. This glaze fires to an opaque black semi-gloss, oxidation or reduction.

Feldspar (Custer)	31.2
Silica	25.1
Whiting	14.6
Kaolin	11.1
Black iron oxide	9.5
Volcanic ash	3.9
Magnesium carbonate	2.8
Bentonite	1.8

SG-178   **Iron-Saturated Base Glaze Cone 9-10**
leadless, opaque, semi-gloss, nontoxic

Mixing. Mix in the manner of SG-1.

Application. Apply in the manner of SG-1.

Firing. Fire in the manner of SG-103.

Fired Results. This glaze fires to a saturated-iron red-brown in oxidation and slightly darker in reduction.

Feldspar (Buckingham)	54.0
Silica	22.5
Kaolin	6.0
Whiting	13.0
Barium carbonate	2.5
Zinc oxide	2.5
Add:	
Red iron oxide	5.0

SG-179   **Dark Brown Stony Matt Glaze Cone 9**
leadless, translucent, dark brown, nontoxic

Mixing. Mix in the manner of SG-1.

Application. Apply in the manner of SG-1.

Firing. Fire in the manner of SG-103.

Fired Results. This glaze fires to a dark brown stony matt in oxidation and darker in reduction.

Tennessee ball clay #1	25.5
Kentucky ball clay #4	19.0
Nepheline syenite	9.0
Bentonite	1.0
Add:	
C.M.C.	1 tsp.

SG-180   **Stony Matt Dark Brown Glaze Cone 9**
leadless, opaque, stony matt, nontoxic

Mixing. Mix in the manner of SG-1.

Application. Apply in the manner of SG-1.

Firing. Fire in the manner of SG-103.

Fired Results. This glaze fires to a dark brown stony matt in oxidation and a grayed darker brown in reduction.

Tennessee ball clay #1	22.0
Kentucky ball clay #4	22.0
Barnard slip	45.5
Nepheline syenite	9.0
Bentonite	1.5
Add:	
C.M.C.	1 tsp.

SG-181   **Chocolate-Brown Smooth-Matt Glaze Cone 9**
alkaline, opaque, smooth matt, nontoxic

Mixing. Mix in the manner of SG-1.

Application. Apply in the manner of SG-1.

Firing. Fire in the manner of SG-103.

Fired Results. This glaze fires to a chocolate-brown smooth matt in oxidation or reduction.

Sodium silicofluoride	10.1
Whiting	3.9
Kaolin	15.8
Kaolin (calcined)	10.8
Silica	59.4
Add:	
Manganese dioxide	20.0

SG-182   **Opaque Brown Gloss Glaze Cone 9**
leadless, opaque, gloss, nontoxic

Mixing. Mix in the manner of SG-1.

Application. Apply in the manner of SG-1.

Firing. Fire in the manner of SG-103.

Fired Results. This glaze fires to an opaque medium brown in oxidation and slightly darker in reduction.

Silica	42.2
Feldspar (Custer)	32.8
Whiting	13.5
Kaolin	11.5
Add:	
Iron oxide	4.2
Rutile	4.2
C.M.C.	1 tsp.

SG-183　**Opaque Yellow-Brown Fluid Matt Glaze　Cone 9**
leadless, opaque, matt, nontoxic

Mixing. Mix in the manner of SG-1.

Application. Apply in the manner of SG-1.

Firing. Fire in the manner of SG-103.

Fired Results. This glaze fires to an opaque yellow-brown matt in oxidation and a mottled darker brown in reduction.

Feldspar (Kingman)	42.3
Kaolin	20.1
Whiting	19.5
Red iron oxide	6.6
Talc	3.2
Bone ash	1.6
Magnesium carbonate	4.7
Bentonite	2.0

SG-184　**Transparent Buff Gloss Glaze　Cone 9**
leadless, transparent, gloss, nontoxic

Mixing. Mix in the manner of SG-1.

Application. Apply in the manner of SG-1.

Firing. Fire in the manner of SG-103.

Fired Results. This glaze fires to a transparent buff gloss in oxidation and lighter buff in reduction with occasional tints of green in the recessed areas of the ware.

Feldspar (Kona F-4)	34.0
Silica	19.0
Dolomite	15.0
Kaolin	9.0
Volcanic ash	10.0
Wood ash	7.0
Magnesium carbonate	3.0
Rutile	1.0
Bentonite	2.0

SG-185　**Opaque Blue Gloss Glaze　Cone 9**
colemanite, opaque, gloss, nontoxic

Mixing. Mix in the manner of SG-1.

Application. Apply in the manner of SG-1.

Firing. Fire in the manner of SG-103.

Fired Results. This glaze fires to an opaque blue gloss in oxidation and a slightly darker blue in reduction which iron spots well on darker bodies.

Feldspar (Custer)	19.2
Colemanite	22.6
Pemco frit #25	15.7
Kaolin	13.4
Silica	29.1

SG-186　**Opaque Light-Blue Semi-Matt Glaze　Cone 9**
leadless, opaque, semi-matt, nontoxic

Mixing. Mix in the manner of SG-1.

Application. Apply in the manner of SG-1.

Firing. Fire in the manner of SG-103.

Fired Results. This glaze fires to a light-blue semi-matt in oxidation or reduction.

Feldspar (Custer)	38.5
Whiting	11.0
Strontium carbonate	10.0
Kaolin	19.7
Silica	15.1
Rutile	4.2
Cobalt carbonate	1.5
Add:	
Bentonite	1.0
C.M.C.	1 tsp.

SG-187　**Opaque Royal-Blue Semi-Matt Glaze　Cone 9**
leadless, opaque, semi-matt, nontoxic

Mixing. Mix in the manner of SG-1.

Application. Apply in the manner of SG-1.

Firing. Fire in the manner of SG-103.

Fired Results. This glaze fires to an opaque royal-blue semi-matt in oxidation or reduction.

Feldspar (Custer)	38.5
Whiting	16.0
Strontium carbonate	5.0
Kaolin	19.7
Silica	15.1
Titanium dioxide	4.5
Cobalt oxide	1.2
Add:	
Bentonite	1.0
C.M.C.	1 tsp.

SG-188 **Opaque Ultramarine-Blue Matt Glaze   Cone 9**
leadless, opaque, matt, nontoxic

Mixing. Mix in the manner of SG-1.

Application. Apply in the manner of SG-1.

Firing. Fire in the manner of SG-103.

Fired Results. This glaze fires to an opaque ultramarine-blue matt in oxidation or reduction.

Feldspar (Custer)	39.0
Silica	29.0
Whiting	19.3
Kaolin	7.7
Red iron oxide	7.0
Ultrox	3.9
Cobalt oxide	0.4
Add:	
Bentonite	1.0
C.M.C.	1 tsp.

SG-189 **Clear Gloss Glaze   Cone 9**
leadless, transparent, gloss, nontoxic

Mixing. Mix in the manner of SG-1.

Application. Apply in the manner of SG-1.

Firing. Fire in the manner of SG-103.

Fired Results. This glaze fires to a clear gloss in oxidation or reduction.

Silica	32.0
Whiting	20.0
Nepheline syenite	33.0
Kaolin	15.0
Add:	
Bentonite	1.0

SG-190 **Clear Gloss Glaze   Cone 9**
leadless, transparent, gloss, nontoxic

Mixing. Mix in the manner of SG-1.

Application. Apply in the manner of SG-1.

Firing. Fire in the manner of SG-103.

Fired Results. This glaze fires to a clear gloss at cone 9 oxidation or reduction.

Bismuth oxide	8.3
Feldspar (Kingman)	23.7
Magnesium carbonate	3.8
Whiting	14.1
Kaolin	15.4
Silica	34.7

SG-191 **Clear Gloss Glaze   Cone 9**
alkaline, transparent, clear gloss, nontoxic

Mixing. Mix in the manner of SG-1.

Application. Apply in the manner of SG-1.

Firing. Fire in the manner of SG-103.

Fired Results. This glaze fires to a clear gloss at cone 9 in oxidation or reduction.

Pemco frit #25	9.5
Lithium carbonate	5.0
Kaolin	24.2
Silica	61.3
Add:	
Bentonite	2.0
C.M.C.	1 tsp.

SG-192 **Clear Gloss Glaze   Cone 9**
alkaline, transparent, clear gloss, nontoxic

Mixing. Mix in the manner of SG-1.

Application. Apply in the manner of SG-1.

Firing. Fire in the manner of SG-103.

Fired Results. This glaze fires to a clear gloss in oxidation or reduction.

Pemco frit #25	14.7
Nepheline syenite	72.1
Whiting	8.2
Kaolin (EPK)	4.8
Add:	
Bentonite	2.0
C.M.C.	1 tsp.

SG-193

Clear Gloss Glaze   Cone 9
leadless, transparent, gloss, nontoxic

Mixing. Mix in the manner of SG-1.

Application. Apply in the manner of SG-1.

Firing. Fire in the manner of SG-103.

Fired Results. This glaze fires to a clear gloss in oxidation or reduction.

Feldspar (Kingman)	20.0
Tennessee ball clay #1	20.0
Whiting	19.0
Silica	30.0
Bentonite	1.0
Add:	
C.M.C.	1 tsp.

SG-194

Clear Gloss Glaze   Cone 9–10
leadless, transparent, gloss, nontoxic

Mixing. Mix in the manner of SG-1.

Application. Apply in the manner of SG-1.

Firing. Fire in the manner of SG-103.

Fired Results. This glaze fires to a clear gloss in oxidation or reduction.

Feldspar (Custer)	44.0
Whiting	20.0
Cornwall stone	20.0
Kaolin	6.0
Kaolin (calcined)	6.0
Zinc oxide	4.0
Add:	
Bentonite	1.0
C.M.C.	1 tsp.

SG-195

Clear Gloss Glaze   Cone 9–10
leadless, transparent, gloss, nontoxic

Mixing. Mix in the manner of SG-1.

Application. Apply in the manner of SG-1.

Firing. Fire in the manner of SG-103.

Fired Results. This glaze fires to a clear gloss glaze in oxidation or reduction.

Feldspar (Kona F-4)	42.0
Colemanite	12.0
Dolomite	6.0
Talc	15.0
Kaolin	5.0
Silica	20.0

SG-196

Clear Gloss Glaze   Cone 9
leadless, transparent, gloss, nontoxic

Mixing. Mix in the manner of SG-1.

Application. Apply in the manner of SG-1.

Firing. Fire in the manner of SG-103.

Fired Results. This glaze fires to a clear gloss in oxidation or reduction.

Cornwall stone	82.0
Whiting	12.0
Colemanite	2.0
Nepheline syenite	4.0
Add:	
Bentonite	2.0
C.M.C.	1 tsp.

SG-197

Clear Gloss Glaze   Cone 9
leadless, transparent, gloss, nontoxic

Mixing. Mix in the manner of SG-1.

Application. Apply in the manner of SG-1.

Firing. Fire in the manner of SG-103.

Fired Results. This glaze fires to a clear gloss in oxidation or reduction.

Feldspar (Kona F-4)	80.0
Whiting	7.0
Strontium carbonate	5.0
Zinc oxide	5.0
Spodumene	3.0
Bentonite	1.0

SG-198

Clear Fluid Gloss Glaze   Cone 9
leadless, transparent, gloss, nontoxic

Mixing. Mix in the manner of SG-1.

Application. Apply in the manner of SG-1.

Firing. Fire in the manner of SG-103.

Fired Results. This glaze fires to a clear fluid gloss in oxidation or reduction.

Nepheline syenite	54.0
Silica	27.0
Whiting	9.0
Magnesium carbonate	5.0
Colemanite	4.0
Bentonite	1.0

SG-199

Clear Gloss Glaze   Cone 9
barium, transparent, gloss, toxic

Mixing. Mix in the manner of SG-3.

Application. Apply in the manner of SG-3.

Firing. Fire in the manner of SG-103.

Fired Results. This glaze fires to a clear gloss in reduction or oxidation.

Feldspar (Kona F-4)	40.0
Silica	26.5
Whiting	6.0
Strontium carbonate	5.0
Barium carbonate	8.0
Colemanite	7.0
Kaolin	3.5
Magnesium carbonate	4.0

SG-200

Clear Semi-Gloss Glaze   Cone 9
leadless, transparent, semi-gloss, nontoxic

Mixing. Mix in the manner of SG-1.

Application. Apply in the manner of SG-1.

Firing. Fire in the manner of SG-103.

Fired Results. This glaze fires to a clear semi-gloss in oxidation or reduction.

Feldspar (Kona F-4)	47.3
Silica	28.0
Whiting	6.0
Strontium carbonate	4.0
Dolomite	6.7
Zinc oxide	5.0
Kaolin (EPK)	1.5
Spodumene	1.4

SG-201

Clear Semi-Gloss Glaze   Cone 9
leadless, transparent, semi-gloss, nontoxic

Mixing. Mix in the manner of SG-1.

Application. Apply in the manner of SG-1.

Firing. Fire in the manner of SG-103.

Fired Results. This glaze fires to a clear semi-gloss in oxidation or reduction.

Feldspar (Custer)	48.6
Silica	19.5
Whiting	13.8
Kaolin	14.3
Spodumene	2.8
Colemanite	2.0
Add:	
C.M.C.	1 tsp.

SG-202

Clear Semi-Gloss Glaze   Cone 9
barium, transparent, semi-gloss, nontoxic

Mixing. Mix in the manner of SG-1.

Application. Apply in the manner of SG-1.

Firing. Fire in the manner of SG-103.

Fired Results. This glaze fires to a clear semi-gloss in oxidation or reduction.

Feldspar (Kona F-4)	48.3
Silica	26.9
Colemanite	13.4
Barium carbonate	6.5
Whiting	2.0
Strontium carbonate	1.9

SG-203 **Gloss Patterned Glaze   Cone 9**
alkaline, translucent, patterned gloss, nontoxic

Mixing. Mix in the manner of SG-1.

Application. Apply in the manner of SG-1.

Firing. Fire in the manner of SG-103.

Fired Results. This glaze fires to a clear patterned gloss
in oxidation or reduction.

Tennessee ball clay #1	50.5
Colemanite	13.0
Whiting	36.5
Add:	
Bentonite	1.5
C.M.C.	1 tsp.

SG-204 **Clear Satin-Matt Glaze   Cone 9**
alkaline-bristol, transparent, clear matt, nontoxic

Mixing. Mix in the manner of SG-1.

Application. Apply in the manner of SG-1.

Firing. Fire in the manner of SG-103.

Fired Results. This glaze fires to a clear satin matt in
oxidation or reduction.

Tennessee ball clay #1	38.4
Kentucky ball clay #4	20.0
Colemanite	8.2
Zinc oxide	31.4
Bentonite	2.0
Add:	
C.M.C.	1 tsp.

SG-205 **Clear Satin Matt   Cone 9**
alkaline, transparent, clear satin matt, nontoxic

Mixing. Mix in the manner of SG-1.

Application. Apply in the manner of SG-1.

Firing. Fire in the manner of SG-103.

Fired Results. This glaze fires to a clear satin matt in
oxidation or reduction.

Pemco frit #54	7.5
Spodumene	47.9
Kaolin	3.5
Silica	41.1
Add:	
Bentonite	2.0
C.M.C.	1 tsp.

SG-206 **Clear Satin-Matt Glaze   Cone 9**
colemanite, transparent, satin matt, nontoxic

Mixing. Mix in the manner of SG-1.

Application. Apply in the manner of SG-1.

Firing. Fire in the manner of SG-103.

Fired Results. This glaze fires to a clear satin matt in
oxidation or reduction.

Colemanite	34.2
Kaolin	10.8
Kaolin (calcined)	15.0
Silica	40.0
Add:	
Bentonite	1.0
C.M.C.	1 tsp.

SG-207 **Opaque Mottled Cream-Matt Glaze   Cone 9**
leadless, opaque, matt, nontoxic

Mixing. Mix in the manner of SG-1.

Application. Apply in the manner of SG-1.

Firing. Fire in the manner of SG-103.

Fired Results. This glaze fires to a mottled cream matt
in oxidation and a grayed-pink cream in reduction.

Feldspar (Custer)	41.6
Kaolin	21.8
Whiting	17.0
Silica	10.0
Ultrox	6.4
Rutile	3.2
Add:	
Bentonite	1.0
C.M.C.	1 tsp.

SG-208   **Opaque Cream-Matt Glaze   Cone 9**
leadless, opaque, matt, nontoxic

Mixing. Mix in the manner of SG-1.

Application. Apply in the manner of SG-1.

Firing. Fire in the manner of SG-103.

Fired Results. This glaze fires to an opaque cream matt in oxidation and a cream-tan matt in reduction which iron spots well over darker clay bodies.

Feldspar (Custer)	41.6
Kaolin	21.8
Whiting	17.0
Silica	10.0
Ultrox	7.7
Magnesium carbonate	1.9

SG-209   **Transparent Yellow-Green Gloss Glaze   Cone 9**
colemanite-barium, transparent, gloss, toxic

Mixing. Mix in the manner of SG-1.

Application. Apply in the manner of SG-1.

Firing. Fire in the manner of SG-103.

Fired Results. This glaze fires to a transparent yellow-green gloss in oxidation and mottled light green in reduction.

Feldspar (Kona F-4)	42.8
Whiting	11.0
Strontium carbonate	6.0
Kaolin	17.0
Silica	9.0
Colemanite	8.2
Barium carbonate	5.8
Green chromium oxide	2.0
Add:	
C.M.C.	1 tsp.

SG-210   **Opaque Yellow-Orange Matt Glaze   Cone 9-10**
Courtesy of Don Curtis, University of Arkansas
leadless, opaque, matt, nontoxic

Mixing. Mix in the manner of SG-1.

Application. Apply in the manner of SG-1.

Firing. Fire in the manner of SG-103.

Fired Results. This glaze fires to an opaque yellow-orange matt in reduction. It is very attractive used with iron or rutile decoration sprayed or brushed over or under the glaze.

Feldspar (Kingman)	50.0
Kaolin (EPK)	24.0
Dolomite	16.0
Whiting	10.0
Tin oxide	5.0
Bone ash	8.0
Red iron oxide	1.0
Rutile	1.0

SG-211   **Opaque Mottled Tan-Rust Fluid Matt Glaze   Cone 9**
leadless, opaque, fluid matt, nontoxic

Mixing. Fire in the manner of SG-1.

Application. Apply in the manner of SG-1.

Firing. Fire in the manner of SG-103.

Fired Results. This glaze fires to an opaque mottled tan-rust in oxidation and a darker tan in reduction which iron spots well over darker clay bodies.

Feldspar (Custer)	44.0
Whiting	20.0
Silica	12.0
Kaolin	10.0
Rutile	8.0
Red iron oxide	3.0
Ultrox	2.0
Magnesium carbonate	2.0

SG-212   **Opaque Rust Matt Glaze   Cone 9**
leadless, opaque, matt, nontoxic

Mixing. Mix in the manner of SG-1.

Application. Apply in the manner of SG-1.

Firing. Fire in the manner of SG-103.

Fired Results. This glaze fires to an opaque rust matt in oxidation and a beautiful charcoal-gray in reduction which iron spots very well over darker clay bodies.

Feldspar (Custer)	47.9
Whiting	19.7
Kaolin (calcined)	13.3
Kaolin	13.3
Red iron oxide	3.2
Ultrox	2.0
Chrome oxide	0.6

SG-213

Tan Streaked Semi-Matt Glaze **Cone 9**
Courtesy of Pal Wright, Ottawa, Kansas
leadless, opaque, semi-matt, nontoxic

Mixing. Mix in the manner of SG-1.

Application. Apply in the manner of SG-1.

Firing. Fire in the manner of SG-103.

Fired Results. This glaze fires to a streaked tan matt in reduction.

Feldspar (Clinchfield)	43.5
Kaolin	20.9
Dolomite	13.9
Whiting	8.6
Tin oxide	4.3
Bone ash	7.0
Red iron oxide	0.9
Rutile	0.9

SG-214

Opaque Tan-Matt Glaze **Cone 9**
leadless, opaque, matt, nontoxic

Mixing. Mix in the manner of SG-1.

Application. Apply in the manner of SG-1.

Firing. Fire in the manner of SG-103.

Fired Results. This glaze fires to an opaque tan in oxidation and an off-white in reduction.

Feldspar (Kona F-4)	26.0
Whiting	20.0
Volcanic ash	19.0
Rutile	10.3
Kaolin	11.3
Silica	11.0
Ultrox	2.4
Add:	
C.M.C.	1 tsp.

SG-215

Translucent Blue-White Gloss Glaze **Cone 9**
leadless, translucent, gloss, nontoxic

Mixing. Mix in the manner of SG-1.

Application. Apply in the manner of SG-1.

Firing. Fire in the manner of SG-103.

Fired Results. This glaze fires to a blue-white translucent gloss in oxidation and a slightly grayed white in reduction.

Feldspar (Custer)	35.2
Spodumene	19.3
Silica	17.3
Colemanite	10.5
Talc	10.1
Ultrox	4.3
Boric acid	3.3

SG-216

Translucent Off-White Gloss Glaze **Cone 9**
leadless, translucent, gloss, nontoxic

Mixing. Mix in the manner of SG-1.

Application. Apply in the manner of SG-1.

Firing. Fire in the manner of SG-103.

Fired Results. This glaze fires to a translucent off-white gloss in oxidation and a darker off-white in reduction.

Cornwall stone	40.0
Silica	26.5
Kaolin	14.5
Whiting	9.0
Dolomite	4.0
Colemanite	3.0
Ultrox	3.0
Add:	
C.M.C.	1 tsp.

SG-217

Translucent White Gloss Glaze **Cone 9**
leadless, translucent, gloss, nontoxic

Mixing. Mix in the manner of SG-1.

Application. Apply in the manner of SG-1.

Firing. Fire in the manner of SG-103.

Fired Results. This glaze fires to a translucent white gloss in oxidation and clear in reduction.

Feldspar (Custer)	81.9
Whiting	8.0
Silica	7.0
Magnesium carbonate	3.1
Add:	
C.M.C.	1 tsp.

SG-218

Translucent White Gloss Glaze   Cone 9
alkaline-frit, translucent, gloss, nontoxic

Mixing. Mix in the manner of SG-1.

Application. Apply in the manner of SG-1.

Firing. Fire in the manner of SG-103.

Fired Results. This glaze fires to a translucent white gloss in oxidation and semitranslucent in reduction.

Pemco frit #54	16.0
Nepheline syenite	55.0
Whiting	29.0
Add:	
Bentonite	2.0
Ultrox	4.0

SG-219

Translucent White Gloss Glaze   Cone 9
alkaline-frit, translucent, gloss, nontoxic

Mixing. Mix in the manner of SG-1.

Application. Apply in the manner of SG-1.

Firing. Fire in the manner of SG-103.

Fired Results. This glaze fires to a translucent cloudy-white gloss in oxidation or reduction.

Pemco frit #54	12.2
Feldspar (Custer)	10.5
Magnesium carbonate	3.5
Wollastonite	10.7
Kaolin	9.7
Kaolin (calcined)	14.8
Silica	38.6

SG-220

Translucent Blue-White Semi-Gloss Glaze   Cone 9
leadless, translucent, semi-gloss, nontoxic

Mixing. Mix in the manner of SG-1.

Application. Apply in the manner of SG-1.

Firing. Fire in the manner of SG-103.

Fired Results. This glaze fires to a translucent blue-white semi-gloss in oxidation or reduction.

Silica	13.8
Feldspar (Kona F-4)	13.8
Kaolin (EPK)	15.9
Zinc oxide	10.9
Ultrox	6.0
Whiting	10.2
Bentonite	1.0

SG-221

Translucent Tan-White Semi-Gloss Glaze   Cone 9
leadless, translucent, semi-gloss, nontoxic

Mixing. Mix in the manner of SG-1.

Application. Apply in the manner of SG-1.

Firing. Fire in the manner of SG-103.

Fired Results. This glaze fires to a translucent tan-white semi-gloss and more gray in reduction.

Nepheline syenite	31.0
Silica	30.0
Whiting	19.0
Kaolin	13.0
Ultrox	5.0
Magnesium carbonate	2.0
Add:	
C.M.C.	1 tsp.

SG-222

Translucent Gray-White Semi-Gloss Glaze   Cone 9
leadless-barium, translucent, semi-gloss, toxic

Mixing. Mix in the manner of SG-3.

Application. Apply in the manner of SG-3.

Firing. Fire in the manner of SG-103.

Fired Results. This glaze fires to a translucent gray-white in oxidation and slightly darker in reduction.

Feldspar (Custer)	46.5
Barium carbonate	15.9
Tennessee ball clay #1	9.7
Silica	6.7
Whiting	6.5
Ultrox	5.9
Talc	5.5
Colemanite	1.8
Rutile	0.5
Add:	
C.M.C.	1 tsp.

SG-223 **Translucent Cloudy-White Semi-Gloss Glaze Cone 9**
leadless, translucent, semi-gloss, nontoxic

Mixing. Mix in the manner of SG-1.

Application. Apply in the manner of SG-1.

Firing. Fire in the manner of SG-103.

Fired Results. This glaze fires to a translucent cloudy white in oxidation and somewhat brighter in reduction.

Feldspar (Custer)	20.0
Colemanite	5.6
Magnesium carbonate	2.4
Whiting	9.4
Kaolin	21.6
Silica	41.0
Add:	
Bentonite	1.0
C.M.C.	1 tsp.

SG-224 **Translucent White Semi-Gloss Glaze Cone 9**
leadless, translucent, semi-gloss, nontoxic

Mixing. Mix in the manner of SG-1.

Application. Apply in the manner of SG-1.

Firing. Fire in the manner of SG-103.

Fired Results. This glaze fires to a translucent white semi-gloss in oxidation or reduction.

Spodumene	31.5
Whiting	18.5
Kaolin	6.1
Silica	43.9
Add:	
Bentonite	1.0
C.M.C.	1 tsp.

SG-225 **Translucent White Semi-Matt Glaze Cone 9**
leadless, translucent, semi-matt, nontoxic

Mixing. Mix in the manner of SG-1.

Application. Apply in the manner of SG-1.

Firing. Fire in the manner of SG-103.

Fired Results. This glaze fires to a translucent white semi-matt in oxidation or reduction.

Feldspar (Custer)	35.0
Kaolin (EPK)	22.0
Dolomite	20.0
Silica	18.0
Whiting	2.0
Talc	3.0
Add:	
Bentonite	1.0
C.M.C.	1 tsp.

SG-226 **Translucent Gray-White Semi-Matt Glaze Cone 9**
leadless, translucent, semi-matt, nontoxic

Mixing. Mix in the manner of SG-1.

Application. Apply in the manner of SG-1.

Firing. Fire in the manner of SG-103.

Fired Results. This glaze fires to a translucent gray-white semi-matt in oxidation or reduction.

Feldspar (Custer)	40.0
Whiting	18.0
Cornwall stone	18.0
Tennessee ball clay #1	20.0
Magnesium carbonate	4.0
Add:	
Bentonite	1.0
C.M.C.	1 tsp.

SG-227 **Translucent White Semi-Matt Glaze Cone 9**
leadless-barium, translucent, semi-matt, nontoxic

Mixing. Mix in the manner of SG-1.

Application. Apply in the manner of SG-1.

Firing. Fire in the manner of SG-103.

Fired Results. This glaze fires to a translucent white in oxidation or reduction and iron spots well.

Feldspar (Custer)	42.2
Silica	26.2
Colemanite	9.8
Dolomite	8.7
Barium carbonate	4.5
Ultrox	4.3
Whiting	2.6
Kaolin	1.8
Add:	
C.M.C.	1 tsp.

SG-228

Translucent Off-White Semi-Matt Glaze   Cone 9
barium, translucent, semi-matt, nontoxic

Mixing. Mix in the manner of SG-1.

Application. Apply in the manner of SG-1.

Firing. Fire in the manner of SG-103.

Fired Results. This glaze fires to a translucent off-white semi-matt in oxidation or reduction.

Nepheline syenite	71.2
Silica	8.4
Kaolin (EPK)	7.0
Dolomite	4.6
Barium carbonate	4.2
Whiting	2.0
Ultrox	2.6
Add:	
C.M.C.	1 tsp.

SG-229

Translucent White Satin-Matt Glaze   Cone 9
leadless, translucent, satin matt, nontoxic

Mixing. Mix in the manner of SG-1.

Application. Apply in the manner of SG-1.

Firing. Fire in the manner of SG-103.

Fired Results. This glaze fires to a translucent white satin matt in oxidation and is clearer in reduction.

Feldspar (Custer)	32.7
Magnesium carbonate	3.3
Wollastonite	23.0
Silica	41.0
Add:	
Bentonite	1.0
C.M.C.	1 tsp.

SG-230

Translucent White Matt Glaze   Cone 9
leadless, translucent, matt, nontoxic

Mixing. Mix in the manner of SG-1.

Application. Apply in the manner of SG-1.

Firing. Fire in the manner of SG-103.

Fired Results. This glaze fires to a translucent white matt in oxidation and a slightly grayed white in reduction.

Cornwall stone	58.0
Whiting	38.0
Magnesium carbonate	4.0
Add:	
C.M.C.	1 tsp.

SG-231

Translucent White Matt Glaze   Cone 9
leadless, translucent, matt, nontoxic

Mixing. Mix in the manner of SG-1.

Application. Apply in the manner of SG-1.

Firing. Fire in the manner of SG-103.

Fired Results. This glaze fires to a translucent white matt in oxidation and a light gray in reduction.

Nepheline syenite	40.0
Feldspar (Custer)	20.0
Whiting	35.0
Dolomite	5.0
Add:	
C.M.C.	1 tsp.

SG-232

Translucent Fluid Matt Glaze   Cone 9
leadless-ash, translucent, matt, nontoxic

Mixing. Mix in the manner of SG-1.

Application. Apply in the manner of SG-1.

Firing. Fire in the manner of SG-103.

Fired Results. This glaze fires to a translucent light tan in oxidation and an off-white in reduction.

Feldspar (Kona F-4)	36.0
Hardwood ash	28.0
Kaolin	14.0
Talc	14.0
Cornwall stone	6.0
Ultrox	2.0
Add:	
C.M.C.	1 tsp.

SG-233

Translucent Patterned Matt Glaze   Cone 9
alkaline, translucent, matt, nontoxic

Mixing. Mix in the manner of SG-1.

Application. Apply in the manner of SG-1.

Firing. Fire in the manner of SG-1.

Fired Results. This glaze fires to a translucent white patterned matt in oxidation and clear in reduction.

Tennessee ball clay #1	52.7
Borax (powdered)	7.6
Lithium carbonate	39.7
Add:	
Bentonite	2.0
C.M.C.	1 tsp.

SG-234

Translucent White Semi-Gloss Glaze   Cone 9
leadless, translucent, semi-gloss, nontoxic

Mixing. Mix in the manner of SG-1.

Application. Apply in the manner of SG-1.

Firing. Fire in the manner of SG-103.

Fired Results. This glaze fires to a translucent white semi-gloss in oxidation or reduction.

Zinc oxide	8.7
Feldspar (potash)	35.3
Strontium carbonate	10.0
Kaolin	10.8
Silica	28.6
Whiting	6.6

SG-235

Opaque White Gloss Glaze   Cone 9
leadless, opaque, gloss, nontoxic

Mixing. Mix in the manner of SG-1.

Application. Apply in the manner of SG-1.

Firing. Fire in the manner of SG-103.

Fired Results. This glaze fires to an opaque white gloss in oxidation or reduction.

Cryolite	12.2
Wollastonite	24.7
Kaolin	12.0
Silica	50.0
Magnesium carbonate	1.2

SG-236

Opaque White Gloss Glaze   Cone 9
leadless, opaque, gloss, nontoxic

Mixing. Mix in the manner of SG-1.

Application. Apply in the manner of SG-1.

Firing. Fire in the manner of SG-103.

Fired Results. This glaze fires to an opaque white gloss in oxidation and an off-white in reduction.

Feldspar (Custer)	31.0
Whiting	5.0
Zinc oxide	12.0
Kaolin	28.2
Silica	20.6
Dolomite	3.2
Add:	
C.M.C.	1 tsp.

SG-237

Opaque White Semi-Gloss Glaze   Cone 9
leadless, opaque, semi-gloss, nontoxic

Mixing. Mix in the manner of SG-1.

Application. Apply in the manner of SG-1.

Firing. Fire in the manner of SG-103.

Fired Results. This glaze fires to an opaque white semi-gloss in oxidation and a slight gray in reduction.

Silica	36.8
Feldspar (Kona F-4)	12.2
Kaolin	15.9
Zinc oxide	10.9
Whiting	10.2
Ultrox	6.0
Magnesium carbonate	2.0

SG-238

Opaque White Semi-Gloss Glaze   Cone 9
leadless, opaque, semi-gloss, nontoxic

Mixing. Mix in the manner of SG-1.

Application. Apply in the manner of SG-1.

Firing. Fire in the manner of SG-103.

Fired Results. This glaze fires to an opaque white semi-gloss in oxidation or reduction. It iron spots well in reduction.

Nepheline syenite	45.0
Silica	28.0
Dolomite	10.0
Whiting	4.0
Strontium carbonate	4.0
Talc	6.0
Kaolin	10.0
Titanium dioxide	2.0
Add:	
Ultrox	4.0
C.M.C.	1 tsp.

SG-239

Opaque White Semi-Gloss Glaze   Cone 9
barium, opaque, semi-gloss, toxic

Mixing. Mix in the manner of SG-3.

Application. Apply in the manner of SG-3.

Firing. Fire in the manner of SG-103.

Fired Results. This glaze fires to an opaque white semi-gloss in oxidation or reduction.

Feldspar (Kingman)	46.5
Barium carbonate	15.4
Tennessee ball clay #1	9.0
Silica	6.5
Whiting	6.5
Ultrox	6.4
Talc	3.5
Colemanite	3.0
Dolomite	1.8
Titanium dioxide	0.5

SG-240

Opaque Mottled White-Tan Matt Glaze   Cone 9
barium, opaque, matt, toxic

Mixing. Mix in the manner of SG-3.

Application. Apply in the manner of SG-3.

Firing. Fire in the manner of SG-103.

Fired Results. This glaze fires to an opaque mottled white-tan in oxidation and a grayed-white in reduction.

Feldspar (Custer)	45.5
Barium carbonate	18.8
Kentucky ball clay #4	8.0
Whiting	6.6
Rutile	8.5
Ultrox	7.6
Bone ash	4.6
Add:	
Bentonite	1.0
C.M.C.	1 tsp.

SG-241

Opaque White Matt Glaze   Cone 9
leadless, opaque, matt, nontoxic

Mixing. Mix in the manner of SG-1.

Application. Apply in the manner of SG-1.

Firing. Fire in the manner of SG-103.

Fired Results. This glaze fires to an opaque white matt in oxidation or reduction.

Feldspar (Custer)	41.8
Silica	18.8
Talc	15.5
Colemanite	10.9
Dolomite	7.5
Kaolin	4.0
Bone ash	1.4
Add:	
Bentonite	1.0
C.M.C.	1 tsp.

SG-242

Opaque White Matt Glaze   Cone 9
leadless, opaque, matt, nontoxic

Mixing. Mix in the manner of SG-1.

Application. Apply in the manner of SG-1.

Firing. Fire in the manner of SG-103.

Fired Results. This glaze fires to an opaque white matt in oxidation or reduction.

Feldspar (Custer)	49.7
Kaolin	27.1
Whiting	20.2
Magnesium carbonate	3.0
Add:	
C.M.C.	1 tsp.

SG-243

Opaque White Matt Glaze   Cone 9
leadless, opaque, matt, nontoxic

Mixing. Mix in the manner of SG-1.

Application. Apply in the manner of SG-1.

Firing. Fire in the manner of SG-103.

Fired Results. This glaze fires to an opaque white matt in oxidation and a gray in reduction.

Nepheline syenite	60.4
Spodumene	13.2
Silica	8.1
Kaolin	6.5
Dolomite	4.9
Whiting	2.6
Ultrox	4.3

SG-244

Opaque Opalescent White Gloss Glaze   Cone 9
leadless, opaque, gloss, nontoxic

Mixing. Mix in the manner of SG-1.

Application. Apply in the manner of SG-1.

Firing. Fire in the manner of SG-103.

Fired Results. This glaze fires to an opaque white gloss in oxidation and a mottled white gloss in reduction.

Nepheline syenite	63.5
Pemco frit #25	14.8
Vanadium pentoxide	6.7
Whiting	3.4
Strontium carbonate	2.0
Kaolin	3.5
Ultrox	4.6
Silica	1.5

SG-245

Opaque White Smooth-Matt Glaze   Cone 9
leadless, opaque, smooth matt, nontoxic

Mixing. Mix in the manner of SG-1.

Application. Apply in the manner of SG-1.

Firing. Fire in the manner of SG-103.

Fired Results. This glaze fires to an opaque white smooth matt in oxidation and a gray in reduction.

Kaolin	32.0
Dolomite	19.0
Feldspar (Custer)	24.0
Silica	6.5
Whiting	5.5
Talc	3.0
Ultrox	1.0
Add:	
C.M.C.	1 tsp.

SG-246

Opaque White Smooth-Matt Glaze   Cone 9
leadless, opaque, smooth matt, nontoxic

Mixing. Mix in the manner of SG-1.

Application. Apply in the manner of SG-1.

Firing. Fire in the manner of SG-103.

Fired Results. This glaze fires to an opaque white smooth matt in oxidation and a gray in reduction.

Feldspar (Custer)	32.0
Dolomite	22.0
Kaolin	22.0
Silica	22.0
Whiting	2.0

SG-247

Opaque Mottled-White Matt Glaze   Cone 9
leadless, opaque, matt, nontoxic

Mixing. Mix in the manner of SG-1.

Application. Apply in the manner of SG-1.

Firing. Fire in the manner of SG-103.

Fired Results. This glaze fires to an opaque mottled-white matt in oxidation and a gray in reduction.

Feldspar (Kingman)	40.0
Dolomite	30.0
Colemanite	20.0
Kaolin	8.0
Whiting	2.0

SG-248

Opaque White Matt Glaze   Cone 9
leadless, opaque, matt, nontoxic

Mixing. Mix in the manner of SG-1.

Application. Apply in the manner of SG-1.

Firing. Fire in the manner of SG-103.

Fired Results. This glaze fires to an opaque white matt in oxidation and a gray-white in reduction.

Zinc oxide	40.4
Feldspar (Custer)	22.6
Silica	17.2
Whiting	12.1
Rutile	5.6
Colemanite	2.0
Add:	
Bentonite	1.0
C.M.C.	1 tsp.

SG-249

Smooth Opaque Matt Glaze   Cone 9
leadless, opaque, cloudy white, slightly toxic

Mixing. Mix in the manner of SG-3.

Application. Apply in the manner of SG-3.

Firing. Fire in the manner of SG-103.

Fired Results. This glaze fires to an opaque smooth matt in oxidation and a gray-white in reduction.

Feldspar (potash)	48.5
Whiting	9.5
Zinc oxide (calcined)	9.9
Kaolin (EPK, calcined)	21.3
Silica	10.7
Add:	
Bentonite	2.0
C.M.C.	1 tsp.

SG-250

Rustic Opaque Matt Glaze   Cone 9
leadless, opaque, matt, nontoxic

Mixing. Mix in the manner of SG-1.

Application. Apply in the manner of SG-1.

Firing. Fire in the manner of SG-103.

Fired Results. This glaze fires to a rustic opaque white matt in oxidation and a gray-white in reduction.

Feldspar (Kingman)	56.5
Whiting	6.5
Zinc oxide	7.6
Kaolin (EPK)	17.5
Silica	10.9
Bentonite	2.0
Add:	
C.M.C.	1 tsp.

SG-251

Opaque Cratered Matt Glaze   Cone 9
leadless, opaque, matt, nontoxic

Mixing. Mix in the manner of SG-1.

Application. Apply in the manner of SG-1.

Firing. Fire in the manner of SG-103.

Fired Results. This glaze fires to an opaque cratered matt in oxidation and a slightly more gray in reduction.

Feldspar (Kingman)	56.7
Zinc oxide	10.6
Kaolin	10.0
Kaolin (calcined)	4.0
Bentonite	1.0
Add:	
C.M.C.	1 tsp.

SG-252

Transparent Yellow Gloss Glaze   Cone 9
leadless, transparent, gloss, nontoxic

Mixing. Mix in the manner of SG-1.

Application. Apply in the manner of SG-1.

Firing. Fire in the manner of SG-1.

Fired Results. This glaze fires to a transparent yellow gloss in oxidation or reduction.

Volcanic ash	70.0
Whiting	20.0
Ultrox	5.0
Magnesium oxide	3.0
Bentonite	2.0
Add:	
C.M.C.	1 tsp.

SG-253

Transparent Yellow Gloss Glaze   Cone 9
leadless, transparent, gloss, nontoxic

Mixing. Mix in the manner of SG-1.

Application. Apply in the manner of SG-1.

Firing. Fire in the manner of SG-103.

Fired Results. This glaze fires to a transparent yellow gloss in oxidation or reduction.

Volcanic ash	58.6
Whiting	28.0
Magnesium carbonate	3.2
Kaolin	8.2
Bentonite	2.0

SG-254

Transparent Yellow Gloss Glaze   Cone 9
leadless, transparent, gloss, nontoxic

Mixing. Mix in the manner of SG-1.

Application. Apply in the manner of SG-1.

Firing. Fire in the manner of SG-103.

Fired Results. This glaze fires to a transparent yellow gloss in oxidation or reduction.

Volcanic ash	55.0
Whiting	24.0
Kaolin	8.9
Calcium carbonate	7.4
Magnesium carbonate	3.1
Add:	
C.M.C.	1 tsp.

SG-255

Oil-Yellow Gloss Glaze   Cone 9
leadless, opaque, gloss, nontoxic

Mixing. Mix in the manner of SG-1.

Application. Apply in the manner of SG-1.

Firing. Fire in the manner of SG-103.

Fired Results. This glaze fires to an opaque yellow gloss in oxidation or reduction.

Nepheline syenite	23.1
Lithium carbonate	17.5
Colemanite	7.3
Wollastonite	6.0
Talc	13.0
Kaolin	6.5
Silica	26.6
Add:	
Vanadium stain	7.5
Bentonite	1.0

SG-256

Bright Yellow Gloss Glaze   Cone 9
leadless, opaque, gloss, nontoxic

Mixing. Mix in the manner of SG-1.

Application. Apply in the manner of SG-1.

Firing. Fire in the manner of SG-103.

Fired Results. This glaze fires to an opaque yellow gloss in oxidation or reduction.

Pemco frit #25	15.0
Nepheline syenite	70.0
Lithium carbonate	3.5
Whiting	6.0
Ultrox	2.0
Kaolin	3.5
Add:	
Vanadium stain	7.5
Bentonite	1.0

SG-257 **Opaque Black Gloss Glaze   Cone 10**
leadless, opaque, gloss, nontoxic

Mixing. Mix in the manner of SG-1.

Application. Apply in the manner of SG-1.

Firing. Fire in the manner of SG-103.

Fired Results. This glaze fires to an opaque black gloss in oxidation or reduction.

Feldspar (Custer)	50.7
Silica	17.3
Whiting	13.4
Red iron oxide	11.6
Kaolin	6.5
Cobalt carbonate	0.5
Add:	
Bentonite	1.0
C.M.C.	1 tsp.

SG-258 **Opaque Metallic-Black Semi-Gloss Glaze   Cone 10**
leadless, opaque, semi-gloss, nontoxic

Mixing. Mix in the manner of SG-1.

Application. Apply in the manner of SG-1.

Firing. Fire in the manner of SG-103.

Fired Results. This glaze fires to an opaque metallic-black semi-gloss in oxidation or reduction.

Silica	25.0
Feldspar (Custer)	20.0
Whiting	18.0
Kaolin (EPK)	18.0
Red iron oxide	15.0
Dolomite	4.0
Add:	
C.M.C.	1 tsp.

SG-259 **Opaque Blue Matt Glaze   Cone 10**
barium, opaque, matt, toxic

Mixing. Mix in the manner of SG-3.

Application. Apply in the manner of SG-3.

Firing. Fire in the manner of SG-103.

Fired Results. This glaze fires to an opaque blue matt in oxidation or reduction.

Nepheline syenite	48.0
Barium carbonate	38.4
Silica	7.5
Tennessee ball clay #1	6.1
Copper carbonate	4.0
Add:	
Bentonite	1.0
C.M.C.	1 tsp.

SG-260 **Opaque Grayed-Blue Matt   Cone 10**
leadless, opaque, matt, toxic

Mixing. Mix in the manner of SG-3.

Application. Apply in the manner of SG-3.

Firing. Fire in the manner of SG-103.

Fired Results. This glaze fires to an opaque gray-blue in oxidation or reduction.

Feldspar (Custer)	46.4
Kaolin (EPK)	24.7
Dolomite	22.0
Whiting	4.6
Colemanite	1.5
Cobalt oxide	0.5
Green chromium oxide	0.3
Add:	
Bentonite	1.0
C.M.C.	1 tsp.

SG-261 **Semi-Opaque Prussian-Blue Matt Glaze   Cone 10**
barium, semi-opaque, matt, toxic

Mixing. Mix in the manner of SG-3.

Application. Apply in the manner of SG-3.

Firing. Fire in the manner of SG-103.

Fired Results. This glaze fires to a semi-opaque Prussian-blue matt in oxidation or reduction.

Nepheline syenite	89.5
Dolomite	18.5
Zinc oxide (calcined)	8.1
Barium carbonate	19.7
Whiting	4.0
Kaolin (EPK)	62.5
Silica	51.5
Copper oxide	2.5
Cobalt	2.5

SG-262

Translucent Turquoise-Blue Matt Glaze   Cone 10
barium, translucent, matt, nontoxic

Mixing. Mix in the manner of SG-1.

Application. Apply in the manner of SG-1.

Firing. Fire in the manner of SG-103.

Fired Results. This glaze fires to a translucent turquoise-blue matt in oxidation or reduction.

Cornwall stone	91.5
Feldspar (Kingman)	89.4
Dolomite	18.5
Barium carbonate	19.5
Whiting	40.0
Kaolin (EPK)	10.5
Cobalt oxide	2.8
Copper carbonate	5.4

SG-263

Opaque Brown Gloss Glaze   Cone
leadless, opaque, gloss, nontoxic

Mixing. Mix in the manner of SG-1.

Application. Apply in the manner of SG-1.

Firing. Fire in the manner of SG-103.

Fired Results. This glaze fires to an opaque brown gloss in oxidation and a slightly metallic dark brown in reduction.

Silica	25.0
Feldspar (Custer)	22.5
Whiting	17.0
Tennessee ball clay #1	12.5
Kentucky ball clay #4	12.5
Red iron oxide	9.0
Bentonite	1.5

SG-264

Opaque Earth-Brown Matt Glaze   Cone 10
leadless-barium, opaque, matt, toxic

Mixing. Mix in the manner of SG-3.

Application. Apply in the manner of SG-3.

Firing. Fire in the manner of SG-103.

Fired Results. This glaze fires to an opaque earthy brown gloss in oxidation and a metallic brown in reduction.

Feldspar (Custer)	33.2
Kaolin	21.7
Silica	16.8
Manganese carbonate	13.0
Whiting	11.5
Ultrox	2.4
Barium carbonate	1.3
Add:	
C.M.C.	1 tsp.

SG-265

Earth Brown Satin-Matt Glaze   Cone 9
barium, translucent, satin matt, toxic

Mixing. Mix in the manner of SG-3.

Application. Apply in the manner of SG-3.

Firing. Fire in the manner of SG-103.

Fired Results. This glaze fires to an earth-brown satin matt in oxidation and an iron-spot brown in reduction.

Feldspar (Custer)	32.0
Dolomite	22.0
Barium carbonate	21.0
Kaolin (EPK)	15.0
Silica	9.0
Red iron oxide	4.5
Rutile	1.0
Add:	
Bentonite	1.0
C.M.C.	1 tsp.

SG-266

Opaque Cordova-Brown Matt Glaze   Cone 10
barium, opaque, matt, toxic

Mixing. Mix in the manner of SG-3.

Application. Apply in the manner of SG-3.

Firing. Fire in the manner of SG-103.

Fired Results. This glaze fires to an opaque cordova-brown in oxidation and a mottled brown in reduction.

Feldspar (Custer)	48.6
Barium carbonate	20.4
Tennessee ball clay #1	9.4
Whiting	8.2
Ultrox	7.6
Red iron oxide	3.9
Rutile	1.9
Add:	
Bentonite	1.0
C.M.C.	1 tsp.

SG-267

Opaque Iron-Brown Gloss Glaze   Cone 10
leadless, opaque, gloss, nontoxic

Mixing. Mix in the manner of SG-1.

Application. Apply in the manner of SG-1.

Firing. Fire in the manner of SG-103.

Fired Results. This glaze fires to an opaque iron-brown gloss in oxidation or reduction.

Feldspar (Custer)	40.4
Silica	25.2
Whiting	15.5
Red iron oxide	9.4
Kaolin (EPK)	8.7
Bentonite	1.0

SG-268

Opaque Khaki-Brown Gloss Glaze   Cone 10
leadless, opaque, gloss, nontoxic

Mixing. Mix in the manner of SG-1.

Application. Apply in the manner of SG-1.

Firing. Fire in the manner of SG-103.

Fired Results. This glaze fires to an opaque khaki-brown gloss in oxidation and a mottled brown in reduction.

Feldspar (Custer)	56.0
Silica	22.4
Red iron oxide	10.0
Whiting	6.1
Kaolin	4.5
Bentonite	1.0
Add:	
C.M.C.	1 tsp.

SG-269

Opaque Khaki-Brown Matt Glaze   Cone 10
leadless, opaque, matt, nontoxic

Mixing. Mix in the manner of SG-1.

Application. Apply in the manner of SG-1.

Firing. Fire in the manner of SG-103.

Fired Results. This glaze fires to a khaki-brown matt in oxidation and a metallic brown in reduction.

Feldspar (Custer)	50.0
Kaolin	18.0
Silica	13.5
Red iron oxide	11.3
Whiting	6.2
Magnesium carbonate	1.8
Add:	
C.M.C.	1 tsp.

SG-270

Opaque Dark Khaki-Brown Matt Glaze   Cone 10
leadless, opaque, matt, nontoxic

Mixing. Mix in the manner of SG-1.

Application. Apply in the manner of SG-1.

Firing. Fire in the manner of SG-103.

Fired Results. This glaze fires to a dark brown in oxidation and a metallic brown in reduction.

Tennessee ball clay #1	24.0
Silica	24.5
Feldspar (Custer)	19.5
Whiting	14.9
Red iron oxide	15.1
Ultrox	2.0
Add:	
Bentonite	1.0
C.M.C.	1 tsp.

SG-271

Opaque Mottled Brown-and-Black Semi-Gloss Glaze   Cone 10
leadless, opaque, semi-gloss, nontoxic

Mixing. Mix in the manner of SG-1.

Application. Apply in the manner of SG-1.

Firing. Fire in the manner of SG-103.

Fired Results. This glaze fires to a mottled brown in oxidation and a metallic brown in reduction.

Feldspar (Kona F-4)	23.4
Boric acid	17.0
Colemanite	6.0
Red iron oxide	23.0
Silica	13.0
Whiting	13.0
Magnesium carbonate	4.0

SG-272

Opaque Mottled Gray-Brown Matt Glaze   Cone 10
barium, opaque, matt, toxic

Mixing. Mix in the manner of SG-3.

Application. Apply in the manner of SG-3.

Firing. Fire in the manner of SG-103.

Fired Results. This glaze fires to a warm tan-brown in oxidation and a mottled gray-brown in reduction.

Feldspar (Custer)	34.2
Nepheline syenite	25.2
Barium carbonate	12.9
Whiting	7.2
Kaolin	7.8
Silica	3.7
Red iron oxide	3.5
Dolomite	3.4
Bentonite	2.0

SG-273

Opaque Yellow-Brown Matt Glaze   Cone 10
leadless, opaque, matt, toxic

Mixing. Mix in the manner of SG-3.

Application. Apply in the manner of SG-3.

Firing. Fire in the manner of SG-103.

Fired Results. This glaze fires to an opaque tan in oxidation and a warm yellow-brown in reduction.

Feldspar (Custer)	29.0
Whiting	23.0
Silica	13.0
Kaolin (EPK)	13.0
Rutile	10.0
Colemanite	5.0
Red iron oxide	5.0
Bentonite	2.0

SG-274

Clear Fluid Gloss Glaze   Cone 10
barium, transparent, gloss, toxic

Mixing. Mix in the manner of SG-3.

Application. Apply in the manner of SG-3.

Firing. Fire in the manner of SG-103.

Fired Results. This glaze fires to a clear fluid gloss in oxidation or reduction.

Whiting	10.0
Colemanite	12.0
Barium carbonate	7.0
Magnesium carbonate	4.0
Feldspar (Custer)	30.0
Silica	32.0
Kaolin	5.0

SG-275

Clear Gloss Glaze   Cone 10
leadless, transparent, gloss, toxic

Mixing. Mix in the manner of SG-3.

Application. Apply in the manner of SG-3.

Firing. Fire in the manner of SG-103.

Fired Results. This glaze fires to a clear gloss in oxidation or reduction.

Cornwall stone	63.4
Colemanite	14.6
Silica	7.8
Whiting	7.6
Kaolin (EPK)	4.7
Ultrox	1.0
Bentonite	1.0

SG-276

Clear Gloss Glaze   Cone 10
leadless, transparent, gloss, nontoxic

Mixing. Mix in the manner of SG-1.

Application. Apply in the manner of SG-1.

Firing. Fire in the manner of SG-103.

Fired Results. This glaze fires to a clear gloss in oxidation or reduction.

Nepheline syenite	55.9
Feldspar (Custer)	23.8
Talc	17.8
Bentonite	2.0
Ultrox	0.5
Add:	
C.M.C.	1 tsp.

SG-277 **Clear Fluid Gloss Glaze   Cone 10**
leadless, transparent, gloss, nontoxic

Mixing. Mix in the manner of SG-1.

Application. Apply in the manner of SG-1.

Firing. Fire in the manner of SG-103.

Fired Results. This glaze fires to a clear gloss in oxidation or reduction.

Nepheline syenite	55.0
Silica	23.7
Colemanite	10.0
Cryolite	6.1
Lithium carbonate	4.0
Magnesium carbonate	1.2
Add:	
Bentonite	1.0
C.M.C.	1 tsp.

SG-278 **Clear Gloss Glaze   Cone 10**
barium, transparent, gloss, nontoxic

Mixing. Mix in the manner of SG-1.

Application. Apply in the manner of SG-1.

Firing. Fire in the manner of SG-103.

Fired Results. This glaze fires to a clear gloss in oxidation or reduction.

Feldspar (Custer)	50.5
Silica	24.4
Whiting	9.0
Strontium carbonate	3.0
Kaolin (EPK)	6.0
Barium carbonate	4.0
Bentonite	1.0
Add:	
C.M.C.	1 tsp.

SG-279 **Clear Gloss Glaze   Cone 10**
leadless, transparent, gloss, nontoxic

Mixing. Mix in the manner of SG-1.

Application. Apply in the manner of SG-1.

Firing. Fire in the manner of SG-103.

Fired Results. This glaze fires to a clear gloss in oxidation or reduction.

Feldspar (Kona F-4)	50.0
Silica	25.0
Whiting	18.9
Kaolin (EPK)	3.7
Dolomite	3.4
Ultrox	0.5
Bentonite	0.5

SG-280 **Clear Gloss Glaze   Cone 10**
leadless, transparent, gloss, nontoxic

Mixing. Mix in the manner of SG-1.

Application. Apply in the manner of SG-1.

Firing. Fire in the manner of SG-103.

Fired Results. This glaze fires to a clear gloss in oxidation or reduction.

Cornwall stone	47.1
Silica	19.0
Kaolin	15.6
Whiting	12.0
Dolomite	5.1
Zinc oxide	1.0

SG-281 **Clear Semi-Gloss Glaze   Cone 10**
barium, transparent, semi-gloss, toxic

Mixing. Mix in the manner of SG-3.

Application. Apply in the manner of SG-3.

Firing. Fire in the manner of SG-103.

Fired Results. This glaze fires to a clear semi-gloss in oxidation or reduction.

Feldspar (Kona F-4)	37.3
Silica	24.3
Colemanite	22.5
Whiting	10.1
Barium carbonate	4.8

SG-282 **Clear Semi-Gloss Glaze Cone 10**
leadless, transparent, semi-gloss, nontoxic

Mixing. Mix in the manner of SG-1.

Application. Apply in the manner of SG-1.

Firing. Fire in the manner of SG-103.

Fired Results. This glaze fires to a clear semi-gloss in oxidation or reduction.

Feldspar (Kingman)	41.0
Nepheline syenite	34.0
Talc	15.0
Kentucky ball clay #4	5.0
Spodumene	3.0
Magnesium carbonate	2.0

SG-283 **Clear Semi-Gloss Glaze Cone 10**
leadless, transparent, semigloss, nontoxic

Mixing. Mix in the manner of SG-1.

Application. Apply in the manner of SG-1.

Firing. Fire in the manner of SG-103.

Fired Results. This glaze fires to a clear semi-gloss in oxidation or reduction.

Feldspar (Custer)	49.5
Spodumene	19.8
Talc	12.3
Tennessee ball clay #1	9.8
Whiting	4.5
Silica	2.0
Zinc oxide	2.0

SG-284 **Clear Buttery Smooth-Matt Glaze Cone 10**
leadless, transparent, smooth matt, nontoxic

Mixing. Mix in the manner of SG-1.

Application. Apply in the manner of SG-1.

Firing. Fire in the manner of SG-103.

Fired Results. This glaze fires to a clear buttery matt in oxidation or reduction.

Feldspar (Kona F-4)	80.0
Whiting	8.0
Kaolin	8.0
Bone ash	2.0
Magnesium carbonate	2.0

SG-285 **Clear Smooth-Matt Glaze Cone 10**
leadless, transparent, smooth matt, nontoxic

Mixing. Mix in the manner of SG-1.

Application. Apply in the manner of SG-1.

Firing. Fire in the manner of SG-103.

Fired Results. This glaze fires to a clear smooth matt in oxidation or reduction.

Cornwall stone	85.0
Whiting	10.0
Magnesium carbonate	5.0

SG-286 **Clear Matt Glaze Cone 10**
leadless, transparent, matt, nontoxic

Mixing. Mix in the manner of SG-1.

Application. Apply in the manner of SG-1.

Firing. Fire in the manner of SG-103.

Fired Results. This glaze fires to a clear matt in oxidation or reduction.

Whiting	26.0
Alumina hydrate	20.0
Kaolin	12.0
Magnesium carbonate	4.0
Silica	38.0

SG-287

Opaque Cream Gloss Glaze   Cone 10
leadless, opaque, gloss, nontoxic

Mixing. Mix in the manner of SG-1.

Application. Apply in the manner of SG-1.

Firing. Fire in the manner of SG-103.

Fired Results. This glaze fires to an opaque cream matt in oxidation or reduction.

Feldspar (Custer)	32.5
Silica	22.1
Ultrox	12.5
Colemanite	11.0
Talc	5.0
Zinc oxide	4.0
Kaolin	4.0
Magnesium carbonate	1.2
Whiting	6.7

SG-288

Opaque Cream Matt Glaze   Cone 10
leadless, opaque, matt, nontoxic

Mixing. Mix in the manner of SG-1.

Application. Apply in the manner of SG-1.

Firing. Fire in the manner of SG-103.

Fired Results. This glaze fires to a cream matt in oxidation and a gray in reduction.

Feldspar (Custer)	40.6
Silica	17.5
Talc	12.5
Colemanite	12.1
Tennessee ball clay #1	8.3
Dolomite	7.7
Iron oxide	1.3
Add:	
Bentonite	1.0

SG-289

Opaque Gray Matt Glaze   Cone 10
barium, opaque, matt, toxic

Mixing. Mix in the manner of SG-3.

Application. Apply in the manner of SG-3.

Firing. Fire in the manner of SG-103.

Fired Results. This glaze fires to a white matt in oxidation and a gray in reduction.

Feldspar (Custer)	35.0
Nepheline syenite	20.0
Cornwall stone	5.0
Barium carbonate	12.0
Whiting	9.6
Kaolin (EPK)	9.1
Dolomite	5.5
Silica	3.8
Add:	
C.M.C.	1 tsp.

SG-290

Translucent Blue-Gray Matt Glaze   Cone 10
barium, translucent, matt, toxic

Mixing. Mix in the manner of SG-3.

Application. Apply in the manner of SG-3.

Firing. Fire in the manner of SG-103.

Fired Results. This glaze fires to a blue matt in oxidation and a blue-gray in reduction.

Feldspar (Custer)	44.5
Barium carbonate	18.6
Tennessee ball clay #1	8.5
Whiting	7.8
Titanium dioxide	7.5
Ultrox	7.2
Bone ash	4.5
Copper carbonate	0.1
Cobalt oxide	0.4
Red iron oxide	0.3

SG-291 **Opaque Blue-Gray Dry Matt Glaze   Cone 10**
barium, opaque, dry matt, toxic

Mixing. Mix in the manner of SG-3.

Application. Apply in the manner of SG-3.

Firing. Fire in the manner of SG-103.

Fired Results. This glaze fires to an off-white matt in oxidation and a blue-gray in reduction.

Feldspar (Kingman)	42.7
Barium carbonate	16.3
Whiting	16.4
Kaolin (EPK)	8.2
Vanadium pentoxide	8.0
Ultrox	6.6
Rutile	1.8
Add:	
C.M.C.	1 tsp.

SG-292 **Opaque Charcoal-Gray Gloss Glaze   Cone 10**
leadless-barium, opaque, gloss, nontoxic

Mixing. Mix in the manner of SG-1.

Application. Apply in the manner of SG-1.

Firing. Fire in the manner of SG-103.

Fired Results. This glaze fires to an opaque charcoal-gray gloss in oxidation and a dark-brown in reduction.

Feldspar (Custer)	34.2
Silica	25.0
Magnesium carbonate	14.0
Whiting	12.2
Tennessee ball clay #1	8.3
Ultrox	3.4
Chromium oxide	2.4
Barium carbonate	1.5
Add:	
C.M.C.	1 tsp.

SG-293 **Opaque Magnesium-Gray Smooth-Matt Glaze   Cone 10**
leadless, opaque, smooth matt, nontoxic

Mixing. Mix in the manner of SG-1.

Application. Apply in the manner of SG-1.

Firing. Fire in the manner of SG-103.

Fired Results. This glaze fires to an opaque light-gray smooth matt in oxidation and slightly darker with iron spottings in reduction.

Feldspar (Kingman)	45.0
Colemanite	15.0
Dolomite	7.0
Talc	15.0
Kaolin	5.0
Silica	20.0
Tin oxide	6.0
Iron chromate	1.5

SG-294 **Opaque Green Matt Glaze   Cone 10**
leadless-barium, opaque, matt, toxic

Mixing. Mix in the manner of SG-3.

Application. Apply in the manner of SG-3.

Firing. Fire in the manner of SG-103.

Fired Results. This glaze fires to a mottled brown-and-green matt in oxidation and darker in reduction.

Feldspar (Kingman)	49.8
Whiting	8.0
Tin oxide	7.9
Barium carbonate	19.9
Kentucky ball clay #4	9.6
Red iron oxide	4.8
Add:	
Bentonite	1.0
C.M.C.	1 tsp.

SG-295 **Transparent Reduction Blue-Green Matt Glaze   Cone 10**
leadless, transparent, matt, nontoxic

Mixing. Mix in the manner of SG-1.

Application. Apply in the manner of SG-1.

Firing. Fire in the manner of SG-103.

Fired Results. This glaze fires to a transparent blue-green matt in reduction. It is tan in oxidation.

Feldspar (Custer)	45.0
Whiting	21.0
Kaolin (EPK)	21.0
Silica	10.0
Red iron oxide	2.0
Bentonite	1.0
Add:	
C.M.C.	1 tsp.

SG-296

Opaque Broken-Orange Matt Glaze   Cone 10
leadless, opaque, matt, nontoxic

Mixing. Mix in the manner of SG-1.

Application. Apply in the manner of SG-1.

Firing. Fire in the manner of SG-103.

Fired Results. This glaze fires to a mottled yellow in oxidation and a mottled orange matt in reduction.

Feldspar (Custer)	48.8
Whiting	17.9
Kaolin	14.9
Rutile	8.8
Ultrox	5.5
Red iron oxide	4.4
Add:	
Bentonite	1.0
C.M.C.	1 tsp.

SG-297

Opaque Earth-Orange Matt Glaze   Cone 10
barium, opaque, matt, toxic

Mixing. Mix in the manner of SG-3.

Application. Apply in the manner of SG-3.

Firing. Fire in the manner of SG-103.

Fired Results. This glaze fires to a mottled earthy orange in oxidation and a mottled off-white and gray in reduction.

Feldspar (Custer)	60.0
Whiting	12.5
Strontium carbonate	1.2
Tennessee ball clay #1	8.7
Barium carbonate	5.6
Kaolin (EPK)	5.6
Rutile	4.2
Magnesium carbonate	2.2
Add:	
C.M.C.	1 tsp.

SG-298

Opaque Mottled Orange-White Semi-Gloss Glaze   Cone 10
leadless, opaque, semi-gloss, nontoxic

Mixing. Mix in the manner of SG-1.

Application. Apply in the manner of SG-1.

Firing. Fire in the manner of SG-103.

Fired Results. This glaze fires to a mottled white and orange in oxidation and a mottled white and tan-orange in reduction.

Feldspar (Kingman)	45.0
Whiting	20.0
Silica	13.0
Kaolin (EPK)	10.0
Rutile	7.0
Lithium carbonate	5.0
Magnesium carbonate	2.0
Add:	
C.M.C.	1 tsp.

SG-299

Opaque Iron-Red Matt Glaze   Cone 10
leadless, opaque, matt, nontoxic

Mixing. Mix in the manner of SG-1.

Application. Apply in the manner of SG-1.

Firing. Fire in the manner of SG-103.

Fired Results. This glaze fires to an opaque iron-red matt in oxidation and slightly darker with touches of mottled gray in reduction.

Feldspar (Custer)	53.0
Talc	4.0
Kaolin (EPK)	25.0
Bone ash	2.0
Whiting	22.3
Red iron oxide	4.1
Add:	
C.M.C.	1 tsp.

SG-300

Opaque Tan Semi-Gloss Glaze   Cone 10
leadless, opaque, semi-gloss, nontoxic

Mixing. Mix in the manner of SG-1.

Application. Apply in the manner of SG-1.

Firing. Fire in the manner of SG-103.

Fired Results. This glaze fires to an opaque tan in oxidation and a tan-gray in reduction.

Feldspar (Custer)	46.3
Whiting	20.0
Strontium carbonate	2.7
Kaolin (EPK)	11.3
Silica	11.3
Rutile	8.2
Add:	
Bentonite	1.0
C.M.C.	1 tsp.

SG-301

Opaque Tan Matt Glaze   Cone 10
barium, opaque, matt, toxic

Mixing. Mix in the manner of SG-3.

Application. Apply in the manner of SG-3.

Firing. Fire in the manner of SG-103.

Fired Results. This glaze fires to an opaque warm-tan matt in oxidation and slightly lighter in reduction. It will iron spot well over darker bodies.

Feldspar (Custer)	44.0
Barium carbonate	19.0
Rutile	13.0
Tennessee ball clay #1	9.0
Whiting	8.0
Ultrox	7.0
Add:	
Bentonite	1.0

SG-302

Opaque Gray-Tan Matt Glaze   Cone 10
barium, opaque, matt, toxic

Mixing. Mix in the manner of SG-3.

Application. Apply in the manner of SG-3.

Firing. Fire in the manner of SG-103.

Fired Results. This glaze fires to an opaque tan matt in oxidation and an opaque gray-tan in reduction. It will iron spot well over darker bodies.

Feldspar (Custer)	47.4
Barium carbonate	19.7
Kentucky ball clay #4	9.3
Whiting	8.3
Rutile	7.8
Ultrox	6.5
Bentonite	1.0
Add:	
C.M.C.	1 tsp.

SG-303

Opaque Mottled-Tan Matt Glaze   Cone 10
leadless-barium, opaque, matt, toxic

Mixing. Mix in the manner of SG-3.

Application. Apply in the manner of SG-3.

Firing. Fire in the manner of SG-103.

Fired Results. This glaze fires to an opaque warm-tan in oxidation and a mottled-tan in reduction.

Feldspar (Kingman)	53.5
Dolomite	10.1
Kentucky ball clay #4	8.6
Whiting	6.3
Ultrox	5.4
Kaolin (EPK)	5.0
Rutile	4.8
Barium carbonate	4.8
Magnesium carbonate	1.6

SG-304

Opaque Mottled-Tan Semi-Gloss Glaze   Cone 10
leadless, opaque, semi-gloss, toxic

Mixing. Mix in the manner of SG-3.

Application. Apply in the manner of SG-3.

Firing. Fire in the manner of SG-103.

Fired Results. This glaze fires to an opaque tan semi-gloss in oxidation and a mottled tan in reduction.

Lincoln clay	30.3
Feldspar (Custer)	25.0
Dolomite	18.4
Volcanic ash	10.0
Colemanite	5.3
Silica	4.7
Bone ash	3.0
Opax	3.3
Add:	
Bentonite	1.0

SG-305

Translucent White Gloss Glaze   Cone 10
leadless, translucent, gloss, nontoxic

Mixing. Mix in the manner of SG-1.

Application. Apply in the manner of SG-1.

Firing. Fire in the manner of SG-103.

Fired Results. This glaze fires to a translucent white gloss in oxidation or reduction.

Feldspar (Custer)	20.0
Magnesium carbonate	13.7
Whiting	11.8
Alumina hydrate	5.7
Kaolin	8.8
Silica	40.0

SG-306

Translucent White Gloss Glaze   Cone 10
leadless-barium, translucent, gloss, toxic

Mixing. Mix in the manner of SG-3.

Application. Apply in the manner of SG-3.

Firing. Fire in the manner of SG-103.

Fired Results. This glaze fires to a translucent white gloss in oxidation and a slightly gray-white in reduction.

Feldspar (Kona F-4)	90.5
Barium carbonate	5.2
Whiting	2.0
Magnesium carbonate	2.3
Add:	
Bentonite	1.0

SG-307

Translucent White Gloss Glaze   Cone 10
leadless-barium, translucent, gloss, toxic

Mixing. Mix in the manner of SG-3.

Application. Apply in the manner of SG-3.

Firing. Fire in the manner of SG-103.

Fired Results. This glaze fires to a translucent white gloss in oxidation or reduction. It will iron spot well in reduction over darker bodies.

Feldspar (Custer)	56.3
Tennessee ball clay #1	12.9
Dolomite	9.5
Whiting	7.5
Kaolin (EPK)	5.4
Barium carbonate	5.1
Ultrox	1.9

SG-308

Translucent White Gloss Glaze   Cone 10
leadless, translucent, gloss, nontoxic

Mixing. Mix in the manner of SG-1.

Application. Apply in the manner of SG-1.

Firing. Fire in the manner of SG-103.

Fired Results. This glaze fires to a translucent white gloss in oxidation and a slightly gray-white in reduction.

Feldspar (Kingman)	54.8
Kaolin	18.9
Whiting	18.3
Silica	4.7
Ultrox	3.3
Add:	
Bentonite	1.0
C.M.C.	1 tsp.

SG-309

Translucent White Gloss Glaze   Cone 10
leadless, translucent, gloss, nontoxic

Mixing. Mix in the manner of SG-1.

Application. Apply in the manner of SG-1.

Firing. Fire in the manner of SG-103.

Fired Results. This glaze fires to a translucent white gloss in oxidation and a translucent buff-white in reduction.

Cornwall stone	45.5
Colemanite	27.5
Silica	18.3
Whiting	7.3
Magnesium carbonate	1.9
Add:	
C.M.C.	1 tsp.

SG-310

Translucent Semi-Gloss Glaze   Cone 10
leadless, translucent, semi-gloss, nontoxic

Mixing. Mix in the manner of SG-1.

Application. Apply in the manner of SG-1.

Firing. Fire in the manner of SG-103.

Fired Results. This glaze fires to a translucent semi-gloss white of a cloudy type in both oxidation and reduction.

Feldspar (Custer)	30.9
Silica	30.7
Whiting	18.5
Kaolin	15.0
Spodumene	2.4
Ultrox	2.5
Add:	
C.M.C.	1 tsp.

SG-311

Translucent Semi-Gloss Glaze   Cone 10
leadless, translucent, semi-gloss, nontoxic

Mixing. Mix in the manner of SG-1.

Application. Apply in the manner of SG-1.

Firing. Fire in the manner of SG-103.

Fired Results. This glaze fires to a translucent cloudy-white semi-gloss in both oxidation and reduction.

Feldspar (Kona F-4)	30.0
Silica	25.0
Zinc oxide	16.5
Kaolin (EPK)	11.5
Whiting	9.7
Spodumene	5.8
Magnesium carbonate	1.5
Add:	
C.M.C.	1 tsp.

SG-312

Translucent Semi-Gloss Glaze   Cone 10
leadless, translucent, semi-gloss, nontoxic

Mixing. Mix in the manner of SG-1.

Application. Apply in the manner of SG-1.

Firing. Fire in the manner of SG-103.

Fired Results. This glaze fires to a translucent cloudy-white in both oxidation and reduction.

Feldspar (Custer)	30.0
Silica	28.0
Whiting	25.0
Kaolin	12.0
Colemanite	5.0
Add:	
Bentonite	1.0
C.M.C.	1 tsp.

SG-313

Translucent Semi-Gloss Glaze   Cone 10
leadless, translucent, semi-gloss, nontoxic

Mixing. Mix in the manner of SG-1.

Application. Apply in the manner of SG-1.

Firing. Fire in the manner of SG-103.

Fired Results. This glaze fires to a translucent white semi-gloss in oxidation or reduction.

Silica	36.0
Feldspar (Custer)	18.0
Zinc oxide	17.0
Kaolin	16.0
Whiting	11.0
Colemanite	2.0
Add:	
Bentonite	1.0
C.M.C.	1 tsp.

SG-314

Translucent Opalescent-White Glaze   Cone 10
leadless, translucent, gloss, nontoxic

Mixing. Mix in the manner of SG-1.

Application. Apply in the manner of SG-1.

Firing. Fire in the manner of SG-103.

Fired Results. This glaze fires to a translucent opalescent white gloss in both oxidation and reduction.

Cornwall stone	59.7
Colemanite	13.6
Silica	7.2
Whiting	7.2
Kaolin (EPK)	4.6
Ultrox	1.8
Titanium dioxide	3.0
Ilmenite	1.9
Bentonite	1.0

SG-315

Translucent Magnesium-White Semi-Matt Glaze   Cone 10
leadless, translucent, semi-matt, nontoxic

Mixing. Mix in the manner of SG-1.

Application. Apply in the manner of SG-1.

Firing. Fire in the manner of SG-103.

Fired Results. This glaze fires to a translucent buttery-white semi-matt in both oxidation and reduction.

Feldspar (Custer)	45.0
Colemanite	14.0
Dolomite	7.0
Talc	15.0
Kaolin	4.0
Silica	20.0
Add:	
Bentonite	1.0

SG-316 **Translucent White Semi-Matt Glaze Cone 10**
leadless, translucent, semi-matt, nontoxic

Mixing. Mix in the manner of SG-1.

Application. Apply in the manner of SG-1.

Firing. Fire in the manner of SG-103.

Fired Results. This glaze fires to a translucent white semi-matt in oxidation or reduction.

Feldspar (Custer)	42.0
Kaolin (EPK)	24.0
Whiting	17.0
Silica	15.0
Ultrox	2.0
Add:	
Bentonite	1.0
C.M.C.	1 tsp.

SG-317 **Translucent White Semi-Matt Glaze Cone 10**
leadless, translucent, semi-matt, nontoxic

Mixing. Mix in the manner of SG-1.

Application. Apply in the manner of SG-1.

Firing. Fire in the manner of SG-103.

Fired Results. This glaze fires to a translucent white semi-matt in both oxidation and reduction.

Feldspar (Custer)	30.1
Silica	27.1
Whiting	27.2
Kaolin	14.0
Ultrox	1.6
Add:	
Bentonite	1.0
C.M.C.	1 tsp.

SG-318 **Translucent White Semi-Matt Glaze Cone 10**
barium, translucent, semi-matt, toxic

Mixing. Mix in the manner of SG-3.

Application. Apply in the manner of SG-3.

Firing. Fire in the manner of SG-103.

Fired Results. This glaze fires to a translucent white semi-matt in both oxidation and reduction.

Feldspar (Custer)	56.2
Barium carbonate	24.9
Whiting	12.4
Bentonite	4.7
Colemanite	1.8
Add:	
C.M.C.	1 tsp.

SG-319 **Opaque White Gloss Glaze Cone 10**
leadless, opaque, gloss, nontoxic

Mixing. Mix in the manner of SG-1.

Application. Apply in the manner of SG-1.

Firing. Fire in the manner of SG-103.

Fired Results. This glaze fires to an opaque white gloss in oxidation and slightly grayer in reduction.

Feldspar (Kingman)	33.4
Silica	23.0
Opax	13.5
Colemanite	11.0
Whiting	5.0
Talc	5.0
Zinc oxide	4.0
Kaolin	4.0

SG-320 **Opaque White Semi-Gloss Glaze Cone 10**
leadless, opaque, semi-gloss, nontoxic

Mixing. Mix in the manner of SG-1.

Application. Apply in the manner of SG-1.

Firing. Fire in the manner of SG-103.

Fired Results. This glaze fires to an opaque white semi-gloss in oxidation and a light gray in reduction.

Feldspar (Custer)	42.8
Silica	19.5
Talc	14.1
Colemanite	11.5
Dolomite	6.8
Kaolin	3.5
Ultrox	1.8
Add:	
C.M.C.	1 tsp.

SG-321 **Opaque White Fluid Semi-Gloss Glaze   Cone 10**
leadless, opaque, semi-gloss, nontoxic

Mixing. Mix in the manner of SG-1.

Application. Apply in the manner of SG-1.

Firing. Fire in the manner of SG-103.

Fired Results. This glaze fires to an opaque white semi-gloss in oxidation and a gray-white in reduction. It tends to be rather fluid in both firings.

Cornwall stone	44.1
Colemanite	43.8
Titanium dioxide	9.5
Kaolin	2.6
Add:	
Bentonite	1.0
C.M.C.	1 tsp.

SG-322 **Opaque White Semi-Gloss Glaze   Cone 10**
leadless, opaque, semi-gloss, nontoxic

Mixing. Mix in the manner of SG-1.

Application. Apply in the manner of SG-1.

Firing. Fire in the manner of SG-103.

Fired Results. This glaze fires to an opaque white semi-gloss in oxidation and a gray-white with good iron spotting qualities in reduction.

Feldspar (Kingman)	30.0
Silica	28.0
Whiting	24.0
Kaolin	13.0
Colemanite	4.0
Bentonite	1.0
Add:	
Ultrox	10.0

SG-323 **Opaque White Semi-Gloss Glaze   Cone 10**
leadless, opaque, semi-gloss, nontoxic

Mixing. Mix in the manner of SG-1.

Application. Apply in the manner of SG-1.

Firing. Fire in the manner of SG-103.

Fired Results. This glaze fires to an opaque white in oxidation with an excellent buttery semi-gloss surface. In reduction it is a gray-white with the same type of surface.

Feldspar (Custer)	46.0
Silica	28.0
Dolomite	10.0
Colemanite	6.0
Whiting	3.0
Kaolin	2.0
Ultrox	5.0
Add:	
C.M.C.	1 tsp.

SG-324 **Opaque White Smooth-Matt Glaze   Cone 10**
leadless, opaque, smooth matt, nontoxic

Mixing. Mix in the manner of SG-1.

Application. Apply in the manner of SG-1.

Firing. Fire in the manner of SG-103.

Fired Results. This glaze fires to an opaque white smooth matt with a nice buttery surface sheen. In reduction it is slightly more gray with the same type of surface.

Feldspar (Kingman)	42.5
Colemanite	12.3
Dolomite	7.5
Talc	14.2
Kaolin	4.7
Silica	18.9

SG-325

Opaque White Semi-Matt Glaze   Cone 10
leadless, opaque, semi-matt, nontoxic

Mixing. Mix in the manner of SG-1.

Application. Apply in the manner of SG-1.

Firing. Fire in the manner of SG-103.

Fired Results. This glaze fires to an opaque white semi-matt in oxidation and a gray-white in reduction.

Feldspar (Kona F-4)	77.0
Whiting	8.0
Kaolin	9.0
Bone ash	3.0
Ultrox	3.0

SG-326

Opaque White Semi-Matt Glaze   Cone 10
barium, opaque, semi-matt, toxic

Mixing. Mix in the manner of SG-3.

Application. Apply in the manner of SG-3.

Firing. Fire in the manner of SG-103.

Fired Results. This glaze fires to an opaque white semi-matt in oxidation and light gray in reduction. This glaze will iron spot very well over any clay body which contains some iron.

Feldspar (Kingman)	52.5
Barium carbonate	21.0
Silica	9.5
Kaolin	9.5
Dolomite	5.5
Bentonite	2.0
Add:	
C.M.C.	1 tsp.

SG-327

Opaque White Semi-Matt Glaze   Cone 10
leadless, opaque, semi-matt, nontoxic

Mixing. Mix in the manner of SG-1.

Application. Apply in the manner of SG-1.

Firing. Fire in the manner of SG-103.

Fired Results. This glaze fires to an opaque white semi-matt in oxidation and a gray-white in reduction.

Feldspar (Custer)	47.2
Silica	14.5
Talc	14.1
Colemanite	11.6
Dolomite	8.0
Kaolin (EPK)	4.0
Bentonite	0.6
Add:	
C.M.C.	1 tsp.

SG-328

Opaque White Matt Glaze   Cone 10
leadless, opaque, matt, nontoxic

Mixing. Mix in the manner of SG-1.

Application. Apply in the manner of SG-1.

Firing. Fire in the manner of SG-103.

Fired Results. This glaze fires to an opaque white matt in oxidation and a warm pink-white in reduction. In both firing atmospheres it has the buttery surface typical of glazes high in magnesium.

Feldspar (Kingman)	61.5
Dolomite	10.0
Ultrox	9.1
Whiting	9.0
Kaolin	5.6
Colemanite	5.4
Add:	
Bentonite	1 tsp.

SG-329 **Opaque White Matt Glaze   Cone 10**
leadless, opaque, matt, nontoxic

Mixing. Mix in the manner of SG-1.

Application. Apply in the manner of SG-1.

Firing. Fire in the manner of SG-103.

Fired Results. This glaze fires to an opaque gray-white matt in oxidation and slightly darker in reduction.

Feldspar (Custer)	60.0
Kaolin	30.0
Talc	4.0
Bone ash	2.6
Whiting	2.3
Magnesium carbonate	1.1
Add:	
C.M.C.	1 tsp.

SG-330 **Opaque White Matt Glaze   Cone 10**
leadless, opaque, matt, nontoxic

Mixing. Mix in the manner of SG-1.

Application. Apply in the manner of SG-1.

Firing. Fire in the manner of SG-103.

Fired Results. This glaze fires to an opaque white matt in oxidation and a gray-white in reduction. It has excellent iron spotting qualities in both firings.

Feldspar (Custer)	60.0
Whiting	20.0
Kaolin	15.0
Ultrox	5.0
Add:	
Bentonite	1.0
C.M.C.	1 tsp.

SG-331 **Opaque White Matt Glaze   Cone 10**
leadless, opaque, matt, nontoxic

Mixing. Mix in the manner of SG-1.

Application. Apply in the manner of SG-1.

Firing. Fire in the manner of SG-103.

Fired Results. This glaze fires to an opaque white matt in oxidation and slightly more gray in reduction.

Feldspar (Custer)	51.3
Talc	9.2
Tennessee ball clay #1	25.1
Kaolin	5.2
Whiting	9.2

SG-332 **Opaque Off-White Matt Glaze   Cone 10**
Courtesy of Gordon Beaver, Kingston, Arkansas
leadless, opaque, matt, nontoxic

Mixing. Mix in the manner of SG-1.

Application. Apply in the manner of SG-1.

Firing. Fire in the manner of SG-103.

Fired Results. In oxidation, this glaze is a nice off-white; in reduction it is a darker off-white. It iron spots well over medium-dark clays.

Feldspar (Custer)	50.0
Kaolin (EPK)	25.0
Dolomite	20.0
Whiting	5.0

SG-333 | **Opaque Mottled-White Matt Glaze   Cone 10**
leadless, opaque, matt, nontoxic

Mixing. Mix in the manner of SG-1.

Application. Apply in the manner of SG-1.

Firing. Fire in the manner of SG-103.

Fired Results. This glaze is a smooth matt white in oxidation and a mottled white matt in reduction.

Kaolin	32.0
Dolomite	30.0
Feldspar (Custer)	24.0
Silica	8.0
Whiting	7.0
Bentonite	1.0
Add:	
C.M.C.	1 tsp.

SG-334 | **Translucent Ochre-Yellow Matt Glaze   Cone 10**
barium, translucent, matt, toxic

Mixing. Mix in the manner of SG-3.

Application. Apply in the manner of SG-3.

Firing. Fire in the manner of SG-103.

Fired Results. This glaze fires to a translucent yellow matt in oxidation and a grayed yellow in reduction.

Feldspar (Custer)	40.0
Barium carbonate	16.4
Whiting	14.6
Tennessee ball clay #1	8.8
Magnesium carbonate	7.8
Ultrox	6.9
Yellow ochre	4.8
Rutile	1.7

SG-335 | **Opaque Waxy-Yellow Matt Glaze   Cone 10**
leadless, opaque, matt, nontoxic

Mixing. Mix in the manner of SG-1.

Application. Apply in the manner of SG-1.

Firing. Fire in the manner of SG-103.

Fired Results. This glaze fires to a light cream-yellow in oxidation and a grayed-yellow in reduction. It iron spots well in heavy reduction.

Feldspar (Custer)	60.0
Whiting	19.4
Kaolin	15.9
Rutile	3.9
Red iron oxide	1.8
Bentonite	1.0
Add:	
C.M.C.	1 tsp.

SG-336 | **Firey-Yellow Matt Glaze   Cone 10**
leadless, opaque, matt, nontoxic

Mixing. Mix in the manner of SG-1.

Application. Apply in the manner of SG-1.

Firing. Fire in the manner of SG-103.

Fired Results. This glaze fires to a light firey-yellow matt in oxidation and a grayed-yellow in reduction.

Feldspar (Kingman)	50.0
Kaolin	50.0
Dolomite	25.0
Whiting	10.0
Tin oxide	5.0
Bone ash	8.0
Red iron oxide	1.0
Rutile	2.0

26
PORCELAIN GLAZES
CONE 10-15

Porcelain glazes as we know them today no doubt had their origin in China. Usually glazes which mature between cone 10–15, can be classified as porcelain glazes even though some porcelain-type glazes are fired at temperatures lower than this.

Porcelain glazes like those in the stoneware range are usually based on a few common compounds: kaolin, silica, feldspar, barium, magnesium, whiting, and calcium. Although using these few elements allows much easier measuring and mixing, caution should be exercised in this critical process to avoid costly mistakes.

The glazes in this chapter are arranged first by cone level, then by color alphabetically, and finally by surface texture, within each color division.

The reader will find lists of possible chemical substitutions in Chapter 34, Dictionary of Clay and Glaze Compounds.

Note. The glazes in this chapter are labeled toxic or nontoxic. Toxic glazes should be carefully handled both in formulation and in application. During preparation the potter should wear a dust mask to prevent inhalation of toxic materials and not allow these materials to come into prolonged contact with the skin. Frequent washing of the hands when handling these glazes is a wise precaution. Toxic glazes should be applied by brushing and dipping—never spraying. For even under the best conditions some inhalation of the toxic mist from the spray is bound to take place or, equally bad, the mist from the spray gun can settle on the skin and be absorbed into the body system.

FORMULAS FOR PORCELAIN GLAZES

PG-1   **Clear Porcelain Gloss Glaze   Cone 10**
feldspathic, transparent, gloss, nontoxic

Mixing. Weigh out the ingredients and mix by using one of the methods outlined in Chapter 17, Glaze Preparation.

Application. Apply to cone 06–04 bisque by brushing, dipping, or spraying. See Chapter 17 for more details.

Firing. Fire in a nonelectric kiln to the cone level indicated in the recipe.

Fired Results. This glaze fires to a clear gloss at cone 10 in oxidation or reduction. It is a good base for most of the high-fire colorants.

Cornwall stone	60.0
Feldspar (Buckingham)	20.0
Whiting	3.0
Colemanite	3.0
Add:	
Bentonite	1.0
C.M.C.	1 tsp.

PG-2

Clear Semi-Gloss Glaze   Cone 10
feldspathic, transparent, semi-gloss, nontoxic

Mixing. Mix in the manner of PG-1.

Application. Apply in the manner of PG-1.

Firing. Fire in the manner of PG-1.

Fired Results. This glaze fires to a clear semi-gloss at cone 10 in oxidation or reduction. It is a good base for most high-fire colorants and can easily be made opaque by the addition of 5%–10% tin oxide or other opacifier.

Silica	32.0
Whiting	20.0
Feldspar (Buckingham)	32.0
Kaolin (Florida)	16.0
Add:	
Bentonite	1.0
C.M.C.	1 tsp.

PG-3

Clear Gloss Glaze   Cone 10
feldspathic, transparent, gloss, nontoxic

Mixing. Mix in the manner of PG-1.

Application. Apply in the manner of PG-1.

Firing. Fire in the manner of PG-1.

Fired Results. This glaze fires to a clear crackle of great beauty and is of the type favored by the ancient potters of China. It is a very good base for most colorants and can be made opaque by the use of 10% tin oxide or other opacifier.

Cornwall stone	87.0
Whiting	13.0
Add:	
Bentonite	1.0
C.M.C.	1 tsp.

PG-4

Opaque White Glaze   Cone 10
feldspathic, opaque, semi-gloss, nontoxic

Mixing. Mix in the manner of PG-1.

Application. Apply in the manner of PG-1.

Firing. Fire in the manner of PG-1.

Fired Results. This glaze fires to a buttery opaque white at cone 10 in oxidation or reduction. It is a good base for most of the high-fire colorants.

Feldspar (Kona F-4)	80.0
Whiting	10.0
Kaolin	9.0
Bone ash	3.0
Add:	
Bentonite	1.0
C.M.C.	1 tsp.

PG-5

Opaque Black Satin-Matt Glaze   Cone 11
feldspathic, opaque, satin matt, nontoxic

Mixing. Mix in the manner of PG-1.

Application. Apply in the manner of PG-1.

Firing. Fire in the manner of PG-1.

Fired Results. This glaze fires to an opaque black satin matt at cone 11, oxidation or reduction.

Silica	30.5
Whiting	26.0
Kaolin (Florida)	13.0
Cobalt oxide	8.5
Iron chromate	8.0
Feldspar (Custer)	7.0
Kaolin (EPK)	7.0
Add:	
Bentonite	1.0
C.M.C.	1 tsp.

PG-6

Mottled Brown-Black Gloss Glaze   Cone 11
feldspathic, opaque, gloss, nontoxic

Mixing. Mix in the manner of PG-1.

Application. Apply in the manner of PG-1.

Firing. Fire in the manner of PG-1.

Fired Results. This glaze fires to a mottled brown-black gloss at cone 11, oxidation or reduction.

Feldspar (Kingman)	55.5
Silica	23.5
Red iron oxide	9.6
Whiting	6.8
Kaolin (Florida)	4.6
Add:	
Bentonite	1.0
C.M.C.	1 tsp.

PG-7 **Opaque Mottled-Brown Matt Glaze Cone 11**
feldspathic, opaque, matt, nontoxic

Mixing. Mix in the manner of PG-1.

Application. Apply in the manner of PG-1.

Firing. Fire in the manner of PG-1.

Fired Results. This glaze fires to an opaque brown in oxidation and a mottled-brown matt in reduction.

Feldspar (Buckingham)	39.4
Silica	24.2
Whiting	17.5
Red iron oxide	9.0
Kaolin (Florida)	9.0
Ultrox	0.9
Add:	
C.M.C.	1 tsp.

PG-8 **Opaque Tan-Brown Semi-Gloss Glaze Cone 11**
feldspathic, opaque, semi-gloss, nontoxic

Mixing. Mix in the manner of PG-1.

Application. Apply in the manner of PG-1.

Firing. Fire in the manner of PG-1.

Fired Results. This glaze fires to a tan in oxidation and a warm brown in reduction at cone 11.

Silica	28.0
Feldspar (Buckingham)	24.9
Kaolin (Florida)	17.7
Whiting	17.5
Rutile	6.0
Tin oxide	2.0
Red iron oxide	2.0
Dolomite	1.9

PG-9 **Clear Fluid Gloss Glaze Cone 11**
feldspathic, transparent, gloss, nontoxic

Mixing. Mix in the manner of PG-1.

Application. Apply in the manner of PG-1.

Firing. Fire in the manner of PG-1.

Fired Results. This glaze fires to a clear fluid gloss at cone 11, oxidation or reduction. It is a good base for most of the high-fire colorants.

Feldspar (Custer)	34.5
Zinc oxide	22.8
Whiting	15.9
Silica	15.9
Feldspar (Kona F-4)	10.9

PG-10 **Clear Gloss Glaze Cone 11**
leadless, transparent, gloss, nontoxic

Mixing. Mix in the manner of PG-1.

Application. Apply in the manner of PG-1.

Firing. Fire in the manner of PG-1.

Fired Results. This glaze fires to a clear gloss in oxidation or reduction.

Silica	44.2
Kaolin (Florida)	27.0
Feldspar (Custer)	16.4
Whiting	11.4
Bentonite	1.0
Add:	
C.M.C.	1 tsp.

PG-11 **Clear Semi-Gloss Glaze Cone 11**
feldspathic, transparent, semi-gloss, nontoxic

Mixing. Mix in the manner of PG-1.

Application. Apply in the manner of PG-1.

Firing. Fire in the manner of PG-1.

Fired Results. This glaze fires to a clear semi-gloss at cone 11, oxidation or reduction.

Silica	32.0
Whiting	21.0
Feldspar (Custer)	33.0
Kaolin (EPK)	14.0

PG-12

Clear Matt Glaze   Cone 11
feldspathic, transparent, matt, nontoxic

Mixing. Mix in the manner of PG-1.

Application. Apply in the manner of PG-1.

Firing. Fire in the manner of PG-1.

Fired Results. This glaze fires to a clear matt in oxidation or reduction.

Feldspar (Kingman)	30.0
Silica	30.0
Whiting	21.2
Feldspar (Buckingham)	10.8
Kaolin	8.0
Add:	
Bentonite	1.0
C.M.C.	1 tsp.

PG-13

Opaque Metallic Purple Semi-Gloss Glaze   Cone 11
feldspathic-ash, opaque, semi-gloss, nontoxic

Mixing. Mix in the manner of PG-1.

Application. Apply in the manner of PG-1.

Firing. Fire in the manner of PG-1.

Fired Results. This glaze fires to an opaque brown semi-gloss in oxidation and a metallic purple semi-gloss in reduction.

Volcanic ash	37.0
Feldspar (Custer)	30.0
Red cone 06 clay	20.0
Hardwood ash	8.0
Red iron oxide	5.0
Add:	
Bentonite	1.0
C.M.C.	1 tsp.

PG-14

Opaque Rust-Brown Gloss Glaze   Cone 11
leadless, opaque, gloss, nontoxic

Mixing. Mix in the manner of PG-1.

Application. Apply in the manner of PG-1.

Firing. Fire in the manner of PG-1.

Fired Results. This glaze fires to a dark brown in oxidation and a rust-earthy brown in reduction with some mottling.

Monmouth clay	40.0
Feldspar (Custer)	20.0
Albany slip	18.0
Feldspar (Kingman)	7.5
Kaolin	6.7
Whiting	6.2
Burnt umber	1.6
Add:	
Bentonite	1.0

PG-15

Opaque Tan Gloss Glaze   Cone 11
feldspathic, opaque, gloss, nontoxic

Mixing. Mix in the manner of PG-1.

Application. Apply in the manner of PG-1.

Firing. Fire in the manner of PG-1.

Fired Results. This glaze fires to an opaque tan gloss in oxidation and slightly darker and mottled in reduction.

Feldspar (Kingman)	54.4
Dolomite	9.3
Tennessee ball clay #4	8.6
Whiting	7.7
Ultrox	5.4
Kaolin (EPK)	5.1
Rutile	4.7
Colemanite	4.8
Add:	
C.M.C.	1 tsp.

PG-16

Opaque Mottled Tan Semi-Gloss Glaze   Cone 11
leadless, opaque, semi-gloss, nontoxic

Mixing. Mix in the manner of PG-1.

Application. Apply in the manner of PG-1.

Firing. Fire in the manner of PG-1.

Fired Results. This glaze fires to an opaque mottled tan in oxidation and a gray-tan in reduction.

Lincoln clay	31.0
Feldspar (Custer)	25.9
Dolomite	18.4
Volcanic ash	10.3
Ledidolite	5.7
Silica	4.0
Bone ash	3.0
Ultrox	1.7

PG-17 **Warm Opaque Tan Semi-Gloss Glaze   Cone 11**
feldspathic, opaque, semi-gloss, nontoxic

Mixing. Mix in the manner of PG-1.

Application. Apply in the manner of PG-1.

Firing. Fire in the manner of PG-1.

Fired Results. This glaze fires to a warm opaque tan semi-gloss in oxidation and slightly darker and more gray in reduction.

Feldspar (Buckingham)	14.8
Feldspar (Custer)	14.8
Feldspar (Kingman)	14.8
Whiting	21.0
Silica	12.6
Kaolin (Florida)	11.6
Tin oxide	7.0
Yellow ochre	2.0
Rutile	1.4

PG-18 **Translucent White Gloss Glaze   Cone 11**
feldspathic, translucent, gloss, nontoxic

Mixing. Mix in the manner of PG-1.

Application. Apply in the manner of PG-1.

Firing. Fire in the manner of PG-1.

Fired Results. This glaze fires to a translucent white gloss in oxidation or reduction.

Silica	35.5
Whiting	21.0
Feldspar (Kingman)	21.1
Kaolin	9.2
Feldspar (Buckingham)	8.2
Bone ash	5.0

PG-19 **Translucent White Satin-Matt Glaze   Cone 11**
feldspathic, translucent, satin matt, nontoxic

Mixing. Mix in the manner of PG-1.

Application. Apply in the manner of PG-1.

Firing. Fire in the manner of PG-1.

Fired Results. This glaze fires to a translucent white satin matt in oxidation or reduction.

Nepheline syenite	39.5
Whiting	7.7
Zinc oxide	2.1
Kaolin (Florida)	19.0
Silica	11.7
Opax	4.0
Bentonite	2.0
Add:	
C.M.C.	1 tsp.

PG-20 **Translucent White Cloudy Matt Glaze   Cone 11**
feldspathic, translucent, matt, nontoxic

Mixing. Mix in the manner of PG-1.

Application. Apply in the manner of PG-1.

Firing. Fire in the manner of PG-1.

Fired Results. This glaze fires to a translucent white matt with cloudy effects in oxidation or reduction at cone 11.

Feldspar (Custer)	56.8
Whiting	23.7
Kaolin	17.0
Bentonite	2.5
Add:	
C.M.C.	1 tsp.

PG-21 **Semi-Opaque White Smooth Gloss Glaze   Cone 11**
feldspathic, semi-opaque, gloss, nontoxic

Mixing. Mix in the manner of PG-1.

Application. Apply in the manner of PG-1.

Firing. Fire in the manner of PG-1.

Fired Results. This glaze fires to a semi-opaque white smooth gloss in oxidation or reduction at cone 11.

Cornwall stone	84.0
Whiting	14.0
Bentonite	2.0

PG-22

Semi-Opaque White Smooth Matt Glaze   Cone 11
feldspathic, semi-opaque, smooth matt, nontoxic

Mixing. Mix in the manner of PG-1.

Application. Apply in the manner of PG-1.

Firing. Fire in the manner of PG-1.

Fired Results. This glaze fires to a semi-opaque white smooth matt with a buttery surface sheen in oxidation or reduction.

Feldspar (Custer)	44.0
Colemanite	14.0
Dolomite	8.0
Talc	14.0
Kaolin (Florida)	5.0
Silica	20.0
Add:	
Bentonite	1.0

PG-23

Milky Opaque Gloss Glaze   Cone 11
colemanite-barium, opaque, gloss, toxic

Mixing. Mix in the manner of PG-1, but handle with care as this glaze contains a toxic chemical.

Application. Apply by brushing or dipping. (See note at the beginning of this chapter.)

Firing. Fire in the manner of PG-1.

Fired Results. This glaze fires to a milky opaque gloss in oxidation or reduction at cone 11.

Whiting	10.0
Colemanite	12.0
Barium carbonate	6.0
Magnesium carbonate	4.0
Feldspar (Custer)	30.0
Silica	32.0
Kaolin	6.0

PG-24

Opaque White Semi-Gloss Glaze   Cone 11
feldspathic, opaque, semi-gloss, nontoxic

Mixing. Mix in the manner of PG-1.

Application. Apply in the manner of PG-1.

Firing. Fire in the manner of PG-1.

Fired Results. This glaze fires to an opaque white semi-gloss in oxidation or reduction.

Feldspar (potash)	35.1
Kaolin (Florida)	9.9
Whiting	13.5
Borax	1.0
Silica	16.2
Zinc oxide	1.8
Zircopax	23.4

PG-25

Opaque White Semi-Matt Glaze   Cone 11
feldspathic, opaque, semi-matt, nontoxic

Mixing. Mix in the manner of PG-1.

Application. Apply in the manner of PG-1.

Firing. Fire in the manner of PG-1.

Fired Results. This glaze fires to an opaque white semi-matt in oxidation or reduction.

Feldspar (Custer)	45.3
Whiting	19.3
Silica	11.6
Kaolin	24.0
Zinc oxide	5.0
Rutile	3.0
Opax	2.0

PG-26

Opaque White Buttery Smooth-Matt Glaze   Cone 11
feldspathic, opaque, smooth matt, nontoxic

Mixing. Mix in the manner of PG-1.

Application. Apply in the manner of PG-1.

Firing. Fire in the manner of PG-1.

Fired Results. This glaze fires to an opaque white smooth matt in oxidation or reduction at cone 11.

Feldspar (Kona F-4)	80.0
Whiting	9.0
Kaolin	9.0
Bone ash	2.0
Add:	
Bentonite	1.0
C.M.C.	1 tsp.

PG-27 **Opaque White Matt Glaze   Cone 11**
feldspathic, opaque, matt, nontoxic

Mixing. Mix in the manner of PG-1.

Application. Apply in the manner of PG-1.

Firing. Fire in the manner of PG-1.

Fired Results. This glaze fires to an opaque white matt in oxidation or reduction at cone 11.

Feldspar (Buckingham)	25.9
Silica	25.5
Talc	18.2
Colemanite	12.3
Dolomite	8.7
Tennessee ball clay #1	9.4

PG-28 **Opaque White Matt Glaze   Cone 11**
leadless, opaque, matt, nontoxic

Mixing. Mix in the manner of PG-1.

Application. Apply in the manner of PG-1.

Firing. Fire in the manner of PG-1.

Fired Results. This glaze fires to an opaque white matt in oxidation or reduction at cone 11. This is a good base for most of the high-fire colorants.

Nepheline syenite	30.6
Kaolin (Florida)	22.2
Silica	15.4
Dolomite	13.6
Zinc oxide	11.3
Whiting	0.7

PG-29 **Opaque Gray-Blue Matt Glaze   Cone 12**
feldspathic, opaque, matt, nontoxic

Mixing. Mix in the manner of PG-1.

Application. Apply in the manner of PG-1.

Firing. Fire in the manner of PG-1.

Fired Results. This glaze fires to an opaque gray-blue matt in oxidation and slightly darker in reduction at cone 12.

Feldspar (Kingman)	48.4
Kaolin (Florida)	23.7
Dolomite	21.2
Whiting	2.4
Colemanite	1.5
Cobalt oxide	0.6
Chromium oxide	0.2

PG-30 **Opaque Brown Matt Glaze   Cone 12**
feldspathic-barium, opaque, matt, toxic

Mixing. Mix in the manner of PG-23.

Application. Apply in the manner of PG-23.

Firing. Fire in the manner of PG-1.

Fired Results. This glaze fires to an opaque brown in oxidation and a mottled brown in reduction.

Feldspar (Custer)	50.1
Barium carbonate	18.9
Kentucky ball clay #4	10.4
Whiting	7.2
Ultrox	7.6
Red iron oxide	3.8
Rutile	2.0
Add:	
C.M.C.	1 tsp.

PG-31 **Clear Gloss Glaze   Cone 12**
leadless, transparent, gloss, nontoxic

Mixing. Mix in the manner of PG-1.

Application. Apply in the manner of PG-1.

Firing. Fire in the manner of PG-1.

Fired Results. This glaze fires to a clear gloss in oxidation or reduction at cone 12.

Silica	44.2
Kaolin	28.0
Feldspar (Kingman)	16.2
Whiting	11.6
Add:	
Bentonite	1.0
C.M.C.	1 tsp.

PG-32

Clear Gloss Glaze   Cone 12
feldspathic, transparent, gloss, nontoxic

Mixing. Mix in the manner of PG-1.

Application. Apply in the manner of PG-1.

Firing. Fire in the manner of PG-1.

Fired Results. This glaze fires to a clear gloss in oxidation or reduction at cone 12.

Feldspar (Kingman)	53.8
Whiting	19.2
Tennessee ball clay #1	19.2
Kaolin (Florida)	4.6
Opax	3.2
Add:	
Bentonite	1.0
C.M.C.	1 tsp.

PG-33

Clear Matt Glaze   Cone 12
feldspathic, transparent, matt, nontoxic

Mixing. Mix in the manner of PG-1.

Application. Apply in the manner of PG-1.

Firing. Fire in the manner of PG-1.

Fired Results. This glaze fires to a clear gloss in oxidation or reduction at cone 12.

Feldspar (Custer)	38.0
Whiting	21.5
Kaolin (Florida)	21.5
Silica	15.5
Titanium oxide	4.5
Add:	
Bentonite	1.0
C.M.C.	1 tsp.

PG-34

Opaque Gray-Tan Semi-Gloss Glaze   Cone 12
feldspathic, opaque, semi-gloss, nontoxic

Mixing. Mix in the manner of PG-1.

Application. Apply in the manner of PG-1.

Firing. Fire in the manner of PG-1.

Fired Results. This glaze fires to an opaque gray-tan in oxidation and darker in reduction.

Feldspar (Custer)	40.0
Hardwood ash (oak)	34.0
Kentucky ball clay #4	24.0
Magnesium carbonate	2.0
Add:	
Bentonite	2.0
C.M.C.	1 tsp.

PG-35

Clear Gloss Glaze   Cone 13
feldspathic, transparent, gloss, nontoxic

Mixing. Mix in the manner of PG-1.

Application. Apply in the manner of PG-1.

Firing. Fire in the manner of PG-1.

Fired Results. This glaze fires to a clear gloss in oxidation or reduction.

Feldspar (Custer)	45.0
Feldspar (Kingman)	40.0
Whiting	14.0
Bentonite	1.0
Add:	
C.M.C.	1 tsp.

PG-36

Clear Semi-Gloss Glaze   Cone 13
feldspathic, transparent, semi-gloss, nontoxic

Mixing. Mix in the manner of PG-1.

Application. Apply in the manner of PG-1.

Firing. Fire in the manner of PG-1.

Fired Results. This glaze fires to a clear semi-gloss in oxidation or reduction.

Feldspar (Custer)	80.0
Whiting	20.0
Add:	
C.M.C.	1 tsp.

PG-37

Clear Smooth Matt Glaze   Cone 13
feldspathic, transparent, matt, nontoxic

Mixing. Mix in the manner of PG-1.

Application. Apply in the manner of PG-1.

Firing. Fire in the manner of PG-1.

Fired Results. This glaze fires to a clear smooth matt in oxidation or reduction.

Feldspar (Custer)	75.0
Whiting	25.0
Add:	
Bentonite	2.0
C.M.C.	1 tsp.

PG-38

Translucent White Gloss Glaze   Cone 13
leadless, translucent, gloss, nontoxic

Mixing. Mix in the manner of PG-1.

Application. Apply in the manner of PG-1.

Firing. Fire in the manner of PG-1.

Fired Results. This glaze fires to a translucent white gloss at cone 13–15 in oxidation or reduction.

Feldspar (Custer)	42.0
Silica	26.0
Whiting	18.0
Tennessee ball clay #1	12.0
Kaolin (EPK)	3.0

PG-39

Translucent White Semi-Gloss Glaze   Cone 13
leadless, translucent, semi-gloss, nontoxic

Mixing. Mix in the manner of PG-1.

Application. Apply in the manner of PG-1.

Firing. Fire in the manner of PG-1.

Fired Results. This glaze fires to a translucent gloss white in oxidation or reduction at cone 13.

Silica	50.0
Kaolin (calcined)	26.0
Feldspar (Custer)	15.0
Dolomite	10.0

PG-40

Opaque Gloss Glaze   Cone 13
leadless, opaque, gloss, nontoxic

Mixing. Mix in the manner of PG-1.

Application. Apply in the manner of PG-1.

Firing. Fire in the manner of PG-1.

Fired Results. This glaze fires to an opaque white in oxidation or reduction at cone 13 and above.

Feldspar (Buckingham)	70.0
Silica	25.0
Kaolin	3.0
Dolomite	2.0

PG-41

Clear Gloss Glaze   Cone 14
feldspathic, transparent, gloss, nontoxic

Mixing. Mix in the manner of PG-1.

Application. Apply in the manner of PG-1.

Firing. Fired in the manner of PG-1.

Fired Results. This glaze fires to a clear gloss in oxidation or reduction.

Feldspar (Custer)	28.0
Whiting	20.0
Kaolin	20.0
Silica	32.0
Add:	
Bentonite	1.0
C.M.C.	1 tsp.

PG-42

Clear Semi-Gloss Glaze   Cone 14
feldspathic, transparent, semi-gloss, nontoxic

Mixing. Mix in the manner of PG-1.

Application. Apply in the manner of PG-1.

Firing. Fire in the manner of PG-1.

Fired Results. This glaze fires to a clear semi-gloss in oxidation or reduction.

Feldspar (Kingman)	26.0
Whiting	22.0
Kaolin	20.0
Silica	32.0

PG-43

Clear Matt Glaze   Cone 14
feldspathic, transparent, matt, nontoxic

Mixing. Mix in the manner of PG-1.

Application. Apply in the manner of PG-1.

Firing. Fire in the manner of PG-1.

Fired Results. This glaze fires to a clear matt in oxidation or reduction.

Feldspar (Kingman)	26.0
Whiting	26.0
Kaolin	20.0
Silica	28.0
Add:	
C.M.C.	1 tsp.

PG-44

Translucent Matt Glaze   Cone 14
feldspathic, transparent, matt, nontoxic

Mixing. Mix in the manner of PG-1.

Application. Apply in the manner of PG-1.

Firing. Fire in the manner of PG-1.

Fired Results. This glaze fires to a translucent matt in oxidation or reduction.

Feldspar (Buckingham)	70.0
Whiting	25.0
Kaolin	5.0

PG-45

Semi-Opaque Gloss Glaze   Cone 14
leadless, semi-opaque, gloss, nontoxic

Mixing. Mix in the manner of PG-1.

Application. Apply in the manner of PG-1.

Firing. Fire in the manner of PG-1.

Fired Results. This glaze fires to a semi-opaque white gloss at cone 14, oxidation or reduction.

Silica	46.0
Feldspar (Custer)	14.0
Alumina oxide	12.0
Whiting	10.0
Feldspar (Buckingham)	10.0
Kaolin (EPK)	8.0
Add:	
C.M.C.	1 tsp.

PG-46

Clear Gloss Glaze   Cone 15
feldspathic, transparent, gloss, nontoxic

Mixing. Mix in the manner of PG-1.

Application. Apply in the manner of PG-1.

Firing. Fire in the manner of PG-1.

Fired Results. This glaze fires to a clear gloss in oxidation or reduction at cone 15.

Feldspar (Kingman)	28.0
Whiting	20.0
Kaolin (Florida)	20.0
Silica	32.0

PG-47 Clear Semi-Gloss Glaze Cone 15

feldspathic, transparent, semi-gloss, nontoxic

Mixing. Mix in the manner of PG-1.

Application. Apply in the manner of PG-1.

Firing. Fire in the manner of PG-1.

Fired Results. This glaze fires to a clear semi-gloss in oxidation or reduction at cone 15.

Feldspar (Kingman)	26.0
Whiting	22.0
Kaolin (Florida)	20.0
Silica	34.0
Add:	
Bentonite	1.0
C.M.C.	1 tsp.

PG-48 Semi-Opaque White Gloss Glaze Cone 15

leadless, semi-opaque, gloss, nontoxic

Mixing. Mix in the manner of PG-1.

Application. Apply in the manner of PG-1.

Firing. Fire in the manner of PG-1.

Fired Results. This glaze fires to a semi-opaque white gloss glaze at cone 15, oxidation or reduction.

Silica	48.0
Feldspar (Custer)	20.0
Alumina oxide	10.0
Kaolin (Florida)	8.0
Add:	
C.M.C.	1 tsp.

PG-49 Translucent Semi-Gloss White Glaze Cone 15

leadless, translucent, semi-gloss, nontoxic

Mixing. Mix in the manner of PG-1.

Application. Apply in the manner of PG-1.

Firing. Fire in the manner of PG-1.

Fired Results. This glaze fires to translucent semi-gloss white in oxidation or reduction at cone 15.

Silica	46.0
Alumina oxide	26.0
Feldspar (Custer)	10.0
Feldspar (Kona F-4)	6.0
Whiting	8.0
Kaolin (Florida, calcined)	4.0
Add:	
Bentonite	1.0
C.M.C.	1 tsp.

PG-50 Translucent White Matt Glaze Cone 15

leadless, translucent, matt, nontoxic

Mixing. Mix in the manner of PG-1.

Application. Apply in the manner of PG-1.

Firing. Fire in the manner of PG-1.

Fired Results. This glaze fires to a translucent white matt in oxidation or reduction.

Silica	46.0
Alumina oxide	28.0
Feldspar (Custer)	8.0
Feldspar (Kona F-4)	4.0
Whiting	10.0
Kaolin (Florida, calcined)	4.0
Add:	
Bentonite	2.0
C.M.C.	1 tsp.

27
CELADON GLAZES
CONE 010-11

For many centuries celadon glazes have been greatly prized for their beautiful cool colors which have a great depth and a changeability of character reminiscent of the hues to be found in a cool body of water. They must be especially formulated and fired in a reducing atmosphere to achieve their particular color characteristics, ranging from cool gray through gray-green and blue-green to olive green. Even grayed blues of great beauty can be produced with the addition of bone ash to the glaze formula in amounts of 4% to 8%. It was in this manner that the Chinese Sung dynasty Chun blue glazes were produced.

The glazes in this chapter range in color to include all types of celadons. They also range in cone level from cone 010 to 11.

For more details on reduction glazes the reader may wish to consult Chapter 16 on Glaze Types under Reduction Glazes.

The glazes in this chapter are arranged first by cone level, then by color, alphabetically, and finally by surface, within each color section.

The reader will find lists of possible chemical substitutions in Chapter 34, Dictionary of Clay and Glaze Compounds.

Note. The glazes in this chapter are labeled toxic or nontoxic. Toxic glazes should be carefully handled both in formulation and in application. During preparation the potter should wear a dust mask to prevent inhalation of toxic materials and not allow these materials to come into prolonged contact with the skin. Frequent washing of the hands when handling these glazes is a wise precaution. Toxic glazes should be applied by brushing and dipping—never spraying. For even under the best conditions some inhalation of the toxic mist from the spray is bound to take place or, equally bad, the mist from the spray gun can settle on the skin and be absorbed into the body system.

FORMULAS FOR CELADON GLAZES

CG-1   **Light Gray-Green Semi-Gloss Celadon Glaze   Cone 010**
alkaline, translucent, semi-gloss, nontoxic

Mixing. Weigh out the ingredients and mix by using one of the methods outlined in Chapter 17, Glaze Preparation.

Application. Apply to cone 06 bisque by brushing, dipping, or spraying. See Chapter 17 for more details.

Firing. Fire in oxidation in a gas kiln to cone 018, then in moderate reduction to cone 010, cool the kiln slowly down to cone 016 with the kiln sealed, then cool normally.

Fired Results. This glaze fires to a gray-green semi-gloss at cone 010 in moderate reduction.

Lithium carbonate	7.5
Pemco frit #54	61.5
Kaolin (Florida)	20.8
Silica	10.2
Add:	
Red iron oxide	2.0
Bentonite	1.0
C.M.C.	1 tsp.

CG-2 **Cloudy Gray-Green Semi-Gloss Celadon Glaze   Cone 04**
alkaline, translucent, semi-gloss, nontoxic

Mixing. Mix in the manner of CG-1.

Application. Apply in the manner of CG-1.

Firing. Fire in oxidation up to cone 012 then reduce the kiln to cone 04. At this point seal the kiln and cool slowly down to cone 010 then cool normally.

Fired Results. This glaze fires to a cloudy gray-green semi-gloss at cone 04 in moderate reduction.

Lepidolite	18.4
Spodumene	34.6
Pemco frit #54	48.0
Add:	
Red iron oxide	2.0
Bentonite	1.0
C.M.C.	1 tsp.

CG-3 **Dark Gray-Green Semi-Gloss Celadon Glaze   Cone 04**
alkaline, translucent, semi-gloss, nontoxic

Mixing. Mix in the manner of CG-1.

Application. Apply in the manner of CG-1.

Firing. Fire in the manner of CG-2.

Fired Results. This glaze fires to a dark gray-green semi-gloss at cone 04 in moderate reduction. It is reminiscent of the celadons produced in Northern China in ancient times.

Lepidolite	20.6
Spodumene	36.2
Hommel frit #14	39.3
Whiting	4.9
Add:	
Red iron oxide	2.0
Bentonite	1.0

CG-4 **Dark Grayed Blue-Green Semi-Gloss Celadon Glaze   Cone 04**
alkaline, translucent, semi-gloss, nontoxic

Mixing. Mix in the manner of CG-1.

Application. Apply in the manner of CG-1.

Firing. Fire in the manner of CG-1.

Fired Results. This glaze fires to a dark grayed blue-green semi-gloss at cone 04 in moderate reduction.

Colemanite	70.0
Kaolin (Florida)	12.0
Silica	18.0
Add:	
Red iron oxide	1.5
Bentonite	1.0
C.M.C.	1 tsp.

CG-5 **Transparent Blue-Green Gloss Celadon Glaze   Cone 01**
alkaline-frit, transparent, gloss, nontoxic

Mixing. Mix in the manner of CG-1.

Application. Apply in the manner of CG-1.

Firing. This glaze should be fired in oxidation up to cone 014, then in moderate reduction up to the indicated cone level, cone 01.

Fired Results. This glaze fires to a transparent blue-green gloss in moderate reduction at cone 01.

Ferro frit #3819	30.4
Hommel frit #14	32.0
Whiting	31.8
Lithium carbonate	5.8
Add:	
Bentonite	2.0
Red iron oxide	2.0
C.M.C.	1 tsp.

CG-6 **Cloudy Translucent Blue-Green Semi-Gloss Celadon Glaze   Cone 01**
colemanite, translucent, semi-gloss, nontoxic

Mixing. Mix in the manner of CG-1.

Application. Apply in the manner of CG-1.

Firing. Fire in the manner of CG-5.

Fired Results. This glaze fires to a cloudy blue-green semi-gloss celadon in moderate reduction at cone 01.

Colemanite	65.0
Kaolin	8.0
Whiting	2.0
Silica	25.0
Add:	
Red iron oxide	2.0
Bentonite	2.0

CG-7 **Translucent Blue-Green Semi-Gloss Celadon Glaze**
Cone 4
colemanite, translucent, semi-gloss, nontoxic

Mixing. Mix in the manner of CG-1.

Application. Apply in the manner of CG-1.

Firing. Fire in oxidation to cone 010, then in moderate reduction to cone 4. Cool the kiln very slowly back down to cone 010 then cool normally.

Fired Results. This glaze fires to a translucent blue-green semi-gloss in moderate reduction at cone 4.

Colemanite	60.0
Kaolin (Florida)	8.0
Whiting	2.0
Silica	28.0
Red iron oxide	2.0
Add:	
Bentonite	2.0
C.M.C.	1 tsp.

CG-8 **Transparent Blue-Green Semi-Gloss Celadon Glaze**
Cone 4
alkaline-frit, transparent, semi-gloss, nontoxic

Mixing. Mix in the manner of CG-1.

Application. Apply in the manner of CG-1.

Firing. Fire in the manner of CG-7.

Fired Results. This glaze fires to a transparent blue-green semi-gloss in moderate reduction at cone 4.

Pemco frit #54	34.0
Pemco frit #25	32.5
Silica	32.0
Red iron oxide	1.5
Add:	
Bentonite	2.0
C.M.C.	1 tsp.

CG-9 **Opaque Grayed Blue-Green Celadon Glaze   Cone 6**
feldspathic, opaque, smooth matt, nontoxic

Mixing. Mix in the manner of CG-1.

Application. Apply in the manner of CG-1.

Firing. Fire in oxidation to cone 010, then in moderate reduction to cone 6. Cool the kiln very slowly back down to cone 010 with kiln sealed, then cool normally.

Fired Results. This glaze fires to a grayed blue-green smooth matt at cone 6.

Feldspar (Kingman)	63.2
Whiting	6.6
Kaolin	5.0
Silica	25.0
Red iron oxide	1.7
Add:	
Bentonite	2.0
C.M.C.	1 tsp.

CG-10 **Opaque Blue Semi-Gloss Celadon Glaze   Cone 7**
feldspathic, opaque, semi-gloss, nontoxic

Mixing. Mix in the manner of CG-1.

Application. Apply in the manner of CG-1.

Firing. Fire in oxidation to cone 08, then slowly in moderate reduction to cone 7. Cool the kiln slowly down to cone 02 in reduction, seal the kiln then cool normally.

Feldspar (Kingman)	40.2
Whiting	15.8
Magnesium carbonate	2.5
Zinc oxide	3.6
Kaolin (Florida)	3.8
Silica	34.1
Add:	
Red iron oxide	1.0
Bone ash	2.0
C.M.C.	1 tsp.

CG-11 **Soft Blue Chün-Type Crackle Celadon Glaze   Cone 8–9**
feldspathic, opaque, semi-gloss, nontoxic

Mixing. Mix in the manner of CG-1.

Application. Apply in the manner of CG-1.

Firing. Allow for a warming-up period of the kiln with only the pilots lit for about one hour. Then fire slowly in oxidation up to cone 015. Fire in moderate reduction up to cone 06 and heavy reduction up to cone 8–9. Seal the kiln and allow to cool slowly back down to cone 6, then cool normally.

Fired Results. This glaze fires to an opaque soft blue of the Chün type favored by the ancient potters of China.

Feldspar (Buckingham)	82.0
Whiting	8.0
Strontium carbonate	1.0
Silica	7.5
Bone ash	1.5
Add:	
Red iron oxide	1.5
Bentonite	1.0
C.M.C.	1 tsp.

CG-12 **Gray-Blue Celadon Glaze   Cone 8**
feldspathic, translucent, gloss, nontoxic

Mixing. Mix in the manner of CG-1.

Application. Apply in the manner of CG-1.

Firing. Fire in the manner of CG-11.

Fired Results. This glaze fires to a gray-blue in moderate reduction at cone 8. The surface is not a high-gloss but rather one of depth.

Feldspar (Kingman)	78.4
Silica	14.0
Whiting	4.8
Red iron oxide	2.2
Opax	0.7
Add:	
Bone ash	2.0
C.M.C.	1 tsp.

CG-13 **Gray-Blue Celadon Glaze   Cone 8**
feldspathic, translucent, semi-gloss, nontoxic

Mixing. Mix in the manner of CG-1.

Application. Apply in the manner of CG-1.

Firing. Fire in the manner of CG-11.

Fired Results. This glaze fires to a gray-blue semi-gloss in moderate reduction at cone 8.

Feldspar (Kingman)	77.4
Silica	14.0
Whiting	5.8
Red iron oxide	2.3
Opax	0.5
Add:	
Bone ash	1.5
C.M.C.	1 tsp.

CG-14 **Soft Light Gray-Blue Crackle Celadon Glaze   Cone 9**
feldspathic-ash, semi-opaque, semi-gloss, nontoxic

Mixing. Mix the ingredients in the manner of CG-1 but see Chapter 29 for the proper method of preparing wood ash for use in this glaze.

Application. This glaze works best when it is applied by spraying. See Chapter 17 on Glaze Preparation for more information about sprayed glazes.

Firing. Fire in the manner of CG-11.

Fired Results. This glaze fires to a soft light gray-blue crackle at cone 9 in heavy reduction.

Feldspar (Buckingham)	80.0
Whiting	7.0
Silica	7.0
Soft wood ash	4.0
Bone ash	2.0
Add:	
Yellow ochre	1.0
Bentonite	1.0
C.M.C.	1 tsp.

CG-15 **Soft Opaque Blue-Gray Matt Celadon Glaze   Cone 9**
feldspathic, opaque, matt, nontoxic

Mixing. Mix in the manner of CG-14.

Application. Apply in the manner of CG-14.

Firing. Fire in the manner of CG-11.

Fired Results. This glaze fires to an opaque soft blue-gray matt at cone 9 reduction.

Nepheline syenite	31.5
Kaolin (Georgia)	21.0
Silica	17.2
Dolomite	13.2
Whiting	7.0
Zinc oxide	6.0
Spodumene	3.1
Red iron oxide	1.0
Add:	
Bone ash	3.0

CG-16 **Gray-Blue Celadon Glaze   Cone 9**
feldspathic, translucent, semi-gloss, nontoxic

Mixing. Mix in the manner of CG-1.

Application. Apply in the manner of CG-1.

Firing. Fire in the manner of CG-11.

Fired Results. This glaze fires to a gray-blue celadon semi-gloss in moderate reduction at cone 9.

Feldspar (Kingman)	77.5
Silica	13.8
Whiting	6.0
Red iron oxide	2.2
Opax	0.5
Add:	
Bone ash	1.0
C.M.C.	1 tsp.

CG-17 **Transparent Greenish Blue Semi-Gloss Celadon Glaze
Cone 9**
lithium-calcium, transparent, semi-gloss, nontoxic

Mixing. Mix in the manner of CG-1.

Application. Apply in the manner of CG-1.

Firing. Fire in oxidation to cone 08, then in moderate reduction to cone 9. Cool the kiln while still reducing back to cone 02, seal it, and then cool normally.

Fired Results. This glaze fires to a transparent greenish blue semi-gloss in moderate reduction at cone 9.

Lithium carbonate	8.5
Whiting	15.8
Kaolin (Florida)	20.5
Silica	55.3
Add:	
Red iron oxide	1.2
Bentonite	2.0
C.M.C.	1 tsp.

CG-18 **Opaque Blue Smooth-Matt Celadon Glaze   Cone 9**
lithium-barium, opaque, smooth matt, toxic

Mixing. Mix in the manner of CG-1.

Application. Apply in the manner of CG-1.

Firing. Fire in the manner of CG-17.

Fired Results. This glaze fires to an opaque blue smooth matt in moderate reduction at cone 9.

Lepidolite	14.8
Spodumene	23.3
Pemco frit #54	8.9
Whiting	8.0
Barium carbonate	16.6
Silica	28.4
Add:	
Red iron oxide	1.1
Bentonite	2.0
C.M.C.	1 tsp.
Bone ash	1.0

CG-19   **Opaque Gray-Blue Semi-Gloss Celadon Glaze   Cone 9**
leadless, opaque, semi-gloss, nontoxic

Mixing. Mix in the manner of CG-1.

Application. Apply in the manner of CG-1.

Firing. Fire in the manner of CG-17.

Fired Results. This glaze fires to an opaque gray-blue semi-gloss at cone 9 reduction.

Pumice	59.4
Whiting	29.0
Magnesium carbonate	3.4
Kaolin (Florida)	8.2
Add:	
Black iron oxide	1.0
Bone ash	2.0
Bentonite	1.0
C.M.C.	1 tsp.

CG-20   **Opaque Blue-Green Satin-Matt Celadon Glaze   Cone 9**
barium, opaque, satin matt, toxic

Mixing. Mix in the manner of CG-1, but handle with care as this glaze contains a toxic chemical.

Application. Apply by brushing or dipping. (See note at the beginning of this chapter.)

Firing. Fire in the manner of CG-17

Fired Results. This glaze fires to an opaque blue-green satin matt at cone 9 reduction.

Pumice	55.0
Whiting	27.0
Barium carbonate	8.0
Kaolin (Florida)	8.0
Magnesium carbonate	2.0
Add:	
Yellow ochre	1.0
Bone ash	2.0
Bentonite	1.0
C.M.C.	1 tsp.

CG-21   **Soft Green-Gray Crackle Celadon Glaze   Cone 9**
feldspathic-ash, opaque, semi-gloss, nontoxic

Mixing. Mix in the manner of CG-14.

Application. Apply in the manner of CG-1.

Firing. Fire in the manner of CG-17.

Fired Results. This glaze fires to a soft green-gray crackle at cone 9 reduction.

Feldspar (Buckingham)	66.0
Kaolin (Florida)	5.0
Whiting	7.0
Silica	12.0
Soft wood ash	6.0
Bone ash	4.0
Add:	
Yellow ochre	1.6

CG-22   **Translucent Soft Blue-White Chün Glaze   Cone 9**
feldspathic-barium, translucent, semi-matt, toxic

Mixing. Mix in the manner of CG-20.

Application. Apply in the manner of CG-20.

Firing. Fire in the manner of CG-17.

Fired Results. This glaze fires to a translucent soft blue-white semi-matt at cone 9 reduction.

Feldspar (Buckingham)	42.1
Silica	27.1
Colemanite	8.9
Dolomite	8.8
Barium carbonate	4.4
Opax	2.5
Whiting	2.7
Kaolin (Georgia)	1.9
Zinc oxide	1.6
Red iron oxide	1.0
Add:	
Bone ash	3.0
Bentonite	1.0
C.M.C.	1 tsp.

CG-23 **Semi-Opaque Blue Semi-Gloss Celadon Glaze** **Cone 9–10**
feldspathic, semi-opaque, semi-gloss, nontoxic

Mixing. Mix in the manner of CG-1.

Application. Apply in the manner of CG-1.

Firing. Fire in the manner of CG-17.

Fired Results. This glaze fires to a semi-opaque blue semi-gloss at cone 9–10 reduction.

Feldspar (Custer)	29.0
Dalton clay	1.9
Whiting	9.0
Dolomite	32.6
Silica	23.3
Red iron oxide	0.7
Opax	1.4
Bentonite	2.0

CG-24 **Opaque Blue Chün Celadon Glaze** **Cone 10**
feldspathic-ash, opaque, semi-gloss, nontoxic

Mixing. Mix in the manner of CG-14.

Application. Apply in the manner of CG-14.

Firing. Fire in the manner of CG-11, but fire to cone 10.

Fired Results. This glaze fires to an opaque blue celadon semi-gloss at cone 10 heavy reduction.

Feldspar (Buckingham)	56.0
Silica	22.0
Whiting	14.0
Soft wood ash	5.0
Bone ash	3.0
Add:	
Yellow ochre	2.3
Bentonite	1.0
C.M.C.	1 tsp.

CG-25 **Soft Gray-Blue Kuan-Chun Glaze** **Cone 10**
feldspathic-ash, opaque, semi-gloss, nontoxic

Mixing. Mix in the manner of CG-14.

Application. Apply in the manner of CG-14.

Firing. Fire in the manner of CG-24.

Fired Results. This glaze fires to a soft blue semi-gloss celadon in cone 10 heavy reduction.

Feldspar (Buckingham)	49.0
Silica	27.0
Whiting	15.0
Soft wood ash	6.0
Bone ash	3.0
Add:	
Yellow ochre	2.5

CG-26 **Soft Blue-Gray Kuan-Chün Glaze** **Cone 10**
feldspathic-ash, opaque, semi-gloss, nontoxic

Mixing. Mix in the manner of CG-14.

Application. Apply in the manner of CG-14.

Firing. Fire in the manner of CG-24.

Fired Results. This glaze fires to an opaque soft blue-gray at cone 10 reduction.

Feldspar (Buckingham)	54.0
Silica	23.5
Whiting	13.5
Soft wood ash	6.0
Bone ash	3.0
Add:	
Yellow ochre	2.5

CG-27 **Soft Blue-Green Kuan-Chün Glaze** **Cone 10**
feldspathic-ash, opaque, semi-gloss, nontoxic

Mixing. Mix in the manner of CG-14.

Application. Apply in the manner of CG-14.

Firing. Fire in the manner of CG-24.

Fired Results. This glaze fires to an opaque soft blue-green at cone 10 reduction.

Feldspar (Buckingham)	56.0
Silica	22.0
Whiting	12.0
Mixed wood ash	6.0
Bone ash	4.0
Add:	
Yellow ochre	2.5

CG-28 **Light Blue-Green Gloss Celadon Glaze   Cone 10**
feldspathic, transparent, gloss, nontoxic

Mixing. Mix in the manner of CG-1.

Application. Apply in the manner of CG-1.

Firing. Fire in the manner of CG-24.

Fired Results. This glaze fires to a light blue-green gloss in moderate to heavy reduction at cone 10.

Feldspar (Kingman)	44.0
Whiting	23.0
Kaolin (EPK)	20.0
Silica	11.0
Red iron oxide	2.0
Add:	
Bentonite	1.0
C.M.C.	1 tsp.

CG-29 **Light Blue-Green Celadon Glaze   Cone 10**
feldspathic, transparent, gloss, nontoxic

Mixing. Mix in the manner of CG-1.

Application. Apply in the manner of CG-1.

Firing. Fire in the manner of CG-24.

Fired Results. This glaze fires to a light blue-green gloss in moderate reduction at cone 10.

Nepheline syenite	42.0
Silica	27.0
Whiting	19.0
Kaolin (Florida)	10.1
Red iron oxide	1.9
Add:	
C.M.C.	1 tsp.

CG-30 **Soft Gray-Green Matt Celadon Glaze   Cone 10**
feldspathic-ash, opaque, matt, nontoxic

Mixing. Mix in the manner of CG-14.

Application. Apply in the manner of CG-14.

Firing. Fire in the manner of CG-24.

Fired Results. This glaze fires to a soft gray-green opaque matt at cone 10 reduction.

Feldspar (Buckingham)	54.0
Silica	24.0
Whiting	13.0
Soft wood ash	6.0
Bone ash	3.0
Add:	
Yellow ochre	2.5

CG-31 **Dark Translucent Semi-Matt Celadon Glaze   Cone 10**
feldspathic, translucent, semi-matt, nontoxic

Mixing. Mix in the manner of CG-1.

Application. Apply in the manner of CG-1.

Firing. Fire in the manner of CG-24.

Fired Results. This glaze fires to a dark translucent semi-matt in moderate reduction at cone 10.

Whiting	30.0
Feldspar (Kingman)	29.3
Kaolin (Florida)	21.0
Silica	17.0
Red iron oxide	2.7
Add:	
Bentonite	1.0
C.M.C.	1 tsp.

CG-32 **Soft Opaque Gray-Blue Celadon Glaze   Cone 10**
feldspathic, opaque, semi-gloss, nontoxic

Mixing. Mix in the manner of CG-1.

Application. Apply in the manner of CG-1.

Firing. Fire in the manner of CG-24.

Fired Results. This glaze fires to an opaque gray-blue semi-gloss at cone 10 reduction.

Silica	37.6
Feldspar (Custer)	32.3
Bone ash	16.0
Kaolin (Florida)	7.9
Whiting	2.0
Strontium carbonate	2.0
Yellow ochre	2.2
Add:	
Bentonite	1.0
C.M.C.	1 tsp.

CG-33

Soft Opaque Blue-Green Celadon Glaze   Cone 10
feldspathic, opaque, semi-gloss, nontoxic

Mixing. Mix in the manner of CG-1.

Application. Apply in the manner of CG-1.

Firing. Fire in the manner of CG-24.

Fired Results. This glaze fires to an opaque soft blue-green semi-gloss at cone 10 reduction.

Silica	40.6
Feldspar (Kingman)	28.2
Bone ash	14.8
Kaolin (Georgia)	12.2
Whiting	2.1
Black iron oxide	1.1
Yellow ochre	1.0
Add:	
Bentonite	1.0
C.M.C.	1 tsp.

CG-34

Soft Opaque Grayed Blue-Green Celadon Glaze   Cone 10
feldspathic, opaque, smooth matt, nontoxic

Mixing. Mix in the manner of CG-1.

Application. Apply in the manner of CG-1.

Firing. Fire in the manner of CG-24.

Fired Results. This glaze fires to a soft opaque grayed blue-green smooth matt at cone 10 reduction.

Silica	32.6
Feldspar (Kingman)	33.0
Bone ash	17.0
Kaolin (Florida)	8.8
Kaolin (Florida, calcined)	7.6
Whiting	3.0
Add:	
Red iron oxide	1.0
Yellow ochre	1.0
Bentonite	1.0
C.M.C.	1 tsp.

CG-35

Light Gray-Green Gloss Celadon Glaze   Cone 11
feldspathic, translucent, gloss, nontoxic

Mixing. Mix in the manner of CG-1.

Application. Apply in the manner of CG-1.

Firing. Fire in the manner of CG-24 but to cone 11.

Fired Results. This glaze fires to a light gray-green gloss in moderate reduction at cone 11.

Silica	36.0
Feldspar (Kingman)	29.9
Whiting	26.9
Kaolin (Florida)	5.4
Red iron oxide	1.5
Add:	
C.M.C.	1 tsp.

CG-36

Slightly Gray-Green Gloss Celadon Glaze   Cone 11
feldspathic, transparent, gloss, nontoxic

Mixing. Mix in the manner of CG-1.

Application. Apply in the manner of CG-1.

Firing. Fire in the manner of CG-24, but to cone 11.

Fired Results. This glaze fires to a slightly gray-green gloss in moderate reduction at cone 11.

Silica	35.5
Whiting	22.2
Feldspar (Buckingham)	26.9
Kaolin (Florida)	9.2
Yellow ochre	5.9
Red iron oxide	0.3
Add:	
Bentonite	1.0
C.M.C.	1 tsp.

28
COPPER
RED GLAZES
CONE 04-10

There has always been an air of mystique or romance surrounding the copper red glaze ever since its discovery in China during the Sung dynasty. This mystique no doubt stems from the fact that the technique for producing this glaze was unknown outside China for centuries, and even today a copper red glaze of true quality is most difficult to achieve and even more elusive when the potter tries to obtain consistent results.

The copper red glaze, sometimes known as *sang de beouf*, ox blood, *rouge flambé*, or flambé red, refers to a type of reduction-fired glaze in which metallic copper becomes suspended in colloidal form in the glaze due to its loss of oxygen during the reducing period. For more information on this complex glaze, consult Suggested Reading.

The glaze formulas in this chapter have been tested and proved to be the most reliable of those available. If the directions are followed faithfully, good results of various shades of copper red should result.

The copper red glazes listed in this chapter are of two types, artificial reduction and true reduction. The first category has a reducing agent added to the glaze in the form of silicon carbide and is fired in an oxidizing atmosphere. The second is fired in a true reducing atmosphere in the kiln. The directions for each glaze should be consulted and read carefully to determine the proper technique for each type.

The glazes in this chapter are listed first by cone level, color from light to dark, and by glaze surface within each color.

The reader will find lists of possible chemical substitutions in Chapter 34, Dictionary of Clay and Glaze Compounds.

Note. The glazes in this chapter are labeled toxic or nontoxic. Toxic glazes should be carefully handled both in formulation and in application. During preparation the potter should wear a dust mask to prevent inhalation of toxic materials and not allow these materials to come into prolonged contact with the skin. Frequent washing of the hands when handling these glazes is a wise precaution. Toxic glazes should be applied by brushing and dipping—never spraying. For even under the best conditions some inhalation of the toxic mist from the spray is bound to take place or, equally bad, the mist from the spray gun can settle on the skin and be absorbed into the body system.

FORMULAS FOR COPPER RED GLAZES

CRG-1   **Artificial Reduction Copper Red Glaze   Cone 04**
lead-alkaline, translucent, gloss, toxic

Mixing. Weigh out the ingredients and mix by grinding in a ball mill. Glazes containing soluble alkalines should either be wet-ground and used immediately or ground dry and only the amount to be used mixed with water. Two hours of grinding, wet or dry, is usually sufficient to get a thorough mix. Glazes which do not contain alkalies may be wet-ground for two hours and stored for future use. Grinding of these glazes also ensures uniformity of color. Handle with care as this glaze contains a toxic chemical.

Application. Apply to cone 06 bisque by dipping or brushing. Brushing of copper reds seems to be less satisfactory than the former two methods. (See note at the beginning of this chapter.) The glaze should be applied to at least 1/16" (1.6mm) in thickness to produce a good copper red.

Ferro frit #3396	27.0
Silica	24.0
White lead	19.0
Ferro frit #3134	14.0
Kaolin (EPK)	10.0
Whiting	3.0
Opax	3.0
Add:	
Tin oxide	1.0
Copper carbonate	0.2
Red iron oxide	0.1
Silicon carbide	0.3
Bentonite	1.0
C.M.C.	1 tsp.

Firing. Fire in oxidation to cone 04, hold the temperature at that point for 20 to 30 minutes, then cool quickly back down to cone 06, then cool in a normal manner. Since this is an artificial reduction glaze, no reducing atmosphere is needed in the kiln.

Fired Results. This glaze fires to a dark blood red at cone 04.

CRG-2

Artificial Reduction Copper Red Glaze   Cone 04
lead-alkaline, opaque, gloss, toxic

Mixing. Mix in the manner of CRG-1.

Application. Apply in the manner of CRG-1.

Firing. Fire in the manner of CRG-1.

Fired Results. This glaze fires to a mottled ox-blood red at cone 04. The mottled colors are usually a mixture of grays and reds in a mottled run pattern.

Ferro frit #3134	35.5
Silica	26.9
White lead	22.3
Kaolin (Florida)	9.8
Tin oxide	2.9
Whiting	1.9
Copper carbonate	6.0
Silicon carbide (200 mesh)	0.4
Add:	
Red iron oxide	0.3
Bentonite	1.0
C.M.C.	1 tsp.

CRG-3

Artificial Reduction Copper Red Glaze   Cone 04–03
lead-alkaline, translucent, gloss, toxic

Mixing. Mix in the manner of CRG-1.

Application. Apply in the manner of CRG-1.

Firing. Fire in the manner of CRG-1.

Fired Results. This glaze fires to a bright mottled blood-red translucent gloss at cone 04. At cone 03 it is slightly darker.

Silica	27.0
White lead	17.0
Red lead	5.0
Ferro frit #3396	15.0
Ferro frit #3134	16.0
Ferro frit #3191	4.0
Zinc oxide	3.0
Whiting	2.0
Add:	
Tin oxide	1.0
Copper carbonate	2.0
Silicon carbide (180–200 mesh)	0.4
Bentonite	2.0
C.M.C.	1 tsp.

CRG-4

Artificial Reduction Copper Red Glaze   Cone 04–03
lead-alkaline, translucent, gloss, toxic

Mixing. Mix in the manner of CRG-1.

Application. Apply in the manner of CRG-1.

Firing. Fire in the manner of CRG-1.

Fired Results. This glaze fires to a medium blood-red at cone 04, slightly darker at cone 03. Red hues of greater depth can be achieved with this glaze when it is applied over a darker body.

White lead	25.0
Kaolin (Florida)	19.0
Silica	18.0
Ferro frit #3196	15.0
Ferro frit #3191	12.0
Ferro frit #3134	9.0
Opax	2.0
Add:	
Tin oxide	1.0
Copper carbonate	1.0
Silicon carbide (200 mesh)	0.3
Bentonite	1.0
C.M.C.	1 tsp.

CRG-5 **Artificial Reduction Copper Red Glaze   Cone 2**
raw alkaline, opaque, gloss, nontoxic

Mixing. This glaze should be wet-ground in a ball mill for two hours and used immediately, or dry-ground for two and one-half hours and stored dry until ready for use.

Application. Apply by brushing, dipping, or spraying.

Firing. Fire in oxidation to cone 2, soak at that temperature for 20 to 30 minutes, cool quickly to cone 01, then cool the kiln in a normal manner.

Fired Results. This glaze fires to a glossy blood red at cone 2. If the glaze has not been properly ground it will be a spotted red.

Feldspar (Kona F-4)	33.0
Borax	28.0
Silica	18.0
Kaolin (EPK)	12.0
Fluorspar	6.0
Tin oxide	2.0
Silicon carbide (200 mesh)	0.5
Copper carbonate	0.5
Red iron oxide	0.5
Add:	
Bentonite	1.0
C.M.C.	1 tsp.

CRG-6 **Artificial Reduction Copper Red Glaze   Cone 2**
raw alkaline, translucent, gloss, nontoxic

Mixing. Mix in the manner of CRG-5.

Application. Apply in the manner of CRG-5.

Firing. Fire in the manner of CRG-5.

Fired Results. This glaze fires to a dark blood red at cone 2 with some mottling and streaking. The results are usually more handsome if this glaze is used over a darker body.

Feldspar (Kona F-4)	34.0
Borax	29.2
Fluorspar	6.6
Kaolin (Florida)	12.4
Silica	17.8
Tin oxide	2.0
Copper carbonate	0.5
Add:	
Red iron oxide	0.5
Silicon carbide (200 mesh)	0.5
Bentonite	1.0
C.M.C.	1 tsp.

CRG-7 **Deep Blood-Red Copper Reduction Glaze   Cone 4**
alkaline, opaque, gloss, nontoxic

Mixing. Mix in the manner of CRG-1.

Application. Apply in the manner of CRG-5.

Firing. Fire in oxidation up to cone 06, moderate reduction to cone 3, and heavy reduction to cone 4. Soak in reduction at that temperature for half an hour, cool the kiln quickly down to cone 1, still maintaining the reducing atmosphere, then cool in a normal manner.

Fired Results. This glaze fires to a deep blood-red at cone 4. It will give a red of even greater depth if used over a darker body.

Silica	30.8
Feldspar (Kona F-4)	27.3
Whiting	12.8
Ferro frit #3134	12.2
Tin oxide	7.8
Kaolin (Florida)	5.6
Dolomite	1.9
Opax	8.0
Copper oxide	7.0
Add:	
Bentonite	1.0
Red iron oxide	0.5
C.M.C.	1 tsp.

CRG-8   **Blood-Red Copper Reduction Glaze   Cone 6**
lead-alkaline, opaque, gloss, toxic

Mixing. Mix in the manner of CRG-5.

Application. Apply in the manner of CRG-1.

Firing. Fire in the manner of CRG-7, but to cone 6.

Fired Results. This glaze fires to a rich blood-red at cone 6.

White lead	11.8
Red lead	11.8
Whiting	5.5
Kaolin	2.8
Silica	29.4
Borax	29.9
Boric acid	4.5
Sodium carbonate	4.4
Tin oxide	1.6
Copper oxide	0.5
Add:	
Bentonite	1.0
Red iron oxide	0.2
C.M.C.	1 tsp.

CRG-9   **Blood-Red Copper Reduction Glaze   Cone 8**
lead-alkaline, opaque, gloss, toxic

Mixing. Mix in the manner of CRG-1.

Application. Apply in the manner of CRG-1.

Firing. Fire in oxidation up to cone 2, moderate reduction to cone 6, and slightly heavier reduction on up to cone 8. Soak in reduction at this temperature for half an hour, then seal the kiln and cool rapidly down to cone 6, then cool normally.

Fired Results. This glaze fires to a blood-red opaque gloss at cone 8. It will give greater depth of color if used over a buff body that has been bisqued to cone 02.

Silica	30.0
Borax	29.0
Red lead	20.1
Whiting	6.1
Boric acid	4.6
Sodium carbonate	4.5
Kaolin (Florida)	3.0
Tin oxide	1.9
Copper carbonate	0.8
Add:	
Bentonite	1.0
C.M.C.	1 tsp.

CRG-10   **Artificial Reduction Copper Red Glaze   Cone 8**
feldspathic, opaque, gloss, nontoxic

Mixing. Mix in the manner of CRG-5.

Application. Apply in the manner of CRG-1.

Firing. Fire in oxidation to cone 8, cool the kiln quickly down to cone 6, then cool normally.

Fired Results. This glaze fires to a mottled medium-red opaque gloss at cone 8.

Feldspar (Kona F-4)	32.8
Sodium carbonate	1.5
Borax	28.4
Whiting	7.3
Kaolin	12.3
Silica	17.7
Tin oxide	1.8
Copper carbonate	0.3
Silicon carbide	0.5

CRG-11   **Ox-Blood Copper Reduction Glaze   Cone 8**
feldspathic, opaque, gloss, toxic

Mixing. Mix in the manner of CRG-5.

Application. Apply in the manner of CRG-1.

Firing. Fire in oxidation to cone 06, moderate reduction to cone 4, heavy reduction to cone 6, and moderate reduction on up to cone 8. Soak at that temperature for half an hour in moderate reduction, then seal the kiln and cool rapidly down to cone 6, then cool normally.

Fired Results. This glaze fires to an ox-blood opaque gloss at cone 8 reduction. Over a buff clay body it will produce a red of greater depth.

Cornwall stone	27.9
Silica	32.5
Zinc oxide	4.0
Barium carbonate	9.3
Sodium carbonate	6.3
Borax	20.0
Copper carbonate	2.0
Tin oxide	2.0
Add:	
Bentonite	1.0
C.M.C.	1tsp.

CRG-12 **Dark Blood-Red Copper Reduction Glaze   Cone 8**
feldspar-alkaline, opaque, gloss, nontoxic

Mixing. Mix in the manner of CRG-5.

Application. Apply in the manner of CRG-5.

Firing. Fire in the manner of CRG-11.

Fired Results. This glaze fires to a dark blood-red opaque gloss at cone 8. Over a darker body it produces a Persian red.

Feldspar (Kona F-4)	21.0
Borax	26.0
Silica	20.1
Kaolin (Georgia)	12.5
Whiting	6.0
Sodium carbonate	2.0
Tin oxide	2.0
Copper carbonate	0.4

CRG-13 **Red-Pink Copper Reduction Glaze   Cone 9**
alkaline, opaque, semi-gloss, nontoxic

Mixing. Mix in the manner of CRG-5.

Application. Apply to the thickness of 1/16'' (1.6mm) by spraying.

Firing. Fire the kiln through a warming-up period of half an hour with only the pilots on. Fire in oxidation up to cone 016, moderate reduction to cone 015, then heavy reduction for one hour, and light reduction the rest of the way up to cone 9. Seal the kiln and cool normally.

Fired Results. This glaze fires to a rich red-pink with darker mottling at cone 9. At a full cone 10 it is a rich dark Persian red.

Feldspar (Kingman)	40.8
Silica	24.5
Ferro frit #3134	7.9
Whiting	7.3
Kaolin (EPK)	4.7
Zinc oxide	3.4
Feldspar (Custer)	2.7
Borax	2.7
Sodium silicate	1.0
Bentonite	1.0
Ferro frit #3819	1.2
Copper carbonate	0.5
Silicon carbide (200 mesh)	0.3
Add:	
C.M.C.	1 tsp.

CRG-14 **Mottled Medium-Red Copper Reduction Glaze   Cone 9**
feldspathic, opaque, gloss, nontoxic

Mixing. Mix in the manner of CRG-5.

Application. Apply in the manner of CRG-5.

Firing. Fire in the manner of CRG-13.

Fired Results. This glaze fires to a mottled medium red at cone 9 reduction.

Silica	36.4
Feldspar (Buckingham)	34.0
Whiting	14.6
Borax (calcined)	12.0
Tin oxide	1.7
Kaolin (calcined)	0.9
Copper carbonate	0.4

CRG-15 **Rose-Red Copper Reduction Glaze   Cone 9**
feldspathic, opaque, smooth matt, nontoxic

Mixing. Mix in the manner of CRG-5.

Application. Apply in the manner of CRG-5.

Firing. Fire in the manner of CRG-13.

Fired Results. This glaze fires to a rose-red smooth matt at cone 9.

Feldspar (Godfrey)	77.8
Colemanite	8.5
Whiting	12.1
Copper oxide	0.4
Tin oxide	1.0
Red iron oxide	0.3
Add:	
Bentonite	1.0
C.M.C.	1 tsp.

CRG-16   **Ruby-Red Copper Reduction Glaze   Cone 9**
alkaline, opaque, gloss, nontoxic

Mixing. Mix in the manner of CRG-5.

Application. Apply in the manner of CRG-5.

Firing. Fire in the manner of CRG-13.

Fired Results. This glaze fires to a bright ruby-red opaque gloss with some mottling at cone 9.

Silica	29.6
Kaolin (EPK)	14.2
Feldspar (Kingman)	13.8
Whiting	8.9
Feldspar (Custer)	8.2
Borax	8.2
Sodium carbonate	5.7
Ferro frit #3134	3.5
Ferro frit #3819	3.4
Zinc oxide	2.1
Tin oxide	1.0
Bentonite	0.5
Copper carbonate	0.4
Silicon carbide (200 mesh)	0.3
Add:	
Red iron oxide	0.5
C.M.C.	1 tsp.

CRG-17   **Garnet-Red Copper Reduction Glaze   Cone 9**
feldspathic, opaque, semi-gloss, nontoxic

Mixing. Mix in the manner of CRG-5.

Application. Apply in the manner of CRG-5.

Firing. Fire in the manner of CRG-13.

Fired Results. This glaze fires to a deep garnet-red semi-gloss at cone 9.

Nepheline syenite	54.2
Sodium carbonate	4.6
Colemanite	12.2
Whiting	6.0
Silica	21.5
Copper oxide	0.2
Tin oxide	1.0
Red iron oxide	0.3
Add:	
Bentonite	1.0
C.M.C.	1 tsp.

CRG-18   **Ox-Blood Copper Reduction Glaze   Cone 9**
feldspathic, opaque, semi-gloss, nontoxic

Mixing. Mix in the manner of CRG-5.

Application. Apply in the manner of CRG-5.

Firing. Fire in the manner of CRG-13.

Fired Results. This glaze fires to an ox-blood semi-gloss at cone 9.

Nepheline syenite	41.8
Feldspar (Buckingham)	9.0
Kaolin (Georgia)	1.9
Silica	22.3
Colemanite	13.0
Whiting	10.4
Copper oxide	0.3
Tin oxide	1.0
Red iron oxide	0.3
Add:	
Bentonite	1.0
C.M.C.	1 tsp.

CRG-19 **Copper Red Reduction Glaze   Cone 9**
feldspathic, opaque, semi-gloss, nontoxic

Mixing. Mix in the manner of CRG-5.

Application. Apply in the manner of CRG-5.

Firing. Fire in the manner of CRG-13.

Fired Results. This glaze fires to a bright candy-apple red with some mottling at cone 9. It can be very effective used over a buff body.

Feldspar (Kona F-4)	44.0
Silica	25.5
Whiting	13.0
Ferro frit #3134	12.5
Kaolin (Florida)	3.5
Tin oxide	1.3
Copper carbonate	0.2
Red iron oxide	0.2
Add:	
Bentonite	1.0
C.M.C.	1 tsp.

CRG-20 **Blood-Red Copper Reduction Glaze   Cone 9**
alkaline, opaque, gloss, nontoxic

Mixing. Mix in the manner of CRG-5.

Application. Apply in the manner of CRG-5.

Firing. Fire in the manner of CRG-13.

Fired Results. This glaze fires to a blood red gloss at cone 9.

Feldspar (Kona F-4)	43.6
Silica	26.0
Whiting	13.6
Ferro frit #3134	12.0
Kaolin (EPK)	2.3
Tin oxide	1.1
Copper carbonate	0.4
Add:	
Bentonite	1.0
C.M.C.	1 tsp.

CRG-21 **Dark Ox-Blood Copper Reduction Glaze   Cone 9**
nepheline syenite, opaque, gloss, nontoxic

Mixing. Mix in the manner of CRG-5.

Application. Apply in the manner of CRG-5.

Firing. Fire in the manner of CRG-13.

Fired Results. This glaze fires to a dark opaque ox-blood gloss at cone 9.

Nepheline syenite	54.2
Colemanite	12.1
Whiting	10.5
Silica	21.5
Copper oxide	0.4
Tin oxide	1.0
Red iron oxide	0.3
Add:	
Bentonite	1.0
C.M.C.	1 tsp.

CRG-22 **Light-Red Copper Reduction Glaze   Cone 9–10**
alkaline, opaque, gloss, nontoxic

Mixing. Mix in the manner of CRG-5.

Application. Apply in the manner of CRG-13.

Firing. Fire in the manner of CRG-13.

Fired Results. This glaze fires to a light-red gloss with darker red mottling at cone 9–10 reduction.

Feldspar (Kingman)	41.4
Silica	23.0
Ferro frit #3134	10.5
Feldspar (Kona F-4)	8.6
Whiting	6.3
Zinc oxide	3.1
Borax (calcined)	2.2
Bentonite	1.6
Tin oxide	1.0
Feldspar (Buckingham)	0.6
Copper carbonate	0.5
Silicon carbide	0.5
Sodium carbonate	0.3
Borax	0.2
Kaolin (Florida)	0.2
Add:	
Red iron oxide	0.2
C.M.C.	1 tsp.

CRG-23 **Medium-Red Copper Reduction Glaze   Cone 9–10**
alkaline, opaque, gloss, nontoxic

Mixing. Mix in the manner of CRG-5.

Application. Apply in the manner of CRG-5.

Firing. Fire in the manner of CRG-13.

Fired Results. This glaze fires to a mottled medium-red opaque gloss at cone 9–10. At a hard cone 10 it is slightly darker.

Feldspar (Kingman)	27.6
Silica	26.2
Kaolin (EPK)	9.4
Ferro frit #3134	8.0
Whiting	6.9
Feldspar (Custer)	5.4
Borax (calcined)	5.4
Sodium carbonate	3.8
Hommel frit #14	3.0
Zinc oxide	2.7
Tin oxide	0.9
Copper carbonate	0.4
Silicon carbide (200 mesh)	0.3
Add:	
Bentonite	1.0
Red iron oxide	0.2
C.M.C.	1 tsp.

CRG-24 **Ox-Blood Copper Reduction Glaze   Cone 9–10**
feldspathic, opaque, gloss, nontoxic

Mixing. Mix in the manner of CRG-5.

Application. Apply in the manner of CRG-5.

Firing. Fire in the manner of CRG-13.

Fired Results. This glaze fires to an opaque ox-blood at cone 9–10.

Feldspar (Kingman)	54.6
Silica	21.2
Ferro frit #3134	11.4
Whiting	5.3
Zinc oxide	3.8
Bentonite	1.6
Tin oxide	1.1
Copper carbonate	0.5
Silicon carbide (200 mesh)	0.3
Add:	
Red iron oxide	0.2

CRG-25 **Dark-Red Copper Reduction Glaze   Cone 9–10**
feldspathic, opaque, gloss, nontoxic

Mixing. Mix in the manner of CRG-5.

Application. Apply in the manner of CRG-5.

Firing. Fire in the manner of CRG-13.

Fired Results. This glaze fires to a dark-red opaque gloss at cone 9–10.

Feldspar (Kingman)	49.7
Silica	22.0
Ferro frit #3134	10.6
Ferro frit #3191	7.2
Whiting	3.3
Zinc oxide	3.1
Bentonite	1.5
Tin oxide	1.5
Copper carbonate	0.5
Silicon carbide (200 mesh)	0.4
Add:	
Red iron oxide	0.2
C.M.C.	1 tsp.

CRG-26

Garnet-Red Copper Reduction Glaze   Cone 9–10
feldspathic, opaque, gloss, nontoxic

Mixing. Mix in the manner of CRG-5.

Application. Apply in the manner of CRG-5.

Firing. Fire in the manner of CRG-13.

Fired Results. This glaze fires to a garnet red at cone 9–10.

Feldspar (Kingman)	36.8
Silica	29.3
Whiting	10.3
Ferro frit #3134	7.1
Kaolin (Georgia)	3.1
Sodium silicate	2.9
Zinc oxide	2.4
Bentonite	1.1
Opax	1.1
Ferro frit #3191	0.6
Borax	0.4
Copper carbonate	0.4
Silicon carbide (200 mesh)	0.2
Add:	
Red iron oxide	0.2

CRG-27

Purple-Red Copper Reduction Glaze   Cone 9–10
feldspathic, opaque, gloss, nontoxic

Mixing. Mix in the manner of CRG-5.

Application. Apply in the manner of CRG-5.

Firing. Fire in the manner of CRG-13.

Fired Results. This glaze fires to an opaque purple-red gloss at cone 9–10.

Silica	32.1
Feldspar (Kingman)	27.6
Whiting	11.1
Borax (calcined)	9.5
Ferro frit #3134	7.1
Kaolin (Georgia)	5.7
Opax	2.7
Ferro frit #3191	1.3
Tin oxide	1.2
Bentonite	1.1
Copper carbonate	0.4
Silicon carbide	0.2
Add:	
Red iron oxide	0.1

CRG-28

Orange-Red Copper Reduction Glaze   Cone 10
feldspathic, opaque, gloss, nontoxic

Mixing. Mix in the manner of CRG-5.

Application. Apply in the manner of CRG-5.

Firing. Fire in the manner of CRG-13 but fire on up to cone 10.

Fired Results. This glaze fires to an orange-red opaque gloss at cone 10.

Feldspar (Buckingham)	78.0
Whiting	12.4
Colemanite	8.0
Tin oxide	1.0
Copper oxide	0.3
Red iron oxide	0.3
Add:	
Bentonite	1.0
C.M.C.	1 tsp.

CRG-29

Orange-Pink Copper Reduction Glaze   Cone 10
feldspathic, opaque, gloss, nontoxic

Mixing. Mix in the manner of CRG-5.

Application. Apply in the manner of CRG-5.

Firing. Fire in the manner of CRG-28.

Fired Results. This glaze fires to an orange-pink much like the "peach bloom" Chinese glaze at cone 10.

Nepheline syenite	41.3
Silica	20.3
Colemanite	11.8
Whiting	11.8
Feldspar (Buckingham)	9.4
Kaolin (Florida)	2.2
Opax	1.4
Tin oxide	1.1
Copper oxide	0.4
Red iron oxide	0.3

CRG-30

Bright Blood-Red Copper Reduction Glaze   Cone 10
alkaline-barium, translucent, gloss, toxic

Mixing. Mix in the manner of CRG-5.

Application. Apply in the manner of CRG-1.

Firing. Fire in the manner of CRG-28.

Fired Results. This glaze fires to a bright blood-red that is somewhat translucent when thin and more opaque when thick. Fire to cone 10.

Feldspar (Buckingham)	31.1
Silica	29.4
Colemanite	14.1
Zinc oxide	5.3
Opax	3.0
Barium carbonate	6.7
Talc	6.4
Copper carbonate	2.0
Tin oxide	1.5
Red iron oxide	0.5
Add:	
Bentonite	1.0
C.M.C.	1 tsp.

CRG-31

Ruby-Red Copper Reduction Glaze   Cone 10
feldspathic, transparent, gloss, nontoxic

Mixing. Mix in the manner of CRG-5.

Application. Apply in the manner of CRG-5.

Firing. Fire in the manner of CRG-28.

Fired Results. This glaze fires to a ruby-red transparent gloss at cone 10. It will give a deeper red if used over a dark body.

Feldspar (Kingman)	51.8
Silica	25.6
Whiting	8.8
Colemanite	6.5
Dolomite	2.3
Opax	2.2
Tin oxide	1.0
Copper carbonate	1.0
Red iron oxide	0.9
Add:	
Bentonite	1.0
C.M.C.	1 tsp.

CRG-32

Rich Dark-Red Copper Reduction Glaze   Cone 10
feldspathic-barium, translucent, gloss, toxic

Mixing. Mix in the manner of CRG-5.

Application. Apply in the manner of CRG-1.

Firing. Fire in the manner of CRG-28.

Fired Results. This glaze fires to a rich dark red, much like the Persian reds, at cone 10.

Feldspar (Buckingham)	42.5
Silica	25.0
Colemanite	17.5
Barium carbonate	10.0
Whiting	2.5
Copper carbonate	1.0
Tin oxide	1.0
Red iron oxide	0.5
Add:	
Bentonite	1.0
C.M.C.	1 tsp.

CRG-33

Grayed-Red Copper Reduction Glaze   Cone 10
alkaline, opaque, gloss, nontoxic

Mixing. Mix in the manner of CRG-5.

Application. Apply in the manner of CRG-5.

Firing. Fire in the manner of CRG-28.

Fired Results. This glaze fires to a darker red with a slightly grayed hue at cone 10. It gives a deeper red over a darker clay body.

Feldspar (Buckingham)	50.5
Feldspar (Kingman)	20.0
Colemanite	10.9
Whiting	7.2
Silica	7.2
Tin oxide	1.1
Copper carbonate	1.1
Add:	
Red iron oxide	0.2
Bentonite	1.0
C.M.C.	1 tsp.

CRG-34 **Deep Ox-Blood Copper Reduction Glaze   Cone 10**
feldspar-colemanite, opaque, semi-matt, nontoxic

Mixing. Mix in the manner of CRG-5.

Application. Apply in the manner of CRG-5.

Firing. Fire in the manner of CRG-28.

Fired Results. This glaze fires to a deep opaque ox-blood semi-matt at cone 10. Over a darker body it is almost a Persian red.

Feldspar (Buckingham)	56.5
Feldspar (Kingman)	20.0
Colemanite	10.5
Whiting	11.4
Copper oxide	0.3
Tin oxide	1.0
Red iron oxide	0.3
Add:	
Bentonite	1.0
C.M.C.	1 tsp.

CRG-35 **Ox-Blood Copper Reduction Glaze   Cone 10**
feldspathic, opaque, gloss, nontoxic

Mixing. Mix in the manner of CRG-5.

Application. Apply in the manner of CRG-5.

Firing. Fire in the manner of CRG-28.

Fired Results. This glaze fires to an ox-blood opaque gloss at cone 10.

Feldspar (Buckingham)	44.1
Silica	28.9
Ferro frit #3134	10.5
Whiting	5.1
Kaolin (Florida)	4.7
Borax	4.6
Zinc oxide	3.5
Bentonite	1.5
Hommel frit #14	1.2
Tin oxide	1.0
Copper carbonate	0.5
Silicon carbide	0.3

CRG-36 **Artificial Reduction Magenta Copper Glaze   Cone 10**
feldspathic, opaque, gloss, nontoxic

Mixing. Mix in the manner of CRG-5.

Application. Apply in the manner of CRG-5.

Firing. Fire in the manner of CRG-28.

Fired Results. This glaze fires to a magenta red at cone 10.

Silica	30.4
Feldspar (Kona F-4)	15.0
Feldspar (Buckingham)	12.6
Ferro frit #3191	21.4
Whiting	5.5
Kaolin (EPK)	4.8
Borax	4.6
Tin oxide	2.2
Ferro frit #3134	1.3
Red iron oxide	0.7
Silicon carbide	0.8
Zinc oxide	0.4
Copper carbonate	0.3
Add:	
Bentonite	1.0
C.M.C.	1 tsp.

29
ASH
GLAZES
CONE 06-10

In ancient times the first pottery ware was unglazed. But in China as the ancient Chinese potters became more proficient at kiln building they developed kilns that would fire to higher temperatures and discovered that their ware was being partially glazed by the ash which drifted through the kiln chamber from the fire box. Thus ash glazing was born.

The value of glazes which incorporate large amounts of plant or wood ash as opposed to those which have been compounded chemically lies in their uniqueness and subtlety. Ash glazes, especially those which are reduction fired to produce broken or mottled surface effects, if properly exploited are very handsome.

In the cone 11 to 13 range most wood ash alone will form a thin, watery type of glaze which is highly durable but not very attractive. It is for this reason that ashes are used mainly as a glaze ingredient rather as a glaze in themselves. The usual starting point for ash glaze test trials is equal parts of ash, feldspar, and clay which usually produces a highly durable, clear gloss glaze. For those who wish to experiment, this basic formula should be kept in mind.

PREPARING ASHES FOR USE

The use of wood or plant ash as a glaze ingredient can never be an exact science for the chemical analysis of ashes tends to vary from one location to another due to the differences in the soil where they grow. Consequently it is wise to gather a large amount (at least 100 pounds/45 kilos) and thoroughly mix it if any consistency is to be achieved in the glaze results. Even a single glaze batch will give varying results as it ages on the shelf.

Some potters prefer to use ashes which have had little or no processing other than sieving through a 60- to 80-mesh screen. This method of preparation leaves the soluble aklalies in the ash and thus tends to give greater variety to the glaze in which it is used. Other potters who wish greater consistency give the gathered ashes more processing. The usual procedure, while not complicated, does involve a great deal of work as follows.

Collect a large amount of the ash, 100 to 200 pounds/45 to 90 kilos, to insure that you will have enough ash to continue the work with one particular glaze composition. Sieve the ashes through an 80- to 100-mesh screen, discarding all material which does not pass through the screen. Place the ashes in a plastic container and add enough water to cover the ashes by several inches. Stir the ash mixture vigorously with a stick to allow any unburned pieces to float to the top to be screened off and discarded. *Never stir the ash liquid with your hand for the solution contains alkalies which are caustic.* Care should also be taken in screening the ashes to avoid breathing the ash dust. Allow the ash and water mixture to stand for two or three hours, then pour off the excess top water. Repeat this washing process at least three times, then place the ashes aside to dry. When the material is dry, screen it through a 100-mesh screen to break up the particles, being careful not to breath the dust. After this final screening the ashes are ready for use or can be stored in containers for future use.

The glazes listed in this chapter take into consideration that ash content varies from place to place and they should perform well if the directions are followed faithfully. If a glaze should fail, decrease the ash content by 5% and increase the flux content by 5% and retest.

The glazes in this chapter are listed first by cone level, then by color, alphabetically within each cone level, and finally by surface within each color.

The reader will find lists of possible chemical substitutions in Chapter 34, Dictionary of Clay and Glaze Compounds.

Note. The glazes in this chapter are labeled toxic or nontoxic. Toxic glazes should be carefully handled both in formulation and in application. During preparation the potter should wear a dust mask to prevent inhalation of toxic materials and not allow these materials to come into prolonged contact with the skin. Frequent washing of the hands when handling these glazes is a wise precaution. Toxic glazes should be applied by brushing and dipping—never spraying. For even under the best conditions some inhalation of the toxic mist from the spray is bound to take place or, equally bad, the mist from the spray gun can settle on the skin and be absorbed into the body system.

FORMULAS FOR ASH GLAZES

AG-1

Translucent Off-White Ash Glaze   Cone 06–04
ash-alkaline, translucent, semi-matt, toxic

Mixing. Weigh out the ingredients and mix by grinding in a ball mill. Glazes containing soluble alkalies such as this one should either be wet-ground and used at once or dry-ground and only the amount to be used mixed with water. Two hours of grinding, wet or dry, is usually sufficient to get a thorough mix and grind of the materials, but handle with care as this glaze contains a toxic chemical.

Application. Apply to cone 06 bisque by brushing or dipping. Dipping however, tends to be more successful with ash glazes. (See note at the beginning of this chapter.) Allow the ware to dry thoroughly before firing.

Firing. Fire in oxidation to cone 06 and cool the kiln normally. This glaze can be fired in reduction but it is less successful than those at higher temperatures. For firing in reduction, first fire in oxidation up to cone 016 then in moderate reduction the rest of the way up to cone 06. Seal the kiln and quickly cool it back down to cone 016, then cool normally.

Fired Results. This glaze fires to an off-white semi-matt in oxidation and slightly darker in reduction.

Hardwood ash	
(unwashed)	50.0
Borax	35.0
Dolomite	5.0
Sodium carbonate	5.0
Colemanite	5.0
Add:	
Bentonite	1.0
C.M.C.	1 tsp.

AG-2

Clear Wood Ash Glaze   Cone 04–02
lead-feldspar, transparent, gloss, toxic

Mixing. As this glaze contains no soluble alkalies it can be wet-ground and stored if the potter desires.

Application. Apply in the manner of AG-1.

Firing. Fire in the manner of AG-1 but to cone 04–02.

Fired Results. This glaze fires to a clear gloss at cone 04–02 in oxidation or reduction. When made opaque it is a mottled gloss.

White lead	46.7
Feldspar (Kona F-4)	27.0
Wood ash (mixed	
and washed)	13.0
Tennessee ball clay #1	12.0
Kaolin (calcined)	1.3
Add:	
Bentonite	2.0
C.M.C.	1 tsp.

AG-3

Translucent Cream Ash Glaze   Cone 04–02
ash-lead, translucent, gloss, toxic

Mixing. Mix in the manner of AG-2.

Application. Apply in the manner of AG-1.

Firing. Fire in the manner of AG-2.

Fired Results. This glaze fires to a translucent cream gloss at cone 04–02. Iron and rutile make good colorants for this glaze. It usually works better if used over a dark clay body.

Mixed hardwood ash (washed)	50.0
Hommel frit #14	35.0
White lead	14.0
Bentonite	1.0
Add:	
C.M.C.	1 tsp.

AG-4

Translucent Off-White Ash Glaze   Cone 04–02
ash-lead, translucent, smooth matt, toxic

Mixing. Mix in the manner of AG-2.

Application. Apply in the manner of AG-1.

Firing. Fire in the manner of AG-2.

Fired Results. This glaze fires to a translucent cloudy off-white smooth matt at cone 04–02. This glaze is not recommended for reduction firing.

White lead	45.7
Feldspar (Custer)	24.5
Kentucky ball clay #4	12.0
Hardwood ash (washed)	15.0
Kaolin (EPK)	1.0
Pemco frit #25	1.0
Add:	
Bentonite	1.0
C.M.C.	1 tsp.

AG-5

Semi-Opaque Off-White Ash Glaze   Cone 04–02
ash-lead, semi-opaque, gloss, toxic

Mixing. Mix in the manner of AG-2.

Application. Apply in the manner of AG-1.

Firing. Fire in the manner of AG-2.

Fired Results. This glaze fires to a semi-opaque off-white gloss at cone 04–02. This is a good base for earth colorants.

Hardwood ash (washed)	50.0
White lead	45.0
Talc	4.0
Bentonite	1.0
Add:	
C.M.C.	1 tsp.

AG-6

Translucent Cloudy-White Ash Glaze   Cone 04
ash-lead, translucent, semi-gloss, toxic

Mixing. Mix in the manner of AG-2.

Application. Apply in the manner of AG-1.

Firing. Fire in the manner of AG-2.

Fired Results. This glaze fires to a translucent cloudy-white semi-gloss at cone 04. It is a good base for earth colorants. It will iron spot well if fired in moderate reduction and if used over a darker clay body.

White lead	30.9
Red lead	13.0
Feldspar (Custer)	26.8
Tennessee ball clay #1	12.1
Kaolin (EPK, calcined)	2.0
Wood ash (washed)	13.4
Colemanite	1.8
Add:	
Bentonite	1.0
C.M.C.	1 tsp.

AG-7 **Mottled Ash Glaze Cone 04**
ash-lead, translucent, gloss, toxic

Mixing. Mix in the manner of AG-2.

Application. Apply in the manner of AG-1.

Firing. Fire in the manner of AG-2.

Fired Results. This glaze fires to a mottled translucent gloss at cone 04. It makes a good color base for any of the colorants that work well in lead glazes.

White lead	25.0
Pemco frit #25	16.0
Feldspar (Custer)	16.0
Tennessee ball clay #1	3.6
Kaolin (Florida)	4.8
Mixed wood ash (unwashed)	6.0
Add:	
Bentonite	1.0
C.M.C.	1 tsp.

AG-8 **Clear Semi-Gloss Ash Glaze Cone 6**
ash-feldspar, transparent, semi-gloss, toxic

Mixing. Mix in the manner of AG-2.

Application. Apply in the manner of AG-1.

Firing. Fire in oxidation or reduction. For reduction fire first in oxidation up to cone 06, moderate reduction to cone 04, and a slightly heavier reduction on up to cone 6. Seal the kiln and cool rapidly down to cone 4, then cool normally.

Fired Results. This glaze fires to a clear semi-gloss at cone 6. It will take opacifiers well and is a good base for the earth colorants iron, rutile, or ilmenite.

Wood ash (washed)	38.0
Feldspar (Custer)	20.0
Whiting	18.0
Talc	13.0
Kaolin (EPK)	9.0
Magnesium carbonate	2.0
Add:	
Bentonite	1.0
C.M.C.	1 tsp.

AG-9 **Semi-Opaque Ash Glaze Cone 6**
ash-feldspar, semi-opaque, stony matt, toxic

Mixing. Mix in the manner of AG-2.

Application. Apply in the manner of AG-1.

Firing. Fire in the manner of AG-8.

Fired Results. This glaze fires to a semi-opaque stony matt at cone 6. At cone 8 it has a smooth buttery surface and is more transparent.

Wood ash (washed)	50.0
Feldspar (Custer)	20.0
Whiting	10.0
Silica	15.0
Kaolin (Florida)	5.0
Nepheline syenite	5.0
Dolomite	3.0
Bentonite	2.0
Add:	
C.M.C.	1 tsp.

AG-10 **Smooth Matt Ash Glaze Cone 6**
ash-feldspar, semi-opaque, smooth matt, toxic

Mixing. Mix in the manner of AG-2.

Application. Apply in the manner of AG-1.

Firing. Fire in the manner of AG-8.

Fired Results. This glaze fires to a semi-opaque smooth matt at cone 6 producing a surface that is smooth and slightly buttery. It iron spots well in reduction.

Feldspar (Kingman)	20.0
Nepheline syenite	20.0
Wood ash (washed)	20.0
Kentucky ball clay #4	10.0
Magnesium carbonate	5.0
Talc	3.0
Bentonite	1.0
Add:	
C.M.C.	1 tsp.

AG-11   **Smooth Matt Ash Glaze   Cone 6**

ash-feldspar, semi-opaque, smooth matt, toxic

Mixing. Mix in the manner of AG-2.

Application. Apply in the manner of AG-1.

Firing. Fire in the manner of AG-8.

Fired Results. This glaze fires to a semi-opaque smooth matt with a slightly buttery finish at cone 6 oxidation or reduction. In reduction it will iron spot well. The best colorants for this glaze are iron, rutile, and ilmenite.

Feldspar (Kingman)	20.0
Nepheline syenite	20.0
Wood ash (washed)	40.0
Kentucky ball clay #4	10.0
Talc	5.0
Magnesium carbonate	5.0
Add:	
Bentonite	1.0
C.M.C.	1 tsp.

AG-12   **Cloudy Off-White Semi-Gloss Ash Glaze   Cone 6**

ash-feldspar, semi-opaque, semi-gloss, toxic

Mixing. Mix in the manner of AG-2.

Application. Apply in the manner of AG-1.

Firing. Fire in the manner of AG-8.

Fired Results. This glaze fires to a cloudy off-white semi-gloss with a slightly buttery finish at cone 6 oxidation or reduction. This glaze will iron spot well if used over a dark clay body.

Feldspar (Kingman)	38.0
Mixed ash (washed)	40.0
Kentucky ball clay #4	18.0
Talc	2.0
Dolomite	2.0
Add:	
Bentonite	1.0
C.M.C.	1 tsp.

AG-13   **Cloudy Semi-Opaque Semi-Gloss Ash Glaze   Cone 8**

ash-feldspar, semi-opaque, semi-gloss, toxic

Mixing. Mix in the manner of AG-2.

Application. Apply in the manner of AG-1.

Firing. Fire in oxidation or reduction. For reduction, first fire in oxidation up to cone 06, moderate reduction up to cone 6, and heavy reduction up to cone 8. Seal the kiln and quickly cool to cone 6 then cool normally.

Fired Results. This glaze fires to a cloudy semi-opaque white semi-gloss at cone 8 oxidation. In reduction it is a tan-white. This glaze is a good base for most of the feldspar colorants, particularly the earth colors which will iron spot well if used over a buff or brown body.

Feldspar (Buckingham)	33.0
Wood ash (washed)	33.0
Tennessee ball clay #1	29.0
Dolomite	2.0
Silica	2.0
Talc	1.0
Add:	
Bentonite	1.0
C.M.C.	1 tsp.

AG-14   **Opaque Semi-Matt Ash Glaze   Cone 8**

ash-feldspar, opaque, semi-matt, toxic

Mixing. Mix in the manner of AG-2.

Application. Apply in the manner of AG-1.

Firing. Fire in the manner of AG-13.

Fired Results. This glaze fires to an opaque cream-white semi-matt at cone 8 oxidation. In reduction it is slightly darker with mottling and iron spotting if it is used over a darker clay body.

Feldspar (Buckingham)	40.0
Wood ash (washed)	40.0
Kentucky ball clay #4	29.0
Talc	1.0
Add:	
Bentonite	1.0
C.M.C.	1 tsp.

AG-15 **Translucent Off-White Semi-Gloss Ash Glaze   Cone 8**
ash-feldspar, translucent, semi-gloss, toxic

Mixing. Mix in the manner of AG-2.

Application. Apply in the manner of AG-1.

Firing. Fire in the manner of AG-13.

Fired Results. This glaze fires to a translucent off-white semi-gloss with a slightly buttery finish at cone 8 oxidation. In reduction it is a light, creamy tan with some mottled areas. It will iron spot well if used over a darker body.

Feldspar (Kona F-4)	34.0
Wood ash (washed)	34.0
Tennessee ball clay #1	30.0
Magnesium carbonate	2.0
Add:	
Bentonite	1.0
C.M.C.	1 tsp.

AG-16 **Light Gray-Green Ash Glaze   Cone 8–9**
Courtesy of Sue Garner, Springfield, Missouri
ash, opaque, matt, toxic

Mixing. Mix in the manner of AG-2.

Application. Apply in the manner of AG-1.

Firing. Fire in the manner of AG-13.

Fired Results. This glaze fires to a light gray-green in reduction and iron spots very well.

Hardwood ash (unwashed)	50.0
Yellow ochre	50.0

AG-17 **Dark-Brown Matt Ash Glaze   Cone 8–10**
ash, opaque, matt, toxic

Mixing. Mix in the manner of AG-2.

Application. Apply in the manner of AG-1.

Firing. Fire in the manner of AG-13, but up to cone 10 if desired.

Fired Results. This glaze fires to a dark brown matt with a slightly buttery finish at cone 8–10 oxidation. In reduction it is a metallic brown-black.

Hardwood ash (washed)	45.0
Yellow ochre	40.0
Whiting	10.0
Dolomite	5.0
Add:	
Bentonite	1.0
C.M.C.	1 tsp.

AG-18 **Light-Green Cigarette-Ash Glaze   Cone 8–10**
ash-feldspathic, opaque, matt, toxic

Mixing. Mix in the manner of AG-2.

Application. Apply in the manner of AG-1.

Firing. Fire in the manner of AG-17.

Fired Results. This glaze fires to a light-green opaque matt at cone 8–10 reduction with good iron spotting over a dark body.

Cigarette ash (unwashed)	24.0
Hardwood ash (unwashed)	40.0
Nepheline syenite	70.0
Talc	30.0
Kaolin	30.0
Add:	
Cobalt oxide	1.0
Green chrome oxide	1.5

AG-19 **Opaque Tan Ash Glaze   Cone 8–10**
ash-feldspar, opaque, semi-matt, toxic

Mixing. Mix in the manner of AG-2.

Application. Apply in the manner of AG-1.

Firing. Fire in the manner of AG-17.

Fired Results. This glaze fires a light-tan opaque semi-matt in oxidation and a darker yellow-tan in reduction with good iron spotting if a buff to brown body is used.

Feldspar (Custer)	39.0
Mixed hardwood ashes (washed)	37.0
Kentucky ball clay #4	19.0
Spodumene	4.0
Magnesium carbonate	1.0

AG-20 **Clear Gloss Ash Glaze   Cone 9**
ash-feldspar, transparent, gloss, toxic

Mixing. Mix in the manner of AG-2.

Application. Apply in the manner of AG-1.

Firing. Fire in the manner of AG-17 but to cone 9.

Fired Results. This glaze fires to a clear gloss at cone 9 oxidation or reduction. It will take opacifiers well and iron spots well if used over a darker body.

Softwood ash (washed)	50.0
Feldspar (Kingman)	24.0
Nepheline syenite	24.0
Bentonite	1.0
Magnesium carbonate	1.0
Add:	
C.M.C.	1 tsp.

AG-21 **Brown Matt Weed-Ash Glaze   Cone 9**
ash, opaque, matt, toxic

Mixing. Mix in the manner of AG-2.

Application. Apply in the manner of AG-1.

Firing. Fire in the manner of AG-20.

Fired Results. This glaze fires to a medium-brown matt in oxidation at cone 9. In reduction it is a metallic brown with good iron spotting.

Weed ash (unwashed)	48.0
Pyrophyllite	48.0
Magnesium carbonate	2.0
Add:	
Bentonite	1.0
C.M.C.	1 tsp.

AG-22 **Creamy-White Mottled Ash Glaze   Cone 9**
ash, opaque, semi-gloss, toxic

Mixing. Mix in the manner of AG-2.

Application. Apply in the manner of AG-1.

Firing. Fire in the manner of AG-20.

Fired Results. This glaze fires to a creamy-white mottled semi-gloss at cone 9 in oxidation or reduction. If used over a dark clay body it will iron spot well.

Plastic vitrox	75.0
Softwood ash (unwashed)	10.0
Hardwood ash (unwashed)	10.0
Jordan clay	4.0
Bentonite	1.0
Add:	
C.M.C.	1 tsp.

AG-23 **Light-Gray Matt Weed-Ash Glaze   Cone 9**
ash, transparent, matt, toxic

Mixing. Mix in the manner of AG-2.

Application. Apply in the manner of AG-1.

Firing. Fire in the manner of AG-20.

Fired Results. This glaze fires to a light-gray matt in oxidation at cone 9. In reduction it is a slightly darker gray with good iron spotting if used over a darker clay body.

Weed ash (unwashed)	50.0
Nepheline syenite	48.0
Magnesium carbonate	2.0
Add:	
Bentonite	1.0
C.M.C.	1 tsp.

AG-24 **Opaque Brown Semi-Matt Ash Glaze   Cone 9–10**
ash-feldspar, opaque, semi-matt, toxic

Mixing. Mix in the manner of AG-2.

Application. Apply in the manner of AG-1.

Firing. Fire in the manner of AG-20, up to cone 10 if desired.

Fired Results. This glaze fires to an opaque brown semi-matt in oxidation at cone 9–10. In reduction it takes on a metallic sheen with iron spotting when used over a darker body.

Mixed ash (washed)	32.0
Tennessee ball clay #1	26.0
Albany slip	5.0
Feldspar (Custer)	31.0
Red iron oxide	1.8
Bentonite	1.2
Dolomite	2.0
Add:	
C.M.C.	1 tsp.

AG-25 **Opaque Stony Matt Ash Glaze Cone 9–10**
ash-feldspar, opaque, stony matt, toxic

Mixing. Mix in the manner of AG-2.

Application. Apply in the manner of AG-1.

Firing. Fire in the manner of AG-24.

Fired Results. This glaze fires to an opaque white stony matt at cone 9–10 in oxidation or reduction. It is a very good base for the earth colorants.

Mixed hardwood ash (unwashed)	35.0
Feldspar (Kingman)	35.0
Kaolin (Georgia)	15.0
Talc	13.0
Magnesium carbonate	2.0
Add:	
Bentonite	1.0
C.M.C.	1 tsp.

AG-26 **Opaque Tan Smooth Matt Ash Glaze Cone 9–10**
ash-feldspar, opaque, smooth matt, toxic

Mixing. Mix in the manner of AG-2.

Application. Apply in the manner of AG-1.

Firing. Fire in the manner of AG-24.

Fired Results. This glaze fires to an opaque tan smooth matt at cone 9–10 in oxidation and slightly darker in reduction with iron spotting if used over a darker body.

Mixed wood ash (unwashed)	25.0
Feldspar (Custer)	32.0
Dolomite	12.0
Kaolin	10.0
Silica	18.0
Magnesium carbonate	2.0
Add:	
Red iron oxide	2.0
Rutile	3.0
C.M.C.	1 tsp.

AG-27 **Soft Satin Matt Ash Glaze Cone 9–10**
ash-feldspar, translucent, satin matt, toxic

Mixing. Mix in the manner of AG-2.

Application. Apply in the manner of AG-1.

Firing. Fire in the manner of AG-24.

Fired Results. This glaze fires to a translucent soft satin matt in oxidation or reduction at cone 9–10. It is a good color base and iron spots well over darker bodies.

Mixed hardwood ash	20.0
Dolomite	14.0
Silica	20.0
Feldspar (Custer)	20.0
Nepheline syenite	14.0
Kaolin (EPK)	10.0
Bentonite	2.0
Add:	
C.M.C.	1 tsp.

AG-28 **Semi-Opaque Semi-Gloss Ash Glaze Cone 9–10**
ash-feldspar, semi-opaque, semi-gloss, toxic

Mixing. Mix in the manner of AG-2.

Application. Apply in the manner of AG-1.

Firing. Fire in the manner of AG-24.

Fired Results. This glaze fires to a semi-opaque semi-gloss which is a slightly cloudy white in cone 9–10 oxidation and a light cloudy cream-white in reduction with some mottled effects and iron spotting when used over a darker clay.

Mixed wood ash	33.0
Tennessee ball clay #1	33.0
Feldspar (Kingman)	33.0
Magnesium carbonate	1.0
Add:	
Bentonite	1.0
C.M.C.	1 tsp.

AG-29

Opaque Off-White Matt Ash Glaze   Cone 9–10
ash-feldspar, opaque, matt, toxic

Mixing. Mix in the manner of AG-2.

Application. Apply in the manner of AG-1.

Firing. Fire in the manner of AG-24.

Fired Results. This glaze fires to an opaque off-white matt in oxidation at cone 9–10. In reduction it is a cream white which will iron spot well over darker bodies. It is also a good base for most colorants.

Mixed ash (unwashed)	35.0
Feldspar (Kingman)	35.0
Kaolin (Florida)	15.0
Talc	13.0
Dolomite	2.0
Add:	
Bentonite	1.0
C.M.C.	1 tsp.

AG-30

Opaque Gloss Coal-Ash Glaze   Cone 10
ash-feldspar, opaque, gloss, toxic

Mixing. Mix in the manner of AG-2.

Application. Apply in the manner of AG-1.

Firing. Fire in the manner of AG-24 but to cone 10.

Fired Results. This glaze fires to an opaque off-white gloss in oxidation at cone 10. In reduction it is a darker off-white with iron spotting and mottling if used over a buff to brown body.

Coal ash	20.5
Kentucky ball clay #4	8.3
Whiting	21.5
Feldspar (Custer)	31.8
Redart clay	3.1
Yellow ochre	1.6
Silica	12.0
Magnesium carbonate	1.2
Add:	
Bentonite	1.0
C.M.C.	1 tsp.

30
SLIP GLAZES
CONE 4-9

As in the case of the ash glazes it was the ancient Chinese potters who first discovered the slip glaze. And again the higher temperature ranges made possible by the advance of kiln technology and firing techniques made the development of these glazes possible. Slip glazes are mostly or in some cases entirely made up of natural clays. And some of the most outstanding of the older Chinese glazes are of this type.

Slip glazes are made of raw natural clays, most of which contain sufficient fluxes in the form of iron, alkalies, or feldspar to act as a glaze without extensive chemical adjustments. Most common clays, in fact, will melt at temperatures around 2300° F./1260° C. and the heavy iron-bearing ones will fuse at temperatures even lower than this.

Slip glazes have several natural advantages that make them worthy of the potter's attention. They are predictable and reliable; they craze very little or not at all; they have a long firing range; they are not expensive to use; and due to their simple composition they are easy to mix. Although the color range is limited to the earth colors — brown, yellow-browns, black, brownish

black, dark brown, and tan — there is quite a variety of color hues possible within this range — especially for the potter who makes rustic-type wares. Even within these limitations the potters of ancient China were able to produce some astoundingly beautiful and subtle colors.

By studious testing of the various slip glazes, even those you might dig locally, the potter can produce some very interesting and unique results. Such testing should also include using these glazes on different types and different colored bodies to determine what temperature they will reach and what color hues can be produced.

The glazes listed in this chapter were especially selected for their beauty and reliability and should perform well under most firing conditions if the directions are followed and the potter is willing to devote a little time to experimentation.

The following glazes are listed first by cone level, then by color, alphabetically, and finally by surface within each color division.

The reader will find list of possible chemical substitutions in Chapter 34, Dictionary of Clay and Glaze Compounds.

Note. The glazes in this chapter are labeled toxic or nontoxic. Toxic glazes should be carefully handled both in formulation and in application. During preparation the potter should wear a dust mask to prevent inhalation of toxic materials and not allow these materials to come into prolonged contact with the skin. Frequent washing of the hands when handling these glazes is a wise precaution. Toxic glazes should be applied by brushing and dipping—never spraying. For even under the best conditions some inhalation of the toxic mist from the spray is bound to take place or, equally bad, the mist from the spray gun can settle on the skin and be absorbed into the body system.

FORMULAS FOR SLIP GLAZES

SLG-1

Beaver-Brown Smooth Matt Slip Glaze Cone 4
slip, semi-opaque, smooth matt, nontoxic

Barnard slip	28.0
Kentucky ball clay #4	27.0
Opax	8.5
Colemanite	36.0
Add:	
Bentonite	1.0
C.M.C.	1 tsp.

Mixing. Weigh out the ingredients and mix by using one of the methods outlined in Chapter 17, Glaze Preparation.

Application. Apply to either hardware or greenware by brushing, dipping, or spraying (do not spray glazes that are toxic). Chapter 17 can be consulted for further information on these three types of application.

Firing. Fire this glaze to cone 4 oxidation.

Fired Results. This glaze fires to a beaver-brown smooth matt at cone 4 oxidation.

SLG-2   **Deep-Brown Satin Matt Slip Glaze   Cone 4**
slip, opaque, satin matt, nontoxic

Mixing. Since this is a glaze that contains soluble sodium, it should either be dry-ground for two hours and only the amount needed mixed with water, or wet-ground and used at once.

Application. Apply in the manner of SLG-1.

Firing. Fire in the manner of SLG-1.

Fired Results. This glaze fires to a deep brown satin matt at cone 4 oxidation.

Barnard slip	38.6
Talc	30.6
Opax	7.8
Sodium bicarbonate	23.0
Add:	
Bentonite	1.0
C.M.C.	1 tsp.

SLG-3   **Metallic-Brown Slip Glaze   Cone 4**
slip-alkaline, translucent, gloss, nontoxic

Mixing. Mix in the manner of SLG-1.

Application. Apply in the manner of SLG-1.

Firing. Fire in the manner of SLG-1.

Fired Results. This glaze fires to a metallic-brown gloss at cone 4 oxidation.

Barnard slip	70.5
Albany slip	11.8
Lithium carbonate	17.2
Opax	0.5
Add:	
Bentonite	1.0
C.M.C.	1 tsp.

SLG-4   **Bean-Pot-Brown Gloss Slip Glaze   Cone 4–6**
slip, transparent, gloss, nontoxic

Mixing. Mix in the manner of SLG-1.

Application. Apply in the manner of SLG-1.

Firing. Fire in oxidation to cone 4–6.

Fired Results. This glaze fires to a gloss deep brown at cone 4–6. This is a very useful glaze for utility ware.

Albany slip	87.5
Nepheline syenite	12.5
Add:	
Bentonite	1.0
C.M.C.	1 tsp.

SLG-5   **Cordova-Brown Gloss Slip Glaze   Cone 4–6**
slip, transparent, gloss, nontoxic

Mixing. Mix in the manner of SLG-1.

Application. Apply in the manner of SLG-1.

Firing. Fire in the manner of SLG-4.

Fired Results. This glaze fires to a cordova-brown gloss at cone 4–6 oxidation. This is a highly stable glaze that is good for utility ware.

Albany slip	82.0
Red iron oxide	13.0
Lithium carbonate	5.0
Add:	
Bentonite	1.0
C.M.C.	1 tsp.

SLG-6   **Antique Golden-Brown Slip Glaze   Cone 4–6**
slip, opaque, semi-gloss, nontoxic

Mixing. Mix in the manner of SLG-1.

Application. Apply in the manner of SLG-1.

Firing. Fire in the manner of SLG-4.

Fired Results. This glaze fires to an antique-brown semi-gloss with hues in the surface.

Albany slip	79.0
Cryolite	20.0
Magnesium carbonate	1.0
Add:	
Bentonite	1.0
C.M.C.	1 tsp.

SLG-7

Moss-Brown Gloss Slip Glaze   Cone 4–6
slip, translucent, gloss, nontoxic

Mixing. Mix in the manner of SLG-1.

Application. Apply in the manner of SLG-1.

Firing. Fire in the manner of SLG-4.

Fired Results. This glaze fires to a moss brown with occasional greenish tints in the surface.

Albany slip	89.0
Lithium carbonate	9.0
Magnesium carbonate	2.0
Add:	
Bentonite	1.0
C.M.C.	1 tsp.

SLG-8

Caramel-Brown Gloss Slip Glaze   Cone 4–6
slip, opaque, gloss, nontoxic

Mixing. Mix in the manner of SLG-1.

Application. Apply in the manner of SLG-1.

Firing. Fire in the manner of SLG-4.

Fired Results. This glaze fires to an opaque caramel gloss at cone 4–6 oxidation.

Albany slip	92.0
Titanium oxide	8.0
Add:	
Rutile	2.0
Bentonite	1.0
C.M.C.	1 tsp.

SLG-9

Chocolate-Brown Matt Slip Glaze   Cone 6
slip, opaque, matt, nontoxic

Mixing. Mix in the manner of SLG-1.

Application. Apply in the manner of SLG-1.

Firing. Fire oxidation to cone 6.

Fired Results. This glaze fires to a chocolate-brown matt at cone 6.

Albany slip	83.0
Lithium carbonate	10.8
Rutile	6.0
Red iron oxide	0.2
Add:	
Bentonite	1.0
C.M.C.	1 tsp.

SLG-10.

Light-Brown Matt Slip Glaze   Cone 6
slip, opaque, matt, nontoxic

Mixing. Mix in the manner of SLG-1.

Application. Apply in the manner of SLG-1.

Firing. Fire in the manner of SLG-9.

Fired Results. This glaze fires to a light-brown matt at cone 6 oxidation.

Albany slip	86.0
Ferro frit #3134	4.2
Wollastonite	9.5
Rutile	0.3
Add:	
Bentonite	1.0
C.M.C.	1 tsp.

SLG-11

Mottled Medium-Brown Slip Glaze   Cone 6
slip, translucent, gloss, toxic

Mixing. Mix in the manner of SLG-1.

Application. Apply in the manner of SLG-1.

Firing. Fire in the manner of SLG-9.

Fired Results. This glaze fires to a medium-brown gloss with some mottling at cone 6 oxidation.

Barnard slip	48.0
Pemco frit #25	7.7
Wollastonite	12.2
Silica	23.0
Barium carbonate	9.1
Add:	
Bentonite	1.0
C.M.C.	1 tsp.

SLG-12

Amber Gloss Slip Glaze   Cone 6–8
slip-alkaline, transparent, gloss, nontoxic

Mixing. Mix in the manner of SLG-2.

Application. Apply in the manner of SLG-1.

Firing. Fire to cone 6–8 oxidation.

Fired Results. This glaze fires to a transparent gloss at cone 6–8.

Native red clay	50.0
Borax	50.0
Add:	
Bentonite	2.0
C.M.C.	1 tsp.

SLG-13   **Clear Slip Glaze   Cone 6–8**
slip-alkaline, transparent, gloss, nontoxic

Mixing. Mix in the manner of SLG-2.

Application. Apply in the manner of SLG-1.

Firing. Fire in the manner of SLG-12.

Fired Results. This glaze fires to a clear gloss at cone 6–8 oxidation.

Cone 06 white clay	50.0
Borax (powdered)	50.0
Add:	
Bentonite	1.0
C.M.C.	1 tsp.

SLG-14   **Bright Red-Black Slip Glaze   Cone 8**
slip, opaque, semi-gloss, nontoxic

Mixing. Mix in the manner of SLG-1.

Application. Apply in the manner of SLG-1.

Firing. Fire to cone 8 oxidation. For reduction firing first fire in oxidation to cone 06, in moderate reduction to cone 6, and in heavy reduction to cone 8. Seal the kiln and allow to cool normally.

Fired Results. This glaze fires to a red-brown in oxidation and a mottled red-black in reduction with some metallic hues apparent in the surface.

Barnard slip	88.0
Whiting	8.0
Rutile	4.0
Add:	
Bentonite	1.0
C.M.C.	1 tsp.

SLG-15   **Red-Brown Matt Slip Glaze   Cone 8**
slip, opaque, matt, nontoxic

Mixing. Mix in the manner of SLG-1.

Application. Apply in the manner of SLG-1.

Firing. Fire in the manner of SLG-14.

Fired Results. This glaze fires to a red-brown in oxidation and a mottled reddish brown-black in reduction. The effect is doubly prominent if used over a dark clay.

Cone 06 red clay	92.0
Whiting	5.0
Talc	3.0

SLG-16   **Transparent Golden-Brown Gloss Slip Glaze   Cone 8**
slip, transparent, gloss, nontoxic

Mixing. Mix in the manner of SLG-1.

Application. Apply in the manner of SLG-1.

Firing. Fire in the manner of SLG-14.

Fired Results. This glaze fires to a golden brown in oxidation and a slightly darker brown with metallic highlights in reduction.

Red clay	80.0
Feldspar (Custer)	18.0
Rutile	2.0
Add:	
C.M.C.	1 tsp.

SLG-17   **Red-Brown Matt Slip Glaze   Cone 8–10**
slip, opaque, matt, nontoxic

Mixing. Mix in the manner of SLG-1.

Application. Apply in the manner of SLG-1.

Firing. Fire in the manner of SLG-14, but this glaze may be fired on up to cone 10 if desired.

Fired Results. This glaze fires to a yellow-brown matt in oxidation and a mottled red-brown in reduction with good iron spotting effects if used over a dark clay body.

Albany slip	52.0
Whiting	18.0
Spodumene	15.0
Red iron oxide	10.0
Rutile	5.0
Add:	
Bentonite	1.0
C.M.C.	1 tsp.

SLG-18   **Oil Spot Slip Glaze   Cone 8–10**
slip, opaque, gloss, nontoxic

Mixing. Mix in the manner of SLG-1.

Application. Apply in the manner of SLG-1.

Firing. Fire in the manner of SLG-17, but give the wares a half hour soaking at the selected cone level 8, 9, or 10, then cool normally with the kiln sealed.

Fired Results. This glaze fires to an oil spot smooth matt at cone 8–10 oxidation and a metallic charcoal-gray in reduction.

Albany slip	72.0
Burnt sienna	8.0
Feldspar (Custer)	5.0
Feldspar (Kingman)	5.0
Red iron oxide	6.0
Hardwood ash (washed)	4.0
Add:	
Bentonite	1.0
C.M.C.	1 tsp.

SLG-19   **Metallic-Black Gloss Slip Glaze   Cone 9**
slip, opaque, gloss, nontoxic

Mixing. This glaze should be wet-ground in a ball mill for at least half an hour to insure the proper mixing of the zinc oxide which occasionally tends to clump in solution.

Application. Apply in the manner of SLG-1.

Firing. Fire in oxidation or reduction. For reduction begin firing in oxidation to cone 06, switch to moderate reduction to cone 6, and continue with slightly heavier reduction to cone 9. Soak at cone 9 and cool normally.

Fired Results. This glaze fires to a metallic black in oxidation with more metallic effects in reduction.

Barnard slip	74.0
Zinc oxide	19.0
Opax	6.0
Add:	
Bentonite	1.0
C.M.C.	1 tsp.

SLG-20   **Black Matt Slip Glaze   Cone 9**
slip, opaque, matt, nontoxic

Mixing. Mix in the manner of SLG-1.

Application. Apply in the manner of SLG-1.

Firing. Fire in the manner of SLG-19.

Fired Results. This glaze fires to a black matt in oxidation. In reduction it is a black matt with occasional metallic hues in the surface.

Barnard slip	73.5
Albany slip	12.4
Lithium carbonate	13.8
Cobalt oxide	0.3
Add:	
Bentonite	1.0
C.M.C.	1 tsp.

SLG-21   **Creamy Tan-Brown Gloss Slip Glaze   Cone 9**
slip, opaque, gloss, nontoxic

Mixing. Mix in the manner of SLG-1.

Application. Apply in the manner of SLG-1.

Firing. Fire in the manner of SLG-19.

Fired Results. This glaze fires to a creamy tan-brown gloss with a slightly buttery quality at cone 9 oxidation. In reduction it is a buff-brown which iron spots well if used over a darker clay body.

Albany slip	80.0
Kaolin (Florida)	8.0
Spodumene	10.0
Magnesium carbonate	2.0

SLG-22   **Date-Brown Matt Slip Glaze   Cone 9**
slip-feldspar, opaque, matt, nontoxic

Mixing. Mix in the manner of SLG-1.

Application. Apply in the manner of SLG-1.

Firing. Fire in the manner of SLG-19.

Fired Results. This glaze fires to a date-brown opaque matt with a slightly buttery finish at cone 9 oxidation. In reduction it is only slightly darker with occasional metallic hues. This is a very good glaze for all types of utility wares.

Barnard slip	35.0
Nepheline syenite	42.0
Talc	10.0
Opax	10.0
Magnesium carbonate	3.0

SLG-23   **Olivewood-Brown Gloss Slip Glaze   Cone 9**
slip, opaque, gloss, nontoxic

Mixing. Mix in the manner of SLG-1.

Application. Apply in the manner of SLG-1.

Firing. Fire in the manner of SLG-19.

Fired Results. This glaze fires to an olivewood-brown opaque gloss with some typical mottling in a cone 9 reduction firing. This glaze is not recommended for oxidation as it tends to be rather muddy.

Albany slip	79.0
Barnard slip	2.0
Kaolin	9.0
Rutile	10.0

SLG-24   **Sudan-Brown Opaque Gloss Slip Glaze   Cone 9**
slip-zinc, opaque, gloss, slightly toxic

Mixing. Mix in the manner of SLG-1.

Application. Apply in the manner of SLG-1.

Firing. Fire in the manner of SLG-19.

Fired Results. This glaze fires to an opaque Sudan-brown gloss in oxidation and slightly darker in reduction at cone 9.

Albany slip	80.0
Zinc oxide	9.0
Kaolin	9.0
Magnesium carbonate	2.0
Add:	
Bentonite	1.0
C.M.C.	1 tsp.

SLG-25   **Opaque Tan Matt Slip Glaze   Cone 9**
slip-feldspar, opaque, matt, slightly toxic

Mixing. Mix in the manner of SLG-1.

Application. Apply in the manner of SLG-1.

Firing. Fire in the manner of SLG-9.

Fired Results. This glaze fires to an opaque tan matt in oxidation or reduction. It will iron spot well if applied over a darker body.

Albany slip	30.0
Nepheline syenite	30.0
Whiting	14.0
Rutile (milled)	10.0
Silica	9.0
Barium carbonate	5.0
Magnesium carbonate	2.0
Add:	
Bentonite	1.0
C.M.C.	1 tsp.

SLG-26   **Mottled Tan Gloss Slip Glaze   Cone 9**
slip, opaque, gloss, nontoxic

Mixing. Mix in the manner of SLG-1.

Application. Apply in the manner of SLG-1.

Firing. Fire in the manner of SLG-19.

Fired Results. This glaze fires to a mottled tan gloss
with streaks of tan and light blue in it. It should only
be fired in reduction for it does not do well in oxidation.

Albany slip	44.0
Wollastonite	25.0
Zinc oxide	28.0
Talc	1.0
Opax	2.0
Add:	
Vanadium pentoxide	5.0
Bentonite	1.0
C.M.C.	1 tsp.

SLG-27   **Textured Tan-and-Brown Matt Slip Glaze   Cone 9**
slip, opaque, matt, nontoxic

Mixing. Mix in the manner of SLG-1.

Application. Apply in the manner of SLG-1.

Firing. Fire in the manner of SLG-19.

Fired Results. This glaze fires to a slightly textured
brown and tan matt at cone 9 reduction—it is not
recommended for oxidation firing.

Albany slip	86.0
Kaolin (Florida)	4.0
Zinc oxide (calcined)	9.0
Magnesium carbonate	1.0
Add:	
Titanium dioxide	2.0
Bentonite	1.0
C.M.C.	1 tsp.

SLG-28   **Rich-Brown Opaque Matt Slip Glaze   Cone 9**
slip-spodumene, opaque, matt, nontoxic

Mixing. Mix in the manner of SLG-1.

Application. Apply in the manner of SLG-1.

Firing. Fire in the manner of SLG-19.

Fired Results. This glaze fires to a light brown in
oxidation and a rich darker earthy brown opaque matt
in reduction at cone 9. At cone 10 it becomes a smooth
satin matt.

Albany slip	67.0
Spodumene	16.0
Whiting	6.0
Rutile	7.0
Red iron oxide	3.0
Magnesium carbonate	1.0
Add:	
Bentonite	1.0
C.M.C.	1 tsp.

SLG-29   **Oil Spot Slip Glaze   Cone 9**
slip, opaque, matt, nontoxic

Mixing. Mix in the manner of SLG-1.

Application. Apply in the manner of SLG-1.

Firing. Fire in the manner of SLG-19. This glaze can
be fired on up to cone 10 if desired.

Fired Results. This glaze fires to a brown oil spot
opaque matt in oxidation and a metallic-black oil spot
in reduction at cone 9–10.

Albany slip	80.0
Red iron oxide	6.0
Rutile	10.0
Feldspar (Kingman)	4.0
Add:	
Bentonite	2.0
C.M.C.	1 tsp.

SLG-30   **Iron-Red Slip Glaze   Cone 9**
slip-feldspar, opaque, semi-gloss, nontoxic

Mixing. Mix in the manner of SLG-1.

Application. Apply in the manner of SLG-1.

Firing. Fire in the manner of SLG-29.

Fired Results. This glaze fires to a khaki brown in oxidation and a rich iron red in reduction at cone 9–10.

Albany slip	64.0
Nepheline syenite	34.0
Rutile	2.0
Add:	
Bentonite	2.0
C.M.C.	1 tsp.

31
SALT AND VAPOR GLAZING

The process of salt glazing of pottery has enjoyed a recent revival by potters after many years of neglect and disdain. Salt glaze itself was first discovered by potters in Medieval Germany sometime in the latter part of the 14th century and is still used by German potters to produce utility ware of high quality. The beer stein so common in that country is a typical example of such ware. And the glaze used on this ware grew in popularity mainly due to its simplicity, its high quality and stability, and its high resistance to chemical attack or weathering. Salt glazing was also quite common in early America for the production of utility ware such as stoneware storage jars.

One of the most attractive features of the salt glazing process is that it can be accomplished entirely in the firing and usually with only one firing — the bisque firing and glaze application are thus eliminated and production time shortened.

The procedure for salt glazing is really quite simple. The pottery in its greenware state is placed in the kiln and fired in oxidation to the maturing point of the clay. At this temperature rock salt (sodium chloride) is thrown into the kiln. (The salt may be moistened which can help break the particles down to a smaller size thereby causing them to melt faster. However the water will cause a small explosion when introduced into the kiln.) The salt plus the moisture given off from the burning fuel spurs a chemical reaction in which the salt turns to sodium hydroxide and hydrochloric acid gas. And due to the high temperature in the kiln chamber the gas chemically unites with the silica and alumina on the surface of the pottery to produce a glaze of high quality.

The process does, however, have its disadvantages. The hydrochloric acid and chlorine gases produced by the salting are poisonous in the gaseous state. Consequently the kiln and studio should be extremely well ventilated to avoid breathing of the vapors. A second disadvantage is that the vapor that glazes the pottery also glazes the interior of the kiln and the kiln furniture and thus renders the kiln useless for other types of firing. And finally the color range possible in salt glazing is somewhat limited.

The best salt glazes are produced in a downdraft kiln which is well vented into a chimney to carry off the harmful gases. Kiln furniture should be painted with a good thick coating of equal parts of aluminum hydrate or fireclay and kaolin held together by a gum additive to prevent vapors from forming glazes on the shelves and post supports. The potter will find that after several salt firings the interior of the kiln will become glazed over and less salt will be needed to produce good results. The fuel used can be either gas, oil, or wood, but the process should not be attempted in an electric kiln as the vapors will quickly destroy the elements.

The firing range for salt glazing is quite wide. Salt glazes may be produced at temperatures ranging from cone 04–12. The temperature used depends entirely upon the maturing point of the clay body, for the sodium gases react with the silica to form a glaze only at the point when the silica is approaching the vitrification state to unite with the other elements in the clay body itself. At lower temperatures, below cone 6, some borax, usually 5%, is added to the salt to give an added "boost" in producing the glazing vapors. Most salt glazing, however, is done at temperatures from cone 6–12.

Almost any clay body will accept a salt glaze, but those with a higher silica content seem to produce better glaze results due to the fact that there is more silica with which the sodium gases can react and unite. In addition the clay body should be smooth and relatively free of rough grog as the glazing vapors will not penetrate and cover up rough and gritty surfaces on the face of the ware. Some potters get around this problem by covering the grogged surface with a grog-free engobe made of the same clay mixture as the body which is applied while the ware is leatherhard.

The reader will find listings of several clay bodies which will work well for salt glazing for cone 04–12 at the end of the chapter.

Color in salt glazed pottery may be obtained by several methods. The most obvious method is to use a colored clay body. For grays, tans, and amber colors, a body with a small percentage of iron should be used. Iron-bearing clays will produce darker browns to black-browns, depending on the percentage of iron in the body. The second method for producing color is through the use of engobes. Any engobe chosen should have some free silica in it to work well and such coloring oxides as cobalt for blue, iron oxide for tan to buff, and rutile for ochre yellows can be used to tint or color the engobes. Some potters even brush water-thinned oxides directly on the clay to produce designs.

Before pottery is placed in the kiln to be salt glazed it must be glazed inside because the sodium vapors will not go down inside the form unless the mouth of the ware is quite wide. Most any good stoneware glaze will work well for this purpose, but the potter should take care to see that the glaze will fit the clay body well. Another point to remember when choosing glazes and colorants is that salt glazing can alter colors as well as textures of some glazes.

The salt glazing process, while not difficult, does have a step-by-step procedure which should be followed if good results are to be obtained:

1. Select a clay body which is high in free silica (at least 10%) for making the pottery.

2. When the pots are almost dry they should be glazed inside and allowed to dry completely before stacking in the kiln. Any of the single-fire glazes listed in Chapter 18 will work well if it is of a comparable cone level to the maturing point of the clay body.

3. When stacking the kiln allow at least 1½″ (3.8 cm) between the pots to allow the sodium vapors to circulate well in the kiln chamber.

4. When stacking, place at least 5 "draw rings" directly in front of the peep hole. These draw rings, made of the same clay as the ware, are necessary to indicate to the potter the progress of the glazing and the growing thickness of the glaze coating of the pots.

5. If a pyrometer is not used, place the cones where they can be seen to indicate when the maturation point has been reached and the salting is to begin. The potter should remember that firing cones are useless after the salting begins for the sodium vapors affect them chemically and they often go down before their normal deformation temperature is reached. This is why the draw rings are necessary.

6. When the kiln is stacked and sealed, fire in oxidation in the normal manner to the cone level of the maturing point of the clay body.

7. When body maturity is reached the salt can be thrown into the kiln chamber. Allow 1 pound/.45 kilo of salt for every 12 cubic feet (.33 cubic meter) of kiln chamber space for each individual salting. As much as 5 pounds/2.25 kilos may be needed for first glaze firing. Either moisten the salt well and pack in small packets of aluminum foil that can be easily pushed through the peep hole or pack it in paper cups to throw into the fire box.

8. Watch the process through the peep hole, when the vapor seems to be clearing, throw more salt into the kiln.

9. After three or four saltings carefully hook one of the red-hot draw rings out of the peep hole, cool it in the water and check to see if the draw ring has a sufficient glaze coating on it. If it has not, continue the salting process until another draw ring indicates that the glazing is sufficient.

10. When the glaze is built up to the potter's satisfaction the firing is stopped and the kiln allowed to cool in the normal manner if tans or browns are desired. However, if gray colors are to be produced the kiln must be cooled rapidly down at least three cones.

VAPOR GLAZING WITHOUT SALT

An alternative method of vapor glazing which is ecologically more attractive when compared to the corrosive vapors formed by salt, is to use the carbonate form of the alkalies. For when these carbonates are used instead of salt, carbon dioxide is released instead of the corrosive and poisonous chlorine gases.

The carbonate mixture used should be prepared in a paste form, wrapped in aluminum foil packets, and introduced into the kiln chamber in the same manner described in the instructions for salt glazing. The mixture includes sodium carbonate, potassium carbonate, and lithium carbonate. Calcium carbonate (whiting) is added in large quantities to act as a dispersing agent for the alkalies. Borax is also used to produce more sodium gas and bentonite is added to aid in converting the dry materials to paste form by the addition of water. Once the mixture is prepared, the same procedure is used as outlined for salt glazing with the same results. The carbonate mix formula is given below:

Sodium carbonate	36.0
Potassium carbonate	8.0
Lithium carbonate	4.0
Borax	3.0
Whiting	48.0
Bentonite	1.0

CHART OF CLAY BODIES SUITABLE FOR SALT GLAZING

The following clay bodies should work well for salt or vapor glazing if the grog content is either excluded entirely or is kept to a very fine mesh (80 to 100 mesh). The clay bodies are listed by cone level from lower to higher temperatures.

Cone 04

ET–2	White throwing body
ET–2	White throwing body
ET–8	Cream throwing body
ET–9	Pink throwing body
ET–10	Buff throwing body
ET–12	Gray throwing body
ET–21	Porcelain-type body
ET–32	Buff throwing body
ET–33	Buff-pink throwing body

Cone 03–1

SST–3	Light red throwing body
SST–6	Buff-white throwing body
SST–8	White throwing body
SST–9	Light red throwing body

Cone 2

SST–10	Cream-tan throwing body
SST–11	Light cool-tan body
SST–12	Cream-tan throwing body
SST–13	Buff throwing body

Cone 3

SST–16	White throwing body
SST–17	Tan throwing body

Cone 4

SST–20	Tan-cream throwing body
SST–23	Tan-buff throwing body

Cone 5

SST–24	Red-brown throwing body
SST–25	White throwing body
SST–26	Medium tan throwing body
SST–28	Dark tan throwing body
ST–5	Tan-gray throwing body

Cone 6

ST–4	Brown throwing body
ST–5	Gray-brown throwing body
ST–6	Speckled-tan throwing body
ST–12	Off-white throwing body
ST–18	Gray-brown throwing body
ST–21	Tan throwing body

Cone 8

ST–25	Tan-cream throwing body
ST–27	Orange-brown throwing body
ST–30	Gray-tan throwing body
ST–31	Warm-gray throwing body
ST–32	Off-white throwing body
ST–37	Buff throwing body
ST–38	Earth-red throwing body
ST–39	Gray throwing body
ST–45	Warm-brown throwing body
ST–51	Gray-tan throwing body

Cone 9

ST–53	Brown throwing body
ST–60	Metallic-brown throwing body
ST–62	Red-brown throwing body
ST–65	Gray throwing body
ST–66	Warm-gray throwing body
ST–69	Orange-brown throwing body

Cone 10

ST–70	Gray-tan throwing body
ST–72	Red-brown throwing body
ST–73	Red-brown throwing body
ST–75	Brown-black throwing body

32
GLAZE DEFECTS
AND ADJUSTMENTS

There are few things in the area of pottery that are more exasperating than having a pot which is well formed come from the kiln marred by some flaw in the glaze. There are generally several logical reasons why these flaws or defects occur. Sometimes there is a single cause but in most cases there are several contributing causes. In many cases the defect may be caused by some error or carelessness in the preparation of the body, or it may be the result of improper firing. More frequently, however, the fault lies in the preparation or improper application of the glaze to the ware. Whatever the causes, it is important for the potter to recognize these flaws and defects, their causes, and the methods to correct them if he wishes to control and perfect his art.

Listed below in alphabetical order are the most common flaws and defects which the potter may encounter. The reader will note that after each defect listed the possible contributing causes are given and the steps that should be taken to correct it.

DESCRIPTION	CAUSE	ADJUSTMENT
Blistering Blistering or bubbling apparent in the glaze or on the surface of the glaze.	1. Gases escaping from the body during glaze firing. 2. Gases escaping from the glaze during firing. 3. Raw alkaline glazes which have sat on the shelf in solution until disassociation has taken place.	1. Fire the bisque a cone or two higher to make the body less porous. 2. Dampen the bisque ware. Fire the kiln more slowly and allow for a soaking period of half an hour at the maturing point to allow the broken bubbles to heal over after the gases have escaped. 3. Grind raw alkaline glazes thoroughly and use them the same day or grind them dry and mix up only the amount needed.
Color Loss Faded areas in the glaze color.	1. Overfiring to the point that disassociation of the coloring oxide takes place.	1. Watch the kiln temperature more carefully to prevent overfiring.
Crazing Cracks formed in the glaze in irregular patterns.	1. Differences in the rate of expansion or contraction of the clay body and the glaze, i.e., the glaze shrinks more than the body of the ware. 2. The glaze coating is too thick. 3. Moisture intake in the pottery after firing—this is known as delayed crazing.	1. Increase the silica content of the clay body by 5% and test the glaze for crazing. 2. Apply the glaze in thinner coats. 3. Use higher fired bisque to retard latent moisture intake.
Crawling Drawing of the glaze into clumps leaving bare areas on the ware.	1. Glazing the ware too thickly. 2. Overfiring the glaze. 3. Firing the kiln too rapidly. 4. Clay content of the glaze too high. 5. Drying the glaze after application too quickly. 6. Lack of adhesiveness and tensile strength in the glaze. 7. Too high tensile strength in the glaze. 8. Flocculation in storage due to soluble alkalies in the glaze. 9. Greasy or dirty bisque. 10. Overloading the glaze with opacifiers or with feldspar. 11. Underfiring. 12. Too smooth a body surface, such as burnished ware. 13. Double glazing where the first glaze is too dry. 14. Using water with a very high mineral content.	1. Use a thinner glaze coat. 2. Fire the glaze one or two cones lower. 3. Fire the kiln more slowly. 4. Decrease the clay content of the glaze recipe by 2% to 3% and test for signs of crawling. 5. Allow the glaze application to dry normally. 6. Use a gum adhesive such as C.M.C. in amounts of one teaspoon per pint/half-liter of glaze. 7. Decrease the gum adhesive content by half. 8. Use glazes with soluble alkalies soon after preparation, or grind and store them dry and mix only the amount needed. 9. Protect bisque ware from contamination by foreign materials before glazing. 10. Decrease the amount of opacifiers or feldspar in the glaze. 11. Check for other signs of underfiring on the piece and determine if a higher firing is needed. 12. Do not finish pottery to a very smooth surface if it is to be glazed. 13. Apply second glaze while the first glaze is still slightly moist. 14. Use water with a lower mineral content.

DESCRIPTION	CAUSE	ADJUSTMENT
Devitrification Areas on the glaze surface which have a frosted crystal-like appearance.	1. Too slow cooling of the kiln. 2. Too much free silica in the glaze. 3. Too high clay content in the glaze recipe.	1. Cool the kiln more quickly after the maturing point of the glaze is reached or after the soaking period, if one is employed. 2. Reduce the amount of free silica content by 5%. 3. Reduce the clay content by 5%.
Excessive Gloss Excessively high shine on the glaze surface.	1. Overfiring. 2. Rapid firing and cooling of the kiln. 3. Excess flux in the glaze recipe. 4. Excess silica in the glaze recipe.	1. Fire one cone lower. 2. Slow down the firing process. 3. Decrease the fluxing agent by 5% or add kaolin in amounts of 2% to 5%. 4. Decrease the silica content in the glaze formula or add kaolin in 2% to 5% amounts.
Glaze Running Glaze runs down the sides of the ware, pooling at the base and leaving thin areas at the top.	1. Overfiring. 2. Insufficient kaolin content in the glaze to stabilize it.	1. Watch the kiln more carefully to prevent overfiring. 2. Increase the kaolin content of the glaze by 2% to 5%.
Overfiring Opaque glazes going translucent or clear, matt glazes going shiny, glazes losing their color, excessive flowing of the glaze, glazes going thin and soaking into the pores of the ware.	1. Overfiring.	1. First check to see if the cone level of the glaze has been exceeded, if this is not the case, the glaze may actually have a lower maturing point than indicated in the formula. If the evidence indicates this, fire one cone lower or two cones lower if necessary.
Pinholing Small pinholes in the surface of the glaze.	1. Air escaping from a porous underfired bisque ware. 2. Excessive grinding of the glaze. 3. Gases escaping from the glaze. 4. Glazes which are too viscous.	1. Fire the bisque one cone higher and dampen the ware before glazing. 2. Grind the glaze for shorter periods of time. 3. Allow for a soaking period of half an hour at the maturing point of the glaze to let these gas holes to heal over. 4. Increase the flux or decrease the clay content by 2% to 5%.
Rough Surface Rough, sandy, or grainy surface on the glaze.	1. Glazing too thin. 2. Underfiring. 3. Insufficient flux in glaze to melt the silica.	1. Apply the glaze more thickly. 2. Fire the glaze ware one or two cones higher. 3. Increase the fluxing agent by 2% to 5%.

DESCRIPTION	CAUSE	ADJUSTMENT
Scumming A frosty scumlike deposit on the surface of the glaze.	1. Soluble salts in the glaze. 2. Sulfur fumes from the fuel where oil or solid fuel is used.	1. Add 2% barium carbonate or a teaspoon of vinegar per pint/half-liter to the glaze mix. 2. Use saggers to protect the pots or try another fuel with a lower sulfur content.
Shivering Glaze breaking away from the body.	1. Takes place when the glaze shrinks more than the glaze, causing a buckling of the glaze.	1. Decrease the silica content of the glaze 5% to 10%.
Speckling Surface marred by specks of nonglaze material.	1. Foreign material getting into the glaze mix. 2. Dust or foreign matter falling on the glazed or bisque ware during the drying process.	1. Protect glaze containers to prevent contamination by foreign materials. 2. Protect ware during drying stages of both bisque and glazing to prevent foreign matter from settling on them.
Underfiring Underfired glazes will usually be opaque with rough gritty surfaces and immature colors as compared to the finished mature glaze.	1. Not firing the glaze to its proper maturing point.	1. Fire the glaze one cone higher and check for signs of underfiring—if they are still present, fire the glaze still higher by stages until the proper maturing point of the glaze is determined.

33
GLAZE COLORANTS

The utilitarian function of a glaze is to provide the pot with a tough, sanitary, easily cleaned surface that will provide a coating impervious to the attacks of acids and wear in general. Due to intensive research carried on by potters over the centuries, particularly in the last two decades, there is a wide variety of colors available to potters today to decorate their wares.

All glaze colorants are obtained from the oxides or carbonates of the common metals such as iron, copper, nickel, zinc, tin, manganese, rutile, and ilmenite. The oxides of the rarer metals, vanadium, cobalt, uranium, cadium, and selenium are also used because there are no inexpensive substitutes that will produce similar results.

In practice it is quite common to use two, sometimes more, of these oxides or carbonates as glaze colorants to obtain more subtle hues or modify harsh colors given by the stronger colorants. Other oxides are often added to promote special effects such as flowing or mottling.

It should be recognized that glaze color is not an absolute science for it is affected by many factors and variables. Clay body color can cause changes and modifications in glazes. For example, a glaze used over a lighter firing body, such as white or cream, will be brighter than a glaze used over a buff or brown body. The temperature of the firing and the atmosphere, whether oxidation or reduction, will alter colors significantly. The coarser coloring oxides like ilmenite, iron, and manganese in granular form will quite often break or bleed through the surface of the glaze to produce spotting and mottled effects. Colorants are also affected by their use with one another and very much by the type of glaze base in which they are used, whether lead, alkaline, feldspar, etc. For these reasons the author feels it wise to list each of the commonly used glaze colorants and their basic characteristics when used alone, in combination with other colorants, or in the different types of

glaze bases. The potter should also know their behavior at different firing levels and atmospheres. They are listed below in alphabetical order.

CHROME OXIDE

Chrome is a rather versatile and somewhat fickle colorant. It can produce red, pink, brown, yellow, or green depending on the type of glaze base, the firing temperature, and the other colorants with which it is combined. Its major characteristics are:
1. In a medium lead glaze with zinc oxide, chrome oxide will produce green.
2. In low-fired lead-base glazes, low in alumina content, it will produce oranges and reds.
3. In low-fired lead glazes which also contain some sodium, brilliant yellows may be produced.
4. Glaze bases which contain zinc will produce brown hues with the addition of chrome oxide.
5. In glaze bases with tin, pinks can be produced.
6. In any base glaze, chrome with cobalt oxide will produce beautiful blue-greens.
7. Above cone 6 chrome tends to be fugitive and will escape from the glaze in vapor form to contaminate other glazes.
8. Chrome, if used with manganese, will produce muddy and dingy colors — this combination should be avoided.
9. Chrome may be used in the form of chrome oxide, potassium bichromate, or lead chromate — *the latter two colorants however are very soluble and poisonous.*

COBALT OXIDE

The most stable and reliable colorant available to the potter is cobalt. It can be used either in oxide or carbonate form — the latter usually being preferred due to its fine particle size which allows more uniform mixing in the glaze base. Its major characteristics are:
1. Cobalt is the strongest colorant in tinting

power of all the glaze colorants. Therefore only very small additions, ½% to 2%, are necessary.
2. It gives similar and uniform color hues in all glaze bases.
3. In alkaline bases the blues are particularly brilliant.
4. When it is used in glazes with some magnesium content, it produces purple-blue colors.
5. The blues produced by cobalt can be modified significantly by the introduction of iron oxide, manganese, magnesium, rutile, ilmenite. nickel, or chrome.
6. Cobalt oxide glazes should be ball milled to insure uniform mixing to prevent mottling or specking.

COPPER OXIDE

Copper, either in the oxide or carbonate form, has been used for many centuries to produce turquoise and green. The Egyptians used it as early as 3000 B.C. in alkaline glaze bases to produce the color we know as Egyptian Blue. It is a strong colorant with the following characteristics:

1. Copper oxide is very soluble in glaze bases and tends to mix thoroughly in the melt to produce strong colors.
2. It is a strong flux and will generally make any base to which it is added more fluid and the surface more brilliant and glossy.
3. Additions of 1% will give a pronounced light green tint to a glaze, 3% will give strong color, and amounts above 5% will give metallic greens to blacks.
4. Copper oxide added to a high alkaline base will produce turquoise blues — this is the only manner in which this color can be produced.
5. In lead-base glazes copper will produce warm, soft greens. These colors are usually better if modified with iron, vanadium, rutile, cobalt, or nickel.
6. Copper used in lead glazes tends to increase the solubility of lead and therefore should not be used on utility ware.
7. In colemanite glazes copper will give blue-green colors reminiscent of the Egyptian Turquoise, but they are less brilliant in hue. These glazes are usually deeper in color if made opaque.
8. In barium-base glazes copper produces a greenish blue of great depth and intensity, but due to the barium content they are usually of the dry-matt type.
9. In feldspar-alkaline reduction glazes copper will produce the famous ox-blood reds discovered by the Chinese.
10. At cone levels above 8 copper loses its stability and tends to become volatile and escape from the glaze in vapor form which can discolor surrounding pieces in the kiln.

ILMENITE

Ilmenite is a metal compound containing titanium and iron in small quantities. Its major characteristics are:
1. Ilmenite is used primarily for its influence on other glaze materials to produce mottling or spotting.
2. It can be used in granular form to produce speckled glazes.
3. At least 3% is needed to produce a good tint in glazes.
4. Ilmenite like rutile will act as an opacifier when used in amounts above 5%.
5. It can be added to clay bodies or engobes in granular form to produce speckled colors beneath transparent glazes.
6. When added to bodies or engobes and fired in reduction it will cause prominent iron spotting.

IRON OXIDE

This is probably the most common of all the glaze colorants. It is usually used in the form of ferric oxide which is red. The variety of colors possible with the use of this oxide are almost infinite. Its major characteristics are:
1. When it is present in the clay body it will affect most glazes used over it.
    A. When clear glazes are used over such a body they will reveal colors of tan, buff, brown, red-brown, or earth yellow, depending on the amount of iron oxide present in the clay body.
    B. When the glaze base used over such a body is high in lead the colors are usually warm in tone.
    C. When the glaze base is alkaline the colors are cooler and tend to be grayed in tone.
    D. In the cone 02–5 range glazes used over such a body will tend to be more grayed and subdued than the lower fired glaze bases.
    E. In the cone 5 and up range colors used over such a body are even more subdued.
2. In lead-base glazes iron will produce warm, soft colors of tan, straw yellow, yellow-brown, amber, red-brown, or mahogany.
    A. In high lead bases at low firing levels, 2% to 4% iron will give brilliant tones of amber.
    B. In high lead glaze bases with 5% to 10% tin oxide creamy yellows with red-brown markings will result, especially if used over textured bodies.
3. In alkaline glazes iron produces cooler colors of tan, yellow, and brown.
4. If iron is used in combination with zinc, colors tend to be rather muddy and dingy.
5. When iron is used in excess of 8%, dark browns to black result. The black colors may be very brilliant in surface — sometimes known

as mirror blacks.

6. If a large amount of iron is used it may tend to crystallize out during the cooling. These effects may be quite attractive in high-lead glazes producing brilliant crystals tinted yellow to red-brown. The aventurine glazes are produced by such a method.

7. Iron may be used to modify other colors. The colors produced by copper, vanadium, and cobalt may be subdued by the addition of 2% iron oxide to produce colors of greater subtlety and depth.

8. Iron may also act as a flux at stoneware temperatures due to its lower melting point.

9. In reduction firing iron may be used to produce gray-green colors known as celadons.

10. In high-fire reduction glazes with considerable alkalie compounds present, iron in amounts of 10% or more will produce colors known as saturated-iron reds with the colors showing up as red to red-brown mottled areas on a darker background.

MANGANESE OXIDE

This colorant may be used either in the form of manganese carbonate or manganese dioxide. When compared to cobalt or copper, manganese is a rather weak colorant, needing at least 3% to produce a good tint. Its major characteristics are:

1. In high-alkaline glazes manganese will produce rich purples.

2. In lead glazes it will produce a soft purple, sometimes tinted with brown.

3. Manganese carbonate is finer in particle size and is usually preferred for glazes.

4. Manganese dioxide due to its particle size is often used in clay bodies to produce spotting by the bleeding-through process at temperatures above cone 4.

5. Manganese in lead glazes may cause blistering if the atmosphere is not an oxidizing one.

6. When combined with iron oxide it will produce rich shades of cool brown.

7. When used with cobalt it will give rich deep shades of violet or plum.

NICKEL OXIDE

Nickel is seldom used by itself due to its fickle nature. Therefore it is commonly used as a modifier for other colorants. Its major characteristics are:

1. Nickel oxide in amounts of 1% will gray and subdue any glaze color.

2. Used alone in amounts up to 1% it will produce a rather attractive gray.

3. Above 1% browns are usually produced with this oxide in any glaze base.

4. Used alone in amounts above 3% nickel tends to promote matt finishes due to its refractory nature.

RUTILE

Rutile is a titanium oxide ore with iron oxide chemically bonded to the titanium. It is used often by potters as a source of titanium where the coloring power of the iron is not objectionable. Its major characteristics are:

1. Rutile as a colorant is rather weak. Usually 3% to 5% is required to give a noticeable tint. Used in such percentages it produces tans to browns.

2. Rutile will produce broken, mottled surface colors.

3. In colemanite glazes the mottling is more pronounced.

4. The mottling effect is more opaque if the glaze base is opaque.

5. In amounts of 5% and over it will act as an opacifier.

6. Used with other colors it has a graying effect.

7. Rutile can be used to promote crystallization in crystalline glazes.

USING SINGLE COLORANTS

The oldest and simplest method of making colored glazes is with the addition of single colorants. By this method the potter can test the true coloring power of the oxide in question.

It is best to start with a good base glaze which is known to perform well, i.e., a glaze which is transparent and colorless. Usually the base glaze is figured as 100% and any addition of colorants is based on amounts (in percentages usually) which are added to the base.

After the base glaze is selected, make separate tests with each of the colorants selected to determine the results of the different percentages of additions to the glaze base. It is always wise to make several tests with differing percentages of the same oxide to determine the strength of the color desired. It is also advisable to run the same set of tests using an opacifier, such as tin oxide or opax, in the same set of tests to determine the reaction of the colorant in an opaque glaze.

Finally the potter should test the various glazes over different colored clay bodies to determine the desired effect, for the glaze colors are often altered by the clay body on which they are applied. Blues and greens, for example, may become dark and rather dingy on a dark-colored clay body.

The percentage chart at the end of the chapter will serve as a guide to the adding of single colorants to all kinds of base glazes.

CHART OF COLORANT BLENDS

While it is possible to produce glazes which are quite attractive by the addition of single colorants, better hues and more subtle colors are possible by the addition of two or more colorants which will react favorably with one another.

The following guide is given to help the potter select combinations intelligently, for not all colorants react favorably with one another.

Chrome + cobalt oxide = blue-green
copper oxide = green
ilmenite = warm green
iron oxide = grayed green
manganese = brown (muddy)
nickel oxide = brown
rutile = warm green
vanadium = yellow green

Cobalt + chrome oxide = blue-green
copper oxide = blue-green
ilmenite = matt gray-blue
iron oxide = grayed blue
manganese oxide = blue-purple
nickel oxide = grayed blue
rutile = warm grayed blue
vanadium = grayed or ochre yellow

Copper + chrome oxide = green
cobalt oxide = blue-green
ilmenite = warm gray-green
iron oxide = warm grayed greens
manganese oxide = brown to metallic black
nickel oxide = grayed greens
rutile = warm matt greens
vanadium = warm yellow-greens

Ilmenite + chrome oxide = warm green
cobalt oxide = matt gray-blue
copper oxide = warm gray-green
iron oxide = tan to spotted brown
manganese oxide = brown to dark brown
nickel oxide = brown
rutile = spotted browns
vanadium = yellow-browns

Iron + chrome oxide = black-green
cobalt oxide = grayed blues
copper oxide = warm green, metallic greens, and black
ilmenite = spotted browns
manganese oxide = browns
nickel oxide = grayed browns

rutile = ochre-browns with mottling
vanadium = ochre-yellows

Manganese + chrome oxide = browns (muddy)
cobalt oxide = blue-purples
copper oxide = brown to black
ilmenite = spotted browns
iron oxide = browns
nickel oxide = gray to brown
rutile = mottled browns
vanadium = yellow-browns

Nickel + chrome oxide = browns (greenish)
cobalt oxide = gray to blue
copper oxide = grayed greens
ilmenite = browns
iron oxide = browns (grayed)
manganese oxide = gray to brown
rutile = brown
vanadium = gray to ochre-browns

Rutile + chrome oxide = warm greens
cobalt oxide = warm mottled blues
copper oxide = warm greens
ilmenite = spotted browns
iron oxide = ochre-browns
manganese oxide = mottled browns
nickel oxide = patterned browns
vanadium = ochre-yellows

Vanadium + chrome oxide = yellow-greens
cobalt oxide = ochre-yellows
copper oxide = warm yellow-greens
ilmenite = yellow-browns
iron oxide = ochre-yellows
manganese oxide = yellow-browns
nickel oxide = gray to ochre-browns
rutile = mottled ochre-yellows

LOW-LEAD GLAZES   CONE 012–2

Chemical	Percentage	Color
Antimony oxide	2.0	light yellow
	4.0	medium yellow
Black iron oxide	2.0	light yellow
	4.0	dark ochre-brown
Burnt sienna	2.0	tan
	4.0	buff-brown
Burnt umber	4.0	brown
	6.0	brown to black
Cadmium sulfide	2.0	light yellow
	4.0	yellow
Chrome oxide	2.0	bright orange
	4.0	deep orange
Cobalt carbonate	1.0	light blue
	2.0	medium blue
Cobalt oxide	0.5	light blue
	1.0	medium blue
Copper carbonate	3.0	light green
	5.0	green
Copper oxide	2.0	light green
	3.0	green
Copper phosphate	1.0	yellow-green
	3.0	green
Crocus martis	3.0	earth yellow
	5.0	buff (spotted)
Ilmenite	1.0	earth yellow
	2.0	buff-yellow
Iron chromate	1.0	bright orange
	3.0	deep orange
Manganese dioxide	3.0	brown to black
	6.0	black
Nickel oxide	2.0	earth yellow
	4.0	buff-yellow
Opax	5.0	yellow-white
	10.0	opaque off-white
Potassium bichromate	2.0	orange-red
	5.0	orange
Red iron oxide	5.0	mottled brown
	10.0	deep brown
Rutile	5.0	earth yellow
	8.0	ochre-yellow
Selenium	2.0	yellow-orange
	5.0	orange
Tin oxide	4.0	cream-white
	8.0	opaque cream-white
Uranium oxide	4.0	orange-red
	6.0	orange
Vanadium oxide	4.0	orange-red
	6.0	orange
Yellow ochre	2.0	earth orange
	5.0	deep earth orange
Zinc oxide	5.0	translucent white
	10.0	opaque white
Zircopax	5.0	translucent white
	10.0	opaque white

ALKALINE GLAZES   CONE 010–04

Chemical	Percentage	Color
Antimony oxide	2.0	light yellow
	4.0	yellow
Black iron oxide	2.0	light amber
	4.0	amber
Burnt sienna	2.0	off-white
	4.0	tan-white
Burnt umber	4.0	tan
	6.0	cool brown
Cadmium sulfide	2.0	white
	4.0	white
Chrome oxide	2.0	light green
	4.0	green
Cobalt carbonate	1.0	light blue
	2.0	blue
Cobalt oxide	0.5	light blue
	1.0	blue
Copper carbonate	3.0	light turquoise
	5.0	turquoise
Copper oxide	2.0	light turquoise
	3.0	blue-green
Copper phosphate	1.0	blue-green
	3.0	dark blue-green
Crocus martis	3.0	mottled buff
	5.0	darker mottled buff
Ilmenite	1.0	light speckled tan
	2.0	speckled tan
Iron chromate	1.0	gray-brown
	3.0	black to brown
Manganese dioxide	3.0	purple-violet
	6.0	purple
Nickel oxide	2.0	gray
	4.0	dark gray
Opax	5.0	translucent white
	10.0	opaque white
Potassium bichromate	2.0	gray-yellow
	5.0	medium gray-yellow
Red iron oxide	5.0	red-brown
	10.0	dark brown
Rutile	5.0	gray-brown
	8.0	dark gray-brown
Selenium	2.0	white
	5.0	off-white
Tin oxide	4.0	translucent white
	8.0	opaque white
Uranium oxide	2.0	off-white
	4.0	light yellow
Vanadium	4.0	light yellow
	6.0	yellow
Yellow ochre	2.0	tan-white
	5.0	translucent white
Zinc oxide	5.0	translucent white
	10.0	opaque white
Zircopax	5.0	translucent white
	10.0	opaque white

413

COLEMANITE GLAZES   CONE 06–02

Chemical	Percentage	Color
Antimony oxide	2.0	grayed yellow
	4.0	cream yellow
Black iron oxide	2.0	tan
	4.0	buff-tan
Burnt sienna	2.0	tan-white
	4.0	tan
Burnt umber	4.0	warm tan
	6.0	tan-brown
Cadmium sulfide	2.0	white
	4.0	white
Chrome oxide	2.0	green
	4.0	deep green
Cobalt carbonate	1.0	blue-purple
	2.0	deep blue
Cobalt oxide	0.5	blue-purple
	1.0	deep blue
Copper carbonate	3.0	light turquoise
	5.0	turquoise
Copper oxide	2.0	light turquoise
	3.0	turquoise
Copper phosphate	1.0	light blue
	3.0	medium blue
Crocus martis	3.0	buff
	5.0	buff-tan
Ilmenite	1.0	off-white
	2.0	tan
Iron chromate	1.0	gray
	3.0	medium gray
Manganese dioxide	3.0	purple
	6.0	deep purple
Nickel oxide	2.0	tan
	4.0	buff-tan
Opax	5.0	translucent white
	10.0	opaque white
Potassium bichromate	2.0	ochre-yellow
	5.0	cool buff-tan
Red iron oxide	5.0	amber brown
	10.0	red-brown
Rutile	5.0	earth pink
	8.0	pink-brown
Selenium	2.0	white
	5.0	white
Tin oxide	4.0	translucent white
	8.0	opaque white
Uranium oxide	2.0	off-white
	4.0	buff
Vanadium oxide	4.0	off-white
	6.0	light yellow
Yellow ochre	2.0	buff-tan
	5.0	buff
Zinc oxide	5.0	translucent white
	10.0	opaque white
Zircopax	5.0	translucent white
	10.0	opaque white

HIGH-LEAD GLAZES CONE 04–2

Chemical	Percentage	Color
Antimony oxide	2.0	white
	4.0	off-white
Black iron oxide	2.0	gray
	4.0	charcoal-gray
Burnt sienna	2.0	tan-white
	4.0	tan
Burnt umber	4.0	off-white
	6.0	cool tan
Cadmium sulfide	2.0	off-white
	4.0	off-white
Chrome oxide	2.0	gray-green
	4.0	dark gray-green
Cobalt carbonate	1.0	light blue
	2.0	blue
Cobalt oxide	0.5	light blue
	1.0	blue
Copper carbonate	1.0	aqua-blue
	3.0	blue-green
Copper oxide	2.0	blue-green
	3.0	medium blue-green
Copper phosphate	1.0	blue-green
	3.0	deep blue-green
Crocus martis	3.0	buff
	5.0	tan
Ilmenite	1.0	off-white
	2.0	tan-white
Iron chromate	1.0	grayed purple
	3.0	purple
Manganese dioxide	3.0	grayed purple
	6.0	dark grayed purple
Nickel oxide	2.0	buff
	4.0	buff-brown
Opax	5.0	translucent white
	10.0	opaque white
Potassium bichromate	2.0	light purple
	5.0	purple
Red iron oxide	5.0	gray-brown
	10.0	brown
Rutile	5.0	mottled white
	8.0	mottled tan
Selenium	2.0	white
	5.0	white
Tin oxide	4.0	translucent white
	8.0	opaque white
Uranium oxide	2.0	light yellow
	4.0	yellow
Vanadium oxide	4.0	cream-white
	6.0	cream
Yellow ochre	2.0	off-white
	5.0	light ochre-yellow
Zinc oxide	5.0	translucent white
	10.0	opaque white
Zircopax	5.0	translucent white
	10.0	opaque white

POTASH GLAZES CONE 4–6

Chemical	Percentage	Color
Antimony oxide	2.0	off-white
	4.0	off-white
Black iron oxide	2.0	light yellow-brown
	4.0	dark ochre-brown
Burnt sienna	2.0	tan
	4.0	buff-tan
Burnt umber	4.0	tan
	6.0	dark tan
Cadmium sulfide	2.0	white
	4.0	white
Chrome oxide	2.0	warm gray
	4.0	dark gray
Cobalt carbonate	1.0	light blue
	2.0	blue
Cobalt oxide	0.5	light blue
	1.0	blue
Copper carbonate	3.0	grayed brown
	6.0	brown
Copper oxide	1.5	grayed brown
	3.0	khaki-brown
Copper phosphate	1.0	blue
	3.0	blue-green
Crocus martis	1.0	tan
	3.0	ochre-brown
Ilmenite	1.0	mottled white
	3.0	mottled tan-white
Iron chromate	1.0	gray
	3.0	gray-tan
Manganese dioxide	3.0	grayed purple
	6.0	greenish gray-purple
Nickel oxide	2.0	warm gray
	4.0	charcoal gray
Opax	5.0	translucent white
	10.0	opaque white
Potassium bichromate	2.0	mottled earth gray
	5.0	mottled off-white
Red iron oxide	5.0	light yellow-brown
	10.0	dark yellow-brown
Rutile	5.0	light earth orange
	8.0	earth orange
Selenium	2.0	white
	5.0	white
Tin oxide	4.0	translucent white
	8.0	opaque white
Vanadium oxide	4.0	off-white
	6.0	yellow-white
Yellow ochre	2.0	tan
	5.0	buff tan
Zinc oxide	5.0	translucent white
	10.0	opaque white
Zircopax	5.0	translucent white
	10.0	opaque white

SPODUMENE GLAZES CONE 8–10 REDUCTION

Chemical	Percentage	Color
Antimony oxide	2.0	gray
	4.0	medium gray
Black iron oxide	2.0	mottled brown
	4.0	mottled dark brown
Burnt sienna	2.0	mottled tan
	4.0	mottled buff-tan
Burnt umber	4.0	mottled tan
	6.0	mottled buff-tan
Cadmium sulfide	2.0	mottled pink
	4.0	mottled pink
Chrome oxide	2.0	metallic gray
	4.0	metallic charcoal
Cobalt carbonate	1.0	mottled blue-gray
	2.0	mottled blue
Cobalt oxide	0.5	mottled blue-gray
	1.0	mottled blue
Copper carbonate	3.0	mottled gray
	6.0	mottled metallic charcoal
Copper oxide	1.5	mottled gray
	3.0	mottled metallic charcoal
Copper phosphate	1.0	mottled blue-gray
	3.0	mottled deep metallic blue
Crocus martis	1.0	mottled tan
	3.0	mottled buff-tan
Ilmenite	1.0	mottled buff
	3.0	mottled buff-brown
Iron chromate	1.0	mottled cool gray
	3.0	mottled charcoal-gray
Manganese dioxide	3.0	mottled gray
	6.0	mottled charcoal gray
Nickel oxide	2.0	warm gray
	4.0	mottled charcoal gray
Opax	5.0	off-white
	10.0	opaque off-white
Potassium bichromate	2.0	mottled gray
	5.0	metallic gray-black
Red iron oxide	5.0	mottled brown
	10.0	brownish black
Rutile	5.0	mottled off-white
	8.0	mottled gray
Selenium	2.0	mottled gray
	5.0	mottled dark gray
Tin oxide	4.0	off-white
	8.0	opaque off-white
Vanadium oxide	4.0	mottled gray
	6.0	medium mottled gray
Yellow ochre	2.0	mottled gray
	5.0	mottled gray-tan
Zinc oxide	5.0	gray-white
	10.0	opaque gray-white
Zircopax	5.0	translucent white
	10.0	opaque white

34
DICTIONARY OF CLAY AND GLAZE COMPOUNDS

Note. Some of the chemicals listed below are potentially dangerous to the health of the potter. This has been noted in relevant entries. Extreme caution should be taken when handling these chemicals. In the entries below, m.p. denotes melting point.

Albany Slip. (m.p. 2264°F./1240°C.) A naturally occurring slip clay found near Albany, New York. It contains silica, alumina, and sufficient fluxes to function as a glaze at cone 6-12. See Chapter 16 on slip glazes for formulas. *See also* the Clay Chart in the Appendix for analysis. Albany slip has no equivalent substitute.

Albite. ($Na_2.Al_2O_3.6SiO_2$) This is another name for pure soda feldspar. Almost any soda feldspar will substitute for it where mentioned in glaze formulas. If potash feldspar is substituted, the color of the resulting glaze will be altered and the maturing point raised. *See* Feldspar.

Aluminum Oxide. (Al_2O_3) (m.p. 3722°F./2050°C.) Sometimes known as alumina, this oxide is used in glazes in amounts up to 10%. It can be introduced into the glaze either through the feldspar or the clay or even separately. It promotes viscosity in the glaze, thus stabilizing it, prevents devitrification during cooling, gives hardness and durability, and promotes matt finishes. Used in moderate amounts it will also help prevent crazing in utilitarian glazes.

Alumina Hydrate. ($Al\,[OH]_3$) (m.p. 3722°F./2050°C.) This chemical is sometimes preferred to the oxide form for its adhesive quality and its ability to remain suspended in the glaze.

Amblygonite. (Li_2O-7.8,Al_2O_3-34.2,SiO_2-2.8,P_2O_5-47.5) This compound is occasionally used to introduce lithium into a glaze. Lepidolite or spodumene can usually be substituted for it on a 2-1 ratio.

Antimonate of Lead. ($3PbO.Sb_2O_3$) (m.p. 1616°–1652°F./880°–900°C.) This compound is a yellow stain or pigment also known as Naples Yellow or sometimes yellow medium or yellow base. It is very poisonous and should be handled with great care. *See* Antimony Oxide for more details.

Antimony Oxide. (Sb_2O_3) (m.p. 1166°F./630°C.) This chemical is used as an opacifier and a colorant to produce yellows. It is very poisonous and slightly soluble. It is sometimes used in cone 06–1 glazes as an opacifier but is more commonly used to make Naples Yellow stain. Its formula is: red lead–15%, antimony oxide–10%, and tin oxide–4%. This mixture is calcined in a crucible to cone 08, wet ground, washed, and then dried. It will produce fairly good yellow colors if used in amounts up to 10%. Larger amounts tend to promote blistering in the glaze. There is no effective substitute.

Ash. *See* wood ash.

Ball Clay. A fine-grained sedimentary clay used in clay bodies to promote plasticity and higher firing ranges. It is also used as a glaze ingredient in higher fired glazes. For glaze use one type will generally substitute for another with very little difference. *See* the Clay Chart in the Appendix for analysis of individual ball clays.

Barium Carbonate. ($BaCO_3$) (m.p. 2480°F./1360°C.) This chemical is a poisonous alkaline earth which is used as a matting agent in lower fired glazes to promote matt finishes and for its effect on colorants such as copper. (Used with either copper carbonate or oxide, it will give intense hues of blue.) At higher temperatures it is a strong flux. In such cases it will give a hardness and brilliance second only to lead glazes. It has no effective substitute.

Barnard Clay. A slip clay similar to Albany slip but with a much higher clay content. *See* the Clay Chart in the Appendix for its analysis.

Bentonite. ($Al_2O_3.4SiO_2.9H_2O$) This compound is a fine-particled derivation of volcanic ash. It is used in clay bodies up to 6% to promote plasticity and in glazes up to 2% to prevent settling. In clay bodies ball clay can be used as a substitute but five times as much is required to produce the same increased plasticity. There is no substitute for bentonite in glaze use.

Bicarbonate of Soda. *See* Sodium Bicarbonate.

Binders. *See* Gums.

Bismuth Oxide. (Bi_2O_3) (m.p. 1517°F./825°C.) This is a metallic element which is sometimes used as a flux to promote longer firing ranges in glazes. It will also lessen the tendency of a glaze to craze. Its action is similar to that of lead but is completely nontoxic. It is not used generally due to its high cost. It has no effective substitute.

Bismuth Subnitrate. ($BiONO_3.H_2O$) (m.p. 1517°F./ 825°C.) This element is used in the production of luster glazes due to its lower melting point. It is usually used in combination with several nitrate elements suspended in a resin solution and fired on top of another harder glaze at a lower temperature—usually around cone 019. It has no effective substitute.

Bone Ash. ($3CaO.P_2O_5$) Sometimes known as calcium phosphate, it is used as a flux in higher fired glazes and as a body flux in porcelain, where it contributes to translucency. It has no effective substitute.

Borax. ($Na_2O.2B_2O_3.10H_2O$) (m.p. 1366°F./741°C.) This sodium borate compound influences most glaze chemicals with a very strong fluxing action. It is a major source of flux in alkaline glazes which are used to produce purple and turquoise. The colors produced with this flux are particularly brilliant but are subject to crazing. Soda ash can generally be substituted for this chemical with few adjustments.

Boric Acid. ($B_2O_3 3H_2O$) This is a flaky soluble alkaline material which is usually used as a flux in alkaline glazes. When used as the only flux in an alkaline glaze it is less likely to cause crazing than sodium fluxes. It has no effective substitute.

Buckingham Feldspar. A potash feldspar. See Feldspar for more information and the Feldspar Chart in the Appendix for its analysis. Custer feldspar is a good substitute if Buckingham is not available.

Burnt Sienna. ($Fe_2O_3.H_2O$ + impurities) This is a hydrated form of iron-manganese ochre much like umber but with a lower manganese content. See Yellow Ochre. It has no accurate substitute.

Burnt Umber. (analysis will vary) This is a naturally occurring hydrated form of iron with a varying manganese content. It is used as a colorant to produce gray-browns. Ochre or sienna can be substituted if a minute amount of manganese dioxide is added to the substitute.

Cadmium Sulfide. (CdS) This compound is used as a low-fire colorant to produce yellows and combinations with selenium to produce reds and oranges. It tends to be fugitive at temperatures above cone 010. It has no effective substitute.

Calcium Borate. See Colemanite.

Calcium Carbonate. See Whiting.

Calcium Fluoride. See Fluorspar.

Calcium Phosphate. See Bone Ash.

Calcium Sulfate. See Gypsum.

China Clay. See Kaolin.

Chromium Oxide. (Cr_2O_3) (m.p. 4418°F./2270°C.) This is a metallic compound used commonly as a colorant to produce greens. Used in combination with tin it will produce pink, and with zinc oxide it will produce brown. Bright reds can also be produced in low-fire high-lead glazes which are low in alumina content. It has no effective substitute.

Clinchfield Feldspar. A potash feldspar. See Feldspar for more information and the Feldspar Chart in the Ap-

pendix for its analysis. Custer feldspar is the best substitute for this compound.

C.M.C. This is a form of gum arabic—a vegetable gum used in glazes as a binder and adhesive to give them a better coating power in the dry state. Mix as follows: Add 25 grams of C.M.C. to 1 quart/.9 liter of water plus 3 to 5 drops of formaldehyde to prevent decomposition. Mix this well and let set for several days. Then shake or stir to get an even consistency. C.M.C. can be used in amounts of 1 teaspoon per 100 grams of glaze. Gum tragacanth will substitute well here but is is more expensive than this commercial variety of gum.

Cobalt Carbonate. ($CoCO_3$) (m.p. 1661°F./905°C.) This compound is used as a colorant to produce blues. It can also be used with manganese, iron chromate, or nickel to produce strong blacks (see the Colorant Charts in the Appendix for percentages). Cobalt oxide can be effectively substituted for it if used in one-half the given amount.

Colemanite. ($2CaO.3B_2O_3.5H_2O$) This is a naturally occurring form of calcium borate. As it is only slightly soluble in water it does not develop the crystals or lumps characteristic of borax glazes. It is widely used as a low-fire flux due to the low fusion point of the boron content. It has the advantage of producing low-fire leadless glazes which tend to craze less than other alkaline types. It tends also to lend a milky blue opalescence to the glaze that employs it as a flux. The commercially sold product Gerstley Borate is a type of colemanite and will substitute well in any glaze recipe which calls for colemanite.

Cobalt Oxide. (CO_3O_4) (m.p. 1661°F./905°C.) This is the major oxide used for producing blues (see the colorant charts in the Appendix for percentages). It is very strong and glazes employing it as a colorant should be ball milled to insure thorough mixing. If cobalt carbonate is substituted for the oxide, double the amount.

Compost Bacterial Tablets. This is a commercial composting bacterial agent used to promote bacterial action in organic materials. It can be used in clay mixtures to promote aging. Beer can also be used for this purpose.

Copper Carbonate. ($CuCO_3$) (m.p. 2100°F./1149°C.) This chemical is used as a major colorant to produce greens, turquoise, and copper reds. For producing turquoise in alkaline glazes and copper reds in reduction glazes the carbonate form is usually preferred to the oxide due to its finer particle size. Copper oxide can be used as a substitute if the amount is reduced by one-half.

Copper Oxide. (CuO) (m.p. 1947°F./1064°C.) This colorant tends to produce greens of a grayish nature when used in lead glazes, turquoise in alkalies, yellow-greens in potash, and blue-greens in barium base glazes. *Lead galzes with copper content should not be used on utility ware because the copper tends to increase the solubility of the lead.* Copper carbonate can be substituted for copper oxide if the amount is doubled.

Copper Phosphate. (CuP_2O_5) This chemical can be used to produce greens, blues, and blue-greens in lead, colemanite, and potash glazes respectively. It has no effective substitute.

Cornwall Stone. (Cornish Stone) This is a feldpathoid used commonly in glazes. It will minimize glaze defects such as crawling or crazing. Its characteristics lie somewhere between kaolin and feldspar. Godfrey spar or Carolina stone can serve as substitutes for it, or failing this, 67 parts feldspar, 22 parts silica, and 11 parts kaolin can be substituted if the above compounds are available. *See* the Feldspar Chart in the Appendix for its analysis.

Chromate of Iron. *See* Iron Chromate.

Crocus Martis. (Fe_2O_3 + impurities) This is a naturally occurring form of iron oxide with other impurities. It can be used in glazes or clay bodies to promote mottled or spotted effects. Used in engobes under reduction glazes it will iron spot exceptionally well. There is no effective substitute.

Cryolite. ($Na_3.AlF_6$) (m.p. 1828°F./998°C.) This is a sodium-aluminum fluoride used mainly to produce crater glazes and crackle effects in other alkaline glazes. The fluorine gas driven off during the firing tends to cause bubbles and blisters in the glaze. If the glaze is not fairly fluid it can also cause pinholes. A soaking period of half an hour will generally get around this difficulty, however. There is no effective substitute.

Cullet. (formulas vary) (m.p. 1202°-1472°F./650°-800°C.) This is glass in various forms, scrap glass that is used to decorate pottery. It can also be used in finely ground form as a glassmaker and flux in glazes. There is no equal substitute.

Cupric or **Cuprous Oxide.** *See* Copper Oxide.

C.W. 5 Ceramic Clay. A stoneware clay which fires in the cone 5–10 range. It fires buff in oxidation and brown in reduction. It is a very good clay for the potter who likes iron spotting in the production of glazes.

Custer Feldspar. This is probably the most commonly used of all the potash feldspar. *See* Feldspar and consult the Feldspar Chart in the Appendix for its analysis. Kingman or Buckingham feldspar is the best substitute if Custer is not available.

Dextrine. This is a vegetable gum which is completely soluble in water. Add about two tablespoons per pint (½ liter of water and a few drops of formaldehyde to prevent decomposition and allow to set for a few hours after a vigorous shaking. Add two tablespoons of the solution to a pint (½ liter) of glaze.

Dolomite. $CaCO_3.MgCO_3$) (m.p. 4658°-5072°F./2570°-2800°C.) This is a double carbonate of calcium and magnesium. It is an inexpensive method of adding calcium and magnesium to glazes to promote that "buttery" smoothness common to magnesium glazes. It can be used in bodies to promote longer and lower firing ranges. One-fourth the amount of each compound, calcium carbonate and magnesium carbonate, can be substituted if dolomite is not available.

Epsom Salts. *See* Magnesium Sulfate.

Eureka Feldspar. This is a potash feldspar. *See* Feldspar for more information and the Feldspar Chart in the Appendix for its analysis. Custer or Kingman feldspar will substitute if Eureka is not available.

Feldspar. (m.p. 2228°F./1220°C.) The feldspars are of two major types: potash ($K_2O.Al_2O_3.6SiO$) and soda- ($NaO.6SiO_2$). Both types tend to vary in content from one location to another. This is the major reason why glaze recipes may need to be altered unless the materials used are identical. Feldspar is a major ingredient of clay bodies and glazes. Potash and soda feldspars can be used interchangeably with the following results: potash feldspar promotes a harder glaze surface, soda feldspar lowers the fusion point of bodies or glazes slightly, and fired colors may be different. *See* the Feldspar Chart in the Appendix for the analysis of each type of feldspar. *See* also Nepheline Syenite and Cornwall Stone.

Ferric Oxide. *See* Iron Oxide.

Ferro Frit #3124. A leadless frit which melts at cone 06. Substitutes: Ferro #3386 or Hommel #285.

Ferro Frit #3134. A borosilicate frit which melts at cone 06. Substitutes: Hommel #14, Hommel #242, or Pemco #54.

Ferro Frit #3223. A borosilicate frit which melts at cone 06. Substitutes: none.

Ferro Frit #3819. A leadless frit which melts at cone 06. Substitutes: Pemco #25 or Hommel #259.

Ferrous Oxide. *See* Iron Oxide.

Fire Clay. (m.p. highly refractory) This is a naturally occurring sedimentary clay prized for its refractory qualities. It is used in clay bodies to promote higher firing ranges for clay bodies. *See* the Clay Chart in the Appendix for its analysis. Fire clays are also listed here by brand name.

Flint. *See* Silica.

Fluorspar. (CaF_2) (m.p. 2372°F./1300°C.) This compound is also called calcium fluoride. It is used as a flux in glazes. It has a tendency to form bubbles, craters, or pinholes unless the glaze is fairly fluid or a soaking period is employed to allow these imperfections to heal over at the melting point. When used with copper it can produce some unusual blue-green colors.

Formaldehyde. (HCHO) (no melting point) This is used in gum solutions to prevent decomposition and spoiling. It should also be used in glazes which employ ball clays, as they sometimes contain organic matter which can sour and cause bubbling of the glaze.

Frits. These are commercially prepared combinations of silica and soluble fluxes melted together and ground to powder to render the fluxes insoluble. Lead compounds are fritted to render them nontoxic. Ferro, Pemco, and Hommel frits are listed in the Appendix under their brand names and by number. *See also* the Lead Silicate entries.

Gerstley Borate. *See* Colemanite.

Glass Cullet. *See* Cullet.

Godfrey Feldspar. A compound very similar to Cornwall stone or Carolina stone. Either one can be substituted for it.

Goldart Clay. This is a stoneware clay that will fire in the cone 06–8 range. At cone 06 it is white, at cone 2 cream, at cone 6 tan, and at cone 8 buff. See the Clay Chart in the Appendix for its analysis. H is sometimes called AF clay.

Gold Chloride. ($AuCl_3$) (m.p. 1292°F./700°C.) This metal compound is used as a lustrous enamel over other glazes. It is usually prepared in liquid form with resin and bismuth as a flux, painted on the ware, then fired to cone 019. Firing must be precise or the gold will turn to a purple color.

Grog. This ground, fired-clay material is used in clay bodies to give them texture and strength during the throwing process, promote drying in heavy wares, increase fired strength, and reduce drying and firing shrinkage.

Ground Glass. *See* Cullet.

Gums. ($CaSO_4$) These are glaze adhesives such as gum arabic, tragacanth, or dextrine. They are used in glazes to promote suspension and strength in the dried glazes.

Gypsum. This calcium compound has limited use in glazes; it is used only in fine granular form to promote the formation of crater effects in a glaze.

Hawthorn Clay. This is a stoneware clay which has a wide firing range of cone 1–14. It produces a family of colors from cream to brown depending on the firing temperature. *See* the Clay Chart in the Appendix for its analysis.

Hematite. *See* Iron Oxide.

Hommel Frit #14. A leadless alkaline frit which melts at cone 06. Substitutes: Ferro #3134, Hommel #259, or Pemco #54.

Hommel Frit #242. A leadless frit which melts around cone 06. Substitutes: Ferro #3134, Hommel #14 or Pemco #54.

Hommel Frit #259. A leadless frit which melts around cone 06. Substitutes: Ferro #3819 or Pemco #25.

Hydrochloric Acid. This aqueous solution of hydrogen chloride is a strong corrosive and should be handled with extreme care.

Ilmenite. ($Fe_2O_3TiO_2$) (m.p. 2489°F./1365°C.) This iron-titanium compound is used as a colorant to produce tans and buffs. It can also be used in granular form to produce speckled glazes. Used in bodies or engobes it promotes iron spotting in reduction glazes. Rutile can be substituted as a poor stand-in as the coloring power of rutile is far weaker than that of ilmenite.

Iron Chromate. ($FeCrO_4$) (m.p. 2818°–3272°F./1548°–1800°C.) This colorant can be used to produce several colors. In low-fire glazes it will produce orange, in alkaline glazes it will produce gray, and in potash and spodumene glazes at high-fire levels it will produce mottled grays. There is no effective substitute for this compound.

Iron Oxide, Black. (FeO) (m.p. 2818°F./1548°C.) This common colorant will give a variety of colors depending on the glaze base used. In most cases its effects are about the same as red iron oxide, *see* next entry. Generally red iron oxide can be substituted for it, though many potters prefer black iron oxide for producing celadon glazes in reduction firing. *See* the Colorant Chart in Chapter 33 for further details.

Iron Oxide, Red. (Fe_2O_3) (m.p. 2818°F./1548°C.) This is the most commonly used form of the iron colorants. It It is used most often to produce tan to brown colors. When used in amounts above 4% it can react as a flux and increase the fluidity of the glaze. Black iron oxide will substitute for it. *See* the Colorant Chart in Chapter 33 for color possibilities.

Jordan Clay. This is a high quality stoneware clay which is used in clay bodies to produce cream- to buff-colored bodies. Monmouth clay is a good substitute. *See* the Clay Chart in the Appendix for its analysis.

Kaolin. ($Al_2O_3.2SiO_2.2H_2O$) (m.p. 3164°–3245°F./1740°–1785°C.) This compound is sometimes called China clay due to its wide use in the production of white clay bodies in a wide temperature range. In glazes it is used as a source of alumina and silica to stabilize the glaze. Used in large amounts it will produce matt glazes. It has no effective substitute. *See* the Clay Chart in the Appendix for the analysis of the different kaolins.

Kentucky Ball Clay #4. This is probably the most popular of all the ball clays. *See* the Clay Chart in the Appendix for its analysis.

Keystone Feldspar. A potash feldspar. *See* Feldspar for more information and the Feldspar Chart in the Appendix for its analysis. Custer Feldspar is a good substitute if Keystone is not available.

Kingman Feldspar. A potash feldspar. *See* Feldspar for more information and the Feldspar Chart in the Appendix for its analysis. Custer feldspar can be easily substituted for it.

Kona A-3 Feldspar. A potash feldspar. *See* Feldspar for more information and the Feldspar Chart in the Appendix for its analysis.

Kona F-4 Feldspar. The most popular soda feldspar. *See* Feldspar for more information and the Feldspar Chart in the Appendix for its analysis.

Lead Antimonate. *See* Antimonate of Lead and Antimony Oxide.

Lead Basilicate. ($PbO.2SiO_2$) (m.p. 1310°–1472°F./710°–800°C.) *See* Lead Silicate.

Lead Carbonate. ($2PbOCO_3.Pb[OH]$) (m.p. 1472°F./800°C.) White lead is the common name for this compound. It is used as a low-fire flux to produce clear, glossy glazes. Unfortunately, as a glaze material it is highly poisonous. It should be handled with caution and not be used to glaze utility wear. Red lead, which is even more toxic, can be substituted if the amount is cut by one-third. Consult the Chapter 33 for colors possible with lead glazes.

Lead Monosilicate. *See* Lead Silicate.

Lead Oxide. (Pb_3O_4) (m.p. 1616°F./880°C.) This lead compound is commonly known as red lead and is also used as a low-fire flux. It is highly toxic, even more so than the white carbonate form, and tends to settle in the glaze solution more readily than the carbonate form. If white lead is substituted, increase the amount by one-third. Consult Chapter 33 for color possibilities with lead glazes.

Lead Sesquisilicate. *See* Lead Silicate.

Lead Silicate. This term refers to a frit of lead and silica which by the fritting process eliminates the toxic effects of the lead. Glazes made with a lead silicate are generally considered "lead safe" and may be used on utility wares. Lead silicates come in three forms: lead bisilicate ($PbO.3SiO_2$) with a melting point of 1310°–1472°F./ 710°–800°C., lead monosilicate ($Pb.SiO_2$) with a melting point of 1238°–1382°F./670°–750°C., and lead sesquisilicate ($2PbO.3SiO_2$) with a melting point of 1274°–1562°F./680°–850°C. All of these frits will form fluid, glossy glazes at the melting point given.

Lepidolite. ($[LiNaK]_2.[Fe]H_2$) (m.p. 2138°F./1170°C.) This lithium-aluminum-silica compound is a important source of alkaline flux at temperatures above cone 4. It promotes tougher and more durable glaze finishes. Good copper blues can be produced in such glazes. It has no effective substitute.

Lime. *See* Whiting.

Lincoln Fire Clay. A very plastic brand of fire clay similar in content to other fire clays. *See* Fire Clay and consult the Clay Chart in the Appendix for fire clay analysis.

Lithium Carbonate. (Li_2CO_3) (m.p. red heat) This compound is the most important and common form of the alkali lithium. It is a major flux for higher fired alkaline glazes. It is less soluble than other alkaline compounds and produces more durable glazes, since greater amounts of silica and whiting can be used in combination with it. The copper blues possible with this compound are very similar to those produced in raw alkaline glazes using soda ash or borax. It can also be used as an auxiliary flux to bring down the melting point of higher fired stoneware glazes by as much as 2 to 3 cones. It is possible to substitute Lepidolite for lithium, but the silica content and alumina content must be altered.

Magnesite. *See* Magnesium Carbonate.

Magnesium Carbonate. ($MgCO_3$) (m.p. 5072°F./2800°C.) This compound is most commonly used in high-fire glazes to produce the buttery surface quality favored by many potters for utility ware. At high temperatures it will function as a slow flux and is then valuable for its "slowing" effect on fluid glazes such as the crystalline type, which cannot employ alumina for this purpose. Dolomite can be substituted for magnesium carbonate if the whiting content is cut by half.

Magnesium Oxide. *See* Magnesium Carbonate.

Magnesium Sulfate. ($MgSO_4.7H_2O$) (m.p. 5072°F./ 2800°C.) This compound is better known as epsom salts. Its major use in glazes is to prevent settling of the heavier contents. It will also thicken glazes for better application. Usually 1% is sufficient for either purpose. Any of the gums or bentonite can be used for this purpose also.

Magnetite. *See* Iron Oxide.

Manganese Carbonate. *See* Manganese Oxide.

Manganese Dioxide. *See* Manganese Oxide.

Manganese Oxide. (MnO) (m.p. 5072°F./2800°C.) This compound is used mainly as a colorant to produce browns, blacks (with cobalt and nickel), and purple in alkaline glazes. When used in amounts exceeding 5% it generally causes blistering of the glaze. It is not generally wise to substitute for any of the manganese compounds. They are listed together for they all decompose to the oxide form at 662°F./350°C., and the oxide form will only melt at 5072°F./2800°C. This compound can be toxic if used in large amounts.

M M Fire Clay. This is a high-quality fire clay used in raku and high-quality stoneware bodies. Most any good fire clay will substitute for another. The potter will find, however, that some are more plastic than others. Lack of plasticity can usually be solved by the addition of ball clay or bentonite.

Monmouth Stoneware Clay. This is a very high quality stoneware clay used in high-fire bodies. Any good cone 12 stoneware clay will substitute for it.

Nepheline Syenite. (m.p. 2233°F./1223°C.) This compound is very similar to the feldspar group and can even be substituted for potash feldspar if the potter wants to lower the firing temperature of a glaze by at least 1 cone, sometimes 2 cones depending on the other contents of the glaze. Glazes using this compound tend to craze less and are more durable in the middle temperature range. *See* the Feldspar Chart in the Appendix for its analysis. The only possible substitute would be soda feldspar, which would raise the maturing point by at least one cone and alter the resulting color. Potash feldspar would raise the temperature also but would do less to alter the resulting color.

Nickel Oxide. (Ni_2O_3) (m.p. 752°F./400°C.) Nickel oxide is used solely as a colorant to produce browns, blue when used with zinc, tan with whiting, and gray-brown in barium glazes. Generally it is used as an auxiliary colorant. It has no equivalent substitute.

Ochre. See Yellow Ochre.

Opax. This is a commercially prepared opacifier with the following analysis: ZrO_2-90.84, SiO_2-6.48, Na_2O-1.11, and Al_2O_3-.91. Possible substitutes are Zircopax, Superpax, and tin oxide.

Oxford Feldspar. This is a potash feldspar. *See* Feldspar. *Also see* the Feldspar Chart in the Appendix for its analysis. Custer feldspar will substitute if Oxford is not available.

Pearl Ash. See Potassium Carbonate.

Pemco Frit #25. A leadless frit which melts in cone 06 range. Substitute: Hommel #14.

Pemco Frit #54. A leadless frit which melts at cone 06. Substitutes: Hommel #259 or Ferro #3134.

Petalite. ($Li_2O.Al_2O_3.8SiO_2O$) This is a lithium-aluminum-silicate which is used primarily in clay bodies for utilitarian ware to reduce thermal expansion and increase the resistance to thermal shock. It is also used in higher fire glazes as a source of lithium and silica. It has no effective substitute.

Pine Lake Fire Clay. A fire clay available in some regions. See Fire Clay and the Clay Chart in the Appendix for analysis.

Plastic Vitrox. This is a complex clay type of material similar to both feldspar and Cornwall stone. It can be substituted for half of either one of these compounds if the potter wants to lower the firing temperature of the glaze by 1 to 2 cones. The color change is minimal. See the Clay Chart in the Appendix for its analysis. The only possible substitutes are Cornwall stone, Carolina stone, or soda feldspar, all of which will raise the melting point of the glaze.

Potash Feldspar. See Feldspar and the Feldspar Chart in the Appendix for further information.

Potassium Carbonate. (K_2CO_3) (m.p. 932°-1067°F./ 500°-575°C.) Commonly known as "pearl ash," this chemical is used mainly for its effect on colorants when used as a low-fire flux. Its effects are similar to those of the other alkalies. This compound should be stored in an airtight container as it tends to absorb moisture. Glazes made with this compound should be used at once due to their highly soluble nature. This compound has no effective substitute.

Potassium Bichromate. ($K_2Cr_2O_7$) (m.p. 1780°F./ 971°C.) This chemical is used solely as a colorant to produce reds, oranges, greens, blues, and grays, depending on the glaze base. See the Colorant Chart in Chapter 33 for specifics. Potassium bichromate is toxic and should be handled with great care. It has no equivalent substitute.

Praseodymium Oxide. (Pr_2O_3)(m.p. 2336°F./1280°C., then disassociates) This is a "rare earth" chemical used as a colorant to produce yellows. It is more stable than vanadium and will take higher firings. When used in frit form with zirconium and silica it will remain stable at all temperatures. Vanadium will substitute if cone 6-7 is not exceeded in the glaze firing.

Pyrophyllite. ($Al_2O_3.4SiO_2.H_2O$) This compound is used mainly in tile clay bodies. Its use in glazes is similar to that of kaolin but it will reduce crazing and thermal expansion better than kaolin. It can also be used in ovenware bodies for the same reasons, but has to be kept below 15% of the body weight due to its highly nonplastic nature. Kaolin can be substituted in an emergency.

Quartz. See Silica.

Redart Clay. This is an iron red clay with a firing range

of cone 04-1. See the Clay Chart in the Appendix for its analysis.

Red Dalton Clay. This is an iron red clay similar in composition to Redart. See the Clay Chart in the Appendix for its analysis.

Red Lead. See Lead Oxide.

Rutile. ($FeTiO_3$) (m.p. 3452°F./1900°C.) This is one of the crystalline forms of titanium. It is used in 1% to 3% amounts to produce tans, but its most common use is to modify the action of other colorants and to produce special effects such as mottling and streaking. Such effects are particularly striking in colemanite glazes. See Chapter 33 on glaze colorants for further details. Titanium dioxide can be substituted if the tan color is not a necessity to the glaze.

Sagger Clay. This clay is a refractory mixture of fire clay and grog, usually in 50-50 proportions. It is used to make saggers in which other wares are fired in an open flame kiln. See the Clay Chart in the Appendix for its analysis.

Salt. See Sodium Chloride.

Sand. Sand of the type found in rivers or the beach can often be used as grog in larger pieces.

Selenium. (Se) This nonmetallic element is used in sodium-fluorine frits, sometimes in combination with cadmium, to produce low-fire reds. It has no equivalent substitute.

Silica. (SiO_2) (m.p. 3119°F./1715°C.) All pottery is literally based on this material in both the clay body and the glazes used. Silica is the glass-forming element that vitrifies to hold the clay together and the element in glazes which melts to form the glass coating we call a glaze. At 3119°F./1715°C. it will form a very hard glass by itself. In glazes, fluxes are added to bring down the melting point. Used with alumina as a stabilizer silica forms a glaze which is tough, durable, and highly resistant to wear. It can be added to the glaze recipe in the form of clay, feldspar, or by itself. If the potter wishes to increase the maturing point of a glaze, silica (also called flint) can be added to the basic formula. It has no substitute.

Silicate of Soda. See Sodium Silicate.

Silicon Carbide. (SiO) (m.p. 3992°F./2200°C.) This highly refractory compound is used mainly in high-fire kiln furniture. When used in alkaline glazes in amounts of 0.5% to 1.0% it can produce artificial reduction copper reds. It has no substitute.

Silver Chloride. (AgCl) This compound is the metallic oxide generally used in the production of local luster glazes. It is usually combined with bismuth in an oil or resin solution to provide an overglaze luster at cone 019. It has no equivalent substitute.

Soapstone. See Talc.

Soda Ash. (Na_2CO_3) (m.p. 887°-932°F./475°-500°C.) This compound is a very active flux for low-temperature glazes, but due to its highly soluble nature it is generally used in frit form to prevent recrystallization in the glaze solution. Glazes which use raw soda ash should be well ground and used immediately or dry-ground and only the amount needed mixed with water. Soda ash is also used in small amounts as a deflocculant in slips and clays to reduce the amount of water needed to make the clay plastic, thus reducing shrinkage of the body from the wet to the dry state. A possible substitution is sodium bicarbonate, but the amount should be doubled.

Sodium Bicarbonate. ($NaHCO_3$) (m.p. $887°$-$932°$F./ $475°$-$500°$C.) This sodium compound is used both in slips as a deflocculant and in low-fire glazes as a flux. Like soda ash it is completely soluble and should be treated in the same manner when used in raw alkaline glazes. Soda ash can be substituted if about half the amount is used.

Sodium Borate. *See* Borax.

Sodium Carbonate. *See* Soda Ash.

Sodium Chloride. (NaCl) (m.p. $1472°$F./$800°$C.) The only use for this compound in pottery is in salt glazing. See Chapter 32 on salt glazing for further details.

Sodium Silicate. ($Na_2O.SiO_2$) (m.p. $1990°$F./$1088°$C.) This liquid compound is usually used as a deflocculant for slips. It greatly reduces the amount of water needed to form casting slips, thus reducing shrinkage. Soda ash or sodium bicarbonate may be substituted in some cases. See each of those entries for details.

Spodumene. ($Li_2O.Al_2O_3.4SiO_2$) (m.p. $1994°$-$2399°$F./ $1090°$-$1315°$C.) This compound is one of the potter's best sources of lithium, which is a very active flux, especially at stoneware levels. Spodumene can be used both in white bodies and glazes where it will lower the vitrification point. It can also be used to replace part or all of the feldspar content to lower the melting point by 1 to 2 cones. Lithium carbonate can be substituted, but it is a tricky process. For every gram substituted add 1 gram of Al_2O_3 and 4 grams of SiO_2.

Steatite. *See* Talc.

Strontium Carbonate. ($SrCO_3$) (m.p. $1472°$-$1832°$F./ $800°$-$1000°$C.) This alkaline earth compound can be used as glaze flux to promote craze resistance and a longer firing range. Its behavior in a glaze is almost identical to that of whiting, which will substitute well for this more expensive compound. The difference in texture, surface, and color will be subtle if substitutions are made.

Talc. ($3MgO.4SiO_2.H_2O$) This compound, which is also known as steatite or soapstone, is an insoluble magnesium compound which is sometimes used in glazes but is more commonly used in cone 04-6 white bodies to lower the maturing point. Used in glazes it will promote a slightly opaque glaze, makes iron produce browns, and alters the intensity of cobalt oxide. It has no equivalent substitute.

Tennessee Ball Clay #1. A high-quality ball clay used both in bodies and in glazes. In clay bodies most any good ball clay will substitute but in glazes the two closest substitutes are Tennessee ball clay #5 or Kentucky ball clay #4. *See* the Clay Chart in the Appendix for its analysis.

Tennessee Ball Clay #5. A high-quality clay used both in bodies and in glazes. In clay bodies most any good ball clay will substitute. In glazes substitute only Tennessee ball clay #1 or Kentucky ball clay #4. *See* the Clay Chart in the Appendix for ball clay analysis.

Tin Oxide. (SnO_2) (m.p. $2066°$F./$1130°$C.) This metallic compound is the most effective of all the opacifiers at all temperature levels. Usually 5% to 8% will opacify any glaze completely. It also acts to stabilize glaze flow. If amounts above 8% are used it should be calcined to red heat to prevent crawling of the fired glaze. Any of the commercial opacifiers such as Opax, Zircopax, or Superpax will substitute but larger percentages will be necessary—usually up to 10% for an opaque glaze. Tin oxide is very expensive, making substitution attractive.

Titanium Oxide. (TiO_2) (m.p. $3362°$F./$1850°$C.) This compound, like tin oxide, can be used as an opacifier. It tends to produce cream colors as compared to the white effects of the tin. It has a mottling effect on colors and glazes very similar to that of rutile. Rutile can be substituted for it if the iron content is not a problem.

Uranium Oxide. (U_3O_8) (m.p. $2300°$F./$1260°$C.) This compound is used as a colorant to produce yellows and orange-reds. Its high cost usually eliminates any advantage it may have since the less costly vanadium, praseodymium, and cadmium-selenium frits are just as effective. Because it is sold as a spent oxide it has a very low radioactivity. For yellows, vanadium or praseodymium will substitute and the cadmium-selenium frits will substitute if oranges or reds are desired.

Vanadium Oxide. (V_2O_5) (m.p. $1265°$F./$685°$C.) This oxide can be used in 5% to 10% amounts to produce yellow. The addition of titanium or tin will favor the production of stronger yellows. The most popular substitute is praseodymium.

Vermiculite. This material, which is highly refractory, is used mainly as an insulating material but can be used as a grog to reduce the weight of heavy ceramic pieces.

Volcanic Ash. This is a glassy compound of volcanic origin. It can be used in large amounts in glazes. *See* the Feldspar Chart in the Appendix for its analysis. It can be substituted for 70% of the feldspar or 30% of the silica content without adverse affects to the glaze. The closest substitutes are Cornwall stone or Carolina stone.

Water Glass. *See* Sodium Silicate.

White Lead. *See* Lead Carbonate.

Whiting. ($CaCO_3$) (m.p. $4658°$F./$2570°$C.) Chemically known as calcium carbonate, this compound is widely used in glazes and bodies. In glazes it is used as a matting agent and stabilizer to make them more durable by producing harder and tougher silicates. At stoneware temperatures it acts as a flux. In bodies it will lower the virtification point and reduce porosity. It can be substituted for by Wollastonite.

Wollastonite. $(CaO.SiO_2)$ (m.p. 2804°F./1540°C.) This compound is sometimes used as a replacement for silica and whiting. It is used mainly to reduce firing shrinkage and improve resistance to thermal shock in both glazes and clay bodies. Whiting may be substituted if an equal amount of silica is also added.

Wood Ash. This compound will vary greatly in content from location to location and from one type of ash to another. Consequently, when it is used some experimentation will be necessary. The usual starting point is 2 parts ash, 2 parts feldspar, and 1 part clay. Nepheline syenite can be substituted for half of the feldspar content to bring down the firing temperature.

Yellow Ochre. $(Fe_2O_3.H_2O)$ A naturally occurring iron earth compound used as a colorant to produce ochre yellows, tans, and browns. Possible substitutes are burnt umber and burnt sienna.

Yellow Base. (m.p. 1652°F./900°C. and up) A glaze stain produced by a calcined mixture of red lead, tin oxide, and antimony oxide. *See* Antimony Oxide.

Zinc Oxide. (ZnO) (m.p. 2480°F./1360°C.) This oxide is used as a flux, opacifier, and color modifier. At high temperatures it is an active flux. When excessive amounts are used in glazes low in alumina it will often produce crystals. It has no equivalent substitute.

Zirconium Oxide. (ZrO_2) (m.p. 4424°F./2440°C.) This compound is generally used in commercially prepared opacifier frits in combination with other compounds. Any commercial opacifier or tin oxide will substitute.

Zircopax. This is a standard commercial opacifier in frit form consisting of zinc, tin, and silica. Opax, Superpax, or tin oxide will substitute well.

APPENDIX

CLAY ANALYSIS CHART (AMERICA)

	SiO_2	Al_2O_3	Fe_2O_3	TiO_2	CaO	MgO	K_2O	Na_2O	MnO	I.L.
Albany slip	57.6	14.6	5.2	0.4	5.8	2.5	3.2	0.8	0.08	9.5
Ball clay	51.9	31.7	0.8	1.5	0.2	0.2	0.9	0.4	—	12.3
Barnard clay	41.4	6.7	29.9	0.2	0.5	0.6	1.0	0.5	3.25	8.4
Bentonite	64.3	20.7	3.4	0.11	0.46	2.26	2.9	—	—	5.15
C W-5 clay	48.8	35.7	1.6	1.8	0.3	0.2	1.0	1.0	—	13.2
Fire clay	58.1	23.1	2.4	1.4	0.8	1.1	1.9	0.3	—	10.5
Goldart	57.3	28.5	1.23	1.98	0.08	0.22	0.88	0.30	—	9.39
Hawthorn	48.4	33.8	1.90	1.00	0.02	0.23	0.94	0.16	—	12.9
Jordan	61.19	20.23	1.73	1.18	0.16	0.52	2.0	0.23	—	6.89
Kaolin (English)	47.25	37.29	0.85	0.05	0.03	0.28	1.8	0.04	—	12.20
Kaolin (Georgia)	49.9	38.9	0.4	1.3	0.1	0.1	0.2	0.2	—	14.21
EPK Kaolin (Florida)	45.91	38.71	0.42	0.34	0.09	0.12	0.22	0.04	—	14.16
Kentucky ball clay #4	52.1	31.2	0.8	1.6	0.4	0.3	1.0	0.3	—	12.4
Monmouth fire clay	50.89	44.95	2.21	0.84	0.11	0.30	0.55	0.01	—	—
Monmouth stoneware clay	56.8	28.5	—	—	0.3	0.3	0.3	0.3	—	12.2
Plastic Vitrox	75.56	14.87	0.09	—	0.22	0.20	6.81	0.29	—	2.04
Redart	64.24	16.41	7.04	1.06	0.23	1.55	0.40	4.07	—	4.78
Red Dalton	63.2	18.3	6.3	1.3	0.3	0.5	1.6	1.2	—	6.4
Sagger	59.4	27.2	0.7	1.6	0.6	0.2	0.7	0.3	—	9.4
Tennessee ball clay #5	53.3	30.1	1.0	1.4	0.3	0.2	1.5	0.8	—	11.4

FELDSPAR ANALYSIS CHART (AMERICA)

	SiO_2	Al_2O_3	Fe_2O_3	CaO	MgO	K_2O	Na_2O	I.L.
Bell	68.3	17.9	0.08	0.4	0.01	10.1	3.1	0.33
Buckingham	65.58	19.6	0.01	0.16	0.2	12.44	2.56	0.32
Carolina stone	72.30	16.23	0.07	0.62	0.01	4.42	4.4	1.06
Chesterfield	70.6	16.3	0.08	0.03	—	8.5	3.75	0.4
Clinchfield	See Custer							
Cornwall stone	71.1	16.8	0.16	1.6	0.05	6.57	2.29	1.25
Custer	68.5	17.5	0.08	0.30	0.01	10.4	3.0	0.3
Eureka	69.8	17.11	0.1	—	—	9.4	3.5	0.2
Keystone	See Custer							
Kingman	66.0	18.7	0.1	0.1	—	12.0	2.8	0.2
Kona A-3	71.6	16.3	0.07	0.4	—	3.7	7.8	0.1
Kona F-4	66.8	19.7	0.04	1.8	—	7.0	4.5	0.2
Nepheline syenite	60.4	23.6	0.08	0.7	0.1	9.8	4.6	0.7
Oxford	69.4	17.04	0.09	0.38	—	7.92	3.22	0.3
Pyrophyllite	73.5	20.0	0.5	0.1	—	1.4	1.2	3.3
Spruce pine #4	67.9	19.01	0.05	1.54	0.01	4.98	6.22	0.08

COMMERCIAL FRIT CHART

Ferro 3124. Borosilicate type used in glazes in the cone 3–5 range.

Ferro 3134. Borosilicate type used in art glazes in the cone 06–04 range.

Ferro 5301. Low-temperature frit used for making crackle glazes in the cone 08–04 range.

Ferro 3150. This frit is usually used as a body flux in low- to medium-temperature clay bodies.

Ferro 3195. Low-temperature alkaline type is used in cone 08–04 glazes.

Ferro 3211. Calcium-boron type used in higher range glazes.

Ferro 3223. Sodium-borosilicate type used in low-temperature glazes in the earthenware range.

Ferro 3304. Lead frit used in cone 08–02 glazes where a lead base is necessary to achieve certain colors that are not possible with the borosilicate-type frit.

Ferro 3386. Potash-sodium-lead borosilicate type used in low-temperature glazes, mainly earthenware.

Ferro 3396. Lead-alkaline-boron type used for low-temperature glazes.

Ferro 3403. Lead frit used in high-temperature earthenware to soft stoneware ranges.

Ferro 3419. Lead-alkaline-silicate type used in the cone 06–04 range.

Ferro 3466. Lead-zinc-silicate type used for medium-temperature-range glazes.

Ferro 3467. Lead-type frit used in high-temperature earthenware to soft stoneware glazes.

Ferro 3496. Medium-lead frit for cone 05–02 glazes. This frit is very good for compounding glazes that are crystal clear for use with overglaze colors.

Ferro 3819. Leadless frit used for low-temperature glazes.

Hommel 13. Sodium-lead-borosilicate type used for low- to medium-temperature glazes.

Hommel 14. Borosilicate type used in art glazes in the cone 06–6 range.

Hommel 22. Lead-borosilicate type used for medium-temperature glazes.

Hommel 61. High-lead type used in cone 08–02 glazes.

Hommel 240. Sodium-lead-borosilicate type used in low- to medium-temperature glazes.

Hommel 242. Borosilicate type used mainly in art glazes for its unusual run effects.

Hommel 259. Leadless type used for low-temperature glazes in the lower earthenware glaze range.

Hommel 265. Lead silicate type used in medium-temperature ranges.

Hommel 266. Alkaline-borosilicate type used in low- to medium-temperature glazes.

Hommel 267. Borosilicate type used in low-temperature glazes.

Hommel 285. Potash-alkaline-borosilicate type used in high-temperature earthenware to soft stoneware glaze ranges.

Pemco 25. Leadless alkaline type used for glazes in the cone 06–02 range.

Pemco Pb-41. Zinc-lead-borosilicate type used for low-temperature glazes where zinc is necessary to effect a color change in other colorants.

Pemco 54. Borosilicate type for partially fritted glazes in the cone 06–04 range.

Pemco Pb-63. High-lead frit used for low-temperature glazes.

Pemco 64. Leadless frit used for low-temperature glazes.

Pemco 67. Potash-sodium-borosilicate type used for glazes in the cone 06–02 range.

Pemco 83. Lead-borosilicate type used for glazes in the cone 08–2 range.

Pemco 283. Leadless alkaline frit used for glazes in the cone 06–2 range.

Pemco 311. Leadless borosilicate type used for glazes in the cone 3–6 range.

Pemco 316. Lead-alkaline-silicate type used for glazes in the medium-temperature range.

Pemco Pb-349. Complicated lead-alkaline type used in glazes in the cone 02–8 range.

Pemco Pb-361. Lead-borosilicate type used in medium-temperature glazes.

Pemco Pb-545. Lead-alumina-silicate type used in stoneware glazes.

Pemco 626. Low-temperature barium-silicate type used for glazes in the cone 06–02 to obtain the unusual barium-blue colors.

Pemco Pb-723. Lead frit used for high-temperature earthenware to soft stoneware glazes.

Pemco Pb-742. High-lead frit used for low-temperature glazes where absolute clearness of the glaze is a necessity.

Pemco 926. Sodium-calcium-alumina-borosilicate type used for glazes in the soft stoneware range.

Pemco 930. Low-temperature strontium-silicate frit for glazes in the cone 06–02 range. This frit will give a durable earthenware or low soft stoneware glaze. It is probably the best frit to use on utilitarian ware in this temperature range.

CHART OF COLORANTS FOR OXIDATION GLAZES

Colorant	Percentage	Fired Result
Cobalt carbonate	½%	medium blue
Cobalt carbonate	1%	strong blue
Cobalt oxide	¼%	medium blue
Cobalt oxide	½%	strong blue
Copper carbonate	2%	light green
Copper carbonate	4%	strong green
Copper oxide	1%	light green
Copper oxide	2%	strong green
Iron oxide	2%	tan
Iron oxide	4%	medium brown
Iron oxide	6%	strong brown
Iron chromate	2%	light gray
Iron chromate	4%	medium gray
Manganese carbonate	2%	light purple
Manganese carbonate	4%	medium purple
Manganese carbonate	6%	dark purple
Chrome oxide	1%	light green
Chrome oxide	2%	green
Rutile	5%	tan
Rutile	8%	strong tan
Nickel oxide	2%	gray-brown
Ilmenite	4%	tan
Ilmenite	6%	strong tan
Vanadium stain	4%	light yellow
Vanadium stain	6%	medium yellow
Vanadium stain	8%	strong yellow

COLORANT COMBINATIONS

Colorant	Percentage	Fired Result
Cobalt carbonate	½%	gray-blue
Iron oxide	2%	
Cobalt carbonate	½%	purple-blue
Manganese carbonate	5%	
Cobalt carbonate	½%	blue-green
Copper carbonate	2%	
Copper carbonate	2%	warm green
Iron oxide	2%	
Copper carbonate	3%	yellow-green
Vanadium	3%	
Copper carbonate	3%	warm green
Rutile	3%	
Cobalt carbonate	½%	warm mottled blue
Rutile	3%	
Vanadium stain	5%	warm ochre yellow
Rutile	4%	
Rutile	4%	spotted medium tan
Crocus martis	3%	
Ilmenite	2%	textured brown
Rutile	2%	
Cobalt carbonate	3%	
Iron oxide	3%	mirror luster black
Manganese carbonate	2½%	

Note. The percentages should always be calculated by the dry body weight of the formula.

CHART OF COLORANTS FOR REDUCTION GLAZES

Colorant	Percentage	Fired Result
Cobalt carbonate	½%	medium blue
Cobalt carbonate	1%	strong blue
Cobalt oxide	¼%	medium blue
Cobalt oxide	½%	strong blue
Copper carbonate	½%	ox-blood red
Copper carbonate	1%	deep blood red
Copper carbonate	2½%	mottled red and black
Manganese carbonate	5%	brown
Ilmenite	3%	spotted brown
Rutile	2%	spotted tan
Iron oxide	1%	celadon
Iron oxide	2%	dark celadon
Iron oxide	3%	dark mottled celadon
Nickel oxide	2%	gray-blue
Iron oxide	10%	saturated-iron red

COLORANT COMBINATIONS

Colorant	Percentage	Fired Result
Cobalt carbonate	½%	turquoise
Chrome oxide	1%	
Cobalt carbonate	½%	patterned blue
Rutile	3%	
Cobalt carbonate	½%	gray-blue
Nickel oxide	1%	
Manganese carbonate	4%	patterned brown
Rutile	4%	
Ilmenite	2%	textured ochre
Rutile	2½%	
Cobalt carbonate	½%	gray-blue
Iron oxide	2%	
Cobalt oxide	1%	
Iron oxide	8%	black
Manganese dioxide	4%	

Note. The percentages should always be calculated by the dry body weight of the formula.

HEAT COLOR/TEMPERATURE CHART

Note. The cones given here and throughout this book refer to Orton Standard cones.

Cone	°Centigrade	°Fahrenheit	Color of heat	Changes in clay	Glaze m.p.
022	605	1121		dehydration	
021	615	1139			
020	650	1202			
019	660	1220			
018	720	1328	dull red		overglaze colors or enamels
017	770	1418			
016	795	1463			
015	805	1481		organic matter in clay burns out	glass slumps
014	830	1526			
013	860	1580			
012	875	1607	cherry red		luster glazes
011	895	1643			
010	905	1661			
09	930	1706	orange		low-fire lead glazes
08	950	1742			
07	990	1815			low-fire earthenware
06	1015	1845		red and native clays mature	
05	1040	1904			
04	1060	1940			
03	1115	2035			
02	1125	2055	yellow	cream and buff clays mature	higher fire earthenwares
01	1145	2090			
1	1160	2120			
2	1165	2130		soft stoneware vitrifies	
3	1170	2138			
4	1190	2174		iron-bearing clay melts	china glazes
5	1204	2201			
6	1230	2245			soft feldspar glazes
7	1250	2283			
8	1260	2300		stoneware clays mature	salt glazes
9	1285	2345	white		stoneware glazes
10	1305	2381		hard stoneware; porcelain begins to vitrify	
11	1325	2417			
12	1335	2435			
13	1350	2465		porcelain matures	porcelain glazes
14	1400	2550			
15	1435	2610			

CLAY ANALYSIS CHART (UNITED KINGDOM)

	SiO_2	Al_2O_3	Fe_2O_3	TiO_2	CaO	MgO	K_2O	Na_2O	MnO	I.L.
Glenboig fire clay	57.0	27.0	2.0	1.0	1.0	—	1.0	1.0	—	14.0
HM. Blue ball clay	53.0	31.0	1.3	1.2	0.3	0.5	3.1	0.5	—	9.1
HM. China clay no. 1	47.1	36.9	1.09	0.23	0.13	0.21	1.7	0.08	—	12.1
HM. China clay no. 2	48.3	36.9	0.75	0.04	0.1	0.1	2.5	0.1	—	11.11
P&S. Basalt	48.6	14.1	11.2	1.6	7.9	10.3	0.6	2.4	0.1	3.8
P&S. Blue ball clay	48.5	33.5	1.0	0.9	0.3	0.3	2.3	0.4	—	12.8
P&S. China clay P. China clay	46.62	38.31	0.38	0.07	0.33	0.25	0.68	0.3	—	13.2
W. ball clay no. 1	52.9	32.6	1.0	1.0	0.2	0.4	2.5	0.4	—	9.0
W. ball clay no. 2	63.3	24.5	1.0	1.3	0.2	0.3	2.5	0.4	—	6.5
W. China clay no. 2	47.7	37.2	0.6	0.03	0.1	0.25	1.84	0.08	—	12.2
WBB. China clay CC	46.8	37.4	0.8	0.1	0.1	0.2	1.7	0.1	—	12.8
WBB. BBV ball clay	71.3	18.8	0.8	1.5	0.2	0.3	1.9	0.3	—	4.9
WBB. TA ball clay	59.8	26.4	1.0	1.4	0.2	0.5	2.4	0.4	—	7.9
WBB. TWVA ball clay	50.5	32.8	1.0	1.0	0.2	0.3	2.2	0.3	—	11.7
WBB. TWVD ball clay	52.9	32.6	1.0	1.0	0.2	0.4	2.5	0.4	—	9.0
WBB. Sanblend	51.04	32.56	0.81	0.93	0.34	0.28	2.53	0.4	—	11.11
WBB. Super Strength BKS. 5	75.4	15.0	0.8	1.3	0.2	0.4	1.9	0.3	—	4.7
WBB. Super Strength NDK	57.2	28.9	1.0	1.1	0.4	0.5	2.6	0.4	—	7.8

The following are suggested near equivalents to the clays employed in the formulas. This list is based upon chemical analyses rather than physical properties.

Albany slip. There is no near equivalent in the U.K., but some estuarian muds will be found to act as passable substitutes. If the clay properties are not required, a ground basalt provides similar reactive effects.

Ball clay. HM. Blue ball clay (ECC Hymod KC) WBB. Sanglend 55.

Barnard clay. There is no near equivalent in the U.K. to imitate the particular combinations of iron and manganese in this clay. However, some of the Staffordshire red clays make passable substitutes.

Bentonite. Most bentonites available in the U.K. have sufficiently high silica contents to be near equivalents.

CW-5 clay. WBB. TWVA ball clay.

Fire clay. A good quality fire clay is required of low iron content. The nearest British fire clay is Blenboig.

Goldart. WBB. Super Strength NDK.

Hawthorn. P&S. Blue ball clay.

Jordan. W. Ball clay no. 2

Kaolin (English). HM. China clay no. 1 (ECC Stannon). WBB. China clay CC. W. China clay no. 2

Kaolin (Georgia). HM. China clay no. 2 (ECC Trevisco).

EPK kaolin (Florida). P&S. China clay. P. China clay.

Kentucky ball clay. HM. Blue ball clay (ECC Hywood KC). WBB. TWVD. Ball clay. W. Ball clay no. 1.

Monmouth fire clay. There is no near equivalent but a high alumina fire clay should be sought.

Monmouth. WBB. TA. Ball clay.

Plastic Vitrox. WBB. BBV. Ball clay. WBB. Super Strength BKS. 5.

Redart and Red Dalton. There are no near equivalents, but red clays like Etruria Marl make passable substitutes.

Sagger. A low-iron-content fire clay is required, like Glenboig. Alternatively, if the chemical nearness is important, WBB. TA. Ball clay is similar.

Tennessee ball clay. HM. Blue ball clay (ECC Hymod KC). WBB. TWVD. Ball clay. W. Ball clay no. 1.

References to the suppliers of the above clays.

HM   Harrison Mayer, Ltd., Meir, Stoke-on-Trent, ST3 7PX

P & S   Podmore & Sons, Ltd., Shelton, Stoke-on-Trent, ST1 4PQ

P   Potclays, Ltd., Brickkiln Lane, Etruria, Stoke-on-Trent

W   Wengers, Ltd., Etruria, Stoke-on-Trent, ST4 7BQ

WBB   Watts Blake Bearne & Co., Ltd., Park House, Courtenay Park, Newton Abbot, TQ12 4PS

FELDSPAR ANALYSIS CHART (UNITED KINGDOM)

The following are suggested near equivalents to the feldspars employed in the formulas. The list is based upon the chemical analysis of feldspars available in the United Kingdom.

American Feldspar	U.K. Feldspar	SiO_2	Al_2O_3	Fe_2O_3	CaO	MgO	K_2O	Na_2O	I.L.
Bell	P&S Potash feldspar	68.2	17.5	0.2	0.25	0.12	10.3	2.5	—
Buckingham	HM Potash feldspar	65.19	18.98	0.12	0.47	—	11.81	2.88	0.36
Carolina stone	P&S Cornish stone	72.9	14.93	0.13	2.06	0.09	3.81	4.0	0.61
	W Mineralised stone	75.4	14.5	0.18	0.25	—	4.3	4.8	—
Chesterfield	F Potash feldspar	70.0	18.0	—	—	—	9.1	3.0	—
Cornwall stone	P Potash feldspar	77.0	15.0	0.15	—	—	8.0	2.5	—
Custer	P&S Potash feldspar	68.2	17.5	0.2	0.25	0.12	10.3	2.5	—
	W Potash feldspar	66.11	18.26	0.1	0.76	0.1	10.38	3.75	—
Eureka	F Blended feldspar	66.0	19.0	—	—	—	9.3	4.6	—
Kingman	HM Potash feldspar	65.19	18.98	0.12	0.47	—	11.81	2.88	0.36
Kona A-3	P&S Cornish stone	72.9	14.93	0.13	2.06	0.09	3.81	4.0	0.61
Kona F-4	F Blended feldspar	66.0	19.0	—	—	—	9.3	4.6	—
Nepheline syenite	HM Nepheline syenite	60.5	23.4	0.07	0.64	0.4	4.63	9.96	0.69
Oxford	F Blended feldspar	66.0	19.0	—	—	—	9.3	4.6	—
Pyrophyllite	F Blended Cornish stone	72.1	16.4	—	1.7	—	4.4	3.6	—
Spruce Pine 4	P Soda feldspar	68.0	19.0	0.15	—	—	3.0	7.5	—

References to the suppliers of the above materials.

F   Ferro (Great Britain) Ltd, Wombourne, Wolverhampton, WV5 8DA
HM   Harrison Mayer Ltd, Meir, Stoke-on-Trent, ST3 7PX
P&S   Podmore & Sons Ltd, Shelton, Stoke-on-Trent, ST1 4PQ
P   Potclays Ltd, Brickkiln Lane, Etruria, Stoke-on-Trent
W   Wengers Ltd, Etruria, Stoke-on-Trent, ST4 7BQ

CHART OF COMMERCIAL FRITS (UNITED KINGDOM)

It is not possible to make an equivalent list of American and U.K. frits because each frit is individual. However, the possible substitute may be arrived at by a careful comparison of the descriptions. The effect will not be vastly different where the amount of frit involved is small.

Ferro (Great Britain) Ltd. Wombourne, Wolverhampton WV5 8DA

Note. The American Ferro frits to which these most nearly correspond are given in parentheses.

201 100	Lead bisilicate, the basic lead frit for low- and middle-temperature glazes.
201 101	Lead sesquisilicate, a basic lead frit with a slightly higher lead content than the bisilicate.
201 102	Standard borax frit for use at all temperatures.
201 103	Low-solubility clear frit for producing clean transparent or coloured glazes in the middle-temperature range.
201 104	Low-expansion leadless frit.
201 105	Alkaline leadless frit for low- and middle-temperature glazes. (3159)
201 106	Super-opaque leadless zircon frit for white glazes (3819)
201 107	High-zinc frit.
201 108	High-lime frit.
3467	Lead frit. (3467)
140 00	Borosilicate frit with high-lime content. (3124)
140 17	Lead frit. (3496)
140 19	Sodium borate frit. (3223)
140 24	Calcium borate frit. (3211)
LHT-596-A	Lead-zinc-silicate frit. (3466)

Harrison Mayer, Ltd. Meir, Stoke-on-Trent, ST3 7PX

36.2.191	Lead bisilicate, the basic lead frit for low- and middle-temperature glazes.
36.2.192	Standard borax frit, calcium-sodium-borosilicate for use at all temperatures.
36.2.193	Alkaline leadless frit. A high-expansion frit for crackle and alkaline effects in low- and middle-temperature glazes.
36.2.194	Standard zircon opaque leadless frit for middle-temperature glazes.
36.2.195	Lead borosilicate. Equivalent to combined lead and borax frits for producing low-solubility glazes.

Podmore & Sons, Ltd. Shelton, Stoke-on-Trent, ST1 4PQ

P 2241	Lead bisilicate, the basic lead frit for low- and middle-temperature glazes.
P 2242	Lead sesquisilicate, a basic lead frit with a slightly higher lead content than the bisilicate and useful in low-temperature glazes.
P 2244	Calcium-borate frit used in stoneware glazes and to give special effects at lower temperatures. High boric oxide content.
P 2245	A general purpose high-expansion alkaline-borosilicate type frit for low- and middle-temperature glazes.
P 2246	Standard borax frit, calcium-sodium-borosilicate for use at all temperatures.
P 2247	Low-expansion alkali-borosilicate for middle- and high-temperature glazes.
P 2248	White opaque zircon-borax frit for middle-temperature opaque glazes.
P 2249	Leadless low-expansion borosilicate frit for middle-temperature glazes where crazing problems are encountered.
P 2250	High-alkali frit. A high-expansion frit for crackle and alkaline effects in low- and middle-temperature glazes.

P 2251　Alkali-borosilicate frit with clean transparency and stability for middle-temperature glazes.

P 2252　Low-expansion borax frit for stoneware glazes.

Potclays Ltd. Brickkiln Lane, Etruria, Stoke-on-Trent

2261　Lead bisilicate, the basic lead frit for low- and middle-temperature glazes.

2262　Lead sesquisilicate, a basic lead frit with a slightly higher lead content than the bisilicate and useful in low-temperature glazes.

2263　Standard borax frit, calcium-sodium-borosilicate for use at all temperatures.

2268　Calcium-borate frit, alkali-calcium-borosilicate for use in middle-temperature and stoneware glazes.

2270　White opaque zircon-borax frit for making opaque low- and middle-temperature glazes.

2275　High-alkali frit. A high-expansion frit for crackle and alkaline effects in low- and middle-temperature glazes.

Wengers, Ltd. Etruria, Stoke-on-Trent, ST4 7BQ

1461 W　Soft borax frit, sodium-borosilicate for low-temperature glazes.

1463 W　Borax frit for middle-temperature and stoneware glazes.

1460 W　Soft alkali-borosilicate for low-temperature glazes.

1455 W　High-alkali frit, sodium-calcium-borosilicate for middle-temperature glazes.

Many formulas in this book contain toxic materials. The obvious ones which should be handled with care during glaze preparation are red lead (lead oxide), white lead (lead carbonate), litharge (yellow lead oxide), lead monosilicate, antimony oxide, barium carbonate, and potassium bicarbonate. Other materials may constitute a health hazard if incorrectly handled. Clay and silica dusts, for example, are so fine that they clog the lungs, causing silicosis. The dust particles are so small as to be invisible in the air. Therefore all glazes in powder form, or when sprayed as fine mist or dried on clothing, benches, and floors constitute a possible hazard. Some of the ceramic materials, while not immediately poisonous, are regarded as sources of toxicity in combination with other materials. Care should be taken with any glazes containing compounds involving antimony, barium, cadmium, chromium, cobalt, copper, lead, nickel, selenium, vanadium, and zinc.

Potters are responsible for the safety of themselves, their employees, and the public on or near their premises. Teachers are responsible for the safety of themselves and their students. The most important legislation in Great Britain was the Health and Safety at Work Act, 1974, but additional directives to teachers are given in the Department of Education and Science Administrative Memoranda numbers 517 and 2/65. A number of other codes of practice and pamphlets on safety are in circulation. Most suppliers of ceramics materials include digests of the relevant literature in their catalogues and give sound advice on the handling of their products.

A knowledge of the hazards involved is the first requisite. Precautions to be taken should include a developed habit of cleanliness including the wearing of protective clothing, the changing of this before eating and drinking, the frequent washing of the protective clothing, the washing down of work surfaces, and the removal of splashes from walls and floors before they are dry. Smoking, eating, or drinking should not take place in the pottery. Facilities for thorough washing of hands, arms, and face after using glazes should be available. When toxic or potentially hazardous glazes are used they should be applied by pouring and dipping rather than spraying or painting. Spraying should not be used for glazes containing raw lead or lead monosilicate or sesquisilicate, antimony oxide, barium carbonate, cadmium compounds, or potassium dichromate. In any case, spraying must be done only in a spraybooth incorporating an extractor system fitted with efficient filters.

Incorrectly fired glazes toxic materials usually evolve into complex silicates where they are inert. However some glazes, especially underfired and low-fired ones, are dissolved by food acids and constitute a health hazard. Glazes on tableware in the United Kingdom are expected to pass the British Standard Specification 4860 which states the permissible limits of metal release from glazed ceramic ware. The British Ceramic Research Association, Queens Road, Penk Hull, Stoke-on-Trent ST4 7LQ will undertake testing at standard fees. Coloured glazes containing lead or cadmium are the most likely to release soluble poisons.

SUGGESTED READING

Note. The books discussed below are listed by content from material for the beginning ceramics student to the advanced professional.

Books

Kenny, John B. *The Complete Book of Pottery Making.* Philadelphia: Chilton Book Co., 1949; 2nd ed., 1976. London: Pitman, 1967.
This is a good book for the beginner. It is very well written and has many illustrations depicting how to choose and prepare clay, as well as forming techniques.

Hofstead, Jolyon. *Step by Step Ceramics.* Racine, Wisconsin: Western Publishing Co., Inc., 1967.
This is a very good paperback which gives the advancing beginner many new ideas of throwing, glazing, firing, and even building a kiln.

Kenny, John B. *Ceramic Design.*
Philadelphia: Chilton Book Co., 1963. London: Pitman, 1964.
This book presents excellent coverage of many ways of working with clay and many illustrations of the process and finished products.

Winterburn, Mollie. *The Technique of Handbuilt Pottery.* New York: Watson-Guptill, 1969. London: Mills and Boon Ltd, 1966.
A great book for beginning students who wish to learn more about handbuilding. It is well written and illustrated.

Sanders, Herbert H. *How to Make Pottery.* New York: Watson-Guptill, 1974.
A good book for advancing beginners. It covers many areas of pottery making and has many good illustrations of technique and finished products.

Kriwanek, Franz F. *Keramos.* Dubuque, Iowa: Kendall-Hunt Publishing Co., 1970.
A good little paperback with an easy approach to most of the areas of pottery.

Ball, Carlton F., and Lovoos, Janice. *Making Pottery Without a Wheel.* New York: Van Nostrand Reinhold, 1965.
This is a very delightful book on the many and unusual ways of building and decorating pottery by hand.

Nelson, Glenn C. *Ceramics.* New York: Holt, Rinehart, and Winston, 1960.
An excellent handbook. It covers a broad area from old to new and is oriented toward beginners.

Reigger, Hal. *Raku: Art and Technique.* New York: Van Nostrand Reinhold, 1970.
This book covers clay and glaze preparation, kiln building, and firing techniques.

Tyler, Christopher and Hirsch, Richard. *Raku: Techniques for Contemporary Potters.* New York: Watson-Guptill, and London: Pitman, 1975.
A well-written study of raku techniques today; beautifully illustrated with some technical information.

Norton, Frederick H. *Ceramics for the Artist Potter.* Cambridge: Addison-Wesley, 1956.
This is a good, comprehensive well-structured handbook for the more advanced student.

Norton, Frederick H. *Elements of Ceramics.* Cambridge, Massachusetts: Addison-Wesley, 1952.
This is a more advanced book for the advanced student of pottery and glazes.

Rhodes, Daniel. *Clay and Glazes for the Potter.* Philadelphia: Chilton Book Co., 1957. London: Pitman, 1967.

This is a good book for the more advanced student who wishes to delve deeper into the nature of clays and glazes.

Rhodes, Daniel. *Stoneware and Porcelain.* Philadelphia: Chilton Book Co., 1959. London: Pitman, 1960.
This book is for the more advanced student who wishes to dig even deeper into the nature of stoneware and porcelain.

Wildenhain, Marguerite. *Pottery: Form and Expression.* New York: Van Nostrand Reinhold, 1959.
This is a truly beautiful book with magnificent pictures of the artist at work as well as ancient and contemporary ceramic work.

Sanders, Herbert H. *Glazes for Special Effects.* New York: Watson-Guptill, 1974.
This great book covers the theory and production of crystalline glazes, copper reduction glazes, ash glazes, and luster decoration.

Grebanier, Joseph. *Chinese Stoneware Glazes.* New York: Watson-Guptill, 1975.
This is an excellent book in which the author presents his re-creations of the glazes used by ancient Chinese potters. It has much useful information and many formulas.

Fournier, Robert. *Illustrated Dictionary of Practical Pottery.* New York: Van Nostrand Reinhold, 1973.
This book is exhaustive and in its coverage of the whole area of pottery and in its detail. There are nearly 1200 entries and nearly 500 illustrations to help the potter. No potter should be without it.

Hamer, Frank. *The Potter's Dictionary of Materials and Techniques.* New York: Watson-Guptill, and London: Pitman, 1975.
Another excellent reference source which completely covers the ceramic field. It would be ideal for the potter to own both Fournier and Hamer.

Periodicals, U.S.A.

Ceramics Monthly, P.O. Box 12448, 1609 Northwest Blvd., Columbus, Ohio 43212.
This is a good pottery magazine with much useful information for both amateurs and professionals. It also contains many advertisements for suppliers and detailed information on art and craft shows around the country where potters can enter and sell their work. No potter, beginner or professional, should be without it.

Craft Horizons, 16 East 52nd Street, New York, N.Y. 10022.
This magazine covers all areas of the craft field including much information for the potter, dealing with contemporary American and international ceramics. It is always well illustrated and thus very inspirational.

Studio Potter, Box 172, Warner, N.H. 03278.
A bi-yearly magazine which combines the best of contemporary ceramics with useful technical information. Extremely well written and designed, this magazine is a must for every potter's library.

Periodicals, U.K.

Ceramic Review, William Blake House, Marshall St., London, W1, England.
Put out by the Craftsmen Potter's Association of Great Britain, this magazine contains much useful information which travels well across the ocean. Many reviews of European shows are also included.

Pottery Quarterly, Northfields Studio, Tring, Hertfordshire, England.
An erratically published little magazine full of useful information.

GLOSSARY/INDEX

Absorbency. The ability to soak up water

Acid. In ceramics, one of the three major families of glaze ingredients. Silica is the acid most important to potters. Neutrals and bases are the other groupings. The acid grouping is called the RO_2 group, which functions mainly as a glass-former

Adjusting: clay bodies, 22–23, 118–119; glazes, 404–407

Aging of clay. Letting clay sit in the wet state to allow bacterial action to improve the plasticity, 23–24

Albany slip, 161–164; glazes, 162–164

Alkali. A flux, as opposed to an acid, or a soluble salt obtained from the ashes of plants

Alkaline: clay, 19; glaze(s), 140–141, 144, 413

Alumina. An oxide, naturally occurring in clays and feldspars, which acts to stabilize a glaze

AMACO commercial glazes, 190, 198

Amphoteric. Capable of reacting chemically either as an acid or as a base

Applying glazes: brushing, 145; dipping, 145; spraying, 145

Ash, preparing for use, 385

Ash glaze. A high-temperature glaze made from wood, plant, or bone ash which contributes silica, alumina, and fluxes such as lime and potash to glazes, 141, 385–393; formulas, 386–393

Aventurine. A glaze giving a glossy, crystalline appearance due to the sparkling particles of iron, copper, or chrome oxide suspended in it

Bacterial growth, 23–24

Ball clay, discussion of, 15, 23

Ball mill. A means of grinding glazes by placing glaze ingredients and a charge of pebbles and water in a porcelain jar (industry uses large metal drums). The jar is then turned, 127, 144

Banding wheel. A turntable which enables a work to be rotated while being shaped

Bat. A disk made of plaster, fired clay, or wood on which clay can be dried, worked, and thrown

Batch formula. A combination of ceramic materials to be weighed out and mixed to produce a glaze

Bentonite, 22, 23; discussion of, 16

Binder, 15; ball clay as a, 15; bentonite as a, 16, 146; borax as a, 146

Bisque (bisc, biscuit). Fired clay which has no glaze, 21

Bisque firing. First firing used to harden the body at about cone 010–06 before glazing

Blistering. A glaze fault with bubbles and cratered surfaces occurring from the gases not being allowed to escape from the glaze before it sets. This can happen by firing too fast, the glaze being applied too thickly, or when lead glazes are subjected to reducing atmospheres, 404

Bloating. The condition of gas bubbles being trapped in the clay body resulting in large blisters or open tears, 118, 404

Boiling glaze, high-fire, 167–168; colorants for, 168; formulas for, 167–168

Bone china. A hard, translucent white china having bone ash as a fluxing agent

Boron glazes, 141

Break-through glazes, 161–166; colorants for, 166; formulas for, 162–166

Bristol glazes, 141

Brushing glazes, 145

Burnishing. Rubbing a green or leatherhard clay object with a smooth tool or the hand to produce a shiny surface

Calcine. To heat to a high temperature without fusing in order to purify a clay or glaze material

Casting clay bodies, 25, 27; earthenware, 31, 40–42; porcelain, 89–91; soft stoneware, 53–55; stoneware, 75–77

Caustic. Capable of destroying or eating away by chemical action

Celadon. A grey-green to blue-green glaze originated in China. The color results from iron oxide fired in reduction; glaze formulas, 365–373

Ceramichrome commercial glazes, 190, 196–198

Chemically combined water (bound water). Water chemically combined in the clay body and the glaze. This water will begin to leave the body as water vapor at about $842°F./450°C.$ and continues through red heat, about $1112°F./600°C.$ There is a loss of weight at this time but little shrinkage

Ch'ing ware. Porcelain from the Manchu dynasty using

ox-blood and peach bloom glazes, produced during the early part of the 18th century

Ch'ing-pai ware. A porcelain from the Sung dynasty which has a suggestion of blue where thick

Chlorine gas, 401

Choosing a clay body, 25

Chrome oxide, discussion of, 408

Chün. An Oriental glaze of an opalescent, thick, cloudy blue or blue-green nature which is sometimes spotted with violet or red-purple. This spotting is due to reduced copper oxide

Clay(s): analysis chart, US, 427; UK, 431; commercial, 25; data on body formulas, 29–30; defects, 118–119; definition of, 14; deposits, 14; native, 18–24; primary, 14; secondary, 14–16; single firing, 146; types, 16–17; used with crackle glazes, 169–170. See also Earthenware; Porcelain; Raku; Soft stoneware; Stoneware

Clay body rating scale, 29

Clay preparation: native, 20–21; body, 25–28

Cobalt oxide, discussion of, 408–409

Coefficient of expansion. The proportion of growth of a material for a given increase in temperature

Coiling. Making clay objects by building with a series of ropes of clay, 20

Colemanite glazes, 414

Colloid. A substance in a state of fine division. The particles range in diameter from about 0.2 to about .005 micron

Color of native clay, 20, 22

Colorants: clay, 22, 116–117; glaze, 16, 408–411, 428–429

Commercial glazes, special effects with, 190–198

Cones. Devices used to measure the heat-work inside a kiln. Made up of differing blends of ceramic materials, cones melt and deform at specific temperatures. All cones referred to in this book are Orton Standard cones; equivalent chart, 430

Copper oxide, discussion of, 409

Copper red glazes, 374–384; formulas, 374–384

Cracking, 118–119

Crackle glazes. Glazes having minute cracks on the surface. These are caused by the different rates of cooling between body and glaze after firing. Crackle is often used for decorative purposes, 141–142, 169–176; Bristol, 141; colorants for, 175–176; formulas for, 170–175; raku, 93

Crater glazes, 177–181; colorants for, 181; formulas for, 177–181

Crawling. Exposure of areas of unglazed clay as the glaze coating separates during firing, 141, 404

Crazing. A mesh of fine cracks in the glaze surface, sometimes considered decorative, 404; in raku glazes, 93; in slip glazes, 394; in underfired ware, 112. See also Crackle

Crystalline glazes. Glazes having clusters of crystals of various shapes and colors embedded in a more uniform and opaque matrix. Iron, lime, zinc, or rutile used in a glaze with an alkaline flux and high silica and low alumina content will normally produce crystals. The cooling cycle must be slow for the development of crystals, 142, 182–185; formulas for, 182–185

Cullet. Broken glass which can be reused. It is used in glazes in powdered form

Cup and spoon measure glazes, 157–160; formulas for, 157–160

Decant. The process of drawing off the top layer of a liquid suspension without disturbing the lower layers

Defects: clay body, 118–119; glaze, 404–407

Deflocculant. A soluable substance, often sodium carbonate or sodium silicate, used in a casting slip to improve suspension

Deformation, 119

Devitrification. The formation of crystals in a glaze during slow cooling, 405

Digging clay, 18, 20

Dipping. Coating a piece of pottery by immersing it in a container of glaze, 145

Draw trial. A piece of clay, usually a ring, taken from the firing kiln to measure the progress of the firing

Drying clay, 27, 118

Duncan Ceramics commercial glazes, 190–196

Dunting. The cracking of a piece of pottery, which can happen either while the kiln is cooling or when the pot has been out of the kiln for hours or even days, 119

Earthenware. A low-temperature porous clay which is often sealed by firing with a covering glaze, 15; clay body formulas, 31–45; discussion of, 16–17; glaze formulas, 199–231; used for cooking pots, 112

Eggshell porcelain. Translucent, thin-walled porcelain

Egyptian paste, 107–111; body formulas, 107–111

Empirical formula. A formula for a glaze explained in molecular proportions

Engobe. Often used interchangeably with slip, an engobe is made up of clay and/or glaze materials and is used as a decorative coating for pottery, 120–126; colorant chart, 126; formulas, 120–126; used in salt glazing, 402

Equivalent weight. A weight that will yield one unit of a component (RO, R_2O_3, or RO_2) in a compound. It is usually the same as the molecular weight of the chemical compound being discussed

Extruding. The forcing of plastic clay through a die for the purpose of shaping it

Faience. Earthenware decorated with opaque, colored glazes

Fat clay. A highly plastic clay

Feldspar chart; US, 426; UK, 432

Feldspathic glazes. Glazes having a relatively high proportion of feldspar. Used on stoneware or porcelain, they are very hard and durable, 142

Filler. A nonplastic material added to clay in order to

make pieces where control of weight and shrinkage is desirable

Fire clay, discussion of 15, 16

Firing native clay, 21–23

Fit. The adjustment between a glaze and the clay body it is used on, 119

Flashing. The impingement of flame on a pot in the kiln, which often causes discoloration of the body or glaze

Flint grog. *See* Silica grog

Floatatives, 145

Floating glaze, 186; formula for, 186

Flocculants. Thickeners; using, 145

Flowing glazes, 142, 187–189; formulas for, 187–189

Flux. A substance which melts and also causes other substances to become fluid, 25; as a glaze component, 140

Formaldehyde, 15

Free silica. Silica that is not attached to another compound in a clay but exists in a separate crystalline state, 112

Frit. Glass that has been melted and reground for use as a basis for glazes, 141; chart: US, 427; UK, 433–434; glaze, 142

Fuse. To become fluid with heat

Fusion point. The temperature at which a ceramic material will melt under heat

Glass cullet. *See* Cullet

Glaze(s): alkaline, 413; ash, 141, 385–393; breakthrough, 161–166; celadon, 465–473; classification, 140–143; colemanite, 414; commercial, 140, 190–198; copper red, 374–384; crackle, 141–142, 169–176; crater, 177–181; crystalline, 182–185; cup and spoon measure, 157–160; defects, 404–407; earthenware, 199–231; floating, 186; flowing, 142, 187–189; high-fire boiling, 167–168; high-lead, 415; low-lead, 412; porcelain, 354–364; potash, 416; preparation, 144–145; salt, 401–403; single-fire, 146–151; slip, 401–403; soft stoneware, 232–283; special-effect, 161–189; spodumene, 417; stoneware, 143, 284–353; types, 140–143; vapor, 401–403; wide-firing-range, 152–156

Glaze firing. The firing cycle at which the glaze materials melt to form a glasslike surface coating

Glaze rating scale, 30

Gram scale. A device used for measuring weight in the metric system

Greenware. Pottery which has not been fired

Grog. A clay body additive that provides both strength and texture to the ware, 25, 27, 28, 119; in salt clay bodies, 401–402

Gums, 145

Hare's fur. A temmoku glaze which resembles hare's fur with streaks of opaque light brown, sometimes with a trace of gray or blue-gray on a background of glassier consistency

High-fire boiling glaze. *See* Boiling glaze, high-fire

Hydrochloric acid, 401

Ilmenite, discussion of, 409

Impurities: granular, 19; in native clay, 14, 15, 19; organic, 19

Interface. The area of contact between the glaze and the clay body

Iron oxide, discussion of, 409, 410

K'ang Hsi ware. Porcelains produced during the Ch'ing dynasty with blue and white, enameled, copper red, ox-blood, and peach bloom glazes

Kaolin, discussion of, 14–15

Kiln. In pottery, an enclosure used to conserve heat while firing ware; salt glazing, 401

Kiln furniture. Refractory shelves and posts used to stack a kiln, 14; salt glazing, 401

Kiln wash. The protective coating that is painted on kiln shelves and floors. It is made up of water and equal parts by weight of kaolin and silica, 14

Lead glazes, 142; high-, 415; low-, 412

Lead poisoning, 141

Leatherhard. Greenware with most of the moisture gone but still soft enough to be carved or burnished easily, 82

Lime content in clay, 19

Lung-chüan ware. Pale, bluish green celadons made in the Chekiang province of China

Luster. Surface decoration achieved by a thin layer of metal deposited on the glaze; glazes, 142–143

Majolica. Low-temperature decorated, tin-glazed earthenware

Manganese oxide, discussion of, 410

Matt glaze. A glaze having a dull rather than a glossy finish, 143

Maturation point. The temperature at which clay and glazes reach their complete hardness, fusion, and stability. Every clay and glaze has its own maturation point; adjusting, 23

Mixing: casting bodies, 27; clay, 25–26; glazes, 144–145; sculpture bodies, 28; throwing bodies, 27

Moisturizing, 23–24

Mold. A form containing a hollow, negative shape. The positive is made by pouring either wet plaster or casting slip into this hollow. The mold is usually made of plaster of paris

Mortar and pestle, 144

Native clays, 18–24

Neutral. One of the three main ingredients necessary for a glaze, the R_2O_3 group. *See* Alumina

Neutral atmosphere. The atmosphere in a kiln between reducing and oxidizing

Nickel oxide, discussion of, 410

Oil of lavender, 142

Oil spot. A temmoku brown-black glaze which has a speckled surface of golden or silvery spots

Opacifier. A material which remains in suspension in a glaze, making it opaque, 93

Opalescence, 141

Open. To make a clay more porous by adding fillers or grog

Opener, 25; coffee grounds, 28, 31; sawdust, 28, 31

Open firing. Ware stacked directly in the combustible firing material

Ovenware: clay body formulas, 113-115; forming, 112; glaze formulas, 113-115; properties of, 112

Overfiring, 405

Overglaze. Decoration applied with overglaze colors on top of an already fired glazed piece. The overglaze firing is at a lower temperature than the glaze fire

Overglaze colors. Colors containing coloring oxides or ceramic stains, a flux, and some type of binder

Ox-blood. A deep-red glaze obtained from reduced copper, 374

Oxidation. Sufficient oxygen in the kiln atmosphere during firing to ensure the complete combustion of the fuel gases; glaze chart, 428

Oxide. Any element combined with oxygen; coloring, 116-117, 408-411

Patina. A shiny surface on ceramic pieces usually due to age. Ceramic sculpture can be given a patina by treatment with wax or oil

Peach bloom. A reduced copper glaze

Peeling. The term used when the slip and the glaze separate from the body. This may happen when slip is put on a body that is too dry or when a glaze is applied too thickly or to a dusty surface

Peep hole. An opening in the kiln wall for the purpose of observing cones or removing draw trials

Pinholing. A glaze defect caused by too rapid firing or by tiny air holes in the clay, 406

Plasticity. The nature of clay which allows it to be manipulated and still maintain its shape without cracking or sagging, 14, 15, 16, 25, 27, 29, 31, 119; adjusting for, 22-23, 82-83; testing for, 20

Porcelain. A hard, white, translucent, nonabsorbent clay body; clay body formulas, 82-92; discussion of, 14, 17; glazes, 143; glaze formulas, 354-364; improving plasticity of, 82-83

Porosity, 119

Porous nature of clay, 16

Potash glazes, 416

Preparing clay. See Clay preparation

Press molding. Taking clay and pressing it between two plaster molds in order to form clay objects, 107

Primary clay, 14

Pug. Mix

Pug mill. A device for mixing plastic clay, 21, 25, 26

Pyrometric cones. See Cones

Raku. Rough Japanese earthenware used originally in the tea ceremony; now adapted to modern uses, 93-106; clay body formulas, 92-97; glaze formulas, 97-106

Rangetop ware: clay body formula, 115; forming, 112; glaze formula, 115; properties of, 112

Raw glaze. A glaze having no fritted materials

Recognizing native clay, 18-19

Red heat. When refractories and ware inside the kiln are glowing red, around cone 010

Reducing agent. An organic material applied with the glaze or introduced into the kiln chamber during firing to induce reduction, 374-376

Reduction. Insufficient oxygen inside the kiln to allow all materials to develop into their oxide form; artificial, 374-376; glaze, discussion of, 143; glaze chart, 429

Refractory. A material which is heat resistant. In a kiln refractory materials include the bricks, shelves, and shelf supports; clay, 14, 15; element in glaze formation, 140

Residual clay. See Primary clay

Resists. Materials such as wax, paraffin, or paper applied to certain areas of a ceramic piece to produce designs

Rouge flambé. A deep-red reduction glaze with areas of green and blue, 374

Running of glaze, 405

Rutile, discussion of, 410

Sagger. A refractory container in which glazed ware is placed to protect it from the direct flame and combustion gases during firing

Salt glaze. A glaze made by throwing salt into a hot kiln. The salt vaporizes and combines with the silica in the clay body to form sodium silicate, a hard, glassy glaze, 143, 401-403; colorants for, 403

Sand. A loose, granular material made up primarily of silica, 19, 25, 27, 28

Sang de boeuf. The French term for ox-blood, 374

Sculpture clay bodies, 25, 28; earthenware, 31, 43-45; porcelain, 91-92; soft stoneware, 77-81; stoneware, 56-57

Scumming. A frosty, scumlike deposit on the surface of a glaze, 117, 406

Secondary clay, 14-16

Settling of glazes, 144-145

Sgraffito. A type of decoration made by scratching through a colored slip so that the contrasting body color beneath will show

Shard. A piece of pottery which has been broken

Shivering. The breaking or pulling away of the glaze from the body due to excess shrinkage of the body, 119, 406

Short clay. A body having no plasticity

Shrinkage. The contraction of clay either in drying or in firing. Stoneware shrinks at about 1652°F./900°C. and earthenware at a slightly lower temperature, 14-17, 21, 23, 27, 31, 119, 146; rating, 29

Silica, as a glaze component, 140, 141, 401
Silica grog. Sand or flint used as an opener
Single firing, 146–151; formula for glazes for, 147–151
Slip. A liquid clay used in mold casting and also as a thin coating over a ceramic body. Slips can cover up surface defects, provide a colored coating for a pot as a background for underglaze brushwork decoration, or furnish a layer through which designs may be cut. *See also* Engobe
Slip clay. Clay that can function as a glaze with few or no additions. Albany and Michigan are examples, 16
Slip glaze, 143, 394–400; formulas, 394–400
Slip method of mixing clay, 25, 26
Slurry. An uneven mixture of plastic clay and water
Soak. The retention of a certain heat in the kiln for a period of time to achieve specific glaze effects, 25, 26
Sodium in Egyptian paste, 107
Soft stoneware: clay body formulas, 46–57; discussion of, 17; glaze formulas, 232–283
Soluble. The ability of going into solution—often referring to fired glazes and their susceptibility to acid attack from foods, 144
Spar. Short for feldspar
Special-effect glazes, 161–189; formulas for, 162–189
Special effects with commercial glazes, 190–198
Speckling. Glaze surface marred by bits of nonglaze material, 406
Spodumene glazes, 417
Spraying. Applying a glaze by using a compressed-air spray machine; glazes, 145
Stabilizer. A material used to reduce extreme variation in the physical condition of another material; ball clay as a, 15; fire clay as a, 15; glaze, 140; kaolin as a, 14
Stain. An inorganic material used in coloring clay bodies and glazes, 127–137; formulas, 127–137
Stoneware. Ware which vitrifies completely between 2240° and 2400°F./1248.5° and 1315.5°C. Clay, feldspar, and quartz are the primary ingredients of stoneware, 15–16; clay body formulas, 58–81; discussion of, 17; glazes, 143; glaze formulas, 284–353. *See also* Soft stoneware

Temmoku. A streaked brown slip glaze of which examples are hare's fur and oil spot
Temperature chart, 430
Temperature range, 29
Testing native clay, 19–22
Thermal shock, 16, 93, 140

Throwing. The process of shaping clay on the potter's wheel
Throwing clay bodies, 25, 27; earthenware, 31–40; porcelain, 82–89; soft stoneware, 46–52; stoneware, 58–81
Ting ware. Porcelain, usually white, made in Sung dynasty China
Tooth. A coarse or rough-grained structure in a clay, 28
Trailing. Using a device, usually a tube, to apply a decorative line of slip to a clay piece
Translucent. Letting light pass through, but not transparent, 82, 93

Underfiring, 406
Underglaze. Colored decoration applied to bisque ware before the glaze is applied

Vapor glaze. *See* Salt glaze
Viscosity. The quality of glaze not to run
Vitreous. The hard, glassy, nonabsorbent quality of a body or glaze, 46
Vitrification. Firing to the point where the ware is at its hardest, most glassy state, 119; in salt firing, 401
Volatilize. Vaporize

Ware. Pottery or porcelain in the green, bisque, or glazed state
Warping. Distortion caused by uneven or rapid drying or uneven firing conditions
Waterglass. Another name for sodium silicate, used as a deflocculant
Water smoking. The first part of the firing cycle, when water is driven from the clay body
Wax resist. Liquid wax applied to greenware or bisque ware to resist a subsequent slip or glaze coating
Wedging. Kneading clay to make a homogeneous mixture and to remove air bubbles, 21, 24
Wet-grind. To grind with water or other liquid in a ball mill, 144
White body. A clay body, often low temperature, which usually contains a high percentage of talc and fires white
White ware. Pottery or china with a white or light cream-color, 14
Wide-firing-range glazes, 152–156; formulas for, 152–156
Wood ash. *See* Ash glaze
Workability. The plastic quality of a clay body

Ying Ch'ing. Porcelain produced during the Sung dynasty which has a suggestion of blue where thick